READINGS IN COUNSELING

READINGS IN
THE APPLIED SOCIAL SCIENCES

This Association Press book is one of a series of "readings" books on the applications of the social sciences in counseling, group work, social work, camping, adult education, religious education, and similar fields. The purpose of these books is to bring together in useful form for students and practitioners selected contributions from many sources. The selection of material for each book is made by an editor who is acquainted with the important literature of the field and has an established place as a practitioner. These carefully assembled and conveniently arranged source materials are intended to aid both laymen and professional workers.

Titles in the series or in preparation include:

Readings in the Development of Settlement Work, edited by Lorene M. Pacey

Readings in Counseling, edited by Karl Zerfoss

Readings in Group Work, edited by Dorothea Sullivan

Readings in Adult Education, edited by Malcolm Knowles

Readings
in Counseling

EDITED BY

Karl Zerfoss

Association Press   New York

Printed in the United States of America
Sowers Printing Company, Lebanon, Pa.
 2

Preface

The idea of the *Readings* grew out of the experience of the editor over a number of years, both in teaching and in contacts with the counseling field. During this time it became increasingly clear that many interested in counseling did not have ready access to the varied resources to be found in the literature. Furthermore, no one source seemed to afford adequate coverage and the task of assembling materials from various sources was practically impossible for most persons in this field.

It is hoped that the *Readings* may help to organize thinking in an area where available resources as related both to theory and to method are of great diversity; may provide a basis for continued study and inquiry; may offer a ready source to which readers can turn for material both significant and difficult to procure and may improve the insight and quality of guidance in general. Perhaps these objectives may be accomplished best by using the *Readings* as a source book.

The selections were chosen with a view to their use by teachers in school and college; Y.M.C.A. and Y.W.C.A. secretaries; leaders of Scouts and Boys' Clubs; ministers and other church workers; playground, physical education, recreation, and camp leaders; industrial personnel workers; and others likewise interested in individualizing their approach to those whom they serve.

The *Readings* have been organized around an outline used currently by the editor in a guidance course. They are concerned with the general aspects of guidance, as to principles, content, and method. In the main the selections apply to adolescents and young adults. In selecting the material it was impossible to eliminate all overlapping, but perhaps some overlapping is desirable, for authors with similar ideas and ap-

v

proaches quite often present them in such varied ways that the issue at hand is emphasized and clarified.

The editor examined much of the literature available. His own point of view, of course, determined the selections used. Among the decisive factors were the convictions that guidance is primarily an emphasis *within* education (or program); that the most constructive guidance approach is one of decentralization of emphasis throughout the experience of constituents; that the major concern of *most* guidance workers is with the "normal problems of normal people" in a preventive or an enrichment role rather than in a curative one; and that along the guidance continuum there is a proper place for all workers, from the generalist to the specialist.

Certain assumptions need to be kept in mind in the examination and use of the *Readings*: first, that the reader will have had some preliminary preparation in the guidance field; second, that the selections included are ones in which the general counselor—especially the nonexpert—will be interested and from which he might profit; and, finally, that the readers will need to transpose some selections from their original context to that in which the application is to be made, since the material relates primarily to basic considerations rather than to the special concerns of particular readers.

The editor wishes to express sincere appreciation to the authors and publishers whose permissions to quote made the book possible. He gratefully acknowledges his indebtedness to George Williams College for the substantial assistance given in the copying of the materials, and to the office staff who did this work. To his wife, Annie Agnew Zerfoss, he is deeply grateful for constant encouragement and effective assistance.

KARL P. ZERFOSS

Chicago, Illinois
September, 1951

Contents

Part I

THE COUNSELING SCENE TODAY

1.

The Need

---

1. PROBLEMS ARE MANY, VARIED, COMPLEX, AND DIFFICULT

People seeking help from a counselor in the course of a typical day are apt to present an amazing variety of complex and difficult problems. For example, a counselor in industry is likely to encounter such questions as the following:

"Can you arrange a transfer for me? My foreman is an awful crank, except to a couple of girls who are always flirting with him."

"My landlord won't fix the plumbing, and I have to move. Will you help me get into the housing project?"

"The matron always gives me the worst uniform in the shop."

"My boy friend writes from a camp in California that he has fallen in love with another girl. What can I do about it?"

"I'll have to quit my job unless you can find nursery care for my four-year-old Sammy. The neighbor won't keep him any longer because he teases her cat."

"I won't work alongside a Negro, and I'm going to quit."

The foremen too bring their problems:

"I'll have to fire Joe unless we can find out why he gripes all the time."

"One of my best workers, Jane, has been off the beam for ten days or so now. Do you think you can find out what's the matter?"

"Absenteeism in my department is the worst in the plant. Can you help me find out why?"

"How can I keep up my workers' morale when half the time the superintendent countermands my orders?"

3

Annette Garrett, *Counseling Methods for Personnel Workers.*
New York: Family Service Association of America, 1945,
pp. 7-8.

2.   THE PERSONAL-SOCIAL NEEDS OF YOUTH

The personal-social needs of high school youth stem from
the growth characteristics of the adolescent and from the kind
of society in which he lives and to which he is expected to
adjust and to contribute. When we talk about the personal-
social needs of an adolescent boy or girl we refer to such
concerns as:

The need for the boy or girl to understand the changes taking
place in his maturing body and to accept the normality of these
changes and of the concomitant interests and urges characteristic
of adolescence.

The need to gain increasing independence from parental and
home controls.

The need to establish satisfying friendships with individuals from
both sex groups and to experience a sense of genuine acceptance
by a group of admired contemporaries.

The need to establish a close relationship with one member of
the opposite sex and to give and receive affection in socially
approved ways.

The need to engage in work which gives him a sense of accomplishment and which he feels contributes to purposes larger than
his own.

These needs have an immediate urgency for boys and girls
of high school age. They represent the so-called "felt" needs.
Any fact of skill or other type of orientation which is recog-
nizable by youth as relating to these needs finds immediate
acceptance and use.

Camilla M. Low, "The Neglect of the Personal-Social Needs
of Youth," *Progressive Education*, Vol. 28, No. 2, November,
1950, pp. 52-53.

3.   NEEDS ARISE OUT OF THE INCREASING COMPLEXITIES
OF MODERN LIFE

Psychologically, a need for guidance is found wherever the
environment is sufficiently complex to permit a variety of

responses and whenever individuals are not equipped to react instinctively to the stimulus of the environment. Among animals and in primitive social orders, the guidance of youth is taken care of by the parents. Even in a fairly advanced civilization which maintains a certain homogeneity, the home can continue to be the chief guidance agency. Thus, in the largely agrarian society which obtained in the United States until approximately 1900, there was no keenly felt need for organized guidance other than that provided by the family.

It is unnecessary to point out that within the last half century our environment has become exceedingly complex. The astonishing development of pure and applied science and the mechanization of industry have led to minute vocational specialization and an infinite number of vocational choices. The growth of huge industries and the pyramiding of the financial structure have led to dense concentration of the population in certain areas and to dependent sociological problems. The attempt of the schools to keep pace with the growing need for social and industrial education has so expanded the curriculum that the pupil is presented with a bewildering array of subject choices, frequently with little or no information concerning those for which he is best fitted. . . .

At the same time the changing environment has placed much greater responsibility upon young people for the making of wise choices, and educational agencies have become aware of large differences among individuals in their potentialities for success in different areas.

> Arthur E. Traxler, *Techniques of Guidance.* New York: Harper and Brothers, 1945, pp. 1-2.

4. The Problems of Older Youth and Young Adults

. . . Older youth and young adults are the growing edge of our culture, and they are advancing through a period which in their own development (in most cases) initiates their adjustment to an occupation and their establishment of a home and intensifies their need for the clarification of life values. The blind drift of social and economic forces tends more and more to obstruct the expression of these basic needs in our society.

> E. G. Williamson, editor, *Trends in Student Personnel Work.*

Minneapolis: The University of Minnesota Press, 1949, p. 49.
(From chapter by Howard Y. McClusky.)

5. The Demand for Guidance Is Wide-Spread

.. All about us is ample evidence that most men are like the
singer of the negro spiritual—"standin' in the need of prayer,"
or some other form of help . . . This evidence of need is of
two sorts and may be obtained by finding the answers to these
questions: (1) What difficulties must men encounter before
they turn to someone or some agency for help? and (2) When
they discover that they are in trouble what do they do about it?

The chaotic situation in world affairs with war selected as
the only means of settling differences; national problems of
unemployment, wretched housing, and poverty amidst plenty;
a country in which the most frequent age of criminals is nine-
teen (the next most frequent being eighteen, then twenty-
one); a demonstrable lack of intelligent life planning on the
part of youth: these are some of the troubles that man has
created for himself. (Homer P. Rainey. *How Fare American
Youth?* New York: D. Appleton-Century Company, Inc., 1938,
p. 159.)

Proof is readily available that man realizes his need of help
and is constantly attempting to do something about it. One
has but to study the advertisements . . . to realize the truth-
fulness of this assertion. "Good money" would not be paid
newspapers and magazines over a period of years if financial
returns were not forthcoming to advertisers of shortcuts to
happiness. Periodicals would not conduct "Advice to the Love-
lorn" columns and other sections dealing with a variety of
personal problems if there were no demand for guidance.

D. Welty Lefever, Archie M. Turrell, Henry I. Weitzel,
Principles and Techniques of Guidance. New York: The
Ronald Press Company, 1941, pp. 3-4.

6. Counseling a "Must" in Secondary Schools

. . . The provision of an adequate guidance and counseling
program is rapidly becoming a "must" for all secondary schools.
These developments are a result of many contributing causes.
As the curriculum has expanded, the need for careful pupil

planning becomes more evident. As the adult culture becomes more and more complex, the pupil's need for more information and assistance becomes evident. As the school begins to individualize its activities, more and more information about pupils is needed. As the school program attempts to become more realistic, it is necessary to know more about pupils and the situations they now face and will face in the future. As we study the needs and problems of pupils we find an over-abundance of unsolved conflicts and difficulties.

> J. Fred Murphy, chairman, "Characteristics of a High School Guidance and Counseling Program," *The North Central Association Quarterly*, Vol. 22, No. 2, October, 1947, p. 220.

7. YOUNG PEOPLE WANT HELP

Youngsters in all parts of the United States were asked: "Would or would not most High School students like to discuss their personal problems with a sympathetic adult who would tell no one?"

68 per cent said: "Yes"
18 per cent said: "No"
14 per cent were: "Undecided"

> Report of Purdue Opinion Poll, Chicago *Sun-Times*, 1948.

8. "NORMAL" STUDENTS HAVE PROBLEMS

Of 259 healthy, "normal" students investigated by the Grant Study (made at Harvard University) in 1938-1942, 232 men, or 90 per cent, either raised problems that they wished to discuss or presented problems which the staff recognized as ones that thorough discussions would help to solve.

> C. W. Heath and L. W. Gregory, "Problems of Normal College Students and Their Families," *School and Society*, May 18, 1946, p. 355.

9. THE NEED AMONG HANDICAPPED CHILDREN IS GREAT

Among Handicapped Children (Under 21) in the U.S.:

Speech defects	4,000,000
Hearing defects	2,000,000
Orthopedically handicapped	510,000

Rheumatic fever, heart disease	500,000
Epileptic	300,000
Cerebral Palsy	200,000
Visual defects	65,000
Total	7,575,000

Reported in the Chicago *Sun,* March 24, 1947.

10. PROBLEMS REVEALED IN THE PUBLIC PRESS

In October, 1948, sixty-five students at George Williams College, Chicago, Illinois, reported having noted in Chicago papers, for one day or so, 261 news items (same item duplicated by the several students) indicating problems of people. The items were tabulated thus for the higher frequencies:

Murder	109
Narcotic addiction	32
Suicide and attempted suicide	29
Divorce	28
Parental difficulties	20
Custody fight	13
Robbery	11
Sex difficulties	11
Child abandonment	8
Total	261

Included in the other items reported were: race prejudice, housing, child cruelty, arson, worry, fantasy, runaway child, and vocational choice.

From class reports as indicated above.

11. MENTAL HEALTH NEEDS IN AMERICA

These are the known facts:

8,000,000 *Americans* suffer from some sort of mental illness.

Over *one-half of all hospital beds* are occupied by 600,000 mentally ill—125,000 new cases are admitted annually.

Doctors report that over *half* the patients who come to them with physical complaints are really suffering from mental or emotional disorders.

Half of all medical discharges from the *army* during World War II were on a neuro-psychiatric basis (nervous and mental illness). Over *one-third* of all Selective Service rejections were for the same cause.

In Illinois, 49,000 persons were under care in nine state hospitals in 1948. The yearly increase is 1,000 to 1,500.

These are the more serious cases, but all through the pattern of society runs the dangerous thread of mental illness in the form of emotional disturbances which cannot be counted.

Every community is affected.

> Publicity material, Illinois Society for Mental Hygiene, 1951. (A selected page.)

12. PEOPLE IN TROUBLE

"My 14-year-old daughter ran away. I am afraid. Can you help me find her?"

"My baby is sick. Where can I get a doctor right away?"

"My boy was killed in France. Will you please show me how to fill out these papers?"

"My wife left me and my six children last Friday. Where can I leave the two who don't go to school?"

"Can you get me into the housing project? The rats run over my children. The roof leaks. Too many people have to use the toilet."

"I want to be a citizen. What should I do?"

> From the Report of a Chicago (Illinois) social settlement, January, 1945.

13. MARITAL DIFFICULTIES

Another class of evidence of the heterosexual adjustment of young adults is impounded in data on marriage and divorce. By the age of twenty-eight the majority of people are married, but in recent years their chances of staying married have seriously declined. In 1937, divorces per 100 marriages were 17.2; in 1940, 16.5; in 1943, 22.8; in 1944, 27.5; and in 1945, 31, or almost one in three marriages. To put it another way, the number of marriages ending in divorce between 1937 and 1945 almost doubled. The dislocation and turmoil of the war are largely responsible for this increase; but if we can judge from the aftermath of World War I, the divorce rate will not return to its pre-war level. Although these statistics apply to all ages

of the married population, they reveal the marital difficulties
of young people because most of the breakups occur within a
few years after marriage.

> E. G. Williamson, editor, *Trends in Student Personnel Work.*
> Minneapolis: The University of Minnesota Press, 1949, p. 47.
> (From chapter by Howard Y. McClusky.)

Individuals in Need: Illustrations

14. THE UNHAPPY CHILD

A teacher discovered among her pupils a child whose home
life was very unhappy. She came to school in a disturbed
frame of mind, and was often rude to her classmates as well
as defiant toward her teacher.

> Joint Committee on Health Problems in Education of the
> N.E.A. and the A.M.A., *Mental Hygiene in the Classroom.*
> Edited by C. V. Hobson, 1939, p. 40.

15. THE CHILD WHO ACTS CLOWNISH

Jerry, in the eighth grade, is constantly doing something to
attract the attention of his classmates. He makes "bright"
remarks during recitation, insists on talking more than his
share of the time, performs antics as he walks around the room
to create a laugh, and even dresses, walks and combs his hair
in an unusual manner to attract attention.

> *Ibid.*, pp. 26-7.

16. THE TIMID CHILD

Jerry, in the sixth grade, is in good health and of average
size. On the playground he shrinks from entering into games
and play because he is afraid of being hurt. If he gets a little
bump he is through. He will not re-enter the game.

> *Ibid.*, p. 51.

17. THE ANTAGONISTIC CHILD

Doris, in the ninth grade, finds it very hard to get her school
work. She is unattractive and has no special talents. She
opposes her classmates on almost every question, and does not

want to do what they want to do. At home her parents are constantly bickering with her.

Ibid., p. 52.

18. SHE NEEDED FRIENDS

A philosophy instructor found that many students brought their personal problems to him—so many that it was often a burden. One young freshman came to him and said that she thought she ought to leave school. Her chief trouble seemed to be that she had no real friends. She was a fair student, agreeable, quiet. She had never had a date. The instructor talked with the dean of women and the head of the residence hall who arranged to move her in with another girl who had overcome the same difficulty the previous year. He also asked two other girls to help this young lady learn how to be more attractive. The plan seemed to work, at least to the extent that she developed some close friendships, had a few dates, and was a much happier young woman.

> Donald J. Shank, editor, *The Teacher as Counselor.* Washington: American Council on Education Series, Vol. vi, No. 10, October, 1948, pp. 5-6.

19. A HEALTH PROBLEM

Mr. "H" is a man of fifty years. He came to me one day and asked if I could provide him with a mouth wash. I examined him and found a badly inflamed condition of the throat. After administering an antiseptic solution, I examined the swelling in his neck and learned of pain in the shoulder. Examination of his teeth showed pyorrhea of the gums. His blood pressure was 20 points high. He was advised to see a dentist who X-rayed his teeth and found several decayed. The teeth were removed and within two months' time this man has regained his normal health.

> Report from an unidentified Y.M.C.A. physical director, 1934.

20. GENERAL DISSATISFACTION

The student was quite agitated after class today and requested an interview. Reported that the previous June, right after exams, he had a severe stomach attack. At first it was said to be an ulcer but later it was called a "nervous upset." Reported a fear and tenseness when about to participate in a class, a conference or such activity. Said he thought there was something really wrong as he had no heart in his work and felt like doing nothing.

From editor's personnel records.

21. POOR ACCEPTANCE BY OTHERS

Jim is not liked by many men in the residence and there have been some complaints about the way he handles people on his job. He does not seem to know how to get along with people and is frequently the object of derision by fellow workers and members, when he is not around.

From a report by one of the editor's students.

22. VOCATIONAL INDECISION

Al came in to discuss his dissatisfaction with his part-time job and his studies.

From editor's personnel records.

23. EMPLOYMENT CONCERN

Syd made an appointment to discuss the possibilities there were for employment.

From editor's personnel records.

---

24. NEEDS MULTIPLIED IN A CHANGING WORLD

When we add to this picture the alterations wrought by a rapidly changing technological society in producing rapid and easy transportation and communication, we see that the additional effect of these changes in our living conditions is staggering. High mobility means ease in getting about and in observing the nature of the environment and experiences of other people. It also operates to raise one's level of expectancy and desire for the better things in life. Rapid communication means that we are immediately in touch with increasingly larger numbers of individuals. Through movies, radio, and television, distant things, people, and ideas enter our immediate experience. International and global problems once far removed are now on our doorsteps. We face the necessity of understanding the institutions and mores of other peoples, together with the need for a better understanding of ourselves and an ability to be able effectively to interpret our own ways to others. Intercultural and interpersonal relationships are now vitally important. We have entered a new era of human destiny.

Our lives today reflect the changing conditions of our times, and there is much confusion concerning what we shall do about many of our most basic problems. Personal insecurities are multiplied by the action of forces beyond our immediate control. Feelings of confusion, insecurity, inadequacy, and frustration are increasingly a part of our lives. The conditions of modern life generate a degree of anxiety which is productive of maladjustment and neurosis.

> Harl R. Douglass, editor, *Education for Life Adjustment.* New York: The Ronald Press Company, 1950, p. 69. (From chapter by A. S. Clayton.)

25. NEW INSIGHT ABOUT THE NEEDS OF YOUTH

With growth in understanding of the dynamic nature of the human personality, *new student needs* are recognized. The social demands of a complex society create problems of adjustment never before experienced. The wider range of individual differences found in the more heterogeneous student population enrolled in our high schools today contrasts sharply with the student personnel characteristics of thirty or even twenty years ago. It is estimated that 70 or 75 per cent of youth of high school age are now enrolled in school, compared with 47 per cent in 1930 and 24 per cent in 1920. This increase in numbers has meant a consequent increase in the range of differences among students and an increase in the variety of student problems. School curricula have expanded, too, creating a wider range of course offerings and raising problems of choice that call for careful educational advising. *New objectives* of the secondary school call for consideration of student needs outside the classroom—physical, social, and emotional needs as well as intellectual or academic development. Guiding and assisting pupil growth in self-realization, in human relationships, in civic responsibility, and in vocational or economic efficiency places new and challenging demands upon teachers and our educational processes. *New tools and procedures* have been devised to deal with new needs and with old needs in new ways. Differential aptitude tests, sociometric measurements, personality diagnosis, group dynamics, and psychotherapy through counseling are some of the developments which enlarge the effectiveness of both teaching and guidance procedures.

> C. Gilbert Wrenn and Willis E. Dugan, *Guidance Procedures in High School.* Minneapolis: The University of Minnesota Press, 1950, p. 2.

26. EDUCATIONAL GUIDANCE A VITAL NEED

While there has always been a need for guidance, certain social and economic changes in the present-day world have increased the need of this phase of education in the public schools. The first of these changes is in the position of the home. In early colonial days, boys and girls grew up in homes where they were trained to share the responsibility of providing food, clothing, and shelter for the family. Labor was unspecialized; each family lived largely to itself, spinning yarn, weaving cloth, dipping candles, repairing and building houses and sheds, and performing other similar duties.

Changed conditions of living, especially in urban sections, have changed the general pattern of early life. There are not many chores for city boys or girls to perform, and in many cases their parents are not at home long enough to train them to perform these tasks. The breakdown of the apprentice system in labor and industry and the increased specialization in these fields has caused much confusion. Young men and women are confronted with a bewildering variety of occupations, and in order to make intelligent choices they must have adequate information about occupations, such as the nature of the work involved, qualifications for employment, the possibilities of securing employment in various fields, and the best training for various types of work.

The boy or girl entering school and coming into contact with new and more formal experiences than those previously encountered in the home and neighborhood will need guidance. There is need for orientation, and help in meeting the strange and sometimes difficult problems of adjusting to new ways of doing things. Through individual guidance, the transfer from the home to the school may be more easily accomplished. The pupil who is transferred from one school environment to another is also likely to need guidance. This individual is faced with the problems of making new friends, or learning slightly different ways of meeting particular situations, and in general, of finding himself in this new situation. Pupils who are maladjusted physically, educationally, morally, or emotionally, are in special need of individual guidance. Even the well-adjusted child who is ambitious to succeed in some vocational endeavor will need help in finding himself in relation to the world of work that he will enter at a later time. When the general question is asked: "Who should receive educational guidance?" the answer is: "Every school pupil."

Wendell W. Cruze, *Educational Psychology.* New York· The Ronald Press Company, 1942, pp. 510-11.

27. PROBLEMS OF STRESS FALL INTO CATEGORIES

The problem of stress outside the college may be rather arbitrarily divided into three categories on no more dynamic basis than immediacy and obviousness. The first category is the temporary crisis situation. The girl is homesick; falls in love; her father dies; her sister has a dangerous operation; she becomes ill herself; or perhaps she merely makes her debut. The second category is the more protracted crisis, so protracted that it is scarcely a "crisis" at all. The parents quarrel; are divorced; are chronically ill. The father has lost his money, necessitating prolonged readjustment of family standards. A difficult grandmother has come to live in the home, and so forth, and so forth. The third category embraces permanent items of strain: a more gifted sibling, markedly rejecting, dominating, or oversolicitous parents, disturbed social or economic adjustment of the family, physical disability, an unusual degree of beauty or homeliness, and the like.

Ruth L. Munroe, *Teaching the Individual.* New York: Columbia University Press, 1942, p. 137.

28. Needs of the Individual and of Society

Need for Guidance from the Standpoint of the Individual.— The amazing and rapid increase in the complexity of industrial and economic life, the changes in the conditions of living, and the phenomenal development of educational facilities beyond the elementary school have greatly increased the dependence of the individual upon outside help, and this dependence is steadily becoming greater. The young person is now confronted with a bewildering complexity of choice, not only of occupations and of jobs within an occupation, but also of future schools and kinds of specialized training for life work. Intelligent choice can result only where the young person has adequate facts and experiences and receives careful counseling at all stages of his progress. These society must provide. Delicate adjustments are necessary in the life of the youth of today that were not necessary half a century or more ago. The individual needs assistance as never before.

*Necessity from the Standpoint of Society.—*Society also has a claim; its very safety and progress demand that each individual be in that place, occupational, civic, and social, where he can contribute to the welfare of others and contribute his best to this welfare. This means that he shall be in an occupation where he will succeed, at least to the extent of making his own living. It means that he shall be so trained that, to the extent that it is possible for him, he will make society better and contribute his bit to improving conditions.

Arthur J. Jones, *Principles of Guidance*, Third Edition. New York: McGraw-Hill Book Company, 1945, pp. 49-50.

29. Need Versus Problem

The terms "need" and "problem" are often used interchangeably but this is the result of superficial thinking or of careless expression. A *need* is a demand of the organism, whether or not acknowledged or understood by the individual. A need is a "construct," or hypothetical concept, of a physiological tension which is electrochemical in nature. The situation which gives rise to the construct may be psychological or social in nature. This tension or need may be instigated from either within or without the organism. It is as real as the physical structure itself although it may not be within the range of conscious awareness.

A problem, on the other hand, is something of which the individual *is* aware and for which he has no immediate solution. Without awareness there is no problem. But the individual may not link a felt problem with a basic need. His problem is that he hates his job, but he may or may not see the relationship between this and his need for social acceptance. If he were socially more secure, the job might be less humiliating. A student is in financial difficulty because he is spending too freely on his acquaintances. This is again the result of his need for acceptance by his peers, a need which is not being satisfied by his mere existence among them. A problem is the outward expression or result of a need. It could be classified as a symptom of some unmet need. If dealt with directly, the results may be only superficial.

There is a current trend therefore toward speaking of needs, a positive concept, rather than of problems which connote a maladjustment and which is essentially negative. We are concerned with the meeting of student *needs,* therefore, and with the contribution of personnel services to meet or satisfy these needs.

> C. Gilbert Wrenn, *Student Personnel Work in College.* New York: The Ronald Press Company, 1951, pp. 13-14.

30. Guidance Is for the Many as Well as for the Few

So it is not surprising that our American civilization is beginning to develop a large number of agencies whose chief purpose it is to *orient* the individual, as he moves among some dozen other institutions whose function it is to teach him, cure him, or correct him, or merely hire him for a money wage. Each of the institutions which yesterday thought of their functions as simple and clear—whether it was to produce glass bottles, or teach arithmetic, or develop swimming skill, or prepare for Heaven—now has this supplementary function of orientation—of the employee who is a puzzled person as well as machine operator, of the child who must learn its social role as well as long division, of the camper whose swimming skill is only one count in the long battle for recognition in the group or freedom from adult surveillance, and of the parishioner who may be anxious enough to serve his God, but is often very unsure whether moving to California or Panama will or will not increase his ability to do so. Each considerable part of the individual life, as student or worker, member of the community or member of a church, is beginning to be seen as a phase of development in which it is possible to give such a wrong emphasis that the whole later pattern of life may be distorted or an opportunity missed to correct some past distortion.

As each familiar situation comes to be seen as a part of life in which significant whole choices—not merely choices of one major subject or another, a commercial course or a general course—are made, we are increasingly seeing guidance, or orientation, as something which everyone needs—as they need food, sleep, education, recreation, and employment. Just as it is no longer invidious to draw one's water from the city supply, and the old distinctions between those with water works of their own and those who drank from the village pump have disappeared and all depend upon a common pure city water supply, so any old ideas that guidance was for the weak, or the stupid, the problem child, the square peg in the round hole are also disappearing. As travelers on a public carrier feel it their right to know at what times bus or train will start, when it will arrive and what is the fare to be paid, so travelers through our modern society are coming to feel that they too are in need of schedules and time tables and every possible device to help them find their way, board the right train, change at the right junction, recognize their stop when they reach it. Those who travel furthermost and oftenest use these devices most. Such devices have become aids to the gifted as well as crutches for the crippled, a common need of all in a changing world.

Rosalind Cassidy and Hilda C. Kozman, *Counseling Girls in a Changing Society.* New York: McGraw-Hill Book Company, Inc., 1947, pp. xvi-xvii. By permission of the publishers.

2.

Types of Problems

---

31. NEEDS IN THE COMMON AREAS OF LIVING

Through all varieties of problems encountered by individuals in common areas of living there run certain types of universal need which can be translated into the chief forms of guidance service to be rendered:

1. The need for *adjustment* in academic, personal, vocational, or avocational problem-situations, requiring professional, individualized aid in making immediate and suitable adjustments at "problem points."

2. The need for *orientation* toward life objectives in problems of career planning, educational programming, and direction toward long-term personal aims and values, requiring professional help in evaluating factors involved in future action.

3. The need for *development* of personal effectiveness and power of self-direction, requiring professional assistance in achieving self-insight and control, and in discovering and undergoing educational experiences essential to personal growth.

> Robert H. Mathewson, *Guidance Policy and Practice.* New York: Harper and Brothers, 1949, p. 45.

32. PROBLEMS LISTED BY YOUTH IN A NATIONAL SURVEY

PHYSICAL PROBLEMS

52%	I want to gain (or lose) weight
24	I'm concerned about improving my figure
37	I want to improve my posture and body build

13   I get tired easily
15   I don't get enough sleep
16   My teeth need attention
12   I have frequent headaches
33   I want to get rid of pimples

SCHOOL PROBLEMS

54%   I wish I knew how to study better
53   I have difficulty keeping my mind on my studies
21   I don't know how to prepare for tests
20   I have too much homework
38   I have difficulty in expressing myself in writing
41   I have difficulty expressing myself in words
40   I would like to know more definitely how I am doing in
      school work

SOCIAL PROBLEMS

54%   They want people to like them more
33   Wish they could converse better
23   Don't know how to act toward people they dislike
42   Wish they were more popular
60   Want to make new friends
36   Want to develop more self-confidence
25   They feel ill at ease at social affairs
32   Want to learn how to dance
21   Want to feel important to society or to their own group
23   They can't live up to the ideals that are set for them

DATING PROBLEMS

Dating problems of boys

41%   I don't have a girl friend
34   I'm bashful about asking girls for dates
23   Is it all right to go places stag?
17   What are good manners on a date?

Dating problems of girls

30%   I don't have a boy friend
23   I'm not popular with boys
36   I don't know how to refuse a date
20   Is it all right to kiss my date the first time we go out?
29   Is it all right to accept "blind dates"?

PERSONAL PROBLEMS

23%	I'm easily excited
33	I have trouble keeping my temper
35	I worry about little things
27	I'm nervous
35	I can't help daydreaming
26	I feel guilty about things I've done
29	My feelings are easily hurt
25	I need to learn not to let people push me around
41	I often do things I later regret
29	I feel I must always be on the go
23	I'm unsure of myself
29	I want to get rid of an undesirable habit

VOCATIONAL PROBLEMS

42%	Want to know what their real interests are
43	Are wondering what career to follow
56	Want to know what kind of work they are best suited for
40	Ask "How much ability do I really have?"
29	Want to know what kind of training different vocations require
27	Wonder what fields are overcrowded

H. H. Remmers and C. G. Hackett, *Let's Listen to Youth.*
Chicago: Science Research Associates, 1950, pp. 30, 32, and
38. (From a nation-wide survey of 18,000 high school
students.)

33. THE PROBLEMS OF YOUTH IN THE Y.M.C.A.

The obvious well-spring of information in the field of
"youth's problems today" is the recent "Grass-Roots Inquiry."
This continent-wide consultation involved more than 10,000
young people and leaders of Y.M.C.A.'s in an attempt to discover the chief problems of young people. *Faith for the Future*
(by Charles Noble and published by Association Press) is
based on the results of this inquiry. . . . The fundamental
problems are focused in eight areas:

1. War and military service
2. Educational and vocational choices
3. Racial, religious, and political differences
4. Proper use of leisure time

5. Mature personality development
6. Moral standards
7. Sex education and preparation for marriage
8. A strong faith in God

> Philip G. Swartz, "Counseling in a Smaller Y.M.C.A.," *Counseling,* April, 1951, p. 1.

34. SOME FINDINGS FROM THE ROSS STUDY

Another recent study of great significance is revealed in *Religious Beliefs of Youth* by Murray G. Ross (Association Press). One part of this survey indicated that "the desire to move up the vocational ladder, to have economic security, to have a fine family and a nice home, and to enjoy the respect of the community is a goal of almost all the youth studied." This same source also points out that "almost three-quarters of the nearly 2,000 young people . . . who responded . . . do not feel their individual lives are very important in the larger scheme of things." The findings of this study suggest that these young people are "clinging to religious concepts which provide little in the way of focus or direction in their lives." Although this is indeed a serious condition, an even more startling conclusion is offered by Mr. Ross when he warns that the group is generally suffering from "a kind of paralysis which prevents them from working through these concepts to find a meaningful and obligating philosophy of life." This latter deficiency makes it almost impossible for the individual to realize fully his potentialities.

> *Ibid.,* p. 1.

35. KINDS OF HELP GIVEN BY FAMILY AGENCIES

Proportion of 30,767 cases in 40 agencies given casework consideration in relation to various categories of problems: Family relations, 48.0 per cent; Economic, 39.1 per cent; Personality adjustment, 25.0 per cent; Physical illness, 22.6 per cent; Mental illness, 7.8 per cent; Educational and vocational guidance, 5.0 per cent; Employment, 16.9 per cent.

> *Highlights,* November, 1950, p. 132. Published by Family Service Association of America, 192 Lexington Ave., New York, N. Y.

36. NORMAL PROBLEMS AMONG COLLEGE MEN

The kinds of problems varied greatly according to individual situations. Most of them centered around social or family relationships. Many men revealed multiple interconnected problems such as personality difficulties, adjustment to family and friends, college finances, and career. Others revealed only isolated problems in a setting of very sound personality. Any classification of problems is somewhat artificial. In Table II, however, are illustrated the types of issues raised, grouped according to certain areas which seemed important.

TABLE II

KINDS OF PROBLEMS RAISED

(Including both self-offered problems and those recognized by the staff.)

Number of Participants

1. Social adjustment (shyness, feelings of inferiority, social sensitivity, making friends, meeting and getting along with girls, immaturity per se, roommates, class dissatisfactions) 113
2. Adjustments to family
   a. Parental discord, separation, divorce, remarriage.... 14
   b. Antagonism to parents, reaction to domination or discipline, family criticism, lack of understanding, family relations in general.............................. 69
   c. Advice concerning physical or mental health of parent 18
   d. Adjustment to death of parent..................... 6
3. Career and life work............................... 67
4. Finances in college................................ 35
5. Need for discussions centering around subject's personality
   a. Emotional instability, tenseness, excitability, fears and concerns, "psychoneurotic" symptoms.............. 50
   b. Discussions of personality in general, integration of personality, handling of arrogance and egotism...... 47
   c. Need for directions, objectives, purpose, and values.. 32
   d. Mood swings 21
   e. Rigidity, "just-so" personality.................... 12
   f. Possible mental illness........................... 6
6. Academic
   a. Adjustment to Harvard, dissatisfactions with Harvard 20
   b. Academic help needed, organization of time and work 14

Number of
Participants

  c. Intellectual lacks for college or career............. 6
  d. Field of concentration (majoring).............. 3
7. Sex
  a. Marriage, love affairs, sex relations.............. 39
  b. Problems arising from masturbation.............. 17
  c. Need for information concerning homosexuality..... 3
  d. Information about venereal disease............... 2
8. Others
  a. Anti-Semitism, Anti-Nazism 8
  b. Religious conflict, search for religious belief........ 8
  c. Alcohol 7
  d. College scrapes 6
  e. General advice needed......................... 6
  f. Help in getting job........................... 5
  g. Stammering, speech 4
  h. Insomnia 3
  i. Handwriting 2
  j. Extracurricular activities 2
  k. Revolt against New England..................... 2
  l. Extreme wealth 1

C. W. Heath and L. W. Gregory, "Problems of Normal College Students and Their Families," *School and Society,* May 18, 1946, p. 356.

37.   Mooney's List of Problem Areas

The Mooney Classification:
  1. Health and Physical Development
  2. Finances, Living Conditions, and Employment
  3. Social and Recreational Activities
  4. Social-Psychological Relations
  5. Personal-Psychological Relations
  6. Courtship, Sex, and Marriage
  7. Home and Family
  8. Morals and Religion
  9. Adjustment to College Work
 10. The Future: Vocational and Educational
 11. Curriculum and Teaching Procedures

Ross L. Mooney, *Mooney Problem Check List.* Bureau of Educational Research, Ohio State University, Columbus, Ohio. Published by the Psychological Corporation, New York, 1950.

38. PROBLEM AREAS FOR HIGH SCHOOL AND COLLEGE GIRLS

Although these persistent problems of living are completely interrelated and in no way separated in the individual's experiencing, it may be helpful in this discussion to view the problem areas of high-school and college girls which define their needs as

Personal living—requiring emotional, mental, and physical health —a system of values, self-management, self-direction.

Personal-social relationships—requiring belongingness, the making and keeping of friends, skills in cooperative social relationships.

Social-civic relationships—requiring participation in group activities, self- and group government, social action.

Vocational or economic relationships—requiring goal and preparation for useful work and opportunity to use this preparation.

> Rosalind Cassidy and Hilda C. Kozman, *Counseling Girls in a Changing Society.* New York: McGraw-Hill Book Company, Inc., 1947, p. 6. By permission of the publishers.

39. PROBLEMS ACCORDING TO YOUTH THEMSELVES

Percentage of youth listing given problems:

Economic security	66.0
Educational and vocational choice	13.1
Home	9.0
Personality adjustment	3.2
Social relations	2.6
Other	5.5
Number of youth included	9,414

(Representative sampling of American Youth.)

> H. M. Bell, *Youth Tell Their Story.* Washington: American Council on Education, 1938, p. 250.

40. PROBLEMS OF ADOLESCENTS IN OUR CULTURE

Margaret Mead, working from the background of her study of Samoan culture, makes certain observations regarding the problems of adolescence in our culture. She feels that we must train our children to choose, teach them how to think, not what to think, and must present them with choices so that they will learn to weigh alternatives. The kinds of choices adolescents and youth face here which are not imposed upon them in many cultures are (1) the choice of vocation; (2) choices growing out of the gap between education of the parents and child; (3) choices of shifts to new occupations— the Negroes' migration to the North, for example; (5) choices involved in movies, stories, etc., which present short cuts to fame such as do not exist in the experience of young people as they struggle to climb upward; (6) moral choices growing out of heterogeneous standards of a complex culture.

She concludes that we pay for these choices by crime and delinquency, conflict and neuroses, and in the lack of coherent tradition. At the same time we, by very virtue of this extensive freedom of choice, offer to each person many possible ways of life, the opportunity for the development of individuality, and personal expression to a high degree. (Margaret Mead, *Coming of Age in Samoa*. New York: William Morrow and Company, Inc., 1928, chap. 14.)

> Paul H. Landis, *Adolescence and Youth*. New York: McGraw-Hill Book Company, Inc., 1947, pp. 74 and 76.

41. Ways in Which People Get "Off the Beam"

Let us attempt a rough and amateurish typology of the various ways in which human beings get "off the beam." There are, first of all, the jams due to *ignorance*. These are manifold and likely to increase in a technological civilization. But these are the counselor's delight, for they can usually be repaired with a minimum of net damage and a maximum of pedagogical satisfaction. Then, secondly, there are jams which come from *deficient judgment*. These are more difficult because they involve the emotions and orectic thinking of the counselee. Thirdly, there are the jams which are due to *undisciplined appetite*. These are still more complicated than the first two because their outward symptoms always mask some inner deterioration of the self. In the fourth place, there are the jams which result from *the clash of aggressive wills* in life's forum or marketplace. In a competitive society, a premium is often placed upon what is plainly one of the most fruitful sources of moral—and emotional—maladjustment. And such cases are exceedingly difficult, for what is desired by the person counseled is a first-aid job, or at least, a rationalization and defense. Jams of the fifth type are due to the fundamental aberrations: (1) evasion of reality; (2) hypersensitivity to rejection; (3) what the medieval moralists called *accidie* (a sour mixture of irritable slothfulness and prideful despair). These latter, by the way, are the typical sins of cheerless respectability.

Notice that in this list there is a common factor, which increases in intensity in rough proportion to the complexity of maladjusted situation. This constant can be identified if one observes that human tragedy is compounded, not by outer circumstances but by *inner estrangement,* alienation from self, one's fellows and from God. Both the biblical myths and modern psychological metaphors agree that this feeling of alienation is the clue to the human predicament.

> Albert C. Outler, *A Christian Context for Counseling.* An Edward W. Hazen Foundation pamphlet, Series III, No. 18, New Haven, Conn., 1945, pp. 8-9.

42. PROBLEMS DEFY CLASSIFICATION

. . Each one of our hundreds of subjects had unique problems and in each case they were complicated by problems raised by home and community conditions, health, parental attitudes, evidence of differential achievement levels, inadequate school offerings, and the many other factors which made each of these even more complex. No two subjects were alike, regardless of the fact that they could be placed under the headings which are currently used in the classification of cases in guidance textbooks. Indeed very few of the problems were simple enough to use the simplest classifications with any degree of validity. Usually there were so many complications that multiple implications and effects could be observed.

As our subjects increased in age their problems frequently changed and increased in number. Occasionally the solution of one problem brought others to solve. The student who, as the result of efforts by the counselors and teachers, had found that school work could be challenging was now faced with the problem of securing financial support for higher education —something which had not caused him any concern up to that time. The youth who had withdrawn from other students, and who had responded to our efforts to help him to overcome his fear of others, became a new problem when his enthusiasm for group activities resulted in neglect of school assignments that were to be done alone. Changes in home situations such as those caused by the failure of a father's business, changes in health conditions, development of a new interest, and countless other factors, brought new problems so frequently that a case could never be closed. Finally, of course, there was the problem of the decision which all our subjects were required to make regardless of their original status—the decision concerning the choice of vocation, or the making of a plan for further education. (Reference then made to ten case studies which are then outlined.)

> John W. M. Rothney and Bert A. Roens, *Guidance of American Youth*. Cambridge: Harvard University Press, 1950, pp. 4-5.

3.

The Opportunity

---

43.   COUNSELING—A NORMAL PART OF ONE'S WORK

The teacher, minister, or other educational leader who would be effective must take steps to include the function of counseling as a normal part of his work. He can accomplish this end in several ways. His contacts with individuals in his work with groups, small and large, can establish confidence that he is a sympathetic, helpful and trustworthy individual. He has the opportunity to observe conduct and to sense personality difficulties in their earlier stages, particularly among children and adolescents. His work makes it natural for him to take the initiative in consultations with such persons on various aspects of the program and of the individual's relation to it, and he can often help with personality difficulties if he conducts these conferences with due attention to the emotional problems involved. He can in public utterance discuss the problems of childhood, adolescence, and adult life in such a way that people come to have confidence that he understands them and could give helpful counsel. The most significant opportunities for such counseling arise in connection with important events in the life of the individual or of the family. He can make it clear that he is willing to talk with individuals in regard to such crucial experiences as the transition at birth, going to school, choosing vocation and mate, making marriage adjustments, preparing for children, adjusting to middle life and old age. He should arrange his office or study in such a way that he is easily and privately available. It is recognized particularly in the case of the minister that he may call on people at times of crisis, and in such circumstances the one who is alert often has exceptional opportunities for personal counsel. In brief, the person uses his contacts with individuals and groups to establish a reputation for his willingness and his ability to counsel.

> Harrison Sacket Elliott and Grace Loucks Elliott, *Solving Personal Problems*. New York: Henry Holt and Company, Inc., 1936, pp. 213-14. By permission of the publishers.

44. WHERE GUIDANCE MAY FUNCTION

The guidance function may be directly achieved by:

1. Dispensing wholesome information about (a) healthful living; (b) educational possibilities; (c) social living; (d) vocational possibilities; and (e) ethical principles.
2. Rendering help with (a) the problems of individuals that are encountered in the normal program activities; and (b) particular emotional and behavior problems.
3. Giving attention to (a) cooperative relations with home, school, and other agencies; (b) resources in vocational placement organizations, child guidance clinics, and mental hygiene associations.

> John W. Fuhrer, "The Administrator and the Guidance Program," *George Williams College Bulletin*, January 15, 1947, p. 3.

45. THE OPPORTUNITIES OF THE PASTOR IN COUNSELING

The pastor calls on a woman of fifty who has just lost her husband. She is somewhat dazed, hurt, grief-stricken. She finds it very difficult to talk, yet she wants to talk. The pastor senses her suffering; he wants to help her. Furthermore, religion is supposed to have an answer for such situations. But the pastor may feel utterly helpless and inadequate. What can one say that really helps in such situations?

The pastor calls at a bedside in a hospital. Previously he has learned from the doctor that the operation was successful, and that the patient should recover in routine fashion. But he finds a woman filled with anxiety and bitterness. She is full of complaints. Why does life have to deal so with her? Why does God permit such experiences? The pastor may feel that he has to answer her questions. But can he? To be sure, he can give intellectual formulations. But can he answer the deeper, vital issues in her life out of which the questions grow? And do his intellectual answers really satisfy; do they bring healing? How can he help her?

A young man calls on the pastor. He is thinking of getting married. In fact he is sure he wants to get married. But he cannot make up his mind between Mary and Jane. It isn't the first time he has been in such a quandary. Two years before another girl broke her engagement to him. He was sure he loved her; now he is almost as sure that he did not love her. Can the pastor help him, he asks?

> Carroll A. Wise, *Pastoral Counseling, Its Theory and Practice.* New York: Harper and Brothers, 1951, pp. 1-2.

46. A GROUP WORKER SENSES NEEDS

1. When the member is confused as to the activity in which he should participate
2. When an individual is rarely seen playing with others
3. When an individual is having difficulties with his leaders
4. When a boy is moody
5. When a boy damages property
6. When an individual shows signs of wanting some one with whom to talk
7. When an individual has a handicap and shows its effect
8. When an individual must be aroused to a problem of which he is unaware

> Reported by a Boys' Club worker-in-training to the editor in 1940.

47. OPPORTUNITIES FOR GUIDANCE ON THE JOB

1. With a young man graduating from high school considering going on to college or to a job
2. With a young man interested in opportunities for a career in physical education
3. With a young man who seeks help in writing a letter to an employer
4. Discussion with a man who needs aid on weight reduction in acceptable way
5. Discussion of question of kind of exercise to take with a member just recovering from an illness

6. Problem of result of a blood test showing positive Wassermann. How to break the news to the man?

    Reported by a Y.M.C.A. physical director-in-training to the editor in 1940.

48.   OPPORTUNITIES REPORTED BY A CHURCH WORKER

1. Sixteen-year-old girl is shy, timid and a poor mixer. She is attractive and of good intelligence. Seems to be well liked by members of the group.
2. An eighteen-year-old boy is loud, not very courteous, aggressive, and almost always attempts to be the life of the party.

    Reported by a group worker-in-training to the editor in 1940.

49.   NEEDS EMERGE IN NORMAL AGENCY CONTACTS

1. Enlisting new members
2. Interviewing new members
3. Assimilating new members
4. Enlisting committeemen
5. Committee, board meetings
6. Coaching committeemen
7. Enlisting leaders for group activities
8. Coaching leaders for group activities
9. Employing secretaries
10. Employing clerical and janitorial staff
11. Discharging people
12. Conferring with staff, coaching staff members, maintaining relations with staff
13. Discovering interests of members
14. Discovering peculiarities of members in activities
15. Following up interests of members
16. Giving physical examinations
17. Discussing problems revealed by physical examinations
18. Prescribing exercise
19. Giving individual instruction
20. Giving psychological tests
21. Discussing psychological test results with applicant
22. Observing behavior of member
23. Holding religious interviews
24. Discussing church membership with members
25. Giving sex information
26. Lending money
27. Extending credit
28. Pacifying folks
29. Finding jobs for men
30. Giving vocational counsel

Guidance Survey in Y.M.C.A., an undated report, *circa* 1934.

50. THERE ARE SOME UNUSUALLY FINE OPPORTUNITIES

Opportunities for guidance present themselves wherever there are people—alone or in groups. Certain operations or activities seem to offer an especially fine chance for guidance practice. Included in these are:

1. The admission and assimilation processes in an agency, school or church
2. The physical examination
3. The testing program
4. Disciplinary situations
5. Individual contacts around programs of all kinds
6. Projects or joint activities in camping, hiking, educational trips, picnics, etc.

From the editor's class lecture.

51. PHYSICAL EDUCATION INSTRUCTORS SEE EVIDENCE OF NEED BELOW THE SURFACE

In a physical education class, where student was a leader of a small group of persistent "trouble makers"; and by the frequent writing of obscene notes, left intentionally, where they would be found . . . Through the girl's constant worry and inquiries about her physical education grades, and demands for the teacher's attention and help in class . . . In a regular individual interview held with all members of a health class . . . In a voluntary conference with the instructor of a health class, following a class discussion of boy-girl relation . . . Through student's refusal to dress in a gymnasium outfit for her physical education class . . . Through a rude remark to the physical education teacher which caused derogatory remarks by other students regarding the girl . . . Through the boy's repeated attempts to avoid choosing a partner in a coeducational social dancing class . . . Through contact with the boy on the football and basketball teams . . . Because of the boy's failure to ask girls to dance in a social dancing class . . . Through repeated "cuts" in physical education and through the teacher's observation of the boy's behavior in class . . . Through the attempt of the physical education staff to arrange a program for the boy which would minimize his handicap and help him to become better adjusted emotionally.

Margaret Leonard *et al.*, "A Project Study of Mental Hygiene," *The Journal of Health and Physical Education*, February, 1942, pp. 76-77, and 117.

52.   INCIDENTAL GUIDANCE SERVICES OF THE TEACHER

The guidance services of teachers must not necessarily be performed in a special period; they may be performed incidentally as a part of the regular work of the teacher. These services must be rendered when they are needed. Preparation for meeting guidance needs of pupils may be made in practically every phase of the school program. They may be made as the teacher assumes the role of instructor in the classroom, as he directs extra-curricular activities, as he assumes responsibility for managing the home room, and as he engages in other duties about the school.

M. L. Goetting, *Teaching in The Secondary School.* New York: Prentice-Hall, Inc., 1942, p. 440. By permission of the publishers.

53.   OPPORTUNITIES ARISE IN THE DAILY ROUTINE

In their counseling role, teachers cover a wide range of contacts, from short, casual conversations to a long series of interviews. These face-to-face contacts grow out of classroom guidance. By showing consideration, recognition of good qualities, and interest, the teacher-counselor gradually builds a good relationship with students out of which a readiness for counseling arises. Instead of having to gain rapport in an interview, as the counselor isolated in a personal office does, the teacher-counselor continues the good relationship he has established in classroom, laboratory, shop, or playground.

Ruth Strang, *The Role of the Teacher in Personnel Work* (Revised). New York: Bureau of Publications, Teachers College, Columbia University, 1946, p. 318.

54.   "NORMAL" PEOPLE ALSO HAVE NEEDS

Counseling Leading to Self-Discovery. Too frequently counselors spend most of their time with students who make trouble and leave the others to take care of themselves. This should not be. The following is an example of a "normal" case—a boy who was unlikely to make trouble for other people because he was so passive. The boy presented no obvious symptoms but came to the counselor of his own accord. He said he wanted "vocational testing," but in back of this request was a desire to map out his life, to get a blueprint or a design for living . . . .

Ibid., pp. 267-68.

55. OPPORTUNITIES ARISE AT BOTH ENRICHMENT AND AT CURATIVE LEVELS

There are two main types of counseling opportunities—(1) those in which every student is helped to develop in his own best way and (2) those in which individuals are helped in some crisis or difficulty. In the first situation counselor and student explore, appraise, and plan. In the second situation they direct their attention to the particular choice to be made or the problem or difficulty to be solved. Included under the second heading are emotional difficulties, problems of boy-girl relationships, family relationships, health, so-called discipline problems, failure in one or more subjects, choice of course and further education, and choice and preparation for a vocation.

Ibid., p. 266.

Part II

THE MEANING OF GUIDANCE

4.

Some Definitions of Guidance

56. Baxter

. . Although definite terms may vary to some extent, it is probably agreed that guidance is intended to *help the child to help himself.*

> Edna D. Baxter, "What Is Guidance?" *Childhood Education.* Association for Childhood Education, Vol. 25, January, 1949, p. 202.

57. Finch and Yowell

The term "guidance" is used to refer to all those services rendered to the individual for the purpose of helping him develop the ability to (a) establish suitable goals for himself and (b) discover and organize the means by which these goals can be reached. More simply, guidance may be looked upon as services provided to help the individual develop the ability to make suitable plans for his own activities.

> F. H. Finch and Velma Yowell, "Guidance for the Exceptional Child," *The Education of Exceptional Children.* The Forty-ninth Yearbook of the National Society for the Study of Education, Part II. Chicago: The University of Chicago Press, 1950, chap. 5, p. 83. By permission of the Society.

58. Williamson and Foley

Counseling has been defined as a face-to-face situation in which, by reason of training, skill, or confidence vested in him by the other, one person helps the second person to face, perceive, clarify, solve, and resolve adjustment problems . . . it rather includes all efforts on the part of both counselor and client to face, clarify, and solve problems. In short, then, counseling is a process which aids an individual to progress in personality growth and integration.

> E. G. Williamson and J. D. Foley, *Counseling and Discipline.* New York: McGraw-Hill Book Company, Inc., 1949, p. 192.

59. MATHEWSON

. . in a broader sense, however, counseling may be thought of as any mode of professional aid extended to the individual through verbal educative means by which the individual is enabled to make improved adjustments and to pursue his individual development more effectively (p. 208).

Guidance . . . has come to be defined as the systematic, professional process of aiding individuals in making their choices, plans, and adjustments; in undertaking effective self-direction; and in meeting those problems of personal living that fall within the sphere of educational responsibility (p. 118).

Guidance and personnel service in education then becomes a phase of the whole educational process of improving the individual's power of adjustment, development, and effective purposing so that he will become more capable of harmonious and creative living. This view is not one of pure individualism; it perceives the person as self-reliant and self-possessed yet socially sensitive and cooperative (p. 119).

> Robert H. Mathewson, *Guidance Policy and Practice.* New York: Harper and Brothers, 1949, pp. 208, 118, and 119.

60. DONAHUE

. . Guidance . . . is the process of assisting an individual to develop insight and ability to adjust to successive events in his life through the appraisal of his capacities, aptitudes, and interests; the understanding of his motivations, emotional reactions, and compensatory behavior; the appreciation of the origin of his attitudes and values and their relationships to the cultural milieu such that he may attain a degree of personality integration permitting the most effective use of his potentialities and the greatest contribution to the society in which he lives.

Wilma T. Donahue, Clyde H. Coombs, and Robert M. W. Travers, editors, *The Measurement of Student Adjustment and Achievement.* Ann Arbor: University of Michigan Press, 1949, p. 73. (From chapter by Wilma T. Donahue.)

61. ZERFOSS

Guidance represents a point of view and method which seek to understand the individual as an unique personality and to aid him to understand himself, and to provide resources and experiences which will contribute most effectively to his total growth. Its purpose is to aid persons to meet more adequately their problems and relationships of life, in such a way that they may attain the greatest degree of self-realization consistent with the common good. Counseling at its best seeks, as it progresses, to enable the individual to become more and more an independently on-going person.

From editor's lecture notes.

62. KOPAS

Guidance is the formally organized effort of an institution set up primarily for the purpose of

A. Helping the individual to
1. Better understand himself and more clearly see his needs, both personal and social.
2. Become more fully aware of the available opportunities for participation.
3. Formulate more effective programs of participation, and
4. More effectively evaluate the results and implications of the reconstructed experience.

B. Helping the group leader to
1. Better understand the individual, his outlook on life, needs, desires, and plans.
2. Become more fully aware of the total influence on his development the "Y" and the more immediate environment have exerted and are exerting.
3. More effectively utilize the club-room experience for promoting in individuals growth in self-direction.

J. S. Kopas, "Six Aspects of Guidance," *A Primer of Guid-*

ance Through Group Work. New York: Association Press, 1940, p. 31.

63. JONES AND HAND

The Meaning of Guidance: Guidance is coming to be regarded as that inseparable aspect of the educational process that is peculiarly concerned with helping individuals discover their needs, assess their potentialities, develop their life purposes, formulate plans of action in the service of these purposes, and proceed to their realization.

> Arthur J. Jones and Harold C. Hand, "Guidance and Purposive Living," *Guidance in Educational Institutions.* Thirty-seventh Yearbook of the National Society for the Study of Education, Part I. Chicago: University of Chicago Press, 1938, chap. 1, pp. 24-25. By permission of the Society.

64. THE INDIVIDUAL AT THE CENTER

. . So, in the long run, individualized education consists of an intellectual and philosophical approach to a basic human problem: interest in, respect for, and assistance to unique personalities.

> Ben D. Wood and Ralph Haefner, *Measuring and Guiding Individual Growth.* New York: Silver Burdett Company, 1948, p. 523.

65. EDUCATION AS GUIDANCE

Let it be reiterated, then, that pupil personnel service is an interim service, brought into the picture to serve pupils and to teach educators they are dealing with individual personalities rather than numbers or names in a roll book. Furthermore, when educators realize that this service is essential in any adequate educational program, the term itself may become obsolete, may drop out of the vocabulary, leaving only the comprehensive term, education. When that happens, education will take its place as an institution of dignity and real effectiveness. Before this happens, however, our educational leaders must learn to look at every pupil as an individual with possibilities and limitations, with intelligence and emotions, with aptitude or ineptitude in one or more directions, with physical characteristics to which the school must give as careful attention as the farmer gives to those of cattle, corn, or chrysanthemums.

> Frank G. Davis, "Pupil Personnel Service in the Public Schools," *Education,* April, 1950, p. 514.

66. GUIDANCE AND EDUCATION MEET

Mental hygiene is really an attitude or point of view which is reflected in all the activities of the school. It strives to attain precisely the same goals that sound education seeks—continuous sturdy growth leading to wholesome personality orientation.

> Paul A. Witty and Charles E. Skinner, editors, *Mental Hygiene in Modern Education.* New York: Rinehart and Company, Inc., 1939, p. 9.

67. GUIDANCE AND EDUCATION CLOSELY RELATED

It [education] is that reconstruction or reorganization of experience which adds to the meaning of experience, and which increases ability to direct the course of subsequent experience.

> John Dewey, *Democracy and Education.* New York: The Macmillan Company, 1920, pp. 89-90.

68. GUIDANCE EPITOMIZES OUR DEMOCRATIC PHILOSOPHY

The point will bear repeating that guidance as defined by those who approach the problem rationally implies first of all recognition and understanding of the individual and creation of conditions that will enable each individual to develop his fullest capacities and ultimately to achieve the maximum possible self-guidance and security both economically and socially. This concept of guidance epitomizes our democratic philosophy. It is as enduring as democracy itself, for basically it is democracy applied to the life of the school.

> A. E. Traxler, *Techniques of Guidance.* New York: Harper and Brothers, 1945, p. 13.

69. NATURE AND MEANING OF MODERN GUIDANCE

Modern education is concerned with the balanced development of all phases of personality, including such emotional control and attitudinal growth as will free the energies of learners from self-concern and will harness their minds and their hands to socially desirable goals. Guidance seeks to individualize education, to arouse a point of view and to provide procedures whereby *each* student will grow in the directions planned for *all.* Guidance is not an activity which differs from education; it is an emphasis in education. Guidance workers are convinced that:

1. Each child is a unique and distinct personality.
2. In a democracy each person is a value.
3. Personality grows through the purposive striving of each individual, through the give and take of individual and environment.
4. Schools must discover and meet the needs of each pupil.
5. It is possible to combine group instruction with satisfactory provision for the personality needs of each individual.
6. Effective guidance demands the cooperative participation of teachers, administrators, and specialists.
7. Effective guidance must make use of all known scientific knowledge about personality and its growth.
8. Effective guidance must be well represented in the budget of a school.

WHAT DO WE MEAN BY GUIDANCE?

Guidance means realizing that each pupil is an individual, not just one of thirty-six pupils in a geometry class. Here is Johnny who can't see the board because he is nearsighted. Here is Susan who can't keep attentive because she is deaf. Here is Tony who had a fight with his brother before he came to school. Here is Willie whose mother scolded him last night and he didn't sleep well. Here is Homer who has never done well in arithmetic, but whose father always wanted to be an engineer. Each pupil is a distinct personality which we must learn to know.

Guidance means accepting each pupil as an independent personality. Perhaps Richard would be a better boy if he were a better performer; he would pass his finals if he were not a nervous overactive child. The teacher must remember that Richard can't be made into a new boy overnight; it takes time to change his personality. The teacher must also remember that to expect a child to act constantly like someone else is to reject his views. Acceptance means taking a child as he is with the firm knowledge that the feeling of being wanted is one of the ways that a child will grow into more desirable patterns of personality.

Guidance means arranging the school environment in the interest of the individual student. Wesley must take a heavy load in order to avoid habits of idleness, and Bob must go to another class for reading instruction. Mary must be coaxed into social activities programs to help overcome her timidity, and Helen must be restrained from overactivity on account of her health.

Guidance means making a systematic study of individuals who deviate from the average. Warm and friendly acceptance of the pupils in class is essential to guidance but is not in itself enough. Teachers in schools must use all the tools of their profession to appraise every aspect of the child's personality, to pry into all the factors that might lead to his improvement. Here was Earl who was well liked by his teachers and by his classmates, who got along well, but somehow reached the tenth grade without actually learning how to read. Harold was labeled a "psychiatric case" and allowed to drift along because he would not re-read books he had read as a child. Good will and enthusiasm must be supplemented by all available scientific tools.

Guidance means helping the individual student to understand himself and to modify his ways of adjusting. Joe has suffered all his life from the fear of stuttering in public. He has avoided all classes in which he might be called upon to make a report. This has gone on throughout his years in junior and senior high school, and into his second year of college. Joe was convinced that he had a speech impediment, and that there was nothing he could do about it but avoid speaking situations. After three weeks of private tutoring, Joe's "handicap" disappeared almost completely and the great burden of the defect which he had sought to conceal dropped from his life. Roger has failed two classes but is still well satisfied with his own abilities and convinced that he has failed because of poor teaching. He must be led to feel that learning is a responsibility of the learner, and that evasion of learning is an escape which will prove costly.

In the long run, guidance cannot improve personalities. It can only help personalities to improve themselves.

Guidance means helping each pupil learn to live as a cooperating member of a family, and of a community. Janet left home and voluntarily sought admission to the detention home because her mother made her cook dinner and wash dishes. Janet must be led to realize that her mother who works all day is also a personality, with her own problems, and with the need for a relaxing and friendly home, that home duties are part of the responsibility of each person, and are also a part of the fun in home living. Alex would not continue his course after a midterm examination because he was convinced that every other member of the class had cheated. He shows the rather frequent attitude of the insecure personality, who finds relief in establishing himself as morally superior to his associates. Teachers and counselors must work with Alex on his sense of values, but more than this, they must help him discover the source of his frustration and the security and joy that come from the attitude of helping and loving other personalities in his group instead of criticizing and condemning them.

Guidance means helping each pupil learn to make the best use of his physical equipment. Warren, a severely disabled spastic child, cockily asserts that no person has physical limitations to his activity. He must be led to accept the realistic judgment that physical capacities are relative and that piano playing is open to him as a hobby but not as a profession. Marie, who is pushing herself into the personality pattern of her attractive and popular friends, must be helped to develop the quiet elegance of her more restrained charm rather than affect the posture, dress, speech, and activities of her friends.

Guidance means helping each pupil make a realistic choice of career. Earl, who loves to tinker with automobiles and radios, must learn the differing requirements of engineering and technology. Albert, a pleasant, handsome, well-coordinated boy who loves people, must learn that it is more valuable for him to become a good barber than for him to keep on trying year after year to get the scholarship necessary for admission to the study of dentistry. Russell gave up school to work in the corner service station, but talks physics and mathematics to his teacher-customers on every possible occasion. He must be encouraged to develop the drive for returning to his engineering education.

> Harl R. Douglass, editor, *Education for Life Adjustment.*
> New York: The Ronald Press Company, 1950, pp. 314-16.
> (From chapter by J. W. McDaniel.)

70. GUIDANCE INVOLVES INSPIRING, DISCIPLINING, AND INFORMING

The baffling, subtle task of the teacher, then, is *guidance.* The child's task is to learn; the teacher's is to guide learning. And since no two children are alike—heredity different, environment different—we see now that the teacher's task is *creative* guidance. The personality that emerges can be thought of as a work of art, the parents and teachers taken together constituting a kind of generalized artist-teacher. Although the teacher, working as artist, has many responsibilities, one above all others pervades his entire work—the guidance of learning and development. To educate is to guide the on-going flow of human experience creatively. But in doing so, the teacher works as artist, not as mere skilled mechanic.

This qualification becomes emphatic when we break down the task of guiding development into its three outstanding aspects:

First: Inspiring: stimulating and energizing human beings, arousing interests and enthusiasms in them, opening vistas of feeling and thought, building attitudes of confidence.

Second: Disciplining: leading young people to manage themselves, building habits of self-appraisal and self-control, creating attitudes of searching self-criticism—in short, developing a person of *disciplined initiative.*

Third: Informing: surrounding children and youth with the sources of the world's best knowledge, gathering and organizing man's most sensitive literary statements; providing access to the materials and discoveries of the natural and physical sciences, opening new vistas on man's knowledge of the universe, the earth and its living creatures; disciplining the use of this knowledge, developing critical attitudes of validity and reliability of the facts, practicing young people in the art of drawing conclusions.

Thus a new conception of education emerges—namely the guidance of learning and development. While the old school was based largely on the teacher's intention to teach, the new school builds on the child's intention to learn. Hence, the threefold task—inspiring learning, disciplining learning, and building the knowledge upon which learning thrives. The key question for the teacher is: What psychological findings will contribute most effectively to guiding learning, and hence to the greatest possible development?

> Lawrence E. Cole and William F. Bruce, *Educational Psychology*. New York: World Book Company, 1950, pp. 573-74.

71.   PERSONNEL WORK PERVADES WHOLE SCHOOL

Obviously personnel work is not an "extra," a fad, or a frill; it is an essential part of good education. It has always been so. Wherever and whenever teachers have been concerned with helping each individual to realize his potentialities, they have exemplified the personnel point of view and rendered guidance services. . . .

Personnel work, in some sort of spiritual way, must pervade the entire school. It ought to be like fresh air—so natural and pervasive a part of our total living that we scarcely ever bother even to talk about it.

> Ruth Strang, *The Role of the Teacher in Personnel Work* (Revised). New York: Bureau of Publications, Teachers College, Columbia University, 1946, p. 29.

72.   GUIDANCE RELATED TO EVERY ASPECT OF THE SCHOOL

Guidance is one of the most difficult of all educational subjects to discuss because there has been, and there continues to be, confusion and uncertainty concerning its nature and functions. Some authorities feel that guidance is as broad as all education and that the whole program of the school should be set up for guidance purposes, whereas others would restrict it to some relatively narrow aspect such as vocational guidance or moral guidance. Some guidance programs consist chiefly of courses in occupational information. The main emphasis in other guidance programs is on the placement of pupils in courses designed to eliminate or reduce failure. Still others stress therapy and the treatment of maladjustment as the central purpose of the counseling relationship. Not infrequently, character building is thought to be the main purpose and function of guidance. Too often, one fears, the guidance program of schools consist of little more than lip service to a nebulous concept which is useful in the publicity relations of the school but which has almost no influence on the lives of the individual pupils. . . .

Ideally conceived, guidance enables each individual to understand his abilities and interests, to develop them as well as possible, to relate them to life goals, and finally to reach a state of complete and mature self-guidance as a desirable citizen of a democratic social order. Guidance is thus vitally related to every aspect of the school—the curriculum, the methods of instruction, the supervision of instruction, disciplinary procedures, attendance, problems of scheduling, the extracurriculum, the health and physical fitness program, and home and community relations. This of course implies the closest kind of cooperation between guidance functionaries and all the other members of the staff. Although guidance is closely related to all areas of the school, those charged with responsibility for the guidance program cannot be specialists in all these fields. Their functions are to collect and systematize accurate information about pupils, to provide an individual counseling service, and to carry on a dynamic educational program among their colleagues and among the pupils and their parents that will lead to intelligent use of the information that the guidance department is able to provide.

A. E. Traxler, *Techniques of Guidance*. New York: Harper and Brothers, 1945, pp. 2-4.

73. GUIDANCE—CENTRAL OR PERIPHERAL?

While the words "guidance" and "counseling" are on the lips of many today, among laymen as well as professionals, there is no generally accepted definition of either. Perhaps such ambiguity interferes with a more adequate guidance program. I have attempted recently to discover the meaning with which these words are used by writers in several fields and agencies.

Guidance to some immediately signifies the use of special services and referrals; it is thought of as something which is added to the ongoing program of the agency in question. In this view experts are responsible for the added contribution, and centralization is the key to operation. On the other hand, there are those who think of guidance as the qualitative aspect of program or as an emphasis within it. Here guidance is the very warp and woof of education or program. This emphasis is carried out by such "generalists" as classroom teachers, YMCA secretaries, playground supervisors and similar workers. Its key is decentralization.

The problem before us is to inquire into the educational philosophy upon which various guidance plans are based, and upon the procedures which arise from such beliefs. While there are few advocates today for either complete decentralization or centralization, marked differences exist in the weight put upon these two positions. It might be possible to arrange a listing of advocates of various guidance plans in such a way as to present almost a continuum from complete (or a high degree of) decentralization to its opposite. However, the great majority of writers in this field recognize the need for some combination of the two emphases. This paper is concerned with discovering the part of the continuum upon which reliance is put for the carrying out of effective guidance. Let line D   E   C represent the total continuum (all guidance possibilities), D decentralization, and C centralization. Then the question is whether reliance is placed in the area DE or in CE and at what point therein. For example, in a guidance program in high school or college, is greatest weight placed upon the curriculum and its regular teachers, or upon special services? Are specialists in the YMCA expected to carry out an adequate guidance program, or is faith also put into the on-going work of the agency? Is trust put upon what takes place in the "side-shows," or upon what goes on in the "big tent"? *Again, it needs to be repeated that the writer is not advocating nor studying an "either—or" situation, for it is conceded almost universally that both general and special services are needed. The question at issue is just where major reliance rests for effective guidance.*

The issue raised here is fundamental to all educational methodology. It is concerned with the relation of peripheral to central processes in education. Just where is dependence for education being put? Today in education, as well as in religion, politics, health, and other areas there is great reliance placed upon special services rather than upon the heart and core of the major experiences of life in such categories. In the economic area we find it necessary to introduce various forms of charity to compensate for unwarranted inadequacies upon the part of citizens. We deplore the fact that mental illness is a most serious menace, yet we generally attempt to combat it by increasing the bed capacity of our institutions or the number of psychiatrists, rather than to seek more basic remediation.

The same issue was raised in an article by Lloyd-Jones (Esther Lloyd-Jones, "Centrifugal and Centripetal Guidance," *Teachers College Record,* October, 1949, pp. 7-13), in which she discussed centrifugal and centripetal guidance. The author seems to advocate a type of guidance program which emphasizes the desirability of using all the central forces of an institution for the development of persons, rather than relying upon an ever increasing number of specialists. The Harvard Report on general education is quoted by her as saying: "All specialism enhances the centrifugal forces in society." (Centrifugal defined by Webster as "that force which tends to impel a thing, or parts of a thing, outward from a center of rotation.") It is the entripetal process, (or, "that which is directed toward the center") which the author advocates. For such a program it is necessary for teachers, specialists, administrators, etc., to work closely together. This seems to be a plea for dependence upon central processes.

The problem here presented is illustrated in the reference to a study of 700 high school seniors in a western state where nearly twice as many reported that they turned to their family and friends as to their teachers and counselors for aid upon vocational and personal problems. *(Newsletter,* Science Research Associates, Chicago, Illinois, January, 1950.) Whether such a fact as this is an occasion for rejoicing or not, depends upon one's adherence to central process or special services for the development of youth.

Lawrence K. Frank, one of the great educators of our time, has "pinpointed" the issue with clarity and deep insight when he writes: "Specifically, I would say that there is no question about the urgent need for specialized service which will provide not only professional guidance but diagnosis and therapy for the many distorted personalities now coming to school and college. But with equal emphasis I would say that we will not be able to do much for the advancement of mental health in the schools unless and until we infuse the whole school program, content of courses, methods of teaching and the individual teacher personalities with an understanding of how they can help the child and the adolescent to grow up and achieve maturity and mental health. This is a goal that cannot be reached quickly, but we can progress in that direction more rapidly if the specialist, namely counselors, guidance experts, psychologists, psychiatrists, social workers, etc., who are concerned with individual clinical problems will recognize the overwhelming importance of helping teachers and parents to gain insight and understanding and to provide what children and youth need for mental health. Unfortunately, many specialists seem to find it necessary to impress teachers and parents with their superior knowledge and professional ability and to make parents feel that they are, of course, utterly incapable of understanding what is involved or of doing anything of significance for children and youth. . . . " (Lawrence K. Frank, Letter to Karl P. Zerfoss, October 3, 1949.)

Karl P. Zerfoss, "Guidance—Central or Peripheral?" Unpublished manuscript, 1951.

5.

The Guidance Point-of-View

---

74. THE GUIDANCE HYPOTHESIS

. . . The guidance worker, when confronted by a child with any kind of problem, takes the view that the conduct in question represents purposive activity of the child. So thinking, he is led to probe for the answers to such important questions as

1. What basic needs of this child are not being met?
2. What are the sources of frustration that are preventing adequate realization of needs?
3. What habits of adjustment has the child developed or what habits is he developing to overcome these frustrations?
4. What better means of meeting needs can be developed for this child?

> Harl R. Douglass, editor, *Education for Life Adjustment.* New York: The Ronald Press Company, 1950, p. 319. (From chapter by J. W. McDaniel.)

75. UNPREJUDICED OBJECTIVITY

The characteristic which Jung calls "unprejudiced objectivity" is a "human quality—a kind of deep self-respect for facts and events and for the person who suffers from them." Only he who can be thus objective can help another to that same sort of facing of his own life and problems. Objectivity does not mean coldness or lack of sympathy and understanding, but it does mean that one does not become involved with his own emotions in the counseling situation. The fact that he maintains an attitude of unprejudiced objectivity does not mean that the counselor has no standards of values and no criteria as to goals of growth, but that he understands that the given conduct under examination is the best the individual has been able to develop to satisfy his intrinsic needs and desires and that he recognizes that when any more adequate medium of satisfaction is discovered, the less mature or the less satisfactory will be given up. He recognizes that to fight against a symptomatic manifestation of behavior is futile except as a better way for the satisfaction of the fundamental motive is found. Such an understanding keeps intact a "psychic rapport" between the counselor and the individual needing help. Any shade of condemnation breaks this atmosphere of objectivity, necessary if help is given by one individual to another, and any manifestation of being shocked at any conduct, however reprehensible, puts up a barrier between them.

Harrison Sacket Elliott and Grace Loucks Elliott, *Solving Personal Problems*. New York: Henry Holt and Company, Inc., 1936, pp. 200-201. Used by permission of the publishers.

76. THE NATURE OF OBJECTIVITY

The ability to take into account the view of other persons, to take their roles, is fundamental to the achievement of "objective" thought. Without this ability the individual is tied down to a limited perspective. Since he has no means of making comparisons and of knowing other points of view, his own perceptions necessarily appear as absolutes. The relativity of things becomes incomprehensible. We have seen an example of this in the child's egocentrism.

Objective thought also requires, as Piaget has demonstrated, that the individual become aware of the mechanisms of his own thought. In order to discount biases, to make allowance for the uniqueness of one's own views, and to examine critically one's own conclusions, the individual must be able to make comparisons and relative judgments. This is impossible so long as there is no awareness of the existence of other possible views. The transition from childish egocentrism to objectivity is therefore also a transition from individualistic, unrealistic thought to socialized thinking.

Alfred R. Lindesmith and Anselm L. Strauss, *Social Psychology*. New York: The Dryden Press, Inc., 1949, pp. 186-87.

77. In Guidance an Adequate Frame of Reference Is Sought

. . The phrase, "personnel philosophy of education," suggests the basic task of making explicit the assumptions about the growth and development of the student so that the guidance worker may begin with a unified, consistent conception of the student as a dynamic organism functioning within a physical and social environment.

For example, the assumptions that make up the "student personnel point of view" constitute the frame of reference in light of which the personnel worker proceeds. For one thing, the broad objectives of general education illustrate such assumptions, for we say that the behavior of the student should be changed, if necessary, so that he will be an effective member of his society and will make the best possible use of his potentialities. Another cluster of propositions relates to the "needs" approach in education. We assume from data drawn from the various sciences that the student has certain purposes, that he encounters difficulties in achieving them, and that to surmount these difficulties he must develop personal resources in the form of skills, knowledge, interests, attitudes, and abilities. Another frame of reference, the concept of the student as a unitary psychobiological organism in interaction with dynamic forces in the environment, has implications for personnel practices and procedures. As a dynamic organism the student responds as a whole being to forces from within and without, yet always in terms of a unique pattern of abilities, interests, and skills. Still other propositions relate to the environment in which the individual lives. Dynamic and changing in nature, the society of the individual is composed of subcultures each one of which imposes its own limitations and opportunities upon him.

A philosophy of personnel work is made up of assumptions, hypotheses, or propositions such as these and is based on data taken from the various descriptive sciences.

Paul J. Brouwer, *Student Personnel Services in General Education*. Washington: American Council on Education, 1949, pp. 275-76. (From chapter by Charles W. Cannom.)

78.   Point of View Dictates Guidance Procedures

. . It (mental hygiene) is rather an attitude and a point of
view that should influence everything the teacher does professionally: her method of asking questions as well as her
manner when accepting answers; the procedure followed in
administering tests and that governing her supervision of playground activities; the appeals by which she stimulates the
pupil's desire to participate in classroom activities and the
measures to which she resorts to bring the unruly into line;
her attitude toward the asocial child, such as the young thief
or the bully, and that toward the unsocial pupil whose timidity
prevents him from mingling with others. Far from being a
distinct group of skills and facts, mental hygiene in the classroom takes on significance only when it is bound up so inextricably with all the teacher does that careful analysis alone
can reveal its exact influence. There is no opposition between
sound educational procedures and mental-hygiene principles;
both are concerned with the adjustment of the present child
and of the adult he will become.

> Harry N. Rivlin, *Educating for Adjustment*. New York:
> Appleton-Century-Crofts, Inc., 1936, pp. 1-2.

79.   The Personnel Worker Must Be Objective
and Realistic

So far as the psychology of the counselor is concerned, we
may summarize our view by saying that the personnel techni-
cian must remain objective and realistic. He must be a searcher
after the "truth" which seeks to learn the actual status of
individual personalities in relation to the realities of the surroundings. He must constantly attempt to build for individual
self-development, realization, and control. Freedom of individual choice and of action is a god before which he must
continually bow. He will be an interpreter and a conveyor
of information and in this respect may have influence upon
his clients, but he will qualify to any necessary extent information which he conveys, and will introduce it in such a way as
to make it serve the general purpose of client education. The
counselor's view must include both the environment and the
individual, and, in a sense, he must understand and interpret

both. To assist the client in objective evaluation of all pertinent facts to the end that the client becomes better informed and more capable of self-adjustment and development is his predominant purpose.

> Robert H. Mathewson, *Guidance Policy and Practice.* New York: Harper and Brothers, 1949, pp. 101-2.

80.   THE MORALISTIC VERSUS THE OBJECTIVE APPROACH

. . Up to the present century the prevailing attitude toward adjustive difficulties has been a *moralistic* one. . . . The gist of this attitude (the moralistic) is that the unsuccessful or unusual person is by deliberation or folly departing from expected standards of conduct. The overaggressive or conceited individual is dismissed as queer or is treated with reprimands or deprivations. The daydreaming boy is described as lazy and is lectured and punished. The fearful girl is told to "snap out of it" and that her difficulties are "only her imagination." Parents, classmates and even teachers often augment the troubles of the unadjusted by subjecting them to social ridicule. The moralistic attitude convinces the sufferer that he is inferior or blameworthy and provides further difficulties to which he must adjust. This point of view is well illustrated by the attitude of an executive who refused the services of a psychiatrist in his establishment, saying that if any of his men were maladjusted all they had to do was to use their common sense and straighten themselves out! The executive believed that if a man were sane the use of "reason" and "will power" was all that was needed; if he were not sane he should be placed in an institution.

Lecturing, punishment and even reassurance have, however, proved to be notably ineffective ways of dealing with adjustment problems. The worrier is not cured by being told that he should not worry. The shiftless individual is aided very little by preaching or retribution. What is needed for the successful treatment of these persons is a scientific understanding of human nature.

In sharp contrast to the moralistic viewpoint, the *objective or psychological attitude* places no blame or judgment upon the individual. Human behavior is the result of causes, just as physical phenomena arise inevitably from certain sufficient antecedents.

> Laurance Frederic Shaffer, *The Psychology of Adjustment.*
> Boston: Houghton Mifflin Company, 1936, pp. 7-8.

81.   THE LANGUAGE OF BEHAVIOR

When a student is not interested in school; when he is restless, inattentive, noisy; when he is lazy, careless, untidy, idle; when he shows off, acts silly, is disobedient; when he lies, cheats, steals; when he engages in masturbation or sex offenses; when he is shy, unsocial, unhappy, depressed, oversensitive, overconscientious—the teacher should ask, "Why?"

> Ruth Strang, *The Role of the Teacher in Personnel Work*
> (Revised). New York: Bureau of Publications, Teachers
> College, Columbia University, 1946, p. 114.

82.   LEARN TO UNDERSTAND NOT TO BLAME

Understanding children . . . helping children: this is not a simple business. But when you realize that, at least you know some things *not* to do:

Don't look for wonders. It took a long time to build up the problem or it took some very major event. You are entitled to a long time to help overcome it. When you hit on the right way of treating him and you follow through, and when all the teachers do, and when the whole school does, the child will improve. But it takes time.

Don't expect the child to know why he is acting the way he is. *You* can understand that there are some basic causes but the child cannot. If you forget this, all you do is talk *at* children. "Why did you hit him? Tell me. Why? Why?" And the poor youngster does not know. You waste your breath. You make him feel more uncomfortable.

But something worse: you can come to believe that he knows but he just won't tell you. He is holding out on you.

> James L. Hymes, Jr., *Teacher Listen—the Children Speak . . .*
> Philadelphia: National Mental Health Foundation, 1949, pp.
> 13-14.

83. SEEK OUT AND REMOVE CAUSES

The individualized treatment or rehabilitation of the student offender whose personality development deviates from the social norms does not ignore the seriousness of the offense nor its effect upon other students and upon the institution itself. But, . . . the main purpose of disciplinary counseling is to alleviate the cause of misbehavior so that these causes will no longer operate, so that *it will no longer be necessary for the student to offend society. The purpose is to cure and not to punish.* The student who gets into difficulties of one sort or another is treated as an individual who needs special teaching assistance, and the whole process is organized to take account of the student's assets and liabilities and thus to effect his rehabilitation within the limits of his potentialities.

> E. G. Williamson and J. D. Foley, *Counseling and Discipline.* New York: McGraw-Hill Book Company, 1949, p. 21.

84. THE SICK NEED HELP

For the counselor who accepts the assumptions of modern psychology, undesirable personality characteristics and anti-social conduct are in most cases sickness. He recognizes that there are those who are deliberately exploiting their fellows for their own advantage, and these he recognizes as the real sinners in our present social life; but these seldom come to him for help. Most people have become sick of soul as others have contracted illness of body. They need, from his point of view, not condemnation for their failures, but help in conquering their inadequacies.

> Harrison Sacket Elliott and Grace Loucks Elliott, *Solving Personal Problems.* New York: Henry Holt and Company, Inc., 1936, p. 302. By permission of the publishers.

85. MENTAL HYGIENE (?) IN THE CLASSROOM

It was Ed. Psych, and Dr. "X" talked about concepts and used texts which have been outmoded for twenty years, and never gave any indication that they weren't the latest and most authentic. He treated the class like eight-year-olds, and gave each student one question (complete with reference attached) to answer during the quarter. Called the roll daily, and gave two tests.

On the day I had to answer my question, two people were ahead of me. The first dared to disagree with the reference cited, and was roundly berated by the prof. Another boy rose to defend him, and he was really put in his place with the prof. turning purple, shouting and waving his arms. The next question was answered by a girl who was interrupted in the middle of her discussion so the prof. could direct a few more insults to the boys, and suggest strongly that they might be happier outside the classroom. It was the most disgraceful exhibition of temper that I've ever seen in any classroom, and the whole class was embarrassed and resentful. When I was called on, I read my question, "What must the teacher do to improve his own mental health?" All hell broke loose, and I was afraid to look at the professor. There was much yelling and stomping, and some clapping, and a lot of laughter. My attitude must have been as bad as that of the other two fellows, for we all got C's, though our test grades were considerably above those of people who got B's.

From the letter of a graduate student to the editor, 1948.

86. THE JUDICIAL TEMPERAMENT

They say in the Boys' Court that this judge has "the judicial temperament." When I asked what that meant they told me this story:

A few weeks ago he sentenced a young offender to a year in the House of Correction. "Thanks, you . . . ," said the boy, over his shoulder, adding a phrase that can't be printed in a family newspaper. The usual procedure in such a case would be an additional six months for contempt of court. The judge merely said, "Here! Come back!" "You think you're a tough guy, don't you?" he asked, after a full minute of quiet appraisal.

"Well, judge," said the boy, "I've never had a break in my life. My father died when I was a kid, and the first time I ever got into trouble I was sent to St. Charles. . . . "

The judge continued the case for three weeks, while the probation department made an investigation. The boy had a record, but most of the charges against him were vagrancy.

He had been all over the map. "You're going to get a break this time," said His Honor, and put him on probation for a year.

> Helen Cody Baker, "No Bad Boys? The Court Helps Prove It," Chicago *Daily News*. (Date unestablished.)

87.   No Guidance Point of View Here!

At the age of 24 I was unhappy in the work I was doing and had a feeling of insecurity and restlessness. I had been in three other jobs since graduating from college and in none of them had I found the satisfaction and pleasure that I felt should go with a job. I had gone into the business world with the feeling that a good income was the first requirement to happiness and that I, too, like many other men could soon command such an income and all the accompanying pleasure. In spite of modest success in this respect I failed to get the satisfaction I wanted and finally decided to call upon a friend of mine who held a very important position in a large national manufacturing concern. Aside from being successful financially this man was a devoted churchman and considered a fine example of the "Christian businessman." I could think of no one more qualified to look at my problems with me than this middle-aged executive.

Without an appointment I went into his office one day and was received most cordially. He offered me a chair in his office which was within easy hearing of several clerical workers in an adjoining room. I briefly outlined my position indicating to him my feeling of insecurity, of being in a job that offered no future, the sense of doing something that was not very important and in general gave him my educational background and experience.

It was a good thing that I had this few minutes at the beginning of our talk, because after that he did all the talking.

As soon as I had finished he began relating his own experiences in his climb to the top, telling of the long hours, overtime work, loyalty to the boss, and all the other qualities that are found in a Horatio Alger book. He seemed to feel that by relating his own experiences he was helping me, when as a matter of fact I was bored and left the office feeling that I had wasted a morning. Never did he attempt to understand any of the underlying causes of my dissatisfaction, nor did he ask any questions that might have thrown light on my situation. He didn't mention my skills, special abilities, home background, personality problems, educational equipment or basic interests. It never occurred to him that I was in the wrong vocation, at least he never mentioned it.

From start to finish he was strictly "old school" in his approach, emphasizing such things as "hard work," "long hours," "not watching the clock," etc. It was his opinion that anyone, if he worked hard enough and applied himself would eventually be "successful."

Within a few minutes I realized he was of no help. He gave advice but had no real insights into my problem. He attempted to sell me on his particular ideas as they related to his life but completely failed to enter into my situation.

From a report by one of the editor's students.

88. Understanding Essential in Guidance of Jack

Jack's starting point seems to be a well developed pattern. In a seemingly very friendly manner, he approaches the adult with an air of wide-eyed, innocent earnestness. He tries to charm adults in a rather seductive manner. He almost purrs when talking or he talks with a tired, whiney, very childish tone. If the adult "falls for" this much he will ask persistent and endless meaningless questions. Behind all this is a great deal of hostility in the form of taunting teasing and scorn. . . .

Fortunately, there were one or two adults at the school, one of whom was his teacher, who were not impressed, fooled or annoyed by his coyness. They treated Jack in a consistently friendly and realistic manner. They made an effort to understand his behavior and thus didn't react to it personally.

From a report by one of the editor's students.

89. The Needs of Pupils Come First

When teachers accept the guidance point of view and carry on their work with the idea of promoting the guidance services of the school, they place the needs of pupils above the demands of subject matter. They cease regarding themselves as subject matter specialists, and they cease trying to make subject matter specialists out of pupils. They do not express the needs of youth in terms of the amount of subject matter that they must master in order to be educated. On the other hand, they consider the needs of youth in terms of the life problems which youth faces. They regard the principal concern of the school in terms of the services rendered to assist youth in meeting life and in making the adjustments demanded by the problems of life. Education thus becomes life, and the chief function of the school is to help pupils make adjustments to the demands of life.

M. L. Goetting, *Teaching in the Secondary School.* New York: Prentice-Hall, Inc., 1942, p. 440. By permission of the publishers.

90. A CREED FOR TODAY

From the psychological point of view all behavior and conscious experience are effects that have their causes. This fundamental article in the psychologist's creed seems trite enough—for every event must have its cause—but the everyday view is really quite different. "I just happened to think of something," we say, or "I just happen to dislike that person," as if such psychological events had no causes. When a person's behavior is objectionable to us, we speak as if he were perverse and that was the end of the matter. The psychologist asks after the causes of the perversity—the motives, the training, the background in the individual's heredity and environment. The psychologist cannot always unravel the tangle of causes, but his creed implies a tolerant and hopeful attitude. So far as he can discover the laws of human nature, he has hope of helping the individual and eventually of bettering the developmental conditions of life so that human behavior can be stepped up to a higher level.

Robert S. Woodworth, *Psychology,* Fourth Edition. New York: Henry Holt and Company, Inc., 1940, p. 599. Used by permission of the publisher.

91. TEACHER LISTEN—THE CHILDREN SPEAK

. . Misconduct is a symptom, not an isolated phenomenon, and symptoms cannot be treated directly. Whispering may arise from an excessive need for attention as part of an egocentric maldevelopment. Boisterous and unruly conduct is frequently a symptom of compensation for inferiority. Cheating is a means of adjusting to lack of success. Truancy is usually a withdrawal from a school situation intolerable to the pupil's motives. The teacher with a psychological viewpoint can remedy some of these problems without more expert assistance by looking for the causes and seeking to remove them. There can be no set formula for treating any conduct problem. Whispering, for example, which is the most common and annoying of pupils' sins against order, may arise from many causes. If a pupil whispers to gain information about a lesson, it is justifiable and should be incorporated in school procedure. A pupil may whisper because he is idle or bored, in which case better motivated work is the remedy. He may whisper to gain the attention of the teacher or pupils, which need should not be suppressed but should be applied to a useful activity that will teach the egocentric child the socialization that he lacks. In many instances an understanding teacher may win over a disorderly pupil by means of a personal attachment, after which his conduct can be directed into constructive channels. The good teacher needs to be extremely resourceful in problems of conduct. No set of tricks of classroom method can replace a fundamental understanding of human nature as a necessary part of the preparation for the teacher's task.

For more serious or persistent conduct problems, clinical assistance is necessary. A few school systems have complete child guidance clinics within their own organizations, while others utilize community resources of this type. Teachers may do a considerable service to mental hygiene by recognizing maladjustments early in their course of development, and by cooperating with clinics in their study and treatment. Children who present problems not commonly considered as disciplinary such as those who are "queer," suspicious, withdrawn or unsocial, may also be discovered by psychologically trained teachers and referred for the clinical help that they need.

Laurance Frederic Shaffer, *The Psychology of Adjustment.* Boston: Houghton Mifflin Company, 1936, pp. 511-12.

92. PSYCHOLOGICAL INSIGHTS UNDERGIRD GUIDANCE POINT OF VIEW

What are some of the strands in the mental hygiene point of view? . . . There are certain psychological foundations which constitute the very base line in this guidance insight. What are they? Or perhaps there is one major from which all others are derived? Perhaps so, but we are safe in naming a number of important ones. First, there is the necessity of understanding rather than blaming, or the objective versus the moralistic point of view. Perhaps next comes the fact of individual differences from which the guidance movement had great stimulus. At this point one needs to know that people vary in every known way—physically, mentally, emotionally, attitudinally, etc. The leader's job requires a modification of program or individual approach to match the variations presented by those with whom he comes in contact . . . Then the dynamics of behavior needs to be understood. This includes a study of the psychology of motivation and adjustment. Behavior is purposive. It is dictated by our desires and wishes working through our total personality. "All the world's a stage and all its men and women merely players," expresses what happens to people who are "working out" their motives. Activities offer important opportunities on this "stage" and we as "producers" and "stage directors" need to understand what people actually are doing there and to cooperate with the process. Finally, there are the facts about the way people learn and grow and there are rules which govern the learning progress. We grow better under some conditions than under others, and it is the job of the good teacher or activity leader to know these rules and conditions.

> Karl P. Zerfoss, "Mental Health in the Activity Program." Lecture notes.

93. NEW WAYS IN TEACHING CHILDREN

Better Guidance in Developing Personality: Our schools have made a number of significant advances in guiding the development of the personality of pupils. (V. V. Anderson, *Psychiatry in Education.* New York: Harper and Brothers, 1932, p. 430.) As an example, emphasis on competition has been reduced. Many teachers attempt to motivate children to compete with their own previous records rather than with their fellow-pupils. This shift of emphasis has tended to reduce the strain and stress that was so noticeable in the old-fashioned school situation. In many cases it also tends to stimulate the children rather than overwhelm them with the difficulties of competition. The attitudes toward discipline have also been changed. Formerly punishment of one sort or another had been used as the most important element in the discipline of children. Children tended to consider such punishment as retaliative, and therefore tended to become antagonistic and rebellious. The teacher has become a director and leader, rather than a taskmaster and disciplinarian. Most important of all, teachers have learned to consider behavior problems from a psychological standpoint. They no longer classify children as "good" or "bad." Nowadays the problem child is considered a psychologically sick child. These changes have influenced teachers to study their children rather than to mold them to their own liking. Instead of rewarding children for their good behavior and punishing them for their undesirable behavior, teachers tend to study each child's capacities and difficulties and then institute proper measures for his best development. The newer attitudes of teachers are well illustrated in their increased demand for college courses on mental hygiene and child development, and in their increased participation in parent-teacher groups and child-study associations.

With this excellent beginning, it is most probable that still further advance will be made in the reorientation of the school from its former status to a place where each child will be adequately studied and treated from the educational, psychological, and psychiatric standpoints.

> Mandel Sherman, "Contributions to Education of Scientific Knowledge in Mental Hygiene," *The Scientific Movement in Education.* Thirty-seventh Yearbook of the National Society for the Study of Education, Part II. Chicago: University of Chicago Press, chap. 35, p. 443. By permission of the Society.

94. EMPHASIS UPON THE WHOLE PERSON

This philosophy imposes upon educational institutions the

obligation to consider the student as a whole—his intellectual capacity and achievement, his emotional make-up, his physical condition, his social relationships, his vocational aptitudes and skills, his moral and religious values, his economic resources, his aesthetic appreciations. It puts emphasis, in brief, upon the development of the student as a person rather than upon his intellectual training alone.

American Council on Education, *The Student Personnel Point of View,* 1937, Series 1, No. 3, p. 1.

95. THE WHOLE CHILD GOES TO SCHOOL

Edith sits at her desk staring into space as if she did not want to see or hear what the teacher or anyone else is saying. This is the same Edith whose father repeatedly berates her for her "dumbness" and whose mother is forever criticizing her manners, her looks, her way of talking until now Edith is afraid of opening her mouth. George, with the sullen face and brooding eyes, is always ready to pick a fight and yell "dirty sheeny"! He is the same George whose mother has always threatened to pack him off to boarding school. Her chief method of punishment has been to "isolate" him. Johnny Jones, who stands up in class and recites in meek and mild fashion, an hour before was screaming in a tantrum on the dining-room floor. He is the same Johnny Jones who, an hour later, angrily throws a rock through the school window and goes undiscovered, throwing the blame on another boy.

What good will it do Edith for her teacher to keep on saying, "Speak up, Edith. Sit up and pay attention. Use your eyes. Use your ears. Use your tongue." Because of the emotions inside her, Edith cannot talk. She cannot bear to look squarely at life and the world around her. Hearing and seeing and talking bring too much hurt.

What good will it do for George to sit on a bench in the principal's outer office hour on end while one person after another walks past and away from him, leaving him isolated and alone? This only makes George the more bitterly in need of letting out the resentment inside him. It only piles up the feelings of being deserted which have already brought him so much hurt.

What good will it do to pat Johnny Jones on the back and praise him for his fine recitation, leaving the sly anger to find its own outlet? What good will come to either Johnny Jones or society if he is left without learning to handle the destructive feelings that lurk inside him?

Edith and George and Johnny and millions of other children come to school bringing their emotions with them as well as their bodies and intellects. Edith and George and Johnny have more serious "problems" than many. But the difference lies in degree, not in essence. We know that we can no longer have our schools work only on the mind and ignore the rest of the child. We have gone far since the days when Mario's mother answered his teacher's request to have Mario bathed, with a note saying, "He comes to school for to teach, teacher. He don't come to school for to smell."

In many classrooms today, teachers are helping to meet children's physical needs. They see to it, for example, that those who require it have midmorning milk or midafternoon rest. They recognize that if a child is physically overtired or undernourished, his school work can be readily affected.

In some classrooms today, teachers are helping also to meet children's emotional needs. So far they are few and far between, these teachers. But here and there they are working, alone or in small groups, courageously moving forward, knowing that if a child is emotionally overwrought or undernourished his schoolwork is affected, as is also his personality and his life.

These teachers realize that a child must feel that he is understood and appreciated for what he is as well as for what he accomplishes. They know that it helps a child to study if he feels that he is *wanted* and *belongs* in his classroom. They know that emotional warmth and protection from coldness is just as important as protection from cold winds and draughts. They know that many a disciplinary problem has yielded when the old punitive disciplinary measures have stopped and the new acceptant measures have begun.

Dorothy W. Baruch, *New Ways in Discipline*. New York: McGraw-Hill Book Company (Whittlesey House), 1949, pp. 215-17.

96. In Disciplinary Counseling as Elsewhere Look at the Whole Person

A basic dimension in any counseling point of view is the underlying philosophy of education in a democratic society. In the present case, the student personnel point of view is the undergirding thought structure of our concept of disciplinary counseling. Adherence to this educational philosophy makes it incumbent upon the institution to regard the student as a dynamic and total personality in process of development, and not as a fragmented or fragmentable individual. Moreover, by this point of view, the student is viewed as, and his efforts evaluated in terms of his status as, an apprentice learner and not as an adult worker-producer in a social or economic enterprise. Thus it follows that, for example, his problem behavior is not evaluated as that of a matured, educationally completed adult but as a beginning learner. Likewise his misbehavior is not viewed as separable from his religious, spiritual, or moral values; nor from his social, scholastic, or residential experiences. In like manner his financial condition and his health are as much a part of him as his tongue with which he talks or his arms with which he works. Fragmentation of these parts of the individual student in *any* kind of counseling tends to inhibit, if not suppress, the individual's unified growth and integration.

> E. G. Williamson and J. D. Foley, *Counseling and Discipline.* New York: McGraw-Hill Book Company, 1949, pp. 196-97.

97. Facts Are Needed to Understand

Knowledge leads to understanding. One teacher said, "I thought John was just lazy, until I learned about the long hours of work he was doing every day at home; then I realized that he was too tired to learn."

Another teacher said, "Two parents were very critical of me and of the school until they saw that I was interested in their child and knew enough about her to help her make the most of herself; then they helped me in many ways."

Another teacher made this comment: "I did not know whether Peter couldn't or wouldn't do the work assigned to children of his age. But when I began to study his mental ability, I found that he was much brighter than his school work indicated."

In every class period the teacher has opportunity to "learn" his students. Their questions, answers, and contributions to discussion, as well as their written work and other kinds of creative work, give a fairly accurate impression of their mental alertness and their special knowledge, skills, or deficiencies. When students are working together on reports or projects, the teacher has a chance to observe how they get along with one another. The approach they make to the teacher gives some indication of their relationship with adults. Their response to failure, to criticism, to difficulty is also significant evidence of their stage of development.

> Ruth Strang, *The Role of the Teacher in Personnel Work.* (Revised). New York: Bureau of Publications, Teachers College, Columbia University, 1946, pp. 113-14.

98. OBJECTIVE AND SUBJECTIVE FACTS ARE IMPORTANT AND INTERRELATED

Every situation has its objective and subjective aspects. A man loses his job. That is an objective fact. His feelings about this event constitute a subjective fact. A man is ill with tuberculosis. That is a medical fact. But every person who has any sort of illness has accompanying it certain feelings about the illness. There are variations in the physical aspects of tuberculosis, but there are many more variations in human reactions to that disease. So we could run the gamut of human experiences and note that every objective experience— marriage, hunger, getting a job, leaving one's children in a day nursery—has its accompanying subjective counterpart of emotional attitudes. Experience and skill lead to more and more awareness of this inter-relationship.

Social workers sometimes contrast what they call the "reality situation" of a client with his emotional problems. This separation is unfortunate because it sometimes leads us to operate as if these two areas were mutually exclusive. The implication is that the emotional components of the situation are not real. Whereas, of course, they certainly are real to the person experiencing them. The way one feels about a situation is as much a fact as the situation itself. To avoid such erroneous implications, we shall, in this discussion, speak instead of the objective aspects and the subjective aspects of a client's situation. Both are always present.

If we seem in our discussion to be directing our attention primarily to subjective aspects, to feelings, attitudes, and emotions, this is because we recognize that they are as important as the objective facts themselves and are much more likely to be overlooked. Our concentration upon them does not imply any lack of appreciation of the significance of the objective facts. We recognize, of course, that over-attention to subjective factors would limit our service to the individual just as much as would lack of appreciation of them. In practice we must be extremely vigilant to give each group of factors its due weight.

A student who applies for a scholarship on the grounds that his father has just retired and is unable to see his son through college may be even more worried over his father's poor health, which necessitated the retirement, than he is over the financial problem. The dean who notes only the latter may be failing to give the boy the help he most urgently needs, or may be giving a scholarship to a boy whose anxieties will prevent his profiting from it.

In seeking to help people even in very simple situations we need to listen not only to their objective requests but also to the undertones which reveal their feelings and give us clues as to perhaps even more serious objective situations not overtly revealed. A man's frequent absences from work may indicate neither unreliability nor laziness but may be due to worry about his wife's illness or to anxiety about pressing debts. In either case the underlying subjective factor, worry, is caused by an objective situation which may not be apparent at once to a personnel manager.

> Annette Garrett, *Interviewing, Its Principles and Methods.* New York: Family Service Association of America, 1942, pp. 13-14.

99. TEACHERS WITH GUIDANCE POINT OF VIEW SEE THINGS IN A DIFFERENT LIGHT

. . . Teachers who possess an understanding of human be-

havior and who have become imbued with the personnel point
of view show a change in attitude toward the "problem child."
They become less concerned with the maladjustment of the
child as a disturbing force in an orderly school life and become
more concerned with it as a destructive force in a child's life.
They see that it is the child and not the school routine which
needs protection from maladjustment. They change from a
policy of attaching blame and punishment to one of seeking
the underlying cause of maladjustment and of trying to correct
or counteract its influence on the child. Discipline as the giving of penalties changes to a form of character education.
Efforts are directed toward helping the pupil attain progressive development through learning to accept responsibility for
his own acts and through substituting self-discipline, or inner
control, for teacher discipline, or outer control. Teachers with
this conception of discipline find what happens to the pupil
to be of greater importance than his immediate adjustment to
school rules and regulations. They are able to shift attention
from making and enforcing rules to enlisting the pupil's conscious cooperation and to creating a school environment more
conducive to the conduct desired.

> Jane Warters, *High School Personnel Work Today.* New
> York: McGraw-Hill Book Company, Inc., 1946, p. 43.

100.   THE CHARACTERISTICS OF UNDERSTANDING TEACHERS

. . teachers who understand children show the following
characteristics: (1) they think of children's behavior as caused
by a series of factors that can be identified and they therefore
believe that boys and girls are understandable and educable;
(2) they are able to accept every child emotionally and to
respect and value him as a human being; (3) they recognize
that every child is unique and therefore they constantly seek
information about each of their pupils that will enable them
to know the factors that are influencing their development
and behavior; (4) they know the common developmental tasks
that all children face during the several phases of their growth
and what complications often arise as individuals with varying
characteristics and backgrounds work at those tasks; (5) they
know the more important generalizations that describe and

explain human growth, development, motivation, learning, and behavior; and (6) they are well accustomed to methods of gathering and organizing relevant information about a child, of finding the scientific principles to which this information points as explaining the particular individual's maturity level and overt actions, and of using these explanatory principles— together with the pertinent data—as the basis for helping the youngster meet his problems of growing up.

> American Council on Education, *Helping Teachers Understand Children,* 1945, pp. 19-20.

101. The Normal Problems of Normal People

Until within comparatively recent times, most of the concrete case data on different kinds of mental deviation and maladjustment accessible to the mental hygienist, educationist, psychologist, sociologist, classroom teacher, or parent, have been based on distinctly pathological types of abnormals, such as mental defectives, psychotics (people subject to some major form of mental disease), pronounced neurotics or psycho-neurotics (persons subject to various kinds of nervous maladies), delinquents, or criminals. The case histories and clinical data from the pens of psychiatrists and clinical psychologists, based on the investigation of this kind of human material, are not lacking in exciting interest, dramatic appeal, and basic significance. They occupy a merited position in the technical literature of psychiatry, clinical psychology, and educational and social pathology. But the great army of lay workers (teachers, parents, ministers, welfare workers, and the like) who are concerned with the welfare of the normal and superior population tend to regard this material as extreme, pathological, and inapplicable to their problems. Much of it is too technical for lay consumption, and it is generally found in technical publications that are inaccessible to the general reader. To the many workers with normal children or adults, data gathered from distinctly abnormal types suffer from apparent extraneousness or "detachment from reality," and therefore do not appear to be applicable to normal deviates. Obviously such data do not supply the most appropriate or challenging type of illustrative material for those engaged in ministering to the mental, social, or educational requirements of the normal population.

Again, the study of mental abnormalities in the distinctly pathological groups sometimes leads the reader to ascribe unwarranted importance to minor mental deviations in normal persons. He may become obsessed with the idea that such deviations are evidence of mental disease, and become unduly concerned about the sanity of such persons, or about his own sanity. Every minor mental aberration is evidence to him of incipient or latent mental disease! Many young cases so diagnosed have passed through the writer's clinics. Who is not familiar with adolescents subject to minor mental maladjustments or transient development instabilities diagnosed as cases of predementia praecox or dementia praecox because of the bias that springs from excessive preoccupation with pathological cases, who failed after many years to develop mental disease? To be sure, a thorough understanding of the abnormal mind contributes to the better understanding of the normal mind. For one thing, it demonstrates that there is no sharp boundary between the normal and the abnormal. But information regarding mental quirks in the normal based wholly on a study of distinctly diseased types of mentality will lead to many mistaken inferences and unjustified conclusions. Records of maladjustments obtained from normal and superior groups, described without attempts at embellishment or exaggeration, will be less thrilling than the fantastic or grotesque symptom-complexes characteristic of the mentally diseased. They will, however, be more "true to life" and of greater practical value for students interested primarily in the conservation of the mental, educational, and social health of normal and well-endowed people, who probably constitute 90 per cent of the total population.

An advantage of familiarity with data secured from the normal population is that they supply indisputable evidence, as suggested above, that normality is a relative term. We find on careful investigation that normal and talented people are not free from personality blemishes. Many normal people, so-called, are subject to the same kinds of mental deviations and idiosyncrasies that afflict the pathological groups, although, of course, the involvements are less extensive and less severe.

Examination of the case histories in this volume discloses the fact that persons at large in society, functioning as normal individuals and filling important positions in life, are subject to an amazing variety of transient or lasting mental disturbances or idiosyncrasies, and that mental maladjustments may be produced by all sorts of processes of conditioning, even the most trivial ones. They offer convincing proof that the most fruitful field of application of mental hygiene principles is preventive and constructive mental health work with the vast army of potentially normal children. . . .

We conclude, therefore, that although the study of psychiatry and the frank psychoses and psychoneuroses is not without value to all those whose work is with the normal population, a more important background of information on maladjustments, quirks, and hampering habits and attitudes for the guidance of such workers will be obtained from the study of case material culled from the "psychopathology of everyday life."

> J. E. Wallace Wallin, *Minor Mental Maladjustments in Normal People.* Durham: Duke University Press, 1939, pp. 1-3.

102. MENTAL HYGIENE IN EVERYDAY LIFE

The Role of the Layman: The practice of mental hygiene is not limited to the work of clinics, or the treatment of maladjusted persons. In a very real sense, everyone is engaged in mental hygiene, whether he intends it or not. In this respect, mental hygiene is like all of the other fields of knowledge that are intimately concerned with human welfare. All of the fire departments of the country could not extinguish the conflagrations that would ensue if persons in general were not careful in preventing fires. Physicians and hospitals would be inadequate to cope with disease if individuals did not assume responsibility for their own health and that of their communities. Similarly, preventive action in mental hygiene is of more fundamental importance than is remedial work to repair damages already done. If all persons who deal with others, especially parents, teachers and employers, governed their influence by principles of mental hygiene, there would be fewer lame and deficient personalities for clinicians to treat. The constructive measures that are applied to create effective personality have been termed *positive mental hygiene*. No unique principles are necessary in this field, for the theories developed throughout this book pertain as much to the psychology of those who adjust well as to those who do so poorly.

It is often asserted that only good intentions and common sense are necessary to bring about successful outcomes in human problems. This is a half-truth. Many well-adjusted persons have lived in the centuries before any scientific study of human nature was begun. Such individuals owed their good fortune to the vague and unanalyzed formulations of mental hygiene principles that have always existed in folklore, religion and tradition. The need for the precise study of human problems exists, none the less. A hundred years ago persons who were ill were bled to cure their ailments. Modern medicine recognizes the futility of this procedure. But children are beaten and scolded even today because parents still in the dark ages of mental hygiene believe that this is an effective way of guiding their conduct. Some of mental hygiene is as old as the Bible and has existed as long as there have been kind and understanding persons. Other principles of equal importance directly contradict the traditional beliefs of even the wisest of grandmothers.

The role of the layman in mental hygiene is exactly analogous to the part that he plays in respect to physical health. Parents and teachers do not treat serious physical illnesses, but must know how to recognize their presence, in order to call on a physician in time. In providing proper diet, sleep, exercise and healthful surrounding, on the other hand, the responsibility of the parent is a primary one. As far as pronounced disorders of behavior are concerned, laymen need only to know how to identify them, to learn to consider them from an objective rather than a moralistic viewpoint, and to seek such expert assistance as may be available. In the everyday problems of the development and training of emotional and other habits, the intelligent and informed parent or teacher can contribute directly to the building of an effective personality. Also, just as parents bind up the child's little wounds of physical injury, so some remedial service may be rendered on the occurrence of simpler and more common maladjustments.

Laurance Frederic Shaffer, *The Psychology of Adjustment.* Boston: Houghton Mifflin Company, 1936, pp. 499-500.

103. GUIDANCE A NATURAL PART OF LIFE

Fundamental assumptions in guidance and personnel work are that individuals require special professional help from time to time in understanding themselves and their situations and in dealing with their problems; that this special help should be essentially educative in nature; that it can supply information about individual personality and about social reality which the individual can get in no other way, except perhaps through a costly process of trial and error, which it is the purpose of the personnel service in part to alleviate or prevent.

To the extent that human nature can be understood and predicted, that information about the environment can be assembled, that people can learn and adapt, and can make plans and have them mature—to this extent the professional personnel worker can aid the individual in learning facts about himself he could not otherwise obtain, in procuring facts about environmental conditions not otherwise available, in relating personal and environmental facts in a more rational and planned manner. All of this can be achieved by a method which places its dependence upon the ability of the individual to learn, to purpose, to decide and to act—for himself.

The individual, it is assumed, cannot do without such help in certain adjustments and problems that occur in his life up to mature adulthood. Assistance with adjustment problems actually is given to all persons from birth onward by parents, relatives, family friends, and well-wishers in the community. The only questions are how intelligent this aid can be, how helpful it will prove to the individual and to society, and under whose auspices it will be conducted.

Robert H. Mathewson, *Guidance Policy and Practice.* New York: Harper and Brothers, 1949, p. 117.

104. GUIDANCE AN EMPHASIS NOT A DEPARTMENT

. . Guidance cannot function as a separate department of

the school. It is not something extra which may be achieved with a special organization and additional personnel. A guidance program cannot be created by administrative decree, nor can it be put into operation merely by the employment of "guidance specialists" or "guidance workers." The guidance point of view must permeate the entire school organization and personnel if an efficient program is to be in operation.

> M. L. Goetting, *Teaching in the Secondary School.* New York: Prentice-Hall, Inc., 1942, p. 439. By permission of the publishers.

105. Guidance Is Not a "Fifth Wheel"

The first demand surely should be the maintenance of a schoolroom which is conducive to healthy personality growth. An atmosphere of friendliness, cooperation, and genuine joy in living is as valuable for emotional hygiene as are sunshine, fresh air, good food and exercise for physical hygiene. The warm, sunny, stable, well-organized, efficiently working personality is not usually the product of intricate psychological manipulation, but of normal growth under generally favorable emotional conditions. . . . Mental hygiene is not a new "subject," to be introduced into a crowded curriculum at certain prescribed periods. Rather, mental hygiene provides a point of view which modifies all the work of the teacher.

> Paul A. Witty and Charles E. Skinner, editors, *Mental Hygiene in Modern Education.* New York: Rinehart and Company, Inc., 1939, pp. 507-8. (From chapter by Goodwin Watson.)

106. The Teacher Has a Positive Role in the Classroom

Thus the usefulness of a mental-hygiene approach is nullified by an overemphasis upon the abnormal. It is now conceded that much of the terminology of abnormal psychology is inappropriate to use in dealing with school children. Teachers appear to need, more than anything else, practical assistance in the subtle but fascinating task of understanding children's problems. Diagnosis is part of expert teaching— and the teacher is precisely the person whose training should enable her to perform this task well. She should have, of course, sufficient acquaintance with symptoms of psychopathy to be able to identify children whose disorders are so acute as to require the services of a psychiatrist. These "cases" should be referred to proper psychiatric agencies. She should try not to neglect any problem child whose condition can be improved in the regular classroom. But her goal is primarily to create classroom conditions wherein mental conflicts and emotional stresses are infrequent and wherein sympathetic and understanding guidance reduces the number and severity of behavior disorders.

> Paul A. Witty and Charles E. Skinner, editors, *Mental Hygiene in Modern Education*. New York: Rinehart and Company, Inc., 1939, p. 10.

107. COUNSELING A UNIVERSAL FUNCTION

The thesis of this paper is that the counseling provided by a well-trained, capable counselor is an educational technique which can benefit *all* students. If counseling is defined not as a therapy for students having difficulties but as an educational situation offering to all students opportunities for development, the part the counselor plays in our educational system becomes quite different from that played in the past. (E. G. Williamson, "Counseling as a Fundamental Process in Education," *Schoolmen's Week Proceedings*. University of Pennsylvania Bulletin, 33rd Joint Meeting, Southeastern Convention District of Pennsylvania State Education Association, 1946.)

From the time a counselee enters the interviewing room, the counselor carefully observes his behavior, both verbal and otherwise, to identify possible problems and when such identifications are made, to treat these problems. The counselee, however, can obtain more in the interview than the alleviation of psychological conflicts and these additional functions of the interview can be listed.

1. The interview offers the counselee an opportunity for establishing a responsible relationship with a respected adult. The intimate contacts most students have are restricted to members of their family or to people in their own age groups and many college students have no more than casual contacts with other mature individuals. A counselor who is willing to discuss in a situation void of emotional tensions and pressures,

a student's political, religious, social or sexual beliefs, and who reacts to the student's statements as an appreciative adult, can provide the student with an experience often obtained by young people out of school and working with adults but frequently not available to college students.

2. The counseling situation provides an opportunity for the student to feel that someone is interested in him as a person. This is particularly a problem in a large school where individual contacts between staff members and students may not be extensive. Knowing that someone is available and willing to engage in a face-to-face conversation offers the student an ego satisfaction often difficult to obtain in many colleges. Assuming a need for affiliation the counseling interview provides an opportunity for the student to gain both social experience and to obtain satisfaction of that need. (H. A. Murray and others, *Explorations in Personality.* New York: Oxford University Press, 1938.)

3. The counseling situation offers the student an opportunity to recognize explicitly his goals and to verbalize the processes which resulted in their selection. Most students are working toward goals they have previously chosen. Frequently they have not defined realistically these goals; often they have not understood the means by which they selected these goals, and usually they know little of the motivations underlying these selections. Although students need not be encouraged to engage in excessive introspection or non-productive self-study, they must be taught the need for understanding their own motives and those of others. By discussing those things for which students are working, and why they are doing this, the counselor can assist the student in understanding his own personal mechanisms and can help the student to evaluate his progress toward his goals. The definition of goals and the clarification of motives are two activities a counselor can engage in with any student.

4. Every student must acquire certain skills and learn certain facts which are most effectively taught through the means of personal interviews. In certain areas, such as the field of occupations, general knowledge teachable in larger groups is desirable, but specialized knowledge, relevant to a single or

only to a few students, is also necessary. This type of information can be taught most effectively by counselors. In group psychotherapy, individual therapy is a necessary adjunct. In group instruction, counseling instruction is frequently needed. This is particularly true where the subject matter of the course relates directly to the life of the student, as it does in courses on marriage and family life, mental hygiene, abnormal psychology, and vocational orientation.

If the counselor attempts to perform these functions, along with his previously recognized ones of helping students solve problems, the techniques used in counseling and the attitudes of the counselor toward counseling will have to be changed. More emphasis must be placed by the counselor on the personal relationship between counselee and counselor. The counselee also will have to perceive that the counselor is not interested in the problem but rather in the student and will have to accept the counselor not as a specialist who defines and helps solve problems but rather as a rational and feeling adult ready to enter into a constructive social-personal relationship with the student.

When doing this type of counseling, the counselor will not have to refrain from talking about himself and can reveal his own attitudes and relate his own experiences. The student will have to see the interview as a give-and-take situation where those exchanges characteristic of most effective social situations prevail. The depth of emotional relationship involved in psychoanalytic transfer is neither necessary nor desired here, but the counselor must assume a personalized, affective role in the counseling situation.

The goals of this type of counseling do not preclude the use of test data. In fact, until students become accustomed to this new educational role of the counselor, tests can provide a convenient and harmless means of establishing the desired relationship. In many schools, all entering freshmen, all juniors, or all the students falling into other categories are given one or more tests for purposes of classification, screening, obtaining norms, or research. Frequently the students tested are invited at the time of the examination to see a counselor to discuss the results of the tests. Many students who have

problems accept these invitations and thus establish contact
with a helpful counselor. Many other students who have no
observable problem also accept the invitation, motivated by
curiosity, a hidden problem or the need for talking with someone. What the counselor does with these latter students
depends upon his view of the counseling situation. If he is a
therapist only, and not an educator, he carefully observes the
student for any problems, and finding none, describes the
test scores and concludes the contact. If he is attempting to
make a counseling interview of this contact, he accepts the
interview as a normal social situation and works toward the
goals already described. . . .

The implications of this educational role of the counselor
are manifold. Obviously, the counseling program and the
instructional program must be closely coordinated. This has
been the practice for several years in the General College of
the University of Minnesota, where students in classes in
vocational orientation and individual orientation have accepted
their counselors in these described roles. More recently, the
course, "Preparation for Marriage," in the College of Science,
Literature and the Arts at Minnesota has made more extensive
use of this relationship. Three of the instructors in this course,
including the Chairman of the Family Life Sequence, hold
appointments as one-half-time counselors in the Student Counseling Bureau. As part of the course work, students have one
or more personal interviews with these instructors and these
interviews are structured as counseling interviews. All data
available to University counselors are in the hands of these
instructors and instruction is individualized and personalized
to the point where student and counselor are participating in
a socially meaningful relationship.

Counselors who are to assume these functions will perhaps
require training not now obtained by most counselors.
Although they must be skilled diagnosticians and therapists,
they must also be sound educators possessing well-thought-out
educational philosophies and having a clear understanding of
the educational problems of normal youth. Obviously, a
greater number of better-qualified counselors than are now
available will be needed if this function of the counselor is
widely recognized.

The hitherto accepted idea that counseling must occur in an office, preferably over a desk, must also be re-examined. Counselors may have to go where students are—to rallies, picnics, camps, and meetings, instead of waiting for students to come to their offices or to a counseling bureau. These counseling offices themselves perhaps should be changed from typical offices to conversation-stimulating situations. An experiment of this sort is already under way where a comfortable interviewing room *without a desk* is in use and interviews conducted in this room are being compared to interviews conducted in the more traditional offices.

Finally, if counselors are to assume this new role, they must create a new stereotype of themselves to be held by educators and students. More of their discussion must concern the "normal" student, more of their concern directed toward the educational problems and dilemmas of society. Following this, counseling as an educational technique need not limit itself to the schools but, like all education, can enter into the community.

> Ralph F. Berdie, "Counseling: An Educational Technique," *Educational and Psychological Measurement,* 9, 1949, pp. 89-94.

108. The School to Train Toward a Personal and Social Maturity

As a mental health objective, socialized individualism is of paramount importance, the individual aspect because it is directly concerned with personal adjustment, and the socialized aspect because it affects relationship with other individualities, and determines the adequacy of one's adjustment to the social scene. Schools are henceforth to study the individual child, evaluate as accurately as possible his potentialities, set up situations that will afford him opportunity to cultivate them, and prepare him as well as possible for intelligent and satisfying participation in the work of the world. They are to train his emotions and his perspectives so that his personality may be an asset rather than a liability in the niche which he is to fill. At the same time, they are to build into the framework of his personality healthful attitudes of sympathy, tolerance,

appreciativeness, liberality, and of his own responsibility as a
social being to the end that his inclinations and faiths shall be
wholesomely and agreeably related to those of his fellows.

> Lawrence A. Averill, *Mental Hygiene for the Classroom
> Teacher*. New York: Pitman Publishing Corporation, 1939,
> p. 197.

109. NOT ONLY ADJUSTMENT BUT ALSO CREATIVITY

Each *culture* has the power: (1) to develop in its children
a characteristic life style. (2) to give them—along with the
meat and drink which sustains life—a set of ideas and beliefs
which govern their behavior. (3) to give them a set of reasons, or rationalizations, which make their way of life seem
right, ultimate, absolute.

Hence, it behooves us to examine our own culture more
searchingly. What has it done to us? What is it doing to our
children?

Are we, as teachers, merely agents hired to pass *on* the
culture, training our charges to adjust and conform to the
accepted mode? Or are we, as their critics and guides, to
assist them to *pass* on the culture, to judge it, to discover ways
and means of improving it?

And which culture? As we examine American culture, we
discover classes, areas, occupations each with its characteristic
influences. How can we see *who* the learner is, or whither he
is bound, until we find ways and means of studying and evaluating this background? And how, indeed, can we take an
objective view of ourselves until we see our place as teacher
in this culture?

While we must recognize frankly the tremendous power of
the culture, we need to guard ourselves from accepting an
environmentalist bias that would leave no hope for individual
initiative and creativeness. Human beings are forever remaking their culture, and we have the opportunity of and responsibility for transforming our American culture in terms of
democracy as it is reinterpreted through social experience.

> Lawrence E. Cole and William F. Bruce, *Educational Psy-
> cology*. New York: World Book Company, 1950, p. 274.

110. A CHRISTIAN CONTEXT FOR COUNSELING

This discussion will undertake the exploration of some of the relations between Christian theology and the theory and practice of counseling. This is an increasingly pressing problem which has been too little reflected upon, not only by theologians but by counselors as well. Modern counseling has a curious lineage. Its hoariest ancestor is the ancient art of sympathy and shared wisdom, which is surely older than written history. Its often none-too-well remembered grandparent is the Christian ethic, with its recognition of and concern for the worth of human persons and its ideal of human community. But its immediate parent is modern psychology, which makes the kindred social sciences its aunts and uncles. Such a heritage creates an understandable confusion and instability in the offspring. The spirit and intent of counseling betrays its ancestry in high religion. But its techniques and middle axioms are predominantly controlled by the materialistic and mechanistic assumptions of the prevailing systems of psychopathology, psychoanalysis and psychiatry. When religious persons have sought to avail themselves of the therapeutic aids of modern psychology they have often found themselves in the anomalous position of trying to adopt methods and reject the assumptions on which those methods *apparently* are based. If we accept the practical insights which behavioristic psychology and psychoanalytic theory admittedly afford us, are we thereby committed to follow them in their conclusions about the nature of the human self, freedom and responsibility, and their positivistic notions of truth and reality? It would indeed be a painful choice if we have to decide between the Christian account of man and his destiny, on the one hand, and the doctrines of modern psychology, on the other. It is the thesis of this essay that no such choice is required of us. Rather, our task is that of assimilating the practical wisdom of the psychologist, however secular and mechanistic his own world-view may be, to the basic and perennial first principles of the Christian faith and Christian theology.

What is wanted is a Christian *context* for counseling. Contemporary Christians cannot afford to ignore the solid growing

results of scientific studies in psychology and sociology nor
can the scientists, for their part, continue to remain complacent about their crude, mechanistic assumptions—the dramatic
news about the atomic bomb adds terrible urgency to the
demand that science submit its awesome powers to the guidance and goals of ethical religion. I cannot pretend to offer
to you the explicit details of a concordat between Christian
theology and modern psychological theory. It will be enough
if I can make you aware of the immense importance of the
task and if I can illustrate some of the ways in which it may
be worked at with good hope of progress.

Consider the counseling situation itself. At its simplest, it
consists of two people, both of whom are concerned to solve
or improve a human situation which is, for some reason or
other, out of balance or control. Who *are* these people? What
qualifies one to help the other and what makes one need help?
What are the limits within which this sort of help is possible?
What are their common goals and what are the norms by
which success or failure may be gauged?

Any effort to give fundamental answers to questions such
as these leads out beyond the ken of mechanism and positive
science and raises issues which are essentially theological in
form, to which theological answers must be given. What does it
mean to be a human person? How are the jams into which we
mortals fall to be accounted for? Is there any clue to the human
predicament which explains the mystery of evil without explaining it away? What are the moral possibilities and responsibilities
when one person undertakes to help another? Is there an honest
way beyond human tragedy? How does one contribute something to the repair and remaking of his social environment?
What sort of education is required to guide a growing person into the most adequate realization of his potentialities?

> Albert C. Outler, *A Christian Context for Counseling.* An
> Edward W. Hazen Foundation pamphlet, Series III, No. 18,
> New Haven, Conn., 1945, pp. 3-4.

111. THE FOUR CORNERS OF THE GUIDANCE BUILDING

. . First, I am convinced that we need sympathetic, trained,
open-minded, patient teachers who believe that individuals
constitute the most important resource of society and that

the primary responsibility of a school and a community is to help those individuals to attain all-around growth—physical, mental, emotional, social, spiritual. . . .

The second corner of the guidance building . . . is, obviously, a means of finding individuals. Those means are fact-finding devices of various types: tests, observations, work accomplished, special achievements—literary, social, citizenship, dramatic, athletic. . . .

A third corner of this guidance building . . . is systematic recording and preservation of data covering the individual's entire school career—from kindergarten through high school and into college. For this purpose cumulative record forms are essential. Even more important is constant review, analysis, and study of the records of individual pupils. To accomplish this basic desideratum of the guidance program, teachers need careful, systematic introduction to records, and to their value and interpretation. . . .

There's a fourth corner of this guidance structure . . . and it is probably the most difficult one of all to achieve. It consists of adjusting school procedures and activities to the facts produced by measurement and accumulated data. It involves diversified curricula, individualized methods, modified grading systems, improved teaching in specific subjects such as reading and arithmetic, more realistic vocational guidance at junior and senior high-school levels, closer parent-teacher relations, and broader community understanding of individual learning problems.

> Ben D. Wood and Ralph Haefner, *Measuring and Guiding Individual Growth.* New York: Silver Burdett Company, 1948, pp. 514-15.

112.   DIFFICULT NOT TO JUMP TO CONCLUSIONS

The reader should be well aware by this time that when he begins to study problems of human behavior, he is getting into the most complex and confusing area of all fields of investigation. Despite this knowledge, he will often read into observed behavior his personal interpretation of the causes of it and the motives that underlie it without sufficient information and understanding to justify his conclusions. He will find that the inhibition of snap judgments about behavior and

the motives that lie behind it is one of the most difficult habits
to acquire in the process of becoming an effective counselor.

> John W. M. Rothney and Bert A. Roens, *Counseling the
> Individual Student*. New York: William Sloane Associates,
> Inc., 1949, pp. 87-88.

113.   POINTS OF VIEW IN THE Y.M.C.A.

Among practitioners in the Y.M.C.A. today there is little
evidence of concern over the dilemma posed by the relationship of "general" (decentralized) and "special" (centralized)
services as they relate to the function of central program in
contrast to peripheral activities. There are substantial grounds
for the conclusion that the majority of Y.M.C.A. secretaries
think of guidance as special activity and not as an integral
phase of total operation.

This same problem arises in other agencies and fields. In a
recent study of this issue on the high school and college levels
(Karl P. Zerfoss, "Guidance—Central or Peripheral." Unpublished article, 1951), the following conclusions were stated:
"(1) Relatively few of the writers in the field are clearly aware
of the dilemma raised . . . (2) Guidance seems to mean some
'special' or 'centralized' effort, often quite apart from the
work of the teacher or other 'generalist.' Two well-known
authorities (A. J. Jones and H. C. Hand, 'Guidance and
Purposive Living,' *Thirty-seventh Yearbook, N.S.S.E.*, Part I.
Bloomington: Public School Publishing Co., 1938, p. 18)
stated that most secondary schools and colleges in America
regard guidance as an 'adjunct specialty.' (3) The idea of
guidance as being an integral phase of effective education is
growing. This is particularly true at the secondary school
level." This concept has a foot-hold in the Y.M.C.A. and seems
to be emphasized especially among the few who are writing
about guidance.

Since approximately eighty percent of the Associations today
have three men or less upon the staff, it is futile in the main,
to talk about providing special services. However, this does
not mean that we must practically abandon hope in guidance
activity for small Associations, as some have proposed. (Philip
G. Swartz, "Counseling in a Smaller Y.M.C.A.," *Counseling*,
April, 1951.) On the contrary, we should bring into adminis-

trative and program leadership secretaries trained in basic guidance insights and skills; and we need to help those staff people now on the job without such equipment to acquire it. In addition to this attention to the personal equipment of the worker we should become more fully aware of and skilled in using the resources inside and outside the Association in the form of other professional people—physicians, ministers, case workers, educators, personnel workers, etc.—and organizations with interests similar to our own. This applies in many of the smaller communities as well as in the larger ones, though in lesser degree.

It is also clear that it is unwise for agencies to expect even the most elaborately conceived plan of special services to be effective if not based in a supporting matrix of sound program. On the other hand, even the most effectively integrated scheme always will call for some special services. Both emphases are definitely needed.

Another conclusion listed in the study by the author already referred to applies in some extent to the Y.M.C.A. Here it was stated that: "The obvious trend toward curriculum reorganization along functional lines is a direct shift to emphasis on central processes rather than a magnification of the 'fringes.'" One of the journals in the secondary school field (J. Fred Murphy, Chairman, "Characteristics of a High School Guidance and Counseling Program." *North Central Quarterly*. October, 1947, pp. 219-247), has pointed up this conclusion in the comment: "In schools where the philosophy of general education has influenced curriculum patterns, resulting in a 'core' or 'common-learnings' or similar programs, *much that previously had been isolated as guidance and counseling has become an integral part of classroom activity. . . .* " (p. 239) Today many an antiquated school curriculum set-up is being made partially tenable by excellent special services. Likewise, often in informal social agencies the program is unsound educationally when examined by modern group work standards and such inadequacies cannot be remedied by anything short of internal changes.

Karl P. Zerfoss, "Guidance Emphasis in the Y.M.C.A.," *Counseling*, September, 1951, pp. 1-4.

114. A Good Counselor Works Himself Out of a Job

The goal of counseling should be to help the individual to take responsibility for his own life and for his share in the social load that must be carried. The goal of medical treatment is not simply to remove the pain, but to help the patient get well so that he no longer needs the doctor; and not only to help him get well, but to lead him to understand himself and the circumstances of life so that he may meet future situations with a better chance of avoiding ill health. Similarly, the goal of counseling is not simply to remove immediate irritating difficulties, but to help the patient get well so that he no longer needs the counselor, and in order that he may meet future difficulties successfully instead of being defeated by them. To achieve this the counselor . . . if he does his work well, will find himself progressively less and less necessary to those he has tried to help. He will be able to gauge his success by the very degree to which he is necessary or unnecessary, and to be unconcerned if his work has been so well done that even the person helped fails to recognize what his contribution has been.

> Harrison Sacket Elliot and Grace Loucks Elliott, *Solving Personal Problems*. New York: Henry Holt and Company, Inc., 1936, p. 223. By permission of the publishers.

115. You Can Learn How to Help

Today's knowledge can not only tell you the fact: children do these things. It can also tell you *why*. Youngsters—at many ages—seek independence. They want to be very "grown-up." They want to be Themselves—with a capital T; personalities; real people in their very own right. Wanting all these so deeply they do often resist adults, rebel at rules, fight. We wish they wouldn't; but children do. They seem to have to, if they are going to grow.

Children want independence. They want love. They want the support of the children around them. They want the sense of doing more, of giving more and learning more. These are some of the *whys* at the roots of behavior. These are the deep urges that all children feel, and they drive children into "bad" deed at times, as well as good. . . .

These *whys*—and new knowledge about how all children tend to behave at different ages—give teachers and parents today more to go on. We can be much smarter disciplinarians. We do not have to get upset over deeds that are natural, over behavior that will pass anyhow, over ways that all children have *because* they are children.

You can feel real confidence that you are right when you are gentle, kindly, not harsh . . . when you do not blame children too much for doing what they have to do. Your children will not carry the burden of being called "bad"—and that is a burden for child or man—when actually they are good, good as growing children.

There is even more you can easily do. Some school activities allow children to be their healthy selves more fully than others: the arts; play with blocks and sand and dolls and puppets; simple spontaneous dramatic play; good vigorous out-of-door life at school; committee work where children do the talking and deciding; active work where all youngsters can feel Big through contributing, each in his own way.

This kind of creative, busy, happy working—plus your good-natured, not-harsh, not-blaming, friendly way—is not just a boon to children. It is a boon to our country. It allows more and more youngsters to grow with peace inside of them. It is good education *and* a good groundwork for decent human relations.

This Is the Task

You want your children to learn, and you want them to live. You want them to get along with people, to get along with themselves. It is a big new task you have. You may be baffled by it at times, and no wonder! It is not easy.

Yet teachers—you—have to do it. Unless you work at it many of today's unhappy and troubled children have no one else to whom to turn. You must be the child's friend. The classroom teacher is one of the child's closest sources of understanding, of friendly guidance and of direction toward good feelings.

It is hard. For not all behavior is a phase; not all difficulties are outgrown; not all trouble is natural and necessary as a

part of growing up. You need a kindly, patient point of view
as a part of your approach to children, but that isn't all.

Some children—many children—you help by not landing too
hard, by waiting for time and growth. But still others have
needs which go beyond this. The children themselves tell you
who they are. They do not use words on paper or words of
the tongue. But the children talk.

They talk with their bodies, with all their behavior, through
everything they do. You have heard it. *(It is a persistent,
demanding, continuous, over-and-over-again note.)* Often you
know easily what it means. Sometimes this body-talk, this
language of behavior is not clear. You have to wait, listen
again, put two and two together the way you do when a baby
first talks. But it is language. Children are asking you to
listen and to help them.

> James L. Hymes, Jr., *Teacher Listen—the Children Speak...*
> Philadelphia: National Mental Health Foundation, 1949,
> pp. 8-10.

116. Genuine Re-Education a Real Possibility

Best contemporary thought seems to be forsaking the idea
that "problem" behavior is usually the expression of bad
heredity and mental deficiency. Instead, it accounts for maladjustment in terms of excessive deprivation, frustration, or
insecurity which denies the child opportunity to fulfill the
basic needs of his developing personality. It does not tend to
classify behavior disorders into genetic types but seeks to
understand in each case the disharmony or imbalance between
the dynamics of the individual and the limiting conditions of
his environment. It believes in the possibility of genuine
re-education, to be accomplished by reconditioning, by adjusting the environment, by enriching and expanding the
child's experience, by aiding the individual in the realization
of worthy behavior goals, and by stimulating him to evolve
new value concepts.

> Daniel A. Prescott, *Emotion and the Educative Process.*
> Washington: American Council on Education, 1938, p. 138.

6.

Variations in the Guidance Approach

A. *The Directive Approach*

117. THE ORIGIN OF DIRECTIVE GUIDANCE

. . Thus, throughout the history of psychiatry, as Appel's review of psychiatric methods indicates, the therapist has assumed the major responsibility for directing the thinking, the emotional life, and, upon occasion, even the daily behavior of the patient. This dominance by the therapist has often been necessary simply because of the psychological and emotional immaturity of the patient, who must early become dependent upon and acquiescent to the counselor. In much the same manner, although with a different emphasis, those engaged in personnel guidance programs have stressed the salutary effects upon human adjustment of supervised activities, planning services, and personal conferences. So it is that psychotherapeutic approaches have gradually evolved, with some momentum it is true, from both psychiatric practice and personnel guidance programs and have in so doing acquired an early historical and psychological emphasis upon the psychologist's directive role in assisting clients to achieve resolutions of troublesome problems. This, briefly speaking, is the origin of directive psychotherapy. (K. E. Appel, "Psychiatric Therapy," chap. 34; J. McV. Hunt, editor, *Personality and the Behavior Disorders.* New York: The Ronald Press Company, 1944.)

> L. A. Pennington and Irwin A. Berg, editors, *An Introduction to Clinical Psychology.* New York: The Ronald Press Company, 1948, p. 443. (From chapter by Fred McKinney.)

118. THE BASIC ASSUMPTIONS IN PRESCRIPTIVE COUNSELING

If permissive counseling may be characterized as student-controlled, prescriptive counseling by contrast is counselor-controlled. This difference is clean-cut when we consider the basic assumptions, the sequence of counseling steps, and the counselor's function in the prescriptive approach.

Basic Assumptions:

1. Prescriptive counseling assumes that the counselor is better able to identify desirable goals for the student than the student himself. Because of his training, his maturity, and his information about the student from personnel materials such as tests, records, and health reports, the counselor can make better judgments than can the student about such matters as the student's vocational choices, life-goals, or relations with others. The student comes to the counselor with a problem. The latter, after careful study of relevant materials, provides him with alternative solutions. The student himself selects from the counselor-chosen alternatives the choice which he wishes to make.

2. The emphasis in prescriptive counseling is upon the intellectual approach to the student's problem. It is assumed that knowledge of alternative choices or solutions will lead to proper choice and hence to changed behavior. In other words, the acceptance of goals is a rational, logical process. A student, for example, desired very much to be a doctor, but obviously lacked the scholastic aptitude and other personal qualifications. If he followed prescriptive methods the counselor would show the student the requirements for medicine, would analyze the student's case material for indications of other vocational potentialities, and would, finally, provide him with the best possible choices which wise and keen insight into the student's situation would provide. Such a procedure, it is presumed, would enable the student (if the counseling was skillful) to "see" these choices as feasible possibilities for him. He would know which choice to make. If he tended to choose erroneously, the counselor would, of course, urge him to try out, at least, that course which seemed to suit his abilities and interests most favorably, emphasizing the necessity, too, of making tentative decisions.

3. Effective counseling demands personnel materials, an assumption related to the process of counseling. The counselor recognizes the limitations of tests and measurements, but they are, nevertheless, indispensable. In making judgments of appropriate choices for the student, in appraising interests, abilities, needs, and the like, the counselor cannot depend upon his "hunches." Personnel materials of all sorts provide the objective data which justify and support his analysis.

4. The counselor carries the burden of responsibility for the solution of the student's problem. In the last analysis, it is his judgments from which the student may choose, his interpretations of personnel data which guide the student's thinking, and his responsibility to stick with the problem until the student sees the light.

> Paul J. Brouwer, *Student Personnel Services in General Education*. Washington: American Council on Education, 1949, pp. 17-18.

119. THE COUNSELOR-CENTERED APPROACH

The first type of counseling which we may consider could well be called counselor-centered. In this type of counseling the significant activities rest with the counselor. The counselor must first of all make a diagnosis and hence an important part of his effort is concentrated on getting information. Much of this is gained from the individual who comes to him for help and more may be gained from others—spouse, parents, friends, commanding officer, physician, and the like. The counselor may gain information not only through interview and inquiry but also through the use of test procedures, measuring ability, personality characteristics, and other aspects of the individual and his adjustment. In order to make a suitable diagnosis the counselor must know the facts about the adjustment problem in question. If a man complains bitterly about his lack of promotion the counselor must know whether or not this complaint is justified. If an individual is upset because he believes his wife is "stepping out" the counselor must know whether this is true or a figment of the man's imagination. If a woman war worker feels that she is unjustly treated by the company, or a service man is uncertain as to whether he should marry now or after the war, the counselor must be able to gather all the facts which are relevant to these complex situations.

The second function of the counselor in this method of dealing with the individual is understanding and interpretation of the data. In order to interpret it correctly the counselor must have not only complete information but a thorough knowledge of the psychology of personality and the psychology of adjustment. He must accept a heavy responsibility for a correct diagnosis and interpretation since a mistake in judgment may cause him to deal with the problem in such a way as to make it worse rather than better. He must have the professional skill to know whether his diagnosis of the situation should be kept to himself or should be revealed and interpreted to the client. If he decides upon the latter he will need skill in handling emotional resistance and must be prepared to find the client upset when truths are unpleasant.

The third function of this type of counselor is to have at hand the solutions for the problems which the client presents. He must know whether marriage is a wise step in this instance, whether divorce is the only solution for the next couple. He must be able to suggest a course of action for the man whose wife is unfaithful, and to advise steps which will lead toward deserved promotion for the war worker. He must have the solution for homesickness and social maladjustment, for bitterness and discouragement. He must basically have the answers to the client's problems.

This counselor-centered type of counseling is typical of much of the work which is carried on today in this field. Experience would indicate that it is characteristic of much psychiatric practice and of much of the counseling work of psychologists and social workers. It is typical of almost all work in the field of vocational guidance and of much of industrial personnel work. Workers in these professional fields usually see the function of the counselor as creating rapport, gathering information, analyzing, diagnosing, interpreting, advising, suggesting, and solving.

Although this is the common procedure in many fields of counseling effort it seems clear that it is definitely inappropriate for the group to whom this paper is directed. In the first place the necessary process of gathering information is not feasible for the wartime counselor because it is too costly in time. In the second place the professional training of most USO workers, clergymen, and other semi-professional counselors is inadequate to make the necessary diagnostic judgments. In the third place this approach to counseling carries definite risk for the client when the counselor has inadequate professional preparation. Serious harm may be done to an individual by giving him prematurely an interpretation of his behavior which he is not prepared to accept. In the fourth place this counseling viewpoint is not at all in accord with the free and non-authoritarian atmosphere in which most of these counselors operate. The USO worker for example, who takes over the responsibility for diagnosing and solving the problems of one of the participants in his group is adopting a viewpoint quite contrary to the democratic and spontaneous atmosphere which prevails or should prevail in the major portion of his work.

> Carl R. Rogers, "A Counseling Viewpoint for the U.S.O. Worker," mimeographed, 1945, pp. 1-2.

120. THE COUNSELOR PRESCRIBES AND DIRECTS

. . By "prescriptive counseling" is meant those practices wherein the counselor makes judgments about the student and endeavors to communicate them to him as effectively as possible in order to influence him to behave in ways *prescribed* by the counselor (but now accepted by the student).

> Paul J. Brouwer, *Student Personnel Services in General Education.* Washington: American Council on Education, 1949, p. 11.

121. DEAN "A" USES DIRECTIVE APPROACH

Imagine that a student, SJ, said exactly the same words with the same inflection to two deans whom we shall call Dean A and Dean B. SJ has come voluntarily to see each dean separately. He has not met either one before.

The dean says: Good morning. Won't you sit down? (SJ sits.) What would you like to talk about?

SJ: There's a little problem I want to talk over with you. I haven't got my high school diploma yet. I came to college under an arrangement whereby I am to get it this June.

For perhaps sentimental reasons I'd like to get my diploma with the rest of my high school class this June. Up until now I'd been planning to take a week off and go home at that time. My home is in Z (a city 700 miles away). I thought at that time I'd also see my draft board because I'm just turning eighteen and will have to register.

I guess I didn't realize the difference between high school and college courses. I didn't realize how important lectures were at college. I'd hate to miss the lectures in biology and in Mr. C's course. . . .

Prescriptive Method. Dean A: Sure, you may go home if you'd like to; nothing in the rules against it. But I wouldn't advise you to. From June 18 to 28 you will have ten free days to see your friends, your draft board, and all that. You won't miss any classes here. You'll not lose out in your work.

SJ: I suppose you're right. But I'd hate to miss graduation— for sentimental reasons, I suppose. Mr. Bixby, the principal, was swell about letting me start college before I officially graduated, and I'd kind of hate to let him down.

Dean A: I know it seems a little as though you're ignoring him. But as you said yourself, college is different from high school. It hardly pays to cut lectures and labs unless absolutely necessary. But, of course, you'll have to decide for yourself whether to stick it out or duck out. It doesn't seem to me that going back to your high school graduation is absolutely necessary, is it, SJ?

SJ: No, I guess not. You're probably right. Well, I'll stick it out until the ten-day vacation between quarters.

Dean A: Good boy. So-long.

(Adapted from materials supplied by Dean of Students, BASIL PILLARD, Antioch College. The contrasting interviews with Deans A and B, assuming the identical initial situation, highlight the different procedures and outcomes when permissive or prescriptive counseling methods are used. See selection 140 for Dean B's nondirective approach.)

Ibid., pp. 11-13.

122. Prescriptive Methods Conform to Popular Approach

Prescriptive methods utilize the more common characteristics in our culture, such as sound judgment, the effective use of objective data, and a keen interest in promoting and prescribing the welfare of others. In addition, prescriptive methods demand knowledge of the materials of counseling, such as tests, anecdotal records, health reports, and academic records. The counselor must be able to use these materials in order to arrive at an accurate appraisal of the student.

Most faculty members traditionally have used prescriptive methods in their counseling work. The usual personnel program, the expectations of the student and his parents, the general didactic emphasis of the college and, perhaps not least, the human proclivity to advice-giving, to prescribing suitable ideas and courses of action to younger or less informed persons, have combined to popularize and structure the prescriptive approach to counseling. It is the usual thing to do.

Ibid., p. 26.

123. Counseling Is More Than Words

For I was hungry and you fed me,
I was thirsty and you gave me drink,
I was a stranger and you entertained me,
I was unclothed and you clothed me,
I was ill and you looked after me,
I was in prison and you visited me.

James Moffatt, *The New Testament: A New Translation.* New York: Harper and Brothers, 1922, Matthew 25: 35-36.

124. Values in the Directive Approach

By way of introduction to *directive techniques,* as they are to be developed here, it is wise to indicate that they are not incompatible with client-centered therapy; nor does their use preclude the counselor from permitting the more garrulous client to continue verbalization during the interview. Today, few if any of the experienced counselors who use the directive approach when it is deemed wise, would interrupt those patients who are "naturals" for the nondirective relationship. The best counseling procedure, therefore, is that which most appropriately utilizes the client's needs to understand himself and to satisfy effectively his motives at a stable and mature level. Direction, for most of the cases treated by the clinical psychologist, will accordingly consist of assistance rendered in speeding the general process of adjustment, and hence will entail more often than not the guidance function rather than outright dominance and control. Indeed, what occurs in a counseling session depends, as Wrenn (C. G. Wrenn, "Client-Centered Counseling," *Educational and Psychological Measurement*. 1946, 6, 439-44), has indicated, upon the nature of the client and the situation. The maturity, intelligence, self-knowledge, extroversion, and stability of the patient, and the urgency and pervasiveness of the problem are among those aspects which structure the therapeutic interview. The personality of the counselor, his training, reputation, methods, and resources are also among those variables that affect the counseling relationship. Psychotherapeutic procedures, directive in nature, accordingly have their place in the resolution of personal problems through the medium of the clinical interview.

> L. A. Pennington and Irwin A. Berg, editors, *An Introduction to Clinical Psychology*. New York: The Ronald Press Company, 1948, pp. 443-44. (From chapter by Fred McKinney.)

125. The Inadequacies of Prescriptive Counseling

Many other counselors, however, use a different approach. When someone comes to them for help they "take over." Like a doctor intent upon making a diagnosis, they ask many questions about the client's problems and symptoms and finally decide just what the trouble is and what caused it. Then, by means of pep talks, subtle suggestions, or logical arguments, they persuade the client to follow definite courses of action that they feel are for his own good. In the extreme of this type of counseling all the client has to do is answer the counselor's questions and follow his recommendations. This kind of counseling is directive and counselor-centered.

More and more counselors are beginning to feel that such

directive techniques, in most circumstances, are not really helpful at all. Sometimes the initial problem that the client brings to the counselor is only a surface symptom of a more deeply underlying maladjustment. For example, it is well known that many students seeking vocational or educational guidance are really troubled by more basic difficulties. Yet, some counselors, because they take the initiative out of the client's hands and concentrate on the first problem presented, may miss this underlying maladjustment entirely.

Sometimes when a counselor takes the responsibility for solving a client's problems he may find the "answers," but at the expense of making the client a more dependent individual. The client may feel inferior because he had to lean on someone also for help. As a result, he may feel less confident to handle future problems on his own.

Some clients secretly resent being told what to do. Although they may listen passively enough, they will not follow the counselor's advice. Perhaps, they have always rebelled against authority. Perhaps they feel their integrity is threatened when they are told what to do. Some clients, believing they have not been given the right advice, shop around until they find a counselor who tells them what they want to hear.

Sometimes clients are unable to follow the suggestions they get from counselors. Advising a depressed person to buck up or an alcoholic to control himself is like telling someone to pull himself up by his bootstraps. People may be able to force themselves into a state of cheerfulness or self-control, but usually for short periods of time only. When the almost inevitable relapse sets in, they are left feeling worse than when they started. They believe they are spineless weaklings without will power.

> Daniel Malamud, "The Counselor Says 'M-HM,'" *Science Monthly*, February 1948, pp. 145-48.

B. The Client-Centered Approach

126. HISTORICAL ORIGINS OF CLIENT-CENTERED COUNSELING

The historical origins of client-centered counseling are found in will therapy by Otto Rank and relationship therapy by

Jessie Taft. Originally a student of Freud's, Rank later differed with him concerning the nature of the therapeutic relationship. He believed that in psychotherapy, as in every other life experience, a conflict exists between the "wills" of the two persons involved. Therefore it was his opinion that the client should be allowed free opportunity to exert his will in dominating the counselor. Rank was much impressed with the notion of birth trauma, a concept which refers to the emotional pain that the separation from the mother is believed to cause the newborn child. He assumed that every life experience duplicates this situation, and that the patient who has not found a successful means of adjusting to this separation suffers a neurosis. For Rank, therefore, each therapy situation was an experience in readjusting to the separation from a person who represented the loved parent. Eventually the ending of treatment was itself thought to have symbolic value as a part of this relationship.

This conception of will therapy was brought to this country by Jessie Taft (J. J. Taft, *The Dynamics of Therapy in a Controlled Relationship*. New York: Macmillan, 1933), a social worker, who translated Rank's writings into English. Taft placed great emphasis on the relationship which exists between the two persons in a therapeutic interview. She believed that this relationship was more important than the decisions or the intellectual explanations of behavior which might be made during therapy. The situation was, therefore, made very permissive, and the client was allowed to express any attitude that he felt.

This point of view spread in this country between 1930 and 1940 so that eventually a number of people were utilizing similar concepts. John Levy's relationship therapy, David Levy's attitude therapy, and Frederick Allen's approach to psychotherapy with children are among the more important examples. Rogers also was influenced by this approach; in 1940 he began to modify the point of view in the direction of an even more permissive relationship. By 1942 his ideas had been sufficiently crystallized to be published in the book entitled *Counseling and Psychotherapy* (C. R. Rogers, *Counseling and Psychotherapy*. Boston: Houghton Mifflin, 1942).

Since that time further developments of the concepts of non-directive therapy have appeared, but its basic principles are essentially unchanged.

> L. A. Pennington and Irwin A. Berg, editors, *An Introduction to Clinical Psychology.* New York: The Ronald Press Company, 1948, pp. 465-66. (From chapter by William U. Snyder.)

127. BROUWER DEFINES PERMISSIVE COUNSELING

. . By "permissive counseling" is meant those practices in which the counselor creates a permissive relation which enables the student freely to express his feelings, emotions, and ideas, to the end that he will be more independent and self-understanding and hence more capable of solving his own problems.

> Paul J. Brouwer, *Student Personnel Services in General Education.* Washington: American Council on Education, 1949, p. 11.

128. THE PHILOSOPHICAL ORIENTATION OF THE COUNSELOR

The primary point of importance here is the attitude held by the counselor toward the worth and the significance of the individual. How do we look upon others? Do we see each person as having worth and dignity in his own right? If we do hold this point of view at the verbal level, to what extent is it operationally evident at the behavior level? Do we tend to treat individuals as persons of worth, or do we subtly devaluate them by our attitudes and behavior? Is our philosophy one in which respect for the individual is uppermost? Do we respect his capacity and his right to self-direction, or do we basically believe that his life would be best guided by us? To what extent do we have a need and a desire to dominate others? Are we willing for the individual to select and choose his own values, or are our actions guided by the conviction (usually unspoken) that he would be happiest if he permitted us to select for him his values and standards and goals? . . .

Perhaps it would summarize the point being made to say that, by use of client-centered techniques, a person can implement his respect for others only so far as that respect is an integral part of his personality make-up; consequently the person whose operational philosophy has already moved in the direction of *feeling* a deep respect for the significance and worth of each person is more readily able to assimilate client-centered techniques which help him to express this feeling. (This whole topic might be helpfully pursued on a deeper level. What permits the therapist to have a deep respect for, and acceptance of, another? In our experience, such a philosophy is most likely to be held by the person who has a basic respect for the worth and significance of himself. One cannot, in all likelihood, accept others unless he has first accepted himself. . . .)

Hence, to put in more summarized or definitive form the attitudinal orientation which appears to be optimal for the client-centered counselor, we may say that the counselor chooses to act consistently upon the hypothesis that the individual has a sufficient capacity to deal constructively with all those aspects of his life which can potentially come into conscious awareness. This means the creation of an interpersonal situation in which material may come into the client's awareness, and a meaningful demonstration of the counselor's acceptance of the client as a person who is competent to direct himself. The counselor acts upon this hypothesis in a specific and operational fashion, being always alert to note those experiences (clinical or research) which contradict this hypothesis as well as those which support it.

> Carl R. Rogers, *Client-Centered Therapy.* Boston: Houghton Mifflin Company, 1951, pp. 20-22 and 23-24.

129. SOME FORMULATIONS OF THE COUNSELOR'S ROLE

As we look back upon the development of the client-centered point of view, we find a steady progression of attempts to formulate what is involved in implementing the basic hypothesis in the interview situation. Some of these are formulations by individual counselors, whereas others have been more generally held. Let us take a few of these concepts and examine them, moving through them to the formulation which appears to be most commonly held at the present time by therapists of this orientation.

In the first place, some counselors—usually those with little specific training—have supposed that the counselor's role in carrying on nondirective counseling was merely to be passive and to adopt a laissez faire policy. Such a counselor has some willingness for the client to be self-directing. He is more inclined to listen than to guide. He tries to avoid imposing his own evaluations upon the client. He finds that a number of his clients gain help for themselves. He feels that his faith in the client's capacity is best exhibited by a passivity which involves a minimum of activity and of emotional reaction on his part. He tries "to stay out of the client's way."

This misconception of the approach has led to considerable failure in counseling—and for good reasons. In the first place, the passivity and seeming lack of interest or involvement is experienced by the client as a rejection, since indifference is in no real way the same as acceptance. In the second place, a laissez faire attitude does not in any way indicate to the client that he is regarded as a person of worth. Hence the counselor who plays a merely passive role, a listening role, may be of assistance to some clients who are desperately in need of emotional catharsis, but by and large his results will be minimal, and many clients will leave both disappointed in their failure to receive help and disgusted with the counselor for having nothing to offer.

Another formulation of the counselor's role is that it is his task to clarify and objectify the client's feelings. The present author, in a paper given in 1940 stated, "As material is given by the client, it is the therapist's function to help him recognize and clarify the emotions which he feels." (Carl R. Rogers, "The Process of Therapy," *Journal Consult. Psychol.*, 1940, 4: p. 162.) This has been a useful concept, and it is partially descriptive of what occurs. It is, however, too intellectualistic, and if taken too literally, may focus the process in the counselor. It can mean that only the counselor knows what the feelings are, and if it acquires this meaning it becomes a subtle lack of respect for the client. . . .

At the present stage of thinking in client-centered therapy, there is another attempt to describe what occurs in the most satisfactory therapeutic relationships, another attempt to describe the way in which the basic hypothesis is implemented. This formulation would state that it is the counselor's function to assume, in so far as he is able, the internal frame of reference of the client, to perceive the world as the client sees it, to perceive the client himself as he is seen by himself, to lay aside all perceptions from the external frame of reference while doing so, and to communicate something of this emphatic understanding to the client. . . .

Another attempt to phrase this point of view has been made by the author. It is as follows:

As time has gone by we have come to put increasing stress upon the "client-centeredness" of the relationship, because it is more effective the more completely the counselor concentrates upon trying to understand the client *as the client seems to himself.* As I look back upon some of our earlier published cases—the case of Herbert Bryan in my book, or Snyder's case of Mr. M.—I realize that we have gradually dropped the vestiges of subtle directiveness which are all too evident in those cases. We have come to recognize that if we can provide understanding of the way the client seems to himself at this moment, he can do the rest. The therapist must lay aside his preoccupation with diagnosis and his diagnostic shrewdness, must discard his tendency to make professional evaluations, must cease his endeavors to formulate an accurate prognosis, must give up the temptation subtly to guide the individual, and must concentrate on one purpose only; that of providing deep understanding and acceptance of the attitudes consciously held at this moment by the client as he explores step by step into the dangerous area which he has been denying to consciousness.

I trust it is evident from this description that this type of relationship can exist only if the counselor is deeply and genuinely able to adopt these attitudes. Client-centered counseling, if it is to be effective, cannot be a trick or a tool. It is not a subtle way of guiding the client while pretending to let him guide himself. To be effective, it must be genuine. It is this sensitive and sincere "client-centeredness" in the therapeutic relationship that I regard as the third characteristic of nondirective therapy which sets it distinctively apart from other approaches. (Carl R. Rogers, "Significant Aspects of Client-Centered Therapy," *American Psychologist,* 1946, 1, pp. 420-21.)

    Ibid., pp. 26-30.

130. A Theory of the Therapist's Role

With this type of material in mind, a possible psychological explanation of the effectiveness of the counselor's role might be developed in these terms. Psychotherapy deals primarily with the organization and the functioning of the self. There are many elements of experience which the self cannot face, cannot clearly perceive, because to face them or admit them would be inconsistent with and threatening to the current organization of self. In client-centered therapy the client finds in the counselor a genuine alter ego in an operational and technical sense—a self which has temporarily divested itself (so far as possible) of its own selfhood, except for the one quality of endeavoring to understand. In the therapeutic experience, to see one's own attitudes, confusions, ambivalences, feelings, and perceptions accurately expressed by another, but stripped of their complications of emotion, is to see oneself objectively, and paves the way for acceptance into the self of all these elements which are now more clearly perceived. Reorganization of the self and more integrated functioning of the self are thus furthered.

Let us try to restate this idea in another way. In the emotional warmth of the relationship with the therapist, the client begins to experience a feeling of safety as he finds that whatever attitude he expresses is understood in almost the same way he perceives it, and is accepted. He then is able to explore, for example, a vague feeling of guiltiness which he has experienced. In this safe relationship he can perceive for the first time the hostile meaning and purpose of certain aspects of his behavior, and can understand why he has felt guilty about it, and why it has been necessary to deny to awareness the meaning of this behavior. But this clearer perception is in itself disrupting and anxiety-creating, not therapeutic. It is evidence to the client that there are disturbing inconsistencies in himself, that he is not what he thinks he is. But as he voices his new perceptions and their attendant anxieties, he finds that this acceptant alter ego, the therapist, this other person who is only partly another person, perceives these experiences too, but with a new quality. The therapist perceives the client's self as the client has known it, and accepts it; he perceives the contradictory aspects which have been denied to awareness and accepts those too as being a part of the client; and both of these acceptances have in them the same warmth and respect. Thus it is that the client, experiencing in another an acceptance of both these aspects of himself, can take toward himself the same attitude. He finds that he too can accept himself even with the additions and alterations that are necessitated by these new perceptions of himself as hostile. He can experience himself as a person having hostile as well as other types of feelings, and can experience himself in this way without guilt. He has been enabled to do this (if our theory is correct) because another person has been able to adopt his frame of reference, to perceive with him, yet to perceive with acceptance and respect.

Ibid., pp. 40-41.

131. CONDITIONS FAVORABLE TO CLIENT-CENTERED THERAPY

If the individual or group is faced by a problem;
If a catalyst-leader provides a permissive atmosphere;
If responsibility is genuinely placed with the individual or group;
If there is basic respect for the capacity of the individual or group;
Then, responsible and adequate analysis of the problem is made;
responsible self-direction occurs;
the creativity, productivity, quality of product exhibited are superior to results of other comparable methods;
individual and group morale and confidence develop.

Ibid., pp. 63-64.

132. CLIENT-CENTERED THERAPY WIDELY APPLICABLE

. . client-centered therapy is very widely applicable—that indeed in one sense it is applicable to all people. An atmosphere of acceptance and respect, of deep understanding, is a good climate for personal growth, and as such applies to our children, our colleagues, our students, as well as to our clients, whether these be "normal," neurotic, or psychotic. This does *not* mean that it will *cure* every psychological condition, and indeed the concept of cure is quite foreign to the approach we have been considering. With some types of individuals hospital care may be necessary, or with others some type of drug therapy may be necessary, and a variety of medical aids may be utilized in psychosomatic conditions. Yet a psychological climate which the individual can use for deeper self-understanding, for a reorganization of self in the direction of more realistic integration, for the development of more comfortable and mature ways of behaving—this is not an opportunity which is of use for some groups and not for others. It would appear rather to be a point of view which might in basic ways be applicable to all individuals, even though it might not resolve all the problems or provide all the help which a particular individual needs.

    Ibid., p. 230.

133.   Conditions Essential for Therapy

It has seemed to us that the client-centered therapist operates primarily upon one central and basic hypothesis which has undergone relatively little change with the years. This hypothesis is that the client has within himself the capacity, latent if not evident, to understand those aspects of his life and of himself which are causing him unhappiness or pain, and the capacity and the tendency to reorganize himself and his relationship to life in the direction of self-actualization and maturity in such a way as to bring a greater degree of internal comfort. The function of the therapist is to create such a psychological atmosphere as will permit this capacity and strength to become effective rather than latent or potential.

How does the therapist implement this function, creating an atmosphere in which self-directive therapy can take place? We have been able, in practice, to create the appropriate conditions with a majority of our clients, and what follows is a current attempt to formulate the essential aspects of the conditions for therapy as they are determined by the therapist.

1. The therapeutic phenomenon seems most likely to occur when the therapist feels, very genuinely and deeply, an attitude of acceptance of and respect for the client *as he is,* with the potentialities inherent in his present state. This means a

respect for the attitudes which the client now has and a continuing acceptance of the attitudes of the moment, whether they veer in the direction of despair, toward constructive courage, or toward a confused ambivalence. This acceptance is probably possible only for the therapist who has integrated into his own philosophy a deep conviction as to the right of the individual to self-direction and self-determination.

It may help to discuss briefly the meaning of the term "respect," as we have been using it. In other orientations there is also respect for the client or patient, but this is usually respect for the person as *un*revealed. It is a respect for something underneath, not respect for the person as he seems to himself at that moment. In client-centered therapy, however, the counselor attitude which we have found most fruitful is a complete acceptance of the person as he seems to himself at that moment. It is only as *he* is dissatisfied with this self that he explores further into his attitudes and feelings.

2. A second and corollary condition making for therapy is the complete willingness of the therapist for the center or locus of evaluation and responsibility to remain with the client. All judgments, all evaluations, all changes in evaluations, are left to the client. The counselor not only avoids voicing any evaluations of the client—or his behavior, or the meaning of his behavior, or the behavior of others—but, by his immersion in the empathic process, tends to avoid *making* these judgments. Likewise responsibility is left with the client—whether it be responsibility for choosing the next topic of his conversation or responsibility for some grave choice with regard to himself and his future. This whole attitude on the part of the therapist is, if it is to be effective, real and not forced. It is a basic willingness to help the client realize his own life in his own terms and an unwillingness to attempt to take over the responsibility for his life or any part of it.

3. A third condition for therapy is the therapist's willingness and sensitive ability to understand the client's thoughts, feelings, and struggles from the client's point of view. This ability to see completely through the client's eyes, to adopt his frame of reference, has seemed to be an important way of implementing the fundamental hypothesis and is the basis for

the use of the term "client-centered." To receive completely what the client is trying to communicate of his feelings even when his communication is confused or incoherent or fragmentary—to be able to enter into the client's private world and see it from *his* point of view—this is what we mean by adopting the client's frame of reference.

4. A fourth condition of therapy is that the counselor use only those techniques which implement these basic attitudes. Techniques are definitely secondary to attitudes, and seemingly poor technique may succeed if attitudes are sound, while we have not found the reverse to hold true. The most helpful techniques have seemed to be those that communicate something of the attitudes which the therapist deeply holds—his acceptance of the person as he is at this moment and his empathic understanding of the client's attitudes as seen from the client's point of view.

5. Perhaps another aspect of the therapist's function should be mentioned. This is the matter of limits. I feel quite uncertain about this, but my present hypothesis is that the therapist sets those limits which make it possible for him to maintain his own attitudes. If I doubt that I could fully accept in play therapy a child who broke up all the furniture, then I think of breaking furniture as a limit I would set upon the child's behavior, so that he might experience complete acceptance within the relationship as defined. If, with an adult client, I question my ability to remain completely accepting and alertly empathic for a two- or three-hour stretch, then I limit the contact to one hour. In general it may be said that these limits apply to behavior. If the therapist finds it necessary to limit the expression of attitudes in their verbal or symbolic form, then it is very doubtful if the client will experience acceptance.

These would seem to us to be the ways in which the therapist carries out his basic hypothesis. In one sense all these conditions are wrongly described, since it is the experiencing of these by the client which is significant for therapy. It could be more truly stated that the conditions of therapy are met when the client experiences the respect and acceptance the therapist has for him, experiences an empathic understanding, experiences the locus of evaluation as residing within himself, experiences no significant limitation on the expression of his attitudes. I have chosen, however, to describe the situation as the counselor perceives it in trying to establish the conditions.

It is doubtless clear that many conditions which have often been regarded as essential are not mentioned, either because they are regarded as unnecessary or because they seem to be detrimental. Included in these unmentioned items are psychological diagnosis of the client; a transference relationship fostered by the therapist; and such therapist intentions as interpretation, advice, guidance, reassurance, and the like.

> Carl R. Rogers, "A Current Formulation of Client-Centered Therapy," *The Social Service Review,* Vol. 24, No. 4, December, 1950, pp. 443-45.

134. CLIENT-CENTERED COUNSELING IN THE HANDLING OF SOCIAL TENSIONS

The central thesis of this pamphlet may be presented very briefly. It is this: In therapeutic work with individuals, inner conflicts and interpersonal conflicts are clearly resolved by client-centered or nondirective psychotherapy in a manner which can be explained only by a reformulation of certain significant psychological principles. There is reason to believe that these principles may apply to group and social conflicts as well as to individual conflict situations.

A METHOD OF DEALING WITH CONFLICTS

Basically, the principles of the client-centered approach are simple, complex though the skills may be in practice. Essentially, the changes . . . are brought about through a therapeutic process in which the counselor's role is best described by the terms *warmth, permissiveness, acceptance, understanding,* and *nondirectiveness.* He bases his work upon his own warm interest in others. He creates a relationship in which the client comes gradually to feel that any expression of attitude, real or false, shallow or deep, socially acceptable or taboo, is permitted. His reaction to the attitudes and feelings expressed is one of acceptance, a willingness for the person to be what he is, to feel what he feels. It is a reaction of empathy, frequently verbalized in responses which reflect and show understanding of attitudes expressed. His work is permeated by an unwillingness to use any procedure or technique which would guide the client or intervene in his affairs. It is a positive conviction that the client has the capacity of responsible choice. Throughout, the counselor's role is that of a catalytic agent, not a forceful reagent. He does not guide or interpret, or persuade or suggest. He creates an atmosphere in which the client can gradually come to be himself.

It is in this atmosphere that the tendency of the individual to be mature, to desire harmonious relations with others, to be responsible and independent, comes to the fore. It is this latent capacity, released by the unusally permissive aspects of the counseling relationship, which provides the motivation for the change which occurs.

What happens, then, in this type of therapeutic situation, to the negative interpersonal attitudes? . . . Some of the steps in the process are not new, but thoroughly familiar. Others have not been examined with the care which they deserve. In the following sections the various phases and characteristics of this process of change in interpersonal attitudes will be considered. . . .

THE CONSTRUCTIVE RESOLUTION OF INTERPERSONAL CONFLICTS

Release: In situations of interpersonal conflict . . . the first step toward solution is the release of tension. The outpouring of negative feelings is known to be the most prominent feature of the beginning of psychotherapy. (Charles A. Curran, *Personality Factors in Counseling.* New York: Gruen and Stratton, 1945; William U. Snyder, "An Investigation of the Nature of Non-Directive Psycho-Therapy," *Journal of General Psychology.* October, 1945, 33: 193-223), and this emotional release reduces the distortion in attitudes which a defensive adjustment has required. Clients not infrequently comment on the difference it makes in their attitudes when they find they can express themselves freely.

Gradual Exploration of Attitudes: Another phase of the total process of resolution of conflicts is the exploration of attitudes. Little by little, as the noncritical and accepting nature of the relationship is realized, the client dares to push his thinking further into areas which he has not fully investigated on a conscious level. He begins to bring into the picture elements which he has previously been reluctant to consider, or has denied completely. It should be mentioned here that our experience would justify no sharp lines of delineation between conscious and unconscious material. There are instead imperceptible gradations from material which is fully conscious and has been previously expressed, to material which has been fully conscious but never expressed, to material which is dimly realized but never fully admitted to consciousness or expressed, to material which has been definitely denied any conscious recognition. It is upon these varying degrees of dimness that the process of exploration throws light. It may be a consideration of different possible attitudes, gradually admitting the deeper and truer one, as in this example.

"You know, some mornings I just hate to go to work. Maybe I'm lazy, and yet maybe I'm afraid to meet people. It's a nice place to work, nice people and all, but I just hate it. Maybe I'm just getting stale, but I think really it comes back to the fact that I don't want to meet people." (George A. Muench, *An Evaluation of Nondirective Psychotherapy by Means of the Rorschach and Other Tests*. Applied Psychology Monograph #13, Stanford University Press, 1947.)

Often the client realizes that he is exploring his own attitudes, and comments upon his discoveries by saying, "I never thought of it that way before." Such an instance is here quoted from an early interview with a client who had many difficulties in social adjustment.

"I used to think at times that it was a good thing I was reserved, but now I realize that my reservedness was actually caused by vindictiveness. If people do something to me, I try to put some vindictive thing on to them. That's the first time I ever thought of it in that way. . . . I tend, I suppose, to blame others for my own inadequacies." (George A. Muench, *An Evaluation of Nondirective Psychotherapy by Means of the Rorschach and Other Tests*. Applied Psychology Monograph #13, Stanford University Press, 1947.)

The Development of Conscious Awareness of Patterns and Motives: The next phase is a crucial one, the development of a conscious awareness of needs, motives, and satisfactions. This is customarily referred to as the development of insight (Carl R. Rogers, "The Development of Insight in a Counseling Relationship," *Journal of Consulting Psychology,* November-December, 1944, 8: pp. 331-341), but for our present purposes I should like to dissect the process and discuss its characteristic aspects.

The client who has been permitted freely to explore his attitudes without any need for defensiveness can gradually admit to conscious consideration various elements from the shadowed areas which he has been unable to inspect before. As the area of conscious awareness widens, he begins to understand more and more incidents in his life, and gradually to recognize the significant patterns of his behavior. In the example which follows, Mr. Dell, a professional man, first admits the truth of a statement he has formerly denied, comes to understand one incident more deeply, and is then able to achieve conscious awareness of a pattern which he can see applies generally to his behavior.

Mr. Dell: My associates described me as a little tin god on wheels, and I didn't like the description . . . (pause; then slowly) but I think it's probably true. (Pause) I've always been so apprehensive and distrustful of others that I'm not able to let the control over things out of my hands. . . . That's the only way I can get any degree of calm or inner peace. (Tells how even when in the hospital for an operation he made all the arrangements) . . . which an ordinary patient would have left to his physician. I had to have it all arranged to summon forces to my aid, even though I was flat on my back. . . . I suppose that that's why I asked that the operation be carried on under a local anesthetic, so that I could be aware of what was going on.

Counselor: You felt you couldn't lose control even during an operation.

Mr. Dell: (Tells of another incident where he insisted upon looking after himself with the notion that he could do it better than anyone else.) So certainly there has been a deep-seated feeling that things were bound to go wrong if I didn't keep the rudder in my own hands.

. . . We know objectively and statistically that these expressions of insight are increasingly frequent once emotional release is achieved. (William U. Snyder, "An Investigation of the Nature of Non-Directive Psycho-Therapy." *Journal of General Psychology*. October, 1945, 33: pp. 193-223; Charles A. Curran, *Personality Factors in Counseling*. New York: Grune and Stratton, 1945, p. 287.) The client becomes aware of the need which is being satisfied by his behavior. He is able to turn the light of conscious thinking upon the devices, often devious, by which he has been keeping a balance, often precarious, in his psychological economy. He draws together these isolated gleams of understanding into more generalized insights until he becomes fully aware of patterns of reactions which have characterized his behavior in many situations. . . .

So important is this process which we have been discussing— the dawning conscious awareness of patterns and motives— that certain little-realized facts about it should be stressed:

(a) *Increasing the field of conscious awareness seems always to reveal the fact that conflict existed or was intensified because significant attitudes were prevented from coming into conscious consideration.* . . .

(b) *Insight develops spontaneously if the permissiveness of the counseling relationship is real and if emotional release has been achieved.* The client has the capacity to come to a profound, accurate, and meaningful awareness of his own hidden motives and patterns. He will arrive at such an awareness, to the extent that his situation requires it, if the therapist maintains the proper psychological atmosphere. This point requires stress because it stands in sharp contrast to the views held by psychoanalysts, who have consistently maintained that the client must be *given* such insight by the expert. Our case records deny this categorically. Curran also supplies some research evidence on this point. [See Curran ref. above, chaps. 3 and 4.] The nondirective therapist maintains that experience shows that the client can arrive at a richer, truer, more sensitive understanding of his own significant patterns than can possibly be given to him by any therapist. This is achieved in spite of the pain and discomfort which often accompanies these discoveries. The distrust of the individual's capacity, so characteristic of psychoanalysis, appears on the basis of our experience to be unfounded.

(c) *The only patterns the client is likely to explore in nondirective therapy, and the only hidden motivations of which he achieves conscious recognition, are those which have a significant influence upon his present behavior.* The point is important because of the stress which some therapies, notably psychoanalysis, place upon past experience. Mr. Winn told of the boyhood experiences that made him regard himself as sexually inferior because those experiences had a direct bearing upon his present tendency to project his problems upon his wife. There were doubtless many other emotionally colored childhood experiences which he did not feel impelled to bring up, because they were not significantly connected with his present problem.

This is one of the reasons why the nondirective approach achieves constructive results quickly. The client explores his present concerns, and gradually unearths related experiences and attitudes, both present and past. He does not embark upon a complete analysis of all his life's behavior, but finds his attention, without any conscious effort, focusing upon those aspects of his life which are relevant to his current mode of behaving. In a permissive situation his conversation turns inevitably to the areas of emotional discomfort.

Changed Frame of Reference: With this much of the therapeutic process traced, the question still remains: how does it actually change adverse interpersonal relationships? The gist of the answer lies in the next two phases.

Full conscious awareness of all the aspects of a given interpersonal conflict supplies a new frame of reference in which the very nature of the problem is radically altered. At the outset, the conflict between the client and other persons seems inevitable and irremediable. As the denied elements are admitted into consideration, the whole picture of the relationship between the self and others undergoes change. The problem that previously seemed insoluble now becomes mutual and soluble. . . .

Miss Taylor's concept of her problem also underwent transformation. At first she conceived it in terms of unreasonable parental domination and control; later she phrased it somewhat after this fashion: "My parents are unreasonably controlling, but my desire to be dependent and my refusal to share my real self with them helped to create the problem." Again, it is perceived as a mutual and much more soluble difficulty.

One might say that most of the difficult problems of relationship, the situations of interpersonal conflict, are never solved as they stand. They are, in fact, usually insoluble as presented. But when they are redefined in the added light provided by the conscious awarenesses which have developed, they become solved in a new frame of reference. The relationship between the self and the other person is perceived in a vastly different fashion.

Conscious Awareness Alters the Concept of Self: Still another way in which interpersonal tensions become resolved is through the alteration which therapy brings about in the concept of the self. The client, as his span of conscious awareness widens, creates a new, a truer, and a more positive concept of himself. In other words, not only does he perceive the relationship between self and others in a new and different fashion, but he forms a new and altered concept of self which still further alters the total frame of reference by changing one of its major terms. Raimy has shown that the individual's views about himself, his perception of his abilities, his worth, his capacity to cope with life change measurably and markedly during therapy. (Victor C. Raimy, *The Self-Concept as a Factor in Counseling and Personality Organization.* Columbus, Ohio: Ohio State University, 1944. Unpublished Ph.D. thesis.) Muench has shown that such alterations produce significant changes in the pattern and structure of the personality as measured by the Rorschach and other tests, given before and after therapy. (George A. Muench, *An Evaluation of Non-directive Therapy by Means of the Rorschach and Other Tests.* Applied Psychology Monograph #13, Standard University Press, 1947).

An example from the case of a young man with many deep problems will illustrate the fashion in which conscious awareness brings an acceptance of the "real" self, and an alteration of the self-concept:

Joe: Then there's the conflict about the pretense of extreme

masculinity and whether I should adopt it or not. I don't believe
I should. I shouldn't work so hard to try to build up my body the
way I've been doing. Getting a sporty car is a little part of that,
too. If I let things be a little more laissez faire, it may work out
better.

Counselor: You feel that perhaps you don't want to work quite
so hard at being masculine.

Joe: I think all the extravagant things I wanted to do I *thought*
were financial, but I think they were a desire to be masculine.
I've wanted an airplane and a yacht and a big library—that last is
a sort of a musty masculinity, but I never intended to read them.
I've always wanted an underground gunroom, too.

Here it is plain that his previous concept of this aspect of
himself is that of an extremely masculine young man, or possibly in his moments of greater awareness, a concept of himself
as being not at all masculine, but putting up a pretense of
masculinity. Increased conscious awareness brings him a new
concept of self as a person with some masculine traits who can
be comfortable in his own natural degree of masculinity. Need
it be pointed out that this more comfortable and truer concept
of self has many implications for his social relationships? It
makes him definitely more easy, less overbearing, less defensive. It has altered in fundamental fashion the very base on
which his interpersonal conflicts have developed.

*A New Course of Consciously Controlled Action Adapted to
Reality:* Finally, the conscious awareness that develop in
therapy release the individual's capacity to exercise conscious
control over his behavior, to move in purposeful directions
based upon a newly achieved integration. Nothing in the
process of therapy is more impressive than the constructive
capacity for wise behavior shown by the individual when he
has accepted and assimiliated the insights he has himself
achieved. This new behavior, let it be emphasized, is not suggested, even in subtle fashion, by the therapist. It results
from the release of the normal forces of growth within the
individual, who now takes constructive steps to deal with the
problem that he has newly formulated. . . .

Miss Taylor, who resented her parents' control, decided with
fear and trembling to try to stand up as an independent person

in her relationship with them. After vacation, she came in to tell of her attempt:

Miss Taylor: I have never gotten along so well with my parents in all my life. I'm so happy about it I don't know what to do. (She tells of an incident in which her father began to criticize her unjustly.) Something happened, though, and I blew up, too. We had a hot and heavy argument for quite a while. After that he never said another thing. I guess he thought I was big enough to stand on my own two feet. All the rest of the time I was home, instead of telling me what to do, he would ask me. I was able to think for myself for the first time in my life at home. It was a funny feeling.

(Later.) You know when I went home, I would never let my parents read my letters. . . . While I was home this summer, though, I decided that I would try it and see what happened. I did, and my goodness, it helped. It seemed to bring us closer together. For the first time in my life, I felt close to both my parents.

A fresh and constructive solution becomes possible when purposes are clear and behavior is subject to conscious control. Miss Taylor was able to build a constructive relationship to her parents because she was no longer fighting herself in them. . . .

It should be pointed out that the reason interpersonal relations improve as a result of this therapeutic process is that they become realistic. As the person faces and accepts himself, he also becomes realistic in relations with others. Problems of interpersonal relationships do not disappear, but they are handled differently. They are dealt with in ways that are straightforward, and solutions are chosen which are in line with real attitudes, and hence are effective. It would appear that satisfactory ways of getting along with another can always be worked out, if the basis of the relationship is the real attitudes which exist.

POSSIBILITIES FOR THE RESOLUTION OF GROUP CONFLICT: A RÉSUMÉ

Clinical evidence indicates that when social tensions and interpersonal conflicts are dealt with nondirectively in a group, the process closely parallels that of nondirective therapy on an individual basis. The phases of the group process, as well as of the individual process, would seem to be: emotional release, gradual exploration of attitudes, growing conscious awareness of denied elements, a changed perception of the problem in an altered frame of reference, a changed concept of the group and the self, a new course of consciously controlled action better adapted to the underlying reality of the situation, and a resulting improvement in social and interpersonal relationships.

In group therapy as in individual therapy, the basic motivation for change appears to be a socially and biologically based preference for harmonious rather than antagonistic relations, for mutuality rather than complete selfishness, for a high degree of individual independence rather than submissiveness. When this motivation is blocked by repressed elements, factors that the group cannot fully face, conflict situations are difficult to resolve. The force that operates to bring about change, in the atmosphere created by a nondirective therapist acting as a catalyst, is the growth capacity of the individual, the tendency toward maturity and socialization which is the mainspring of human life, group or individual.

These are only clinical hypotheses. The reason for burdening this paper with so much of clinical illustration is to stress the point that we are as yet only at the stage of clinical observation and description. This clinical experience points to possibilities of an exciting nature, but they are as yet only possibilities.

TWO LONG-RANGE IMPLICATIONS

As clinical experience with client-centered therapy is examined and evaluated, its phenomena seem to assume ever greater significance, and at least two long-range implications become worthy of special consideration.

As we examine and try to evaluate our clinical experience with client-centered therapy, the phenomenon of the reorganization of attitudes and the redirection of behavior by the individual assumes greater and greater importance. This phenomenon seems to find inadequate explanation in terms of the mechanistic type of determinism which is the predominant philosophical background to most psychological work. The capacity of the individual to reorganize his atti-

tudes and behavior determined by his own insight into the
factors of his experience is an impressive capacity. It involves
a basic spontaneity which we have been loath to admit into
our scientific thinking. Allport has pointed out that in other
areas besides therapy we have given too little attention to the
volitional factor.

The clinical experience could be summarized by saying that
the behavior of the human organism may be determined by
the external influences to which it has been exposed, *but it
may also be determined by the creative and integrative insight
of the organism itself.* This ability of the person to discover
new meaning in the forces which impinge upon him and in
the past experiences which have been controlling him and the
ability consciously to alter his behavior in the light of this
new meaning have a profound significance for our thinking
which has not been fully realized. We need to revise the philosophical basis of our work to a point where it can admit that
there exist within the individual forces that can exercise a
creative and significant influence upon behavior, which is not
predictable through knowledge of prior influences and conditionings. The forces released through a catalytic process of
therapy are not adequately accounted for by a knowledge of
the individual's previous conditionings, but only if we grant
the presence of a capacity for integration and redirection
within the organism. This capacity for volitional control is a
force which we must take into account in any psychological
equation.

In applying this thought to the situations of interpersonal
and social conflict with which we have been concerned, a
significant implication is evident. A client-centered therapeutic
approach offers the possibility of a solution of social conflict,
not through the discouragingly slow process of trying to
change individuals from without, but through the release of
integrative and constructive forces *within* such individuals and
groups. As we have seen from the clinical illustrations, the
"cure" for a husband's supicion of his wife, or a union leader's
bitterness toward management, lies not in some more powerful
psychological pressure which can be brought to bear by others,
but within the individual himself, through the release of con-

structive forces by procedures we are already beginning to understand. It also appears possible that the "cure" for hatred between Jews and non-Jews, between Negro and white, lies not in the external psychological forces which can be brought to bear, but lies within the fearful and antagonistic groups themselves. It is within the situations in which we find discord and bitterness that we may also find the positive and creative and integrative strengths which may be released through a catalytic type of therapy to bring about a resolution of the conflicts. This is the note of hope which we feel is justified by our experience with a client-centered therapy in individual and group situations.

> Carl R. Rogers, *Dealing With Social Tensions*. Danville, Ill.: The Interstate, Printers and Publishers, 1948, pp. 1-30. (Most of the illustrations and material on group therapy were omitted.)

OTHER INTERPRETATIONS OF CLIENT-CENTERED THERAPY

135. BUTLER AND SEEMAN

The method of psychotherapy with which we are particularly concerned in this discussion is client-centered therapy. Such therapy is based upon certain premises about the nature of personality and the conditions under which personality reorganization takes place. It asserts that an individual who is aware of his own attitudes and motivations is likely to be an integrated person. Client-centered therapy further postulates that an individual has within himself the capacity and resources to develop this self-understanding, and that therapy should provide the conditions under which these resources may be released. The significance of the client-centered approach to counseling seems to revolve about what has been called the internal frame of reference. This is the application in counseling and psychotherapy of a principle often discussed in psychology; that behavior is a result of the way in which an individual thinks about himself, his relationship to others, and his environment. In client-centered counseling, therefore, one of the essential tasks of the counselor is to set up a psychological climate in which the client is enabled to perceive himself, his relationship with others, and his environment in a way that will allow maximum opportunity for him to face his worries, fears, and tensions, and to deal with them in a creative and constructive fashion. It is one of the central tenets of a client-centered counselor that such a psychological climate can be established if, and only if, he consistently behaves in the counseling situation in ways which have been characterized as warm, permissive, and accepting. It is important to note that the counselor must not only be warm, permissive, and accepting from his own standpoint, but from the viewpoint of the client as well. This means that the counselor must genuinely possess these attitudes. If he acts them out mechanically without actually possessing them, his true attitudes of the moment, whatever they may be, are inevitably expressed by non-verbal signs such as: posture, expression, inflection of the voice, and so forth. The client will see the inconsistency between the verbal and the non-verbal expressions, and while he may not interpret them correctly, he will surely interpret them. Since such inconsistencies are often ambiguous, he will interpret them in terms of his own characteristics rather than those of the counselor, and in a way detrimental to the establishment of a good counseling relationship.

Once the pre-conditions of effective client-centered counseling have been established, it is possible to make full use of the internal frame of reference. By this is meant that the counselor, in addition to expressing permissiveness and acceptance of the client as he is *now*, at this very moment, actively endeavors to understand as fully as possible, just what the client is feeling now, how he perceives himself, others, and his environment. It is important to add, that this understanding is not based on a series of inferences of what the client has said but on what the client has expressed, both verbally and non-verbally. In other words, the counselor is endeavoring to understand the client and his world, in the client's own terms. In addition, he is trying to communicate this understanding to the client. It might be remarked at this point that communication to the client of the counselor's understanding is delivered, not by means of a flat statement but frequently with an inquiring kind of inflection which asks rather than insists that the client is being understood.

One of the main hypotheses of the client-centered counselor is that if he has been able: (1) to create the proper psychological atmosphere (2) to understand the client in the client's own terms, and (3) to communicate his understanding, then the client will be enabled to look squarely at himself as he is with what he feels are both his good and bad characteristics. It is this process of facing himself, of admitting his attitudes into awareness that allows him to reorganize his way of seeing himself and his world in the direction of greater emotional freedom and maturity.

An examination of the hypotheses and methods of client-centered therapy will show that they deal basically with the nature and conditions of human learning. If we rephrase the main principle of client-centered therapy specifically as a postulate regarding learning, we may state it as follows: an individual has the maximum opportunity for learning about himself and his environment in a permissive, understanding atmosphere where he is free to go at his own pace and on his own terms. This hypothesis, though it has been applied chiefly to psychotherapy as a special instance of learning, should also be applicable to other situations which are characterized by learning processes. Since in guidance one of the major tasks is to facilitate the student's learning about himself, it follows that the principles of client-centered therapy should be applicable in this field.

In the psychological setting here described distinctions between psychotechnology and psychotherapy disappear. The main question becomes, "In what ways does the student wish to explore his attitudes, his capacities, and his goals?" The question of whether tests should be used or not becomes superfluous. If the student wishes to use tests, then these become one of the tools of which he may come to learn about himself more fully. What is important to note here is that tests then become a tool primarily for the counselee rather than the counselor, and this is so because the essential responsibility for selecting methods of exploration of his problem rests with the student. Since this may in some respects be regarded as a radical departure from current practices with regard to the use of tests, the question may seriously be raised regarding the student's ability to use tests and scores wisely. The evidence available on this point indicates that where students are given responsibility for choosing kinds of tests they wish to take, choices are overwhelmingly in the direction of selections appropriate to their needs. The implications of such evidence is that self-evaluation by the student is not only sound in principle, but also can be applied successfully in practice.

> John M. Butler and Julius Seeman, "Client-Centered Therapy and the Field of Guidance," *Education*, April, 1950, pp. 519-21.

136. SNYDER

Client-centered therapy as developed by Carl R. Rogers is a relatively new technique which has for its historical antecedents the methods of will therapy by Otto Rank and relationship therapy by Jessie Taft. The method consists of counselor-techniques of clarifying the feelings which the client expresses, simple acceptance of what the client says, and explaining the roles of counselor and client. It is essentially *client*-centered, and the counselor continually tries to keep the orientation centered upon the client's own feelings, rather than upon his symptoms. He also tries constantly to keep the responsibility for leading the direction of the interview in the hands of the client himself. In addition to these more positive techniques just mentioned, the counselor avoids certain techniques which are characteristic of some types of counseling situations. He does not give advice or offer criticism. He avoids even the most subtle forms of persuasion, and tries to avoid making interpretations—in the sense of proposing his own explanations for the client's behavior. The counselor seldom gives information; he carefully avoids probing and the asking of direct questions. His use of reassurance and approval is greatly limited and carefully controlled.

The client-centered technique is based upon the belief that the client will make the most satisfactory progress if the counseling situation is one in which he is freed from the usual inhibiting factors and from emotional blocks that prevent him from working out the most effective means for meeting his life problems. It is also based upon the tenet that the client is capable of such growth; that this growth is likely to be prevented if techniques of direction are used.

> L. A. Pennington and Irwin A. Berg, editors, *An Introduction to Clinical Psychology.* New York: The Ronald Press Company, 1948, pp. 495-96. (From chapter by William U. Snyder.)

137. WOODWORTH AND MARQUIS

Nondirective counseling sounds like a contradiction in terms, for what can a counselor do except counsel and direct the maladjusted client who comes to him for help? What can a therapist do except to diagnose the patient's trouble and help him to eliminate the bad motive that is causing the trouble? What, indeed, except to help the client bring to light the good motive, the constructive forces within him, the *vis medicatrix naturae* or "healing power of nature" on which any physician really must rely in combating a disease? The nondirective or client-centered counselors trust the client's will and power to find his own way out of his trouble, if only they supply a psychological atmosphere of warmth and understanding, a "permissive" atmosphere in which he is free to express his thoughts and feelings. The client talks about himself, at first at a relatively superficial level. The counselor, avoiding both praise and blame, reflects back to the client what he has revealed of his motives and thus stimulates the client to go further and deeper in exploring himself. Constructive motives gradually come into view and assert their power so that the client freely chooses a better course than the one he has been blindly following. The task of the counselor in such a series of interviews is by no means easy, for he has to lay aside the superior attitude of the professional expert and meet the client on the client's own ground. The client may at times feel that the counselor is not taking hold as he should, yet he comes back for further interviews because he finds the oppressive load of frustration growing lighter from week to week. (Carl R. Rogers, *Counseling and Psychotherapy.* Boston: Houghton Mifflin, 1942; "Significant Aspects of Client-Centered Therapy," *American Psychologist*, 1946, I, pp. 415-22; Carl R. Rogers and

J. L. Wallen, *Counseling with Returned Servicemen.* New York: McGraw-Hill, 1946.)

Robert S. Woodworth and Donald G. Marquis, *Psychology,* Fifth Edition. New York: Henry Holt and Company, Inc., 1947, p. 397. By permission of the publishers.

138.   Brouwer

The aim of permissive, nondirective counseling is, according to Rogers, to help the student "to become a better organized person, oriented around healthy goals which (he) has clearly seen and definitely chosen." (Carl R. Rogers, *Counseling and Psychotherapy.* New York: Houghton Mifflin Co., 1942, p. 227.) It aims to provide the student with a "united purpose, the courage to meet life and the obstacles which it presents. . . . Consequently, the client takes from his counseling contacts, not necessarily a neat solution for each of his problems, but the ability to meet his problems in a constructive way. . . . " (See p. 218 in reference above.)

Rogers defines effective counseling as a "definitely structured, permissive relationship which allows the client to gain an understanding of himself to a degree which enables him to take positive steps in the light of his new orientation. This hypothesis has a natural corollary, that all the techniques used should aim toward developing this free and permissive relationship, this understanding of self in the counseling and other relationships, and this tendency toward positive, self-initiated actions." (See page 18 in reference above.)

Basic Assumptions. This definition may be made more explicit by indicating the basic assumptions involved in it. The first three relate to the way in which change in behavior occurs; the second three, to the process of counseling.

1. The individual is assumed to have a strong, impelling "drive toward growth, health, and adjustment." The problem which the student faces is *his* problem which *he* wants more than anyone else to overcome. Counseling is, therefore, an effort to free the individual to solve his own problem in his own way. . . .

2. The feelings and emotions in the problem situation are

more significant than the intellectual elements when change in behavior occurs. . . .

4. A permissive relation with the counselor "frees" the student to attack his real problem. In such a relation, the counselor generally responds to feeling instead of to content. . . .

5. Counseling is itself a growth experience. . . .

6. Certain conditions must be met before this permissive approach is feasible. Permissive counseling is not a panacea but, like prescriptive counseling . . . a method of counseling which functions only under certain conditions. The prime requisite for a counseling relation which calls for permissive methods is that the student is under stress to solve a problem. The stress is so great that the student is willing to express his feelings freely about it, regardless of the pain which such expression may bring with it. . . .

In permissive counseling, the faculty member plays a unique role. By responding to feeling, not content, he mirrors the student's feelings and emotions. He does not add to, nor subtract from, the feeling; he does not affect the kind or intensity of feeling. In a sense, he reflects, mirror-fashion, what the student *is* so that the counselee can see himself more realistically. . . .

The counselor lets "a person talk and puts in comments that keep it going instead of stewing in a circle." His comments are responses to feeling. The counselor is "someone to talk to so I can make up my mind." The student makes the decisions; the counselor creates the atmosphere in which the troubled student is free to decide. The counselor supplies friendliness, a genuine warmth, and responsiveness without maudlin sympathy. He is neither judge nor advocate, but allows the free expression of any feelings, no matter how hostile, aggressive, or guilty. He controls the situation only by setting up certain limits beyond which the student cannot go; for example, he limits the time of each interview, and he refuses to allow the student to draw him into argument, debate, or discussion of personal views. Finally, he keeps the counseling situation free from coercion or pressure.

Paul J. Brouwer, *Student Personnel Services in General*

Education. Washington: American Council on Education, 1949, pp. 13-17.

139.   TOWLE RAISES QUESTIONS RELATED TO CLIENT-CENTERED
              EMPHASIS IN SOCIAL WORK

Social workers encounter both adults and children whose growth is obstructed through adversities which deprive and frustrate them. They encounter them often when regressive impulses are in operation, when dependency is in the foreground, when assertive strivings toward independence are weak, distorted, or in abeyance. In such instances often they find that the valid dependency of the moment must be fully and freely met in order that he may again move forward. This implies nurturing services and a giving relationship. Often the strengths, the inner and outer resources, that he brings to the situation must be identified, affirmed, and used. The individual may not need this help, but often the renewal of capacity for self-help is contingent upon the social worker's doing something to and for the individual at the start. Social workers also encounter people who long have been so deprived and frustrated that the growth impulses are submerged or under-developed. They will need help to become more independent, and they may or may not be able to use help to attain a more socialized maturity or to recapture their former competence.

A second concept is that of individual difference. Individuals differ widely in physical energy, in intellectual capacity, in emotional state, in motivation in their lives in general, and in seeking help. They differ widely in their needs, in their adaptations, and in the success or failure of those adaptations. This is a decisive point, for it means that they differ widely in the degree of satisfaction or dissatisfaction which they bring to the helping experience in which they vary in capacity to endure demand, to face reality, to become self-evaluative, to endure pain in the interest of attaining a better social adaptation. They differ widely in social norms by which realistically to evaluate their own responses. They differ widely in knowledge and reality "know-how" with which to meet actual-life demands. Furthermore, their life-situations vary greatly—from being poverty-stricken to rich in resources, material and otherwise; from presenting slight to overwhelming pressures and demands. One individual's emotional disturbance may be commensurate and healthy, another's incommensurate and sick. One individual's maladjustment may be normal, another's a symptom of deep mental ills, organic and/or functional.

This factor of difference in individual and in situation makes essential differential study and differential diagnosis for differential treatment if the individual is to be helped. Furthermore, this factor of difference in individual and in situation makes for different demands in terms of knowledge and skill on the part of workers and in terms of kinds of services as determined by agency function and resources. Hence our practice of differentiated assignment and referral. Social work therefore cannot entertain the possibility of a therapy for all men to be practiced by all workers. A social worker's activity may be directive or nondirective or more often a flexible interplay of both. And herein lies social work's major claim to being client-centered. We would consider it truly worker-centered if what was done was foreordained, prescribed without close reference to individual difference.

Third, we operate on the assumption that the worker is responsible to conduct the helping process. Because he exerts, for the client's welfare, those controls implicit in professional responsibility, it does not follow that the relationship is a controlling one.

It does mean, however, that social case work is worker-centered in that the worker does some thinking about the client. Certain knowledge is attained through professional education for this purpose. A social case worker cannot take responsibility for helping a person without taking responsibility also for evaluating him in the context of his life-situation. It is only as the social worker evaluates precisely that the client may be helped to become self-evaluative and self-directive. For example: A worker might set in operation a therapeutic interview in which the client is talking freely, even precipitously. The comments of acknowledgment which he, the worker, makes if selected without evaluation might touch repetitively on basic conflicts in such a way as to obstruct self-evaluation, through strengthening defenses, thus increasing projections and rationalization. Or they might crash defenses, leaving the client helpless and confused and more incapable than formerly of self-evaluation. The social case worker fears empathy without evaluation. Because a social case worker evaluates the client, it does not follow that he takes over the evaluative process. It merely means that he has the where-withal with which either to help the client evaluate himself or to know whether the client's evaluations are realistic. The social norms, the reality demands against which a client evaluates himself, may have at times to be injected by a worker.

Fourth, when a client enters a helping relationship, it is inescapable that something is done "to and for him," even though one might wish that "he do" entirely "to and for himself." Even in those instances where a worker is non-directive, he exerts an influence on the one who has turned to him for help. Passivity, nondirection, can do a great deal to the person. The trouble is that "it does" irresponsibly rather than responsibly. Some years ago social case workers found, during an extensive phase of passivity, that the client with his feelers out for the response of the worker often became more disturbed than relieved, more coerced than freed. Not getting a response, he talked compulsively and repetitively in endless circles, or he became immersed in understanding the worker rather than himself. The worker's uniqueness aroused anxiety which he strove to dispel through attempts to know the worker when he might better have been focused on under-standing himself. In some instances he felt that the worker was indifferent, in which event he may have been driven to great lengths to provoke a response, frequently outreaching his defenses in talking and in acting out. Or, feeling the worker to be indifferent, he felt rejected, thus experiencing a repetitive rather than a corrective relationship. Hence depen-dencies and hostilities mounted. The relationship became increasingly complicated and often was terminated with more frustration for the client than self-realization.

The worker-client relationship in case work is a working-together to some purpose. Its characteristics are its confidential nature, its respectful nature, and its dispassionate quality. On the part of the worker it involves not just "thinking about" the client but a thinking and feeling with but not like him. Between client and worker it is a feeling-, thinking-, and doing-together to some purpose. Help for the client derives through the opportunity, in time of trouble when he is disturbed, confused, and in conflict, to experience the response of a worker who sees his problem differently, who feels it differently, but who sympathetically understands. In some ways the relationship repeats former relationships. It repeats, however, with a difference; and that difference is decisive, for it constitutes the corrective element. He wants and needs to find in the worker relatedness to, rather than identification with, or a reflection of his feelings, attitudes, and responses. . . .

The worker's initial mode of working is to bring a well-ingrained positive attitude to the client, an attitude that an applicant for help is eligible for service until proved ineligible, an applicant for help is competent until proved incompetent. When a social worker does not equate a need for help with weakness, he does not focus narrowly on the problem and what is wrong with the person (the pathology). When he does not equate a need for help with weakness, he is not fearful of his helping efforts, but instead he will focus on what help is wanted, needed, and can be used. He will focus also on what this person brings to the situation to use in his own behalf. Thus underlying strengths are discerned rather than merely the dependency and confusion, which are in the foreground.

As the worker focuses on determination of need with readiness to meet it, the client experiences social acceptance of his need. Instead of engendering greater needfulness, the worker's attitude will tend to ease humiliation and restore self-respect, at which point seemingly pathological projections and rationalizations may subside. Instead of being driven defensively to exaggerate his problem or to minimize it, the client is encouraged to present it realistically. Because of a change in feeling about himself, the client may be able to view the problem more realistically, and this often is a first step toward its solution.

Charlotte Towle, "Client-Centered Case Work," *The Social Service Review,* Vol. 24, No. 4, December, 1950, pp. 452-54.

140. DEAN "B" USES PERMISSIVE APPROACH

(Adapted from materials supplied by Dean of Students Basil Pillard, Antioch College. The contrasting interviews with Deans A and B, assuming the identical initial situation, highlight the different procedures and outcome when permissive or prescriptive counseling methods are used. See selection 121 for Dean A's directive approach.)

Imagine that a student, SJ, said exactly the same words with the same inflection to two deans whom we shall call Dean A and Dean B. SJ has come voluntarily to see each dean separately. He has not met either one before.

The dean says: Good morning. Won't you sit down? (SJ sits.) What would you like to talk about?

SJ: There's a little problem I want to talk over with you. I haven't got my high school diploma yet. I came to college under an arrangement whereby I am to get it this June.

For perhaps sentimental reasons I'd like to get my diploma with the rest of my high school class this June. Up until now I'd been planning to take a week off and go home at that time. My home is in Z (a city 700 miles away). I thought at that time I'd also see my draft board because I'm just turning eighteen and will have to register.

I guess I didn't realize the difference between high school and college courses. I didn't realize how important lectures were at college. I'd hate to miss the lectures in biology and in Mr. C's course.

Permissive Method. Dean B: You're beginning to feel that if you take a week of the quarter to go home, it will put you behind the eight-ball.

SJ: That's it. I just don't know what to do, and I thought I'd ask you to advise me.

Dean B: Well, I think that's a choice you'll want to make for yourself. You're free to go home if you want. Perhaps, if we talk it over a little more, you'll see more clearly what is best.

SJ: How long do we get off between the spring and summer quarters?

Dean B: You'll get about ten days—from June 18 to the 28th.

SJ: Oh, that's quite a long time. I would like to get back and see my high school class. There are a lot of fellows who will be drafted, and I may not see them again. But now I'm inclined to stay here and go home in between quarters. I couldn't afford to go home both times. If I went for graduation, I know I'd feel pressed and that I was missing out here.

Dean B: You'd like to go, but you wouldn't have such a good time knowing what you were missing here.

SJ: You know, the more I think it over, the more I feel it would be foolish to go. I think I'd feel much better to wait and take the time between quarters. I think that's what I'll do.

Dean B: You're beginning to feel sure that the decision you've made will work out better?

SJ: Yes; well, thanks very much. I guess I just needed to talk it over and get it straight in my own mind. I see it more clearly now. Thanks a lot.

Dean B: You're quite welcome.

> Paul J. Brouwer, *Student Personnel Services in General Education.* Washington: American Council on Education, 1949, pp. 11-13.

141. THE POWER IN THE HUMAN SOUL

"There is power in the human soul," said the Lord,
 "When you break through and set it free.
  Like the power of the atom.
  More powerful than the atom,
  It can control the atom,
  The only thing in the world that can.
  I told you that the atom is the greatest force in the
    world save one.
  That one is the human soul."

> Hermann Hagedorn, *The Bomb That Fell on America.* New York: Association Press, 1948, p. 44.

142. STRENGTH IS FROM WITHIN

Emory Alvord after thirty years of Agricultural Missions with the Bantu in Africa said: "I believe more firmly than ever in the infinite potential in people—any people, all people. But their improvement must come always from within themselves."

> Liston Pope and Clarence W. Hall, "The Man Who Founded a People," *Christian Herald,* March, 1951, p. 96.

143. The Door Opens from Within

William Holman Hunt, great English artist of the Pre-Raphaelite school, painted a garden scene which was hung in the Royal Academy in London. The painting, appropriately called "The Light of the World," shows the Master standing in the garden at night, holding a lantern. He is knocking on the door and awaiting an answer from within.

A critic looked at the painting, turned to Mr. Hunt and said: "Lovely painting, Mr. Hunt, but you've forgotten something. That door upon which the Master is knocking . . . is it never to be opened? You've forgotten to put a knob on the door."

Mr. Hunt smiled with great understanding. "My friend, that door on which the Master is knocking is not just an ordinary door. It is the door to the human heart. It needs no knob, for it can only be opened from within."

> A. O. Malmberg, "Human Relations and Business Success," *Guideposts,* No. 52, 1947, p. 4.

144. Contrast of Directive and Nondirective Approaches
Techniques Most Frequently Employed (Table 5)

(Numbers in parentheses indicate frequency per interview)

Directive Counselor Group:

1. Asks highly specific questions, delimiting answers to yes, no, or specific information. (34.1)
2. Explains, discusses, or gives information related to the problem or treatment. (20.3)
3. Indicates topic of conversation but leaves development to client. (13.3)
4. Proposes client activity. (9.4)
5. Recognizes the subject content of what the client has just said. (6.1)
6. Marshals the evidence and persuades the client to undertake the proposed action. (5.3)
7. Points out a problem or condition needing correction. (3.7)

Nondirective Counselor Group:

1. Recognizes in some way the feeling or attitude which the client has just expressed. (10.3)
2. Interprets or recognizes feelings or attitudes expressed by

general demeanor, specific behavior, or earlier statements. (9.3)

3. Indicates topic of conversation but leaves development to client. (6.3)
4. Recognizes the subject content of what the client has just said. (6.0)
5. Asks highly specific questions, delimiting answer to yes, no, or specific information. (4.6)
6. Explains, discusses, or gives information related to the problem or treatment. (3.9)
7. Defines the interview situation in terms of the client's responsibility for using it. (1.9)

From Table 5 we might draw certain tentative conclusions based, it must be remembered, on study of a very small number of interviews, whose value, however, is enhanced by the fact that they are completely recorded through electrical recording devices. It might be said that counseling of the directive sort is characterized by many highly specific questions to which specific answers are expected, and by information and explanation given by the counselor. These two techniques account for more than half of the counselor's part in this type of treatment interviewing. The counselor further gives the client opportunity to express his attitudes on specified topics, and points out to the client problems and conditions which he, the counselor, has observed to be in need of correction. He clarifies or restates or recognizes the subject content of what the client has told him. He endeavors to bring about change by proposing the action the client should take, and by bringing to bear both evidence and personal influence to insure that such action will be taken.

On the other hand, counseling of the non-directive sort is characterized by a preponderance of client activity, the client doing most of the talking about his problems. The counselor's primary techniques are those which help the client more clearly to recognize and understand his feelings, attitudes, and reaction patterns, and which encourage the client to talk about them. One half of the counselor items fall into these categories. The counselor may further achieve this aim by restating or clarifying the subject content of the client's conversation. Not infrequently he gives the client opportunity to express his feelings on specified topics. Less frequently he asks specific questions of an information-getting sort. Occasionally he gives information or explanations related to the client's situation. Although not the type of technique which could be used frequently, there is considerable redefinition of the interviewing situation as being primarily the client's situation, to use for his own growth.

> Carl R. Rogers, *Counseling and Psychotherapy*. Boston: Houghton Mifflin Company, 1942, pp. 123-24.

145. BASIC DIFFERENCES BETWEEN PRESCRIPTIVE AND PERMISSIVE METHODS

How Is Behavior Changed? One basic difference between prescriptive and permissive methods lies in a difference in belief as to how changes in behavior are most efficiently brought about. Permissive counseling assumes that the individual has a strong drive toward goals; when his realization of his goals is inadequate or when he cannot reach them because he is immobilized by fears, anxieties, or frustrations, maladjustment occurs. Through the permissive relation with the counselor he clarifies his goals, understands himself more clearly, and is able to reorganize his feelings and emotions so that he is enabled to move forward once again toward achieving his goals. In this way, behavior changes—learning occurs and educational objectives are realized.

Prescriptive counseling, on the contrary, assumes that growth occurs through intellectual understanding of inadequacies in present goals. A student aspires to leadership in extra-class activities but lacks the potentialities to be a leader. The counselor, after making a careful valuation of the student's potentialities, points out to him the unrealistic nature of his goal and provides him with alternative objectives more compatible with his abilities. The student, recognizing the validity of the counselor's appraisal, accepts his judgment, changes his goals, and finds new activities more consistent with his abilities. His behavior has changed—the educational objective of orienting the student to himself and the world about him has been realized.

When Is Counseling Needed? A second basic difference

between these points of view relates to the conditions which prevail when counseling is needed. Permissive counseling operates most effectively when definite preliminary conditions have been met. For example, the student faces a serious problem which he feels incapable of solving. Prescriptive counseling is applicable at any time, whether or not students face serious problems or are unaware of their problems. In fact, in the judgment of the counselor, a student may be "riding for a fall" so that the counselor's intervention is an obligation. For example, a student inadvertently or ignorantly has signed up for too heavy a load of courses. The counselor feels sure the student is doomed to fail. He accordingly steps into the life of the student, as it were, and discusses the probabilities of failure. In other instances, the counselor meets students routinely to discuss their plans, problems, and interests. Not only when students are psychologically prepared to change their behavior, therefore, is prescriptive counseling applicable.

What Is the Counselor's Role? A third point of opposition involves the role of the counselor. By implication, the prescriptive counselor "knows best" because he has judgments and advice to make on the basis of personnel data, experience, and insights not understandable or available to the student. Hence he is justified in intervening in the student's life, in determining the best possible alternative goals for the student. On the other hand, the permissive counselor provides no answers about what is right or best for the student. He scrupulously avoids projecting his own judgments and opinions into the discussion. His sole purpose is, by skilled questions and comments and by the creation of a permissive counseling relation, to help the student to solve his own problems.

What Is the Aim? A fourth basic difference exists in the fundamental aim of the counseling process. In prescriptive counseling, the faculty member aims to change the student's behavior in ways which he, the counselor, thinks desirable. He prescribes the alternatives and urges the selection of the most appropriate one. He is thus constantly called upon to make value-judgments about desirable goals for another person and about courses of action designed to achieve their goals. Nevertheless, he aims also as counselor to leave the choices up to the student in order that the latter may become more mature and independent. But the student's choices must be right in the eyes of the counselor, or further counseling, further efforts to "win over" the student, are necessary. The basic aim of prescriptive counseling is, therefore, to secure development along lines judged or prescribed by the counselor.

Permissive counseling, on the other hand, aims to provide the student with the opportunity to find his own goals and achieve them, regardless of what these goals may be. The emphasis is entirely on the growth of the student, not on the particular pattern of behavior which such growth brings with it.

> Paul J. Brouwer, *Student Personnel Services in General Education.* Washington: American Council on Education, 1949, pp. 18-20.

C. *The Co-operative Approach*

146. HELPING THE COUNSELEE WITHOUT INTRUSION

In helping the individual, the counselor is confronted with this paradoxical situation: The client needs the counselor's aid and yet must, in the end, be his own judge and mediator. Moreover, the counselor realizes that, eclectic as he may be, he must see the situation and the client through the lens of his own concepts and outlook upon life and, therefore, can never be completely detached. Remembering the fact that the client must be his own arbiter as a unque and a free man, the counselor asks: "How can I give him the help he needs without intrusion?" This is the basic methodological problem.

The theory that the problem-situation is a field, in the context of which both client and counselor are involved, permits us to see client and counselor as *joint investigators and evaluators,* both contributing their points of view to the problem-situation and striving to evaluate them realistically. Thus the interpretations of the counselor are considered coequal with those of the client, and both are treated in an objective manner. Ultimately, of course, it is the client who chooses what it is that he will do as a result of the joint evaluation.

In the process of joint study of the factors in the problem-situation the counselor must, as we have seen, decide upon the degree of responsibility which he is going to assume and ask the client to assume. In this judgment, he is guided by the principle of all education—that he is arranging experiences so that the counselee is not being indoctrinated or imposed upon but is learning facts, conditions, and relationships which he assimilates and judges before crystallizing his own opinion and plan of action. The counselor's judgment of degree of responsibility to be assumed by him is not rigidly fixed beforehand nor is it completely arbitrary. Instead, it is based upon the emergent characteristics of the problem-situation, which predominantly include the needs of the client.

One counselor testifies that he judges the client's readiness to engage in a free evaluation of the problem-situation, including comments by the counselor, by evidence that the client is actively working on his own problem or plan of action, thus being in a state of ongoing and dynamic self-direction in which he can assimilate and take into account external comments without being unduly influenced by them. The counselor sums it up this way: "When the client shifts from 'what am I *supposed* to do?' to 'what I *can* do,' then I know we can exchange opinions without harm."

> Robert H. Mathewson, *Guidance Policy and Practice.* New York: Harper and Brothers, 1949, pp. 201-2.

147. Guidance as Co-operative Experience

The co-operative method seems to be consistent with a sound interpretation of the nature of man, especially with respect to the way he learns and grows. It avoids the once discarded theory of unfoldment from within. Instead, this point of view is based on the belief that it is through dynamic interaction, between man and his environment, that the various adjustments of life are worked out. It is held that the counselor's function is not merely to dislodge an obstruction in the client's emotional life, for the reason that after such dislodgment the client must then create a solution, in the process of which the counselor has an obligation to contribute something of significance. It is just at this point that the essence of the co-operative method is often misinterpreted. The counselor contributes, but in a co-operative and "give and take" fashion. His participation is not similar to a clerk's, for example, who places groceries from the shelves in the customer's bag, but more like a mother helping her daughter in cooking. She makes a suggestion about the heat here, or about some seasoning there, or the two may discuss other steps to be taken in the process. The identity of the mother's contribution is lost in the child's creation, but it still affects the outcome.

Often the solution worked out by the client is a new creation. It is not something he stumbles upon or discovers ready-made but that which he and others have created. In such an act there is mutuality, wherein the client is affected by the counselor, who in turn is influenced by the client. Naturally, it is the client who is being counseled, but effective and mature counselors show the marks of those with whom they have worked. They become more understanding, wise, humble, and able thereby.

The following experience concerns a mechanical adjustment which does not allow for the wide variations usually characteristic of human relations, but it somewhat roughly illustrates what I mean by creativity through a cooperative experience.

A skilled and resourceful workman, with whom I had been conferring whenever help was needed in making various articles around the house, suggested how a clothes hanger might be repaired. I followed his plan but did all the work myself, and to some extent in my own way. The outcome was due to him and to me. Without both of us nothing would have happened. Together we created an arrangement which met my need for a hanger, and gave me real satisfaction. The experience illustrates anew the place of the leader, be he teacher, parent, counselor, or friend.

Co-operative adventures require the best from both parties in the transaction. Intellectual skill, a significant part of man's total equipment, is an essential element in this process. After emotional channels are cleared there must be a meeting of minds for the creation of the best possible solution. There are many human problems which have a number of solutions or several of varying merit. Such situations require intellectual effort and often joint thinking. To suggest that this is true is not to disparage the client, but to recognize the need and value of co-operative endeavor. But this is not to claim that counseling is merely an intellectual exercise. Neither is it all in the realm of feeling and emotion, but rather the function of a total personality. . . .

Recently there has come to my attention an analogy or two which, it seems to me, epitomizes the issue of the place of the leader in the counseling relationship. I refer to the processes of catalysis and photosynthesis. Webster defines catalysis as "a chemical change effected in a compound by an agent that itself remains stable." This idea seems to be in line with the nondirective view, where the counselor's function is a kind of contact action. In Photosynthesis the energy of light is needed to set off the process of food manufacture in plants. Here the light *enters into* the action, but does not dominate it. It is an instance of an activation which enriches the counselee's decisions and actions without dominating them. This is exactly what is suggested as the essence of the co-operative approach, which is further illuminated by another analogy. At some point in the production of gasoline from crude oil a catalytic agent is introduced and, after doing its work, is reclaimed for later use. However, in co-operative counseling the agent's contribution (the counselor's) cannot be reclaimed, for it has entered into and become a part of whatever reaction may have occurred in the life of the client.

Counseling As a Process

Recently the interview has been emphasized practically to the exclusion of other important phases in the total process which constitutes a counseling experience. I feel this is an unwarranted distortion. The interview alone does not constitute counseling. It is an important tool but only one among a number of others. The counselor deludes himself and cheats his client who claims he can do a sound job without taking into account the matrix in which the individual has his being.

It is not often that the counselor may say that any series of interviews, let alone any single session, accomplished the mission in hand. During a series of conferences the client is subject to a number of influences lying outside of the counselor. Even should the client come to an acceptable solution while actually in the counselor's presence, that does not demonstrate the all importance of that particular interview-session. Perhaps it was only the moment when many forces came to fruition.

When it is conclusively demonstrated that clients may be counseled with little reference to the surroundings in which their lives are set, the task will be greatly simplified. However, until such a time, a good counselor will seek to know all that he can about the client. This would include knowledge of test results, background material about home, school, church—the standard data which the case work method requires. This is not to say that then the counselor should take the initiative in working out a diagnosis, followed by a plan of treatment independent of the client. Nor should he press the client to do so alone or in collaboration. However, if the latter desires to work on the problem with him, the counselor would be informed sufficiently to carry his load in the process but without becoming a dictator. I would prefer to depend upon the solution to a problem which is arrived at by an adequate counselor and an earnest client, working together with pertinent facts at hand, than upon the results of a process dominated by some undefined inner force, which is released whenever the client's emotional blockings have been cleared by the catalytic-like participation of the counselor.

Illustrations

The following situations seem to me to illustrate quite well the fact that sound counseling usually implies a process in which the interview finds its normal place.

The first relates to a young woman who entered college upon completion of high school. She was somewhat ungainly, self-conscious, and ill-at-ease. During the first year she found it necessary to work at a taxing and routine job to meet expenses. However, counseling was continued with her, which included many conferences; help in getting a better job and with supervision upon it; counsel about personal appearance; aid from the college physician; help upon habits of work and study; and special attention from her instructors. These contacts were continued over a period of three years. The student did very satisfactory work at the college and on her part-time job during her last year. Her health and personal appearance improved. Upon graduation she secured a desirable position, from which she since has been promoted. No one is able to say just when she came to herself, for it happened over a period of time and through the agency of many people. During the three years she learned to work co-operatively with several counselors. The causes of her growth were legion. She both gave and received.

The second illustration concerns a young married man who had entered college from a full-time position in a social agency. He was high in scholastic aptitude and quite capable in program promotion, but he had difficulty in getting along with others on the job. This pattern was continued in college but with decreasing intensity. All during his residence counseling was maintained through interviews and other activities. Instructors, other students and employers co-operated in the process. During the time a psychiatrist was suggested. Later the student voluntarily discussed this visit to the specialist with his college counselor. Upon graduation he secured a position where his personality and that of his employer were not well matched. However, he remained at his post several years and was given increases in salary. Just recently he has been promoted to a better job and one of considerable responsibility, where a major requirement is getting along with others. All of his emotional problems have not been solved, but now he is having greater success in a more demanding situation than he experienced previously in a lesser one. Here was a situation where both the client and his counselors were active. The client sought the kind of help he received. He made many decisions while at the institution, but in all of them there were bits of information and insight co-operatively contributed from many sources.

Such situations as these are representative of a vast number of similar ones. They point to the principle of sharing in problem solving, and to the necessity for dealing with individuals in their total environment rather than in the vacuum-like setting of the interview. And further, they point up the necessity for the evaluation of counseling by an appraisal of counselee adjustment over a period of time, rather than the mere avowal of improvement by the client, and that within a relatively short span of time.

The Co-operative Approach Applicable to Other Human Relationships

It is my belief that the co-operative approach is not limited alone to the counselor-client relationship. It may apply to contacts between parent and child, leader and group member, or teacher and student. This would be true only of the most basic aspects of these relationships, and of those which represent such counseling at its best. The training of the parent, leader, or teacher in the co-operative approach would be a necessity. Of these relationships, that of counselor-client is the most artificial and occurs much less frequently. This relationship is surely not some esoteric ritual which cannot be learned by parent and teacher; and it could hardly be one which only a counselor—made of the same stuff as the others— is ordained to use. All of these approaches are but forms of an educational process which is characterized by respect for persons, and belief in their creative power, as well as in their ability to co-operate with others for self-development consistent with the common good.

Karl P. Zerfoss, "Counseling as Co-operative Experience," *Counseling*, May, 1949, pp. 1-4.

148.   GUIDED GROWTH

And next it is guided growth. One recognizes of course that development is largely self-development, that every youth is primarily responsible for his own growth, and yet others may share profoundly in guiding him in his adjustment to his environment. I suggest at this point, the relevance of that lovely but neglected old word *nurture*. Nurture conveys about all that one human being can do for another human being. It connotes the soil, the sun, the rain, the wind, and also time, by all of which nature nurtures the seed up, first the blade, then the ear, and then full fruitage. No conception of the educational process which posits mere natural growth without nurture, however modern its dress, can ever give us a true educational process. It commits us to the jungle instead of to the garden. You can never have a garden without a gardener for the nurture of boys and girls any more than you can have a garden of daffodils without a roughened tender hand that loves them up to their blossoming. In between laissez faire and indoctrination lives the art of nurture, the art of guidance. Guided growth is the essence of the educational process.

> Richard H. Edwards, *The Place of Persons in the Educational Process*. Chambersburg, Pa.: The Kerr Printing Company, 1933, pp. 3-4.

149. JOHN DEWEY DISCUSSES THE CO-OPERATIVE APPROACH

The teacher's business is to see that the occasion is taken advantage of. Since freedom resides in the operations of intelligent observation and judgment by which a purpose is developed, guidance given by the teacher to the exercise of the pupils' intelligence is an aid to freedom, not a restriction upon it. Sometimes teachers seem to be afraid even to make suggestions to the members of a group as to what they should do. I have heard of cases in which children are surrounded with objects and materials and then left entirely to themselves, the teacher being loath to suggest even what might be done with the materials lest freedom be infringed upon. Why, then, even supply materials, since they are a source of some suggestion or other? But what is more important is that the suggestion upon which pupils act must in any case come from somewhere. It is impossible to understand why a suggestion from one who has a larger experience and a wider horizon should not be at least as valid as a suggestion arising from some more or less accidental source.

It is possible of course to abuse the office, and to force the activity of the young into channels which express the teacher's purpose rather than that of the pupils. But the way to avoid this danger is not for the adult to withdraw entirely. The way is, first, for the teacher to be intelligently aware of the capacities, needs, and past experiences of those under instruction, and, secondly, to allow the suggestion made to develop into a plan and project by means of the further suggestions contributed and organized into a whole by the members of the group. The plan, in other words, is a co-operative enterprise, not a dictation. The teacher's suggestion is not a mold for a cast-iron result but is a starting point to be developed into a plan through contributions from the experience of all engaged in the learning process. The development occurs through reciprocal give-and-take, the teacher taking but not being afraid also to give. The essential point is that the purpose grow and take shape through the process of social intelligence.

> John Dewey, *Experience and Education*. New York: The Macmillan Co., 1938, pp. 84-85.

MATHEWSON INTERPRETS GUIDANCE AS CO-OPERATIVE EXPERIENCE

150.   JOINT ACTION

Throughout this activity of varying participation and responsibility, exercised reciprocally by the participants, the process as a whole is still regarded by both counselor and client as a cooperative, joint one. When the problem-situation is so conceived, interpretative, informative, or other types of aid introduced by the counselor will be seen in their proper context as a contribution to joint action upon the problem-situation and not as any attempt to dominate the scene.

> Robert H. Mathewson, *Guidance Policy and Practice*. New York: Harper and Brothers, 1949, p. 199.

151.   METHOD IS SECONDARY

The problem-situation in counseling may be comprehended as the total complex of personal and non-personal, individual and situational factors which comprise a distinct "situation in itself," *centering around the client with his problems and the counselor with his modes of assistance.* Such a perception of the problem-situation permits us to view the task of dealing with it, and with all constituent aspects, not as exclusively counselor-centered, nor as entirely client-centered, but as a cooperative study of the factors in the field, both participants being regarded as existing within the field.

Within this field or problem-situation there may be fluctuations of attention, and emphasis upon one or the other of the participants and upon one or the other pertinent factors as the need demands. If the problem-situation is seen as a field, involving both participants and all subjective and objective factors, the versatile employment of appropriate professional techniques of any kind can occur without conflict of philosophy in fulfilling the main functions of counseling practice. Allegiance, then, is not to any method as such but to an ideal of counseling practice embodying universally recognized responsibilities.

This conception does not for a moment rule out or subordinate the emotional, or non-rational, elements of client psychology. It merely attempts to bring out into the open, in full view of both participants in the cooperative venture, such factors as can be correlated, thought about, and deliberately acted upon. Subjective elements which must be "mulled over" by the client can be treated in just that way and still be recognized as part of the problem-situation. No single aspect of the client's situation or its treatment need be neglected in such a view of the counseling process. Moreover, the great fluidity and flexibility which is granted to the process by virtue of this concept would seem to be not the least of its advantages.

Thus regarded, the joint focus upon the problem-situation by both participants is kaleidoscopic, all the known factors constantly shifting and rearranging themselves as they are perceived and weighed by counselor and client together. As the process continues, the more pertinent key factors begin to appear, and possible means of dealing with them begin to suggest themselves.

Ibid., pp. 195-96.

152. A LEARNING SITUATION

. . Perhaps a better designation of the counselor's role would be that of professional and personal socio-psychological interpreter, who is a cooperant, with the client, in mutual review and analysis of the problem-situation. In this relationship the client will play the role of cooperative investigator with accent upon the learning phase. He learns about himself, about his environment, and about more effective ways of developing himself and adjusting to his environment. The counselor will also be a learner but, in addition, will have a responsibility to deal with the situation and with the client in such a way that maximum learning takes place and will continue to take place on the part of the counselee. In a way, then, he will be a teacher-guide, but in a unique sense which none of our present designations adequately covers.

Ibid., pp. 206-7.

153. Co-Participants

The client-counselor relationship in the counseling process is that of co-operative investigation, focusing upon the objectification of facts in the total field of the problem-situation, with the client assuming a role of inquirer-learner and the counselor that of guide-interpreter-aide, both being co-participants in the investigative process.

Ibid., p. 208.

154. A Consultant-Interpreter-Guide

Our examination of the role of the counselor leads to the ultimate conclusion that the counselor accepts an *educative* function as the heart and core of his work. He is a professional practitioner; he is able to aid the client in appraising his personality; he is informed of environmental fact pertinent to client problems. The counselor does not prescribe, does not provide welfare, does not propagate a faith. As a consultant-interpreter-guide, he attempts to enlarge the individual consciousness and power of self-evaluation and of self-direction while simultaneously aiding the individual to adjust and orient himself in his immediate situation. According to the need of the client, the professional practitioner may have the client accept a great deal of immediate responsibility for self-appraisal and self-aid in the problem-situation, or he may himself assume substantial responsibility for conveying information to the client, evaluating pertinent factors, and interpreting related data.

Ibid., p. 209.

155. MUTUALITY THE ESSENTIAL BASIS OF HUMAN FELLOWSHIP

Thus it discovered that the essential basis of human fellowship is neither justice nor pity, but *mutuality*. The patterns of relation in a truly good family are more nearly the norm of Christian fellowship than any ideological utopia in which abstract justice is the ideal. This verdict has been confirmed both by modern existential philosophy and modern counseling theory. Mutuality between counselor and the person counseled means that the counselor must carefully refrain from violating the freedom, dignity or creativity of the person counseled, no matter how sure he may be that his advice is infallible. But if this limits the scope of counseling, it enriches its spirit.

In "I-Thou" relations, what does mutuality require of us? In the first place, it calls for a solid *sense of security*. The child psychologists have told us about the elemental need of the infant and young child for emotional security. We need not accept the hypothesis that emotional patterns are *irrevocably* fixed in childhood in order to agree that a sense of security is *sine qua non* for effectual human living. To feel that one is wanted, that one really "belongs" and shares in the circle of life around him—all this is indispensable to a poise and unanxious adjustment to one's social situation. This circle-of-belonging needs to be enlarged as life develops until at last man comes to feel that he is "at home in the universe," that God loves him, accepts him pretty much as he is and regards his sharing in the divine purposes with neither cynicism nor condescension. The primary cause of insecurity is the suspicion that one is unloved. A man is literally lost when he does not have an active sense of being beloved by other persons and by God, not because of what he can do, but because of who he is. The good counselor is one who can give such an authentic sense of security to the person counseled, or can at least allay the loneliness of the unloved.

A second thing that is required, if a human relation is to be mutual, is *objective recognition* of a person's own peculiar gifts and skills. In a good family, the members know what each other can do and give encouragement and praise to a job well done, rather than making unrealistic demands from motives of family pride or utility. This is not a mark of indulgent love. It simply means that mutuality does not call for identical ability nor literal equality. The important thing, in any group, is that each one can feel that his gifts matter to the whole and that his status does not depend upon any competitive ranking.

The third prerequisite for mutuality is *liberty*. Human liberty, or moral freedom, does not mean the power to alter natural processes or to act by sheer caprice. It means the capacity, consciously and responsibly, to participate in decisive events in such a way as to feel uncoerced and at least partly responsible for the outcome. There can be no mutuality of persons where this kind of freedom is infringed. . . .

The Christian ideal of human fellowship, then, is built upon the three pillars of security-in-love, recognition-of-personal-worth, and the essential inviolability of each human soul. The first steps in enduring friendships are those which lessen aggression, express respect, reveal real interest in what one can do, and surround one with unobtrusive affection.

The implications of all this are of paramount importance for good counseling. It means that the good counselor is concerned about the basic causes of the feeling of insecurity of the person counseled, seeks to discover and appreciate his gifts and is sensitive to any infraction of his moral freedom. It means that the counselor can do nothing for the person counseled *against* his will, that no solution is a good one if its acceptance is forced. Our efforts at analysis and persuasion may go just as far as they remain persuasive and do not become interventive. The counselor must not only be willing for the person counseled to reject patently good advice; he must, with all the skill and patience he can muster, help him to discover *for himself* the right path forward. When another person stands before you, in admitted distress, it is often difficult to realize that this same person, whose weakness is so plain, is the only person in the world, or out of it, who can choose his way and walk in it. Yet this is actually the case. God surrounds him with His providence and prevenient grace. We may give him all the help we can, but we must avoid, as we would shun sacrilege, the effort to tinker with his soul or to haul him, with no matter how well-intentioned dominance, up to the altar or into the ark.

Jesus did a superb job of counseling with his twelve apostles. He gave them a sense of security. He had a strange confidence in their gifts, he was patient with their purblindness and their repeated failures to comprehend. He loved them without condescension, which made it possible for him to rebuke them without hesitation. He worked at the social and economic problems which confronted him, but most of all, he worked at the inner transformation that would give them new freedom and new power in a hostile world. His affection for them was uncalculated; yet it did not blind him to their faults. But just as he would not call upon his miraculous power to inaugurate the Kingdom or to perform selfish miracles, so also he was willing and able to wait until the leaven of truth worked in their hearts. He even lost one of them. But he taught mankind something that we may one day learn, that mutuality amongst men and mutuality between God and man is the highest and fullest human blessedness and joy.

Albert C. Outler, *A Christian Context for Counseling*. An Edward W. Hazen Foundation pamphlet, Series III, No. 18, New Haven, Conn., 1945, pp. 11-13.

156. A JOINT ENTERPRISE

    .. When any master holds
Twixt chin and hand a violin of mine,
He will be glad that Stradivari lived,
Made violins, and made them of the best.
The masters only know whose work is good:
They will choose mine, and while God gives them skill
I give them instruments to play upon,
God choosing me to help Him. . . .
. . . my work is mine,
And, heresy or not, if my hand slacked
I should rob God—since He is fullest good—
Leaving a blank instead of violins.
I say, not God Himself can make man's best
Without best men to help Him . . . .

George Eliot, "Stradivari," *Poems*. New York: P. F. Collier and Son, undated, pp. 360-61.

157. TOGETHER

What can I give to youth that youth can not get for itself?
I can not hold up truth before them
Or point to it on a safe shelf
Saying: "Here it is! Take and see that it is good!"
(I am not sure enough myself)

If I should try to play the priest or pedant
They would surely find me out
For they have keen eyes for truth
Have youth.

But I may invite them
Saying: "I am not wholly blind—
Come, let us see what we can find!"

By E. K. L., (other data unknown).

D. *The Eclectic Approach*

158. THERE IS NO ONE BEST WAY

. . Experience has shown that relatively few students are
in situations demanding exclusively permissive methods in
counseling. However, experience in the Study has shown
repeatedly both that permissive methods should be used more
often than they are and, second, that effective counseling
utilizes both the permissive and prescriptive approaches. . . .

The most effective counseling seems to be that which adapts
its methods to the demands of the situation. There is no one
best way. It is not permissive versus prescriptive counseling,
but rather both, as techniques to achieve the objectives for
which each is best suited.

> Paul J. Brouwer, *Student Personnel Services in General
> Education.* Washington: American Council on Education,
> 1949, pp. 22 and 26.

159. MATHEWSON DISCUSSES THE ECLECTIC OUTLOOK

The position may be taken that the characteristics of counseling will differ according to varying needs of the clients
and diversified institutional policies and that it will be very
difficult, if not impossible, to comprise all counseling proce-

dures within a common pattern. This pluralistic and completely eclectic outlook must be recognized as having a certain validity. It preserves freedom in meeting client needs in pragmatic ways and resists the dominance of any "authoritative" or "approved" methodology.

Robert H. Mathewson, *Guidance Policy and Practice*. New York: Harper and Brothers, 1949, p. 193.

160. "ADAPTIVE" COUNSELING

While it is true that some counseling is necessarily directive in nature and requires of the counselor a diagnosis and prescription, yet it is also true that such situations are relatively few as compared with situations calling for an artistic blending of directive and nondirective procedures. Clinical research into counseling procedures, whether in college, in industry, in social case work, or in child guidance, reveals unmistakably that a purely directive approach very infrequently promotes growth and may in fact retard it by preventing an individual from solving his own problems. On the other hand, the purely nondirective approach seems to be necessary chiefly when emotional stress is so intense as to preclude a rational analysis of the situation. The normal, healthy student, temporarily disturbed, can usually draw profit from a counseling situation in which he is permitted to express his feelings without fear of censure. But if he is not neurotic, and the average student certainly is not, it is also possible to assist him by providing the information necessary for making rational choices. A great deal of the emotional tension of the college student is occasioned by his lack of experience and understanding. And if the counselor is convinced that the student is emotionally ready to accept his explanations and to look at the situation from a rational point of view, he should be ready to give the student the benefit of his more mature understanding. He must, however, carefully avoid "talking down" to the student, giving information before the student has asked for it, blocking the student in his attempts to express his own opinions and emotions, and providing explanations which might upset the student and so intensify his maladjustment.

Counseling in which directive and nondirective techniques

are both used in their appropriate place we shall call, for want of a better term, "adaptive counseling." By adaptive counseling we mean counseling which aims to help the student to help himself. It is characterized by an adaptation of procedure to meet the particular needs of the student as they are revealed in the counseling interview. Hence, if the student is emotionally upset, he is encouraged to express his feelings and emotions. If he is in need of information and advice, and is emotionally as well as intellectually ready to receive it, it is given to him.

> Paul J. Brouwer, *Student Personnel Services in General Education.* Washington: American Council on Education, 1949, pp. 230-31. (From chapter by Sister Annette.)

161. DOGMATISM AS TO METHOD IS OUT OF PLACE

The viewpoint of the future, in addition to assuming that an over-all emphasis is necessary, will follow Thorne's lead in advocating variation, under certain conditions or in certain situations with the same client, in the degree of responsibility, the amount of attention to attitude versus content, and the degree of intellectual versus expressive manipulations of attitudes. This point of view will provide much more concrete and more generalizable descriptions of the conditions under which these variations can take place. Let me anticipate one possibility. We may find that when the counselor-client relationship has emphasized the responsibility of the client and has stimulated him to considerable expressive response, then the counselor's taking responsibility for stimulating him to intellectual manipulation of his attitudes may produce effective results.

I should like to conclude this discussion by emphasizing that at the present time there is no basis for a dogmatic stand on these issues of counseling methods. What we need is open-minded attempts at discriminating studies that will provide a basis for sound conclusions.

> E. G. Williamson, editor, *Trends in Student Personnel Work.* Minneapolis: The University of Minnesota Press, 1949, p. 128. (From chapter by Edward S. Bordin.)

162. HAMRIN AND PAULSON ON ECLECTIC COUNSELING

Eclectic counseling, as indicated in earlier chapters, operates on the premises and uses the techniques which best suit individual situations. There is no "one" way for a counselor to help every counselee who comes to his office. An immature freshman who does not know whether to take Latin or home economics needs one kind of assistance; an immature but more knowing senior who is making poor social adjustments needs another. The boy whose parents are pushing him too hard will usually not be helped unless his parents are assisted to gain an understanding of his abilities and limitations. On the other hand, the brilliant, overbearing girl needs something more than knowledge of her academic abilities to get along with herself and with other people. For all such individuals, eclectic counseling has possibilities of helpfulness even though it does not attempt to be all things to all counselees.

The Credo of Eclectic Counseling: While eclectic counseling, as the name implies, chooses its techniques from other types of counseling, its adherents have a well-defined philosophy. Eclectic counselors, in other words, make choices that are purposeful and not haphazard.

Responsibility of the Individual. Every counselor pursuing the eclectic way recognizes that each individual must assume responsibility for his own life. This counselor, too, has his own decisions and adjustments to make to keep on an even keel. If the counselor is living his own life fully, he has neither the time nor inclination to assume full responsibility for the life of any other person.

As the eclectic counselor grows in experience, he realizes that many of the young people who come to him are neither ready to assume full responsibility for themselves nor able alone to solve their problems through self-understanding or action. In such instances, the eclectic counselor must assume some initiative or provide suggestions. . . .

One of the eclectic counselor's first duties to his counselee is to ask himself if the school is at fault in the counselee's situation. However, when the counselor has assumed the initiative so that a change in program is effected or the understanding of teachers is enlisted, the pupil's responsibility in the new situation increases, for then he must take increased control of his own activities. If he does not, the adjustments by the school personnel will have been futile.

In helping young people to assume responsibility for themselves, the eclectic counselor employs the basic assumption of nondirective counseling that each individual has the capacity to solve most of his problems. At the same time, the eclectic counselor proceeds along clinical lines when he believes this approach to be most advantageous to the adjustment of the individual counselee.

Preparation for the interview. In making a practice of preparing for interviews, the eclectic counselor perhaps departs furthest from the philosophy of nondirective counseling. The eclectic counselor prepares for the interview by studying all the information he has about the counselee. He may at times plan certain steps to be taken in the interview. Such preparation is essential in routine educational and vocational planning.

When the counselor is asked to see a pupil, either at the pupil's or a teacher's request, he will be wise to look over the pupil's cumulative record ahead of time, for this record throws light on the pupil and his present problems. If the pupil has been interviewed before, the counselor will also want to look over his notes made during the previous interview, because even though the pupil may have been interviewed some time before, he will understandably expect to be remembered. Also, if the counselor has looked over these notes, he will save time by not duplicating questions in the forthcoming interview.

The counselor's responsibility for preparing for the interview extends further than studying data about the counselee. At times he will need to know community resources, to line up helpful books to suggest, or to consult teachers about possible adjustments the school can make.

The attitude of the counselor. Though the counselor prepares for the interview, he does not face the counselee with strong and predetermined convictions about the counselee's probable problem. Instead he is open-minded and helps the counselee to explore the problem. If the counselor enters the interview with an open-minded attitude, he will often hear facts, catch inferences, and detect attitudes which may modify his interpretations of accumulated data or alter his expectations based upon such data. . . .

In this connection, it should be pointed out, an open mind about the significance of data does not mean that the counselor cannot have ideas about the counselee's problem. Nor does the fact that responsibility for making decisions rests with the counselee bar the counselor from judiciously expressing his own ideas. The counselee who comes to the counselor wondering about meteorology as a career has perhaps had his attention directed to that vocation by a parent, teacher, or friend. It is not necessarily his idea just because he utters it. The counselor has as much right to suggest alternatives as have the pupil's relatives and friends. Usually, the counselor can make more astute suggestions than they can.

Choice of technique in counseling. The careful reader may at this point raise the question of how often the authors of this book, in their eclectic approach, have selected techniques from the Rogers approach and applied those techniques to the cases cited. In this connection, the authors emphasize that the counseling they describe deals primarily with problems of educational and vocational planning, and with problems normally encountered in personal and social adjustment and in maturation. Problems of maladjustment requiring psychotherapy are not within the province of most school counselors. These counselors must have adequate psychological training to recognize serious maladjustments, but once they recognize the existence of such maladjustments, they should call in workers trained in psychotherapy. It is in the field of psychotherapy that Rogers' techniques are most useful.

School counselors, however, have many boys and girls who desire to relieve their pent-up feelings in individual conferences. Counselors probably need to use attitude-centered counseling more often in dealing with counselees who seek their help or who are referred by teachers for specific problems than in dealing with counselees who are interviewed as part of a planned over-all guidance program.

In this book, the authors wish to give primary emphasis to

those counseling methods which can be classed as explanatory, informative, and educative in character. When the counselor employs these methods, the interview becomes a learning situation through which the counselee becomes not only better informed about his present difficulty or situation but also better able to handle a new difficulty when it arises.

Self-understanding is essential before the interview can be fruitful as a learning situation. Self-understanding may result from the opportunity for the counselee to tell his story to an attentive, understanding, and permissive listener who, by accepting and reflecting the counselee's attitudes, promotes the desired self-understanding. Self-understanding may also result from the counselee's gaining information about himself from objective data and about his community. Self-understanding should lead the counselee to reorient his goals and actions or to confirm a course previously set. Because in certain situations the school and not the adolescent must do the reorienting, the action may be taken not by the counselee but by the counselor for the counselee. . . .

The eclectic approach selects the methods of the clinical approach when the interview's purpose is to use test data, social history, and knowledge of community resources in helping the counselee to solve his problem. It selects the methods of the attitude-centered approach when the purpose of the interview is to allow the counselee the opportunity to express his feelings. Taking into account the values of the Rogers technique, the eclectic approach recognizes the fact that often the counselee himself has more resources for growth than have been utilized and that his expression of emotionalized attitudes may be a helpful part of much good counseling. The eclectic approach derives from both the clinical and attitude-centered approaches the belief that the counselee rather than the counselor does most of the talking and that at all times the counselee makes the decisions and assumes responsibility for himself and for his future. Thus counselees may have the benefits of several techniques through the eclectic approach since " 'Tis neither this nor that, but both and more."

Shirley A. Hamrin and Blanche B. Paulson, *Counseling*

Adolescents. Chicago: Science Research Associates, Inc., 1950, pp. 82-88.

163. AREAS OF AGREEMENT IN GUIDANCE

Our discussion has illustrated one reason why people get the impression that there is little agreement among various exponents of psychotherapy. We found it difficult to keep attention centered on our wide area of agreement, and seemed irresistibly drawn to the one point of controversy. On that issue of "non-intervention" we seem to have reached the conclusion that psychoanalysis did give much of the initial impetus toward a relationship in which the therapist tries not to let his own values influence the patient, and that the past twenty years have seen all other psychotherapies move toward much the same ideal.

We found reason to agree with Dr. Chassell's observation that if we were to apply to our colleagues the distinction, so important with patients, between what they tell us and what they do, we might find that agreement is greater in practice than in theory. Despite the various names under which we work and our various backgrounds of training we all seem agreed upon many essentials of psychotherapeutic practice.

First, we have found no apparent disagreement on objectives. We all hope to increase the client's capacity to deal with reality, to work, to love, and find meaning in life. For all of us the relationship of therapist and client has been a central factor. We have stressed the need to provide a security which fosters spontaneity. We have seen the treatment relationship as social adjustment under artificially simple conditions, but as a step in socialization. We have recognized that as the therapist meets the oft-used patterns of the patient in an unexpected, fresh and revealing way, the patient is stimulated to new growth. We have urged that the therapist must so understand his own needs as to prevent their unconscious domination of the relationship. Our relationship with the client is an identification controlled in the client's best interests.

We have all stressed, as a third area of agreement, the importance of keeping responsibility for choice on the client. Growth occurs especially as he becomes able to achieve "inte-

gration of will," making his own decisions and carrying out
the implications of new insights earnestly, responsibly, and
with increasing independence. As Dr. Allen put it, "It is what
(clients) do about themselves that is therapy."

A fourth concept which has seemingly been accepted by
us is that good psychotherapy enlarges the client's understanding of himself. We encourage but do not guide expression.
We direct attention to dreams, to art, to phantasy, to verbal
sequences and to behavior. We try to help the individual
accept responsibility for more of his feelings than he previously
could. We recognize that interpretation of his past may be
useful if it illumines for the client his tendencies in the present.
The psychoanalyst says, "Where was id, there shall ego be."
The analytical psychologist accepts this and adds, at least
for some persons, "Keep working at that synthetic, creative,
partly spontaneous process of growth whereby each realizes
his unique indivisible individuality." Every psychotherapy
assumes that in the client there are important impulses and
connections, some half-conscious, some repudiated, some unconscious, which need to be assimilated in a more complete
and truer self-awareness.

We have agreed, negatively, not to try to treat symptoms
in superficial isolation from the structure of the personality.
We do not believe that mere catharsis of feelings is therapeutic. We distrust advice and exhortation. We have agreed
further, I think, that our techniques cannot be uniform and
rigid, but vary with the age, problems and potentialities of
the individual client and with the unique personality of the
therapist.

Finally, we all have recognized that what the therapist can
contribute depends in large measure upon his own character.
He should be mature, objective, constant, with insight into
his own problems and freedom to live with integrity. "A therapist has nothing to offer but himself."

Goodwin Watson, "Areas of Agreement in Psychotherapy,"
The American Journal of Orthopsychiatry, Vol. 10, 1940,
pp. 708-9.

164. THE GUIDANCE CONTINUUM

. . Many group leaders and counselors adopt an authoritative method. They tell the pupils in their classes, the members
of their groups, the people in their congregations, or the
individuals with whom they counsel, what to do. Success in
this type of counseling depends upon the degree to which the
authority is implicitly accepted.

A second type of approach is similar to the first. Where
groups or individuals will not accept authority, the leader or
counselor use suggestion and persuasion. Salesmen use the
method of persuasion. Many teachers in their teaching, and
ministers in their preaching, use a method comparable with
that of the salesman. The evangelists among the preachers
have been particularly skilled in this art. Suggestion is a
similar technique, in which resistance is overcome not by
pressing the idea too directly but by giving the individual a
chance to accept it as his own. The leader of this type of
group discussion goes through a process by which the members seem to reach for themselves the conclusion at which he
wishes them to arrive.

"Personal work," as it has been conducted in the church,
has largely been of the persuasion type. The purpose of this
type of work was to induce the individual to give up a life
of wickedness and sin and to become a Christian or to join
the church. Personal counseling on lifework has often aimed
at persuading the individual to give up a worldly career and
to serve the Lord by becoming a minister or missionary.

Such counseling has not been confined to the church. Various business concerns have sent representatives to the colleges
to seek out likely candidates and to induce them to enter their
particular line of work at home and abroad. Many physicians
and psychiatrists use this technique. They suggest to the
patient what they want him to accept as to his health or his
conduct; or they tell him that there is really nothing the
matter with him and that he is really feeling good, even though
he thinks he is ill; or that he is quite capable of undertaking
the responsibility he has been evading and that he would
find great satisfaction in assuming it. The work of the Christian Science practitioners is largely conducted by suggestion,

with certain elements of authority and persuasion entering into the process. The practices of Couéism and of similar cults are forms of autosuggestion: a method of persuading one's self that there is really nothing the matter and that "every day in every way one is getting better and better."

The third technique is in contrast with the two discussed above. The leader or teacher assumes at first an authoritative relation to the group members in order to give them confidence in themselves and in order temporarily to furnish protection from harmful action; but he sets in motion processes for transferring responsibility little by little to the group itself. He takes care from the first to have the class or group work with him on all the plans he makes for it and to share with him in any decisions. At first in such a process the leader is carrying most of the responsibility himself, but he progressively increases the share carried by the group as rapidly as they are able and willing to accept it. Graduation from such a process comes when the group no longer need the leader to direct them, when they are willing and competent to take charge of their own activities and need the leader only as a resource. So boys' and girls' clubs, accustomed to completely authoritative control and direction, may reach, after several years of such a process of progressive liberation, the point at which they can become self-governing clubs; and classes in school start in the early years, controlled and directed chiefly by teachers, to reach the place in senior high school, in upper class college or in graduate work, where they can take a large degree of the initiative and responsibility for themselves.

Personal counseling also may follow the process involving progress from authority to freedom. Some consultants on children's problems take at first authoritative direction of the parents who are having difficulty, and give them what one such child psychologist calls "sailing orders." As soon as such a counselor has gained the parents' confidence as a result of improvements wrought through his advice, he tries to develop in the parents insight and understanding and to consult with them on future problems. Increasingly he provides the parents with a basis for the understanding and the skill to handle their own problems until they reach the place where they can take responsibility themselves and need only to consult him on the more difficult problems that arise. Some psychologists and other counselors use a similar procedure in their efforts to help the individual with his own problem. They study the problem carefully and work out such adjustments in school or in work, in social affairs or in home relations, as will relieve the difficulty and enable the counselee to meet life more successfully. With a measure of success as a basis, they continue the consultations, working with him on future problems, but seeking to lead him toward a better understanding of himself and of his perplexity and toward an increasing responsibility for decisions made. The individual is "cured" when he reaches the point at which he feels able to handle his own problems, and finds himself competent to do so. He has in the procedure learned how to deal with himself in meeting the situations of life and he has developed an understanding of life situations and a certain skill in meeting them.

A fourth type of counseling corresponds to the freer forms of education. In this type of work with groups, the teacher or leader becomes the director of a process and a resource of information and experience; but he throws the responsibility for participating in and carrying out the process directly on the group. He feels responsible for seeing that the educative process is carried out effectively, but does not attempt to influence its outcome. Group discussion, where the leader confines himself to a chairman's functions, is another illustration of the type. If the group is facing some problems of conduct, or some social situation such as that involved in social events and relations, in economic, political, or interracial affairs, the leader seeks to ensure that the members of the group understand and face squarely the issues involved, that they canvass and foresee the probable consequences of various possible courses of action, and that they make their decision with an adequate basis in information and experience and with due attention to the personal and social values at stake; but he believes that each group has to make its own decisions. Consequently, he is concerned with the adequacy of the process rather than with the outcome, trusting the outcome, even though it differ from his private judgment, if the process has been carried on with fundamental thoroughness.

The same procedure may be followed also in personal counseling. In such a process, the counselor feels that the individual must work out his own solution to his problems, and that he is really a chairman of the process by which the individual is finding his way. He listens patiently, taking only such part as will further the process of exploration. He makes available information or experience of others which may help the individual understand himself, and he co-operates with the counselee as he is seeking to formulate for himself any stages in his progress; but upon the whole, he allows the counselee to find his own solution.

The foregoing review indicates that the methods of personal counseling might be arranged on a scale grading from those in which the counselor takes complete control and gives authoritative answers in the counseling process to those at the other extreme where the maximum of responsibility is thrown upon the counselee to work out his own problems and make his own decisions. In the latter instance the counselor furnishes the occasion for his staying at the process and gives him some help and direction in the problem-solving process. Counselors differ most, then, in the degree to which they take authority and responsibility for the person who comes to them.

> Harrison Sacket Elliott and Grace Loucks Elliott, *Solving Personal Problems.* New York: Henry Holt and Company, 1936, pp. 216-21. By permission of the publishers.

165.   SKILLFUL COUNSELING REQUIRES KNOWLEDGE OF VARYING PROCEDURES

In summary, the emphasis on the non-directive procedure has been stimulating to the field of counseling but it is not a new one nor is it simple. We must give more attention to the client and less to the counselor, but client-centered counseling is not one part of a dichotomy. It is a continuum. Skillful counseling consists of knowing *when* to use the varying procedures that are available along this continuum. And this versatility means adding more emphasis to certain areas of a professional training program, training that will contribute to the psychological insight and skill needed for the extreme of client-centered counseling called non-directive.

C. Gilbert Wrenn, "Client-Centered Counseling," *Journal of Educational and Psychological Measurement*, Winter, 1946, p. 444.

7.

The Sphere of the General Counselor

166. All Counselors Need Adequate Training

The temptation to play God is universal, and all persons in all ages have felt the urge (although they may not have recognized it as such) to direct the lives and juggle the destinies of their fellowmen. Such an urge is at times compounded of the need to satisfy certain instinctive cravings for power; at others, of the need to shut our eyes to the desirability of a bit of personal housecleaning through the device of busying ourselves in directing other people how to put their houses in order. But let the ingredients of this urge to play God be what they may, the fact remains that with an intensity varying according to our personal psychology, this temptation to tell others what to do is present in us all—psychiatrists included. Such being the case, the only safeguard to an unwise or even destructive use of that urge lies in obtaining all the experience and training in the manipulation of human destinies which modern science makes available.

The trouble with this suggestion is that so little of that knowledge is in existence, and even the psychiatrist in his more reflective moments stands humbly on the threshold of the great dark places which are as yet unfilled in man's understanding of man.

Admittedly, training and the opportunity for becoming proficient in the meagre amount of knowledge about human behavior that is available are both difficult and tedious to obtain, and it is understandable that many who at the outset were willing to seek that training grew discouraged. Certainly, psychiatrists have no monopoly on such knowledge and most of them welcome the contributions and assistance of scientific disciplines in allied fields. There is, they recognize, more than one way to skin a cat, and the readjustment of human lives is not a goal that is to be won by the utilization of any single technic alone. No, the psychiatrist not only does not object to sharing the field of human adjustment with vocational guidance experts and counselors, but he is eager for their help, *providing they are properly prepared in a technical and temperamental sense for the delicate task they would undertake.*

It is only when certain clergymen, YM and YWCA representatives, volunteer and professionally untrained social workers, vocational guidance experts, educational (and personal) counselors, and a host of other well-meaning individuals whose principal qualifications are sympathy and a desire to be of help—it is only when such persons either see no need for special training in the field of human behavior or else, seeing it, decline to procure that training that the psychiatrist makes just complaint over the dangers to happiness and efficiency in clients which are not less grave dangers merely because they do not become immediately apparent.

> George K. Pratt, "Seeing the Individual Whole," *Occupations*, Vol. 13, No. 2, November, 1934, pp. 110-11.

167. GUIDANCE SHOULD STRESS PREVENTION AND CREATIVITY

The scope of mental hygiene in the classroom. The teacher who defines mental hygiene on the basis of the case studies of child guidance clinic patients is bound to misinterpret the goals, the procedures, and the scope of mental hygiene in education. The children who are being treated by the clinic are no more typical of the students who fill our classrooms in the elementary and secondary schools than the characters on the front pages of newspapers are representative of the general run of American citizenry. Naturally, mental hygiene is interested in the better adjustment of these children with serious behavior problems, and it admits readily that such children require, and deserve, specialized psychiatric, psychological, and sociological assistance far beyond that which is necessary for the average, or normal, student. However, mental hygiene is concerned even more with the attempt at arresting undesirable abnormalities in behavior patterns by aiding the normal child to live a wholesome emotional life.

To limit the educational applications of mental hygiene to the re-education of maladjusted children is to lose sight of the greatest contribution that the school can make to the improvement of emotional and mental health. It is futile to set up excellent clinics and then to allow schools to perpetuate undesirable practices which are responsible, in part, for the necessity for clinics. Emotional disturbances must be treated at their source. The case records of emotionally maladjusted adults offer abundant evidence of the childhood background of many adult difficulties. If we could convert every teacher, every parent, and every pediatrician to a sympathetic understanding of the problems related to the child's emotional adjustment, we should be able to prevent many serious adjustment problems of later life. Childhood has been referred to repeatedly as the golden period for mental hygiene. The teacher therefore becomes one of the vanguard in the fight for the better emotional health of the general population.

Even this conception of mental hygiene is narrow if it leads to the teacher's thinking of himself as a one-man psychological clinic. Such a teacher easily falls into the error of looking for symptoms of maladjustment in every child. This approach is unsatisfactory not only because it may lead to serious misinterpretations of normal reactions, but also because it blinds the teacher to a more significant phase of mental hygiene; namely, the role of the classroom itself as a vital factor in the child's emotional development.

If the teacher can maintain a classroom atmosphere in which students gain a feeling of security, he accomplishes more for their sound emotional health than he can by practicing amateur psychiatry. It is the teacher's contribution to evaluate his methods of discipline, his teaching practices, and the procedures of class management in terms of their effect on the students' emotional health.

Paul A. Witty and Charles E. Skinner, editors, *Mental Hygiene in Modern Education*. New York: Rinehart and Company, Inc., 1939, pp. 476-77. (From chapter by Harry N. Rivlin.)

168. EVERYDAY PROCESSES HOPE OF THE FUTURE

It is the quiet, devoted work of some parents and some teachers, patiently, day by day, helping children to meet the tasks of life with courage and with adequacy, giving them a sense of belonging and being loved and accepted, which offers the major hope for the future.

Lawrence K. Frank, "Mental Health in Schools," *Education,* Vol. 66, No. 9, May, 1946, p. 555.

169. THE TEACHER IS MORE THAN AN INSTRUCTOR

The classroom teacher must be brought to an appreciation of the fact that, except in unusual cases, all children of reasonably normal intelligence who develop school or subject-matter aversions, behavior difficulties, or personality defects are harboring unhygienic emotional attitudes which can be corrected, or at least greatly ameliorated, by the sympathetic efforts of the school people themselves, notably the *teachers.*

The function of the classroom teacher in a complex age can no longer be restricted to the performance of the conventional instructional and supervisory duties. Increasingly, her province will have to be broadened to include a considerable area of social work, since, after all, teaching is and should be considered social work in the best sense of the term. Even after visiting teachers have become more numerous in the community than they now are, there will still remain a vast deal of contact work and actual consultative work which only the classroom teacher can be expected to undertake in the interest of promoting the better adjustment of individual pupils to the activities, the ideals, and the general atmosphere of the school.

Lawrence A. Averill, "Case Studies in the Schools," *Mental Hygiene,* Vol. 25, January, 1941, pp. 55-56.

170. THE PARENT AND TEACHER ESSENTIAL IN
CHILD'S DEVELOPMENT

These considerations explain why health care, physical and mental, has lagged and why the task is so difficult because parents, especially mothers, must be given renewed confidence and helpful guidance for doing what only mothers can and must do in the family. Today so many women have lost confidence in themselves, largely because they feel that only the trained specialist, pediatrician, nurse, nutritionist, psychiatrist, psychologist, educator, can do anything of significance for children.

It becomes necessary therefore to make a specific effort to reassure mothers, to explain to them their immense responsibilities and their equally great opportunities to foster and maintain the health and personality of their children. What takes place in the home and family in these daily activities of housekeeping and the baby and child care and rearing is the focus of preventive medicine and mental hygiene. Through these homely, seemingly trivial practices, the mother stands guard over and actively promotes the health, physical and mental, of her family, especially her children, as no physician, nurse, or other specialist can or will. These are the basic processes of preventive medicine and mental hygiene, and of culturization, through which as a people we can even more effectively discard those traditional beliefs and practices that foster human defeat and distortion, replacing them with new conceptions and practices that will more effectively advance our cherished values and aspirations.

In the same way it is being discovered that for continuing health care and mental hygiene for children, the schools are the chief agency. Not the clinics and the many specialists who can diagnose and treat the various ills, defects, and handicaps, but the school personnel, especially the classroom teacher. What she does to and for children, as one personality acting, reacting, and inter-reacting with members of the class is the active, daily process of mental hygiene.

But teachers are in many cases much like mothers today. They have been impressed by the specialized knowledge and training of the physicians, the nurses, the social workers, the psychiatrists, the psychologists, and other professionals, and so many have lost confidence in themselves as teachers to do what only teachers can and must do for growing children.

The teacher in the classroom is the strategic person for mental health because he is the only one in the position to do what must be done to help children and youth grow up and achieve maturity with some degree of sanity and of adequacy for social living. But teachers themselves must realize and accept this by revising their image of themselves and by redefining their roles and their functions in the light of these larger opportunities before them to make their work more significant socially and more interesting and absorbing professionally.

> Lawrence K. Frank, "Mental Health in Schools," *Education,* Vol. 66, No. 9, May, 1946, pp. 547-48.

171. CLASSROOM TEACHER KEY TO EFFECTIVE GUIDANCE

Some teachers have always done guidance work. Those who have shared the warmth of their personalities, given of themselves freely because of their interest in and love for children and youth, and been seriously concerned for each individual under their tutelage have been guiding children's emotional and social growth as well as their educational growth.

The classroom teacher holds the key to the effective guidance program. The best efforts of the wisest experts may be futile unless the teachers are a recognized part of this work. It is common knowledge that the teacher's personality will have a direct effect on children within only a few weeks or months after the school year has begun. . . .

Just as the teacher needs the kind of school in which she feels relaxed and able to do her best work in teaching, so do children need the kind of classroom emotional climate in which they may learn to the best of their abilities. They need to feel accepted as they are, if they are to learn a balance between freedom for the benefit of self and restraint for the benefit of the group.

> Edna D. Baxter, "What Is Guidance?" *Childhood Education,* Vol. 25, January, 1949, pp. 203-4.

172. THE COUNSELOR AS AN UNDERSTANDING FRIEND

Anyone who is poorly adjusted to a life situation may find a useful suggestion in the proverb that "two heads are better than one." What he needs is not advice altogether. He needs the chance to use his own head in explaining the problem to an understanding friend, and if the friend does not understand the whole difficulty instantly, so much the better. The person who is in difficulty will understand it better himself after making it plain to his friend. Silent brooding over a troublesome personal matter is almost sure to give a distorted view. Minor maladjustments usually clear up in a confidential talk with a friend, without calling on the professional counselor. More difficult problems, however, do require the assistance of the expert. "Giving advice" is not exactly what the counselor does, for he is careful to leave the individual a large share in solving his own problem and planning his own further course of action. The counselor, from his experience with similar problems, can see the ins and outs of the present problems better than anyone who is new to this type of difficulty. The counselor sees the situation objectively while the individual personally concerned is likely to be biased and emotional. When the emotional disturbance cuts deeply into the personality and upsets the individual's life with nameless fears and fixed ideas, the expert with experience in this type of cases is the psychiatrist.

> Robert S. Woodworth, *Psychology*, Fourth Edition. New York: Henry Holt and Company, Inc., 1940, p. 603. By permission of the publishers.

173. Don't Push the Teacher Around

I wonder if it does not indicate the need, on the part of all of us who are trying to steer people in the direction of the help they should have, of a great deal more humility than we sometimes exercise. Here is where teamwork is so important, because unless the physician, the nurse, the social worker, the clergyman, the lawyer, and the teacher work together, we will achieve very little. Unless they work with sympathy, unless they work quietly, and unless they work lovingly with the parent, they will have the parent all ready for help, and then six months later, the matter having gone up through a hierarchy and down through a hierarchy, comes a report from a child-guidance clinic or worker couched in language that neither the teacher nor the parent can understand or knows how to apply to the situation in question....

You see the teacher often feels left out, feels inferior. Perhaps we teachers have brought that on ourselves. Perhaps we are inferior, but you won't get us to be any better by making us think that we are. You see, we don't know the lingo of the psychiatrist. We don't know the lingo of the psychiatric social worker. We do, however, spend five or six hours a day five days a week with the stuff of life, the children, so you had better use us, and learn to speak a common language with us, and not make us feel, as so many teachers do, that they are sort of pushed over to one side as a group that really does not know and does not understand.

> Alice V. Keliher, "The Professional Person—a Mental Hygiene Resource: In Education," *Mental Hygiene,* Vol. 34, No. 2, April, 1950, pp. 277-78.

174. THE ALERT TEACHER READS THE SIGNS

The classroom offers the most promising place for mental health programs in view of the difficulties of family life today. If the teachers will more clearly recognize in their pupils these idiomatic personality make-ups and needs that have emerged from family backgrounds and more effectively interpret what the child is telling us daily in his speech, his conduct, his displays of emotion, in everything he does, just as each profession has learned to look for and interpret the different symptoms and indicators, so teachers can become more sensitive to the appearance and meaning of children's behavior.

Day by day the child exposes his individual personality make-up and feelings—his "private world," which give the observant teacher clues to what is going on inside and what he needs. This does not mean that teachers should become amateur psychiatrists, attempting to diagnose and treat personality problems. It means that, as teachers, they can and should be alert to what the child is telling them in these various indirect or overt but disguised expressions so that they can deal with the child as a personality, not as a passive doll to be taught or disciplined for showing any resistance, inattention, or disorder.

Everything a child does is meaningful. His way of sitting and standing, of writing and speaking, his errors and mistakes in school work are symptomatic, not merely of inattention and lack of effort, but more often of a fundamental confusion in his whole orientation to life. Likewise, his free drawing or painting or modeling, his story-telling and other activities such as reactions to classmates, are also revealing to the observant eye of how he thinks, believes, and feels toward life. . . .

Primarily mental health in the schools is the responsibility and the opportunity of educators, particularly of classroom and other teachers (physical education, art, and shop), to do to and for pupils what they can uniquely do. Moreover, the most promising practices and methods for fostering mental health in the schools are coming from the experiments and new programs being developed by teachers themselves. The psychiatrists, the psychologists, and others have much to contribute to education and have indeed helped in many of these new programs. But the responsibility is that of the educators, and the methods and procedures which will effectively guard the mental health of school children are essentially group and individual classroom procedures and relationships.

> Lawrence K. Frank, "Mental Health in Schools," *Education,* Vol. 66, No. 9, May, 1946, pp. 551-53.

175. CO-OPERATION WITH THE SPECIALIST

Sometimes it is possible to refer children needing special help to a psychological counselor, visiting teacher, or a psychiatric clinic. There are several reasons, however, why this is not the most satisfactory solution. One such reason is that there are not now enough competent professional counselors to take care of more than a small fraction of the youngsters who need help. A second consideration is that the teacher has a background of experience with the pupil which might prove helpful. Then, too, pupils already have a relationship with the teacher—if this can be made therapeutically effective. Many pupils and their parents object to any procedure, such as reference to a specialist, which seems to single the child out as undesirably different from his fellows.

The best procedure, in many cases, is that in which the teacher undertakes treatment of the problem pupil, with some expert—perhaps a psychological counselor employed by the schools—to whom to turn for guidance. Thus the wisdom of the specially trained counselor is made available to the teacher and helps to prepare him for more skillful handling of the next case.

> Paul A. Witty and Charles E. Skinner, editors, *Mental Hygiene in Modern Education*. New York: Rinehart and Company, Inc., 1939, p. 517. (From chapter by Goodwin Watson.)

176. BOTH TEACHER AND SPECIALIST HAVE IMPORTANT ROLES

The most heated discussions center in the question "Who should perform the personnel functions?" Three points of view are expressed in the literature: (1) the class teacher should provide all personnel services; (2) personnel work is primarily the function of the specialist, with the teachers performing only minor supplementary functions; (3) there are personnel services to be performed by every staff member, but every staff member is not qualified to perform every personnel service. According to this last point of view, there are levels of personnel work of varying degrees of complexity. Certain services can be performed by every teacher; certain services should be performed only by the teachers selected and trained for them; and certain services should be performed only by the specialists.

The second point of view—personnel work is the function of the specialist—is held by only a few authorities and is held with respect to college, not high-school, personnel work. The scarcity of specialists and the tremendous expense of any plan based on this point of view make it unlikely that many schools will consider adopting it.

The first point of view represents an ideal situation, an educational Utopia, and, like all other Utopias, ideally desirable but not practicable. Many arguments are advanced in support of this perfect plan: To separate instructional and guidance work is to deny the whole-child concept. Three-fourths of our high schools are too small to be able to afford the services of the guidance specialist. In the small high school the teacher knows the child so well that the specialized personnel worker is not needed. In any high school, large or small, the teacher is the school person most intimately conversant with the pupil and hence should be charged with his guidance as well as with his instruction. Guidance specialists have made important contributions to educational reform; but these workers are no longer needed because in the new curriculum plans aims are not confined to subject fields but embrace other objectives, including those of personnel work. . . .

To dream of an ideal situation in which the guidance specialist is not provided because not needed is only to dream. Therefore, it is the third point of view that the schools must act upon if they wish to provide strong, effective personnel programs. Any plan based on this point of view is not a perfect scheme; for it is the mean, the practicable point of view. . . . In these proposals both the class teacher and the guidance specialist are given important roles in the program of personnel work. The specialist is there to coordinate the work, to implement new theories, and to supplement the services of the class teacher. This is the desired situation toward which we are working, a situation in which students find the services of specialists available, in which they are served by good teachers who in certain guidance areas are also good personnel workers.

> Jane Warters. *High School Personnel Work Today.* New York: McGraw-Hill Book Company, Inc., 1946, pp. 26-27.

177. Even Improved Curriculum Requires the Specialist

More speedy progress toward the desired ideal situation in which every teacher has an important role in personnel work is being made possible by the work in curriculum revision. In the new curriculum plans, aims are formulated that are not confined to subject fields but are defined in terms of social functionalism and of the optimum development of the individual. More unified experiences are being provided with a wider variety of and greater continuity of learning experiences. Increased attention is being given to the development of the attitudes and skills considered essential for democratic living. And development in self-direction is being made possible through greater participation by pupils in planning and evaluating their experiences. In brief, the principal objective in the new curriculum is to produce the kind of behavior changes needed in meeting both individual needs and social demands.

The socializing of the high schools has not moved so fast that all teachers may now be considered personnel workers. Many teachers continue to be more subject- than pupil-conscious. And, in spite of the tremendous amount of work that has been done in curriculum revision, the great majority of high schools are still without any special provision for individual differences. When the time does finally come when all teachers will be as well trained and as much concerned for the guidance as for the instruction of their pupils, there will still be services needed to supplement and to strengthen the work of the teacher-counselors. No matter how much the curriculum may be improved, there will always be additional services possible to help young people to attain a higher degree of social usefulness and personal happiness. As in the past, so in the future, specialized personnel workers will have a distinct purpose in seeking to discover, to supply, and to improve these services.

Ibid., pp. 29-30.

178. THE SPHERE OF THE GENERAL COUNSELOR

. . Among the general counselors are included social workers, Y.M.C.A. and Y.W.C.A. secretaries, Scout and Boys' Club workers, pastors, religious leaders, teachers and other educational workers. Bone has characterized this group as one whose members employ counseling ". . . as a part of a more inclusive responsibility in those professions whose chief business is with persons." (From the introduction by Harry Bone to *The Art of Counseling,* by Rollo May.) This concept of the general counselor has its counterpart in the school field. Recently Jager has used the term "guidance generalist" in referring to the guidance work which classroom teachers do as contrasted with the practice of specialists. . . .

In the first place, it is assumed that generalists and specialists alike are attempting to aid individuals to make more adequate adjustments in their own lives and to build a society which favors the good of all. This is a team job where both generalists and specialists are needed. Much of the work of psychiatry, for example, is futile because there is not enough of a supporting structure among parents, teachers and informal agency workers. The specialist cannot "go it alone"; and, on the other hand, the generalist often cannot go far enough by himself. The number of psychiatrists today is totally inadequate to meet the needs of the time. Much of the work of these specialists is at the curative level because of the great pressure for human relief. Not enough attention is given to the prevention of maladjustments and comparatively little effort is directed by these specialists to the direct enrichment of human life, which probably is the most needed and fruitful area of work now open to educational leaders. . . .

The work of the general counselors, as discussed here, is thought of as an extension along the guidance continuum in the direction of normal educational processes and away from specialization. There seems, then, to be real need for the general counselor, who, while working on his program in a sound educational manner, does as much individual work as his ability permits and who cooperates intelligently with specialists in the community. Dr. L. Clovis Hirning, acting chief psychiatrist at Grasslands Hospital, recognizes this need for team play when he writes: "And in my opinion the hope of the future with respect to the psychiatric ills of mankind does not lie within traditional limitations of psychiatric practice or solely in the hands of the formally recognized psychiatrists. That others besides psychiatrists are dealing with problems of personality, adjustment and mental illness, particularly in the preventive aspects of these conditions, is an inevitable and desirable development—but a precarious one. The amplification and standardization of the training of such individuals is one of the very important educational problems of today." ("Sound Trends and Appropriate Ambitions in the Counseling Movement," *Teachers College Record*, October, 1944, pp. 25-33.)

Dr. Harry Bone, a consulting psychologist, in his introduction to "The Art of Counseling," by Rollo May, has made an outstanding contribution to the clarification of the role of the general counselor. He considers counseling to fall between the field of education and the work of the consulting psychologist. He elaborates upon the idea thus: "The educator (secular or religious) deals with 'normal' individuals and is concerned with the processes of growth and development—intellectual, moral or religious. The consulting psychologist deals chiefly with corrective or re-educational problems in individuals who have become involved in serious difficulties or adjustment and who often require extended individual treatment. However, no categorical distinction can be made between the needs of individuals for 'education' and for 're-education' respectively. Remedial and disciplinary problems are a 'statistically normal' part of the educator's routine, and the consulting psychologist makes more or less use of positive educational procedures. . . . *The counselor deals with problems which are too complicated to be solved incidentally in the ordinary course of educational procedure, but not so serious as to require the particular specialized services of a consulting psychologist. . . .*" (Rollo May, *The Art of Counseling*, Introduction.)

Rollo May, at another time, supplementing Bone's contribution, indicated other important distinctions between counseling and the more specialized approaches: "One central distinction is that psychotherapy (and, in this instance, psychiatry as well) deals with irrational and unconscious material, whereas counseling does not. That is to say, material comes directly into counseling only when the client himself is able to bring it up and is also able to deal with it to an extent rationally and consciously. . . . Another distinction between psychotherapy and counseling is in degree of intensity as indicated by the number of interviews." (Rollo May, "The Present Function of Counseling," *Teachers College Record*, October, 1944, pp. 13-14.)

Perhaps several comments on Bone's and May's views are in order, especially as they relate to workers in the agencies of informal education. There is a sense in which guidance is given through the on-going agency program (or "education," as Bone designates it). This will be good guidance to the extent that it is sound program. Here is where program (education) and guidance coincide. But no program, however adequate, will be able to meet. all the needs of those who participate, so it is necessary to introduce an emphasis within the program and alongside of it to take care of these special needs. Here, then, the supervisor or leader needs to assume the role of the general counselor and to operate as has been described above. This does not mean, though, that agency program personnel should be unskilled in individual guidance techniques. It is only that they must give their main attention to the group aspects of program while reserving some specific time for attention to individuals. Likewise, the more highly trained counselor may not be giving his complete attention to individual work in all cases. He may specialize but also carry some relation to group processes. However, in some agencies there may be greater specialization, which makes possible the use of one or more counselors who give their entire time to the problems of individuals. These counselors may be trained case workers or consulting psychologists, if not highly skilled general counselors.

If prevention is important in mental hygiene strategy, program leaders and general counselors have important places indeed. It is in their operations that incipient trouble may be discovered and dealt with. It is here that individuals may learn constructive ways of working out their own motives and wishes. And it is here, too, that the specialists will find a laboratory where clients may reconstruct unsatisfactory life patterns.

All of this presupposes adequate training upon the part of the program staff and general counselors. It is not alone enough for these workers to be skilled in program matters, even if they give little time to individualized work. At least they need to have the guidance point of view. This involves, among other considerations, insight about the place of the counselor and counselee in the guidance process; facts about individual differences and modifications in approach which these differences dictate; facts about motivation and the adjustments related thereto; and knowledge of how people learn and grow. A true guidance point of view requires in all of these ways not only knowledge but also experience and insight in practical application. . . .

. . . Knowledge and insight basic to sound judgment may be widened and deepened by actual practice upon the job, by careful reading, by observation and by discussion with other workers or through formal study. A counselor should

[*Continued on page* 184]

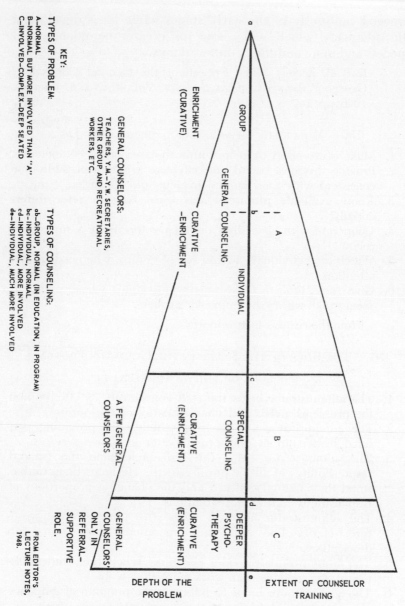

179. Graphic Picture of the Counselor's Sphere

proceed cautiously in the early stages while he is developing the adequacy which will allow for greater confidence and success and more ambitious undertakings.

> Karl P. Zerfoss, "The Sphere of the General Counselor," *George Williams College Bulletin*, Vol. 40, No. 4, January, 1946, pp. 1-4.

180.   WHAT THE GENERAL COUNSELOR MAY DO

1. Make every effort to keep within the area of his competence.
2. Provide the most sound and effective program possible—one consistent with good mental hygiene and education.
3. Know available resources and learn how to refer differentially.
4. Cooperate with specialists on their referrals in a supportive role.
5. Watch for individuals, in and out of groups, who need special attention.
6. Give some time to these needy individuals whose problems seem to fall within the counselor's sphere.

From the editor's lecture notes.

181.   THE ROLE OF THE STAFF IN THE GUIDANCE PROGRAM

I.   THE ROLE OF THE ADMINISTRATOR

1. The administrator helps the staff concentrate its attention on the problems, needs and characteristics of the pupils.
2. The administrator has the responsibility for providing personal leadership in developing better guidance services.
3. The administrator helps the staff understand the "shared responsibility" of all for pupil growth. He helps them understand their mutual concern and the changing proportions of responsibility in different situations.
4. The administrator helps to define the administrative structure, clarify line and staff operations, and define job descriptions.
5. The administrator provides the time, scheduling, and facilities so staff members can work more effectively.
6. The administrator helps to interpret the program of guidance services to the school and to the community.
7. The administrator helps by providing in-service training facilities to assist teachers and counselors acquire greater skill and security.

8. The administrator helps the staff organize the guidance program to provide maximum improvement through the utilization of the guidance program.
9. The administrator selects competent counselors and places them in an educational setting so they can operate effectively.

II.   THE ROLE OF THE TEACHER

1. Teachers, as teachers, are primarily concerned with the problems and needs of their pupils.
2. Teachers are the first line of detection of the emerging maladjustments of pupils.
3. Teachers have an opportunity to provide most of the school situations for maximum pupil development.
4. Teachers have an opportunity to implement many of the decisions made as a result of the pupils' contacts with counselors.
5. Teachers have an opportunity to provide many group therapy activities.
6. Teachers have an opportunity to provide many instructional services closely related to the needs and problems of the pupils.
7. Teachers have an opportunity to acquire much information and many insights about pupils and their experiences.
8. Teachers develop many effective contacts with parents and community agencies. These contacts have important possibilities in the complete guidance program.
9. Teachers have many personal contacts with pupils. These "rapport" relationships place them in an extremely strategic position to help children.

III.   THE ROLE OF THE COUNSELOR

1. The counselor has a designated responsibility for counseling. Much of this counseling is supplemental to the work of the teachers in helping pupils with their problems and their plans.
2. The counselor accumulates and organizes basic data about pupils for staff use.
3. The counselor helps teachers with pupil problems which the teachers find difficult.
4. The counselor helps the staff organize their contacts with parents.
5. The counselor helps the staff to identify and utilize community referral resources.

6. The counselor helps teachers develop instructional activities more closely related to guidance needs of pupils.
7. The counselor helps the staff develop many of the important guidance services of the school: orientation activities, placement services, testing programs, pupil personnel records, follow-up services, etc.
8. The counselor helps the staff gather, organize and use educational and occupational information needed by teachers.
9. The counselor helps the staff carry on research and evaluation studies.

   Institute of Counseling, Testing and Guidance, Michigan State College, East Lansing (mimeographed), 1950.

182. CONTINUOUS COUNSELOR GROWTH IS ESSENTIAL

Counselors should work within the limits of their professional competence. No professional clinical counselor ever completes his training. No matter how intensive and wide-ranging his academic education in theory, or how solid and extensive his observations and preliminary internship and later practice, he continues to find himself baffled by his limitations in insight, his ignorance of methods, and his awkwardness in handling such counseling tools as are available to him. With every fresh counselee he faces new and complex situations. The multitudinous factors of human motivation and behavior interact in many different ways and in varied combinations to produce problems requiring counselor help for their solution. While the problems of two or more students may, on the surface, seem to be identical and their anxieties and resultant actions may appear to be similar, careful diagnosis will show them to be quite different both in their causes and in possible solutions. The counselor's humility of self-recognized ignorance is, therefore, of continuing importance. It must be a rational humility, however, an objective admission of limitation in the face of infinite complexity. It must never develop into an emotional sense of inferiority which leads to self-recrimination, depression, and overtimidity about undertaking responsibility for handling new cases. When this happens, the counselor is himself ready for psychotherapy.

With sound analytical modesty, a counselor will continue to grow in effective power and skill. He will set up for himself a rough scale of levels of competence somewhat on the pattern of those described in Chap. 1 of this book. He will peg himself at what he realistically conceives to be his present level. He will look back over his training and experience to see how far he has come. He will try to identify his limitations and his gaps. He will look ahead and plan means of removing the one and filling up the other. And especially he will continually widen his acquaintance with all available nearby specialzed clinical resources which he may consult or to which he may refer his counselee for supplementary aid or for deeper diagnosis and therapy.

> Milton E. Hahn and Malcolm S. MacLean, *General Clinical Counseling.* New York: McGraw-Hill Book Company, Inc., 1950, pp. 36-37. By permission of the publishers.

Part III

UNDERSTANDING THE INDIVIDUAL

8.

Individual Differences

183. THE SIGNIFICANCE OF INDIVIDUAL DIFFERENCES
A CORNERSTONE OF GUIDANCE

The recognition of the significance of individual differences is one of the principal tenets of the personnel point of view. It is a fundamental principle of personnel work in a democracy. If here, as in certain European countries, the primary function of personnel work were selection, individual differences would continue to receive attention only to the extent that they relate to group interests. But in a democracy the primary function is to secure the recognition of and provision for individual needs, abilities, and interests not in order that pupils may serve as more useful means to the ends of the state but in order to secure the optimum development of the individual. In this country the individual is still the primary end of education. On this point our various philosophies of education are in complete agreement.

Jane Warters, *High School Personnel Work Today.* New York: McGraw-Hill Book Company, Inc., 1946, p. 37.

184. HUMAN VARIATION AS OLD AS THE HILLS

Ways of looking at human differences. Thoughtful persons in all periods of history have been confronted with the facts of individual differences. The philosopher in ancient Athens, like the philosopher in twentieth-century America, was sure to see among his neighbors persons ranging all the way from stupidity to genius, from meanness to magnanimity, from emotional stability to psychotic disintegration. The schoolmaster in Rome, like the schoolmaster in Chicago, noted that some children found it difficult or impossible to master the tasks assigned to them, whereas a few forged far ahead of the rest. The church fathers were continually baffled by the problems of heretics. The builders of democracy found it necessary to give considerable thought to the creation of institutions which would prevent the strong from taking advantage of the weak. Planners of cooperative societies found that motivation differed so widely in members of the group that the same situation brought out very diverse reactions from different individuals.

> Leona E. Tyler, *The Psychology of Human Differences.*
> New York: Appleton-Century-Crofts, Inc., 1947, p. 3.

185. DISCOVERING HIDDEN APTITUDES

. . . If a teacher is really to accomplish anything, she must know each child's characteristics. And (still more important) she must have some understanding of the underlying developmental trends and their causes. Only then can she bring it about that each child finds interests congruent with his abilities, friends suitable to him, attitudes and ambitions best in accord with his potentialities. With such understanding, she may do marvelous things. To bring Mary from shy diffidence into leadership in a previously undiscovered ability, transform James from a rebel into helper, or give Henry the guidance and stimulation which years later make him prominent in his community and grateful to his old teacher—these are experiences which can be as thrilling as a prospector's discovery of gold.

> Sidney L. Pressey and Francis P. Robinson., *Psychology and the New Education*, (Revised). New York: Harper and Brothers, 1944, p. 319.

186. VARIATIONS IN PEOPLE A CHALLENGE

Children are of many types. Types common enough and problem-presenting enough to need special comment are the brilliant and the dull, those emotionally unstable or greatly handicapped, and those who are persistently delinquent. A realistic understanding of the average child in his true "averageness" is also very important.

With thirty million pupils in the schools, each presenting his or her own individual problem an impossible dilemma seems presented. But this dilemma should be regarded as only a challenge to American resourcefulness and ingenuity.

Ibid., pp. 360-61.

187. A Unique Self Develops

In the interaction of individual-and-environment every male and female organism develops a unique personality. Each individual has a different biological endowment, a different biological self; each one interacts in a different field of forces— his particular environment—and develops a social self peculiar to him. This development is directed by a self-ideal or super-self, which is the individual's conscious and unconscious conception of what he ought to be and do. These selves have different needs. For example, a child's need for approval, his biological urge to eat a forbidden cooky, and his growing awareness of how he ought to behave create a conflict in him. Living is a continuum of problem situations. As the individual meets and solves them he develops behavior patterns, habits of responding, attitudes—toward himself, toward others, toward life. The configuration of attitudes he develops is his personality. The configuration is not a static design but dynamically reorganized according to how further conflicts or problem situations are met and resolved. No two individuals develop the same changing configuration of attitudes, for elements in the hereditary endowment, past experiences, and environment of each one are different. A unique self develops, a total personality constantly seeking unity through harmonizing the demands of the biological self, the social self, and the self-ideal.

Rosalind Cassidy and Hilda C. Kozman, *Counseling Girls in a Changing Society*. New York: McGraw-Hill Book Company, Inc., 1947, pp. 11-12. By permission of the publishers.

188. Every Individual Differs from Every Other Individual

Educators have the findings from a vast body of research testifying to the fact that every individual differs from every

other individual. They also have the evidence before
their own eyes. Jane and Susan are both fifteen years old.
But Jane is 5 feet 2, postpubescent, "going steady," well nourished, and independent of her parents, while Susan is 5 feet 7,
pubescent, not interested in boys "that way," probably undernourished, and mama's "baby girl." These are far from complete descriptions of Jane and Susan, but they are sufficient
to make concrete the fact that each individual's growth is in
a unique pattern.

No two individuals develop the same personality because
elements in the heredity, past experiences, and environment
of each one are different. The behavior patterns of each one
are dynamically organized and reorganized in responses particular to the individual. Courage, neatness, punctuality,
recklessness, graciousness, and all the other words we have
for designating the ways people behave do not serve to
describe the behavior of any one person as different from the
behavior of other persons until we know enough about the
individual to say in what ways he is courageous, neat, punc-
tual, and so on, and understand how these ways of responding
are interrelated in the behavior we observe.

Ibid., p. 117.

189. The Individual Not a Law to Himself

But the fact that individual differences are manifested in
every conceivable psychological dimension does not invalidate
the general principles governing the function in question—
does not make each individual a law unto himself. For
example, individual differences in auditory and visual thresh-
olds or various kinds of color blindness do not work against
the validity of general principles underlying vision and audi-
tion. Nor do the "peculiar channels" of perceptual patterns
laid down in past experience and directed by the "particular
innate affective and impulsive tendencies of the individual"
violate the "configurational tendencies which appear in all
individuals at all times" in the perceptual process. The fact
that some of Pavlov's dogs went to sleep during his conditioning experiments does not invalidate the principles of conditioning.

Muzafer, Sherif. *An Outline of Social Psychology.* New York: Harper and Brothers, 1948, p. 434.

190. PEOPLE ARE BOTH ALIKE AND DIFFERENT

In daily life we get along quite well by making two contrary assumptions regarding our fellow men: first, that they are all much alike, and second, that each one is different. When several people are looking at the same scene, we assume that they see about alike; and when they are listening to the same speech we assume that they all hear and understand about alike. And so they do, but only in a general way. One person has better eyes than another and sees the scene more distinctly, or he may have his own special interests and for that reason notice details that others overlook. One person, more than another, has the background for understanding a speech in all its implications. Such differences between individuals are often brought home to us forcibly, and we readily admit that social life has much more spice because individuals differ. At the same time social life would be impossible except for common interests and except for the fact that we all see, hear, think and feel pretty much alike under the same circumstances.

Robert S. Woodworth, *Psychology,* Fourth Edition. New York: Henry Holt and Company, Inc., 1940, p. 54. By permission of the publishers.

191. NO NEW PRINCIPLES NEEDED

In dealing with individual differences in social reactions, no new principles are necessary. In the same way that the principles valid in general psychology are valid in social psychology, so principles governing the individual differences in any field of psychology are valid in dealing with social differences. Whatever is found concerning individual differences in the course of research in genetics, child psychology, the psychology of perception, learning, motivation, affectivity, attitude formation and change, etc., can be extended to individual differences in social psychology. And the really established data of clinical psychologists and psychiatrists, whose concern necessarily is with the individual life history are valid material for us. . . .

Muzafer Sherif, *An Outline of Social Psychology.* New York: Harper and Brothers, 1948, p. 428.

192. PROBLEM OF INDIVIDUAL DIFFERENCES AFFECTED BY TESTING MOVEMENT AND INCREASED ENROLMENTS

Essentially the problem of individual differences in education is that of the adjustment of human beings who vary widely from one another to the organized institution called the school.

That persons differ from one another has, of course, been familiar for long enough. But within recent years two influences have been working together to throw the problem of individual differences into high relief in educational thought and practice.

The first of these has been the rise of the testing movement. The most ordinary observation makes it quite clear that people vary in many respects. But even quite careful observation unchecked by any objective scheme of reference fails to bring home to one the extent of such variations. Few of us become well acquainted with more than a comparatively small number of persons. It is known that we tend to select our close acquaintances from those who are not too extremely different from ourselves. And even when we are brought professionally into contact with large haphazard groups, our relationship with them tends to be so superficial that we are unaware of many of their personal characteristics and easily fail to recognize how widely they may vary from our own. Not till uniform and standardized instruments of measurement and comparison became available could the extent of individual differences within such groups as we find in our public school be appreciated. Even yet many teachers who have been informed as to the facts have failed imaginatively to realize them or to grasp the necessity of taking action with regard to them.

In the second place, concurrently with the rise of the testing movement there has come about an enormous increase in school populations. Many of those who, a generation ago, would hardly have continued beyond the first few grades now remain until the end of high school. In not a few localities, practically all persons of high-school age are now enrolled. Moreover, there is a strong and growing tendency to project attendance for two years beyond the twelfth grade. All this means that the schools, as part of their regular responsibility, have to deal with human types once rarities within their walls. The increase in school population has been much more rapid than that of the population of the country as a whole, with the inevitable result of an increasingly wide radiation and differentiation of human capacity within it. So these two influences—the retention of great numbers who have previously not continued in school, and the emergence and general use of instruments capable of revealing the situation far more clearly than heretofore—have focused attention upon the problem of individual differences.

> James L. Mursell, *Educational Psychology*. New York: W. W. Norton and Company, Inc., 1939, pp. 91-92. By permission of the publishers.

193. Some of the Facts About Individual Variation

Individuals differ in every ability that has ever been tested. Adults differ, ten-year-olds differ, newborn babies differ. They differ widely but not wildly. The first regularity to notice is that the *range* of any ability (the whole distance from the best to the poorest) is limited. The range of reaction time to sound, after a little practice, extends from about 1/10 to about 2/10 of a second. The time for naming 40 easy opposites ranged in a large group of women college students from 35 to 80 seconds. In a memory test these same students studied a list of 25 unrelated words for one minute and then wrote down all the words they could remember. The range extended from 6 to 18 words. (F. E. Carothers, "Psychological Examinations of College Students," *Arch. Psychology*, 1922, No. 46.)

The range, we say, is limited. But the limits are not exact and sharp. If more individuals are tested, someone may be found to fall somewhat outside the range as previously determined. And the range will change with conditions, as with practice. If you test 100 students in a certain ability, the scores scatter over a certain range. Train them and test again; all the individuals have probably improved, so that the range has moved in the direction of greater ability. It may have become somewhat wider or narrower; in any case it will still be considerable; for though training and education may increase everyone's ability they do not destroy individual differences.

Robert S. Woodworth, *Psychology*, Fourth Edition. New York: Henry Holt and Company, Inc., 1940, pp. 60-61. By permission of the publishers.

194. EARLY VARIATIONS AMONG CHILDREN

Individual variations in the rate and pattern of growth and maturation from birth through adolescence are wide. In this day of extreme consciousness of developmental norms, many a mother must have wasted hours worrying because the babies in her book and the baby next door crawled and had teeth at an age at which her child merely sat and smiled at her in toothless glee. Gesell, who has given such intensive study to the process of growth and maturation, dispels the notion of uniformity of growth with one stroke: "The growth career of each individual infant assumes a distinctive pattern." In this respect, even identical twins are not perfectly identical. Children vary not only in the age at which growth and coordinations occur, but also in the general interrelatedness of various motor performances. Five children observed extensively and analyzed from motion pictures at age one kept the same rank order in such discrete measures as general bodily control, manual dexterity, reach-grasp time, creeping speed, near-step, and one-step. From his observations, Gesell believes that every infant has a characteristic "motor habitude" which expresses itself in postural demeanor and modes of movement. It has been discovered, of course, that modes of movement and posture are also influenced by cultural factors of the group in which a child develops.

The differences in the age, rate, and growth and maturation of the body and sexual functions during adolescence are striking. The age of puberty for normal healthy girls may vary from as early as 9 to as late as 20 years. As we saw . . . such variations have their inevitable psychological consequences.

Muzafer Sherif, *An Outline of Social Psychology*. New York: Harper and Brothers, 1948, pp. 433-34.

195. Characteristics in Which Differences Have Been Measured

Many types of measurement have been made on human beings. First, it is obvious to all of us that human individuals are not the same in size and shape. We have learned to expect and to make at least some provision for this kind of variation, though the army still sometimes has trouble fitting out the new recruit whose shoes are size 13, and women find that both the 32's and the 46's are sometimes hard to obtain at dress shops. Much first-rate work has been done in the field of anthropometric measurements. Not only gross height and weight, but the exact sizes of most of the individual parts of the body have been measured. Second, measurements have been made of the physiological processes, or the way various organ systems of the body function. Basal metabolism, the amount of calcium, sugar, acid, and haemoglobin in the blood, respiratory rate, pulse rate, and concentrations of acid and of urea in the urine are physiological characteristics in which individuals have been found to show definite, measurable differences. Third, accurate measurements have been made of motor capacities including such things as reaction time, speed of tapping, steadiness, and swiftness of blow. Fourth, much work on the measurement of sensory and perceptual differences has come from psychological laboratories. We know that individuals vary as to the keenness of their vision, hearing, and sense of smell. Some are much better than others at analyzing and remembering complex patterns of lines, colors, or sounds. Fifth, general intelligence differences have been analyzed. In the complex combination of memory, judgment, and problem-solving which intelligence tests involve, wide, consistent, and practically important differences have been identified. Sixth, there are differences in achievement and knowledge among individuals who have had the same opportunity to learn. Hundreds of school studies are available showing the wide range of achievement found in any school grade. Seventh, vocational interests have been shown to be susceptible to measurement. Finally, considerable progress has been made in the measurement of attitudes, beliefs, opinions, and personality adjustment. Each of these techniques breaks new ground for research.

> Leona E. Tyler, *The Psychology of Human Differences.*
> New York: Appleton-Century-Crofts, Inc., 1947, pp. 20-21.

196.   VARIATIONS IN ABILITY ARE WIDE AND QUANTITATIVE

Variations in a single trait—physical, mental or emotional— are very large. One baby at birth may weigh five times as much as another. One man may be a third taller than another, and in extreme instances, twice as tall. One child in a sixth-grade class may be at the second-grade level in reading ability, while another child in the same class may be able to read as well as a typical high-school senior. And so it is with all forms of academic achievement.

Human beings obviously differ widely in intelligence. Contrast, for example, the behavior of a low-grade idiot with that of a genius such as Einstein or John Dewey. The low-grade idiot cannot walk, cannot use words meaningfully, cannot dress himself, cannot feed himself. At the opposite pole stands the genius whose mental capacity is so great that he seems almost to transcend the usual limitations of the human mind.

A similar picture presents itself with respect to emotional stability. At one extreme stands the individual who is calm, poised, well-controlled in practically every situation—the sort of person who is said to have ice-water in his veins. At the opposite end of the distribution stands the insane individual who has lost control over his behavior. In fact, he is so exceptional that it is not at all strange that earlier generations were convinced that such persons were inhabited by evil spirits.

With respect to the four fundamental needs of all human beings, it is important to keep in mind that the variations in the strength of these needs are considerable. One man may be consumed by insatiable ambition, while another, perhaps even a member of the same family, may be easygoing, casual, lazy. One man may have a very strong desire to be in the limelight, to get acclaim from his fellows, while another is much happier when he is alone and unnoticed. One man may be confident and another insecure. One man may possess relatively strong physiological drives which in another are relatively weak.

Differences in abilities usually quantitative. When a human ability is measured, the differences in that ability are usually quantitative rather than qualitative. There is a continuity of scores from the lowest to the highest. For example, men are neither tall nor short in the sense that tall men and short men represent qualitative differences. Differences in intelligence are also quantitative. If one were to compare two ten-year-old boys one of whom had the intellectual capacity of an imbecile and the other of a young genius, the difference would appear so striking that it might appear on the surface that the two differed qualitatively. However, if the mental capacities of ten thousand ten-year-old boys were measured, the resultant scores would constitute a continuous series, and, as in the case of height, the gradations would be very fine.

A similar situation probably exists with respect to emotional stability. It is unscientific to classify human beings into a dichotomy: the sane and the insane. If a large representative group of individuals of college age were measured for emotional stability, the distribution would approximate the normal curve.

At the extreme right of the distribution, we have those who are exceptionally well adjusted. This small group includes those few individuals who meet nearly every crisis calmly. Their breaking-point is very high. Just below them will come those who are very well adjusted—individuals who meet life's problems and solve them with relatively little difficulty. In the center we have the large average group to which the majority belongs. Individuals in this group experience frustrations and conflicts, disappointments and emotional disturbances, but they always succeed in finding socially acceptable means of reducing tension. Below the average group are those who are emotionally maladjusted. Persons in this group experience considerable tension. In serious cases this tension is persistent.

Herbert A. Carroll, *Mental Hygiene*. New York: Prentice-Hall, Inc., 1947, pp. 65-67. By permission of the publishers.

197. HUMAN BEINGS VARY IN THEIR RATE OF ENERGY OUTPUT

The rate of energy expenditure varies among individuals and may vary for a given person from time to time. The durable human machine does not operate at the same speed for all persons. This second principle is important because it is one possible basis for differences in energy, enthusiasm, and speed of reaction among students. The program of activity which completely exhausts one student may leave another unaffected. One student may habitually be alert, quick-acting, energetic; another apparently sluggish, and slow-thinking. Yet in terms of individual rates of energy expenditure that have nothing to do with physical fitness, intelligence, or motivation, the first student may be simply one with a high rate of energy output, the second with a low rate. They may be equally motivated, equally intelligent, and equally healthy. Each student—and each faculty member—possesses a characteristic rate of energy expenditure that is peculiar to his own body.

Paul J. Brouwer, *Student Personnel Services in General Education*. Washington: American Council on Education, 1949, p. 258. (From chapter by Florence I. Mahoney.)

198. VARIATION IN FAMILY AND COMMUNITY CULTURAL PATTERNS IMPORTANT

In this discussion of the culture which the student brings to college, it should be clear that a knowledge of the composition pattern of student bodies is essential to an understanding of the mores. The geographical districts from which students come, the ancestor patterns, family culture, parental domination, socio-economic level, minority cultures represented, racial patterns, and other mores of the culture from which they come are all factors in understanding a student body and in creating the best adjustments for each student. The basic needs of young people for response, recognition, and security are evident in the "ways of doing things" and are often evident in a manner peculiar to the family and community cultural patterns which have become a part of them.

Janet A. Kelley, *College Life and the Mores*. New York: Bureau of Publications, Teachers College, Columbia University, 1949, p. 32.

199. VARIATIONS IN SOCIAL STATUS AND SOCIAL MOBILITY

The college dean or college president needs to understand the part that social status and social mobility play in the lives of his students. He may be dealing with students who come from middle- and upper-class families and are assured of maintaining their status. Or he may be dealing with the lower-class students who are working to rise in the social scale. Or he may have both types of student on his campus. Especially in the guidance and advisory program of the college should these matters be considered. No student can be helped by a counselor if he is thought of merely as a combination of abilities. His social past and his social goals must come in for consideration. The college administrator should have a clear picture of where his institution fits into the social system, what social groups it serves, and how it can serve these groups in promoting democracy and social solidarity.

> W. L. Warner, R. J. Havighurst, and Martin B. Loeb, *Who Shall Be Educated?* New York: Harper and Brothers, 1944, pp. 168-69.

200. INDIVIDUAL DIFFERENCES IN SOCIAL RELATIONS

There are Frenchmen and Frenchmen; there are Britishers and Britishers, in spite of the common features that give them their distinctive characteristics as Frenchmen or as Britishers. Likewise, there are Catholics and Catholics, Mohammedans and Mohammedans. The same may be said of radicals and conservatives. A certain individual will go all the way for the values he stands for as a group member; another will not do more than five miles for them; still a third will break down in the first mile. One will express the views which he has derived from his group and his loyalties toward it with his characteristic zeal and enthusiasm; another with disinterested coolness. And there are all gradations between these two extremes. In short, there are individual differences in the reactions of people even to what constitutes their common social bonds as members of the same group.

. . . Certainly, there are individual differences in hunger, sex, or any other motive for that matter. There are individual differences in group interaction—for example, in the time and amount of interaction which are necessary before a given individual becomes a part of the group. Some individuals are reticent and some are more forward. There are individual differences in the intensity and expression of prejudice and other attitudes.

> Muzafer Sherif, *An Outline of Social Psychology.* New York: Harper and Brothers, 1948, p. 427.

201. SAMPLES OF VARIATIONS IN SOCIAL REACTIONS

Individual variations are found in infants' earliest reactions to social stimuli. Infants under a year vary widely in respect to the amount and frequency of smiling, laughing, and crying. It is interesting to note that the consistency in the amount of crying of individual infants is greater in the second half-year of life, when social factors come to the fore with greater potency, than in the first half-year of life. Individual variations in emotional susceptibility and irritability are observed in babies in the first two years of life. Children of the same age vary in their responses to play material—in their enjoyment, handling, and constructiveness of various kinds of play—in the frequency with which they become engaged in fights with other children, in the amount and kind of sympathy displayed —in short, along almost any dimension.

> *Ibid.,* p. 436.

202. PHYSICAL CHANGES AND SOCIAL ADJUSTMENT

Careful research has indicated the nature and extent of individual differences in physical and mental development during the period of adolescence. It is now known that some young people enter puberty as early as the age of twelve while others do not begin this important stage of their development until they approach the seventeenth year. These individual differences are all the more significant since maturation of the sex glands is closely associated with growth in stature, appearance of hair on the body, and change in voice. This means that boys differ tremendously with respect to the age at which they acquire the characteristics commonly associated with manhood.

While a great deal is known about the physical changes associated with puberty, comparatively few data are available dealing with the problem of individual social adjustment arising out of the divergent individual growth patterns. Indeed, in recent years there has been a tendency to minimize the adjustments demanded of adolescents because no physical basis has been found to justify the conception of this period as one of "storm and stress." A study of physical changes alone during the period of adolescence cannot furnish a basis for understanding behavior of individuals. The dynamic aspects of behavior incidental to growing up are not the physical changes themselves but rather the manner in which the relationships surrounding the individual change as his individual growth pattern evolves.

The data to be presented . . . will show clearly that many young men do face acute personality adjustments during the period of adolescence. These adjustments arise out of the social situation surrounding the individual and are acute because they sometimes demand a complete change in the conception of self.

> C. Ward Crampton and E. DeAlton Partridge, "Social Adjustments Associated With Individual Differences Among Adolescent Boys," *The Journal of Educational Sociology,* Vol. 12, No. 2, October, 1938, pp. 66-67.

203. INDIVIDUAL VARIATIONS RELATED TO SOCIAL SETTING

. . . social reactions even of individuals of the same culture are subject to variations. It is evident that reactions of the individual will reveal his unique personal characteristics as well as the common characteristics of his group and culture. Individual variations . . . are due to the combined effects of heredity and environment (both physical and cultural). As we proceed to more complex levels of psychological functioning, the modifiability of the organism by the environmental forces becomes more decisive. The level of behavior which is our main concern, i.e., the social level, is probably the most complex. Hence, in determining the individual's whole person, in his experience and behavior in diverse situations, environmental factors are most potent. No one is born a Protestant or a Catholic, a conservative or a radical, an individualist or a collectivist. He becomes one. To be sure, there may be potentialities in him which make him more or less susceptible to becoming a good or bad Protestant, radical, or individualist.

But these potentialities are not sufficient *in themselves* to
make the individual behave in this or that way and to this
or that degree. These potentialities blossom or are transformed
or deflected or blocked by the circumstances he goes through
in a particular environmental setting. Many a man in the
Middle Ages who lived and died with a sense of security—
but hardly revealed individuality—might have developed into
an ardent individualist, as his offspring did, had he lived
after the industrial revolution in Europe. Today there are
fully outgoing individuals heavily engaged in politics and engineering who are offspring of the Hindu whose philosophy of
life is depicted as a complete introvert withdrawal from nature
and life.

These general remarks are made to emphasize the fact that
the individual variations in social behavior acquire real meaning only when taken in relation to the social setting which
contributes so decisively to their appearance. The necessity
of relating items of individual behavior to the social setting
in which they occur has become widely established in psychology in recent years, especially under the impact of the
comparative material presented by social scientists. As psychologists, we must be more specific and carry the analysis
further to the level of single individuals.

Individual variations taken in the abstract have little meaning in themselves. They make sense only in relation to the
appropriate *reference scale*. This idea is not an academic
novelty. People usually make their judgments and appraisals
on the basis of an established range of relationships. To
illustrate with a tangible example: When people see a man
and a woman of the same height (say, 5 feet 9 inches) side
by side and appraise their statures, they usually judge the
man as medium and the woman as tall, even though both are
of equal height. And they have good reason to do so. They
do not take the absolute values of stature as the basis of their
judgment. Whether they realize it or not, appropriate masculine or femine scales of stature (between their averages
there is a difference of four inches) form the basis of their
appraisal.

Muzafer Sherif, *An Outline of Social Psychology.* New York: Harper and Brothers, 1948, pp. 442-43.

204. KNOWLEDGE OF VARIATIONS HAS PRACTICAL SIGNIFICANCE

The study of individual differences has already contributed much to the fund of dependable information on the basis of which we can improve our political, industrial, and educational procedures. Wherever we are confronted with the problem of selecting men for certain duties, or guiding individuals into the tasks which suit them best, the methods of analyzing human characteristics which have been described are applicable. Wherever it is desirable to improve the relationships between groups of people, between men and women, between neighbor and neighbor, between nation and nation, the knowledge we now have and are acquiring about the ways in which the groups differ and the range of variability within each group can make for understanding. Wherever it is important to make *changes* in people, to educate them, to modify undesirable attitudes and prejudices, or to improve their adjustment toward life and society, the habit of thinking in terms of the place each individual occupies in a distribution helps us to adapt our instruction to the actual persons we are instructing. An informed tolerance is a natural outgrowth of a thoroughgoing acceptance of the findings of differential psychology. This alone, an attitude of live and let live, were it to become at all widespread, would work a great improvement in human living.

Leona E. Tyler, *The Psychology of Human Differences.* New York: Appleton-Century-Crofts, Inc., 1947, pp. 406-7.

205. THE INDIVIDUAL AS THE UNIT OF EDUCATION

. . *The individual is the unit of education—the individual with his unique set of needs, interests, and abilities.* While we may not understand him completely, we do know that, like the force called electricity, he is a reality. And it is this reality that all of us in education must face.

Is it enough, though, merely to understand that boys and girls differ one from the other in physical traits, in mental characteristics, in emotional tendencies? Can we be satisfied merely to analyze, to list, to describe the peculiarities that compose individuals? No. If we are to perform our whole duty, we must take two additional steps. First, we must learn to use measuring and recording techniques to analyze continuously the changing abilities of developing individuals. Second, and far more complex, we must provide each individual with such guidance that he will select from the activities offered in schools and colleges a rich and full set of experiences which will stimulate his latent abilities, meet his individual tastes, and develop to the full his peculiar talents. To provide this form of guidance constitutes the most challenging issue before our schools today.

> Ben D. Wood and Ralph Haefner, *Measuring and Guiding Individual Growth*. New York: Silver Burdett Company, 1948, p. 225.

206.   Mass Procedures No Substitute for Individual Attention

If you have ever waited at a busy corner to meet a friend, you may have mused on the extent to which the passing individuals are so much alike and yet so different. But if your friend came along as you were musing, dressed like the others, of the same general height and body build, and perhaps of the same general color of complexion, you recognized that person as *distinctly* your friend. And if for a moment you were not quite sure, his voice, his smile, the clasp of his hand, and a moment of conversation removed all doubt. He was, and is, the only Bob Jones. "No one just like him," you say.

No two human beings have ever been found to be alike. No scientific investigations of human behavior—even those of so-called "identical twins" (R. W. Burnham, "Case Studies of Identical Twins," *Pedagogical Seminary and Journal of Genetic Psychology*, Vol. 56, Second half, June, 1940), have resulted in the finding of individuals completely similar in structure or behavior. The most startling fact about the members of the largest group of individuals with as near common heredity and environment as it has been possible to study, the Dionne quintuplets (W. E. Blatz, *Collected Studies on the Dionne Quintuplets*. Toronto: University of Toronto Press, 1937), is the extent to which they differ in performance and behavior. The observations of writers throughout the ages concerning individuality are being confirmed as we count, measure, manipulate, and give new labels to individual characteristics. Though the observations have been made by a Plato, a Shakespeare, or a factor analyst with his punched-card equipment, the results vary only in slight degree. There are no two persons alike. Allport (G. W. Allport, *Personality, A Psychological Interpretation.* New York: Henry Holt & Company, 1937), states the case as follows:

"The outstanding characteristic of man is his individuality. He is a unique creation of the forces of nature. Separated spatially from all other men he behaves throughout his own particular span of life in his own distinctive fashion. It is not upon the cell nor upon the single organ, nor upon the group, nor upon the species that nature has centered her most lavish concern, but rather upon the integral organization of life processes into the amazingly stable and self-contained system of the individual living creature."

Allport goes on to point out that the general laws of science have value in depicting the common ground upon which all individual minds meet, but that this common ground is really a no man's land. "When the investigator turns his eyes upon the individual he finds that in him all laws are modified."

The counselor who is well trained only in the use of devices for obtaining *mass* data finds too often that his generalizations leave him completely at a loss as to what to do with the local lad who is driving his teacher to distraction, the adolescent girl who is "boy crazy," and the sophomore who is in an academic slump. The counselor who is thoroughly familiar with the literature of experimentation in guidance may be thoroughly bewildered when he has to get down to cases because the *generalizations* apply to so few of them. When the counselor has computed the correlation coefficients between scores on his *tests,* he will often find himself with a problem rather than a solution. When his *group* guidance program is completed, he will find that the need for individual guidance is ever more evident. When he learns about the group, he will find that he must learn more about each individual as a person-in-a-situation. (The references cited at the end of this chapter will be helpful to those who may be disturbed by the apparent conflict between the emphasis upon the individual as an individual and the need for continuous consideration of him as a person-in-a-situation. Note that the procedures recommended in this volume are intended to supplement, not replace, the many excellent group study and instructional procedures which have been devised. There need be no conflict between emphasis upon work with individuals and emphasis upon work with groups if extremes in either procedure are avoided. . . .) Rarely will he be able to justify the existence of his position on the educational scene until he gets down to cases.

Despite the wide acceptance of facts and theories about the extent and importance of individuality as indicated by the frequency of reference to it by educators, there is still too little done for, with, and about, the individual. Despite the incontrovertible evidence of the uniqueness of each person, there is increasing emphasis in education upon *class* instruction, *group* testing, *mass* experimentation and *group* guidance. And despite the evidence concerning the complexity of each unique human organism, there is still much emphasis upon the development of techniques for handling larger and larger groups more efficiently and too little emphasis on methods of working with the individual. Those who develop and encourage the use of such practices ignore, or make only half gestures toward, the fact that the welfare of the mass may be determined primarily by the combination of the welfares of those who compose the group. They do so despite their verbal assurances that our practices and objectives in education have validity primarily when they further the development of each person.

Mass procedures, no matter how well-intentioned, must fail to accomplish the objectives of education unless they are supplemented by adequate attention to the individual. In spite of the ever-increasing efficiency of administrative and organizational devices developed for the management and instruction of groups, it seems unlikely that they will ever become adequate substitutes for the counseling process in which an informed and trained person works with another person, provides him with information that can be interpreted in terms of his personal needs and accomplishments, and assists him to make his own decisions. It is not likely that administrative devices for management of *groups* will ever properly provide for the needs of the individual; semi-individual devices will seldom be sufficient; no substitute will be adequate.

> John W. M. Rothney and Bert A. Roens, *Counseling the Individual Student*. New York: William Sloane Associates, Inc., 1949, pp. 10-12.

207. THE SOCIAL IMPLICATIONS OF GROWTH

It is quite evident on the basis of these data that some of the most significant things about growing up are associated with the social implications of growth. Careful research is needed to determine the nature of these social implications and the way in which they affect the behavior of the individual. It is quite probable that the problems faced by girls as they grow into maturity are quite different from those found in these letters. For example, girls in modern society would not be so anxious to develop muscles and grow tall. Not as many of them would ask for help in putting on weight.

Evidently much of the behavior of young people during the period of adolescence can be traced to problems they face in defining themselves according to how others react to them, or how they think they appear to those about them. Adults who deal with young people can be more skillful if the social implications of individual difference are recognized.

No doubt in many cases the problems of growing boys are accentuated by the nature and administration of the educational program to which they are exposed. For example, the common desire to be six feet tall and possess a body like a Grecian god may be partly the result of the requirements placed upon young people in a physical-education program. Some boys, because of the nature of their inherited characteristics, can never achieve what they have come to feel is an acceptable physique. The more persistently that ideal is kept before them, the more opportunity there is for mental conflict to arise in the minds of those who can never hope to attain it. That this happens in many cases can be seen in the great number of letters received from boys seeking help in this connection. The seriousness of the problem to these boys can be judged by the earnestness with which they write.

> C. Ward Crampton and E. DeAlton Partridge, "Social Adjustments Associated with Individual Differences Among Adolescent Boys," *The Journal of Educational Sociology*, Vol. 12, No. 2, October, 1938, pp. 71-72.

208. PROGRAM ADAPTED TO INDIVIDUAL DIFFERENCES

Twins "A" and "B"—"A" is one of a pair of identical twins— that is, who are supposed to be identical from the embryological point of view. Perhaps this assumption is what steered me off my course. It was not until two years had passed that I realized that I had two totally different individuals to deal with; two individuals who despite their being identical twins had altogether different reactions to the same situations. The difference was subtle, therefore easily missed. Twin "A" was lighter of build than twin "B." Twin "A" held recognition in far stronger esteem. He, unlike "B," was more intent upon receiving reward other than the intrinsic worth of sport. Twin "A" was more nervous, high strung, and easily upset. I should have spent more time with him just before meets in order to quiet him. Instead I gave both twins the same amount of counsel. Twin "A" was prone to emotional outbursts which came unexpectedly and at moments when they were most upsetting to the rest of the squad. I should have shown more patience with him in the process of learning new moves on the apparatus. I should have given him more encouragement because, unlike his brother, he was nourished by praise, and criticism had to be muffled and subtle. During their freshman year, these differences did not emerge very strongly. It was in the sophomore year when the strain of competition, the longer hours of practice, the greatly augmented amount of rapport resulting from one year's experience, brought the differences to the front and clarified the necessity for totally different treatment of "A."

Ruth Ann—This past winter in teaching social dance and physical fitness, I had the opportunity to observe several types

of difference: Ruth Ann was an industrial girl with a personality difference. She registered with her club members for
the beginners' Social Dance Class. She was not attractive; did
not have a pleasing personality; was hard to get along with;
and was not totally accepted by her club members. Each
week during some part of the lesson, after I had finished
demonstrating and explaining a new step to the class, she
would interrupt any number of times usually to this effect,
"Say, you said we should start on our right foot for the man's
part, and you started on your left." Her comments were always
directed toward something I had not done correctly. All
through the lesson Ruth Ann would complain to or nag those
around her; this was annoying to me as well as to her partners.
Each time the girls would change partners Ruth Ann was left
without one. As an instructor, I became concerned about this
girl, realizing something had to be done or the whole teaching
procedure would lose its effect. I realized the girl wanted
attention; wanted to be accepted by the group and desired
friends. Her dancing skill was not poor, but there was much
room for improvement. In wanting her to have a wholesome
experience in the class, I got information about Ruth Ann
from one of the secretaries and made it a point to have
friendly but impersonal chats before or after class with her;
got her confidence and let her know that I was interested in
helping her. I changed my teaching procedure by including
a new system of getting dance partners after each dance to
insure that Ruth Ann would get a partner each time. In doing
all demonstrations of new material I did them slowly and
carefully in front of her. Wherever I needed a partner to
demonstrate or emphasize a particular step, I would always
use her once or twice during the evening. Each time I observed
her dancing I found some good point to comment on. This
change in procedure helped Ruth Ann without hindering
others of the group.

Don, a large 17-year-old, didn't seem at all interested in the
ordinary camp activities and could very seldom be found with
the rest of the boys of his cabin. Observation disclosed the
fact that everything that he did was some sort of self-initiated
project. Sometimes he worked alone and other times he

encouraged others to work with him. The leader immediately
began to encourage and commend him for the things which
he was doing and gradually, through suggestion and guidance,
led him into some real worth-while things in camp. He finally
worked out two projects in which he got a great deal of satisfaction and which incidentally proved helpful to the entire
camp and thus gained wider recognition for him. I think it
is quite obvious that a mistake would have been made, to
attempt to make Don conform to the group.

Frank was just an ordinary boy of 15. He came to camp
with one thing in mind, and that was to fish. He had his rod
and reels, tackle box, and the enthusiasm of a veteran fisher-
man; but he knew nothing about fishing. Fishing by the
campers was not very popular and no provision had been made
for instruction and equipment. However, the leader set about
to see that Frank was taken care of. The procedure was to
help him develop a program for himself so that he would get
both personal satisfaction for himself and a sharing experience
with his group. The end result was that Frank had his opportunity, learned how to use the equipment which he had to
the best advantage, learned something about the habits of
fish, constructed a creditable minnow trap and a minnow box
for the use of all campers, was able to draw other boys to
himself, and best of all, learned how to swim well enough to
pass the boat test so that he could take the boat out alone.

Tony was a boy very much retarded in school. Very little
could be found for him to do around the agency because he
was too slow for any team or group games. He came to my
clay-modeling class at my suggestion. I realized that clay
work was an individual skill and that he could take as long
as he wanted without holding anybody else back. He came
regularly for weeks and just observed. Then one afternoon
when I was called out of the room, he made one of the best
elephants in clay I have ever seen. He surprised me with it
when I returned to the room. All the other boys started to
make elephants but none could compare with Tony's skill.
They went to him for aid and he was pleased to help them
shape the head or the body. This boy found a new interest in
which his retardedness made little if any difference in clay
work.

Pat and *Jo*, two friends of thirteen years of age, are always saying there are too many girls in the room to sew and that they would be able to do much better work alone. One day I missed them from the group and inquired where they were. The girls replied that they were in the Crafts' closet. After a few minutes I stuck my head in the door and found Pat sewing and Jo sweeping the floor. Pat said, "Close the door, please, so the other girls won't come in." I replied, "All right, but would one of you like to take attendance for me in a few minutes?" Pat answered that she would and Jo volunteered to help me clean up the craft room after class. I find that both girls come from large families where they have no privacy. Pat lives with ten others in four rooms, while Jo shares a room with two sisters and a brother. The two girls are very much liked by the group and the other girls do not object to their using the closet as a private sewing room. The door is kept open and the girls alternate from one room to the other. Here, there is a definite need for something of their own. They now seem to enjoy sewing much better and are much happier with this arrangement.

Unpublished reports; furnished the editor as class assignments, 1942

9.

Motivation

A. The General Problem

209. No Established Psychology of Motivation

. . In spite of the promising beginnings of some excellent research material, there is as yet no established psychology of motivation—motivation, especially on the human level, being one of the most difficult problems of the whole discipline. The complexity of the problem becomes even more intricate when motivation is considered in social psychology, for here it necessarily involves the impact of diverse groups (small and large) and culture on the individual.

> Muzafer Sherif, *An Outline of Social Psychology*. New York: Harper and Brothers, 1948, p. 9.

210. What Does Man Want?—A Basic Question

The most profound question we can ask about the human being is: What motivates him? What drives him on? What does he want? What does he struggle for? Variants of these questions are: What does man want out of life? What makes life worth living? What makes him happy or unhappy? Is man motivated primarily by selfish or by unselfish ends? Does he seek the good or does he prefer evil?

> Maurice J. Shore, *et al.*, *Twentieth Century Mental Hygiene*. New York: Social Sciences Publishers, 1950, p. 347. (From chapter by A. H. Maslow.)

211. Motive Defined

As a preliminary statement in advance of complete investigation a motive may be defined as that which arouses, sustains, and directs activity.

Laurence Frederic Shaffer, *The Psychology of Adjustment.* Boston: Houghton Mifflin Company, 1936, p. 84.

212. MOTIVE THE GENERIC TERM

. . . *Whether directed toward food, clothing, shelter, the opposite sex, or toward status, power, social distinction, recognition, trifles concerning dress, decoration, and etiquette, these are all cases of motivated behavior—motives.* We shall use the term *motives as a generic term to cover all the different cases and kinds of goal-directed (motivated) behavior.* We need such a collective term to cover the different kinds of motivated behavior—needs (drives) originating and embedded in the functioning of the organism of the individual, "derived drives" based on them, socially acquired desires, wishes, aspirations, ambitions, directed toward certain goals or values, etc.

Muzafer Sherif, *An Outline of Social Psychology.* New York: Harper and Brothers, 1948, p. 11.

213. A VOCABULARY APPROPRIATE TO THE DISCUSSION OF MOTIVATION

A varied and somewhat confusing list of terms descriptive of motivation has come into use, in part reflecting the different schools of psychology. Thus, a behaviorist is likely to describe motivation in words differing from those of a psychoanalyst, even in a case in which there is no disagreement over facts. In what follows, we have attempted to use a set of terms as "neutral" as possible, that is, terms which are closely related to a matter-of-fact or naturalistic description of motivation as we find it. The following definitions are adhered to in the discussion:

Motivation: A very general term for describing need-satisfying and goal-seeking behavior. It includes physiological drives, unconscious motives, clearly formulated purposes, ideals, etc.

Motives: A very general term for whatever states or events within the organism (under appropriate circumstances) initiate activity or regulate activity in relation to a goal. Hence mo-

tives include *drives, needs, urges, impulses, sets, predisposi-
tions, values, purposes,* etc. The word *need* is most nearly
synonymous with *motive.*

Incentive: An object or situation in the environment capable
of satisfying an aroused motive. Food is an incentive in relation to hunger as a motive. A safe place is an incentive in
relation to pain as a motive. *Reward* and *goal-object* are
synonymous for incentive, but the word *goal* is used somewhat
differently. We may think of the incentive as something which
can be manipulated by the teacher in a direct manner not
possible with motives.

Goal: the goal of the learner is the end-state which gives
direction to motivated behavior. It must always be defined
according to the aroused motives of the learner. Because the
acceptability and satisfying consequences of an incentive depend in part upon the goal-expectations of the learner, the
incentive and the learner's goals have to be distinguished. The
goal is what the learner is seeking rather than the incentive
that the teacher is providing. They may have much or little
in common.

Level of Aspiration: A goal that the individual sets himself,
which he expects to reach or wishes very much to reach.

Intrinsic and Extrinsic Relations Between Tasks and Goals:
The relationship between goals and the learning tasks related
to them may be described as intrinsic or extrinsic, depending
upon the logical relationship between the task and the goal.

The relation between task and goal may be said to be
intrinsic if the incentive conditions are functionally or organically related to the activity. Thus the satisfaction derived
from hearing a program over a self-constructed radio set is a
satisfaction derived from putting the radio to its intended use.
This is an intrinsic satisfaction, because the goal is inherent
in the successful completion of the task of construction.

The relation between task and goal may be said to be
extrinsic if the incentive conditions are artificially or arbitrarily
related to the task. Thus, if a prize is to be awarded to the
first boy to complete his radio, the desire for the prize is
extrinsically related to the task of radio-building.

Because motivational situations are complex, the relation

between task and goal is often at once intrinsic and extrinsic.

A few additional technical terms will be introduced as needed, but the above basic vocabulary suffices to avoid confusion at the outset. It should be pointed out that allowance is made for motives which are not clear to the learner, referred to as unconscious motives. By recognizing that motives are often disguised, we avoid the pitfalls which arise from taking stated purposes and ideals at their face values. Over-emphasis upon verbally acknowledged motives leads to moralizing about behavior instead of making a more penetrating psychological analysis.

Ernest R. Hilgard and David H. Russell, "Motivation in School Learning," *Learning and Instruction*. Forty-ninth Yearbook of the National Society for the Study of Education, Part I. Chicago: University of Chicago Press, 1950, chap. 2, pp. 38-39. By permission of the Society.

214. BEYOND SYMPTOMS LIE MOTIVES

It is first of all fundamental to recognize the inadequacy of simply treating symptoms without consideration of the underlying situation and the possible effect of the treatment upon it. The pupil who is belligerent, morose, daydreaming, or truant is not adequately dealt with if punished for his aggression, berated for his moodiness, rudely interrupted in his "wool-gathering," or pursued by the attendance officer; instead, the treatment may in each instance aggravate the basic difficulty. The important questions are: What frustration or confusion is causing the aggressiveness or moodiness or the real or imaginary flight from the schoolroom? How may that situation be cleared up? Can a reasonable satisfaction of the frustrated interests be somehow secured? Or may the interests need reconstitution, and the level of aspiration need to be changed? These problems, not the symptoms, require attention.

Sidney L. Pressey and Francis P. Robinson, *Psychology and the New Education*. New York: Harper and Brothers, 1944, p. 189.

215. WATCH FOR A VARIETY OF SYMPTOMS

Whether the problem that centers the attention of the

counselor is poor posture, failing academic work, fatigue, truancy, the selection of a program of studies, or chronic fainting spells, one fact is the same in each case: the girl needs help. She needs help in helping herself. The only other generalization that can be made is that each girl requires a different kind of help, because each is showing a behavior that is symptomatic of a need, a need unique to her own particular, individual configuration of causes.

> Rosalind Cassidy and Hilda C. Kozman, *Counseling Girls in a Changing Society.* New York: McGraw-Hill Book Company, Inc., 1947, pp. 3-4. By permission of the publishers.

216.   SHAFFER: BEHAVIOR IS PURPOSIVE

Popular curiosity is not satisfied with a description of how a man performs an act; it also wants to know *why* he does it. The significance of motives, desires or urges is recognized in many fields as in industry, in law, in sport and in education. Why do men work? Economists, political theorists and psychologists have given various answers. It is suggested that men work because they have an instinct to do so, or because they must work to earn food and shelter, or because they seek social approbation, or so that they will not be scorned and derided. Why do people play baseball or congregate to see others play? Why does the school pupil conform to the rules and learn his lessons? Why does he not just sit there, failing to react to the instructive situations provided for him? Such questions as these indicate the widespread interest in motive and the necessity of making a thorough investigation of the problem.

In the treatment of adjustment problems the discovery of motives has been especially fruitful. James is the school bully. On the playground and before and after school he may be found vigorously bossing the smaller boys, mauling them, fighting when he is sure to win. Why does he do it? What is there in it for him? Virginia has run away from home three times. Her parents are in good circumstances and seem interested in her welfare, yet she persists in trying to get away. A study of her motives is necessary in order to understand the problem and assist in its solution. The practical problems of the psychological practitioner have been greatly clarified by the concept that all behavior, no matter how strange, has its motives. Only since this dynamic concept has entered psychology has much progress been made in the solution of adjustment difficulties.

Laurence Frederic Shaffer, *The Psychology of Adjustment.* Boston: Houghton Mifflin Company, 1936, pp. 83-84.

217. BEHAVIOR NEVER UNCAUSED

Fundamental to the counselor's understanding of inconsistent human actions is his realization that, although behavior is often irrational, it is never uncaused. A woman who is late for her dental appointment may "explain" her tardiness as due to transportation difficulties, whereas in fact she may have so dreaded going that she didn't allow herself enough time. All behavior, reasonable or unreasonable, is motivated, though frequently it is difficult or even impossible to discover what the real motives are. Sometimes we can uncover in ourselves or in others what is back of our unusual behavior, and at other times, though it is not possible to discover them specifically, we accept the fact that hidden motives are present and we believe that, were we all-knowing, we could find an adequate explanation.

In practice most of us do accept the principle that every human action has its sufficient motives. This is shown by our readiness to ask for and offer explanations. If a friend does something unusual, we ask at once, "What made him do that?" and quickly we think of a possible cause for his behavior. "He has a fever." "He is still mad because the boss gave him an awful bawling out." "She is upset because she is going to have a baby." "She is terribly jealous, you know."

Annette Garrett, *Counseling Methods for Personnel Workers.* New York: Family Service Association of America, 1945, pp. 17-18.

218. THE COUNSELOR NEEDS TO UNDERSTAND THE DEEPER LEVELS OF BEHAVIOR

Another factor which affects the selection of a counselor is the adequacy of his information, beliefs, and concepts regard-

ing human behavior. We have defined counseling as interaction between two persons; the interaction is governed and
made to serve educational ends by the counselor. The effectiveness of such control of the interaction depends, consequently, upon the counselor's understanding of the *process* of
interaction. He must have concepts of human behavior which
guide him in his questions, which inhibit certain responses,
and which clarify his understanding of how he as counselor
may utilize this knowledge for the student's growth.

Such an understanding of behavior implies more than
common sense in dealing with people. Of course, common
sense is not to be minimized. No doubt many teachers inadvertently are acceptable counselors because their own adjustment to life is mentally healthful and because they seem to
have an intuitive understanding of people. This, however, is
insufficient. The cooperating colleges are attempting to con-
ceptualize this common sense and to add to it the refinements
necessary to better understanding of the deeper levels of
counseling work.

Insufficient insight into human nature on the part of the
counselor is well illustrated in the following story: A professor
of mathematics is talking with a girl who is rather spoiled.
She came in for help on rather obvious problems, hoping to
get him to do the problems for her. The professor (1) shows
her how and then tells her to do her own. She fiddles around
and says she can't get them. This has happened two or three
times. Finally, she goes into a childish rage. (2) He tells her
she is acting like a child. Then she angrily leaves the room.

The professor seemed unaware that this girl's behavior was
saying, "I don't want to assume responsibility for my own
work." If he had had this insight, he would have acted differently, perhaps (1) refusing to show her how to work the
problems until she recognized her basic problem—the desire
to evade responsibility—or, perhaps (2) helping her to see
that she went into a childish rage because this technique had
been helpful to her in the past. At any rate, the counselor's
inability to interpret the student's behavior prevented this
counseling experience from being a source of growth toward
maturity for the student. Common sense told him that she was

acting like a child, but it could not tell him why. Counselors need to develop the ability to react, not to surface manifestations alone, but to underlying feelings and emotions which usually control behavior.

> Paul J. Brouwer, *Student Personnel Services in General Education.* Washington: American Council on Education, 1949, pp. 28-29.

219. THE STEREOSCOPIC POINT OF VIEW

Teachers see behavior from what might be called a stereoscopic point of view. This means that behavior is viewed with one eye, so to speak, as overt and, with the other, as the product of certain known feelings, drives, wants, needs. This stereoscopic point of view thus reveals behavior in its depth and refers all outward behavior to the inner states which cause it. Behavior is thus the expression of inner states as they are conceptually understood by the observer. It helps in answering the questions "What lies behind this behavior? What does this behavior mean to this student? What is he in effect saying about himself by acting as he does?"...

Teachers of the Cooperative Study who have attempted to apply these concepts have first of all become much more sensitive to the cause of behavior in the classroom. By seeing behavior stereoscopically, they have found that the interaction within the classroom reveals the personality. For instance, a student comes to the teacher and says bluntly that he cannot do the work. From a stereoscopic point of view this student, in effect, may be saying a number of things, such as, "In the presence of my classmates, I feel stupid and intellectually outclassed. If I tell you about it, maybe you will help me in some way." Or, "I really think I could do this work very easily, but I want you to think that I am having a great deal of difficulty with it because if you will think this, I shall not have to work so hard." Or, "For some reason I haven't the nerve to speak up in class as much as I feel I should in order to do work which meets with your approval. If I speak to you about it, therefore, you may pay more attention to me."

> *Ibid.*, pp. 149-51.

220. What's Behind the Child Behind the Book

. . . What is behind the child behind the book? How happy
is he? How does he feel about life? What conflicts are bewildering or embittering him? What thwartings is he undergoing in the achievement of his extra-school goals and
purposes, and of his in-school goals and purposes?
If he is ill-behaved, why is he ill-behaved? How can
he be helped to improve conduct? If he is timid, or
introverted, or negative, or afraid of life, how can the factors
that are eventuating in these unfortunate attitudes be controlled? If he is a braggart, or a bully, or an unhealthy seeker
after the limelight, or a pseudo-delinquent, what forces are
impelling him and how may they be counteracted? If he is
lazy, or a daydreamer, or a hopeless procrastinator, what
unsatisfied desires are activating him and how can he be dis-
possessed of them, or how can they be redirected into more
desirable channels? If his total influence in the school setting
is disruptive, if he is an actual or a potential center of dis-
affection in the ranks of his mates, what motives are back of
his conduct and how can he be helped to adjust positively and
aggressively to the schoolroom situation and to the community
or the home situation?

Questions such as these are baffling a great many classroom
teachers today.

> Lawrence A. Averill, "Case Studies in the Schools," *Mental
> Hygiene,* Vol. 25, January, 1941, p. 43.

221. Motivation Essential for Learning and Growth

The whole conception which we have been building up of
the relationship between the individual and the world about
him, and of the emergence of new patterns of insight and
response, clearly implies that dynamic factors are of the first
importance. No living creature, all the way from the amoeba
to man, is ever passively acted upon by the environment. He
is active with respect to it; he makes choices; he selects
certain features in it which determine his responses; he modifies and alters it; and in and through these choices, these selections, and these responses, he himself is changed. This, indeed,
is the fundamental characteristic of being alive at all and of

manifesting that sequential process, so different from the series of physical causes and effects, which is called behavior. Moreover, the importance of energy, or drive, or will, or the presence and operation of a goal, is recognized tacitly or explicitly in all the vast range of experimental work on learning. Even when this specific factor is not under investigation, provision is always made for it. . . . the human subject must have a task set before him which he is at least willing to undertake.

> James L. Mursell, *Educational Psychology*. New York: W. W. Norton and Company, Inc., 1939, p. 291. By permission of the publishers.

222. THE BASIC PATTERN OF MOTIVATION

If we do not fully understand the forces underlying biological self-maintenance, we understand still less the forces tending to psychological integrity. However, they would appear to be an extension of homeostatic strivings, in that the individual generally tends to function psychologically in such a way as to meet his biological needs and avoid unpleasant frustration. In any event, it is generally agreed that the organism does strive toward the maintenance of both biological and psychological integrity.

We have already seen that the self is the reference point around which our psychological functions are integrated. Hence any injury to the self is an injury to the individual's center of adjustive operations. Thus the individual strives to maintain his self-integrity. In fact, we seem justified in considering the maintenance of the self to be the psychological counterpart of physiological equilibrium. From this viewpoint, self-maintenance—both psychological and biological—represents the dynamic force tending to psychobiological unity and constitutes our basic pattern of motivation.

As in the case of biological needs, there is a wide variety of psychological needs involved in self-maintenance. But whereas biological needs are relatively fixed, psychological needs are capable of almost infinite extensions and variations. This does not mean that certain psychological needs such as security, affection, and social approval are not basic and fundamental to healthy personality development, but merely that the precise nature of these needs and their operation in adult behavior are more subject to social modifications. In the societies which encourage the acquisition of material possessions and a position of power or dominance in the group, most of the members come to feel a need for acquiring material possessions and for achieving a position of power. In a communal society, these psychological motives may be so rare as to be considered abnormal. For example, among the Arapesh, men regard leadership as a nuisance or burden rather than an opportunity for glory and self-enhancement, and they gladly avoid it whenever they can. (Mead.)

But despite the existence of wide individual and group differences in psychological motives, there do seem to be certain general psychological needs which are relatively common to most socio-cultural conditions throughout the world and hence which are fairly common among all people. However, the strength of these needs may vary considerably from one group to another and among the individuals within a given group.

James C. Coleman, *Abnormal Psychology and Modern Life.* Chicago: Scott, Foresman and Company, 1950, p. 66.

223. BEHAVIOR AS STRESS-RELIEVING ACTIVITY

More recently we have come to realize that man's behavior is a reflection of his striving for various forms of satisfaction. One does not have to be an avowed behaviorist to observe that the individual is after all in dynamic relation to his environment, being to a large extent dependent upon it for those organic and social satisfactions which the very nature of his organism demands for its integrity. To be explicit, man has certain legitimate *wants* or *needs* which in the nature of the case give direction to his actions and which explain in the fundamental sense, why he acts at all. As Thurstone (L. L. Thurstone, *The Nature of Intelligence.* New York: Harcourt, Brace and Company, 1924, pp. xiii-xiv.) puts it, "It is this shift of interest from the stimulus-response relation to the wants of the living self that marks the fundamental difference between what we know as the old and the new in psychology."...

It would probably be fair to say that it is these related concepts of fundamental *wants* and organism *tensions* that have led us to a conception of human dynamics that bids fair, in the light of present knowledge, to supersede all others in logical validity. If man is characterized by a variety of basic "needs" which demand satisfaction, their frustration will obviously set up desires or tensions of various kinds which call for release or, we might say, restoration to equilibrium. This line of reasoning indicates then that the individual is literally driven to action in favor of responses calculated to relieve his strains and stresses; it suggests that he must strive for a balanced realization of his life needs in order to prevent personal disintegration. . . .

> Louis P. Thorpe, *Psychological Foundations of Personality.* New York: McGraw-Hill Book Company, 1938, p. 204.

224. The Insistent Nature of Needs

. . . Each individual is driven in his behavior to seek satisfactions to basic needs which have their origin in physiological processes, psychosomatic processes, and social conditions. The needs for food, water, activity, and rest are primarily physiological. The needs for being valued by others, for feeling like others, and for affectional relations are social in their context. Finally, each person is driven to make some sense out of the scheme of things and of his place in it—the need for a philosophy of life which gives him a sense of his own value and maintains his self-respect.

When needs are frustrated, the individual makes strong, even violent efforts, to satisfy them. If he does not feel that he "belongs" to or is valued by a group, he makes strenuous efforts to win them or defiantly rejects them. In this light, for example, attention-getting behavior of insecure persons becomes clear. When his needs are satisfied, the person is happy, creative, and capable of expending his energy constructively.

> Paul J. Brouwer, *Student Personnel Services in General Education.* Washington: American Council on Education, 1949, pp. 161-62.

225. Needs Denied May Bring Frustration

The structure and dynamic processes of the human organism

imply the need for certain things, for certain conditions and for certain activities of the body if physical and mental health are to be maintained. The structure and processes of society imply certain knowledges, skills, and functional relationships as necessary to the individual if he is to be effective and adjusted. As he grows up, the experiences of life are sure to raise questions in the mind of each individual about his personal role and about the meaning of life; therefore, each one needs to arrive at a satisfactory mental organization or assimilation of his experiences. Thus, the structure of the organism, the processes of society, and the nature of a person's experiences contrive to give rise to a series of needs, of quasi-needs, and of operational concepts which must be met if wholesome personality development is to be achieved.

These needs are the basis of permanent adjustment problems which all of us face. They are more or less continuously with us. Our behavior is patterned in accordance with what experience has shown us to be the most satisfactory means of working them out, but, as conditions around us vary and change, we are continuously under the necessity of modifying our behavior. These needs become sources of unpleasant affect and even of serious personality maladjustments if they are not met adequately. Furthermore, our society is rich in circumstances which deny to individuals the fulfillment of one or several of these needs and quasi-needs for periods of varying length—this is what has happened to the thousands of maladjusted school children. There is a serious disharmony between the needs which they feel to be vital to themselves and the experiences of life as they meet them. . . .

. . . a few sociologists have come to understand that frequently society itself is at fault when human beings misbehave. By denying to individuals the opportunity to satisfy basic human needs, society creates the psychic and emotional maladjustments which underlie some of the most critical problems that society then seeks to remedy by punishment or reeducation. There is evidence here that society should seek consciously to reorganize itself in such a manner as to make available to each individual the opportunity to satisfy his basic personality needs. (L. K. Frank, "Society As the Patient,"

American Journal of Sociology, XLII. November, 1936, pp. 335-44.)

> Daniel A. Prescott, *Emotion and the Educative Process.* Washington: American Council on Education, 1938, pp. 111-12.

226. ASSUMPTIONS REGARDING THE NATURE OF GROWTH AND DEVELOPMENT

A. *Each individual has basic personality needs which he continuously seeks to satisfy.*

1. Basic personality needs arise from the interaction between forces within the individual (as a psychobiological organism) and forces without the individual in his physical and social environment.
2. Needs may be classified into three categories:
   (a) Physiological needs
   (b) Social needs
   (c) Ego or integrative needs.
3. While each individual has the same type of need—e.g., the physiological need for food, the social need for "belonging"— each individual manifests a unique "pattern of reactivity" as he seeks to satisfy his needs. The pattern of reactivity, giving the individual his peculiar personality, results from the interaction between inner and outer forces.
4. The frustration of the individual's efforts to satisfy his basic needs is the source of maladjustment.
   (a) The desire to satisfy needs is a force, a drive, an immutable urge which compels the individual to seek satisfaction.
   (b) When a need is frustrated—e.g., the social need for being valued by others is frustrated by the individual's being rejected because of his family, color, creed, ugliness, or whatever—the energy, the force, which drives toward the satisfaction is then spent in some other way— by his rejecting others in turn, hating, etc., or by his sublimating this energy into such socially approved channels as pro-Negro agitation, art, or other means for "winning" valuation by others.
   (c) Needs when frustrated too much or for too long lead to physical death—the needs for water, food, etc.—or personality disintegration—the needs for a philosophy of life, a feeling of likeness to others, etc.

5. The appropriate satisfaction of basic needs promotes health, mental and physical, and the growth of the personality in effective, happy living.

6. Needs rarely exist singly but seem to function in clusters whose membership varies from situation to situation—e.g., the need for affectional relations and the need for status are related in the behavior of the student who changed her grade report card from F's to B's because her mother "expected" her to do good work even though she was incapable of better than average scholastic achievement.

B. *As the individual grows up in his culture, he must achieve certain developmental or growth tasks.*

1. The developmental or growth task is imposed by the culture —most boys in our culture are expected to learn how to earn a livelihood as adults; both boys and girls are "expected" to come to terms with their sex roles in socially appropriate ways; and so on.

2. The developmental tasks are constructs or arbitrary abstractions to help in understanding the personality as a resultant of inner (psychosomatic) and outer (cultural) forces. They represent points or areas where the forces of society and the drives within the individual meet to contend for control or, so to speak, to find a way of cooperating. When social forces overpower the individual, he loses his identity and his self-esteem; when inner forces dominate the individual, he may be antisocial and punished by society in accord with his age and violation of the social mores.

3. The objective of the individual in the developmental task, therefore, is so to harmonize inner and outer forces in his behavior that he is at once self-respecting and socially approved and successful. Such harmony is achieved through the gradual process of socialization whereby the individual internalizes the requirements imposed on him by society so that they become his requirements of himself—e.g., the infant begins necessarily dependent upon others; later this dependence is centered in emotional terms on the parent (usually the mother); in adolescence and finally as an adult he is expected to lose this emotional dependence gradually and be able to stand on his own feet. During this process, if his growth (i.e., his achievement of the developmental task of securing independence) is normal and healthy, he internalizes (makes his own) the expectations of him as an adult in the

culture and thus finds it comfortable to live up to his own standards of independence.

4. The developmental tasks are areas of personality adjustment which are convenient to an understanding of the individual because:
   (a) The definition by the culture of *what the individual ought to be* is crucial in its significance to the personality, and
   (b) The definition by the individual of *what he wants to be* is crucial to his personality adjustment.
      1. The *culture,* for example, defines independence from parents—it imposes upon the individual the task of becoming emotionally weaned.
      2. The *individual* defines, for example, his philosophy of life—it must represent a scheme of values suitable to *his* way of living.

5. The developmental tasks are—
   (a) Independence from parents
   (b) Social adequacy and emotional security
   (c) Heterosexual adjustment
   (d) Vocational orientation
   (e) Philosophy of life
   (f) Self-acceptance (self-evaluation)—
      1. Body processes
      2. Sex role
      3. Social value of body
   (g) Goals and aspirations
   (h) Sense of humor and insight

6. The developmental tasks are not discrete entities but areas of personality adjustment which often overlap—e.g., the task of achieving independence from parents involves the task of making appropriate heterosexual adjustments (finding relations with the opposite sex outside the home). Both tasks are intimately related to physiological maturity and other factors in physical and mental growth.

Paul J. Brouwer, *Student Personnel Services in General Education.* Washington: American Council on Education, 1949, pp. 310-13.

227. CRUZE: THE MOTIVATION HYPOTHESIS

Motivation: Motives are the causes of behavior, the *why* of activity. The problem of motivation is not limited to the fields of psychology and education. In practically all fields of human endeavor one may find interest in the forces behind human behavior. In industry, personnel men are employed to seek for more effective means of motivating employees. In the field of sports, coaches use every known means of urging their players to put forth their best efforts. In the field of crime detection, the discovery of the motive is one of the first problems to be solved by the officers in charge. Many questions of law and justice must await the establishment of motives before they can be answered. As an example, the only difference between man-slaughter and first degree murder is a difference in the motives responsible for the behavior.

The problem of the motivation of human behavior is very complex. The doctrine of instincts, first emphasized by William James (W. James, "What Is an Instinct?" *Scribner's Magazine*, 1887, Vol. 30, pp. 433-51 and "Some Human Instincts," *Popular Science Monthly*, 1887, Vol. 31, pp. 160-70 and 666-81), has ceased to be useful in present-day psychological discussions of human motivation. The inclusion of the period of infancy and early childhood in the field of psychological research, with the result that the so-called instincts were observed in the process of being learned, was primarily responsible for the breakdown of this doctrine. Since then, a new terminology has come into use in an attempt to describe new concepts and to provide a satisfactory explanation of human behavior. Generally speaking, there seems to be a distinct tendency to do away with the older and more elaborate terminology and to make use of the simpler terms of *drive* and *motive*.

The objective point of view conceives of the human organism as a complex system of physiological functions. This system remains in a state of relative equilibrium until some energy change, either from within or without, tends to disturb the equilibrium and upset its balance. When such a change takes place in an organism, the organism becomes active in an attempt to reestablish the state of relative equilibrium through the modification or elimination of the stimulating energy change. The energy change which stimulates the organism in this way is known as a motive or drive. Such a concept of motivation should prove to be more useful to education than the rather complicated instinct hypothesis.

In early infancy the stimuli which produce physiological tensions are primarily organic and the responses initiated by them are, as a general rule, random mass activity which shows little or no evidence of specific direction. With increasing development, however, these organic drives are extended and modified by the process of learning, and the individual becomes sensitive to stimuli which were unable to upset the balance of the organism in infancy. As this elaboration of the fundamental drives takes place there is also an increase in the specificity of responses. The individual responds with well-directed activity, designed to restore the state of equilibrium, instead of random mass activity.

Since the individual develops in a social environment, it is customary to speak of these more elaborate drives as social drives, as contrasted with the simpler organic drives which operate in infancy. These social drives, as a general rule, are of much greater importance in formal education than are the simpler organic drives which must be satisfied if the organism is to continue to live.

> Wendel W. Cruze, *Educational Psychology*. New York: The Ronald Press Company, 1942, pp. 269-70.

228. WANTS AND PURPOSES PERSIST AND CONTROL

The Power of Motives: In beginning your study of motives, look about you at the men and women in your community. Look at history also. Our forefathers cleared the American continent with ax and plow, hammer and saw, using their own muscles in grueling, unending labor. History had never seen such conquest of the land. What drove them on?

What was the power that made such labor, such courage, and such persistence possible? What drove the Jim Fiskes and Jim Hills, the Commodore Vanderbilts, the Carnegies, Fricks, Rockefellers, Armours, and Morgans to corner the land and the railroads, the iron, coal, and oil, the meat and the banks of our country? It must have been some very strong motive power!

It is said that Thomas Edison, the wizard who invented

many of our electrical devices, slept only four hours a day, spent seventy years of eager excitement in his laboratory. What motive power! Charles Peirce, thought by many to be America's greatest philosopher, chose to spend many years of his life isolated in a tiny garret in his Pennsylvania house, writing, writing, and rewriting one of the greatest treatises in the history of thought. Why? What drove him on and on, even though not one page of what he wrote was published in his lifetime for others to see?

On every Main Street in America life histories are being written of heroic sacrifice and unremitting toil as well as dreadful exploitation and debauchery. What causes men to do the things they do, say the things they say, or keep from doing some things others think they should do? How do motives become so powerful?

The Genesis of Motives and Purposes: One idea stands out whenever one looks into the doings of men: *motive power*, or simply *motive*. These men whose deeds, good or bad, got them into history, all *wanted something* intensely. They were *moved* by desires. They had purposes. The Robber Barons?— money and power and luxury. The inventor?—the satisfaction of giving mankind a better way of life, as well as money and prestige for himself and family, and the sheer joy of study and work. The philosospher and the scientists and artists in all mediums?—the glorious excitement of creative discovery and achievement. The gangster in plain murder or theft, or in disguised form in politics, business, or labor?—money, luxury, power, conspicuous notoriety or publicity, the sheer excitement of action and the competition of combat. The sacrificing mother?—the joy in her home and the fine development of her children. The moment-by-moment behavior of each was propelled by *what he wanted most*. As the years passed, these specific desires were transformed into deep-lying *purposes*.

So it is in the kaleidoscopic shifting of the events of our daily lives. In a flash-like process each face-to-face situation is sized up, either by child or adult, the words spoken, in a frame of frowns, smiles, or other angry or friendly gestures, bringing about a response from the other person. Behavior generates behavior. Immediate *wants, desires,* expressing the drive of a more remote and cumulating purpose, are the motive power of both appraisal and action. *What men want most determines, in the long run, what they feel and think and do.*

> Lawrence E. Cole and William F. Bruce, *Educational Psychology.* New York: World Book Company, 1950, pp. 231-32.

229. ANDERSON'S CONCLUSION ON MOTIVATION

In human beings, energy is increasingly directed toward goals and objects in the environment and becomes more and more patterned. The term *motivation* covers the forces which impel, lead, or force the activity of persons into one direction rather than another. Activity itself is a basic and fundamental characteristic of the human being as an energy system. Within the larger energy system arc sub-centers of energy which may block one another, or may work together, and which are called *tension systems.*

A tension system involves (1) some impulsion or need within the organism, (2) an object or goal outside toward which energy is directed, and (3) some process of reduction of tension, or satiation, when the goal or object is attained. To describe goals and objects in this reciprocal relation involves the concept of *valence,* which refers to the mutual attractiveness between a need and an object or goal. The organism is within a *field of forces* which is enclosed by a boundary and which may contain both a number of objects with valences and a number of barriers which temporarily block access to them. What the person does depends upon interaction within and with the field of forces. Because he is surrounded by different objects and goals with different valences, *conflict* arises. Out of conflict comes the necessity of choice between alternative lines of action. A characteristic of the person's reactions in a conflict situation is an *oscillation,* or a shifting back and forth from one alternative to another, prior to the decision or action which terminates the disturbance between the tension systems.

While this description is largely in terms of a momentary conflict, actually (because of the progressive organization of behavior) many problems of motivation concern action over a long period of time. A human develops interests and goals which can be described as orderly displays of energy. Self-control and self-management depend on effective organization of energy and the capacity to work for remote goals. The motivated person is persistent, and the strength of his persistence or motivation can be measured by the obstructions he overcomes, by his resistance to distraction, and by his return to primary activities after interruptions.

Any discussion of motivation must consider the relation of the person to others. Many persons are concerned in some way or other either with managing other persons or with being managed by them. Traditional views stress discipline, fear, and punishment. But modern research has made it more and more clear that indirect methods, which use praise and positive modes of stimulation, are as effective or even more effective than direct negative methods, which tend to tear down the personality. Some methods of handling specific situations result in more compliance and more response on the part of others than do other methods; in general, these involve positive, unhurried, encouraging, and specific types of direction.

The human being lives not only by suggestions, commands and directions; he also lives in a world of atmosphere and contexts, in which he reacts to the total stream of stimulation about him. As attention goes to atmosphere and context, new phases of adjustment come into clear relief. There is a place not only for specific incentives but also for the improvement and modification of the framework within which behavior occurs.

> John E. Anderson, *The Psychology of Development and Personal Adjustment.* New York: Henry Holt and Company, Inc., 1949, pp. 256-57. By permission of the publishers.

230. SHAFFER DISCUSSES THE FREUDIAN CONCEPT OF MOTIVATION

A neat way of dispatching the problem of motive, formerly much utilized, was to ascribe a motivating power to instincts. The boy is described as fighting and bullying because of an "instinct of pugnacity." The man works because of an "instinct of workmanship"; we congregate because of an "instinct of gregariousness." A previous examination of this doctrine has already concluded that instinct is not a helpful or explanatory concept in relation to original nature. It is of no more value in connection with motive. . . .

The psychoanalytic school of psychology has always stressed the importance and universality of motive and has made an important contribution by doing so. The various psycho-analytic theories, however, ascribe all motivation to the operation of a single instinct or to a pair of instincts of an antagonistic nature. These theories are sometimes helpful in describing human nature and in the solution of practical problems, but they are subject to criticism as being too vague in some cases and too limited in others. They are derived from a mentalist rather than from an objective approach and are open to all of the objections to instinct theories in general. The most influential of the monistic instinct theories is that of Jung, who describes the "libido" as a single all-important life urge, supplying the energy for all activities. . . .

Among the dualistic doctrines of instinct the most important is that of Freud. It is difficult to state, since he has changed his theory several times, although change itself is not to be criticized, being the essence of scientific growth. Freud's chief instinct, which he has not varied, is a concept of libido which, unlike Jung, he defines more specifically as the sexual instinct, the term sexual being used in a broad sense. At an earlier period Freud contrasted the "ego-instincts" or tendency to self-preservation, with libido. This is simply a restatement of the ancient dichotomy of self-preservation and race-preservation. . . . More recently Freud has decided that the energy of the ego-tendencies is essentially the same as that of libido, hence the two are grouped together as "Eros" or the life instinct which he now places against a balancing "death or destructive instinct." The originator of psychoanalysis has also achieved another opposed pair, the "pleasure principle" and the "reality principle" which act according to the psychological definition of motive in initiating and directing activity. Other writers have proposed further pairs of antagonistic instincts. Adler stresses the ego-instinct or urge to individual superiority, counteracting it with a weaker social instinct.

Trotter, in a view almost opposite, emphasizes the herd instrinct (of conformity) opposed to a weaker self-assertive tendency.

It is true that sex, self-assertion and conformity are important human motives, but no one or two of them can be sufficient to explain all behavior, nor is any of them ultimate and unanalyzable. These are complicated motives, not primitive but in large part due to the learning processes of the individual. The dualistic conceptions of motive are of doubtful value because of their over-simplification and because they easily lead to animistic thinking. While psychoanalysts claim that they do not conceive of libido as an inner *daemon*, they speak of it as "moving," and "attaching itself" to various situations as only a separate living thing could, or at times of its "flowing," being "dammed up" and possessing more or less "adhesivencss" as if it were a physical fluid. Not by such romantic hypotheses, but by the objective observation of the physiological processes of the animal, is the problem of motivation to be settled.

Laurence Frederic Shaffer, *The Psychology of Adjustment*. Boston: Houghton Mifflin Company, 1936, pp. 84-86.

231. CONFLICTING VIEWS OF PERSONALITY DYNAMICS

We come now to a concluding statement of the consequences of the existence of fundamental needs in man. But first we shall endeavor to summarize the conflicting views touching on contrasted conceptions of the foundations of personality dynamics. While no competent student would claim for a moment that our knowledge along this line is anywhere near complete, a number of groups seem to feel that they do not fall far short of holding the key to an explanation of behavior motivation. Thus one rather heterogeneous school of thought holds that we behave as we do because of the presence of irreducible inner mechanisms. They are inclined to attribute attitudes, abilities, character, and conduct, and even personality qualities, to the workings of these innate forces variously called instincts, urges, complexes, will power, and, more recently, motives, drives, tissue needs, visceral tensions, and the like. This group includes the resourceful psychoanalysts with all their impressive sounding explanations (mechanisms), as well as an appreciable percentage of psychiatrists and psychologists, objective and otherwise. It numbers among its followers chemically "minded" endocrinologists and biologically trained maturationists. All look for the foundations of personality *within* the human organism.

A second group feels that an individual's habit, conduct, dispositions, views on life, and character qualities are often all the inevitable results of responses to environmental patterns. This is the view of many sociologists and certainly of environmentalistic psychologists, such as the behaviorists, for example. These groups recognize the presence of fundamental organic mechanisms, but hold that the social environment is the superior influence in shaping character and personality. They make much of studies focusing on the influences of the home, the school, the church, the gang, the movies, and community factors in general.

A slight variation on this group is the one which looks for an explanation of human behavior with all its indoctrinated beliefs, manners, customs, codes, and rituals, to the cultural mores of different societies. Students of society contend that, owing to the rigidity and authoritative nature of most systems of group mores, individual personalities are essentially products of their requirements. (L. P. Thorpe, "The Influence of Mores in Education," *Educational Administration and Supervision,* 1936, 22: 289-98.) Furthermore, it has been shown that a typical child's general character pattern adapts itself to the requirements of each social group of which he becomes a member even temporarily. (H. Hartshorne, *Character in Human Relations.* New York: Charles Scribner's Sons, 1932, pp. 213-14.) From this the inference is drawn that group mores are stronger behavior determiners than are any known inner drives. May (M. A. May, "The Foundations of Personality," *Psychology at Work,* New York: McGraw-Hill Book Company, Inc., 1932, pp. 92-101), who has discussed these conflicting views most adequately, suggests that, since none of them can possibly be regarded as possessing final knowledge concerning the psychological foundations of personality, we might well pool the contributions of each in an effort to construct a more adequate picture of the dynamics problem. Believing as he does that "The problem of human behavior is not only one of mutual adjustments between the organism and its social environment, *but also between the inner mechanisms of the organism and social traditions,*" May advocates a broad conception of personality foundations which includes both the contributions of biological scientists with their inner-mechanism explanations of such organic processes as eating, sleeping, mating, fighting, and the like, and the findings of environmentalists interested in disclosing the modifying effects of social endorsements and cultural traditions. We should like to join with May in this comprehensive approach.

Louis P. Thorpe, *Psychological Foundations of Personality.* New York: McGraw-Hill Book Company, 1938, pp. 222-24.

B. *The Various Motives*

232. WHAT PEOPLE IN OUR CULTURE WANT

The adolescent-youth group wants what all people in our culture want: (1) recognition and status, (2) respect and social favor, (3) response and happy social interaction, (4) security and group acceptance, (5) experience and expression, (6) achievement and success, (7) happiness and freedom. They are not abnormal creatures caught in the emerging tumult of physiological development, but rapidly maturing social creatures quickened by their awareness of the demands of group life in which they are becoming full participants. They want what all people want. The problem of the school and the home and, in fact, of all social groups is to create situations in which these basic wants of adolescents and young people find satisfaction, or else to remove them from the sphere of adult values.

All civilizations are dominated by certain major patterns. These group-wide values become powerful motivating forces of individuals developing in them. Culture may shape personality in the direction of contemplation and withdrawal from an active attack upon social problems. Much of Oriental philosophy historically has been of this character. In our own culture some of the major compulsives which explain the direction personality formation and individual wants take are (1) the competition-success pattern; (2) the desire for bigness, strength, growth, greatness; (3) individual freedom and personal expression; (4) the notion of progress, reform, improvement, and change; (5) epicureanism, the desire of pleasure, sensuous enjoyment.

There are others no doubt, but these seem to be at the forefront in the value scheme of our urban-industrial civilization. . . . We are not assuming that these values are peculiar to adolescence or to youth. They are peculiar to our civilization and affect all age groups. They are of unique significance at the period of adolescence and youth because in his struggle to attain maturity, he must strive toward their realization.

Paul H. Landis, *Adolescence and Youth*. New York: McGraw-Hill Book Company, Inc., 1947, pp. 89-90.

233. THOMAS'S FOUR WISHES

Consider now the more complex forms of social motivation. W. I. Thomas developed a classification of motives which has been of considerable use to sociologists and anthropologists. *We recognize full well that this classification is not a complete explanation of every problem of motivation, and that it is by no means universally accepted—no such classification is—but it will prove useful for our analysis of social psychology.*

According to Thomas, there are four wishes or desires which are so fundamental that they probably include all the others— the desire (1) for new experience, (2) for security, (3) for response, and (4) for recognition. (W. I. Thomas, *The Unadjusted Girl*. Boston: Little, Brown & Company, 1923.)

1. The desire for *new experience* expresses itself in courage, advance, attack, and pursuit. It implies, therefore, motion, change, danger, or instability. It satisfies the love of adventure, which is present in such activities as gambling. It also satisfies such curiosity as occurs when we are creating or building something or solving a problem.

2. The desire for *security* is opposed to the desire for new experience. It expresses itself in timidity, avoidance, and flight. The desire for security makes a person cautious, con-

servative, and apprehensive, tending to regular habits, systematic work, and the accumulation of property.

3. The desire for *response* causes people to seek intimate contacts with other people. It is the most social of the four wishes, and contains both a sexual and a gregarious (crowd) element.

4. The desire for *recognition* is expressed in the general struggle of men for position in their social group. It makes people desire a recognized and advantageous social status. The desire for recognition includes such feelings as "vanity" and "ambition."

> Steuart H. Britt, *Social Psychology of Modern Life* (Revised). New York: Rinehart and Company, Inc., 1949, pp. 106-7.

234. The Main Springs of Action: Shaffer

The study of complex motives, sentiments and purposes has taken us far from the elementary biological drives that impel the organism to activity. A restatement of these fundamentals is desirable to prevent our being lost in a maze of verbal fancies. Primarily, the sources of activity are stimuli, especially those internal stimuli that take the form of visceral tensions. Drives such as those of hunger and sex, which are very directly visceral, are among the strongest of animal motives. Those visceral tensions that are native responses to overstimulation are emotion tensions. From these sources, and from primary adience, spring the strong universal motives such as mastery, social approval and conformity. These motives are drives that have been modified through learning by the extension of the range of stimuli that will arouse them and by the refinement of the activity resulting. Under normal conditions of life, physiological needs having been satisfied, the conditioned emotional motives, with adience and sex, are probably the most important sources of human activity. The complexity of human motivation, however, should not be ignored by the acceptance of any simplified scheme of a few motives. Habits, sentiments and purposes, all forms of learned behavior, also function as springs of human action, but they do so only through the operation of the "lower" fundamental drives of physiological and emotional tensions.

Laurence Frederic Shaffer, *The Psychology of Adjustment.* Boston: Houghton Mifflin Company, 1936, p. 111.

235. MAN'S SOCIAL NEEDS

Behavior does not occur in the absence of what have been variously called drives, impulses, urges, motives, cravings, desires, wishes, and needs. (For convenience we shall make no attempt to distinguish between these terms but shall refer in most instances to such impelling or directing aspects of behavior simply as needs.) . . .

Authorities do not completely agree as to which are the basic needs, that is, those which must be met by the environment in order for the individual to be happy and efficient. Concerning the importance of certain organic needs—for air, food, liquid, proper temperature, rest, sleep, and elimination—there is little difference of opinion; nor is the physiological basis of the activity drive and the sex drive denied. There is less agreement concerning the so-called personality needs. Of these, perhaps the most important are:

The need for affection—to live in a relationship of reciprocated warm regard with one or more individuals.

The need for belonging—to feel that one is an accepted, valued member of a group.

The need for independence—to be able to make one's own decisions and carry out one's own purposes.

The need for social approval—to feel that one's personality and one's actions are respected and admired by others.

The need for maintaining self-esteem—to feel that one's conduct comes up to certain inner standards and thus merits one's own respect. (Any listing of basic needs is to some extent arbitrary. Other formulations may be found in D. A. Prescott, *Emotion and the Educative Process,* 1938; G. B. Watson and R. B. Spence, *Educational Problems for Psychological Study,* 1930; and K. Young, *Personality and Problems of Adjustment,* 1940.)

Arthur I. Gates, Arthur T. Jersild, T. R. McConnell, and Robert C. Challman, *Educational Psychology.* New York: The Macmillan Company, 1942, pp. 628-29.

236. Mathewson Lists the Motives

At the foundation of all individual need are those basic requirements having to do with physical survival and growth: food, clothing, shelter, security, health, affection, freedom of action, sensation, activity, favorable environment for growth.

Beyond these fundamental needs may be recognized certain human desires and urges commonly motivating individuals in our society, some of which may be thought of as primarily "personal" in their orientation and others as primarily "social."

Common motivating urges having a strong personal accent are: the desires for physical well-being; movement and activity; ego preservation and satisfaction; sex relations; fun and recreation; release, escape, rest; adventure and new experience. Among other common motivating tendencies, more strongly related to social considerations (although no sharp demarcation can really be made between those designated as personal and those thought of as social), may be included such motivations as: recognition; power; prestige; order; social cooperation.

Both the personal and the social streams of motivation converge when we think of drives and strivings of the personality toward harmonious life adjustment in all areas of living, for personal growth toward an ideal, for a feeling of adequacy to circumstances, and for the attainment of general capability in relation to social demands.

Murray's well-known list of more than two dozen fundamental psychological needs includes such items as: aggression, affiliation, achievement, recognition, construction, order, passivity, sex, autonomy, seclusion.

Motivations like these seem to be basic and common and to be manifested in all life situations and conditions, in one form or another or in one combination or another. Needs of this kind must be considered by the educator and the personnel worker as providing the fundamental individual motivations to be taken into account in all problems.

Robert Hendry Mathewson, *Guidance Policy and Practice.* New York: Harper and Brothers, 1949, pp. 40-41.

237. Our Deepest Personality Needs

In order to understand how we get to be what we are, not only must we be able to interpret various styles of behavior, but we must also discover what each person wants most out of life and to what degree he is able to gain what he most desires. Each of us must be able to satisfy all three of our deepest personality needs. We must all have some security, some love, and some success. These needs exercise an enormous influence upon our behavior, upon the values that we accept, even upon the life purposes that we develop. They affect our attitudes toward ourselves, toward others, and toward the world in general.

Security is not something that we can set out to achieve. An infant could not be said consciously to desire security; yet without adequate care and protection, its welfare, certainly, and even its life might be endangered. Security, however, transcends physical safety. A person must have adequate food, shelter, and clothing to keep alive, but he also needs the confidence that he is a person who will be equal to life's demands, one who can manage his emotional adjustments and social relationships in a mature manner, who will be equal to taking in his stride, without being too seriously retarded, the normal number of frustrations that come to all of us.

Emotional starvation is just as real as physical starvation. In order to grow emotionally, an individual must feel that he is a worth-while person, that he is needed somewhere by someone, that there is a place for him in his family group, in his social group, in a vocation, and in the world. He must have, permeating all that he is and does, the certainity that he can confidently look himself and other people in the face. Then he knows security. Superficial observers describe it as self-confidence or self-respect. An individual with security might describe it as the background against which his life is lived.

Such security an individual first gains, or fails to gain, from his family group. He can be said to have security in his home if he feels accepted there, if he knows that due consideration is given to his welfare and to his desires, if he can talk over with his parents his actions, his interests, his hopes, and his points of view. Even though his parents may disapprove of his actions and disagree with his opinions, he knows that he will be understood, respected, and loved. Ideally, a person should be able to count on similar treatment from his school, his social group, and later from his employers.

Closely related to the need for security is the need for achievement, or for success. Individuals feel useless, develop a sense of not being needed, unless they have opportunities for achievement. Because no one can survive too much failure or defeat, every person must sometimes have the satisfaction of personal achievement; he must know the feeling of usefulness that is gained from the knowledge that there is something which he does well and for which he is appreciated. However, success must not come too easily. If genuine satisfaction is to be gained by its achievement, failure must be present as a possibility. A satisfactory life seems to be compounded of both success and failure, with the success requiring real efforts for its attainment and the failure not so frequent an experience as to cause despair.

Finally, there is the need for love, which is to be interpreted in its broadest sense as applying to the general tone of the environment in which a person lives and works. Everyone wants to feel that someone is interested in and concerned about him, that he matters to someone. This kind of experience can spur any of us to greater achievement. It is never too late for those who have missed it to learn their own worth by having someone believe in and appreciate them. . . .

Each of us is attempting to satisfy these needs in his own way. We are all different in that for each of us the keystone of our action is determined in some manner or style characteristic of us as individuals. For some individuals recognized success is more important than anything else in life; therefore the struggle to be superior, the fear of being second-rate, is the clue to an understanding of their life plan. Of this group, some people may feel that a large amount of success compensates for having less love than other people. When a person's drive for success is much stronger than his drive for security, he may be willing to adventure into new experiences, to take big risks on the chance of achieving success. Such individuals are valuable for social progress.

Persons to whom security is most important may plod along without much drive toward brilliant successes. They may not need or want them. Nor are they particularly interested in new experiences. A seemingly permanent security is more important to them than what seems like a transient success or an uncertain adventure. They desire lives in which they can know a maximum of such security.

In still other individuals, the desire to love and to be loved overshadows all other drives. Security, adventure, and success are less important to them than the knowledge that somewhere and by someone they are wanted, needed, and loved. They have achieved what is of most value to them in life if they can feel that they belong somewhere.

The behavior of each individual can, to some degree, be interpreted in terms of the relative importance of these personality needs in his life. It is comparatively seldom that one need completely dominates an individual's actions; it is because of this fact that certain actions are sometimes hard to explain. However, a great many puzzling behavior manifestations can be interpreted through an individual's attempts to satisfy the needs that are most important to him.

Esther Lloyd-Jones and Ruth Fedder, *Coming of Age.* New York: McGraw-Hill Book Company, Inc., 1941, pp. 23-26.

238. THE EMOTIONAL FOOD MEN LIVE BY

What are the emotional foods that every human being must have regardless of age? What are the basic emotional requirements that must come to every small infant, to every growing child, to every adult?

In the first place, there must be *affection* and a lot of it. Real down-to-earth, sincere loving. The kind that carries conviction through body-warmth, through touch, through the good, mellow ring in the voice, through the fond look that says as clearly as words, "I love you for what you are, beyond any nasty thing you might do. I love you because you are you."

Closely allied with being loved should come the sure knowledge of *belonging*, of *being wanted*, the glow of knowing oneself to be part of some bigger whole. *Our* town, *our* school, *our* work, *our* family—all bring the sound of togetherness, of being united with others, not isolated or alone.

Every human being needs also to have the nourishment of *pleasure that comes through his senses.* Color, balanced form and beauty to meet the eye, harmonious sounds to meet the ear. The hearty enjoyment of touch and taste and smell. And finally, the realization that the pleasurable sensations of sex can be right and fine and a part of the spirit as well as of the body.

Everyone must feel that he is capable of *achievement.* He needs to develop the ultimate conviction, strong within him, that he *can* do things, that he is adequate to meet life's demands. He needs also the satisfaction of knowing that he can gain from others *recognition* for what he does.

And most important, each and every one of us must have *acceptance* and *understanding.* We need desperately to be able to share our thoughts and feelings with some one person, or several, who really understands. We long to shed all hypocrisy and pretense and to lay aside defensiveness and affectation. We yearn for the deep relief of knowing that we can be ourselves with honest freedom, secure in knowledge that says, "This person is *with* me. He *accepts* how I feel!"

Too few of us ever have this kind of understanding. And so certain parts of us must stay on guard, fearful of discovery, hurt in the sense of aloneness, and often resentful that no one can see what we really are.

As an individual's basic needs are satisfied, he can develop a sense of his own SELFHOOD. *I am I; and I am somehow a worthwhile person. I can relate myself to others with something good to give them. Because I am worth while they will want to relate themselves to me.*

In contrast, if basic needs are unsatisfied, SELFISHNESS replaces the sense of one's own sure and good and fruitful identity. *I'm worth so little I can't take for granted that anyone will like me. I'll have to watch out for and defend myself and clutch for straws and grab with gnawing, hungry greed whatever crumbs I can.*

If any of the basic elements of emotional nourishment are missing, a human being suffers. We, who are already grown, know this. When we feel a lack of love, we become hurt and frightened and often resentful. "You're a brute not to love me. I hate you. I'll make you sorry; you just wait and see."

When we feel a lack of being wanted, we turn touchy and apprehensive and often vindictive. "If you won't have me, I won't have you."

When bodily pleasure has been made ugly and wrong so that it fails to bring vivid satisfactions, we may grow to feel unworthy and cringing. We may become afraid of ourselves and of our own impulses as well as of temptation. And, in addition, we may feel irritable and upset.

When we are unable to gain a sense of achievement in life, as when we feel incapable of carrying out tasks that lie before us, we also are bothered. Anyone who has tried a job that's too hard for him knows this only too well. Whenever a person is expected to do things which he is actually not able to do, he feels lost. He feels overpowered and small and helpless. Panicky, perhaps, and embittered. "I'm incapable. So what's the use?"

Similarly, if the recognition we crave is denied us, resentment mounts. A person may say, "I don't care anyway. So-and-so's praise isn't worth having." But, underneath, he still mutters, "I'd like to do something to get even. . . ."

> Dorothy W. Baruch, *New Ways in Discipline*. New York: McGraw-Hill Book Company, 1949, pp. 13-15.

239. KELIHER DISCUSSES NEEDS

Next to the need for physical survival one of the most fundamental needs of man is *human response*. There are many tangents in our needs for comradeship, for friendliness, for understanding, for belonging, for giving. Again their titles and classifications are not of primary concern. The fundamental thing is that there is in every one of us this strong human need to give and to receive response. And though this need may change the channels through which it finds outlet, it remains a lifetime need for all human beings. The infant needs to know it is loved. It learns this through physical contact, tone of voice, and the many minute acts which build into a matrix of parental love. In young childhood, in later childhood, in adolescence, in adulthood, the same need con-

tinues, imperative as ever, but its expression is usually chan-
neled into ways approved by the adult and child group in
which the individual lives. What if this imperative need is
denied? What if a child is born unwanted? What if he is
separated from his family and lives an institutional life, unloved? What if the avenues of expression between parents
and children are blocked? Then the child behaves psychologically in much the same way that he behaves physically
when he is hungry for food. Lacking human response he may
seek substitutes which he will beg or steal. He will respond
deeply, loyally, often pathetically, to the human being who
extends to him warmth, understanding, and love. Much of his
behavior will be directed to getting attention from people.
He may use negative and combative means to get attention—
or he may directly invite positive responses. The underlying
need is the same.

People cannot stand being ignored. The adult, even with
all of the many experiences he has to fill his life, cannot endure
being slighted. Children and young people can stand even
less the absence of response. There are pathetic youngsters
who would rather be beaten than ignored altogether. Or they
may find that they can get attention by being "naughty,"
"rowdy," "rude," or "disobedient" when they have not obtained human response in legitimate and satisfying ways. In
high school these may be the youngsters who play the "show-
off" role, who are violent non-conformists for the attention it
brings. Under it all they are likely to be very lonely, using
their combative behavior to conceal their real need.

There are other youngsters whose many experiences with
human response have been unsatisfying. Perhaps they have
not been ignored, but have met ridicule, belittling, contempt,
or punishment as human response. One high school girl said,
during a troublesome conflict of her group with authorities:
"The way we act is just a covering. We don't dare act the
way we feel. We'd be laughed at." In fear of meeting the
ridicule they had come to know as their portion, this group
had buried its real feeling under a sham of contempt for
authority.

We not only need and crave human response; we want that
response to be sincere. We want it to be a response to *us as*

we are, for what we are, not to us as means to the ends others have in view. How often are students merely vehicles for curriculum content! How often is the response between teacher and student best characterized as that relationship that exists between puppeteer and puppet! The ability of young people to scrutinize the sincerity of the response they get is well illustrated by the statement of a high school girl about student participation in school administration: "It's all very well to go through the show of asking our advice about running the school. But we know when the asking is sincere, and when, on the other hand, nothing will be done about the things we advise."

Many times when a child fails to find sincere and deep outlets for his need for human response he dries the corn cobs and grinds the bitter earth of superficial, shallow, or tawdry relationships. The need is there. It must be met. It will be met. And the child will use what he finds in life, what we provide for him, as his material for meeting this need.

Another set of needs clusters around the universal human desire for *status,* for recognition, for being looked upon by fellow men as a desirable and desired member of the group. If we were trying to be exact, there would be times when it would be hard to separate these status needs from needs for human response. . . . Status in social groups, status in studies, status in athletics, status in dress, status in all of those things our society has made important, as well as status in the affection of others—these are imperatives for emotional health just as are food and drink for the physical health of the human being. . . .

Another group of needs involves what we might call expressions of *power.* Power over things, power over ideas, power over natural forces, power over people. Here we might also group the creative needs, for power over pen, brush, and string may represent this craving of man to be larger than—in a sense the creator of—the things and people about him. Many think that needs for power arise only as needs for response and status are violated. In our culture some feeling of power seems urgent. Here again it is impossible to really pull out these particular needs and separate them from the three groups we have already talked about. No one need is a separate entity, operating separately. Each is dependent on the others. All working harmoniously and in balance produce what we call the "well-adjusted personality." The denial of any or all of them produces the maladjustments and unhappiness which trouble us greatly.

Another need, closely tied with all the others, and often classified as a physical need, is the need for sex expression. It is the order of all life that it produce a generation to replace itself. Most species have no will in this matter. To those of us who enjoy some privilege of choice it is interesting to reflect on the inevitability of the cycle by which life in the insect world, the plant and animal world, is lived for the production of new life. Never left to chance, some instinct wills that the salmon will spawn, that the queen bee will deposit her eggs, that the flower will disappear, leaving the fruit to grow and ripen. In man the imperative is as great. The difference is that he has more power to control his behavior by will and that his intelligence has helped him find controls over natural forces. He has therefore been able to surround his process of reproduction with feeling. At the same time he has built customs and taboos around sex expression and in many parts of the world he has been forced to learn to wait for the expression of sex until such time and in such channels as his society dictates. But no dictate, however strong, can obliterate this need. The need for sex has not been left to chance. It is firmly and deeply imbedded in every human being. Like the hunger need, like the response need, like any of the other urgent needs, the sex need must find expression. Civilized man has learned to channel the expression, has been forced to learn to make many substitutes, has found ways partially to sublimate it through other activities. But the same thing that happens when the need for food is denied occurs when this need is driven back and permitted no outlet. Some are almost impelled by circumstances to steal their experience, to take it by force, or again, to find it in the tawdriness of bitter dirt or shallow substitutions.

> Paul A. Witty and Charles E. Skinner, editors, *Mental Hygiene in Modern Education*. New York: Rinehart and Company, Inc., 1939, pp. 242-46. (From chapter by Alice V. Keliher.)

240. The Springs of Human Behavior, Both Normal and Abnormal

The conservation of mental health is largely a problem of providing satisfactory outlets for the individual's basic urges, providing a balanced or harmonious adjustment of the various urges to one another, and adjusting the individual's egocentric drives to the cultural demands of the family and the community.

Why do people behave as they do? The answer involves a consideration of stimuli, drives, goals, and purposes. All behavior is, essentially, motivational or goal-seeking in nature. It is a purposive response to a great variety of internal and external stimuli. Human reaction tendencies and behavior patterns are the joint product of the dynamic interaction of the interrelated cravings and needs of the total organism in specific environmental and cultural situations.

The basic stimuli that incite, sustain, and direct behavior are variously referred to as strivings, desires, tensions, excitements, drives, urges, needs, propensities, dispositions, impulses, instincts, instinctual cravings, and ego satisfactions. Any reaction pattern may be regarded as basic that results from fundamental organic needs or from persistently recurrent stimulations that require organic adjustments. Motives and goals may be regarded as drives of a more complex nature and are the product of processes of learning. Motives are at the basis of beliefs, attitudes, and habits. Strong habits, both intellectual and emotional, result from strong motivations. Attitudes and habits, in turn, become motives to action.

The individual's springs to action may operate consciously or unconsciously; they may be native or acquired; they may be, in whole or in part, physiological, psychological, or social; but they never operate as isolated entities. Rather, they operate as dynamic, interdependent factors or constitutents of the total personality in a total environmental situation. The strength of the different cravings and motivations is determined by the needs of the organism as a whole—in the light of past experiences and in particular environmental settings.

The basic physiological drives, innate in nature, related to states of tension and disequilibrium, include hunger (visceral tension) and thirst, elimination activities, removal of sensory irritants or evading painful stimuli (avoidant reactions), seeking pleasure- or satisfaction-yielding experiences (adient reactions), the drives for self-preservation and for propagation (the sex urge), general random or spontaneous activities (from an excess of kinetic energy), the desire for relaxation, rest, and sleep as means of obtaining relief from fatigue or exhaustion. To these fundamental adjustment needs should be added transient or permanent primary automatic activities—"inherited reflexes," as they are called—such as the movements of the lungs (breathing) and of the heart (circulation), the pupillary reaction to changes in illumination or distance, and various mechanical and nonvoluntary responses to external stimuli, such as the eyewink, the knee jerk, coughing, and sneezing.

The concept of human instinctive activities, in the sense of unlearned or inherited complex, coordinated responses to external stimuli, has been largely abandoned by the psychologists of the present generation. The word "instinct" has been replaced by the words "drive," "urge," and "propensity"; but most of the reaction patterns designated by these terms are the result of conditioning and habit formation rather than of inheritance.

The psychological and social drives to action—for our purpose, it is unnecessary to distinguish sharply between the two—include a great variety of goal-seeking activities, such as the desire for affectional, social, physical, and economic security; the need for recognition, prestige, and social status (a condition denominated by yet other terms, such as "ego satisfaction" and "mastery motive"), with the attendant drives toward successful achievement, self-realization, self-assertiveness, and dominance; the desire for acceptance by the group, with the attendant tendencies toward adaptation, conformity, and submissiveness; the urge for acquiring new experiences or adventures; the passion for accumulating possessions; the drive to rid oneself of the feelings of frustration, conflict, and inadequacy by developing counterbalancing superiorities, or by adopting, consciously or unconsciously, various kinds of escape or defense mechanisms, or by rationalizing behavior responses on fictitious levels of aspiration or in terms of spurious goals.

The satisfactory adjustment and resolution of the individual's basic psychosomatic needs and urges are prime conditions for the attainment and preservation of mental integration and soundness. The failure to achieve inner harmony among the individual's ambivalent (incompatible, antagonistic) tendencies, and to reconcile them with the folkways and mores of society, will tend to produce personality modifications or distortions of varying kinds and degrees, depending upon the nature and severity of the intellectual and especially of the emotional conflicts involved and the degree of success of the individual's pattern of response to the conflicts. For better or for worse, man lives in a ready-made society. His ego satisfactions must be realized in a social order of exacting laws, codes, and conventions that impose rigid controls and restrictions upon his liberty of action in the interest of the common good. The demands for conformity mean inhibition, suppression, repression, or sublimation (elevation, refinement) of egocentric trends. Some of the social barriers to rampant individualism are inescapable and insurmountable and will produce unadjusted behavior if the individual is unable to readjust his needs in conformity with recognized social goals. It is the conflicts with implacable cultural demands that constitute the real source of the more severe emotional conflicts and maladjustive response patterns. . . .

J. E. Wallace Wallin, *Personality Maladjustments and Mental Hygiene.* New York: McGraw-Hill Book Company, Inc., 1949, pp. 30-32. By permission of the publishers.

241. Needs and Drives Central in Life

Man seems always to have been concerned with drives and motives. In our language, a surprising number of words refer to action and need. Some (such as will, drive, motive, force, and emotion) relate to the display of energy, and some (such as needs, wants, desires, and wishes) relate to what the organism seeks from its environment.

From birth onward, human beings show tendencies to some types of action rather than others. Thus, the hungry infant cries, and, if held on his mother's lap, makes seeking movements. An older child when hungry goes to the pantry or

cookie jar, which at other times is neglected. From the standpoint of the individual concerned, these tendencies are *needs*—
the child feels hungry and values food highly. From the observer's standpoint, these tendencies are *drives*—the child seeks
food and goes to the cookie jar rather than to the radio, or
in more general terms, his behavior goes in one direction rather
than another. In some situations the behavior in response to
a need is very specific and precise; in other situations it is
somewhat erratic and aimless, even though it may termi-
nate at a specific object or goal.

A hungry person sometimes goes to a cookie jar, sometimes
to a hamburger stand, and sometimes to a dining room or
restaurant for a meal. If a cookie jar is in the room, he may
go to it; if there is none, he may cross the street for a soda.
The action that occurs when a need is felt depends partly
upon the nature of the need itself, and partly upon the facilities available in the environment. There is, then, always a
double relation between the *need*, which sets the framework
within which behavior will occur, and the *environment*, which
determines the manner in which it can be met.

The many needs and drives of the human being may be
grouped into a few main categories. One group, concerned
primarily with the *maintenance of life itself*, are called *appetites*. Included in these are hunger, thirst, elimination, and
the fatigue which leads to rest and sleep. Because of their
close relation to survival, on occasion they will take precedence
over all other demands.

A second group of needs and drives concern the *reproduction of the race*. While these drives are latent in the newborn
infant, they do not appear in full force until late adolescence
and early maturity. Included in this group are the attachments
for the opposite sex that result in mating and the maternal
and paternal impulses that lead to the care of the offspring.

A third group of needs and drives center about *association
with other persons*. Some animals are essentially solitary, like
those of the cat family, while others are gregarious or social,
like the dogs or apes. Human beings are social in their nature.
For young children, isolation or separation from the group is
a powerful punishment, and for criminals, solitary confinement
ranks next to death itself. The needs and drives in this group

cannot be as sharply separated from one another as can the appetites.

A fourth group of needs and drives center about *curiosity and manipulation*. The very young infant is curious about his environment and seeks to manipulate the objects it contains. When old enough to walk, he is "in everything" about the house and is constantly playing with whatever is available. In later life these needs and drives are reflected in our quest for knowledge, our scientific inquiry, and our invention.

From the outset of life, then, man is a kind of creature that is interested in his own preservation, is concerned with the reproduction of his race, is social and gregarious, and is curious about his environment and manipulative of the objects it contains.

But motivation or directed behavior is not entirely a matter of a need and an object or goal that will satisfy the need. It also involves other persons who interpose various blocks or who exercise various degrees of supervision or control. In history, control over others was first exercised almost entirely through the direct application of force. Fear and punishment were used as primary devices for motivation. Slowly and over a long time, man has learned that other types of motivation are effective. The human race has developed various types of indirect control in which men are led or guided, not forced.

A life of terror under harsh external controls is not conducive to the best development of man. As man groped his way along, he gradually discovered that if the individual had some degree of security and some confidence in his environment, his productivity and happiness increased. A concept of *self-directed activity* emerges which leads man to create and to make great contributions to human welfare. Thus, the problem of outer control moves over into the area of self-control.

John E. Anderson, *The Psychology of Development and Personal Adjustment.* New York: Henry Holt and Company, Inc., 1949, pp. 232-34. By permission of the publishers.

242. Basic Personality Needs and Developmental Tasks

All human beings in our culture appear to have certain basic needs, the satisfaction of which is necessary for normal and happy development. Some of these needs are physical; others are mental and spiritual. . . .

One basic human need is the need to be accepted as a unique individual, different from every other person in the world, yet sharing with others a common human nature. This is a need which is often misunderstood and one which is frequently thwarted by parents and teachers. A common misunderstanding of this need is to suppose that such acceptance means condoning misbehavior or encouraging the student in his eccentricities or in his unsocial conduct. This is a wholly erroneous notion. To accept each person as a unique individual means simply that we allow him to grow at his own rate and to develop his natural talents and abilities according to his idiomatic pattern. It means that we refrain from setting up an image of what we would like him to be and from bending our efforts to make him conform. It means, rather, that we assist him to understand himself, his possibilities and his limitations, and in the light of such understanding help him to select, of his own volition, appropriate goals and the means which are adequate for attaining them. Necessarily the student will need instruction as a basis for understanding himself and for coming into contact with authentic values, but in the last analysis the choices to be made must be made by the student himself. Parents who have preconceived ideas that their son should be a doctor, or a Phi Beta Kappa, or a social leader in college, and who exert moral pressure on him to conform to their image of him, may place serious obstacles in the way of his developing his potentialities and may precipitate a situation in which the student cannot develop a sense of personal worth. Teachers, too, may deprive a student of this necessary sense of personal worth by failing to recognize his dignity as a person and by making their acceptance of him depend upon his academic achievement alone.

A sense of personal worth and significance is a *conditio sine qua non* of successful adjustment. Its presence or absence in a particular student may be the result of many other factors besides those mentioned above. One of the most important of these factors is the feeling of belonging. Unless a person can feel that he is a valued member of the groups in which he participates, he will feel insignificant and will take refuge in defense mechanisms and compensations. The reasons why some students are rejected by their fellows are not always apparent to the faculty observer, and teachers who see students only in the classroom may be naively unaware that such a condition exists. Yet rejection by the group may be the clue to such varied behavior as chronic complaining, attention-getting behavior, habitual tardiness or absence, "A" chasing, withdrawal and daydreaming, scholastic failure, violations of regulations and rules, and other kinds of delinquency and unsocial conduct. The way in which a student will react to this treatment will vary according to his temperament and background. Hence, no one behavior pattern can be considered symptomatic.

Another need, the importance of which can scarcely be over-estimated, is that of receiving and giving affection. This is a need which is common to people of all ages, but is particularly insistent at those periods of life when difficult decisions and adjustments must be made. The bitterness of defeat and the anguish of failure become more bearable when they are shared with someone who loves and accepts one. Likewise, success and achievement become worth striving for if their attainment can be joyously shared with another person. In infancy and childhood, and even up until late adolescence, this need should be met by the parents at least, although the teacher too, ideally, should by her friendliness and acceptance of the child provide an emotional undercurrent of security on the basis of which her classroom instruction can be assimilated. There is considerable evidence that if this need is not met in early childhood, particularly by the mother, there may remain with the individual throughout the entire life-cycle a subtle unhappiness in human relations occasioned by a sense of insecurity. It is also evident that the way in which a person meets a new and challenging situation, such as being away from home for the first time, having to meet new people, adjusting to the social stratification usually present on the college campus, or receiving lower grades than he has received before, is influenced to a considerable degree by his earlier experiences of security and insecurity as well as by his present opportunity of receiving and giving affection.

Another need related to the acquisition of a sense of personal worth is the need for a feeling of adequacy on the basis of satisfactory accomplishment. If this need is met very successfully, it may result in overcoming or preventing the personality defects which result from insecurity, but it can never serve as a completely satisfying compensation. There are eminently successful students on every college campus who outwardly appear happy and extroverted, but who are inwardly seething with emotional problems and are obsessed with anxiety and insecurity. Some of these people even become leaders, but their lives are unbalanced and lack significant purpose, and they characteristically sacrifice every other value in life to the acquisition of personal prestige and success.

Students also have a need to maintain in their lives a balance between rest and activity. Consequently, overstimulation as well as understimulation may be mentally unhealthy. Students differ just as much in energy output as in other physiologically conditioned traits and the same expenditure of time and effort should not be expected of everyone. Two students of equal intelligence and ability, both of whom are in perfect health, may both work up to their capacity and yet achieve quite different results. These differences do not indicate, necessarily, that one student is lazy and the other conscientious or that one lacks well-defined goals while the other possesses them. They may simply indicate that the two students differ physiologically in metabolic rate, and, while differing in achievement, they may both be working up to capacity.

Counselors might well cultivate a sensitivity to indexes of energy output, since extreme deviations from the average indicate frequently a condition of serious maladjustment. Some students are continually borrowing on tomorrow's energy and are in a constant state of anxiety and tension, yet do not accomplish a great deal. Their lives are filled with unrelated activities, all of which seem to them equally important, and as a result they are constantly at war with time. Yet in spite of an enormous expenditure of energy the student may still feel frustrated and blocked. He may even succumb to a "nervous breakdown," the explanation of which is not as simple as that of "overwork." It is caused not merely by overwork, but by overwork which does not result in anything significant. It results, as a rule, from a feeling of futility, which in turn has been due to a lack of clearly defined or realistic goals. Such a neurosis might conceivably have been prevented by skillful counseling in which the student is given an opportunity to consolidate his varied activities and experiences into a significant and orderly whole, and in which the student constructs for himself a definite hierarchy of values. It is essential to the development of an integrated personality that there be but one central goal at any one time, yet many college students are unable to acquire this singleness of purpose, partly because of social factors existing on the campus, partly because of a disintegrated curriculum, and partly because of their own personal limitations.

In our culture there are, at every age level, certain "developmental tasks" which apparently must be solved satisfactorily before the individual can successfully attain to the next stage of maturity. For example, the preschool child has the developmental task of establishing a secure and wholesome relationship with its mother, and if this relationship is not established at the appropriate time in the life of the child, he will have greater difficulties than other people in forming warm and congenial relations with persons outside of his home, a condition which may persist throughout the entire life-cycle. Likewise, the preschool child must accept his sex, and parents who either openly or subtly give their child the impression that they would be more pleased if he were of the opposite sex, may make it difficult, if not impossible, for him to meet this task. The great tragedy of this failure may not become apparent until the age of adolescence when it reveals itself in a repudiation of the masculine or feminine role with a resultant maladjustment in nearly all areas of life.

Similarly, there are developmental tasks which must be solved during the primary school years, as, for example, learning the rudiments of reading so that this skill can be used as a tool in subsequent learning. The long-run effect of failing to solve this task is to inhibit the child's development in almost

every area of academic achievement. Some academic problems
of the college student can be traced to this source.

Pubescence and adolescence bring in their wake a complicated and challenging array of developmental tasks, the
successful solution of which is powerfully influenced by the
way in which tasks appropriate to earlier age levels have been
solved. In general, the best preparation for a happy adolescence is a happy childhood, and the best preparation for a
happy maturity is a happy adolescence. Notable exceptions to
this rule do occur, but when they occur they are outstandingly
atypical. Many people have failed to solve the developmental
tasks of adolescence by the time they have reached college,
even though they are physiologically mature. Some students,
for example, are still tied psychologically to their mothers'
apron strings; they have not been able to substitute the healthy
independence and self-determination characteristic of maturity for the comforting security of complete dependence characteristic of infancy and childhood. Often such people are
superior students and are well accepted by the college faculty
to whom they are, as a rule, deferential and submissive. It is
evident, in a good many of such instances, that the student is
using his teachers or counselors as parental substitutes and
manifests toward them the same dependence as he does toward his parents. Other students, on the contrary, may still
be psychologically at an early stage of adolescence in which,
characteristically, there is a rejection of adult standards and
of authority, regardless of how legitimate such authority may
be. Unfortunately, the college years are rather late for going
through this stage unscathed, and the student who possesses
this immature pattern is likely to be the bane not only of the
adults whom he rejects, but of his fellow-students as well.
Skillful nondirective counseling is almost always desirable for
students subjected to emotional hazards of this kind.

Some students, too, arrive in college without having learned
to be poised and at ease in their social relations with members
of both their own and of the opposite sex, without having
developed habits of appropriate grooming, and without having accepted emotionally such basic realities as the social
position of their families and the assets and liabilities of their
own appearance and of their abilities and talents. As a result,

their entire first year in college may be predominantly focused on the solution of these tasks, often at the expense of their scholastic achievement. Teachers who are realistic in their attitude toward students are aware of the fact that academic achievement, important as it no doubt is, is not the whole of life. And, consequently, a student who devotes all of his energy to scholastic achievement may (although not inevitably) develop an unfortunate one-sideness of outlook and become seriously unbalanced.

Another developmental task which becomes particularly insistent in late adolescence and early maturity is that of developing a consistent and all-embracing philosophy of life. Not that this philosophy will be fully developed during this period, since, of course, this is a major problem of the entire life-cycle, but at least the first steps must be taken in the proper direction at this period of life. Otherwise, significant achievement of any kind is impossible. Biographical and auto-biographical literature, as well as adolescent diaries and creative works of various kinds, give overwhelming corroboration to our statement of the importance of meeting this developmental task successfully. . . .

The solution of this problem becomes particularly difficult for students when the several teachers with whom they are studying vary radically in their religious beliefs and philosophies of life, or when the objectives and the philosophy of the college community are opposed to those of their parents and of their home communities. Serious problems in this area frequently call for very skillful nondirective counseling as well as for instruction and advice.

Paul J. Brouwer, *Student Personnel Services in General Education.* Washington: American Council on Education, 1949, pp. 232-39. (From chapter by Sister Annette.)

243. THE CHILD'S NEEDS AS FACTORS IN DEVELOPMENT

Some psychologists regard the "needs" of the child as "appetites"; some as "drives" urging the child toward desired goals; some speak of them as the "well-springs" of behavior, the "urges," the "instincts," the "fountains of life." Whatever simile may be used to describe their exact nature, they are certainly dynamic factors in personality development.

Children are sometimes quite conscious of the existence of their own needs, as when, for instance, they are hungry for food. More often, however, they are not aware of them; the child who is striving to satisfy his needs for self-assertion does not usually realize why he behaves as he does.

Briefly, there are three main types of needs: the *physiological*, the *social*, and the *self* (ego) needs. (These basic needs have been clearly outlined by Prescott in *Emotion and the Educative Process*, American Council on Education, Washington, D. C., 1938.) The *physiological* (or somatic) needs are fundamental. In order to live and grow, the child, like all other animals, must be protected or able to protect himself from the common dangers. In addition to this primitive need for self-protection, there are the need for food and drink, the need for exercise, and the need for rest and sleep. So much is obvious. The metabolism and the biochemical balance of the body must be maintained at all cost. . . .

The *social* needs of the child are as simple to understand as his physiological needs. Essentially there are two kinds of emotional needs which can be satisfied only by the social milieu. The first is the need for personal love and affection. The child needs to feel that his parents—or someone—loves him for himself alone. He is to some extent appreciated because of *who* he is. (See, for instance, the distinctions made by J. S. Plant in *Personality and the Cultural Pattern*, The Commonwealth Fund, New York, 1937.) This affection gives him a deep and lasting sense of security.

The second is the need for acceptance and approval by the group, for appreciation by others because of *what* he is. Sometimes this is in direct conflict with the first. The mother's love for her son, for instance, may be so possessive, powerful, and at the time, so completely satisfying to the child, that he does not feel the need for acceptance by the group. To this extent his personality development will be warped.

The need for social status and social approval shows itself constantly in children at school. Some children will go to great lengths to gain a cherished recognition. If they cannot achieve it by legitimate behavior, they sometimes try behavior that is unacceptable or even antisocial. The boy who wins the admiration of at least some of the class by his effrontery and rudeness to the teacher is doubtless in this category. The desire for status in the social group, and the sense of "belonging" which this brings, are powerful motives that are present in everyone.

The *self* (or ego) needs of the child can readily be appreciated by adults. We all need some self-respect. We all like to feel that we are worthy people, and that we are filling our place in the world in a satisfactory way. We are important because of what we can achieve and contribute. We want our fair share of success, and, in addition to any social satisfaction and increased status which success may bring to us, we get personal satisfaction from a job well done.

Most of us feel the need to assert ourselves a little now and then, to be dominant in certain situations, and so add to our self-respect. Equally important is our need for new experiences. The thrill of adventure, travel, or exploration, even when the exploring is limited to new fields of knowledge investigated for the first time in school or library, persists throughout life. If it does not, we are in danger of failing to achieve the fullest type of personality development. Of special interest to education are the natural demands for spontaneity, for creative expression, and for harmonious appreciation and integration of our various experiences.

The child experiences the same type of personal self-needs, and he should have all the opportunity possible to satisfy them.

Although most of these personality needs are present from an early age, the attempts which the child makes to satisfy them will vary with his development and will be modified by his growth and by his learning. The new-born baby suckles when he is hungry; the five-year-old has learned to use his knife and fork as a means to satisfy his appetite; the ten-year-old is learning a great deal about the necessity of manners and social amenities. Similarly, the egocentricity of the young child, his emphasis on the self-needs, become broadened later into the feeling of self-confidence and the achievement of individual satisfactions through co-operation with the group.

So far the emphasis has been placed on the urgency of satisfying all the interrelated personality needs of the child, without over-emphasis or slighting of any one need. It will be obvious, however, that this satisfaction of the basic needs must be achieved with full consideration of the needs of other persons. Not till then will wholesome personality development take place. In other words, not only must the needs of the child be met by his environment, but the child must meet the requirements set by the people and institutions about him.

> J. D. M. Griffin, S. R. Laycock, and W. Line, *Mental Hygiene*. New York: American Book Company, 1940, pp. 17-21. (Permission to quote granted by W. J. Gage and Co. Ltd., Toronto.)

244. THREE BASIC FACTORS IN PERSONALITY DEVELOPMENT

The basic factor in personality development or maladjustment, the soil in which personality grows or for lack of which it becomes stunted or dies, is security. The word is not synonymous with safety, because some individuals may find security under conditions which to others are dangerous. Security has to do with guarantees to the individual's ability to keep alive, and not only to keep alive physically, through having enough to eat, a place to sleep and clothing to wear but to keep alive emotionally, through maintaining self-respect, through being needed in the world, being given a place in the social relationships of home, vocation, and society at large. When an individual's basic security is threatened, either he succumbs and withdraws from the relationships associated with the threat which developed his paralyzing fears, or he adopts aggressive and fighting characteristics to protect himself in the face of the dangers he believes to be imminent.

Threats to security in relation to parents or home are important factors in the behavior difficulties of children. A child may be born into a family situation where he is unwelcome or where his advent arouses jealousies on the part of one or the other parent or on the part of brothers or sisters. In another home the parents, in order to make a child conform to their wishes, use as punishment the threat that he cannot be mother's or father's little child any longer. A common illusion of the child, that he is adopted and does not really belong to his father and mother, is exaggerated under these circumstances and produces inner emotional conflict. There is no more cruel threat to a child than that of being rejected by parents and denied the home security. . . .

A second and closely related factor in personality development is success or achievement. As security is represented as the soil necessary for growth, so success might be likened to the rain. There is a point beyond which an individual cannot stand defeat and will give up under the blasting experiences of life just as the plant withers under continued drought. But too easy success also is harmful, and is usually achieved under conditions in which one is protected from the ordinary difficulties of making good. Easy success tends to develop an exaggerated sense of importance and to unfit one for life's everyday concerns. Life is made up of success and failure, of achievement and disappointment; every success has its elements of inadequacy. Personality develops best in surroundings which require effort for success and in which failure is a possibility, but where the individual can succeed sufficiently to give him a sense of achievement and of being useful to his world.

Where individuals have no chance for achievement in home and vocation, in social life and in community enterprises, they develop the sense of not being needed, of being useless. For this reason the dole never solves the problem of unemployment. Even though one be assured of food, clothing and shelter, he still faces the demoralizing fact that he seems not to be needed in the world's work, and he has none of the satisfaction and consequent growth which comes through useful work well done. When a man begins to doubt his usefulness in the world, the foundation is laid for personality maladjustment. . . .

A third factor in the development of personality is the social atmosphere in which the individual lives and works, and which may well be likened to the sunshine of the plant-world. To a human being the warmth of relationship to others of his kind is as important as the sunshine to the plant. To be of worth to others, to have others care what happens to him, to have their goodwill and the love of family and friends, produces an atmosphere in which personality blossoms forth; to be deprived of the concern and care of one's fellows, to be robbed of the goodwill and love of family and friends, is to become stunted in personality, withered, deformed. Even the feeling of success or failure is determined as much by the attitude of others towards one's endeavor as by intrinsic accomplishment. Social approval or disapproval is a large factor in determining the kind of conduct in which an individual engages.

> Harrison Sacket Elliott and Grace Loucks Elliott, *Solving Personal Problems*. New York: Henry Holt and Company, Inc., 1936, pp. 49-57. By permission of the publishers.

Discussion of the Motivation Problem

245. NEEDS MAY BE UNCONSCIOUS

The individual is frequently unaware or only partially aware of what his needs and goals really are. Many physiological needs operate entirely on a nonconscious level; others enter awareness as conscious desires or wishes only when they become pressing. We are not ordinarily aware of our need for air until breathing is hindered in some way. Even here, the degree of awareness may vary. We may mutter something about how stuffy it is and proceed to loosen our collars or open a window. But if all air is cut off and we are in danger of suffocation, then the awareness is immediate and vivid and more drastic action may be undertaken to restore our physiological equilibrium.

Basic psychological needs such as those for security, adequacy, social approval, and self-esteem ordinarily operate on relatively unconscious levels. By this is meant that the individual has little, if any, awareness of such needs, even though his behavior may be largely determined by them. Thus he may show off, join exclusive clubs, and even get married for reasons of which he is unaware. Of course he may think up good reasons to justify his behavior, but these may not be the real reasons at all.

The degree of insight or awareness into the motivation underlying one's behavior may vary considerably from one particular behavior pattern to another and from person to person. However, our typical lack of insight into our own motivations is clearly indicated by a mass of clinical and experimental evidence.

> James C. Coleman, *Abnormal Psychology and Modern Life*. Chicago: Scott, Foresman and Company, 1950, pp. 69-70.

246. Recognize Unconscious Motivations

The reasons underlying some forms of human behavior are obvious both to the actor and to outside observers. Sometimes they are concealed from outsiders but are recognized more or less clearly by the actor. Sometimes they are unknown even to him. For example, a man applying for a job insults his prospective employer. How can such behavior be understood? Did he not know he was being insulting? Or didn't he know that an insult would prevent his being hired? Or didn't he really want the job? Or what? In seeking to explain his failure to get the job, he might say, "The foreman was unreasonable." But very likely he would himself be aware of the unsatisfactoriness of such an explanation. Often people who behave in some such irrational way as this are as much puzzled by their behavior as is anyone else.

We can sympathize more readily with such a person's bewilderment if we realize that there is much of our own behavior we find hard to explain. Our glib rationalizations do not satisfy even ourselves. Why do we sometimes fly into a rage if we are kept waiting for a minute when at other times we'll wait in line fairly patiently for half an hour? Why do we sometimes punish a child severely for a slight fault and at other times let more severe misbehavior go unremarked? Why do some people in particular "get our goats"?

If we knew all, we would doubtless understand all. Bizarre behavior, like more usual behavior, has its causes, but sometimes they are deeply hidden. In dealing with others it is seldom possible or essential to understand fully the causes of their actions. It is essential, however, to realize that their behavior is motivated. Its source may lie hidden in the depths of their personalities where neither they nor we can readily discover it. In a complex personality with its many interconnected causal chains, the factors underlying a given bit of behavior are usually many and varied. A single cause cannot be isolated, and to attempt to force the individual to name one is to demand the impossible. He will be forced to resort to an inadequate rationalization.

The recognition that much human motivation is unconscious will enable the interviewer to be more tolerant, less condemna-

tory, and thus better able to help his client effectively. Instead
of becoming impatient with rationalizations, he will realize
that motives which the client disguises even to himself are
probably sources of deep and painful anxiety to him.

Unconscious motivation is much more common than we
ordinarily recognize in our attempt to understand people. We
seek too often for intellectual *grounds* for behavior rather than
for psychological *causes* rooted in feelings and emotions.
"Drives" are emotional affairs, and actions controlled by them
have their source in feeling rather than in intellect. A person
who apparently likes, but really dislikes, another "forgets" a
luncheon engagement with him, and in extenuation pleads a
busy day. A man fired from a job because of incompetence
"explains" that the work was too heavy for him. Why a client
says certain things and leaves others unsaid, why a child with
a high I.Q. flunks in school, why a wife who effusively protests
her love for her husband continually belittles him, are questions whose answers are to be sought not in intellectual but
emotional terms. Explanations such as, "He's deceitful," "He's
lazy," "She's just being modest about him," are obviously
inadequate. Yet for many people such remarks conclude the
discussion and block any real understanding.

> Annette Garrett, *Interviewing, Its Principles and Methods.*
> New York: Family Service Association of America, 1942,
> pp. 12-13.

247.   Behavior Complicated by Unconscious Motives

. . . Our purpose is rather to show that there are drives in
each of us, drives which are the resultants of our needs, drives
which impel us to create our life goals, set up tensions within
us when needs are unfulfilled, and force us relentlessly to pursue these goals. The fact that these needs often operate unconsciously complicates human behavior. We may be quite unaware of the needs which direct certain of our actions. The
teacher knows how often in the classroom or around the
school a youngster will get into some kind of mischief, and will
become, without apparent reason, sullen, combative, retaliative, aggressive, boisterous, untruthful. Oftentimes when the
teacher talks to this youngster and asks him why, he says quite
truthfully, "I don't know." Many a battle between teacher

and child has resulted from this question and this answer. The teacher insists on an answer, the child insists that he does not know. Many a teacher has lost the opportunity to serve the child because he has alienated him by such a battle. The child often really does not know and is confused and troubled by the question. Our best course, perhaps, is to look to see how often in ourselves there are these same movements of sullenness, combativeness, retaliation, aggressiveness, and then to ask, "How did this happen to me?" Was it perhaps that the person we loved seemed unappreciative or unresponsive at some point? Was it perhaps that we had been reprimanded by the principal in the presence of other teachers? Was it perhaps that we had to face financial hazards and had to recognize our lack of power over economic forces? Was it perhaps a more persistent, longer-lived, more deeply imbedded disappointment that the life we had always visualized as just around the corner has never been realized? Or was it just perhaps that we had gotten up late and hadn't had time to eat our breakfast? These and a thousand other reasons could be traced back to their origins in some of our fundamental human needs, and much of our behavior would become clear on the basis of such an explanation. Are the needs of youngsters so different from our own? Let us watch carefully the next infant and child we see. For example, let us watch children of different ages and then look at the adolescents in the classroom to see whether the same needs which drive our lives to some degree and in some combinations do not drive the lives of all human beings of all ages. Will it not be true with all of these that their needs determine their goals and thus their behavior?

> Paul A. Witty and Charles E. Skinner, editors, *Mental Hygiene in Modern Education.* New York: Rinehart and Company, Inc., 1939, pp. 246-47. (From chapter by Alice V. Keliher.)

248. Look for Causes

Visit his home, if you can. Talk with his parents. Talk with teachers. Study what records there are. See the youngster in all the places you can: in the lunchroom, on the playground, on the street, in clubs, at home. The more you know about him the more surely you will be able to help.

Sometimes you will be lucky. Sometimes, those few times when there is some single new pressure, you may spot it quickly. Often a new pressure like this is short-lived. Then you don't have to worry too much. Often such a cause will disappear soon and then the behavior will improve of its own accord. This can help you to relax. You can know that this "bad" behavior probably will not last forever.

This is good luck, however. Many times you won't be able, right away, to find a simple cause. All you will know is that something is wrong, something is bearing down on the youngster and the only way he has for handling it is to hit out at the world.

You don't expect this good luck, for example, when the trouble goes far back. Then the cause is always less specific. Almost never is it some one event that you can put your finger on or some one specific change that you can easily see. A great many things have overwhelmed the child. He can't get back at them; they arc too much for him. But he can hit out at children or at animals and that somehow makes him feel better inside. He is mad at the world or afraid of the world and what it may do to him. He protects himself in this funny way.

This is slow-going but you have to keep *searching* for causes. And the more you see the more sympathetic you will become.

James L. Hymes, Jr., *Teacher Listen—the Children Speak* ... Philadelphia: National Mental Health Foundation, 1949, pp. 15-17.

249. AVOID PROBING FOR MOTIVES

The wise counselor remembers that his counselee's motives may be conscious or unconscious. Even when they are conscious, the employee may be unwilling or unable to reveal them. Although he may know very well his reasons for being upset and nervous, his reasons for quitting the job, for disliking the foreman, or for being unable to do his work adequately, he may be unwilling to share these reasons with the counselor. Perhaps he isn't certain that the counselor can be trusted. Perhaps he fears the counselor will condemn him or try to change him when this isn't at all what he wants. At other times the counselee may be unconscious of his motives. They may spring from conflicts within himself of which he is not aware. Sometimes, for example, the underlying motive for an action is socially unacceptable and would be condemned by the person himself were he conscious of it. In such cases he cannot allow himself to become aware of his real motive. The alcoholic, the "accident prone," or the chronic absentee frequently cannot tell the counselor the motives for his behavior because he has successfully concealed them even from himself. It is obvious that when motivation is thus unconscious, it is futile to argue with the individual on a conscious, rational basis. Since his real reasons are unknown even to himself, logic doesn't reach them, and the behavior continues to the bewilderment of both himself and the counselor.

The counselor should bear in mind, then, when someone comes to him for help, that the account the counselee gives of his difficulties may be inadequate in one or several areas. He may have concealed relevant facts because of timidity or fear, or he may well be quite unconscious of the real causative factors underlying his difficulties.

In the first type of situation the counselor can often help reduce the timidity or fear by his own friendly receptiveness. He can make it clear that he is not a policeman who will punish or a judge who will condemn, but a friendly counselor whose primary interest lies in helping the employee to work out a solution of his problem in a way that is most in keeping with his own fundamental desires.

In the second type of case the counselor, through receptive listening and intelligent questioning, can often help the counselee to discern more clearly the real nature of his problem and to plan more objectively for its solution.

This does not mean that a counselor needs to explore the depths of his counselee's personality, but the fact that he knows of the existence of unconscious motivation will warn him of the futility of argument and advice. In special cases, this recognition will lead him to refer the employee to specialists who are better equipped to be helpful in that area. It is unwise for a counselor ever to "probe" for the motives of a person who comes to him for assistance. If he has established a good relationship with his counselee, he will gradually gain a better understanding of the latter's underlying interests and purposes. But such understanding is never gained through "digging."

> Annette Garrett, *Counseling Methods for Personnel Workers*. New York: Family Service Association of America, 1945, pp. 18-19.

250. WORKING WITH THE NEEDS OF THE CHILD

Rooted in the physiological needs of our very tissues, motives become refined, directed, and socialized as the developing organism comes to terms with his family, his peers, his culture. The struggle to compensate for deficits, to release tensions, to achieve balance, is the main business of the individual.

The concepts of needs, motives, and power of self-balance will furnish the key for the analyses of learning, perceiving, and thinking; and the importance of a clear foundation at this point cannot be overemphasized. We shall observe that the way in which the family and the culture handle the needs of the individual determines whether he is strongly motivated or apathetic, curious and persistent, or indifferent and giving up easily; *which* motive ranks highest in his life style. The teacher who understands the child can *utilize* the needs the child brings with him, *evoke* and *strengthen* his motivation toward socially significant goals, and *guide* him toward that mature and balanced integration of motives which is our goal.

The teacher can do this only if he learns to discover and understand the motivations the child brings with him. If he undertakes such a study, he will learn to respect that homeostatic "wisdom of the body" which struggles to balance deficits and to achieve an optimum growth. By working with these needs the teacher possesses a power that would otherwise be lost. What *we* think the child needs is not enough; what society believes he *ought* to want is not enough. What he *is* must be our concern.

> Lawrence E. Cole and William F. Bruce, *Educational Psychology*. New York: World Book Company, 1950, p. 230.

251. GETTING AT THE BOTTOM OF THINGS

Behavior expresses underlying feelings. Behavior changes as feelings change. This fact is too often forgotten by group leaders. People act as if they could change or modify behavior the way one can change the position of a marionette on a puppet stage. They say: "Don't bite your nails. Sit straight. Be nice to your mother. Go to sleep. Why do you always forget your pencil? Be quiet. You have no reason for acting that way. Behave yourself. You must have confidence in me. Don't lie!" It doesn't work!

There is a purpose back of every action—inner feeling seeking expression. The action may seem to be the very worst way in the world to satisfy the feelings, but that is what the action is for just the same. The reasons are not always visible, since they very often lie within the unconscious. There is "purpose" in nail-biting, but it is not to make the nails shorter. We would not dream of saying: "Why are you having a temperature?" or "Stop bleeding." But we do feel free to say "Stop crying." Why does it seem ridiculous to say "Stop bleeding," and perfectly all right to say "Stop crying?" Why is it so easy to see the purpose in a boy's going to the soda-fountain and so difficult to see his purpose in nail-biting? "Because," one may say, "you cannot stop the blood from running but you can stop the tears; there is some sense in eating ice-cream but none in chewing nails."

We recognize physical pain much easier than emotional pain; we recognize physical hunger more than emotional hunger. One is as real as the other. Crying is a form of behavior. It has a reason and a purpose. One cannot hope to get at the reason by stopping the crying. Nevertheless, one says, if you tell a youngster to stop crying, he will stop. But just what has been accomplished by stopping it? Have you now any better understanding? Do you know more than before what was causing it? Did forceful stopping cure the cause?

If we ignore the fact that behavior is purposive and unconsciously controlled, we may train young people to repress their real feelings, to conform to our standards, and to conform later to any kind of life that is based on regimentation, obedience, and repression of real feelings.

Many group leaders, on first realizing that there are reasons for everything, conclude that they must first find out "the facts" before acting. They say: I never do anything rash, I always get my facts first.

How do they go about doing that?

They go to the group member and say: Why do you come late; Why do you always forget your notebook; Why do you fight; Why are you crying? Leaders who ask these questions are assuming that people always know the reasons for their behavior. Since this is not true, the leaders are often frustrated by defensive answers, by "lying," or by "stubbornness." Although leaders who ask the "why" questions consider themselves above those who always say "don't," the difference is not as great as they like to think.

There is not much difference between "Don't bite your nails," and "Why do you bite your nails?" Actually the child does not know why and will sometimes tell us so. The reasons for it lie within the individual. All we can say here is that nail-biting represents some kind of inner tension.

About all one can do in a group situation is to ask oneself: What does this mean, why is this child so tense, so restless? If one is a knowing observer, he will probably find other symptoms of tension besides nail-biting. The various symptoms together may tell him something about the person. Often he will need help from experts.

Rudolph M. Wittenberg, *So You Want to Help People.* New York: Association Press, 1947, pp. 12-13.

252.   No General Rule for Motivating People

If there is any conclusion from recent research of which a teacher may be sure, it is that there is no known formula or infallible set of procedures to motivate all pupils at all times. Enough evidence has been accumulated to suggest that the whole motivational setting is more important than isolated attempts to energize learning and that certain incentives sometimes used by schools, such as sarcasm, grades, and honor rolls are of doubtful value or even of definite harm. Because an incentive is effective does not necessarily mean that it is good, as seen in the larger context. The evidence seems rather clear, too, that motivation is not something applied apart from the learning situation but is an intrinsic part of it.

> Ernest R. Hilgard and David H. Russell, "Motivation in School Learning," *Learning and Instruction,* Forty-ninth Yearbook of the National Society for the Study of Education, Part I. Chicago: University of Chicago Press, 1950, chap. 2, p. 37. By permission of the Society.

253. THE EXPERTS DIFFER

The best known basic tendencies are naturally those most often faced by the psychoanalysts and other psychotherapists. About these there have been many arguments, with various writers pushing one or another basic need as a particular favorite. As the smoke of battle dies down, it seems apparent that they were all partially correct. Sex, self-esteem, inferiority feelings, isolation, anxiety, love, self-actualization—all these seem to impel various human beings at various times. Some writers have eclectically listed them all, not in any particular order or relationship, but with the implication that these impulses are equally valid and equally strong and are essentially independent of each other. (Thorndike, W. I. Thomas, Woodworth, Murray, and others.)

Others have presented these needs in some sort of structured and organized relationship (Goldstein, Angyal, Maslow) implying that needs are related to each other; that one depends upon another; that they are arranged in a hierarchy; that the emergence of one depends upon the gratification of another; and finally that there are some empirical justifications for the old, dogmatically based division of needs and impulses into "higher" and "lower." Thus, if physiological, safety, love, esteem, and self-actualizing needs are, in that order, prepotent, i.e., demand prior gratification, then it can be meaningful to say that physiological needs are more powerful and more basic than the love needs, but that the love needs are "higher" than the physiological needs because, e.g., they are a later phyletic and ontogenetic development, they require more preconditions; they are more sensitive, they require better conditions of life, etc.

> Maurice J. Shore, *et al., Twentieth Century Mental Hygiene.*

New York: Social Sciences Publishers, 1950, pp. 354-55.
(From chapter by A. H. Maslow.)

254. REASONS FOR CONFUSION IN AREA OF MOTIVATION

Before going further, let us consider some of the reasons
for confusion in the area of motivation:

1. Motivation is difficult, first of all, because it is primarily
concerned with the "whys" rather than the "hows" or "whats"
of behavior. That is, it is concerned with *explanation* rather
than *description*. And, as any scientist or philosopher knows
only too well, the search for causes is one of his most puzzling
and frustrating activities—at the same time that it is fascinating and important.

2. Motives are never directly observable, in the sense that
emotions, learning, memory, or even intelligence are observable. Motives are always inferred or hypothesized from behavior. If an individual seeks out people and seems to enjoy
being with them, we say he has a sociability or affiliation
motive. If he persistently amasses goods and wealth, we posit
an "acquisitive drive."

The trouble is, people sometimes do the same thing for
different reasons. Of five people attending church, one is
devoutly religious, another wishes to show off her new spring
outfit, another hopes to make good business connections, another is escaping from a noisy household, and still another
seeks enjoyment in the music. Conversely, persons similarly
motivated may behave differently. Two individuals each intent
upon recognition may seek it in widely different ways—one
through boasting, let us say, and the other through writing
or scientific research.

Perhaps, of course, we should not hypothesize motives at all.
But psychologists seem forced to do so for both theoretical
and practical reasons.

3. Psychologists and other students of motivation are un-
clear as to the meaning of terms they use. Is a motive an
"inner push," like an instinct? Or is it in some measure a
response to external stimuli? Do motives operate all the time,
or do they come into play only at certain times or in certain
situations? Should we think of motives as broad dynamic

tendencies like "prestige-seeking" and "gregariousness"? Or are they more specific, like "seeking prestige in my community" and "wanting to be with my old friends"? Again, are motives separate from, or do they overlap, attitudes, habits, interests, emotions, and other processes? Agreement will have to be reached on such matters before real progress can be made.

4. Motives may be primarily physiological or primarily social in origin, or, more likely, a combination of the two. The disentangling of these strands is always difficult. . . .

5. Assuming that motives exist, they undoubtedly occur in mixtures and fusions which vary greatly among individuals and in the same individual from one time to another.

Despite this impressive array of difficulties, the social psychologist refuses to be discouraged. He realizes that social behavior cannot be understood and predicted on the basis of motives alone—even if he were sure he had accurate data on them. But, equally, he knows that one cannot interpret social behavior realistically without taking into account the dynamic, energetic, goal-seeking behavior of individuals. Like the educator, the clinician, the advertiser, the newspaper editor, and the politician, the social psychologist cannot understand, predict, or influence human behavior without a fairly adequate knowledge of motives. And the social psychologist, as a scientist, has the even more difficult job of trying to present a systematic theory of motivation.

S. Stansfeld Sargent, *Social Psychology.* New York: The Ronald Press Company, 1950, pp. 158-59.

255.   A New Theory of Motivation Is in the Making

For full understanding of the current state of affairs in the field of motivation, a brief historical-philosophical note will be helpful. Why do official psychological and social science lack a guiding theory of motivation? We seem now to be in the midst of an interregnum. The instinct theory of the past is dead, and the theory of the future is only now being hammered out. The instinct theory was attacked on so many grounds, and was killed so dead that the motivation problem itself was thrown out along with the outworn answer to it.

At least in part, this was due to the prevailing cultural temper which was very mechanistic, very atomistic, and anti-purposive.

Now that the excitement of the instinct controversy is allayed, it is again possible to see some of the merits of the instinct theory. True, it was a poor answer, logically, semantically, empirically, but at least it faced certain essential facts of motivation squarely and honestly. It accepted the fact that man was a self-mover; that his own nature, as well as his environment help to decide his behavior; that behavior is senseless unless one understands its motivation and its goals (if indeed these be separate); and that on the whole, organisms left to their own resources, often display a kind of "wisdom" or a biological efficiency that needs explaining. . . .

All these researches tend to create an atmosphere of greater rather than lesser trust in the organism, and increased rather than decreased respect for its powers of self-government. We must come away from such experimentations with the suspicion that one of the most helpful things we can do for an organism is to leave it alone as much as possible, to allow it to develop in its own style, and by its own laws, and to restrict our help to answering its freely uttered requests for protection, help, materials, etc. The psychotherapist, social worker, and the progressive teacher will have already recognized this as a fairly good definition of the so-called "permissive regime" which puts the burden of proof upon the one who denies or frustrates or neglects the demands of the organisms.

> Maurice J. Shore, *et al., Twentieth Century Mental Hygiene.* New York: Social Sciences Publishers, 1950, pp. 350-51 and 352-53. (From chapter by A. H. Maslow.)

256. Sargent's Summary of Motivation

It is difficult to treat motivation in a way which is satisfying to the scientist, though we have made progress since the days of instinct doctrines. Scientists are fairly well agreed as to the tissue needs of the human organism and their function in producing activity. Furthermore, in satisfying his bodily drives, a child acquires a number of "sets" toward people, things, and activities which may be called "sociogenic motives" (e.g., affiliation, prestige-seeking, acquisitiveness, etc.). These sets are or become more or less generalized, and energize behavior when evoked by appropriate incentives. No known physiological basis for sociogenic motives exists. Morgan's hypothesis that a "central motive state" underlies all drives and motives is plausible, but evidence for it has not yet been obtained. . . .

It is impossible to draw up a satisfactory classification of human motives for several reasons: motives are inferred rather than directly observed; wide individual differences exist; attitudes, interests, values, and emotions have motivational character, along with what we call "drives" and "motives." Despite these difficulties, it is worth while for the social psychologist to try to identify the tensions, or needs, which seem to underlie various kinds of goal-directed behavior. If he has studied his individuals carefully, the motives he infers will help him predict their social behavior, individually or as a group. For social behavior is a function of individuals in a social situation, and motives make up the most dynamic aspect of those individuals.

S. Stansfeld Sargent, *Social Psychology*. New York: The Ronald Press Company, 1950, pp. 173-74.

257. CONSIDER THE NEEDS OF THE WHOLE PERSON

. . . Not only do many needs jointly produce our behavior, but our needs affect each other and vary a great deal in different situations as a result of the high degree of interdependency among them. At the metabolic level, deprivation of carbohydrates causes an increased hunger for proteins from which the body may manufacture part of its sugar requirements. (Masserman.) On a higher motivational level, individuals may eat too much in an attempt to compensate for other life frustrations, or they may engage in promiscuous sexual behavior to increase their feelings of adequacy and of being loved and wanted by others. Similarly, increased social approval or self-esteem may partially compensate for sexual or other frustrations. Consequently, the motivation underlying a particular behavior pattern may be extremely difficult to understand unless we view it always as an interaction of biological, psychological, and sociological factors.

James C. Coleman, *Abnormal Psychology and Modern Life*. Chicago: Scott, Foresman and Company, 1950, p. 68.

258. Personality and Motivation

Among the needs listed by Prescott (Daniel A. Prescott, *Emotion and the Educative Process.* Washington: American Council on Education, 1938), there is a set called *ego-integrative*. That is, the child needs some internal organization within his motivational system in order that he may achieve a sense of inner harmony. In this connection we think of the role of religion, or philosophy of life, or a set of values. The enjoyment of music and the arts, satisfying work experiences, and comfortable relations with other people, all contribute to this general well-being of the person. An adequate description of the individual's ego-integrative needs and his ways of satisfying them would add up to a description of his personality.

Calling attention to ego-integrative needs shows that it is a mistake to think of motivation only in relation to the completion of isolated assignments or tasks. The whole motivational system of the learner is important: how immediate goals are set in relation to remote goals, how successes and failures are reacted to. When his systems of goals and values are understood, the individual child takes on fresh meaning to the teacher.

Because of their different personalities, children respond differently to praise and reproof, to activities done individually and those done in groups, to tasks requiring precision as against tasks requiring strength, and so on. Which athletic event proves satisfying is not merely a matter of muscular skill and endurance but reflects attitudes toward competition, toward pain, toward delight in or fear of bodily contact, and so on. Motivation cannot be divorced from the whole personality of the child.

> Ernest R. Hilgard and David H. Russell, "Motivation in School Learning," *Learning and Instruction,* Forty-ninth Yearbook of the National Society for the Study of Education, Part I. Chicago: University of Chicago Press, 1950, chap. 2, p. 44. By permission of the Society.

259. All Needs Are Interrelated

The needs of developing children fall naturally into three categories representing three major aspects of the life of a person. These categories of need can be called: (1) physiological, when describing needs that spring primarily out of structure and dynamic biochemical equilibria; (2) social or status needs, when describing the relationships that it is essential to establish with other persons in our culture; and (3) ego or integrative needs, when describing needs for experience and for the organization and symbolization of experience through which the individual will discover his role in life and learn to play it in such an effective manner as to develop a sense of worthy selfhood. . . .

There is always the serious danger of misunderstandings when a schematic classification is presented; perhaps this danger is less for persons who thoughtfully doubt the schematic organization than for those who accept it readily. The latter tend to make of a tentative classification scheme a system of definite knowledge into which observed facts must be fitted. A formal appeal is hereby made that the material to follow be regarded merely as an attempt to examine the objectives of behavior in functional terms, to understand what it is that is really "making the wheels go round" in human behavior. It is not an attempt to set up a rigid framework of concepts into which all behavior must be fitted. The categories which have been set up and the more specific needs within them will not be found to be mutually exclusive, independent, instinctive drives, each seeking satisfaction through a specific pattern of behavior. Behavior has a unity which far transcends this. What one does at a given moment may be an attempt to satisfy, at the same time, half a dozen different needs distributed through all three categories; but this behavior cannot be divided up into so and so many units of effort for each need. Therefore, it must be understood clearly that the various needs described do not operate independently of each other—a functional interrelationship between them is evident everywhere. The satisfaction of one need may contribute or be prerequisite to the satisfaction of another. The satisfaction of one need may also place the individual in a situation that will give rise to another. A vital point to remember is that needs are basically related to culture and vary from culture to culture. Particularly in matters involving social relationships are cultural factors important in defining needs; indeed cultural forces even give rise to new needs from time to time.

Daniel Alfred Prescott, *Emotion and the Educative Process.* Washington: American Council on Education, 1938, pp. 113-14.

260. NORMATIVE AND PSYCHOLOGICAL NEEDS

Children need optimal health; they need vocational preparation. Here we are talking about what, in the opinion of adults, children ought to have, but seldom if ever strive to get. Children need recreation; they need rewarding social contacts. Now, we are talking about what, in their own living, children very often strive to get, whether adults like it or not.

The needs of the first class, like the need for optimal health, are only projected requirements. They are projected into children by adults, and they do no more than reflect the values of adults. One may call them "normative needs" because they serve the one purpose of expressing social norms or standards. The important thing to be said here about normative needs is that they lack motive power. This is evident in the fact that we attribute them even to lifeless things, as when it is said of a house that it "needs" paint.

The needs of the other class, like the need for rewarding social contacts, are not at all merely projected requirements that serve only to reflect adult values. They are positive conditions that exist in children and, as such, they help to create child values. The already common name for them is "psychological needs." The point in calling these needs psychological is not that they are always known to the individual who has them. The point is simply that, as states of the person they belong to the network of psychological determinants. When they get linked with goals in the environmental part of this network, directed actions occur. Then, psychological needs become charged, as normative needs never do, with motive power.

The time was when the curriculum was based rigidly upon normative needs. Adults decreed that children needed—ought to have—a knowledge of Latin, mastery of the multiplication tables, a nice appreciation of Tennyson, proper manners, in short, "the cultural heritage," and, for good measure, periodical spankings. Educators undertook to see to it that children got these things. They tutored and implored with an awful sense of obligation, but without any regard for psychological needs. This worked out poorly, as we know. So often, normative needs ran counter to psychological needs, and the sure outcome was that children were unhappier than they deserved to be. Moreover, it is said that, for lack of "motivation," they took in little at a slow rate and then lost much of what they got, so that room was left for better education in behalf of normative needs.

A reaction set in early in the present century when Dewey started his experimental school. The new idea was to base the curriculum upon the psychological needs of children, and so to make education "child centered." Children were not to be frustrated by arbitrary rules and assignments. They were to be happy and well adjusted. But that is not all. In the end, the important normative needs were to be met because "motivation" would, it was thought, guarantee high and efficient intake of the skills, ideas, attitudes, and the like that children ought to have.

Actually, this has all been easier said—*ad nauseam*—than done. But there is no denying that "the new education" has taken hold. At least, the principle that the curriculum should be geared to the psychological needs of children is generally accepted. Let us be clear about the claims, already touched upon here, that are urged in support of this principle. Primarily, there are two. The one is that heed for psychological needs in the planning and management of the curriculum will promote the happiness and personal well-being of individual children. The other is that this strategy will lead to the fulfillment of the really important normative needs of children, and so bring about the realization by the schools of their broader, social objectives.

> Herbert F. Wright, "How the Psychology of Motivation Is Related to Curriculum Development," *The Journal of Educational Psychology*, March, 1948, pp. 149-51.

261. Precipitating Versus Basic Cause

One other distinction must be clearly made. Where there has been a long-lasting and cumulative stress, a comparatively minor or insignificant event may set off a maladjustment. This minor event is called the *precipitating cause*. Often it receives publicity because it makes a good story, but to the student of behavior, it is only the final event in a long series of events which constitute the real stresses. For example, a recent newspaper item told of a seventeen-year-old boy who shot his stepfather in an argument over a dance; actually there had been very strict discipline and much emotional difficulty in the family for many years. Another item some months ago told of a divorce secured by a woman because her husband struck her in a "tiff" over a bridge game; actually, in the divorce action, many difficulties of long duration were brought out. The argument over the dance and the "tiff" over bridge are precipitating causes; the underlying causes lie deep in the relations between the persons and the frustrations and barriers about them. Ordinary people live through many arguments without committing murder or getting divorces.

> John E. Anderson, *The Psychology of Development and Personal Adjustment.* New York: Henry Holt and Company, Inc., 1949, pp. 424-25. By permission of the publishers.

262. SUB-CULTURES COMPLICATE MOTIVATIONS

When we talk about motivation or motives we are talking about any of the circumstances which result in the energizing, selecting, or directing of conduct. Physiological needs and drives, incentives, goals, wishes, purposes, interests, rewards, punishments, fears—all must be considered. Some of these depend upon the fact that children are young mammals, with the biological needs common to their kind. Some depend upon the fact that the children we know grow up in our culture, where from the earliest days certain demands have been made upon them, certain roles assigned to them. The cultural consequences are made more baffling because the different sub-cultures in our country expect different things of children. (W. Allison Davis and Robert J. Havighurst, *Father of the Man: How Your Child Gets His Personality.* Boston: Houghton Mifflin Company, 1947.)

> Ernest R. Hilgard and David H. Russell, "Motivation in School Learning," *Learning and Instruction*, Forty-ninth

Yearbook of the National Society for the Study of Education, Part I. Chicago: University of Chicago Press, 1950, chap. 2, pp. 37-38. By permission of the Society.

263. MOST ACTIVITY RESULTS FROM MIXED MOTIVES

Motives are powerfully influenced by experience and training. It is well to warn the reader against thinking that human motives frequently appear in pure form. Most activity results from mixed motives. The motives are not only mixed by virtue of the fact that one stimulation brings out two or more motives at the same time; they are mixed by virtue of the fact that the motives are satisfied repeatedly in certain particular ways and not in others, so that a motive which was once *non-specific* becomes connected with *particular* kinds of stimuli. The child builds up, therefore, a *habitual* way of satisfying a motive. Later on, new motives are aroused and connected with the object which has already proved so satisfying; additional motives get hooked up to these. A man who has a splendid collection of Chinese paintings has built up, in connection with this hobby, all sorts of satisfactions, personal and social, aesthetic and intellectual. The pictures mean so much to him that almost no aspect of his life is untouched by this special craving. Human motivation is infinitely complex. Its web is of a delicate, intricate pattern. The study of the elementary forms of motivation is important, but equally important in the understanding of human motivation is the recognition of the diversity, richness, and many-sidedness of the motives as they express themselves day by day.

Gardner Murphy, *A Briefer General Psychology.* New York: Harper and Brothers, 1935, pp. 68-69.

264. THE GREAT INFLUENCE OF FREUD

The real revolution of our time has nothing to do with the Communists. It is a deeper and more permanent revolution, and it has been so successful that we have scarcely noticed it.

Sitting in a restaurant the other morning, I heard one waitress say to another: "There's nothing wrong with Linda, except anxiety." And the other waitress nodded gravely in agreement.

Our speech, as well as our thinking has become permeated with slogans and mottos of this revolution. Even the most simple and uninstructed among us constantly use such phrases as "inferiority complex," "neurotic," "unconscious," and "frustration."

Most of these phrases are used inaccurately; nor are they well understood by the people who fling them around with the greatest abandon. But the fact remains that 50 years ago, not one of them was established in the language of mankind.

Freud has been the arch-revolutionist of our age, not Marx or Lenin. And this revolution in our concept of thinking about the human being has been accomplished without shedding a drop of blood or committing a single act of injustice.

Not everything that Freud believed has turned out to be true, and his followers have continually modified his views. But his basic assumption—that a personality is like an iceberg of which we know only the top fragment—is receiving more confirmation every year.

Subconscious. There is no other way to explain why people act as they do, except by trying to understand the deeply-hidden drives that move them. And there is no way to stop them from driving others and themselves to destruction except by trying to get them to understand their own unconscious motives.

It is as simple and profound as that. It is so simple that anyone with an open mind can see the evidence, and so profound that it may take another 100 years before we perfect the technique. When this happens, totalitarianism will no longer be a threat, because the minds of men will not be receptive toward these hostile, hysterical ideas.

The religious mystic tells us to look into our own hearts to solve the problems of the world; with a somewhat different vocabulary, this is what the new revolution tells us, also. Until she learns to do this, Linda is irrevocably stuck with her "anxiety," and we with ours.

> Sydney J. Harris, "Freud Is Father of Our Age." From column: "Strictly Personal," Chicago: The Chicago *Daily News,* May 25, 1951.

265. CHALLENGE TO USUAL CONCEPT OF MOTIVATION

The idea of need or drive, as used by social psychologists, is not necessarily a biological one. It is customary to distinguish between (a) biological and (b) social needs. The former exist because living organisms must do certain things in order to survive and perpetuate themselves. These needs have to do with nourishment, elimination, breathing, sexual activity, warmth, shelter, and so on. They are frequently referred to as "primary," basic," biogenic," or "innate," and constitute some of the necessary conditions of human life. To call them "biological" is accurate and permissible if we bear in mind that specific patterns of behavior associated with them are usually not inherited, and that social pressures—ideals and the like—may lead men to act contrary to their biological needs; for example, fasting, sexual continence, suicide. To call these needs "primary" seems to imply that social needs are derived from them. There is no point, for example, in assuming that the social need for clean white tablecloths is derived from the biological need for nourishment. Moreover, the assumption implicit in such terms as basic, primary, and the like is that biological needs are more important than social needs in human behavior. This assumption is unwarranted. Who, for example, would risk the assertion that the primary need for nourishment is a more important factor in the behavior of the American people than the "derived" needs for a certain standard of living and for social status?

In contrast to the unlearned biological needs are the "acquired," "derived," "social," "secondary," or "sociogenic" ones. These are endless in number for almost any human wish, desire, aspiration, or ambition may be so designated. There have been many attempts to classify social needs into relatively few basic types. Thomas and Znaniecki, for example, have suggested four fundamental wishes: for security, new experience, response, and recognition. The classification of human behavior into categories corresponding to assumed needs, wishes, or drives does not explain the behavior. Thus, if a husband is said to be unfaithful to his wife because of the "wish for new experience" and another husband is faithful because of the "wish for security," we must still ask why one is unfaithful and the other is not. To label behavior in such terms is quite arbitrarily to impute abstract and unverifiable motives, which are conceived as the forces or causative agents behind the overt acts. The need is first inferred from the act and then is used to explain it. Such explanations are circular or tautological because they do nothing which a simple description of the behavior does not accomplish. It may also be noted that referring to social needs as "derived needs" is misleading, since it implies that they are built on and are extensions of biological ones. This has never been demonstrated and its validity is improbable.

In a certain sense this entire book has to do with human needs, for any description or analysis of such matters as the nature of the self, of communication, or of the enacting of roles carries with it implications regarding the nature of human wants and the activities from which satisfactions are derived. Needs represent a relationship between organism and environment and are relative to both the state of the organism and the nature of the environment. The development of verbal behavior conditions the emergence of entirely new needs and new satisfactions. Thus, each of the unique features of modern, urban, technological civilization has ushered in its appropriate and unique needs. Some cosmopolites feel a need to live in cities of more than a million people; others may have a specific need to live only in New York City or to live in the country even if they must work in the city.

The development of the refinements of symbol manipulation has led to the need for intelligence, for rationality, for explanations of natural phenomena and of one's own actions. The prescience of old age and death creates the need for orienting oneself to these realities. The unanswerable questions that can be asked about the origin, ultimate meaning, and destiny of man have led to the development of the needs that are satisfied by religious and philosophical doctrines. The formulation of standards and values produces the desire to be honest, loyal, reliable, and so forth.

Alfred R. Lindesmith and Anselm L. Strauss, *Social Psychology*. New York: The Dryden Press, 1949, pp. 522-24.

10.

Adjustment

---

266. Adjustment Mechanisms Provide Flexibility

When an individual is motivated toward a goal which he cannot achieve because of external or internal factors, he resorts to one or more adjustment mechanisms. An adjustment mechanism is a device used to achieve an indirect satisfaction of a need in order that tension may be reduced and self-respect maintained. Since frustrations are experienced by everyone and since everyone is compelled to maintain his ego, it follows that everyone makes use of adjustment mechanisms. They are our protection against the impact of a not always friendly environment; they are to some extent a buffer between the present and the experiences of the past. They provide an important part of the resiliency which every individual needs; without them, flexibility would be impossible.

It is clear, then, that the mechanisms . . . are not to be considered as harmful in themselves. They constitute desirable, even necessary, methods of dealing with frustrations. They lead to behavior disorders only when carried to extremes.

Herbert Carroll, *Mental Hygiene.* New York: Prentice-Hall, Inc., 1947, p. 134. By permission of the publishers.

267. The Adjustment Process

If the motives of organisms were all immediately and easily satisfied, there would be no need for adjustment. Various hindrances, however, tend to thwart the direct satisfaction of motives. . . . The human, impelled by such motives as those of mastery or social approval, is frequently unable to reduce his drives immediately. He meets with thwarting in the form of

material obstacles, of competition from other similarly motivated individuals, and of hindrances resulting from his own
lack of ability. But a strong motive, once aroused, tends to
keep the individual in a state of activity. Stimulated by the
drive-tension, the individual makes one reaction after another
until at length some response is found which will reduce the
drive. This exploratory activity which begins when a drive is
aroused and ends when the drive is extinguished is probably
the most general pattern of animal and human behavior. It may
be termed the *adjustment process.*

> Laurance Frederic Shaffer. *The Psychology of Adjustment.*
> Boston: Houghton Mifflin Company, 1936, p. 113.

268.   THE PATTERN OF ADJUSTMENT

The process of adjustment may be pictured as shown in
Figure 16. An individual is proceeding in a course of motivated behavior (1) toward an end-result (4). When thwarted
or blocked, he makes varied responses (2) until by some action (3) he overcomes the obstacle and proceeds as before.
The principal steps in the adjustment sequence are therefore
the existence of a *motive,* the operation of some *thwarting*
which prevents its immediate satisfaction, giving rise to *varied
response* leading eventually to tension reduction or *solution.*

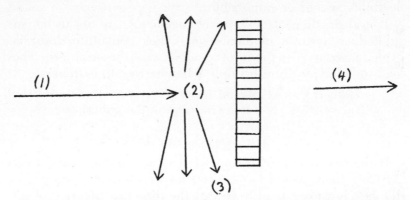

Figure 16.   The Pattern of Adjustment (Dashiell, *Fundamentals of Objective Psychology.* Houghton Mifflin Co., 1928.)

Ibid., p. 116.

269. Sequence in the Adjustment Process

The adjustive process may be described in the following somewhat oversimplified fashion: (1) Every individual has inherent qualities which impel him to activity. These needs, drives, or motives are the basis of all behavior. (2) Behavior is directed toward goals, the attainment of which satisfies the needs or motives of the individual. (3) But, if progress toward a goal is thwarted, disorganization of the personality results unless there is (a) a new course of action in an attempt to overcome or by-pass the thwarting barrier and reach the goal, or (b) modification, shifting, or replacement of the goal until satisfying progress toward a goal becomes possible. These processes go on persistently. Actions that result in satisfying achievement are repeated until the development of the organism or changes in the environment require new action patterns. Actions that fail to bring the individual closer to his goals are abandoned (if their results are recognized) and replaced. Those instances in which complete blocking occurs—in which the individual experiences repeated failures and finds no means of progress toward acceptable goals—lead to the disintegration of personality. This description of the adjustive process does not emphasize sufficiently the fact that the needs, drives, motives, and goals of the individual change. They are constantly subjected to the combined influences of maturation and experience. Furthermore, there are usually a variety of ways by which any given need can be satisfied, and to this must be added another fact that is of prime importance—the individual has the capacity for altering his level of aspiration upward or downward in the light of the degree of success he is experiencing. Thus, every person is confronted with the necessity of making repeated choices and evolving plans for action through which whatever choices he makes are to be achieved.

F. H. Finch and Velma Yowell, "Guidance for the Exceptional Child," *The Education of Exceptional Children,* Forty-ninth Yearbook of the National Society for the Study of Education, Part II. Chicago: The University of Chicago Press, 1950, chap. 5, pp. 85-86. By permission of the Society.

270. FRUSTRATION OF MOTIVES—A SUMMARY

Along with motives themselves, another dynamic factor influencing social behavior is frustration of motives. Following the clinicians, we described the "defense mechanisms" which serve to guide and channel behavior arising from frustration and conflict. The major mechanisms—repression, rationalization, displacement, projection, regression, fantasy, identification, compensation, sublimation—are learned in social contexts and produce behavior which is primarily social. To some extent, also, they are perpetuated by social influences. For example, in our society, people are expected to rationalize. Demagogues encourage displacement by suggesting scapegoats upon whom our anger and hostility can be vented. Social taboos upon sex and aggression facilitate repression, which in turn often leads to other kinds of mechanisms.

A systematic interpretation of reaction to frustration is proposed, according to the sequence: frustration, emotion, mechanism, overt behavior. The blocking of a strong motive arouses a pronounced emotional reaction, typically anger or fear, which impels the individual toward overt behavior. Anger tends to produce aggression and fear withdrawal, but the precise pattern of overt behavior is also determined by the mechanism employed and by the individual's perception of the situation. Some persons have learned to repress, displace, regress, rationalize, and so on and are predisposed toward one or another of these mechanisms. However, whether or not a mechanism is employed also depends on the social situation as the individual interprets it. Thus, in the presence of superiors one is more likely to repress; of inferiors, to displace; of sympathetic friends, to rationalize.

The frustration-aggression hypothesis is criticized as too general. Sometimes frustration evokes anxiety or insecurity feelings which eventuate, via mechanisms like compensation, fantasy, identification, or sublimation, in nonaggressive behavior. Whether or not aggression occurs depends upon the nature of the frustration, the emotion aroused, and the mechanism called into play. Each phase of the reaction to frustration is affected by past learning and by perception of the immediate situation.

To understand and to predict reaction to frustration, all these factors must be taken into account.

The significance of frustration as a determinant of social behavior is underscored by several students of child development. They find the origins of much neurotic and antisocial behavior in the intense and prolonged frustrations which sometimes occur during infancy.

> S. Stansfeld Sargent, *Social Psychology*. New York: The Ronald Press Company, 1950, pp. 198-99.

271. THREE CLASSES OF THWARTING FACTORS

. . . As long as established habits function smoothly no adjustment need be made. When a motive is aroused in a situation for which no ready-made solution exists, thwarting may be said to occur and diffused activity is the result.

Factors that thwart human urges may be divided, conveniently though arbitrarily, into three general classes. The simplest type of thwarting exists when a drive is blocked by an *environmental obstacle*. The cat's thwarting is obviously environmental. If a man's newspaper is not delivered on time or if his automobile stalls in the street, his activities suffer blocking because of material circumstances. The sex drives of prisoners are thwarted by the fact that no persons of the opposite sex are attainable. Laws and customs of society and the activities of other persons, form environmental difficulties and arouse adjustive behavior.

A second class of thwarting is that which occurs because of some *personal defect* of the individual. For the sex motives of a young man to be thwarted because he lives on a lonely farm would be manifestly environmental; for these motives to be thwarted because he is so ugly, uncouth or stupid that girls avoid him would illustrate blocking by personal defect. Physical defects such as lameness or ugliness, mental defects, social defects such as lack of position or education, provide many of the obstacles which prevent the direct satisfaction of motives. It is obvious that environmental and personal thwartings are interdependent. A person of little ability or training in any given trait will succumb to a very small material obstacle. If an individual has high personal endowment, a very great obstacle may be overcome easily. The importance of the distinction between thwarting by environmental obstacle and by personal defect lies in the responses of the individual to his situation. If a person recognizes a thwarting as due to external causes the adjustive attempts are likely to be calm and constructive. Recognition of personal defect, however, implies a helplessness, a lack of available appropriate habits or qualities. An emotional response, typically of the fear type, is therefore aroused. This general condition of inner turmoil renders responses less effective and increases the need for adjustment. Another view of the role of personal defect in blocking is that it arouses a secondary chain of adjustive procedures. A personal defect means a thwarting of the strong and important self motives and leads to vigorous attempts to reduce the intense emotional tensions engendered.

A motive may also be blocked by *conflict with antagonistic motive*. A young woman much in love with a married man suffers from the thwarting of sex, by conflict with the social-approval motive. . . . The term conflict means that the individual confronts a complex situation to different aspects of which he has learned to make antagonistic responses. To the love aspect of the situation the young woman of the illustration has a tendency to make an approaching response toward the person she loves. The social-approval aspect of the situation directs her to make an avoidant response. Since the two antagonistic responses cannot be made at the same time the tension remains unreduced and adjustive activity is demanded. In a thwarting situation of the environmental type the individual has no adequate habit by which to respond. In the conflict situation, on the other hand, he has too many habits and the adjustment must be a selection or a compromise.

Varied Response.   The varied responses to a situation have often been termed *trial and error* reactions. . . .

So far varied response has been considered as a series of muscular activities, but this is not always the case. Instead of making physical attempts a man may indicate his trials by words or other symbols, and even judge on the basis of his past learning whether an indicated trial would be successful or not. If you are confronted with the problem of discovering the best way into town, you do not rush down one street after another trying to find the way by muscular exertion. You try the routes by naming them or by the use of other symbols such as gestures, postures and attitudes, or else seek the aid of the more obvious symbolism of maps, guidebooks or spoken advice. This process of thinking or reasoning is mental or symbolic adjustment and often leads to greater effectiveness in living. . . .

Efficiency in adjustment depends in great degree on the ability of an individual to continue varying his responses until success is achieved. In many instances, found both in the laboratory and in everyday life, the adjustment process is hindered by excessive persistence in an unadaptive mode of activity. This tendency to be unable to vary behavior sufficiently results in what have been termed *persistent nonadjustive reactions*.

> Laurance Frederic Shaffer, *The Psychology of Adjustment*. Boston: Houghton Mifflin Company, 1936, pp. 117-21.

272. HEALTHY FORMS OF ADJUSTING

In a complex environment such as that in which people live in the present age, it is impossible for all of us to achieve our goals. . . .

Thwartings are, then, inevitable. . . . In general, adjustment to thwarting may take place in any one of at least three different ways: (1) by direct attack; (2) by compensation; and (3) by flight. The first of these is by all odds the preferable one from the standpoint of the preservation of the mental health of the individual. As its name suggests, it demands the unflinching facing of reality and the persistent confronting of one's obstacles with an aggressive determination to conquer them. It suggests the axiomatic perseverance of the traveler who, finding his way barred by a towering wall that he could not scale, tunnel under, nor pass around, retracted his steps across the world and so came out on the other side of his obstacle! . . . There are undoubtedly plenty of people in the world who keep on attempting the impossible, even after they learn, or ought to have learned, that they can never succeed in their present attempts. For such people, a substitute or escape form of release becomes imperative.

. . . (2) *Adjustment by Compensation.* Direct attack upon
our problems, in the belief that with determination and aggressiveness they can be resolved and happiness or success
achieved, is the normal, healthy attitude for any individual to
assume. Lacking the character or the moral fiber to persist in
frontal attack, and still chafing against thwartings of fundamental urges, or perhaps honestly convinced that the battle
cannot be won, an individual may adopt some form of compensatory activity which will bring satisfaction of a different
sort, and in so doing spare her ego. Within certain limits compensation is distinctly valuable and all normal people unques-
tionably profit considerably from its operation. If one cannot
achieve her desires in one direction, she can often change their
nature or direction, or substitute some other within reach, and
so achieve satisfaction and do no violence to her self-feeling.

There are so many cravings that beset us that it is humanly
impossible to satisfy them all; indeed, if all of them could be
satisfied, life would tend to become unstimulating and unin-
teresting. We learn rather early in life, if we are completely
sane, that nobody is so fortunate as to realize all his goals, but
that each individual finds happiness in the successful driving
toward a few worthwhile objectives, and in frictionless resig-
nation from the pursuit of others that are beyond reach. In this
counter-balancing of substituted successes and renounced
goals, most individuals at length achieve their serenity and adjustment.

As illustrations of the compensatory mechanism, one might
mention the young woman who, denied the boon of good looks,
patiently sets herself the task of developing an attractive personality, or a warm and friendly heart, or a challenging intellect, and so arrives at substitute happiness; the poorly en-
dowed high school boy who, unable to impress his personality
through his classroom performance, wins his way through the
cultivation of a good-natured disposition, or attractive social
graces, or compelling athletic prowess, and the like; the family
man who, unsuccessful and impractical in his business, finds
happiness and serenity in being the sort of husband and father
that endears him to the whole family circle, and who does not
resent some other man's success in making a fortune in the

business world; the married woman who, denied children that she has dreamed of mothering, directs her energies into social settlement work, child welfare activities, or into vicariously mothering the children of others, or, if she has the talent, even into the creative channels of literature or art; the bereaved wife who seeks solace and substitute happiness in her gardens, or charities, or music; the humble religionist who finds in his faith a compensating joy for all the things he has lost or lacks; the woman teacher who, without family of her own, is happy and content in her ministry to the children of others, or in such other sublimated experiences as she learns to substitute for those denied her.

These are all examples of healthy, sane forms of compensatory experience which enriches life and brings joy and peace to the individual. In each case there has been thwarting of fundamental cravings: cravings for good looks, good scholarship, wealth and business success, children, preservation of the family circle. Deprived of these objectives, one may yet know compensatory forms of personal expenditure of energy and purpose.

> Lawrence A. Averill, *Mental Hygiene for the Classroom Teacher*. New York: Pitman Publishing Corporation, 1939, pp. 28-34. (Selected.)

273. ADJUSTIVE BEHAVIOR AND ITS MECHANISMS

Mechanisms of Adjusting. The process of integrating seems to work in a "normal" way when the environment permits the individual need fulfillment through purposeful action. This is true with reservations. A girl develops a need to own a much-admired dress in a shop window. She purposes to get it; she may have the money; she may have to save for it; she may have to wait until payday; then she buys it. Her tensions are resolved in the satisfaction of wearing the new garment. But suppose, as she is figuring out how to buy the dress, she realizes that buying it means she cannot go to the beach for that week's vacation with her friends. She has desire, she has purpose in relation to the dress and going to the beach. There may be other demands upon her pocketbook—her room rent, her laundry bill. What does she do? How do human beings get themselves out

of such predicaments? How are tensions arising out of conflicting needs resolved? Obviously, they cannot all be resolved by
taking the direct road to need fulfillment.

Psychologists have made the many ways taken to meet conflicting desires familiar to us through such terms as "rationalization," "substitution," "projection," "sublimation," "identification," "compensation," "regression," and many more. These
ways fall into three general types, as shown in behavior. One
type is an aggressive attack on an environment in which an
individual is blocked, is too much frustrated in fulfilling his
wishes, urges, and desires. Attention getting, bullying, dominating others are forms of attack behavior. They are forms
frequently taken by persons who feel insecure, inferior, or
frustrated. If the girl who wanted the new dress had stolen
the money to buy it, that would have been an attack on an environment that did not permit her to satisfy her need.

Another type of behavior is withdrawal from an unsatisfactory environment. Daydreaming and passivity are familiar
forms. The girl might have satisfied her need for the dress
through fantasy. If she could not buy the dress, she could have
used the adjustive mechanism of withdrawal to maintain satisfactory relationships with her environment, to relieve tensions. There is danger, however, that withdrawal from an unsatisfactory real world into an inner world of fantasy, where the
individual has the most beautiful dresses in the world, will
lead to poorer adjustment. In that case, the girl does not solve
her problems by facing them in the real world; she escapes into
a world of fantasy where the problems vanish away.

The third type of adjustive behavior is "substituting" and
there are many forms. Some of these are satisfying needs
vicariously through identification with another person who has
or achieves what is desired; rationalizing—a very familiar form
being, "Oh, well, it isn't any good anyway"; substituting behavior patterns suitable to a younger person when the individual cannot meet a situation at his level of development; sublimating a need for fulfillment in one way into fulfillment in a
different way.

It is important to realize that these ways of adjusting—attack, withdrawal, and substituting—all function in the biolog-

ical process of integrating as means of releasing tensions. They are normal roads to need fulfillment as long as they serve to bring about better adjustment to the environment. When they become defense mechanisms, they are dangerous to satisfactory personality development because they result in poorer adjustment to the environment.

"Problem" Behavior. "Problem" behavior, evidenced in attack, withdrawal, or substituting, shows that individuals are disturbed and seeking a way out of their difficulties. It may or may not be evidence that the ways of adjusting are being used as defense weapons in situations the individual cannot or will not face directly. If persistently manifested, it may be the sign that the individual is taking an escape route to avoid facing his problems. On the other hand, resort to aggression, rebellion, lying, daydreaming, and so on, may simply be signs of immaturity, signs that the individual has not yet learned to take the way leading toward more satisfactory adjustment. These behaviors all too frequently point to an environment that is too coercive, too authoritarian, too insecure. The individual is restricted in meeting his needs, to the degree that he becomes afraid or rebellious and is compelled; he must act in ways to save himself from disintegration. He withdraws or becomes aggressive or makes some kind of substitution for an unsatisfying situation.

If we think of Gesell and Ilg's concept of growth as a spiral movement toward the next stage of development, this helps us to see attack, withdrawal, or substituting behavior as signs of immaturity. The growing individual has new needs, faces new demands from the environment continuously as he moves toward the next stage in his development. He must learn new patterns of responding and in learning them moves from instability in their use toward stability. As the new ways of behaving are established he depends less and less on earlier learned responses, which brought satisfactory adjustment. Behavior must be interpreted in the light of where the individual is in his progress toward maturity as well as in relation to environmental restrictions and demands before it can be labeled "problem" behavior in the limited sense that educators are apt to use the term. For example, if a small child lies his way out of a difficulty, this does not mean, *ipso facto,* a disintegrating personality, but if an adult habitually uses this same device, we have reason to look upon the behavior as an attempt to escape from reality and to search for evidences of personality disturbance. We can consider such an individual immature.

> Rosalind Cassidy and Hilda C. Kozman, *Counseling Girls in a Changing Society.* New York: McGraw-Hill Book Company, 1947, pp. 121-24. By permission of the publishers.

274. Adjustment Mechanisms—Good and Bad

The methods of meeting conflict and responding to group pressures are many and various. If a problem can be met with fair readiness in a reasonable time, the person advances. If he is frustrated or continually blocked, various types of substitute activities and emotional outlets appear, especially when pressures are continued over a period of time and cumulate. We are not primarily concerned with reactions to single or momentary situations, because most persons are likely at one time or another to exhibit almost every type of normal and abnormal behavior. We are greatly concerned with that behavior which, in the face of continued frustration, becomes such an organized habit or method of meeting problems that it interferes with or destroys the person's flexibility and adaptability. In good adjustment, the person becomes free of the tension produced by the situation and moves on in a relaxed way to meet new problems. In inadequate adjustment, the situation retains its tension-producing character because it is dodged or avoided, and it continues to dominate the person.

Some of the outlets discussed center about tension or oscillation and consist either of procrastinating the situation or of anticipating it by worries and anxieties. The next group of reactions is the aggressive group. In these reactions, the person attacks the situation with devices of various degrees of complexity and social acceptability. These devices vary from simple aggression, through superiority attitudes and peculiar abilities, to the substitute activities in which the person sublimates the basic tension. The latter is a desirable form of outlet in that the result is socially acceptable and in many instances, after a time, will lead the person back to good adjustment.

The next reactions are projective, in that they mean either a denial of the situation or a covering up in order to avoid a tension-producing situation. The person may make defensive actions, may rationalize or make excuses, may separate his behavior into logic-tight compartments, may develop an inferiority attitude, or may go so far as to develop an inferiority complex, in which his feelings of inadequacy spread over many situations.

The next group of reactions are escape reactions or retreats from reality, in which the person moves out of the field of forces into an area in which his tensions can be satisfied indirectly. He may use literature and art as forms of escape; he may identify himself with various characters, either fictional or real; he may solve his problems by daydreaming or fantasy; he may go into an unreal world with drugs; or he may develop a physical disability by means of which he avoids his problem but maintains his self-respect and the respect of the group.

Next come the reactions in which difficulties are projected upon other persons or objects. These projective reactions may be exaggerated into extremes which greatly distort reality and may result in delusional systems. Finally, there are regressions to more primitive and immature modes of reaction, and the breaking apart of the bonds of the personality, so that the person is dissociated and needs special treatment.

From the practical standpoint, the problems of meeting reality and of adequate adjustment are problems of learning to face the situations which exist, to distinguish between the significant and the insignificant, and to work out a way of life in the midst of many pressures. The person who has not mastered these processes cannot acquire them in a moment, as they involve a substantial re-education and a reorganization of his way of life. They involve attacking the problems of life in a straightforward, rather frank, direct, and flexible way, rather than bowing under every wind that blows or becoming rigid and abnormal in meeting pressures. The adjusted personality is one that remains flexible and open and moves from one circumstance to another, without too many tag ends of emotional response carrying over into the new situations from the old.

> John E. Anderson, *The Psychology of Development and Personal Adjustment.* New York: Henry Holt and Company, Inc., 1949, pp. 477-79. By permission of the publishers.

275.   SOME ADJUSTMENTS LEAD TO WARPED AND DWARFED PERSONALITIES

The great majority of individuals have the capacity to develop reasonably wholesome and desirable personalities, but the circumstances of life which many have had to meet have warped or dwarfed them. Instead of learning wholesome ways of meeting the situations of life, such persons have developed undesirable personality characteristics which bring difficulty to themselves and make them a problem to others.

Unsatisfactory conduct patterns are of two distinct and opposite types. Some persons meet the situations of life by various kinds of withdrawing behavior, others by different forms of aggression. One type of person runs away from and avoids responsibilities and difficulties; the other meets them by fighting and aggression. One has subnormal temperature and the other fever. Each type of conduct has an extended repertory. The withdrawing type includes the individual who is sensitive and easily hurt, who is extremely good, who withdraws within himself and pouts, or works out his problems in a dream world. IIe may actually run away from responsibility and become a truant at school, give up a job, desert his family, get sick, or in extreme cases commit suicide. The aggressive individual, on the other hand, shows off, bluffs, makes dogmatic or sarcastic statements, develops temper tantrums, is the bully, carries a chip on his shoulder, fights at the drop of a hat, or develops more serious forms of criminal conduct.

These two opposite types of conduct are symptomatic of the same kind of difficulty. In animal and primitive life, the individual in the presence of danger runs, and if cornered fights; but our social mores put so great a disapproval upon cowardice that the tendency in our life is to fight instead of to run, and those who do not fight have to find respectable and approved ways of giving up. But it must not be supposed that the individual who fights is always courageous, and the one who gives up is always a coward. Extreme aggression is often a cover for fear; the bully is always a coward at heart. Dogmatic assertion looks like assurance, but it is often a cover for uncertainty. The more dogmatically a person protests, the less sure he is likely to be of himself and of what he asserts.

The conduct-patterns of warped and dwarfed personalities will not be understood if it is supposed they are deliberately adopted. The individual has hit upon them in his efforts to meet situations he did not succeed in managing in more normal ways. Those patterns which are most persistent usually had their origin in infancy and early childhood, before the age of rational choice of ways of behaving. In infancy and childhood one develops his basic ways of meeting life's situations, attitudes which may be called a "style of life," (This phrase is the one used by Alfred Adler) or styles of life. The fundamental skills and the basic attitudes are developed in these earlier years, so that by adolescence the individual's patterns for meeting life are for the most part formed. . . .

It must also be recognized that however undesirable a pattern of conduct may seem to be, it nevertheless has positive value to the one who uses it. It is his way of protecting himself in the presence of difficulty, or it is in some way useful in getting him what he wants or in getting him out of what he would avoid. No one would say glasses are desirable, but they are essential to seeing for the person with poor eyes and they have positive value to him. Walking on crutches is hardly a desirable method of getting around, but for the lame man they may be essential. No one will give up glasses or crutches unless he has found a better way of seeing or walking. So the various behavior patterns are aids that the individual has adopted in order to get around in life, and he will give them up only as he finds some other way which gives him more security, success, and satisfaction. Human behavior is thus recognized as purposive, in that it is developed through the experience of the individual as he finds his way around the world, and is of some use in the individual's adaptation to his surroundings.

Harrison Sacket Elliott and Grace Loucks Elliott, *Solving Personal Problems*. New York: Henry Holt and Company, Inc., 1936, pp. 41-44. By permission of the publishers.

276.   Nature of the Solution of Difficulties in the Adjusted and Unadjusted

In general, the well-balanced, efficient person attempts to solve his problems in a frank, straightforward manner. He first tries to understand the facts of life and then faces them squarely as they are, no matter how disagreeable or forbidding they may be. He meets his obstacles openly, candidly, and unemotionally, or under conditions of emotional control. He attempts to make a direct frontal attack on the problem itself, instead of trying to side-step or evade it or run away from it. Before reaching a decision or making a response, he tries to size up the whole situation and to evaluate its components, relations, and interrelations, so that he will be able to react to the situation in its entirety after due consideration of all the important relevant facts and circumstances. Another way of emphasizing these traits is to say that the well-adjusted person, in the handling of his problems of adjustment to his inner or outer world, tries to maintain a thoroughly objective or scientific attitude, the scientific attitude being merely the perfection of the objective method of approach in the solution of problems. He is objective-minded. He keeps his attention focused on the objective aspects of his problems—the objective adjustments that he must make, the tasks he must perform—instead of becoming preoccupied with his subjective states—his feelings, timidities, diffidences, prejudices, caprices, egocentric trends, and imagination. If he becomes subjective-minded, he focuses attention on himself merely in order to arrive at an accurate appraisal of his assets and deficits or to obtain self-understanding. In addition to all this, the well-adjusted person tries to respond in a manner reasonably consistent with the social goals and standards of the community and not too inconsistent with his own convictions and personal integrity.

The outcome in the case of most normal persons who thus attack the vicissitudes and exigencies of life and who have reached the age of discretion and are fairly well adjusted is a reasonably satisfactory or victorious solution of life's ordinary problems and often of the more baffling ones also.

But the unadjusted or maladjusted or inefficient individual, instead of attacking his problems in a forthright, objective manner, resorts to a great variety of subterfuges, tricks, and blinds for concealing his failures, shortcomings, or dissatisfactions or for dodging reality and retreating from the ugly facts of life into an illusory, subjective nirvana of security. The numerous response mechanisms that unadjusted persons adopt for solving their problems are probably only variant behavior patterns for cloaking their inadequacies, for disguising their feelings, for evading their responsibilities, and for finding security and satisfaction in deceptive compromises. All of them can be classed as defense mechanisms which the individual consciously or unconsciously adopts to hide, avoid, or overcome his real or imagined deficiencies.

From the mental-health point of view, response mechanisms such as these, when frequently used as a means of escape from difficulties or as a means of solving shortcomings, are inimical to the preservation of mental efficiency and often are disruptive of mental integrity. To be sure, they often appear outwardly successful, for they enable the individual to "get by" temporarily. They may enable him to attain his immediate goals, however inferior or unworthy they may be, or however undesirable the means used to attain them, although frequently the immediate outcomes spell disappointment and frank failure. Even where some form of compromise solution yields temporary satisfaction, the ultimate effect is frequently ruinous to the individual's well-being. Transient victories are often obliterated by the ultimate boomerang of defeat. In the end these deceptive mechanisms may generate a host of mental conflicts and difficulties, which may lead to further dissatisfactions, other unhealthy or inadequate modes of response, mental distortions, and sometimes, eventually, nervous or mental derailments, such as frank neuroses or psychoses.

J. E. Wallace Wallin, *Personality Maladjustments and Mental Hygiene.* New York: McGraw-Hill Book Company, Inc., 1949, pp. 263-64. By permission of the publishers.

277. A Boy Learned the Hard Way

As far back as I can remember I have always been threatened by my father in regard to failing in school. He often reminded me that if I ever flunked a course he would put me in a reform school on a charge of negligent behavior or something similar to that. I have never feared this threat, but I did not want to experience the consequences, i.e.,—the losing of my parental home; respect; being an outcast; and not being able to finish school. Sometimes I "prayed" for leniency (in trying to atone for my neglect), but for the most part managed to keep well up to "par" all through grammar school and high school.

Consequently, when I entered college I had a very good background and concrete basis for this fear. During the first quarter I failed one of my courses. I felt the full force of this long-lived fear. I became moody and downhearted upon receiving the notice, and for a week I thought about this catastrophe. However, I obtained relief through criticism of the teacher's methods and the material presented and also of my parent's attitude. I now realize that my own negligence created a distaste for the material and the teacher, but I still defend my opinion concerning my parent's (father's) attitude.

My father is a person who cannot accept defeat without a display of temper, and many rash acts. I cannot discuss my school grades with him because he is pleasant only when the marks are good. He does not want to hear the bad side. I have always believed that I could do much better in school and live a more rational social life if I could openly discuss both sides of the question with my father and obtain his help and cooperation in overcoming my weak points.

Needless to say, I have not told him of this loss of credit, and I am not sure if I am ever going to tell him.

The most harmful outcome of this fear is the habitual practice of lying, which I have developed to a fine degree.

Written by a student in one of the editor's classes.

278. The New Student Faces Adjustment Problems

Adjustments vary in nature and in quality. Some persons successfully adapt themselves to their surroundings, others acquire unfortunate habits of conduct which hinder rather than aid the eventual satisfactory solution of their difficulties. Each autumn thousands of freshmen arrive at the colleges and universities. In a new environment many adjustive problems confront them. Most of these students adjust satisfactorily. They find new friends, cultivate new interests and participate in new activities that serve as outlets to their needs and drives. Other freshmen fare less well. Some become seclusive and shun the situations that compel them to adjust. A few will become homesick, seeking the satisfactions that have been hitherto cherished instead of acquiring new ones. A number will adjust by showing off or by becoming eccentric, gaining in this way a certain notice and distinction that they fail to attain in more usual channels.

Laurance Frederic Shaffer, *The Psychology of Adjustment.* Boston: Houghton Mifflin Company, 1936, p. 4.

279. ILLUSTRATION OF POOR ADJUSTMENT

We do not have to go to the psychological laboratory to find evidence as to the nature of adjustive behavior. The pattern can be found in innumerable real-life situations. . . . If a clerk in an office is severely reprimanded by his employer, adjustive behavior is demanded. An emotional tension is aroused by the thwarting of mastery and approval motivation. Since the clerk may not be able to combat the situation directly, he tends to discover other tension-reducing outlets. He may curse under his breath, imagine what he would do if he were in the employer's place, or plan a brilliant retort that he is unable to make overtly. The clerk may reduce his tension by a brisk walk around the block or by soundly and unnecessarily spanking his eldest child when he arrives at home, or by quarreling with his wife. In the broad biological sense these behaviors are not adaptive for they do not solve any problem or assist the individual in overcoming his difficulty. But in the individual and psychological sense these are adjustive, for they satisfy or reduce a drive. Such adjustments may be termed inadequate, substitute or unreal, but they are adjustments none the less. They arise in the same manner and follow the same sequence as do the more effectively adjustive behaviors.

Ibid., pp. 115-16.

280. SHAFFER DEFINES GOOD ADJUSTMENT

. . . When the inter-related motives of a person are satisfied without undue emphasis or slighting of any one motive, and when this is achieved with consideration for the adjustments of other persons, then a state of good adjustment may be said to exist.

Ibid., p. 138.

281. ADJUSTMENT IN A CHANGING WORLD

As he grows, every individual has to adjust his behavior to the demands of his time and place. Adjustment has become a key concept in our educational thinking. We conceive of the person as an active, striving organism which seeks its own maintenance and the satisfaction of basic urges and needs. We believe that the growing individual needs to have experiences which enable him to solve the problems which arise as he grows in ability to handle his own adjustments.

We are no longer satisfied with the view that the child is a passive receptacle into which can be poured the knowledge and skills which an adult authority establishes as desirable. To-day we prefer to understand the growth of the child toward maturity as an active rather than a passive process and as a process in which the child learns to perform in certain ways because he is a selective organism making adjustments to his own problems. The conception of education as adjustment means that the educator plays a *positive*, contributory, and indispensable role in guiding the growth of the young. He is seen as the intermediary between the needs and problems of the young and the conditions of the community in which these needs and problems are to be solved. The educator is called upon to guide, clarify, interpret, and balance the socialization process and to participate actively in community groups so that the community may become increasingly a good community for the young. The teacher, far from being released of the responsibility for planning, creating, and appraising the educational process, is of determining importance in the whole enterprise.

Harl R. Douglass, editor, *Education for Life Adjustment.*

New York: The Ronald Press Company, 1950, p. 68. (From chapter by A. S. Clayton.)

282. GROWTH THROUGH ADJUSTMENT

EXPERIENCING DESIRABLE HABITS OF ADJUSTMENT

Growing up is necessarily a process in which boys and girls experience thwartings and frustrations. Environmental restrictions, personal inadequacies, conflicting urges, and educational deficiencies may block the ready achievement of demanded goals. As a consequence, the adolescent may adopt a problem-solving attitude and seek to realign himself toward the overcoming of an obstacle. Or he may set up an adequate alternative outcome and seek its fulfillment. But the individual may also learn some other less desirable way of responding to his frustrations. He may escape into a world of fantasy; he may develop ailments which remove him from control over his problem; he may rationalize, fight, lie, steal, play truant from school, or worry and fret about his unfortunate condition. In any event he learns some way of responding which becomes a resource for action when another frustration occurs. Habits of adjustment or maladjustment are continually being formed.

Boys and girls need an opportunity to study the processes by which habits and dispositions are formed in the process of satisfying basic needs. They need to understand that their individual problems are not unique or abnormal and that all individuals encounter similar difficulties. They need experiences in recreating behavior patterns so as to achieve self-understanding and an ability to apply healthy solutions to personal problems. Lessons in preventive and therapeutic mental health are vital necessities in an education for life adjustment.

EXPANDING FRUSTRATION TOLERANCE

Understanding the process of adjustment is essential to the promotion of mental and social health, yet in itself is not sufficient. As we have already noted, experiences in frustration are an inevitable part of the process of attaining maturity, for the growing individual must learn how to respond to his needs in socially accepted fashion. He must learn to control and channel his impulses so that others accord him approval and respect.

Furthermore, feelings of insecurity, conflict, and frustration are increasingly prevalent because of the changes which have occurred in our society. Feelings of anxiety are multiplied in a corporate, industrial, urban, interdependent, dynamic social order. As these characteristics of our culture are enduring and permanent, we should expect that anxiety and frustration will continue to be common in the lives of all of us.

These observations lead us to believe that acquiring an ability to withstand thwartings, insecurities, and privations is essential to mental and social health. The modern citizen needs a series of controlled experiences in which he enlarges his ability to accept and assimilate frustration. He needs a high degree of frustration tolerance so that he may recognize blockings of his needs and still be able to maintain himself at a high level of personal efficiency. It should be noticed that we are not suggesting a return to the older doctrine of a mental state cultivated by the formal disciplining of a particular capacity. Instead, we are suggesting that a realistic view of contemporary living conditions shows that basic needs may not be satisfied to the degree that an individual feels adequate. The individual needs to learn to endure frustrations.

DEVELOPING A DISCIPLINED PERSONALITY

Boys and girls need to grow in ability to withstand the effects of frustration. They also need opportunities to undertake considered action and to persist in the presence of difficulties, distractions, and setbacks interfering with the achievement of chosen ends. Since most of our undertakings involve other persons, growth should include the ability to withhold one's immediate and ego-serving tendencies in favor of a conjoint working toward the solution. Becoming a mature person consists in achieving a discipline which makes our behavior thoughtful, persistent, and sensitive to the reactions of others. Adjusting to life situations means learning ways of contributing constructive endeavor to problems in which others are involved.

The discipline which should be encouraged in the modern

school is not merely a matter of the maintenance of law and order, or of providing suitable punishment, or of providing for the orderly acquisition of formal subject matter. Boys and girls need a discipline for the democratic solving of meaningful problems. Such a positive discipline is essential to successful schooling because contemporary life imposes demands for thoughtful group deliberation and endeavor. The problems of delinquency, marital incompatibility, and community planning, to mention a few, require a disciplined citizen who knows what he is about, how to engage in fruitful cooperative action, and how to persevere over a long pull in the face of difficulty and confusion. Constructive, group-centered discipline is an essential in attaining maturity.

Ibid., pp. 74-76.

283. HELPING THE CHILD TO ADJUST

Study? Search? Wait? And Do Nothing?

No! You don't have to know causes finally and exactly before you can begin to help the child. There are lots of things you can do, even while you are looking.

The biggest thing: Give him ways to get back at the world . . . ways that are safe and possible.

You have to be creative here. There are no golden tricks. What you can do depends on the age of the child; it depends on you, and on the classroom, and the space and time you have. But you can use your curriculum, the regular daily program you have, to help his feelings come out in more acceptable ways.

It is this kind of thing: You know how sometimes you would like to bang the table when you are mad . . . how you could kick something when you are feeling angry . . . how you want to strike out wildly when you are frightened? These children need opportunities—acceptable, safe, and possible— to do this too. It makes them feel better inside and they need to hit children less.

You can think of possibilities that fit you and that fit into your class program. More shop work and more nails to hit perhaps? A punching bag that the child can sock? More clay to pound? Games where roughhouse is O.K.? More out-of-door play where shouting is not a crime? Dolls the child can boss around in play? More top-of-the-voice singing of lively songs?

Or perhaps your children can make puppets? (Then the puppet is the bossy bully one.) Or children sometimes can express their feelings through little plays they make up, plays in which some of the characters are bossy. Or they can tell stories or write themes on "Once when I was angry . . . " and topics like that.

There are rhythms or art or speech or dramatics or English. But it depends on how you use them. You will have to work out your own ideas but all the activities where hitting-punching-squeezing and talking-big fit into your curriculum will usually help a child like this.

What Is Progress?

Think through what progress you expect from a youngster like this. You mustn't hope that he will move from hitting to not-hitting all at once. That is too abrupt.

There are some in-between steps.

When a child is improving, when he is hitting less, he may threaten more. He may talk about hitting. He may use more bad language. Or he may bully with words but not with his hands. These are all good signs. They are signs that you are really on the right track. . . .

You know that you are dealing with an unhappy child. You know that there are reasons now why he has to act the way he does. But you are bringing nearer the day when he will feel safe with people and safe with the world.

> James L. Hymes, Jr., *Teacher Listen—the Children Speak . . .*
> Philadelphia: National Mental Health Foundation, 1949,
> pp. 15-17.

11.

Relation of the Individual and His Environment

A. The General Problem

284. SOCIAL ASPECTS PARAMOUNT

It should always be remembered that the interactive process in and through which mental development takes place is carried on with reference to the whole of the individual's effective environment. To be sure, this is obvious from the very nature of interaction itself, for clearly in any such transaction between himself and the world about him the learner could not, even if he would, isolate himself from any influence which plays upon him from any source. It is obvious, too, on the basis of everyday common sense. Everybody knows that a job of learning is affected by far more than the contents of the book being studied, or the arrangement of the instrument on which skill is being acquired. Such a job is affected by the conditions of the room, by the presence or absence of other people, by the notice they take of what one is doing, by recent annoyances, by anticipated pleasures or pains—in short, by the entire setting of one's life. When a learning experiment is organized in the laboratory, every effort is made to hold general environmental conditions constant for all the subjects. And when a person is trying to learn something in a more ordinary situation, he does not consider it strange to seek a total setting favorable for the task, both as regards time, place, and social arrangements.

Obvious as this proposition may be, its implications are surprisingly overlooked in much of the work of the traditional school. Considerable attention is paid to securing good textbooks, to making sure that desks and seats are of suitable construction and dimensions, and that proper arrangements are made for lighting, heat, and ventilation. The teacher, too, may plan the lesson as a carefully considered series of verbal and visual stimuli. But there the positive attempt to control environmental factors all too often ends. Certain influences of paramount importance to the pupil, and therefore of paramount effect upon his learning, are disregarded, or considered only in a negative sense. These are the social aspects of the situation. The class group is administered chiefly with a view to preventing what are regarded as disturbances. The pupils are treated as though their home relationships, their friendships with and antipathies to their schoolfellows, and, indeed, the whole scheme of their social *milieu*, were entirely irrelevant.

> James L. Mursell, *Educational Psychology*. New York: W. W. Norton and Company, Inc., 1939, pp. 265-66. By permission of the publishers.

285. THE ORGANISMIC CONCEPT

. . The concept of the whole individual, the organismic point of view, seems relatively simple on the surface and yet it is a psychobiological principle requiring a full appreciation of the complex interactions of the zoological and psychological aspects of the individual to produce "mentally integrated behavior" and the relationship of this constantly changing adjusting individual to the world in general. (Billings, E. G., *A Handbook of Elementary Psychobiology and Psychiatry*. New York: Macmillan Co., 1939). The resultant integrate represents the whole individual and, so defined by Warren (Warren, H. C., ed., *Dictionary of Psychology*. New York: Houghton-Mifflin, 1934), the whole is more than the sum of its parts. Further, however, it is that which, in action, gives an individual his own particular behavioral characteristics and personality dynamics and through interaction with the environment determines "the meanings of things in his life." Psychobiology gives us an understanding of the living changing individual with certain inherent capacities and traits, and with certain tendencies toward feeling, doing, and reacting—an understanding of the host, if you will, to which certain life experiences have been attached. It is this individual host, possessing his own basic or innate tendencies which have been modified and conditioned through past experience and present circumstances, who must be understood and interpreted, if he is to have realistic assistance in the solution of his problems. The host is the basic entity which must be reckoned with in all types of guidance, specialized or total, group or individual, normal or abnormal. It is the host who is experiencing the social, personal, vocational, educational, economic, religious, marital, health, or mental problems; therefore, one of the basic requisites of an adequate training program is a series of courses which will provide knowledge of the nature of the host and his behavior.

This emphasis on the particularity of the host by no means denies the importance of the extrinsic experiential factors in the total reaction pattern. The social milieu, in which the individual lives, made up of such factors as the family relationships of which he is a part, the financial status of the family, the accidents and health hazards which threaten him, the academic recognition which he has won, the kind of work he has done, the values of the culture in which he lives, the nature of the economy, and many others, all determine his life meanings. The guidance worker must then be prepared to accumulate the facts regarding the individual's family, his school life, his personal relationships, his financial resources, his social opportunities, and so forth, if he is to evaluate the meanings of these experiences, the frustrations and satisfactions which they bring to the individual, and the attitudes and interests which they engender in him.

> Wilma T. Donahue, Clyde H. Coombs, and Robert M. W. Travers, editors, *The Measurement of Student Adjustment and Achievement*. Ann Arbor: University of Michigan Press, 1949, pp. 73-74. (From chapter by Wilma T. Donahue.)

286. IMPLICATIONS OF ORGANISMIC THEORY

The guidance practitioner who embraces *organismic* theory does not picture a detached individual to be "fitted into" a purely patterned environment but an individual-situation matrix that may be altered, developed, redirected, dissolved. The individual is both stable and fluid and so is the environment; consequently "adjustability" is possible, like a hat to the head if it does not quite fit. One phase of personality may be apparently a poor "fit," e.g., "aptitude," but another phase e.g., "motivation," may make up for this and bring about tolerable total adjustment. Flexibility of individual and environment results in many rough approximations which might seem impossible on a purely predictive basis.

Yet there is such a thing as one environment being "more favorable" for an individual than another. In youth, favorable individual-environment contexts can be tried out and explored. The same thing can be done in adult life, in part, through counseling, but the difficulty is greater because more definite and fixed interrelations have been established between individual and environment. The individual has many "roles," in the center of which is the "self," and as these roles become established and ingrained, one cannot be changed without influencing the others. Regardless of physical and physiological factors, there is less psychological flexibility in the life of the older person.

From considerations such as these, related to the adoption of the organismic point of view, we may derive a number of conceptions bearing upon guidance and educational practice, like the following:

1. The need for continuous guidance service from kindergarten to, and through, college and adult education is reinforced. Since individuals "grow into" situational contexts, it is better that they adjust and develop in the formative years in such a way that individual-environmental relationships are as favorable as possible. Developmental education is better than remedial education, continuous guidance better than "emergency point" guidance.

2. The individual-environment situation is sufficiently fluid so that much leeway for adjustment is provided for self-directive individuals. Conditions do not admit of determinative predictions but allow for flexible adjustments on the part of intelligent individuals in changing situations. Emphasis should be upon self-understanding, environmental knowledge, ways of relating the self to situations, and self-direction in changing

conditions. Feelings of wider freedom should be released by this process.

3. Various roles which the individual plays in the total scheme of his life derive their color and meaning from each of the other roles and from the pattern of living as a whole, including the values primarily served. Thus, no phase of adjustment, such as vocational adjustment, can be considered in isolation. If education and guidance are properly to prepare and orient individuals, their all-around development must be considered. This means that general orientation and development will involve specializations with an important but not a dominant part; utilitarian values will not be exclusively served; many modes of "success" will be recognized.

4. Since individual and environment are inextricably bound together, education should proceed in a realistic context in which community resources and community-centered education are utilized to the utmost. Education and guidance will be concerned with assisting the community in providing those conditions most suitable for individual development and in helping to develop the kind of individuals best suited to progressive interaction with the community environment. Environment, as well as individual, will be recognized as adaptable. Thus a spirit of industrious and forward-looking optimism and experimentation should pervade a community with an organismic view of life. Fixed limits and an artificial stability and security would be foreign to its beliefs.

5. Individuals and situations should be considered "organically" affiliated to a greater extent. There should be greater tendency to "make something of" the community, area, or region where the individual lives (in company with other cooperative individuals) and less tendency to seek far afield for conditions and opportunities.

6. "Organic" ties will be felt not only with community and region but with the nation and the world. Greater sensitivity to interrelationships should be felt throughout society but in a cooperative and collaborative sense.

If organismic theory were accepted, education and guidance would be focused upon individual and social development in the fullest and most comprehensive sense; individuals would be accorded respect for their own unique worth; artificial limitations would not be placed before individual advance; a new sense of freedom might be experienced throughout society.

> Robert Hendry Mathewson, *Guidance Policy and Practice.*
> New York: Harper and Brothers, 1949, pp. 221-24.

287. THE RECIPROCAL ACTION OF THE INDIVIDUAL AND HIS ENVIRONMENT

Moreover, as we understand more clearly the relation of culture and personality and see how "culture coerces the individual and by that coercion distorts the individual who in turn changes the culture so far as his opportunities and capacities will permit," then we will realize that the nature and quality of a society are determined by the personalities who make up that society and these in turn are created by what the family and other agencies of child rearing and education do to and for the child.

> Lawrence K. Frank, "Freud's Influence on Western Thinking and Culture," *American Journal of Orthopsychiatry*, Vol. 10, 1940, p. 882.

288. MAN IS ONE AND INDIVISIBLE

The very foundation of modern psychiatric belief rests on the assumption that it is impossible to lift a single area of an individual's life (such as his vocational fumblings) out of the matrix of the whole and treat that area as a separate, detached, and unrelated part. Rather does the psychiatrist insist that the intellectual, physical, emotional, and work activities of a human being are merely ramifying aspects of one indivisible reactive whole, and that this constitutes a dynamic and ever changing integration, sensitively responding and adjusting itself to each of the myriad forces that continuously play upon it.

> George K. Pratt, "Seeing The Individual Whole," *Occupations*, Vol. 13, No. 2, November, 1934, p. 108.

289. CONSIDER THE WHOLE OF ONE'S LIFE PATTERN

. . It is never possible adequately to deal with any human being unless one takes into consideration the pattern of his life as a whole. This is fully recognized by competent psychiatrists, workers with delinquents, and others. If only one separate segment of an individual's relationships and activities is considered, there will always be factors in his behavior which are not understood and therefore are liable to be improperly treated. A young man comes late to his work. Is it because he spent most of the night in dissipation, or because his wife was sick and needed his services? If we think of nothing at all but his job, it does not seem to matter. But clearly his deserts, and the prospects of his being a valuable employee, are entirely different in the two cases. This simple illustration clearly shows the importance of understanding any person as completely as possible if we wish to do the right thing for him and to get the best results with him.

> James L. Mursell, *Educational Psychology*. New York: W. W. Norton and Company, Inc., 1939, pp. 284-85. By permission of the publishers.

290. INTERRELATION BETWEEN THE CULTURAL AND PSYCHOLOGICAL

Our current interest in culture not only does not in any way represent a trend away from psychological concepts but, in fact, is evidence of our ability to integrate both psychological and cultural contributions within the framework of our practice. At one time we emphasized environmental and social factors; then, the psychological. Now we are seeing more realistically the dynamic interrelationship of both. It may be that our capacity for integration and seeing the whole will best make explicit the interrelation that implicitly exists between the cultural and the psychological.

> William Gioseffi, "The Relationship of Culture to the Principles of Social Casework," *Social Casework*, Vol. 32, No. 5, May, 1951, p. 196.

291. UNITY OF THE INDIVIDUAL-AND-ENVIRONMENT

Growth is the result of the interaction of internal and external factors. The environment has its characteristics and so has the individual, but each changes and is changed by the other. In and through the interaction between the two, the individual becomes a person, and the kind of person he becomes depends in great measure upon cultural factors. Our young people, growing up in a democracy, become different persons than if they grew up in a totalitarian state; growing up in the United States they become different persons than they would be growing up in China or the Solomon Islands. But this is only half the story. Human beings have an ability greater than other biological creatures to shape their environment. They do not have to go all the way in the adjustments between the two that must take place. We do not live as cave men. The phrase "Necessity is the mother of invention" has a deep meaning biologically as well as socially. Out of human needs arise goals, purposes, to seek and find better means of meeting those needs. In goal seeking and goal attaining the individual is changed by and changes his environment.

> Rosalind Cassidy and Hilda C. Kozman, *Counseling Girls in a Changing Society*. New York: McGraw-Hill Book Company, Inc., 1947, pp. 10-11. By permission of the publishers.

292. UNDERSTANDING THE INDIVIDUAL ALONE NOT ENOUGH

The individual is thus visualized in a dynamic and functional relationship with a changing environment which he both influences and is influenced by. Any educative process, and the guidance phases of such a process, cannot therefore overlook the fact that his adjustment and development depend upon not only an understanding of the individual (and action by him) but an understanding of the environment and action in that environment. The educative character and the developmental influence of the environment, in other words, cannot be neglected in any comprehensive educational program. (In depicting a social psychological view of the self, interactive with an environment of which it is a part, Woodard makes an excellent summary of the developmental process whereby social disciplines are internalized, relying heavily upon Mead's formulations.)

> Robert H. Mathewson, *Guidance Policy and Practice*. New York: Harper and Brothers, 1949, p. 30.

293. MAN RESPONDS TO THE ENVIRONMENT AS A WHOLE

The individual is not a disembodied mind, nor is he a body

without a mind. He is a psychobiological organism in constant interaction with a complex array of environmental forces. As an organism he necessarily responds to his environment as a "whole being." Sometimes we break up this essential oneness for purposes of study or special training and talk of intellectual discipline or of the student's physiological needs. In the classroom, for example, intellectual activity takes precedence over everything else as the student gains experience in reasoning, recalling, abstracting, and appreciating. But even in the classroom intellectual activity is never completely separated from emotional and physiological experience, as we see when fatigue affects the ability of the student to concentrate or emotional disturbances vitiate his interest in study. All of the various disciplines, such as physiology, language, morals, æsthetics, and religion, are interpreted in terms of the individual's adjustment to a dynamic environment. Regardless of the different valuation of learning by doing or learning by reading and meditating, whatever the individual does has potential educative value for him and will necessarily be integrated within himself. Emotional, intellectual, and physical experiences are still experiences inherently containing educational significance.

> Paul J. Brouwer, *Student Personnel Services in General Education.* Washington: American Council on Education, 1949, p. 280. (From chapter by Charles W. Cannom.)

B.   *Specific Relation to Guidance Procedure*

294.   SOCIETY AS PATIENT

The chief job of the psychiatrist has been, is, and always will be the treatment of those individuals whose maladjustment, in part at least, is the result of the sorry state of the social order, whose illnesses are reactions to the stresses in their environment. . . . To many people, reduction of stress and increase in support by changes that can be made in the environment are as important of mental health as the making of changes in the personality. Psychiatry is proving to be a social science as well as a medical science.

William C. Menninger, *Psychiatry*. Ithaca: Cornell University Press, 1948, pp. 93-94.

295. GUIDANCE AT THE GRASS-ROOTS

Unaided by the school and other social institutions, mental hygiene clinics and hospitals for the mentally ill can never solve the problems created by emotional difficulties. Agencies like the child guidance clinic deal with the end product of a long series of mistakes—mistakes made by the child, his parents, his school, his community, and society. It is futile to attempt to prevent maladjustment solely by giving expert care to those people who are already in serious difficulty. As long as the school, for example, is allowed to continue procedures which breed and nurture instability, the clinics will never want for patients. As long as there are parents who project their own emotional problems into the lives of their children, we shall have emotional problems among children. Similarly, we can expect no miraculous reduction in the incidence of emotional disorders so long as our society continues to tolerate economic and social conditions which add to the emotional problems of our fellows.

Paul A. Witty and Charles E. Skinner, editors, *Mental Hygiene in Modern Education*. New York: Rinehart and Company, Inc., 1939, p. 475. (From chapter by Harry N. Rivlin.)

296. HEALTHY INDIVIDUALS IN A HEALTHY SOCIETY

Like many other developing fields of professional endeavor, guidance has suffered somewhat from compartmentalized specialization. There are those who say that guidance in this age is impossible until the social and economic problems of our time are settled satisfactorily enough to permit of the unhampered development of personality. For the sake of guidance itself they would have no guidance at all until the united efforts of those interested had achieved this desideratum. On the other hand there are others who accept the present social order and who believe that all our effort should be put into perfecting those psychological techniques which will make personnel work ever more successful. Whatever they may say, they act as if applying the right tests and other tricks of the trade would fit an individual to live and work in our kind of a world regardless of its problems and imperfections.

Both of these extremes should be rejected. Personal adjustment cannot be effected merely by the use of the psychological tools, nor can it be secured without them. The social situation must be taken into account for it too often introduces elements that neglected will negate the best work a guidance or personnel worker can do.

> Edmund De S. Brunner, "The Social Scene and Personal Adjustment," *Occupations*, April, 1939, p. 581.

297. Need to Improve the Culture

Today we must face the task of reconstructing our culture and creating our own design for living, in which the age-old cruelties, frustrations, and deprivations may, we must hope, be mitigated, if not eliminated. For that task we have need of more understanding of personality and culture and, above all, of faith in the value of human life which the new culture must serve. Until the culture makes the conservation of human values the dominant theme, the individual cannot, or will not, find his fulfillment.

> Lawrence K. Frank, "Society As the Patient," *The American Journal of Sociology*, Vol. 42, November, 1936, p. 344.

298. Social Conditions May Stack the Cards

. . . But we may anticipate sufficiently to state that this research, as well as our other studies, shows that it is at the door of our whole society that we must finally lay the blame for our present criminal situation.

From a dozen different sources come the influences that pull down faster than any single social agency can build up. New recruits to crime are being created steadily. There is, therefore, doubt as to how much of a wedge can be made by any case method as long as social conditions stack the cards so heavily against success. With feebleminded, psychotic, or delinquent parents, crowded and dirty homes in a congested, criminalistic neighborhood, poor recreations, few substitutive outlets, and a current rather demoralized ideology—indeed a lack of all that enriches life—how many children can be expected to emerge into the light to take their place with their more fortunate brothers? If we are willing to let millions of our young citizens subsist at these low levels, how can we wonder if they turn against us to wrest from their environment what they can by fair means or foul?

. . . Less unjust social and economic conditions may be the only way out, and until a better social order exists, crime will probably flourish and society continue to pay the price.

> William Healey, Augusta F. Bronner, and Myra E. Shimberg, "The Close of Another Chapter in Crimnology," *Mental Hygiene*, Vol. 19, No. 2, April, 1935, p. 221.

299. PERSONALITY PROBLEMS DO NOT OCCUR IN A VACUUM

Gradually we have discovered for ourselves that all social issues have a direct and important bearing on mental health and that ultimately a frank avowal of the social responsibility of the psychiatrist is required. Understandably this is a disquieting concept; although each day every psychiatrist must certainly see the destructive influences on his patients of the harsh, restrictive environment, we cling tenaciously to the notion that we can isolate the clinical experience from the social.

May I illustrate with a quite simple example: A young Negro girl came to the clinic last year complaining of feelings of inadequacy and failure and an accompanying sense of doom. She is eighteen, quite lovely looking and a painter of more than passing talent. She lives in a deteriorated neighborhood in Harlem, in a tenement flat of four rooms, with her widowed mother, a fairly undisciplined older sister, two younger brothers, an uncle and a boarder. She attends college at night and in the day is employed as a part-time domestic. In addition, since her mother works and the older sister is irresponsible, she takes the larger share of the care of the house. She is engaged to a veteran who too works during the day and goes to college at night. Her consistently repeated complaints were, in the first place, that she never had any privacy; that this lack drove her to compromise solutions, especially in her relationships with her fiancé, which often offended her and sometimes carried her beyond her own concept of responsible behavior; that she could only paint at odd moments and then under adverse circumstances; that she never had a few dollars ahead since their rent was exorbitant and the cost of living, especially in Harlem for a Negro, was so excessive—and, like a constant recurring theme through it all, her resentment at being a Negro and forced to live and work as a member of an out-group.

I should not like to use this simplified story to do anything more than point up the skein that runs through it, of severe social repression, poverty, inadequate housing, unequal opportunities for recreation and suitable cultural activities and, above all, membership in a minority group and all that is implied by that.

To be sure, there are in this girl severe emotional distortions which do not reflect in any apparent ways such factors as these. We must be careful, however, that lacking such evidence we do not assume that the problems of the personality occur in a social vacuum; those important determinants of character and personality which result from the earliest childhood experiences and which are reflected in the inner dynamics of the person also reflect the impact of social reality on parents, teachers and other key persons in the child's life. There is no separation between personality and society but rather an ever-present continuum of forces mutually interacting. . . .

And as a mental hygiene society you, like such societies throughout the land, must come to be the real watchdogs of the mental health of your community. You must, of course, support as vigorously as you possibly can the efforts to improve mental hospitals, to encourage more and better training facilities, to strengthen all the facilities for the care of the emotionally ill. But I believe that, beyond this, a mental hygiene society must interest itself in working for better housing; it must be aware of what is going on in the schools and recreation centers and in the homes of people; it must press for the legislation necessary to insure equal opportunities of work, education and medical care for all: in short, everything that affects mental health is the proper concern of a mental hygiene society. I look on such societies as social action groups, broad in their concept of mental health, daring in the execution of such social action.

Sol W. Ginsburg, "Mental Health and Social Issues of Our

Times," *The American Journal of Orthopsychiatry*, Vol. 20,
No. 2, April, 1950, pp. 272-73 and 279.

300. SOCIAL CONDITIONS AND THE GUIDANCE PROCESS

The social, economic, and political conditions characterizing
the society have a tremendous bearing upon the guidance
process and upon the institutions which support it.

Unless the socio-economic environment really provides the
freedom of choice and the variety of opportunity which the
counseling situation presumes, then it is obvious that any
guidance service will be virtually devoid of significance. This
consideration is by no means a theoretical one but was shown
to have the utmost practicality during the depression of the
thirties. There was little point in counseling individuals toward lines of vocational pursuit when outlets in these activities did not exist.

Among the most significant of all aspects of the social setting
are the values which pervade it. A guidance process dominated
by high purpose will have little significance in a culture which
condones widespread economic insecurity and exalts values of
prestige, cutthroat competition, undue reliance upon social
welfare benefits, and mechanistic conceptions of personality.

It will be difficult for the guidance practitioner and his client
to transcend (even in the realm of deep subjectivity) the prevalent conditions and values of the society in which they are
living. Indeed, it is part of the personnel function to assist the
client in adjusting to these conditions so far as possible in a
manner consistent with moral and spiritual sanctions. Socio-
economic realities must be taken into account in aiding individuals in their planning, adjustment, and development; yet,
at the same time, both client and counselor can participate
individually, and through appropriate institutional means, in
the development of the society in directions favorable to individual welfare. . . .

We may sum up the foregoing views upon the relationship
of the guidance process to the social setting in three related
propositions, as follows:

1.   The guidance process will have significance only in an
environment in which there is reasonable freedom of choice

and in which alternative choices and opportunities are available.

2. Values which the environment emphasizes and reinforces will condition the psychology of client and counselor alike. Insofar as these values are favorable, the guidance and educative process will be advanced, but insofar as they are inimical to basic individual and social development, the educational and personnel service process will be stultified.

3. In order to make good their own activities and, more basically, to fulfill the individual and social needs which these activities are designed to meet, it will be essential, therefore, for education and its component feature of guidance to participate in, and perhaps take the lead in, a process of social education which will attempt to aid the community of individuals in the study of their own needs and of the social factors which bear upon human development and adjustment.

Robert Hendry Mathewson, *Guidance Policy and Practice.* New York: Harper and Brothers, 1949, pp. 81-83.

301. Significance of the Interrelation of Personal and Social Problems

Sound help for individuals involves full recognition of the interrelation of individual and social problems. The difficulties of the individual reflect directly the problems of the society in which he has grown up and of the social order in which he lives. Human beings differ greatly one from another. Some are happy, outgoing creatures who get along well with others, who meet their life situations positively and wholesomely; others have personality traits which make their associations with others difficult, and which prevent their taking a suitable place in the life of which they are a part. Such unfortunate characteristics are not inevitable and in most cases they need not be permanent. Whether an individual's style of life is desirable or undesirable, he has developed it in his efforts to meet the situations of life; his difficulties usually grow out of the effort to adjust himself to unhealthy or anti-social conditions in home, school, or community.

A child is born into a home; his first and often his most basic personality characteristics are developed in the effort to get along with parents and brothers and sisters. As he grows older, he must negotiate the world outside the home—the street, the traffic, the weather, the seasons; relations with playmates, tradesmen, teachers, policemen—and in so doing he develops the characteristics which he finds enable him to get along successfully in these various relationships. In adult life dependence upon social relations continues. Even physical survival involves a certain amount of adjustment to the practices of the group, and certainly emotional well-being requires such an adjustment. In the presence of too great a threat of being rejected by one's fellows, of being cut off from social approval and fellowship, and of being denied opportunity for life and achievement, neurotic and other undesirable personality characteristics develop. Many of any given individual's traits probably would not have been developed had he been born into a different kind of home, attended a different kind of school, or followed a different vocation. The basis for the most significant work in solving personal problems is a recognition of the social origin of personality characteristics.

To say that characteristics of personality are social in their origin does not mean that individuals are molded as plastic clay by their environment. Some persons resist the mores; others learn to take responsibility for transforming their environment; but the great majority yield to accepted ways of living. Yet whatever habits the individual man develops— whether those of the rebel, the conformist, or the reconstructionist—he is able to keep alive and to grow in proportion as he learns successful methods of living in relation to the material and human aspects of his environment. Being born into our present individualistic, competitive, and predatory society, the human young learn from their elders the characteristic behavior of that society and develop the conduct patterns necessary to protect themselves and to get along in this sort of world. In a social order built more fully upon respect for the welfare of others and with larger provision for co-operative effort for the common good children would as easily develop the attitudes and habits suited to such a society. In other words, adults set the type of social life and children have to adjust themselves to the standards which adults maintain; and by the time they are old enough to take control, they have so adopted the customs of their elders that they perpetuate for their children the life to which they have become habituated. Social idealists who believe in an educational method have often gone about their task the wrong way around. They have centered their attention upon children in an effort to train them to be adults of a different kind, whereas they might better have focused that attention upon adults, to the end that children might be given a social environment of a different kind in which to grow up.

> Harrison Sacket Elliott and Grace Loucks Elliott, *Solving Personal Problems.* New York: Henry Holt and Company, Inc., 1936, pp. 3-6. By permission of the publishers.

302. MAKE LIFE SAFE FOR THE HEALTHY CHILD

We are now working toward, and fighting for, a world in which the harvest of democracy may be reaped. In order to make the world safe for democracy, we must make democracy safe for the healthy child. In order to ban autocracy, exploitation, and inequality in the world, we must realize that the first inequality in life is that of child and adult. Human childhood is long, so that parents and schools may have time to accept the child's personality in trust and to help it to be human in the best sense known to us. This long childhood exposes the child to grave anxieties and to a lasting sense of insecurity which, if unduly and senselessly intensified, persists in the adult in the form of vague anxiety—anxiety which, in turn, contributes specifically to the tension of personal, political, and even international life. This long childhood exposes adults, in turn, to the temptation to exploit thoughtlessly and often cruelly the child's dependence by making him pay for the psychological debts owed to them by others, by making him the victim of tensions which they will not, or dare not, correct in themselves or in their surroundings. We have learned not to stunt a child's growing body with child labor; we must now learn not to break his growing spirit by making him the victim of our anxieties.

> Milton J. E. Senn, editor, *The Healthy Personality.* New

York: Josiah Macy, Jr. Foundation, 1950, pp. 145-46. (From chapter by Erik H. Erickson.)

303. GREAT POWER IN WHOLESOME CONDITIONS

If the teacher has succeeded . . . in building up a generally enjoyable school-world for children, with a curriculum which embodies their own purposes and group relationships which give emotional security, many of the individual adjustment problems will take care of themselves. When a child suffers some physical injury, the doctor and hospital staff do not heal the hurt, but usually try only to provide the best conditions for the organism to heal itself. There is a natural equilibrium of personality, as there is normal physical functioning, and both tend to restore themselves under generally wholesome conditions. Sometimes a youngster who has been regarded as a serious problem seems "transformed" in another class where a better teacher, without knowing anything about his problem past, has given him work that is better suited to his interests and capacities, and a responsible status in a co-operative group. As plants, pale and drooping from lack of light, when put out in the sun straighten up without stakes and color up without paint, so pupils may respond to "social belonging" without specific correction of their defensive faults.

> Paul A. Witty and Charles E. Skinner, editors, *Mental Hygiene in Modern Education.* New York: Rinehart and Company, Inc., 1939, p. 516. (From chapter by Goodwin Watson.)

304. DON'T PILE ON THE PRESSURE

I believe the compulsion is heavy upon us all to prevent another war which will increase tensions, heighten conflicts and exhaust the bodies of men beyond the point of any reasonable chance for self direction. Religion and education cannot escape their obligation to work unceasingly to prevent such calamity, even though they may be diligent, if it comes, in attempting to pick up the broken pieces. Such first-aid is a form of counseling but not at its best, for it should be more concerned with the creative and preventative aspects of human living, while necessarily giving time at the curative level. This point has been made very clear recently by Jesse F. Binford, Executive Director of the Juvenile Protective Association of Chicago. In commenting upon the "curfew law" recently passed by the Chicago City Council as a means of combating delinquency, she has this to say:

"Are we going to provide adequate housing for families so that they can make and have the kind of homes children will want to spend their evenings in? Are we going to make it impossible for boys and girls under eighteen to work at jobs that keep them out late, or even all night? Are we going to open more and even all of our schools as community centers instead of waiting to build a few more recreation centers? Are we ever going to enforce our laws prohibiting minors drinking or working or finding their recreation in our 10,000 taverns? Are parents going to be home at night so that the children will not be alone?" (Jessie F. Binford, *Chicago Daily News*, February 9, 1948.)

This same issue arises in your school and mine. Do we have such a wholesome atmosphere in our agencies that a minimum of frustration is produced, with a maximum of satisfaction and positive behavior? Is our grading system, our method of discipline, our curriculum itself, and our relation with our students so wholesome, and so emotionally mature that help is given in bringing out the best in everyone? Or, are these processes so out of line that we spend a great share of time in counseling with individuals who are thrown into confusion by the system itself?

From the editor's lecture notes.

305. COUNSELING INFLUENCED BY ESPRIT DE CORPS

Counseling in a college community is deeply conditioned by the community's inner temper and *esprit de corps*. If we are to deal constructively with the human problems of men and women whose lives have been deeply etched by the acids of war, we shall be seriously handicapped if the spirit of our school or college is philistine or secular or atomistic. On the other hand, counseling which goes on in an atmosphere of liberty, democracy and creativity is doubly effective. The counselor's stake in the reform of education, then, is obvious. The education of yesterday is literally not good enough for tomorrow. The curricula of our schools and colleges will have to be reorganized. But, certainly as important, we have got to dedicate ourselves to the task of building human community in a world shattered by violence and scarred by the malignant wounds of war; and this calls for the truth and power of Christian faith. If our schools and colleges can be made into communities of common concern for truth and goodness, they will be the seedbeds for men and women of real quality, fit for the challenges of the era upon whose threshold we stand.

> Albert C. Outler, *A Christian Context for Counseling.* An Edward W. Hazen Foundation pamphlet, Series III, No. 18, New Haven, Conn., 1945, p. 18.

306. Sound Personality Calls for Sound Society

Corrective helping of children to help themselves is not the end aim of guidance. It is possible to observe the beginnings of emotional, educational, and social frustrations before patterns of anti-social behavior become fixed. The *preventive* values of guidance are just beginning to be emphasized and there is increasing interest in those techniques and methods which will reach children and prevent maladjustment. The early formative years are the most propitious for preventive guidance.

However, if we are to survive the threats of our atomic age, it is not enough to correct the beginnings of maladjustment or even to prevent them. The school and the home and the community are challenged today to build positive programs of child guidance which will develop strong, healthy personalities who can withstand not only the social pitfalls they are facing and will face but who may exert also a dynamic force on their child society.

Children of today need guidance in the development of that kind of emotional and social strength which will give them a sense of direction so that they may grow in self-government and be a positive influence. This kind of *developmental* guidance is concerned not only with the individual in the group but with the emotional and social strength of the group as a whole.

Edna D. Baxter, "What Is Guidance?" *Childhood Education,* Vol. 25, January, 1949, pp. 202-3.

307. THE IMPORTANCE OF ENVIRONMENT IN MAN'S DEVELOPMENT

This theory also promises experimental support for those optimistic social theorists who assume that people can be improved in their innermost nature by a better environment. Man becomes more loving (friendly, affectionate, congenial, cooperative, protecting) if his fears are removed. He becomes more self-and-other-respecting (more autonomous, independent, courageous, less dominating, tyrannical, sadistic) if his love needs are satisfied. And finally, if he is allowed to respect himself, he becomes more capable of actualizing his best potentialities, i.e., he becomes an individual in the fullest and finest sense. Therefore, any social developments which help to achieve these psychological desiderata (such as improved education, world organization, labor unions, and housing or removal of injustices based on sex, religion or racial differences) may be expected, from current motivation theory, to change human nature in its *essential* character.

Maurice J. Shore, *et al., Twentieth Century Mental Hygiene.* New York: Social Sciences Publishers, 1950, pp. 355-56. (From chapter by A. H. Maslow.)

308. PSYCHOLOGIZING IS NOT ENOUGH

As counselors, we are prone to limit our attention to the demands of society on the individual. We aid in the gaining of insight to the end that the client understands and accepts his feelings toward his problems and is enabled to take concrete steps toward their solution. We are suggesting that the counselor's responsibility also includes helping his client examine the structure of the society out of which his difficulties have arisen, and to form some judgment concerning the role that the client can play in reshaping his environment.

Robert L. Weislogel, "Counseling in a Social Framework," *Counseling,* April, 1948, p. 3.

309. Good Counselors Never Complacent About Unjust and Inadequate Environment

To recognize the importance of the relation between serious personal problems and the environment with which the individual must cope, is to make it impossible for anyone interested in solving those problems to be complacent in the presence of unjust and anti-social conditions in home, community, or society at large. For in the presence of such conditions only the rugged personalities have hope of healthy survival. Many a difficulty of the individual caused by unhealthy social conditions is unnecessary, just as much sickness caused by unhealthy physical surroundings is preventable. The solution of many personal problems will never be possible until we have so remade economic, political, and other aspects of our social relations that the rank and file of human beings have a chance to meet life situations positively and wholesomely. Therefore those who would help individuals must give attention to changing home, school, community, and wider social conditions which are causing or accentuating individual problems. The person who is interested in individual welfare must necessarily co-operate actively in efforts for social amelioration and social reconstruction.

Harrison Sacket Elliott and Grace Loucks Elliott, *Solving Personal Problems*. New York: Henry Holt and Company, Inc., 1936, p. 8. By permission of the publishers.

12.

Major Assumptions and Principles

A. *Organization and Method*

310. EMERGING TRENDS IN GUIDANCE

1. The first trend is one toward more adequate training of guidance personnel. . . .
2. The second trend is toward making guidance an all-faculty function and toward co-operation between guidance specialists and classroom teachers. . . .
3. The third trend is toward close co-operation of the guidance services of the school with the home and other agencies in the community. . . .
4. The fourth trend is toward the orderly accumulation and recording of a variety of information concerning each individual. . . .
5. The fifth trend is toward increased use of objective measures in guidance programs. . . .
6. The sixth trend is toward differential prediction of success on the basis of test batteries that yield comparable scores in broad areas. . . .
7. The seventh trend is toward increased interest in the use of improved techniques in the appraisal of personal qualities of pupils and the treatment of maladjustment. . . .
8. The eighth trend is toward a middle position between directive and non-directive guidance. . . .
9. The ninth trend is toward recognition of relationship between remedial work and guidance. . . .
10. The tenth trend is toward the use of improved case-study

techniques, both for purposes of better understanding of individual pupils and for in-service training of teachers. . . .

11. The eleventh trend in guidance is toward the availability and use of better sources of occupational information. . . .

12. The twelfth trend in guidance programs is toward the use of follow-up studies.

> Arthur E. Traxler, "Emerging Trends in Guidance," *The School Review*, Vol. 58, No. 1, January, 1950, pp. 14-23.

311. Basic Assumptions in Organization of Guidance

The author has been guided by five basic assumptions in the preparation of this book. These, in fact, summarize the essentials in his point of view regarding guidance services in smaller schools. . . .

1. *Guidance work is not confined to "guidance experts."* It is undoubtedly true that the professionally trained guidance worker has a distinct place in the American educational system. However, because of the lack of facilities available to more than 75 per cent of the high schools, his services as an individual cannot be obtained. The universities and other institutions which can afford to employ a staff of workers are, by their very nature, committed to conduct the basic research in the field of guidance. It is to those individuals who have facilities available that the task of the development and evaluation of guidance techniques falls. In much the same manner that the engineers of an automotive manufacturing concern develop and design a new car, so should our institutions of higher learning develop and design tools for guidance workers. But that does not give those who are in our higher institutions a franchise for the application of guidance techniques. As the local mechanic is able to apply his knowledge and to make repairs upon a car designed by professionals, so can the local educator make use of guidance practices which have been developed by experts. Just as there are certain principles governing the repair of a car which carry over from one make to another, so are there educational principles which are true and can be used regardless of the size of the school, regardless of its location.

2. *An effective guidance program is possible in a small school.* Throughout the country for the past ten years ever-increasing numbers of small schools have proved this assumption. Within this book no technique will be found which has not been shown in actual practice to be useful and effective in a small school.

3. *Guidance services cannot be superimposed upon a school but must become through a process of gradual growth an integral part of the school's program.* No one would buy a new furnace and expect it to heat the school building unless it were connected to the radiators. No one can go into the open market and buy a guidance program and expect it to work without connecting it to the school's program. It is true that it is possible to buy things which aid in the construction of an effective guidance program, but regardless of the amount of money spent, the guidance program is doomed to failure unless it is the result of a gradual growth in the mission of the school and a broadening of the point of view of those charged with administering the school's instructional program.

4. *When establishing a guidance program the range of services should be limited to functions which can be performed adequately by the available personnel.* We would not ask a music teacher to begin giving private lessons on the harp or xylophone if he did not have the necessary training for teaching those instruments. It is standard educational practice to ask our teachers to do only those things for which they have the requisite skill. So, too, in guidance, it is unwise to ask an untrained teacher to do individual counseling. Rather he should do those things for which he has the skill. It may be cataloguing occupational information or preparing cumulative records or arranging a series of career conferences. There is enough to be done in the organization of a guidance program so that all teachers can cooperate by doing things for which they are prepared.

5. *The development of the program is dependent upon the speed with which the staff acquires skill in handling additional guidance tools.* Beware of the guidance program that blooms into full flower without adequate roots of training and study. The concept that guidance work can be done by anybody is

just as false as the concept that it is limited to guidance experts. Guidance work can be done by those who train themselves and only after they have acquired basic knowledge should they proceed into the field of individual counseling.

> Clifford P. Froehlich, *Guidance Services in Smaller Schools.* New York: McGraw-Hill Book Company, Inc., 1950, pp. 7-8.

B. *Psychological Insight*

312. UNDERSTANDING REQUIRES MORE THAN KNOWING

In the relationship between interviewer and interviewee, intellectual understanding is clearly insufficient unless it is accompanied by emotional understanding as well. Intellectual knowledge may suffice for mathematics or logic, but to understand intellectually the successive movements of dancing or skiing does not qualify one as a good dancer or skier. Similarly, in our relationships with other human beings, intellectual understanding is barren unless accompanied by emotional understanding. To know about emotions and feelings is not enough. One should be able to "sense" their existence and their degree and quality. Such ability does not come merely from reading a book such as this or merely from classroom study but requires the constant application of theoretical knowledge in practical day-to-day contact with human beings and their objective and subjective problems.

> Annette Garrett, *Interviewing: Its Principles and Methods.* New York: Family Service Association of America, 1942, pp. 24-25.

313. WHEN COUNSELING IS IN ORDER

Personality is the expression of the life of the total organism in its relation to its total environment, particularly in relation to other persons. Each person is motivated by deep physical, emotional and spiritual needs which may be frustrated or satisfied. Wholesome satisfaction in relationship to other persons leads to growth and integration. Failure to receive wholesome satisfaction creates tensions such as anxiety, resentment and guilt. Various psychological processes are set in motion to counteract this emotional pain. When a person becomes aware of these tensions and seeks help, counseling may be in order. Counseling seeks to utilize the resources of personality, to work through tension-producing experiences and to help the person grow to a new level of strength and maturity.

> Carroll A. Wise, *Pastoral Counseling, Its Theory and Practice*. New York: Harper and Brothers, 1951, p. 38.

314. WITH THESE PERSONS: BE CAUTIOUS!

There are certain persons with whom the pastor should be very cautious in proceeding in a counseling relationship.

One of these is the person who has physical complaints. In such situations, the pastor should insist on a good medical examination. The person may have another problem, related or unrelated to the physical complaint, which is within the scope of the pastor and outside the province of the physician. However, if the person's emotional conflicts are causing extreme or serious physical symptoms, or if the person is unaware of any problems except the symptoms themselves, he should be referred to psychiatric help. The pastor should maintain an interest as a pastor, but not try to counsel with such persons unless they are also under the care of a physician.

A second group of persons requiring caution are those who have had sudden changes of personality. Sometimes these changes of personality have religious coloring; sometimes they do not. Ministers are often misled by the religious side of the picture. Sudden changes of personality which create problems in the relationships of the individual to others or which affect his general adjustments adversely, are not to be taken lightly. They may have a physical basis, as in general paresis. Or they may have a psychological basis. Only a psychiatric study can determine this.

A third group are those who show marked symptoms of mental illness, such as depression, overactivity, a fear of impending catastrophe or death, delusions of grandeur or persecution, and others. Persons with bizarre religious ideas should be included here. Such ideas are the reflection of an emotional condition which is too severe for counseling, and they cannot be helped by any rational approach to the ideas. The clergyman should know the community resources available for such persons, and should co-operate with those institutions and with the family of the person in getting adequate treatment. He should also be aware of the great danger of suicide in depressed persons.

A fourth group, the neurotic, is difficult to discuss unless one thinks in purely static terms. Certainly the average pastor is not trained, nor does he have time, to counsel with persons who have a deep neurosis, such as a strong compulsion or a well-developed hysteria. On the other hand, most people in our culture have mild neurotic tendencies. With some of these some ministers can be of help with others they cannot. In some neurotics, as in some psychotics, there is a danger involved in bringing to the surface the strong hostility which they experience. Some people with strong neurotic drives will set up a relationship on the basis of their needs that only a trained person can handle. . . .

A fifth group constitutes those who have a long history of repeated failures and who have learned nothing from their experience. Strangely enough, the clergyman has been very much interested in many of this group. They present an appealing situation, they often have so much of good about them, they are usually very optimistic about themselves and assure the helper that it will never happen again, they come begging for help but often experience a marked inability to take any responsibility for themselves or to face their problems and feelings realistically; they are sometimes experts in intellectualizing their problems and trying to solve it on that basis, they are likely to seek protection and sympathy rather than any relationship that aims at inner change. In this group fall various specific persons and problems; the alcoholic, the homosexual or person afflicted with other sexual perversions (masturbation is not here considered a perversion), criminals, and many others whose activities never bring them into contact with the law, but who live irresponsible, unproductive lives, always meaning to do better but never getting around to it.

We are not saying here that these persons cannot be helped. Certainly some of them can be. But there are real difficulties involved. The minister is well-advised not to attempt counseling with any who represent extreme forms of this reaction unless he has special training and is thus qualified. The lack of conscience or of inner control that is found in many of these people is not easily remedied. With persons falling in a milder form of this pattern some clergymen can be of considerable help. The spontaneous changes in such persons that occasionally occur in religious conversions present problems that we cannot discuss here.

The sixth group is the involutional, the person at the change of life. Physicians feel that most of the problems of this age are grounded in physiological processes. Many psychiatrists feel that while physiological processes are a factor, many of the emotional problems grow out of unsolved situations at some earlier level. Certainly, the general medical opinion makes it difficult to counsel with many of these people. The idea that their problem is physical is a very welcome relief from responsibility, even though inwardly they know it is not entirely true. On the other hand, they frequently come to the pastor with feelings of guilt on which they seek relief. Sometimes they come with marriage problems. In the milder forms, an understanding pastor with some training can be of considerable help. With the extreme forms of this reaction, there are grave difficulties involved in counseling and also the danger of suicide. These persons should be referred to psychiatric help.

Carroll A. Wise, *Pastoral Counseling, Its Theory and Practice*. New York: Harper and Brothers, 1951, pp. 108-11.

315. The Personality Gestalt

The dependence of effective counseling upon the concept of the total interrelatedness of the personality has been earlier suggested. This concept and how we arrived at it is so important that it should be given more careful attention. It is not enough to say that we must deal with a dynamic totality; we must also know just what has been the trend toward an understanding of this concept. "Personality is today conceived of in terms of structures rather than traits. There is an attempt to study the individual as a whole, rather than to isolate very small elements for study. Behavior is considered as an interaction of person and situation, rather than as a property of the person alone." (Lee J. Cronbach, "A Validation Design for Qualitative Studies of Personality," *Journal of Consulting Psychology,* November-December, 1948, p. 365.) What has been the development of this modern concept?

It has been mentioned that psychoanalysis has made a very large contribution to clinical counseling. This is true because psychoanalysis first emphasized certain factors now widely accepted by all who deal with individuals in counseling terms. The proposal that adult peculiarities or characteristics have their origins in childhood experiences is now a part of orthodox child psychology, yet it was first emphasized by Sigmund Freud in his early work in psychoanalysis. . . . As a result of a great deal of experience in relating this theory to individual cases, he developed the concept of a psychogenetic origin of many types of adult behavior. This is now an accepted tenet of all psychotherapy, and yet it had its birth only some fifty years ago. Similarly, we now accept the theory that many drives and desires are repressed only to appear later in forms of behavior different from that in which the original drive would normally be expressed. This is so commonly accepted an hypothesis that many mechanisms of behavior, labeled rationalization, compensation, or projection, are commonly referred to by laymen. Perhaps most of all Freud contributed to the idea that the individual is a total functioning organism and that to understand the totality we must understand each given part of the whole and each past experience. The direct line of development of the nondirective concept in counseling, as systematized and promoted by Carl R. Rogers, is traced back through Jessie Taft and Otto Rank to Sigmund Freud.

Henry Murray in his excellent volume *Explorations in Personality* stands as an exponent of what might be called the school of dynamic psychology. In this exposition he is concerned with the point of view in psychology which he calls the point of view of the "centralists" as opposed to that of the "peripheralists." Murray attempts to prove that those who have studied personality in terms of its peripheral or exterior manifestations have been guilty of studying it piecemeal. Such psychologists are to be contrasted with those who have studied the personality as a dynamic whole and who are more concerned with internal drive than they are with external manifestations. This centralist or dynamic point of view in psychology contends that no segment can be seen or understood in isolation from the whole. This is to say that no partial knowledge of a man, such as his scores on an intelligence test or the results of a test of basal metabolism, can be understood apart from the balance of the psychophysical organism which we call a personality. Murray contends that while it is true that we know much better how to measure accurately the peripheral factors than the central factors, the most significant factors *are* the central ones, that is, those of drive and of integration.

Without identifying oneself with any particular school, it is possible to hold the point of view that the personality is a dynamic whole and that the part must be seen in relation to the whole. When this view prevails, any items of case history or any test datum gains its significance from the context within which it exists. This would also imply that no element of the human personality is static. When any element of the situation changes, some phase of the total personality, and therefore the pattern itself, changes. This makes clinical counseling a far more complex and at the same time a far more meaningful operation. The weight of empirical evidence is in the direction of a dynamic, that is, changeable, totality within which the various known characteristics of behavior exist. One cannot take any number of specific facts about the person and add them up in a quantitative fashion to secure a meaningful understanding of the whole. By the same token, the interpretation of specific information about the individual must always be referred back to the clinician's concept of the total personality, even though only dimly understood. For this reason, clinical counseling is dependent upon a combination of judgment and experience, which may be called trained insight. This insight must accompany even the best technical skills in the interpretation of measurement data or the interpretation of a particular behavior cue observed in the interview. There is in good counseling a certain exercise of social sensitivity not all of which can be easily analyzed and put into words.

C. Gilbert Wrenn, *Student Personnel Work in College*. New York: The Ronald Press Company, 1951, pp. 65-67.

316. THE MODERN VIEW OF PERSONALITY

The personnel worker's concept of counseling and his choice of technics depend upon his theory of personality. From the modern view of personality come ideas that give direction to the counseling process:

1. The idea of motivation—the individual's desire for self-actualization, his need to make his life as "good" or complete as possible.

2. The idea of conscious and unconscious drives to action. Behavior that is consciously motivated is likely to be reasonable and consistent; behavior that is instigated by the unconscious is likely to be irrational and unpredictable. Blindly repressed desires may give rise to inner conflicts or illness. This does not mean that a person should express his every desire, but rather that he consciously decides not to do things that are detrimental to himself or to others.

3. The idea of purpose or goal which gives direction to and integrates a person's behavior trends.

4. The idea of the dynamic organization of personality.

5. The idea of untapped resources for self-realization within the individual which can be released and will sometimes produce psychological miracles. The counselor assumes that the individual has resources for growth within himself and that, when conditions are favorable, he can move toward a better, more complete self-realization.

6. The idea of the many-sided aspects of personality and its continuity from birth to death.

7. The idea of "the language of behavior"—behavior as an expression of inner need.

8. The idea that we are products of our time—that there are cultural causes of behavior and that favorable cultural conditions make good personal development possible.

> Ruth Strang, *Counseling Technics in College and Secondary School* (Revised). New York: Harper and Brothers, 1949, pp. 16-17.

317. ESSENTIAL INSIGHTS

At least five principles are particularly pertinent to teachers in meeting their classroom guidance responsibilities:

1. *Behavior is caused.* Teachers who understand their students will interpret each individual's present behavior in terms of that individual's past experiences, home and family influences, health, personal needs, interests, and goals. Present behavior, however undesirable or annoying, is symptomatic. Rather than punish or treat the symptoms, teachers should search out underlying causes, conditions, or unmet needs that produce the observed behavior. This view of human behavior and action implies that all types of student behavior can be understood and guided only in the light of underlying causes and conditions.

2. *Causes are complex.* It is seldom that only one factor or condition is responsible for a personal difficulty. A number of underlying causes or conditions usually contribute to a single behavior problem.

3. *A pattern of data is needed.* To understand a student effectively a comprehensive picture of him must be obtained. Information gained from a cross-section analysis of his present needs, abilities, and interests must be supplemented by a developmental record of his individual growth. In fact, to know any student as a total personality teachers need more information than is contained in the usual school record of scholastic achievement and test scores. They need a cumulative record identifying growth and change in all dimensions of the child's personality and environment.

4. *Treatment is a cooperative process.* The case study conference is a cooperative approach utilizing the reports, anecdotes, and experiences of all teachers and other trained staff members in a careful analysis of an individual student. The pooling of pertinent information and the weighing of judgments in arriving at specific recommendations in a planned program of therapy are constructive trends in school guidance procedures.

5. *Therapy is continuous.* Recommendations for remedial treatment or action in assisting each child to achieve an optimum adjustment represent only a starting point. A follow-up study of the *effects* of such courses of action is needed, for new facts may come to light and changes in treatment or further courses of action may be found desirable. The successful guid-

ance of an individual student demands patient follow-up and continued attention to the changing pattern of his life.

> C. Gilbert Wrenn and Willis E. Dugan, *Guidance Procedures in High School*. Minneapolis: The University of Minnesota Press, 1950, pp. 17-18.

318. SOME BASIC ASSUMPTIONS OR PRINCIPLES OF WHICH THE COUNSELOR NEEDS TO BE AWARE

1. An atmosphere of acceptance and permissiveness is highly desirable.
2. An objective attitude is essential. Attempt is made at understanding, not blaming; the purposiveness of behavior is recognized as well as the fact that often individuals are unaware of the reasons for their behavior; the psychology of motivation is taken into account along with the adjustment mechanisms which are called into action whenever conflict occurs.
3. Individuals have greater ability at self-guidance than is generally supposed.
4. The counselor has a vital contribution to make in the counseling process although it is the counselee who has the major role in this relationship.
5. The fact that individuals differ in all respects is kept constantly in mind.
6. The psychology of the development of the individual—how he learns and grows—is taken into account. This involves a recognition of the influence upon the individual of environment and culture.

> From the editor's class notes.

319. GUIDES IN PRACTICE OF SOCIAL WORK

Along with the accumulated knowledge in helping people over the years, family service workers have absorbed in their training much that has been distilled from psychiatry, sociology, anthropology, medicine, and economics. In contrast to the primitive and often "paternalistic" ways in which people were helped out of trouble 50 or 75 years ago, the family service counselor has definite precepts which he applies to any seeking aid, such as:

1. Each person has a potential for living a reasonably happy, productive life in harmony with himself and the demands of society.

2. Each person is of equal importance—regardless of race, creed, color or education.

3. Each person can, in the end, make his own best decisions and in a free society must be able or enabled to guide his own life.

4. People are not born good or bad, honest or criminal, kind or cruel.

5. People can adapt and change—life is a process of continual growth.

6. There must be warmth, understanding and acceptance for a person seeking help.

7. The family, as the primary social unit, is the basic area of concern since here most of the personality, social attitudes and patterns of living are shaped.

> Family Service Association of America. News release, June 7, 1951.

320. BASIC GUIDANCE PRINCIPLES

Without subscribing to any particular point of view in counseling, there are certain basic principles which underlie effective counseling which may be used as guides. Counseling is most effective:

a. when a student comes to the counselor with the feeling that he needs help;

b. when a permissive atmosphere is created in the interview so that the student feels free to express his feelings without being criticized or censored;

c. when the counseling situation is regarded as a cooperative relationship in which the counselor and the counselee participate in a mutual search for a solution of the student's problems;

d. when the counselor avoids moralizing and negative comment to the student with regard to his behavior;

e. when the counselor permits the student to discover his own insight into his problems rather than telling him what is wrong;

f. when the individual's total personality adjustment is kept in mind when dealing with any one specific problem;

g. when the counselor has sufficient background and maturity to recognize the implications of the student's decisions and plans, and brings these to the student's attention at appropriate points in the interview;

h. when the counselor consistently employs the policy of encouraging the student to freely express his attitudes and feelings;

i. when the counselor consistently avoids the possibility of being placed on the defensive during the interview;

j. when the counselor guards against the student's becoming too dependent upon him;

k. when the counselor has thought through the problem of human values (the ends for which we live), and their relationships to individual adjustment;

l. when the counselor consistently strives to help the counselee discover the cause and effect relationship between his problems and conditions in himself and in his environment which brought about the problem;

m. when counseling results in a program of action enabling the student to adopt more effective ways of living.

Hugh M. Bell, "Counseling and Guidance," *The American College,* New York: Philosophical Library, pp. 289-90.

321. Principles of Positive Mental Hygiene

1. *Maintenance of good physical health*
   "Mental and physical health are inseparable."

2. *An objective attitude*
   "Objectivity is the habit of attacking problems directly and rationally . . . being guided by facts rather than primarily by desires."

3. *Insight into one's own conduct*
   ". . . perception of relationships between one's drives, situations and responses. Insight is the opposite of self-deceit and rationalization."

4. *A confidential relationship with some other person*

5. *Attention to the present situation or problem*

6. *A sense of humor—of the ridiculous*
   "Don't take yourself too seriously. Laugh at your own mistakes. Relieves tension." Akin to attitude of humility.
7. *Planned activity*
   "Do something—don't just mope."
8. *Satisfying work*
   "The sense of satisfaction and completeness that comes from the successful conclusion of work is one of the greatest integrating forces in human lives."
9. *Rest and recreation*
   Principle of alternation of work and rest.
10. *Normal social participation*
    Counter balances too great an emphasis on egocentric tendencies.

> Laurance Frederic Shaffer, *The Psychology of Adjustment.* Boston: Houghton Mifflin, 1936, pp. 535-40. (Adapted.)

322. NEW INSIGHTS ABOUT HUMAN NATURE

Of greatest importance is this fact: concepts regarding human development have been extraordinarily enriched over what now seem the superficial understandings of a few years ago.

In the first place, recent research regarding physical growth is showing much more clearly than heretofore the interrelation of physical growth and growth of personality. Continuing studies of the same individuals over a period of years as regards the complex and marvelous changes in physique from infancy to maturity, and coincident detailed observation of changes in each youngster's behavior have revealed relationships formerly obscured by averaging or by roughness in methods of investigation. The new knowledge of psychological development is founded on new knowledge of physical growth and change.

A second contribution of recent years to the understanding of human development concerns emotional dynamics. Not intellectual but emotional growth and change have come to be seen as of central importance. A young person's feelings, not his understandings—and feelings which he himself usually does not at all understand—are the forces which really move

him and which determine the direction in which he moves.
Usually these forces are quite as uncomprehended by the
adults who have contact with him. But if a teacher *can* understand them, she gains insights into her pupils' problems which
are invaluable.

In the third place, there is increasing emphasis on and understanding of social development through childhood and
adolescence, and also the effects of the total social and cultural
environment on development. The distinctive fact about a human being is after all not that he is a biological organism; the
distinctive fact is that he is a social being. His growth is not
so much a physical as a social growth. The world he lives in
is not so much a physical as a social world. And the newer
studies of what may be called the social psychology of childhood and youth are therefore important not only for their
originality and their remaking of that topic. They have much
broader import—they must be considered also in connection
with study of the growth and change of interests and ideals,
and of the total personality.

Finally, in psychology and also in the world everywhere,
there has come to be a new appreciation of the importance of
attitudes and ideals and concepts as to value. To no person is
the world a flat, colorless, undifferentiated mass in which
everything is of equal worth. Everyone regards certain people,
things, and ideas favorably and opposes others, considers certain acts right and others wrong, some things beautiful and
others hideous; there may be some ideas and ideals to which
he would devote a lifetime or even give his life. The development, through childhood and youth, of attitudes and ideas as
to what is right and beautiful and true is indeed a topic of
importance—a topic the comparative neglect of which, in both
psychology and education, has been unfortunate indeed.

> Sidney L. Pressey and Francis P. Robinson, *Psychology and
> the New Education (Revised).* New York: Harper and Broth-
> ers, 1944, pp. 1-2.

323. LEVELS OF UNDERSTANDING

Three Levels of Understanding

In the diagnosis of student problems there are various levels of understanding. There is, for example, the level at which we simply classify the student's problem by putting it into a convenient pigeonhole, as shown in the following excerpt:

Mary Jane repeatedly fails to hand in her papers on time although I have warned her that she is likely to fail on this account. When she is called to task, Mary Jane acknowledges her fault, but immediately starts to excuse herself. Her most frequent complaint is that she cannot study because her roommate has the radio turned on all the time. I am convinced that this is just a "rationalization" since her roommate makes the same complaint about her. In fact, I have had occasion to observe that it is usually Mary Jane herself who turns on the radio, and consequently I do not take her complaints very seriously.

The above excerpt illustrates the first level of understanding. Characteristic of this level is a lack of insight into casual relationships. It is important merely as a first step in the direction of understanding the real nature of the problem, but in itself it is psychologically insignificant.

In the second level of understanding there is at least a superficial attempt to determine cause-and-effect relations. Some typical diagnoses falling under this heading might read: "low grades because of poor ability"; or "has become a 'grind' as a compensation for being unpopular with other students." The following excerpt from a counselor's report is illustrative of this level:

John does not seem to associate very much with the boys of his class. Every time I see him he is alone. So far as I know, he has never attended a class meeting, gone to a school party, or eaten lunch with other students. Since he is supporting himself by working outside of school hours, perhaps he has not had time to become acquainted. Or perhaps the fact that he comes from a lower social class than the other boys prevents him from being accepted.

This second level of diagnosis is somewhat deeper than the first and serves, in many instances, as the basis for making environmental changes which will help the student to adjust. Nevertheless, it is well to remember that diagnoses of this type are often superficial and in the case of serious emotional maladjustment are likely to be wholly inadequate. There is a tendency, in this type of diagnosis, to oversimplify the problem and to attribute it to a single cause. Moreover, this type of diagnosis does not include an understanding of the most important factor in the case, namely, what the life-situation or pattern of behavior means to the student himself. For example, in the diagnosis "low grades because of poor ability" we still want to know what this situation means to the student—does he feel threatened with the loss of love from his parents, or with economic insecurity; or does he feel that lack of success in college is not very important anyway for success in life, or that he now has a weapon with which to force his parents to accept his own choice of an occupation or goal? Fortunately, the solution of most student problems does not require such a deep understanding, although the number that does call for such analysis has probably been greatly underestimated.

If we would really understand a student, we must know the goals around which his personality is organized, the values of life which to him are significant, and what people or institutions claim his loyalty and love. This is the third level of understanding. The value of any particular bit of information about a student, therefore, lies in the degree to which it ties in with other facts about him and throws light upon the meaning of his life-situation in terms of what he values.

An understanding of such meaning in the life of the student cannot be procured as readily from objective tests, questionnaires, inventories, and the like, as from nonstandardized sources, such as interviews, creative art and literature, psychodramatics, and expressive and projective techniques. And the interpretation and use of these nonobjective sources of information in such a way as to promote the growth of a student presupposes a counselor with considerable psychological interest and insight and with a deep respect for human personality.

To understand a person then, we need to know much more than his personality traits and characteristic behavior. We need to know why these traits have been acquired and what ends his behavior is intended to serve. And only when we understand the motivation of a life and its "pattern of reactivity" can we formulate hypotheses concerning the ways in which an individual can and will change as a result of his collegiate experience.

> Paul J. Brouwer, *Student Personnel Services in General Education*. Washington: American Council on Education, 1949, pp. 226-28. (From chapter by Sister Annette.)

324. GROWTH IS A PRODUCT OF THE YEARS

There can be no conclusion to a discussion of the art of helping any more than there can be a last chapter in the art of living; for living continues as long as life, and life touches life subtly and unmeasurably down through the generations. Forever, while man is part of the universe, the process of adjustment will endure, always involving new relationships and new situations, shaping and changing him and carrying with it ever the issue of happiness or trouble.

Each one of us, limited though his days may be, is caught up in the sweep of this vast ebb and flow of life. Nature working within him expresses herself in terms of her own timelessness. She is unhurried. Growth is a product of the years. Man, being but part of the whole, may become impatient, content with what would be incomplete. Nature is comprehensive and eternal.

To have grasped this lesson is to have made a beginning of learning the art of helping. We are continually seeking the immediate. We search for panaceas and we want instantaneous change. In a few days we would make different a human being who for three or four decades has been evolving to what he is. Yet if the body develops so slowly that in age one can recognize the youth, how can we expect greater rapidity in the transformation of personality which must express itself through the body and which is influenced by it.

Unfortunately, our very books contribute to the illusion that change in man is an easy and an expeditious process. When in three or four hundred pages the biography of a lifetime may be reviewed, the years themselves seem to take on a kind of cinematographic speed and unconsciously we come to expect the same instantaneous development in the people about us. . . .

Nor can it be said that after one, two, or three years an individual has achieved a permanent adjustment. There is no such thing as permanency in adjustment, for adjustment is constant change. Always a new crisis is arising, a new event occurring; and the whole struggle must be gone over with again. Not until the whole of a man's career is reviewed can a verdict be announced. While life is being lived, one can only say that thus far the individual has succeeded in overcoming his difficulties and in building wisely for the future.

> Karl deSchweinitz, *The Art of Helping People Out of Trouble*. Boston: Houghton Mifflin Company, 1924, pp. 224-26.

325. The Marks of a Well-Integrated Person

A genuine sense of freedom, a positive sense that one is able to so order his life that he may achieve a higher degree of joy for himself and others, is a mark of a well-integrated, mature person. It is one of the goals of counseling. It comes, not through processes of reason, but by the elimination of anxiety, guilt and resentment and the release of the positive qualities of faith, hope and love for actual living. It is not the intellectual acceptance of ideas which are conceived to be the "truth," but the emotional acceptance of the relationships and conditions that make for growth and wholeness of personality that lead to genuine freedom. Freedom and responsibility are the functions of an ever maturing self.

> Carroll A. Wise, *Pastoral Counseling, Its Theory and Practice*. New York: Harper and Brothers, 1951, p. 23.

326. The "Spiritual" Is Related to the Whole Personality

The pastor who would help people must learn to relate religious processes to the total life processes of the personality, not just to a side that is called "spiritual." The spiritual aspects of personality are the meaning that the total experience has for the person-as-a-whole. Such meaning, whether positive or negative, and the response a person makes to it, is the major inner determinant of personality.

> *Ibid.*, p. 19.

327. DANGER IN UNDIRECTED EXPRESSION OF FEELINGS

There is, however, a danger in allowing the client undirected expression of his feelings. They may be due not to a recent upsetting experience but to a long chain of experiences going back into the remote past. These early experiences may have become twisted and distorted and inter-related with other things through the years so that mere talking does not bring relief. His need to talk may not be occasional but constant, and if the interviewer encourages too much release of feeling, areas may be opened up with which both interviewer and client are unequipped to cope. In general, catharsis through talking is more effective the more the disturbing feeling is related to a fairly recent experience, and it becomes of dubious value the more the feeling is due to long repressed experiences. If a difficult situation may be immediately aired, the danger of its being pushed from consciousness but remaining an active source of anxiety is lessened. If a person has had a hairbreadth automobile escape, he feels better if he can talk about it a lot for a while, for then its importance gradually wanes and is forgotten. Particularly with children it is helpful to remember that if they do have a traumatic experience—an accident, an operation, a sex assault—the more immediately they can be helped to express their feelings about it, the less will it be in danger of becoming a source of neurotic conflict.

> Annette Garrett, *Interviewing, Its Principles and Methods.*
> New York: Family Service Association of America, 1942,
> p. 35.

328. THE RELATION OF RELIGIOUS AND EMOTIONAL PROBLEMS

Where a religious question is not grounded in an emotional conflict people will find the usual educational activities of the church supplying their needs. On the other hand, persons who are in emotional conflict will find the usual educational activities of the church unavailable for them. By this it is meant that these activities will not meet their needs. Their needs will not be met until the conflict which is at the bottom of the problem is worked out.

It is my conviction that the majority of the problems expressing themselves in religious terms arise as a result of emotional conflict rather than on a strictly intellectual basis. Sometimes they arise because of a lack of experiences which give a groundwork for religious interpretation. The real meaning of religious creeds and ideas can be grasped only by persons who have experienced within their own lives the realities to which these interpretations point. Religious experience produces the interpretation; the interpretation never produces the experience.

The handling of these emotionally-rooted religious problems is not essentially different from handling problems in other areas of life which are rooted in emotional conflict. The relationship between the counselor and the counselee is of great importance. The attitude of the counselor toward religion and religious faith is very significant. Many nonreligious counselors recognize this difficulty and feel an embarrassment within themselves when religious issues are met. They are very quick to want to refer such persons to ministers or religious counselors. On the other hand, some psychologists do successful work on this level and help many of their clients to gain rather profound religious insights.

There is a temptation here for the religiously trained counselor. Usually such a person having studied extensively in the field of religion has developed his own point of view intellectually. His emotional attitudes toward religion may have kept pace with his intellectual growth, or as is frequently the case, his intellectual growth may have far outstripped his emotional development. The more immature he is emotionally the more he will feel the necessity to fit the individual into his own scheme of thinking. The emotionally mature religious worker will be able to allow the person freedom to work out his own religious faith. It is only that faith which each person works out for himself that will function for both the growth and the integration of personality, or for the salvation of the person.

Carroll A. Wise, *Pastoral Counseling, Its Theory and Practice.* New York: Harper and Brothers, 1951, pp. 219-20.

329. Some Insights and Suggestions

. . .

3. The problem as presented will seem to the person in

trouble insoluble. That's why he is in trouble. A ready acceptance of the picture as he sees it would close the case. Try to see other people in each of the predicaments and see how they might solve them. All problems are essentially subjective.

4. Expect resistance in dealing with problems most deeply concerned. Suspect resistance in tardiness, absence from appointment, talk about irrelevant matters, sudden break in the conversation, sudden forgetting in the middle of a sentence or argument, counter-attacks on counselor or others. . . .

. . .

7. Expect patterns. Among the more common are dependence, fear of the new, avoidance of people, breakdowns, running away from a situation, projecting the blame onto an individual of a given type, displacement making a mountain out of a given sort of molehill, etc.

8. Do not give advice. Give the experience of yourself and others so far as it is useful, taking particular care to emphasize the differences in the situation faced by the counselee. No two persons have faced exactly the same situation. What the counselee needs is ability to handle situations himself, not advice to follow.

9. Be sure all available evidence is provided. If the problem is vocational, it requires extensive occupational information. Health, religion, scholastic and social guidance each have bodies of essential data. Experts may be utilized. . . .

. . .

11. Avoid being maneuvered into emotional behavior. Patients will endeavor to arouse sympathy, to shock you, to hurt you with cutting phrases, to inflate your vanity, to get caresses, to make you pity and care for them, to win rebukes, to provoke outbursts of your own ideas, etc. Objectivity takes constant defense.

12. Take no chances on physical condition. Insist upon reliable examination and treatment. Do not take counselee's word alone.

13. Take no chances on mental examination. Secure adequate

tests of intelligence or other relevant abilities—do not take merely impressions of friends or teachers.

14. Begin at some point where the counselee feels a difficulty. It may not be the root of the problem but it is the only place at which help is really wanted. It will probably lead to the major problems.

15. So far as possible where mutual adjustment is involved, work out a solution in the presence of all persons concerned. While conferences with child and parent, e.g., may be held separately it is usually desirable to have a joint conference in which all the cards are on the table and everyone clearly understands the viewpoint of every other one.

16. It is usually desirable to observe a problem child in his normal environment in the classroom, in his home, and particularly on the street and playground.

17. It is seldom possible to depend exclusively upon the readjustment of the persons and objects in the environment, or upon the new insight and attitude of the person being advised. Both are usually in need of some readjustment. . . .

. . .

20. Do not use the term "psychoanalyze" and do not attempt the psychoanalytic technique. Use experts if necessary. . . .

. . .

22. It is sometimes necessary to study other persons than the one immediately involved. A problem child means at least one and probably two problem parents.

23. Try to provide opportunities for success at interesting and socially approved enterprises.

24. Avoid dependence upon verbal solutions. Get proposed solutions tested out in action.

25. Avoid pet theories, cure-alls, standard suspicions. Hunt for exceptions to theories, especially to new ones.

26. Don't try to save your own face. In many respects you may be less well adjusted than the counselee. Grow with him, don't reach down a helping hand from too high up. . . .

. . .

28. Avoid letting the plans focus on too distant goals without adequate attention to immediate steps. Help the counselee plan on improving adjustment this week, not console himself with phantasy. The past and future exist to enrich the present.

29. Seek to develop a process which will operate in new situations, as well as to secure adjustment of the present one. Experience is continuous, not discrete.

30. Even when simple Anglo-Saxon monosyllables in active illustrative form have been used, it is usually safe to assume that the "understanding" or "reaction" of the person to whom you are talking is in large measure an unknown variable.

31. Use great care to be fair to a point of view you do not support. State it as its enthusiastic advocates would like to hear it stated. To do less is unfair and, incidentally, far less effective.

32. Watch for budding stereotypes. When you find yourself getting an "intuition" in advance of investigation, which classifies a certain person or type of behavior, note it. It may mislead you often if not discounted.

33. Single experiences do not afford ground for generalization. Vivid incidents are particularly to be distrusted. Habitual and recurring behavior is the significant source of data.

34. Regard evidence skeptically, with due regard for the legal "rules of evidence." Remember the large error in first-hand observation and the untrustworthiness of circumstantial evidence. What A tells you about B is as much or more information about A. In scientific records, confirmation by two or three disinterested persons is desirable.

35. Occasionally overhaul your motives in the counseling. Give due weight to the vicarious thrill of hearing about misdeeds, the sense of mastery, the delight in secret intimacy, the desire for affection and trust from the young, the enjoyment of a reputation. Try to keep these in proper proportion to the desire for the welfare of the counselee.

36. Avoid the tendency to encourage and discourage in accord with a pattern of behavior which *you* like best. Let each individual become what is best for him. Particularly

avoid embodying your preferences in the sanctity of "race experience."

37. Encourage independence, doing what you do not approve, if it seem best to the counselee. Give as little help as is absolutely required. Constantly reduce this. If pupils constantly come back for more, consider yourself unsuccessful. Substitute self-confidence for confidence in you. The person who can get along without you is better off than any whom you "help."

38. Do not mistake the children who cause teachers trouble for the "problem children."

39. Keep confidences inviolate.

> Goodwin Watson and Ralph B. Spence, *Educational Problems for Psychological Study.* New York: The Macmillan Company, 1930, pp. 339-43. (Selected.)

330.   AVOID LABELING AND SHOWING-OFF

A more serious damage is sometimes done by persons inadequately trained in psychology who go about diagnosing and labeling the maladjustments of their acquaintances. This is, of course, a compensatory mechanism, for asserting the person's own superiority, a form of showing off. One who has learned a really psychological attitude will keep his guesses to himself, and will try to help maladjusted individuals to make better responses. Considerable good may be accomplished by inviting a shy, seclusive person to a party and seeing that he has a good time; much harm may be done by summarily labeling him an "introvert."

> Laurance Frederic Shaffer, *The Psychology of Adjustment.* Boston: Houghton Mifflin Company, 1936, p. 535.

C.   *Combination of Principles*

331.   ESSENTIAL PRINCIPLES

. . . The guidance principles here presented are useful, regardless of the point of view or method with which they may be allied. These principles have been derived from a variety of sources. . . .

PRINCIPLES PARTICULARLY RELATED TO BASIC ASSUMPTIONS

Guidance is a lifelong process. . . .

The Guidance Service should be extended to all, not simply to the obviously maladjusted. . . .

"Guiding" in the absence of data is quackery. . . .

Special training is needed to do guidance work. . . .

PRINCIPLES RELATED TO OUTCOMES PROJECTED FOR THE STUDENT

Guidance seeks to assist the individual in becoming progressively more able to guide himself. . . .

Provision must be made for all of the interrelated aspects of guidance. . . .

Any aspect of guidance may serve as an avenue of approach, or means of developing rapport. . . .

Each student should have some one individual in the school who is responsible for his guidance. . . .

A code of ethics should be rigorously observed by the guidance worker. . . .

PRINCIPLES RELATED PARTICULARLY TO THE
IMPLEMENTING OF GUIDANCE

Guidance activities are of two kinds: group and individual—not all workers are equally competent in both fields. . . .

When two or more individuals are engaged in guidance, some one should "head up" the work. . . .

Guidance workers should be assigned to students on some definite basis. . . .

Acquaintance with all available guidance agencies or services is essential to the counselor.

> D. Welty Lefever, Archie M. Turrell, Henry I. Weitzel, *Principles and Techniques of Guidance.* New York: The Ronald Press Company, 1941, pp. 31-51. (Discussion under each principle was omitted.)

332. PRINCIPLES BASIC TO GUIDANCE VIEWPOINT

1. Personnel work is concerned with the student as an individual. . . .

2. Individual differences in student needs, abilities, and interests must be recognized and provided for as far as possible by the school.

3. Personnel work is concerned with the whole student.

4. Personnel services are for all students, not for the maladjusted student alone. To serve all students, the work must be preventive, diagnostic, remedial, and developmental.

5. Personnel work is concerned largely with choices to be made and with adjustments in terms of the individual.

6. Personnel work implies counsel but not compulsion.

7. Personnel work seeks to assist the individual to become progressively more able to help himself.

8. Personnel work is a gradual and continuous process. The belief is rapidly growing stronger that this process should continue beyond the school years, that personnel services should be made available to the individual as long as he may need them.

9. Personnel workers need professional knowledge and training in the use of specialized techniques for a more adequate understanding of individual students.

10. Organization is needed to make personnel work effective.

Other principles are stated by some authors just as forcefully as are these ten. Because they are not generally accepted by other authorities, they are not included in this list.

Jane Warters, *High School Personnel Work Today*. New York: McGraw-Hill Book Company, 1946, p. 31.

333. SOME CURRENT ISSUES IN GUIDANCE

1. Shall the guidance program be geared to all the children or shall it concern itself primarily with problem children?

2. Is guidance exclusively a job for experts or can it be entrusted to non-experts?

3. In most situations that employ expensive experts, should the expert's employment be justified on the basis of the number of cases which he can carry or should his case load be held to a portion of his time so that he will have at least as large a portion of time to devote to consultations with teachers concerning

the problems which they have in their relationships with youngsters? . . .

. . .

5. To what extent should the guidance program be focused on vocational guidance, and to what extent on social-emotional development of students?

6. Is guidance primarily a matter of individual counseling; is it primarily accomplished through group work; or does it need a balanced combination?

7. Should group guidance be conceived more importantly as guidance classes and discussion groups or as guided group living and actual guided social experience?

8. Can behavior best be guided by having young people live in school and college environments under the control of adult rules and standards, or by having students participate in the development control, and direction of their own group life?

9. Is guidance a matter for junior and senior high school and college only, or should guidance be thought of as continuous from preschool to adult educational levels?

10. Should the school take responsibility for guidance of youth or should the school recognize that it must cooperate with the home and community in providing for the guidance of youth?

11. Should guidance workers consider their job school-limited, or should they see that school and community must work together cooperatively in the guidance of youth?

12. If all teachers are to be encouraged to be guidance workers, to learn more about guidance, to be "the pivots in schools and colleges on which guidance programs will turn," is it necessary to have specialized guidance staff? . . .

. . .

14. Should we stand for bifurcation of the guidance program along sex lines, or should we wipe out sex considerations in our organizational plans for guidance?

Esther Lloyd-Jones, "Some Current Issues in Guidance," *Teachers College Record,* November, 1947, pp. 77-88. (Only paragraph headings were included.)

334. FUNDAMENTAL BELIEFS

It is apparent that the guidance work done by individuals and organizations is built on a number of fundamental propositions which are basic in their technique and method of approach. . . .

1. *Is there not fairly general recognition of guidance as a process?*

The most effective guidance is that which takes into account the changes of age and environment in a constantly changing society. This means that it is not a service which begins and terminates at a specified time or place. Guidance must take into account the development and experience of the individual. It is a process that takes place over a period of time.

2. *Is not guidance conceived to be for the many rather than the few?*

Historically many guidance services developed to care for certain maladjusted individuals. A desire to develop as far as possible *each* individual's potentialities and to prevent such maladjustment has led to the conviction that such a service must be for the many rather than the few.

3. *Should not guidance seek to assist the individual to become progressively more able to guide himself?*

In very few instances indeed, if any at all, would organizations or individuals concerned with guidance even tolerate, let alone rely upon, a dictatorial point of view as a guiding principle. There is in this country a growing feeling of respect for the individual and a growing belief that all guidance resources should be used to help the individual to help himself. That means they should not be used to tell a person what to do or to dictate a course of action. In a democratic society, the right of each individual to choose for himself needs to be carefully safeguarded.

4. *Is there not a growing recognition of varied approaches in guidance?*

The guidance process in its different phases receives varying emphases as it concerns itself with different individuals. These phases of the guidance process involve, with different emphases, physical and mental health, education, vocation,

economic status, social and emotional factors, etc. The extent
to which an individual should attempt to get help from individuals or organizations interested in these different phases
must depend upon the individual's needs and his recognition
of his needs.

5. *Are not all aspects of guidance functionally interdependent?*

Since all phases of guidance are interrelated, dependent in
each case upon the individual, no pattern or self-limiting form
of guidance is possible. For the benefit of the individual, all
guidance agencies must understand each other and work together. For example, though an individual may seem to be
concerned with only one phase of the guidance process, a consideration of health factors may very easily involve social, emotional, educational, and vocational consideration. Failure to
regard all factors means failure to assist or properly guide that
individual.

6. *Is not the bearing of social factors beyond individual control
receiving greater attention?*

A growing appreciation of the weight of social factors seems
apparent. Recognition and appreciation of the effect of immediate as well as more remote social situations must enter
into any guidance procedure to make it effective toward the
goal of self guidance. This calls for great flexibility of guidance techniques. Dealing with the social situation at times becomes a primary procedure, and at other times it is only supplementary to that of dealing with the individual.

7. *Is there a growing recognition of the ethical implications of
guidance?*

Respect for the individual's personality, confidential handling of the counseling relationship, and determination to utilize
all resources in his interest, are cardinal obligations. In respect
of the relationship with colleagues, mutual respect and modes
of collaboration should be such as to enhance the quality of
the services rendered, and the welfare of the persons served.
In respect of the public, the obligation precludes any false
claim or misrepresentation as to what can be contributed, on
the basis of known techniques, and implies support of those
public policies which contribute to human welfare.

8. *Is not the need for training increasingly recognized?*

All organizations and individuals concerned with the guidance task are insistent that it be done well. There seems also to be a growing recognition that people doing guidance work need special training to do it most effectively. At present, the extent of training varies widely, from thorough training in a single field for the specialist, to a broader training for many who may do their guidance work more incidentally. Good training is demonstrated, in part, by the extent to which the guidance worker makes intelligent use of other competent individuals and agencies in the accomplishment of the guidance task.

9. *Is there not a growing desire and need to know what resources are available?*

The inter-relationships which exist in the guidance process necessarily involve dangers of overlapping as agencies and individuals attempt to function. Those who face their work professionally desire to understand the other person's part in this program. This understanding is not desired in order to supplant the other person or agency, but rather intelligently to supplement what the other can and does efficiently.

> Council of Guidance and Personnel Associations. Fundamental Beliefs, adopted at Cleveland Conference, 1939.

335.   EMPHASIS NOT ALONE UPON THE VOCATIONAL

One of the most deep-seated of all cleavages among practitioners results from differences of opinion as to whether guidance is to be confined to "vocational" guidance, whether it shall cover "personal" guidance in all aspects, or whether it shall be a synthesis of these two.

Traditionally, guidance in the schools and elsewhere has been vocational guidance in large part. The founder of guidance dealt in vocational counseling, the association of workers was called the National Vocational Guidance Association, the section in the United States Office of Education charged with furthering guidance in the nation's schools was named the Division of Occupational Information and Guidance, and departments of universities devoted to the training of technicians have listed their offerings as "educational and vocational guidance." (John M. Brewer and others, *History of Vocational Guidance*. New York: Harper and Brothers, 1942.) (L. S. Hawkins, H. A. Jager, and G. M. Ruch, *Occupational Information and Guidance: Organization and Administration*. Vocational Division Bulletin No. 204, Occupational Information and Guidance Series, No. 1, U. S. Department of the Interior, Office of Education, Washington, 1939.)

Outside of education, in the marts of trade and of professional life, vocational guidance has also been stressed. A common expression typifying the usual point of view sees guidance as essential in order to "keep square pegs out of round holes." The need for selection of employees in business and industrial establishments, the admission of youth into the differentiated curricula of colleges, the allocation of man power in civilian life and in the armed services during the war, the practices associated with the vocational placement of individuals through public employment offices, the selection of apprentices for training programs, the advisement of veterans prior to induction into training or placement on the job—these have all been social activities of the highest importance in which the desirability of guidance primarily of a vocational nature has naturally and rightfully been stressed.

Concurrent with this emphasis upon vocational guidance, especially in recent decades, has been a parallel interest in the adjustment and development of the individual, as a person, for his own sake and in his own right. This interest has primarily actuated people like progressive educators, mental hygienists, psychiatrists, and clinical psychologists. While fully aware of the dependence of individual development on environmental influences and recognizing social requirements and demands, this school of thought has been actively concerned with the growth of individual personality. It has been more interested in personal development than in vocational choice. (Lois H. Meek, and others, *Personal-Social Development of Boys and Girls*. New York: D. Appleton-Century Co., 1940.) (Paul Witty, and others, "Mental Health in the Classroom," *Thirteenth Yearbook, the Department of Supervisors and Directors of Instruction*, National Education Association, Washington, 1940.)

Such an emphasis has not been confined exclusively to pedagogues. Essentially this same philosophy has appeared in the principles underlying the practices of modern industrial psychology, which has sought the solution of many problems of management in a philosophy that accepts the right of the individual to recognition, approval, and favorable conditions for self-development.

We are now at a stage where a fruitful synthesis of these two trends is not only possible but essential. Without in any way impairing the legitimate and necessary extension of activity in that phase of guidance having to do with vocational choice and adjustment, we can view this phase as being applicable to the all-round favorable development of individuals, of social groups, and of communities. In individual and in community alike, the occupational phase of human living is of central importance, yet it must be seen in the total organic context of life in general—the life of the family, of the person outside of his vocation, of the citizen. It is a favorable *total* balance of development which is sought, and in this over-all balance the aspect of occupational choice and adjustment must loom large.

> Robert H. Mathewson, *Guidance Policy and Practice*. New York: Harper and Brothers, 1949, pp. 237-39.

336. Some Basic Principles

Guidance work is not "telling" students what they should do. It is more than a testing program, a homeroom, or a vocations class, although these may be *parts* of a guidance program. The modern concept of guidance is that of a program of services designed to individualize the school experiences of the student and to assist him to become the most effective person possible.

Some specific principles of guidance are:

1. Guidance is concerned with the "whole" student, not with his intellectual life alone.

2. Guidance is concerned with *all* students, not only with special or "problem" students.

3. Guidance is concerned primarily with prevention rather than cure.

4. Guidance is more than just the activity of a specialist; it involves the whole school staff.

5. Guidance is concerned with the choices and decisions to be made by the student.

6. Guidance is concerned with developing student self-understanding and self-determination.

7. Guidance is "counsel"—not "compulsion."

8. Guidance is a continuous process throughout the school life of each student.

> C. Gilbert Wrenn and Willis E. Dugan, *Guidance Procedures in High School.* Minneapolis: The University of Minnesota Press, 1950, pp. 2-3.

Part IV

WORKING WITH THE INDIVIDUAL

13.

Intensive Study of the Individual

---

337. Shaffer on Origin and Nature of Case Study

The Method of Case Study. The case history of an individual is a description of his environment and background and of the influences that have affected his development. The method of case study is very largely a contribution to psychology from the field of social work. Toward the end of the last century social workers began making systematic investigations of the applicants to family relief organizations. At first these studies were made to determine if the client was "worthy," and if other means of assistance were not available. From this beginning, the case study gradually developed into a method for understanding the individual or the family group, in order to administer the kind of aid most needed and ultimately to restore self-help through guidance and training. When psychiatry, psychology and social work became combined in the form of the child guidance clinic, social workers naturally fell heir to the task of gathering most of the case histories, a role for which they had already developed techniques.

The case study method found ready acceptance among psychiatrists and psychologists, for it offered a practical means for applying the genetic point of view. The psychiatrist in practice and the psychologist in theory had come to recognize the incompleteness of a diagnosis based only on the present condition of an individual without inquiry into the development of his traits. Since personality and behavior are the result of an individual's past experiences and adjustments, the value of the developmental history is obvious. The mental hygiene movement has had a reciprocal influence on social case work in general. All branches of social work now conceive their objectives in terms of the personality adjustments of their clients.

Case study data are here distinguished as the facts obtained principally from sources other than the subject himself. These data come from observations made of the subject and of his surroundings, and from the reports of others concerning him. The chief sources of information are interviews with the parents of the subject and with other members of his family, with his employers, his teachers and his associates. Records of schools, courts and of social agencies are utilized when these are available and pertinent. Objective observations of the assets and defects of the individual's environment are also made. The case history method is too little used by psychoanalysts and by many psychiatrists and psychologists who work alone, either because they are not equipped to carry it out, or because they deny its value. On the other hand, some social agencies overemphasize the outside study and place too little value on the individual's own account of his problems and attitudes.

> Laurance Frederic Shaffer, *The Psychology of Adjustment.*
> Boston: Houghton Mifflin Company, 1936, pp. 445-47.

338.   CASE STUDY A SPECIALIZED FORM OF RECORD KEEPING

The case study is an old method which has been rediscovered and adapted to the complex business of modern counseling. Strictly speaking, it is not a tool or technique in quite the same sense as are statistics, anecdotal records, or psychological tests. Its major function is to bring together the information collected by the other tools and their techniques in such a manner that these data can be systematically reviewed and analyzed and clinical weightings assigned them. Basically it is an individualized, discriminating, systematically planned method of record keeping and interpretation.

> Milton E. Hahn and Malcolm S. MacLean, *General Clinical Counseling.* New York: McGraw-Hill Book Company, Inc., 1950, pp. 135-36. By permission of the publishers.

339.   TECHNIQUES FOR THE STUDY OF INDIVIDUAL CHILDREN

The best method for an intensive study of individuals is what may be called the "case study" method, the purpose of which is to assure that so far as possible all important sources of information are tapped and types of information gathered, and all this information so organized and interrelated that the person studied is clearly seen as a dynamic individual trying to adjust to a particular and understood environment. Although some of the work of gathering this information is of a quite routine nature, the major objective of the case study method —to see the individual as a whole, in his world—should never be forgotten. A complete case study usually cannot be made for every child in the classroom; however, teachers should be familiar enough with case study methods to be able to use them for children who especially need individual study. And teachers should have the case study point of view, should realize that such study is necessary for real understanding of a child.

> Sidney L. Pressey and Francis P. Robinson, *Psychology and the New Education (Revised)*. New York: Harper and Brothers, 1944, p. 321.

340. The Case History Method

. . . The psychologist is forced to adopt a substitute for the true developmental method by reconstructing the individual's developmental history as well as can be done from the memory of the individual and his associates and from whatever records have been preserved. This *case history method* has obvious disadvantages, much like those of the anecdotal method. It depends largely on fallible memory of incidents that were not scientifically observed in the first place. But it seems to be the only way to make a start toward answering some very important questions.

The case history method, up to the present time, has been employed mostly with individuals whose behavior is undesirable in some respect. When a person has broken down mentally, the psychiatrist with the assistance of a social worker obtains information on this person's heredity and family environment, noting such conditions as are believed to be important. The patient's own story is taken down and the attempt is made to get back to earlier emotional conflicts which may have a bearing on his present trouble. When a child presents a serious behavior problem—such as stealing, overaggressiveness, destructive "meanness," or shyness and dependence—he may be taken to a child guidance clinic, where a staff of experts considers his history from several points of view, medical, psychological and social. These experts approach the child in a friendly spirit, and make him see they are not trying to "get something on him," but wish to help him by first understanding him. They need co-operation from him and from his parents, and their inquiries must be conducted with tact as well as skill. They work on the assumption that the child's misconduct has causes which should be discovered, causes lying in his environment and in his own limitations.

The guidance clinic does more than reconstruct the history of the case to date. In co-operation with the home and the school, it tries an experiment on the child, by way of treatment. Any treatment of such a case is experimental in some degree, since there is no certainty of success. The case history and present state of the child suggest some cause of the misconduct and the treatment tests this hypothesis by altering certain conditions of the child's life. The hypothesis may be that the child is spoiled or overprotected or denied affection at home, or that his school placement is above or below his mental age, or that his silly behavior, enuresis, fussy eating habits or temper tantrums are just his way of bidding for attention. Treatment in line with any such hypothesis evidently calls for co-operation from parents or teachers. If the treatment succeeds, the hypothesis works and is verified to that extent; if the treatment fails, some other hypothesis must be given a trial.

Case histories of outstandingly fine or successful persons are decidedly lacking so far. The behavior clinics are conducted for the benefit of those who have got into trouble; and the adult, unless he has got into trouble of some sort, is sensitive about being probed. If we could tell in advance that a given newborn baby was going to become great or fine, we could study his development as it proceeded. A biography, written long afterward, is almost sure to be meager and unpsychological in its account of the subject's early development. Now that many children, including some of great promise, are being studied, we may hope in time to possess some authentic developmental biographies of normal and superior people.

> Robert S. Woodworth, *Psychology,* Fourth Edition. New York: Henry Holt and Company, Inc., 1940, pp. 13-15. By permission of the publishers.

341. The Limitations of the Case Study

The limitations of case studies are essentially limitations of the persons who make them. A person who does case work ought to be mature. This kind of maturity has nothing to do with age but rather with adjustment in the major areas of his life: in the family, in his work, and in relation to sex and society. Unless a person is fairly well adjusted, he cannot do effective case work. Persons who have worked through their own difficulties are often especially helpful to other people because they have profited by their own experience. Another difficulty within the case worker is a tendency to impose his own inclinations: a teacher has a tendency to teach; a preacher, to preach; a mother, to be oversolicitous. The bias of the worker, already discussed in connection with the interview, must be recognized. Most serious is the limited ability of teacher-counselors to interpret and unify the data collected and to use it for the good of the student.

In addition to difficulties within the worker, there are inaccuracies of memory. Many details of family history and early development are lost in the fog of faulty observation and memory. Case studies, however, are gaining precision through the use of standardized tests, better technics of interviewing and of reporting observations, and the inclusion of other relevant quantitative data. At best, case history data are fragmentary; they do not give a complete picture of the individual. Some significant information has been withheld, some overlooked, some rejected by the worker as of little worth.

> Ruth Strang, *The Role of the Teacher in Personnel Work.* New York: Bureau of Publications, Teachers College, Columbia University, 1946, pp. 467-68.

342. Need to Check Conclusions From Case Data

The Method of Case Study. Unfortunately the entire adjustive processes of humans are not amenable to study by the more exact research techniques. To impose a high degree of experimental control in the lives of individuals while studying their adjustments would destroy the reality of the situations to which they are compelled to adjust, and hence make the results of experiment inapplicable to the problems involved in everyday difficulties. Also, the causes of an adjustment usually lie in the entire life history of the individual and by the time he comes to the psychologist's attention it is too late to apply control or even measurement to many of his past experiences. To surmount this difficulty, the case method must be employed. A large number of cases of maladjustment which resemble each other as to symptoms are investigated to discover the probable antecedents and most effective curative measures. . . .

The case study method is in accord with the universal steps of scientific procedure. The accumulation of data, analysis, making an hypothesis, and its practical use in prediction, represent the same sequence as was illustrated by the example from physics. The chief defect of the case method is in its manner of securing data. Most of its observations are obtained from the recall of experiences long past made either by the subject or by other persons. The unreliability of remembering must be recognized as a factor limiting the usefulness of case study. This error can be minimized by using objective methods as much as possible and by securing confirming reports from many persons. If the case method were used alone, almost any hypothesis could be based on it. The scientific psychologist regards conclusions from case data as valid only when they are compatible with the results of the more exact techniques of experiment and measurement.

> Laurance Frederic Shaffer, *The Psychology of Adjustment.*
> Boston: Houghton Mifflin Company, 1936, pp. 14 and 16.

343.   A Comprehensive and Difficult Undertaking

The pupil cannot be understood unless he is known. And he cannot be known unless information is had about him, not incomplete and perhaps inaccurate information gathered at random, but comprehensive information systematically gathered and carefully appraised for reliability and significance. To be usable, the information collected must be accurate. To provide a clear, vivid picture of the whole person, it must be significant and comprehensive. To relate the story of the pupil's school life, it must be summarized in a dynamic and unified manner. To show trends and growth, it must be recorded regularly and continuously. And finally, to maintain the unity of the story and to save much waste, the information gathered in one school must be summarized and sent to the next school or other service agency.

> Jane Warters, *High School Personnel Work Today.* New York: McGraw-Hill Book Company, Inc., 1946, pp. 60-61.

344. Means for Securing the Information Needed

The means used for collecting the information needed are described in the literature as analytical and diagnostic techniques. The most common of these are tests, records of achievement, records of activities, questionnaires, check lists, autobiographical sketches, diary records, time-distribution sheets, interviews, records of informal conversations with the student or with those who know him, anecdotal records, records of observation, interest inventories, and health records.

> *Ibid.,* pp. 62-63.

345. Wide Sample of Data From the Case Study

Modern education recognizes each child as a distinct total personality, living in a complex world which in manifold ways is shaping him. His behavior as a pupil in class is only one part of his total life, and the school is only one special environment of the many environments in which he lives. To do its job, the school must extend beyond itself.

For adequate study of the child, the school must know three things with which it often does not now concern itself; it must know at least a little about the home and neighborhood from which the child comes, about his family, and about his life outside of school. A systematic scheme of case study, comprehending these neglected areas of information, is desirable if children are to be really understood. And sources of information beyond the school are obviously necessary if such information is to be had. From all this information, the child as a dynamic personality, trying bravely to make good in his world, may at last be seen. It is impossible thus to see him unless these steps are taken.

Sidney L. Pressey and Francis P. Robinson, *Psychology and the New Education (Revised)*. New York: Harper and Brothers, 1944, p. 360.

346. A COMPREHENSIVE SAMPLING OF FACTS NEEDED

Information needed. To understand students in all dimensions of their personality and environment a comprehensive sampling of facts about each student is needed. Information that is of value for instructional and guidance purposes, and that should be contained in the cumulative record, includes the following:

Areas of Information	*Means of Appraisal*
1. Scholastic aptitude	Previous grades, psychological tests of ability and achievement.
2. Scholastic achievement and basic skills	Previous grades, standardized and teacher-made achievement tests, survey and diagnostic tests of basic skills, school activities, and work experience.
3. Special abilities: clerical, mathematical, artistic, and the like	Special aptitude tests, interviews, evaluation of previous achievement or performance (work experience, hobbies, extracurricular activities).
4. Interests and plans	Autobiographies, interest inventories or tests, stated interests, interviews, previous achievement, and both work and leisure activities.
5. Health and physical status	Physical examination, health history, observation, attendance record and nurse follow-up, and family consultation.

6. Home and family relationships	Observation, anecdotes, rating scales, interviews, autobiographies, themes, check lists and adjustment inventories, reports from employers, group workers,
7. Emotional stability and social adjustment	or group leaders, and parent conferences.
8. Attitudes	Student questionnaires, home contacts, interviews, themes, autobiographies and other documentary information, and standardized rating scales.
9. Work experience	Record of employer, reports of vocational counselor, interviews, and student questionnaires.

C. Gilbert Wrenn and Willis E. Dugan, *Guidance Procedures in High School*. Minneapolis: The University of Minnesota Press, 1950, pp. 18-19.

347. WARTER'S SUGGESTIONS ON INFORMATION NEEDED

What information should personnel workers have on their records? For good personnel work they need such information as the following:

1. *Identifying data*—such information as name, address, age, date of birth, and the like. The addition of a photograph is desirable.

2. *Scholastic-achievement data*—including information on progress toward such objectives as appreciations, understandings, creative expression, and good work habits, as well as information concerning acquisition of information, techniques, and skills.

3. *Psychological data*—information concerning intelligence, special aptitudes, interests, attitudes, and personality traits.

4. *Physical data*—health history; medical and dental data; and general information about health, physical characteristics, appearance, and the student's attitude toward them.

5. *Mental-health data*—information concerning emotional

adjustment, personal competence and confidence, significant limitations, and symptoms of conflict.

6. *Data on use of free time*—information concerning free-time activities and interests in and outside school, membership in organized and unorganized groups, role and adjustment in these groups, social competence and confidence.

7. *Socio-economic data*—information about parents' background, occupation, and education; home and family conditions and influence; significant factors in neighborhood and other social environments.

8. *Data on nonscholastic achievement in and outside school* —information concerning significant experiences, notable accomplishments, special honors, and leadership roles.

9. Information concerning *in- and out-of-school employment,* gainful and nongainful.

10. Information concerning *educational and vocational plans.*

> Jane Warters, *High School Personnel Work Today.* New York: McGraw-Hill Book Company, Inc., 1946, p. 62.

348. CONTENTS OF A CASE STUDY

The minimum contents of a case study *adequate for diagnosing* include the following:—(Adapted from Ruth Strang's *Counseling Technics in College and Secondary School,* Chap. 3, Harper & Brothers, New York, 1937, and Arthur E. Traxler's *Case Study Procedures in Guidance,* Educational Records Bureau, New York, December, 1937 [mimeograph].)

Family history including education, occupation, and financial status of parents and siblings, and the psychological relationships among members of the family and neighborhood relationships.

School history of the student, including his scholastic progress and adjustments to teachers and students, record of participation in activities, the type and name of school attended, study habits, and cumulative record of psychological tests.

Health record, including history of serious illnesses and the physician's report of his present status.

Vocational and work experiences and record of past and present occupational ambitions and plans, including plans and financial resources for occupational training.

Social-recreational interests and habits, including type and frequency of participation.

E. G. Williamson, *How to Counsel Students.* New York: Mc-Graw-Hill Book Company, Inc., 1939, p. 67.

349. SHAFFER'S CASE STUDY OUTLINE

An Outline for Case Study. A synopsis of the principal areas usually covered by a case history may assist in understanding the clinical approach. It may be of value to teachers and parents who will not make complete professional studies alone, but who may be called upon to co-operate in the formulation of a case study. To enumerate all of the factors that are included in case histories is impossible, for any competent attempt to do so would be a book in itself. The outline below is intended only to suggest the scope of case study, especially to those who have no training in social case work. For convenience, some data not usually gathered by the social worker have been included, such as the results of the physical examination and of mental and educational tests.

Not all of the points enumerated in the outline are investigated in every case, while in some instances detailed accounts are made of matters touched on only lightly here. The important function of a case history is to gather all of the pertinent data. It is desirable, therefore, to keep the method of case study flexible. The study of a maladjustment cannot be crammed into any set scheme of case history. Instead, the method of approach must be modified to meet the problems offered by the individual. In some clinics a shorter history is prepared, an experienced social worker judging what is pertinent to the case. This is time-saving, but has the disadvantage of neglecting facts that may become significant as study and treatment progress. It is better to gather too much information than too little. Most of the outline which follows is designed for child cases, since a full case study is most useful with children. For adults an adaptation of some sections is necessary, but the childhood experiences and parental attitudes even of grown persons are not to be ignored.

CASE HISTORY OUTLINE

A. *Identifying Data.*

Name. Address. Date of report. Date of birth (verify from records). Age. Place of birth. Sex. Race. Nationality. Marital status. Occupation. By whom referred.

B. *Statement of the Problem.*

1. *The "Complaint Problem."* Why was the subject referred for study? How do parents, teachers, etc., conceive his problem? Give in the words of the person referring.

2. *Worker's Statement of Nature of Problem.* Exactly what behavior does the subject show that merits study? Cite specific examples. To what situations does he respond by this behavior?

3. *History of the Problem.* When was this behavior first noted? Has the subject reacted similarly at any previous time? Under what circumstances? Are there recurring patterns of response to recurring frustrations?

C. *Family and Social Environment.*

(Little emphasis is placed on heredity and much on environmental influences.)

1. *Persons in the Home.* For each of the following persons, give: age; education; health; outstanding personality traits; social behavior; adjustments to each other; attitude toward the person being studied; and other pertinent facts.
   a. Father.
   b. Mother.
   c. Step-parents, if any.
   d. Siblings—ages; position in family; comparative strength, health, and school accomplishments; any facts of favoritism.
   e. Grandparents—direct effect on the subject through home contacts, if any; indirect effect through the formation of the traits of the parents.
   f. Other relatives, if of direct or indirect influence.
   g. Boarders, or other unrelated persons residing in the home.
   h. Parent's associates, close friends, visitors, if pertinent.

2. *Home Attitudes.* What are the attitudes of the persons in the home, individually and collectively, toward the subject and his problems?

3. *Control and Discipline.* How is the subject managed by his parents? Is he given responsibilities? What methods of punishment are employed? Are parents in agreement as to control?

4. *Economic Status of the Family.* What is the general economic level? Have there been any marked economic changes?

5. *Cultural Status of the Family.* What is their regard for education, books, cultural advantages?

6. *Language Spoken in the Home.* What language? Quality?

7. *Neighborhood.* General social, economic and cultural conditions.

D. *Physical Conditions and History.*

1. *Physical Examination.* When made? How do the patient's size, development and strength compare with norms? General constitution. Defects of vision or hearing. Neurological findings. Endocrine disturbances. Infectious conditions. Teeth, nose and throat. Special tests.

2. *Physical Development.* What has been the course of development of size and strength? Have any anomalies of growth been present? General disease history. Injuries. Right or left-handed? Have any changes in handedness been made?

3. *Conditions Especially Related to Adjustment.* Disorders of the nervous system, chorea, encephalitis, etc. Any "spells," seizures, convulsions, etc. Sleepwalking. Physical symptoms of probable hysterical basis, such as aches, "nervous indigestion." "Nervousness." "Nervous breakdowns."

4. *Sex Development.* Age of puberty. Any other pertinent facts.

E. *Developmental History.*

1. *Prenatal Period and Birth.* Mother's health during pregnancy; condition of birth; birth injuries; normal or premature birth.

2. *Early Developmental Signs.* Age at which weaned; age of teething; ages of holding head erect, standing and walking; age of talking; age of learning to read; control of elimination; self-help in feeding, dressing, etc.

3. *Intellectual Development.* Results of mental tests administered at present time. Records of previous tests. Any indica-

tions of general mental superiority or defect. Special talents or disabilities.

4. *Speech Development.* Record of any speech defects.
5. *Emotional Development.*
   a. Rage behavior. Tantrums; modified forms of rage. How frequent? in what situations?
   b. Fear behavior. General fears; shyness. Specific fears; situations feared most; experiences conditioning these fears. Night terrors.
   c. Love behavior. Attachments to parents or others. Dependence.
   d. Emotional balance. Overemotional or apathetic. Any tendency to elation and depression. Periodicy of emotional behavior.
6. *Social Development.* Extent of social experiences. Successes or failures in group adjustment.

F. *Educational History.*
   1. *School Progress.* Age entered school. Acceleration or retardation. Special classes. Trend of school marks. In the case of adults: success at school; units completed.
   2. *Educational Status.* Results of educational achievement tests. Special abilities or disabilities.
   3. *School Adjustment.* Conduct and discipline problems. Attitude toward school. Truancy.
   4. *Educational Plans and Ambitions.* Are there discrepancies between plans and abilities?

G. *Economic History.*
   1. *Occupation.* Exact nature of the work done. Rewards. Success or failure in work. Attitude toward occupation.
   2. *Occupational History.* Positions. Dates. Salaries. Success or failure. Reasons for leaving a job.
   3. *Vocational Plans and Ambitions.* Are the ambitions attainable with the subject's ability and opportunities?

H. *Legal History.*
   1. *Delinquencies, Court Records* (if any). Exact nature of the delinquent behavior. What steps were taken? What is the effect of these experiences on the subject's attitude?

I. *Habits, Adjustments and Satisfactions.*
   1. *Routine Habits.* Routine of work, recreation, eating, sleeping. A typical time schedule is sometimes helpful.

2. *Play, Hobbies and Interests.* Are recreations typically social or solitary? What does the subject voluntarily do for pleasure? Special skills and interests in hobbies. Reading. What kind of books? Movies, and other organized recreation.
3. *Imaginative Satisfactions.* Wishes, daydreams, remote ambitions.
4. *Sex Habits.* Sex knowledge, experience and interest. Masturbation. Attitude toward the opposite sex. Attitude toward sex questions.
5. *Social Habits.* Does the subject have few or many friends? How does he get along with his associates? Leader or dependent? What are his typical social contacts and activities?

Laurance Frederic Shaffer, *The Psychology of Adjustment.* Boston: Houghton Mifflin Company, 1936, pp. 447-51.

350. Means for Discovering Individual Patterns

Since the individualizing of all school activities is the goal of guidance, the discovery of individual problems and adjustment patterns is a principal concern of teachers and specialists. Diagnostic tools actually used vary in different situations but include all the following:

Observation. A prime diagnostic tool is observation of the child in the classroom, on the playground, alone, in close social groups, in his own home, and in any other type of activity in which the child may be engaged. This observation may be a fairly casual observation by the teacher or any other observer. It may, however, be highly systematic and detailed observation which looks for such characteristics as health habits, speech habits, social relationship habits, study habits, emotional habits, cleanliness, clothing, posture, physique, appearance, coordination, cooperation, play behavior, and a host of other detailed responses. Such observation is often the means for getting a clue as to a particular need or a particular frustration of a child.

Physical Examinations. Such examinations range all the way from a simple measurement of height and weight to complete clinical examinations including neurological and endocrinological tests. Experienced psychologists will never pass judgment on the causation of a particular problem without first having the child undergo an adequate physical examination.

School Records. The study of records will include scholarship records, health reports, records of tests which have been given, and anecdotal reports of behavior characteristics during each school year. Such records will also include family history, developmental records of the individual child, and judgments and reports from previous teachers and other workers who have known the child.

Direct Interviews with the Child. The use made of direct interviews varies, of course, with the age and condition of the child. Generally, however, direct interviews will help to define the problem and to locate factors connected with it, especially to help determine the emotional significance of these factors. . . .

Case Studies. The most complete form of investigation of an individual problem is the case study. These studies record and analyze all the results of observation, school records, home visits, individual examinations, test scores, and the like. Systematic ways of obtaining and recording data are employed. Specific clues as to the handling of children are more likely to be gleaned from such thorough investigation than from the more casual investigation of teachers, administrators, or specialists.

Home Visits. Either as a part of the case study procedure or as a less complete investigation, home visits are frequently utilized in obtaining pictures of the total environment of the child. The extra-school background of the child influences his or her growth and behavior—physical, emotional, intellectual and social.

Autobiographies. Pupil autobiographies, which may be obtained either individually or from groups of pupils, are very frequent sources of good insights into the problems and factors related to these problems of individual children. Such autobiographies are easily obtained by skilled teachers and may become very useful parts of the guidance folder.

Harl R. Douglass, editor, *Education for Life Adjustment.* New York: The Ronald Press Company, 1950, pp. 319-21. (From chapter by J. W. McDaniel.)

351. TOOLS FOR APPRAISAL

Securing the information. Many tools for appraisal have been developed, of which tests are but one. In the typical small high school, where the appraisal techniques of tests and records are usually at a minimum, the main information available about a student often is limited to a scholastic aptitude (intelligence) test score and a record of school achievement. Such a narrow range of understanding can be enlarged by planned use of a variety of simple techniques:

1. *The cumulative record.* The folder-type guidance record aids teachers in their study of the individual by providing a thorough picture of his past performance and development. Such a record system may be inaugurated in the ninth grade and developed progressively for the entire school by setting it in motion for each successive ninth-grade group.

2. *The pupil questionnaire.* A mimeographed questionnaire will provide basic facts about home and family, out-of-school interests and activities, educational and vocational plans, work experience, attitudes, and self-ratings.

3. *Psychological tests.* At least two measures of scholastic aptitude, supplemented by tests of reading skills, measures of scholastic achievement, and an inventory of interests, should be obtained in the high school.

4. *Observation reports and anecdotes.* Teacher reports, in terms of objective anecdotes about actual pupil performance and behavior, both good and bad, represent a desirable addition to the understanding of pupils.

5. *Autobiographies.* Student autobiographies often are introduced in English classes as projects in the development of pupil self-appraisal and clarification of plans. Such personal reports, which should be treated always as confidential, may be used in connection with a cumulative record to establish a more complete understanding of the individual.

6. *Interviews.* The interview is the most effective single technique for obtaining a clearer picture of student plans, attitudes, and adjustment. It is helpful for such specific purposes as (a) securing information from the student, (b) giv-

ing needed information, and (c) assisting pupils in the solution of problems.

7.   *Case study.*   The case study is the most comprehensive technique for the study of an individual. There are two types of case studies: (a) the abbreviated case study provided for all pupils by the developmental picture contained in the cumulative record, and (b) the intensive case history of a particular student, supplemented by careful interpretation of all collected facts and recommendations for treatment. The counselor, the teachers, and whatever other specially trained workers are available pool their efforts in this unified study of an individual.

> C. Gilbert Wrenn and Willis E. Dugan, *Guidance Procedures in High School.* Minneapolis: The University of Minnesota Press, 1950, pp. 19-20.

352.   Sources of Analytical Data

These sources of analytical data include: Reports of psychometrists who administer psychological and aptitude tests and who also observe significant behavior indicative of attitudes, emotions, and ambitions.

Teachers who may have observed significant behavior indicative of emotions, attitudes, interests, and aptitudes.

Parents who often unconsciously reveal the cause of behavior problems in students by describing attitudes and modes of family discipline and regulation.

Other counselors who contribute their own understanding and tentative diagnoses of the student's personality and significant observations of the student's behavior and attitudes.

Specialized personnel officers (in the fields of health, extra-curricular activities, finance and part-time employment, and speech, reading, and study disabilities) who may have observed the student's behavior in different situations and interviews and thereby have formed impressions of his personality and qualifications which yield insight into attitudes not revealed in the counselor's interviews.

Comments by the student's associates which yield insight into his frame of mind not otherwise revealed.

Finally there is one of the most important of all sources of analytical data—the counselor's interview with the student. In the process of talking with the student, the skilled counselor has an opportunity to direct and phrase his questions and comments in such a way as to sample and reveal subtle attitudes, prejudices, beliefs, and interests of the student which may not be analyzed by objective techniques. The effective counselor assimilates available data *before* the interview and then seeks for supplemental and explanatory data by means of interviewing discussions with the students. These data are so individualistic in terms of each student that no standardized descriptions can be made. But this source of analytical data is one of the most important.

E. G. Williamson, *How To Counsel Students.* New York: McGraw-Hill Book Company, Inc., 1939, pp. 63-64.

353. The Teacher's Use of the Case Study

The developmental record is an abbreviated case study kept for all students. The case study is a more comprehensive, unified study of individuals who present baffling complexity of behavior. Both attempt to interpret and synthesize the facts and impressions collected about individuals. By making a few intensive case studies the teacher gains a better understanding of all students and of the complexity of factors that may influence an individual's behavior. He also understands better the significance of the case studies made by specialists with whom he works.

The *case history* is a comprehensive factual account of the individual's development. The *case study*, as its name implies, includes interpretation and integration of the case history data and recommendations based on this study. It is much easier to write a case history than to make a case study. In making case studies teachers should have the opportunity of working closely with trained case workers. Thus they will avoid the grave danger of trying to use clinical methods for which they do not have sufficient background. Making a case study is more like painting a picture than like putting together a jigsaw puzzle.

Ruth Strang, *The Role of the Teacher in Personnel Work.* New York: Bureau of Publications, Teachers College, Columbia University, 1946, pp. 432-33.

354. Possibilities and Limitations of Teachers in Use of the Case Study

Case Study Procedures.—Frequently information about students is needed which cannot be obtained from the student alone. Various other sources and individuals must be consulted. Social background, home conditions, and other environmental factors must be considered. Sometimes case studies need to be made. The case study represents one of the major strategies of guidance. It may be defined as a technique or method of bringing together all pertinent information about a student in forming a unified background for interpreting his needs and treating his difficulties. Needs and difficulties should be broadly conceived; even the best adjusted students have definite needs and encounter difficulties in connection with their class and extra-class work, which case study procedures would reveal.

A case history, therefore, would be useful for every student in the school. If such were available we would have rather complete information concerning the "whole" individual. Such information would assist teachers in becoming aware of student needs, facilitate remedial instruction, and reveal facts that would call forth sympathy instead of apathy and indifference.

Case studies, however, cannot be made for all the students in most secondary schools. Lack of time, if nothing else, will prevent it. It has been estimated that at least 150 hours may easily be spent in preparing a single case study. But time is not the only limiting factor. Most teachers are not prepared to make case studies. Adequate training for this technique is required. Data must be complete within the scope determined for the study. *The misuse of confidential information must also be prevented.*

Case studies are of two kinds: those made for "ordinary" students and those developed for the seriously maladjusted. The first of these can, and should, be compiled by properly prepared teachers; the second should be reserved for the guidance expert. (The Personal Information Form on pages 241-244 is omitted above.)

D. Welty Lefever, Archie M. Turrell, and Henry I. Weitzel,

Principles and Techniques of Guidance. New York: The Ronald Press Company, 1941, pp. 240 and 245.

355. OLSON'S VIEW OF THE CASE STUDY

The techniques and data employed in a case study vary according to the purposes and occasion. Thus the need for comprehensiveness is less when a teacher attempts to locate the process by which an otherwise able child regularly secures an incorrect solution in arithmetic than when a group in a clinic attempts to understand an undesirable trend in the personality of a child and to make recommendations for its elimination. If the problem is guidance into a vocation, the data are somewhat different than if the problem is one of direction into further educational opportunity. Much or little evidence may be required, depending upon the nature of the problem and the seriousness of the consequences that may flow from the decision. Illustrations of the case method applied to educational disabilities may be found in (1) Harry J. Baker, *Educational Disability and Case Studies in Remedial Teaching.* Bloomington, Illinois: The Public School Publishing Company, 1929, 172 p., and (2) Marion Monroe, *Children Who Cannot Read.* Chicago: The University of Chicago Press, 1932, 205 p.

The person engaged in case study realizes that every type of behavior has a past, a present, and a future. If one wishes to modify the future, he does so in part by understanding the dynamics of forces operative in the past and present. A complete account requires some information concerning hereditary factors as revealed in the grandparents, parents, and collaterals. A history of health and disease, and of traumatic emotional and social episodes, is standard practice. An adequate case study usually includes a rather comprehensive appraisal of the child's present status. The measures of status commonly include a physical examination, mental tests, measures of educational achievement, diagnostic tests, and examinations of special interests, attitudes, and aptitudes.

A major instrument in case-study technique is the interview. The interview may be with the individual directly concerned or with a person bearing some relationship to him. In the case of young children, the interview is sometimes implemented with plastic and construction materials, paint, or toys. . . .

The ideal clinical study utilizes the technical refinements growing out of every field of investigation. With all the evidence at hand, decisions, recommendations, and treatment are based upon a synthesis of the material in harmony with available knowledge. In cases of uncertainty, treatment hypotheses are tentatively held to be confirmed or disproved by subsequent events. The formula for clinical practice is simple in broad outline, but enormously complex and technical in detail. The task in case work is to change the child who presents the problem, change the environment, or change both. The change of the child through personal or milieu therapy may require a variety of special knowledge and skills.

In some instances, a particular worker in a definite specialty or position is the responsible agent in case-study procedure. Depending upon the problem, the person may be counselor, physician, minister, nurse, psychologist, teacher, social worker, psychiatrist, personnel officer, speech specialist, principal, dean, or registrar. It is probable that every practitioner in the field of human relations can use case methods with profit.

Since case studies, regardless of the point of contact with the individual, always present ramifications in every direction, successful procedure rests heavily on the breadth and depth of insight of the person or persons conducting them.

> Willard C. Olson, "General Methods—Case Study," *The Scientific Movement in Education.* Thirty-seventh Yearbook of the National Society for the Study of Education, Part II. Chicago: The University of Chicago Press, 1938, chap. 27, pp. 329-31. By permission of the Society.

356. Knowing Individuals in the Group and Out

Your first effort should be directed toward getting acquainted with the pupils in your group and helping them to get acquainted with each other. This is basic. You can't be of any help to these boys and girls unless you know them. And it is necessary to know all of them, for probably the shy, retiring ones will need your help the most. Mary's absence is just troublesome until you know that her mother is fatally ill; then

Mary's problem becomes one requiring not scolding but understanding. Immediately you smooth the way for her by explaining to the other teachers, and Mary finds school a place where people are helpful and kind. Jack's unkempt appearance is revolting until one day you happen to visit the truck farm on the edge of town where he lives, and you wonder that he has the stamina to get to school at all.

But how much can a teacher-adviser be expected to know about individual pupils? Social case workers, clinical psychologists, and psychiatrists have set up standards for knowing individuals which are beyond anything a classroom teacher can attain. A case as handled by a social worker may run into one hundred pages of typed case notes. A case as handled by a vocational counselor in the Veterans Administration counseling centers may involve six or eight hours of testing and several hours of interviewing. A psychiatrist or a psychoanalyst may spend from one hundred to two hundred hours going into the patient's past and advising him.

Teacher-advisers are working at a different level of case work, a level which means knowing and aiding more persons, but persons with less serious problems. Nevertheless, they need to make every effort to know their advisees, for to give guidance "off the cuff," on the basis of hunches and sketchy data, is to be in the class with phrenologists, crystal gazers, and other charlatans.

The teacher-adviser is in a somewhat better position than that of the clinical worker in two ways: (1) The teacher lives with the pupils for a period of time every day, and thereby has an opportunity to know them well. Of course those teachers who are trained to observe and to interpret behavior learn more about their pupils than other teachers who are not alert to notice individuals. And the longer the teacher continues with his pupils, and the fewer different pupils he teaches per day, the better he can know them. (2) The school has, or can have, in its cumulative records a simple case history of each pupil from the time he entered kindergarten until he gets into secondary school. Thus a development record, covering physical, social, mental, and emotional growth, much more accurate than anything the social worker or clinical worker could get in an

hour's interview, is at hand in the school files for the adviser
to use.

Barbara H. Wright, *Practical Handbook for Group Guidance.* Chicago: Science Research Associates, 1948, pp. 141-42.

14.

Interviewing

357. Why People Seek Interviews

How the counselor will carry on the personal interview depends partly upon the reason the individual comes for the consultation and partly upon the attitude he takes toward the counselor. There are the persons who seek counsel simply because they have formed the habit of depending upon others for the answers to all their questions. They are the ones who follow mechanically the advice of the physician on the health problems of their children and have to call him up in regard to each small detail; who trust the bank to decide about their investments and who let the insurance agent work out insurance plans for them; who buy the car a friend recommends and who choose a vacation spot at somebody else's suggestion; who vote the way their favorite newspaper directs and who accept implicitly what the minister declares to be the correct rule of faith and practice. They want the counselor to reply directly: "I advise you to do thus and so on this matter." Then there are those who come because they have never learned how to work out problems for themselves, and find themselves unable to come to a decision. They are bewildered by the complexity of even simple problems, now one course of action appealing to them and then another, so that they find themselves swinging back and forth, wavering and unable to take any position at all. They come to the counselor to be straightened out in their thinking about their problem and to be helped to a definite decision. They need someone to direct their fundamental thinking procedure. There are still others who face decisions in areas with which they are unfamiliar and in which they have insufficient data for making a reliable decision. They come to

399

get help in supplementing their knowledge and experience. There are others who have formed the habit of looking at a question from several points of view and of bringing various opinions to bear upon it before making a decision. They come to get the counselor's viewpoint on a problem, that they may compare it with that of others and so have a wider perspective from which to make up their own minds. There are the persons who find that they can think more clearly and can make up their minds more effectively when they talk a question over with someone else instead of depending upon talking it over with themselves in personal reflection. They use the counselor chiefly as an occasion for reflecting aloud on their problems and as check on the accuracy of their thinking.

> Harrison Sacket Elliott and Grace Loucks Elliott, *Solving Personal Problems*. New York: Henry Holt and Company, Inc., 1936, pp. 225-27. By permission of the publishers.

358. PURPOSES OF THE INTERVIEW

Assuming that the general purpose is that of helping the counselee solve the problem at hand and to aid him in learning how to meet such issues in the future, there are other and more specific purposes with which an interview might be concerned:

(a) To allow the counselee to relieve tension by talking his problem out, to ventilate, to desensitize, as in catharsis; to use counselor as a sounding board or mirror.

(b) To discover facts, insights, attitudes, etc., which counselor and counselee both use in their attempt to understand the situation more fully and from which (along with such data secured elsewhere) interpretations and next steps may be determined upon.

(c) To inform counselee of certain facts or decisions or to raise certain questions or issues.

(d) To afford mutual sharing of ideas, problems, issues; as enrichment level, or as high practice of friendship.

> The editor's class notes.

359. VARIOUS TYPES OF CONTACTS

1. (a) Counselee on own initiative approaches counselor directly and requests aid or conference or upon referral of another person.

   (b) Same except no definite request is made. Counselee makes overtures vaguely or in round about way.

2. (a) Counselor on own initiative approaches counselee directly, converses or arranges conference or through request of another person.

   (b) Same except approach is indirect, incidental, but on counselor's initiative.

   (c) Counselor takes the initiative but works behind the scene entirely and through another or others who may employ any of approaches listed above.

3. Accidental and unplanned contact. Either one may take the lead in arranging for the conversation or it may develop so naturally that neither party seems to direct it.

   The editor's class notes.

360. INTERVIEW NOT THE SOLE PROCEDURE IN GUIDANCE

Another prevalent misconception with regard to counseling is that it involves only one procedure—the interview. But counseling is not synonymous with interviewing, nor is interviewing equivalent to counseling. Of a more complex and specialized nature, counseling includes more than the interview. Among other things it includes record keeping, observation, and other analytical and diagnostic techniques of which the interview is only one. It includes study of all available information on the student; it includes discovery of school and community resources of possible usefulness to the case; and it includes conferences with others to check soundness of judgments made and to secure general and technical information and advice on the case. Counseling begins before the student enters the conference room, and it may continue long after he leaves it.

Jane Warters, *High School Personnel Work Today*. New York: McGraw-Hill Book Company, Inc., 1946, p. 83.

361.   We Talk Too Much

Many of us are so eager to be helpful that we talk too much and too soon, only to discover that what we have been saying has gone in one ear and out the other.

This tendency becomes clearer when we feel called upon to have "a good talk" with Johnny. He has done something wrong and we decide that what he needs is a spanking or a good talking to. The difference between the two is not very great. The physical pain is not usually important, what matters is the emotional hurt—the fear, humiliation, guilt. These effects are more fundamental, deeper reaching, and more damaging than a slap given in anger. The tongue lashing can do more harm than the old-fashioned spanking. Much has been said against physical punishment; perhaps the warnings should have stressed the danger to the nervous system as well as to the body. Today we look on people who use the strap as barbarians. While this is progress, the things we continue to do with our tongues are as cruel.

> Rudolph M. Wittenberg, *So You Want To Help People*. New York: Association Press, 1947, p. 98.

362.   General Suggestions—Strang

No formula, of course, can be given which, if followed, will enable the teacher to do successful interviewing. The interview is far too individual and flexible a process for that. Its course is steered by continuous sensitivity to what the person being interviewed is thinking and feeling. . . .

A few general suggestions, however, should help teachers to improve the quality of their interviews.

1.   *Listen.*   Almost invariably teachers talk too much in the interview. Being in the habit of teaching, they teach. Instead, they should take the attitude of learners; they should listen intently and learn. Problems are sometimes solved without the interviewer saying a word. Worries are often objectified, relationships clarified, by the student's talking while the teacher listens.

2.   *Accept and try to understand.*   The teacher should also curb his reformer tendencies and accept the student as he is —his hostility, his unacceptable ways of meeting life's prob-

lems, his liabilities as well as his assets. The student wants to be understood—not to be judged, labeled, scolded, or praised. In any interview, the teacher should start where the student is.

3. *Share responsibility.* The interview has aptly been called a "joint quest." It is neither wholly "client-centered" nor "counselor-centered." The student has information and resources that the interviewer does not possess. Similarly, the interviewer has information and resources that the less mature individual lacks. The two pool their resources. In this relationship of mutual trust and confidence, the student is stimulated to use his powers of self-analysis and constructive planning to best advantage. But the creative interviewer does more than this; he goes beyond the limited insights many students are able to achieve alone; he helps them to arrive at a better decision or plan.

4. *Have the necessary information.* In many types of interview progress depends on having the facts with which to think straight. Lacking knowledge of the principles of mental hygiene, educational opportunities, social trends or conditions related to the student's life, the requirements of different vocations, or other necessary information, the teacher-counselor cannot serve as a resource when the student has reached the limits of his own ability to understand and handle the situation.

5. *Have faith.* Faith is a bridge between what the individual now is and what he can become. The interviewer's well-founded faith in the student's ability to make the best of himself leads him on. It helps him to see himself in a new light and to take a more hopeful view of the future.

Ruth Strang. *The Role of the Teacher in Personnel Work.* New York: Bureau of Publications, Teachers College, Columbia University, 1946, pp. 406-7.

363. AN OUTLINE FOR THE INTERVIEW

I. Introduction—(Steps leading to the interview)
   1. Preliminary preparation
      a. Securing of all possible background facts.
      b. Arranging for the most favorable setting.
      c. Adjusting one's mental attitude.

2. Approach to the counselee
   a. Friendly and cheerful greeting.
   b. Securing of rapport.
      Means to use—discussing matters of mutual inter-
      est, showing friendly interest in counselee's gen-
      eral affairs, casual talk to put him at ease, refer-
      ences to his past experiences, references to affairs
      with which he is related.

II. Development of the Interview
   1. Revealing the purpose of the interview
      Statement of problem or purpose by counselee or coun-
      selor.
   2. Analysis of this topic or problem
      Means to use—getting at all the facts, searching to dis-
      cover whether apparent problem is real one, seeking
      underlying causes, ascertaining and understanding
      counselee's point of view.
         (Thru this part of interview counselor needs to listen
         carefully, encouraging counselee to talk; yet it is
         important to keep interview in control, guiding it
         skillfully to attain desired ends.)
   3. Turning point
      This is vague, hard to define, and not always present.
      It represents usually the turning toward the solution;
      it may be the point at which the counselee gives evi-
      dence of new insight or a changed attitude, or becomes
      willing to consider or begin constructive measures of
      solution. *It marks progress from the investigation of
      problem to its solution.*
   4. Working out a constructive solution
      Means to use—discussing possible alternatives, giving
      counselee insight into problem, motivating him, sug-
      gesting positive lines of action, encouraging his initia-
      tive and sense of responsibility.
         (Thru this part of the interview responsibility must
         be shifted to counselee and self-guidance stimulated;
         any plan should be as far as possible his own—no
         solution of the counselor should be forced on him.)

III. Conclusion of the Interview
1. Giving final words of encouragement and stimulation.
2. Stressing definite progress gained.
3. Planning for future interviews or follow-up.
   Source unknown, in editor's files.

364. STAGES IN THE INTERVIEW

1. The counselor prepares for the interview. . . .
2. The counselor seeks to make it possible and easy for the counselee to make full use of the counseling situation. This is often described as establishing rapport and defining the situation. . . .
3. The counselor seeks to free the student from any tensions and fears that may be blocking the way to clear understanding and to constructive action. . . .
4. The counselor helps the student to gain self-understanding. . . .
5. The problem is identified and examined. . . .
6. The course of action is planned. . . .
7. The selected course of action is carried out. . . .
8. Referral may be made to other workers. . . .
9. The case is followed up. . . .
10. A record is made of the case.

> Jane Warters, *High School Personnel Work Today.* New York: McGraw-Hill Book Company, Inc., 1946, pp. 84-89. (Adapted.)

365. TECHNIQUES I USE IN INTERVIEWING[1]

Since I interview for varied purposes, I use many techniques.
    However, a few general principles seem to govern what I do:
During an interview, I try to observe the *total child,* and do a
    little "inferential reading" of what I observe.
I always try to look *with* the child at his problem rather than
    at him. I mean this quite literally. I find that fixing a steady
    gaze on him is not conducive to good rapport.

---

[1] The author has previously acknowledged his indebtedness to Miss Ruth Westover, Counselor, Mt. Clemens High School, Mt. Clemens, Mich., for information concerning the guidance program in her school.

I use a meandering, "off-focus" approach to the actual problem. Sometimes it takes two or three interviews before we
are ready to look at the real problem.

I encourage a long-range point of view whenever possible, for
I find that children often let immediate circumstances be-
cloud the ultimate outcome.

I try to give the child feelings of courage, cooperation, adequacy, and understanding of self and others; and alleviate
feelings of fear, hostility, helplessness, and alienation from
self and others.

I know that I can work no miracles. Sometimes all I can do
is give a little comfort, but I do what I can.

I try to remember that there are no "cut-and-dried" answers
in this business of human relations.

> Clifford P. Froehlich, *Guidance Services in Smaller Schools.*
> New York: McGraw-Hill Book Company, Inc., 1950,
> pp. 210-11.

366. PRACTICAL SUGGESTIONS

Let us assume that you have been approached on some
problem of a nature upon which you feel able to give assistance, or that it is a situation where you do not know at the
time the full nature of the problem. Also assume that while
you do not plan to continue in the relationship, if it proves to
be "beyond your depth" as a general counselor, you will work
with the counselee to the limit of your competency. The following suggestions are made in this connection:

1. *Counselor needs to vary his procedure to take into account
   individual differences in the counselee.*

   Counselors need to note difference in interviews where
   counselee has insight and where insight is lacking; where
   counselees vary from the neurotic person to the well-adjusted. The counselor's method of approach and carry
   through must take these differences and others into account.

2. *Counselor needs to strive for rapport with counselee.*
   a. Meaning of rapport: "harmony of relation," "mutual
      confidence."

    b. Ways of establishing rapport in the interviews:
      1. Show genuine confidence and interest.
      2. Begin conversation on familiar ground; on pleasant subject. Learn something of counselee before conference. Might get some identification through reference to a mutual friend or common interest.
      3. Give counselee a chance to talk at points of *his own* greatest interest.
      4. Assure counselee the security which the following give (do not over-stress):
        a. Conference is confidential
        b. Will not press for facts
        c. No ridicule, blame, "lifting of eyebrows," etc.

3. A feeling of leisure is often desirable. At least counselee needs to feel that there is adequate time available for his situation to be considered. However, some terminal arrangements are quite in order, agreed upon beforehand. As a general thing it is unwise for a counselor to get into the habit of having long drawn out sessions when less time would be effective. Some counselors encourage frequent return of counselees and lengthy discussions to the harm of the counselee's independence.

4. The counselor with too much observable technique, too many forms, too business-like, may not make good progress. Needs to be friendly, genuine, easy in manner. To formalize an interview is "as much out of place as to copy a love letter from a manual."

5. In most interviews there needs to be some issue, some problem, some cruciality. Often a counselee is not fully aware of the problem. Sometimes he may only need help in discovering what the problem is. Or he may be aware of the problem and need aid in handling it. In such cases he may come directly to the issue, or he may hesitate to come out with it. Sometimes he will indicate what it is only in the last minute or two of the interview period. In such a situation another conference period may be in order.

6. Consider the scheduled and the unscheduled interview. In the scheduled the counselee may come with an approach

all worked out and counselor may do the same. This may make for too much rigidity, or it may set up a readiness on part of both which will assist in rapport and thus facilitate the discussion.

7. The matter of time and place for the conference is important.
   a. Is the conference room comfortable?
   b. Is the manner of seating appropriate?
   c. Do interruptions occur? (phone, callers)
   d. Is conference too close to or too far away from precipitating incident?
   e. Are either too tired to carry on adequately?
   f. Is there protection against "gossiping or framing" in room location and accessibility?
   g. Has too much secrecy been made of conference?

8. Avoid argument of any kind. An interview is no place for debate, although participants may disagree.

9. Counselor needs to do some recording, usually soon after the interview. In some cases it may be done during the interview. Note the *habit* of recording. Reveals an objective or guidance point of view.

10. Practice the art of listening in the interview. Note difference between "passive" and "creative" listening. In latter, counselor is silent vocally, but alert in posture of body, head, eyes, etc., which encourages the counselee.

11. *Control of the interview:* If one had an unlimited amount of time this would not be too great an issue but the general counselor has limits imposed by his position, so some control is needed. The counselor may need to direct the conversation from a start to some conclusion, and such a role may be agreed upon at outset. If only one session is to be held, then some direction clearly is needed. If counselee assumes control, so much the better. Even here counselor may become active in assisting. If several sessions are to be available, some plan needs to be made so the job at hand may be accomplished in alloted period. But counselor cannot force progress. He has to be flexible enough to adjust to counselee's desires and rate of progress.

12. *Interview pattern:* Here counselor should be flexible but follow *some* pattern. Note Rogers' pattern: (or phases as he calls them) (1) Catharsis and release, (2) Self-understanding and insight, (3) Action.

13. *At the end of the interview:*
    a. If counselee gives the signal—in arising, in remarks, etc.,—counselor follows suit.
    b. Counselor may have to take the initiative with such questions as:
       1. Now have we covered everything?
       2. What do we need to talk about next time?
       3. Is there anything else you care to bring up? (If not, you are finished. If so, set next time.)
       4. How may we summarize what has been covered?
    c. Final Steps   [one.
       1. Try to close with pleasant topic or a constructive
       2. Agree upon next steps—what to do before next conference, such as reading, testing, etc.

    From editor's class notes.

367. Talking Things Over With the Child[1]

Have you noticed how many difficulties can be overcome—what real friendships are made—how it relieves your mind—when you have a chance to "talk things over?" One of the most successful techniques for guiding the growth of the individual and for developing sympathetic understanding between pupil and teacher is the personal interview, the simple process of "talking things over."

Establishing Right Relationships

For the alert teacher there are many opportunities for informal contacts which influence pupil behavior and personal well-being. A friendly comment on the new dress, accompanied by "Did you make it yourself?" may open the way for much genuine individual counseling. Interest in a student's talent or hobby may develop a relationship which will encourage the student to want to talk things over. "I like the way you handled

---

[1] Bernice Miller, "Talking Things Over With the Child."

that problem in your meeting," or "It was good of you to help
Dora track down that information in the library,"—those are the
kinds of appreciative comments by which sensitive teachers
can lay the foundation for later effective guidance work.

In fact the classroom teacher is in a far more enviable position than the counselor whose contacts with the boys and girls
he interviews are relatively infrequent. The teacher does not
have to worry about developing rapport at the time an important interview is being held. The process of fashioning a
relationship of mutual trust goes on in a score of daily situations which bring teacher and pupil together and help them
understand and appreciate each other. Being able to talk
things over with a child at the time he is troubled and needs
help most depends upon how carefully the teacher has utilized
every contact with the child to build confidence. Once rapport
has been established on an enduring basis, teacher and child
can tackle problems together without hesitancy or fear of misunderstanding.

Informal Interviews

The frequent contacts the classroom teacher has with children also give her advantage. It is often unnecessary for the
teacher to schedule a formal conference with a child. A for-
tuitous meeting during a study period or after a club meeting,
for example, may provide the psychological time and place
for a significant conference. A sensitive teacher can capitalize
on chance meetings for much valuable counseling. Dick or Sue
may hesitate to ask for a formal conference with you, but in
general conversation they may tentatively insert feelers which
you will recognize as bids for help. While the counselor seldom
has the opportunity to engage in unplanned interviews, the
teacher can probably do his counseling most effectively
through contacts which appear to the child to be casual.

Planned Interviews

All boys and girls are faced with some problems which can
only be met on an individual basis. If all counseling were left
to chance, certain children might be overlooked and denied
the help they need. For this reason some planned scheme of
individual counseling is necessary.

There are many purposes for which planned conferences may be called, such as to discuss the results on a standardized test, to gain certain information for the cumulative record, to work out a program of studies for the coming semester. Whatever the starting point or obvious purposes may be, other matters relating to the child's more personal problems may be opened up. A skillful teacher can guide the interview into channels which will help the child with those problems which concern him most. Interviews should not be limited to dealing with disciplinary situations or problems of scholastic achievement. Often those who do not show exaggerated outward signs of having problems are most in need of counseling. All pupils should have the opportunity to "talk things over."

Finding Time to Talk Things Over

It is sometimes difficult to find the time to meet with pupils on an individual basis. What arrangements can be made? Because time and privacy are both essential our school dismisses classes early at set intervals to provide school time for counseling. But even if no administrative adjustments were made, all guidance-minded teachers would sandwich in as much individual counseling—both casual and planned—as they could find time for.

A Few Hints to Help Make an Interview Successful

"Guided conversation" demands preparation on the part of the teacher-adviser. The more you know about the individual student, the more you can help him. Consult the cumulative record folder for home background, health record, outside activities, school record, personality indications. Jot down or make mental note of the significant factors and possible approaches. Can a record of irregular attendance or poor scholarship be traced to health difficulties?— To too many outside activities?— To lack of parental interest in school success? Talk with his other teachers about him and find out whether he is working up to ability, how he adjusts to group situations or to authority, what his personal handicaps or special talents are. Then you can better fit this "jig-saw puzzle" of the whole person together.

Privacy during the conference means much to the student. He may like the importance of an appointed time set aside for himself. If you are businesslike, yet friendly and informal, he is likely to respond. Let him pull up a chair alongside of you or across from you. Do not appear to be crowded for time. Give him your full attention. Be sincerely interested in him as a person. Then you have a basis for mutual self-confidence.

The initiative in the conference will probably be yours. Open with some topic you have in common or some accomplishment of his. Possibly you can directly approach the designated problem for the conference. And remember that the sincerity of your interest will work wonders. But do not expect to analyze and solve all his problems in this initial approach.

Because the general purpose of individual counseling is to help the student gain personal insight, together you may analyze the problem, its pros and cons. But let the student do the talking. Help him bring to light the true facts. Study with him the basic problems underlying his attitudes and reactions. You do not accomplish this by being didactic, by your very manner and mental hygiene approach give him the feeling of security he needs. As you discuss scholastic success or vocational plans or his part-time job, in that process you can help him make personality adjustments by seeing himself as he really is. Above all, let him make his own decisions.

Try to give the student a feeling of satisfaction from this conference. This may result from just talking the matter over together—or from having a definite planned course of action —or from some pamphlet or reference which he may find helpful.

When he leaves, give the student the impression that he can always come to you—that you are always interested in seeing more of him. Continued interest is essential. Pupil growth and development take time.

Though you may wish to remember certain facts that are developed, it is much wiser to record them after the conference. On some few occasions when planning together you might say, "Let us make a note of this for future reference." The signed and dated record of the conference should include attitudes, personal information, plans or decisions made.

If this record is filed in the cumulative record, you have a basis for follow-up conferences.

Clifford P. Froehlich, *Guidance Services in Smaller Schools.* New York: McGraw-Hill Book Company, Inc., 1950, pp. 215-18.

368. INTERVIEWING DISCUSSED—SHAFFER

The interview. The direct psychiatric or psychological interview with the patient is the most significant of all of the procedures employed in the mental hygiene case study. Only from the individual himself can be obtained an understanding of his motives, attitudes, emotional trends, attachments, adjustments and degree of integration. Interviews are both *diagnostic* and *remedial*, in that they serve to determine the nature of the patient's difficulties and also to assist him in correcting them. The diagnostic and remedial functions are inseparable in practice. The interviewer continues to gain insight into the patient's condition all through the process of treatment. Only for purposes of description can these two functions be considered apart. The diagnostic aspect will be considered first.

The aim of the diagnostic interview is to get the subject to reveal the significant facts about his personality and his adjustments. This is hindered by a number of factors to which the psychoanalytic term *resistance* may be applied. The simplest type of resistance consists of diffidence toward the interviewer and lack of confidence in him, which must be overcome at the beginning of the interviews. Another relatively simple resistance is caused by feelings of guilt, shame and social disapproval with which the subject regards the behavior being investigated. A more serious resistance is found when repression has caused the forgetting of experiences that were important in the development of the maladjustment. A still more difficult resistance to overcome is lack of insight. In many cases the subject is unable to tell his history clearly because he has never understood the sources or significance of his behavior, since it was acquired by entirely blind trial and error learning. A lack of integration also hinders the direct examination, for this condition prevents the subject from seeing his problem as a whole and from discriminating the significant aspects of it.

The first task of the interviewer is to establish *rapport* with the subject, which serves to weaken his various resistances. Rapport implies a condition of confidence, trust and friendship, and the creation of a positive emotional response on the part of the subject toward the examiner. This consideration is of such paramount importance that the first interview or even several interviews may be spent solely in establishing rapport. All procedures of a well-conducted interview should assist rapport, but at the outset some special devices are often useful. The interviewer should know something in advance about the characteristics of the subject, and may begin by asking him about matters in which he is interested or proficient, rather than to bring up at once painful topics relating to the adjustment problem. The interviewer should show that he is interested in and knows about the things that the subject values. This will give him the status of a collaborator. A species of "identification" assists in beginning an interview, which may be accomplished by referring to friends and experiences that the interviewer and subject have in common. A little flattery or humor is not out of place in getting the subject into a suitable mood.

The personal characteristics of the interviewer are very important both in the process of establishing rapport and in the subsequent procedures. The interviewer must be a well-adjusted person himself, in order to avoid making personal emotional reactions to various aspects of the subject's experiences. The interviewer should not give obvious praise or condemnation of the conduct of his patient, nor show surprise or disgust at any disclosure. The interviewer must secure the respect of the subject without overawing him. He must be friendly, cordial and genuinely interested in the individual and his problems. It is necessary to have the patience to listen to a long-drawn-out tale of woe without restlessness or boredom. The qualities that make an efficient interviewer are so fundamental that persons have to be selected for this task as well as trained for it.

The opinion of most experienced workers, and also a number of experimental findings, favor letting the patient tell his own story first, with as few questions and comments as possible. A free unguided narrative expresses more ideas, and is less likely to contain errors than are the answers to direct questions. The interviewer may encourage the subject over difficulties with reassurances and with such comment as "Isn't that interesting!" or "And then what did you do?" The free narrative approach adds to rapport, for, having told his story, the subject feels that the interviewer is an "insider" and has less resistance to direct questions than if these had been asked at the outset. In listening to the subject's story, the interviewer is alert to catch many significant indications of areas of maladjustment that are not revealed by the story's obvious content. Any part of the narrative to which the subject reacts emotionally or at which he shows a reluctance to proceed, is likely to be important. Topics on which the subject seems to rationalize or to defend his own conduct too warmly indicate sore spots in his adjustive attitudes and warrant further investigation. The discovery of the situations that are emotional stimuli for the individual is of as much value for the mental hygiene study as is the tabulation of the objective facts of his past experiences.

Direct questioning is possible after the subject's confidence has been gained securely. The questions arise from the issues suggested by the case history and the free narrative, or are formulated by the interviewer according to his knowledge of the problems involved. If the patient seems to be withholding segments of information likely to be significant, questioning may be directed toward such matters, often by a round-about route that will make the approach easier. Common precipitating causes of maladjustment such as family circumstances, social relationships, economic troubles and love and sex relationships are thoroughly canvassed. Predisposing factors, including childhood emotional experiences, the development of independence, and the subject's attitudes toward his parents, are explored as fully as possible. A successful study of personality cannot be done in a hurry. The best clinical practice, unless prevented by considerations of expense, allows the subject to take his own time. Dependence is placed on the development of rapport that will eventually permit the subject to make a full disclosure, rather than on persistent or harassing questioning.

Laurance Frederic Shaffer, *The Psychology of Adjustment.* Boston: Houghton Mifflin Company, 1936, pp. 456-59.

369. STEPS IN THE INTERVIEW

While variations and adaptations will be necessary, suited both to the personal development of the counselee and to the character of his problem, the counselor will usually find useful a procedure somewhat as follows. The first step necessary is to give the person full opportunity to state his problem and to say what he wants from the counselor. The counselor should be an understanding listener, not breaking in until the person has time to tell what is on his mind and heart. . . .

In whatever form the individual brings his problem, it is important next for the counselor to get him to look at it in relation to the circumstances out of which it has arisen and in relation to his own personality needs; in other words to make a more adequate analysis of his problem and to come to a better understanding of it. If the individual comes for authoritative advice as to what to do, he will usually give only partial data concerning the situation and the factors, personal and environmental, which make up the problem for him; and it will help him and the counselor to explore the situation further. If he comes for further information on a problem of which he feels his knowledge to be too incomplete for a trustworthy decision, such information can be supplied intelligently only when the counselor fully understands the problem, and can be applied by the counselee only as it is given in terms of the situation he is facing. If the individual is baffled by his problem and cannot make up his mind, it is particularly important that he first understand the situation he is facing. If he is an independent individual who has come to get the counselor's viewpoint on his problem for comparison with others, the counselor obviously cannot answer him intelligently without understanding thoroughly the situation he is facing. . . .

The third step in the interview is to get out into the open all possible suggestions as to what the counselee might do in the situation he is facing, and particularly to find out why each has appealed to him as a possible answer to his problem. In order to widen his outlook and to bring into the discussion answers to his question which he may not have dared to look at, it will be well for the counselor to find out what the counselee has known other people to do in similar situations and why he thinks they adopted those solutions to their problem. . . .

If the counselor knows of other possible solutions which the counselee has not considered, he should introduce them at this time for consideration along with the proposals of the counselee. . . .

The next stage in the consultation is to explore with the consultant the reasons why one alternative appeals to him and another does not; particularly the conflicting reasons which constitute his real problem in coming to a decision. . . .

Usually another stage in the conference is desirable, namely, a consideration of the exact point at which the counselee expects to begin in trying out his conclusion or decision. "What are the next steps?" This could be the question used at the close of any interview in focusing attention on the next thing to be done; but it is particularly important where a decision has been arrived at, either tentatively or with some finality, to be sure that the plan of attack is really put into effect and tested and possibly revised on the basis of further reflection and in the crucible of experience.

Harrison Sacket Elliott and Grace Loucks Elliott, *Solving Personal Problems*. New York: Henry Holt and Company, Inc., 1936, pp. 228-35. By permission of the publishers.

370. INTERVIEWING STUDENTS

Frequently it is advisable to confer with students immediately when their desire for help is indicated and to allow time for unhurried discussion. However, many teacher-counselors find it necessary to schedule interviews and at the outset to put some reasonable limit upon their duration. It is also wise to provide for the emergency situation which calls for a conference then and there, when the student need is such that to delay would be to lose the proper moment. During the discussions care needs to be taken to avoid interruptions. Often colleagues, other students, secretarial personnel, or the telephone are the chief offenders. Usually such breaks are both annoying and unnecessary. At times they may be quite harmful in their effects. Much might be said about the physical setting of the interview which undoubtedly has some influence upon outcomes. The pleasantness of the conference room, the seating of the counselee, and other such items, while of some consequence, are really only secondary.

It is more important to provide a setting in which the counselor may give his undivided attention to the person before him. This requires creative or active listening where the interviewer lays his own problems aside for a while to give himself to his visitor as fully as possible. When the counselor thus gives himself, when he attempts to see things through the eyes of the student, sympathetically yet objectively, he creates an atmosphere and an opportunity highly favorable to good outcomes. Carl Rogers (*Counseling and Psychotherapy*. New York: Houghton Mifflin Company, 1942) has suggested some of the marks of the wholesome atmosphere which is needed for effective results. He included such factors as "warmth and responsiveness," "permissiveness," and "lack of pressure and coercion." In such a setting the student usually will be able to express himself, to reveal his feelings and troubles, or to share his ideas. The counselor likewise should be able to do his part more effectively under such conditions. The counselor and student, taking advantage of the good start they thus have together, then may go forward upon the cooperative venture of dealing with the issue at hand. Here the counselor aids the student to say what is on his mind, to express his feelings, to state his questions, or to talk aloud in trying to formulate the ones which elude him. Together they explore the facts involved, seek new information, and formulate ideas both as to the causation and solution. Sometimes all this may be done in one interview. At other times several discussions may be required. With self-guidance as the objective, the wise counselor will be able to keep perspective. He seeks to make himself unnecessary, but not without contributing something of value to the one who stopped to talk awhile. At times the counselor's greatest contribution may be that of an appropriate referral, which may be to some office of specialized service, to a colleague upon the campus, or to an appropriate person or agency in the community. Usually it is best to work through the organized counseling service of one's institution on these referrals.

Often it is advisable to make some preparation for an interview. At such times the teacher-counselor should seek to secure personnel data from institutional sources to supplement whatever the student may have furnished. When a colleague is known to have worked with the same student, a sharing of information and insight often is quite helpful. In general, the counselor should not take notes during an interview unless he is jotting down some step which he has agreed to take.

In closing the interview it is good practice to review, or have the student do so, what has been accomplished; to set the time for another conference if needed; to decide what is to be done before the next one; or to discuss a desired referral. The counselor should attempt to have the conference end on an encouraging or positive note.

> Donald J. Shank, Chairman, *The Teacher as Counselor.* Washington: The American Council on Education, October, 1948, pp. 23-24. (From chapter by Karl P. Zerfoss.)

Suggestions On Interviewing — Garrett

371. First Purpose of the Interview

. . . The interviewer is sometimes so anxious to help that he rushes ahead without first obtaining a sound understanding of the situation. That such a procedure can be destructive rather than helpful should be clear. To advise a boy to continue in high school without first obtaining knowledge of his interests and abilities is obviously unwise. The first and basic purpose of interviewing is to obtain understanding of the problem, of the situation, and of the client who has come for help.

> Annette Garrett, *Interviewing: Its Principles and Methods.* New York: Family Service Association of America, 1942, p. 26.

372.   Pressure for Information Unwise

Another caution to be kept in mind throughout is that although the interviewer should be clearly aware of his purposes it is not always wise to seek to realize them by direct action. Even where considerable information is desired, it is often best obtained by encouraging the client to talk freely of his problem rather than by asking such pointed questions as, "Were you fired from your last job?" People are sensitive about their personal life, family skeletons, poverty, past mistakes, and so on, and early flat-footed inquiry may only alienate a client and cause him to erect protective barriers against what may well seem to him unwarranted intrusion. Once convinced of the worker's sensitive understanding, of his desire to know not out of wanton curiosity but only in order to help, and of the confidential nature of the relationship, the client will welcome an opportunity to talk about things which earlier he would have suppressed.

Ibid., p. 26.

373.   It's Important Who Initiates Conference

Every interview has, to begin with, its manifest purpose. If an agency has initiated an interview and called someone in, the person interviewed can usually be put most quickly at his ease—relieved of uncertainty in the face of the unknown—and the interview most quickly advanced, by a straightforward statement in terms the client can readily grasp of the interviewer's purpose in asking him to come in for a consultation. Where the interviewee asks for the appointment, the situation is a little different. In such cases, rather than greet him with a barrage of questions, it is better to let him state in his own words his problem and his purpose in coming in for an interview. Sometimes the client is nervous and incoherent, but he is most quickly reassured if he is allowed to begin the interview in his own way. Often the interviewer can learn much from the very hesitancy and indirect way in which the client approaches the account of his difficulty.

Ibid., p. 28.

374. The Value in Talking It Out

An experienced interviewer will always keep in mind the possibility that his client is suffering from some trouble more difficult than he realizes or is able to state. He will endeavor by various methods to put his client at ease, to stimulate him to talk relatively freely about his problem, and to help him to organize his own confused thoughts and feelings about his difficulties. Sometimes talking about the situation to a sympathetic listener will itself lead to a satisfactory conclusion. The client's thoughts may thus be organized so clearly that he sees himself what action he should take. His fears and hesitancies may be removed and he may be encouraged to take whatever action is necessary. More often, perhaps, just talking is not enough and help of other sorts will be required.

Ibid., p. 29.

375. Danger in Probing Too Far

It is of course possible to probe too far. Some sleeping dogs should be left undisturbed. This is particularly true when the interviewer is not equipped to deal with them should they be aroused. Even a skilled interviewer should use a good deal of discretion and wisdom in going beneath the surface.

Ibid., p. 29.

376. Counselor Flexibility Desirable

The fact that interviews bring to light new knowledge of purposes and needs as well as new information about the relevant facts implies that the interviewer should not let his plan of action be unalterably fixed in advance or determined early in the interview. A certain amount of flexibility is always desirable.

Ibid., p. 29.

377. The First Step in the Interview

The first step in an interview is to help the interviewee relax and feel fairly comfortable. Naturally this is difficult to accomplish unless the interviewer himself is relaxed. Sometimes the client can quickly be put at ease by letting him state his

purpose in coming, sometimes by giving him a brief account
of why he was asked to come. In either case, an advisable next
step is to encourage him to talk, and then to listen carefully
while he speaks of what is on the "top" of his mind in connection with the interview.

Ibid., p. 36.

378.   QUESTIONING TOO LITTLE OR TOO MUCH

Most people tend to ask either too many questions or too
few. Each interviewer should study his own tendency and seek
to curb it. Too many questions will confuse and block the
client, while too few may place too much of the burden of
the interview on him and may leave salient areas unexplored.

Ibid., p. 38.

379.   GOOD STRATEGY

In general, we seem to get further by being encouraging and
sympathetic, by leading the client to talk freely, than by trying
to drag information out of him by belaboring him with questions.

Ibid., p. 39.

380.   SKILL IN INTERVIEWING A LEARNED ART

Although the most skilful interviewing gives the appearance
of being a smooth and spontaneous interchange between the
interviewer and the interviewee, the skill thus revealed is obtained only through careful study and years of practice. For
purposes of study it is possible to break down an interview
into a number of component factors and discuss each separately. In actual interviewing, of course, no such sharp breaks
occur, but we must make them in analysis if our discussion is
not to be so general as to be relatively valueless. The interviewer must become conscious of the various subtleties in interviewing before he can absorb them into his spontaneous responses. First recognized in theory, they later become so much
a part of the worker's skill that they are utilized naturally at
each step without conscious notice. We hear much of the intuitive skill of the trained interviewer. But back of such skill
lies much study of the various processes and inter-relation-

ships involved in interviewing. The skilful skier is unconscious of the many movements integrated in his smooth flight, but earlier he had to learn them painfully one by one and then learn to combine them into a harmonious co-ordinated whole.

Ibid., p. 30.

381. How Does It Look to Him?

. . . When an interviewer realizes that a client's point of reference seems like the reasonable one to him, it becomes clear that it is important to attempt to understand how the situation looks from his viewpoint and why that seems to him to be the only correct way of looking at things. If we attempt to do this before trying to persuade him to what seems to us a more logical point of view, we have made a faint beginning of understanding him.

Ibid., p. 32.

382. Behavior Sometimes a Cover-Up

That people do not always say what they mean or act as they feel is continually apparent in interviewing. For example, case workers in relief agencies repeatedly have the experience of having a client storm into the office belligerently demanding immediate financial support, only to have him reveal when met with kindness that underneath he is really frightened, ashamed of his poverty, and pleading for understanding of the mess in which he finds himself.

Ibid., p. 32.

383. The Active Listener

One type of observation occurs through listening. This is one of the fundamental operations of interviewing, and it goes without saying that a good interviewer is a good listener. But what constitutes a good listener? One who frequently interrupts to say what he would have done under similar circumstances is not a good listener, but neither is he who sits like a bump on a log. Absence of response may easily seem to the talker to reflect absence of interest. Everyone knows from his own experience in telling a story that people like a listener

who indicates by brief relevant comments or questions that
he has grasped the essential points of one's tale, and who adds
illuminating comments on certain significant features of one's
account that had not been stressed and might well have been
overlooked by an inattentive listener. This attention to important details that had not been emphasized gives the story-
teller the stimulating feeling that the listener not only wants
to, but does understand, to an unusual degree, what he is
trying to say.

Ibid., p. 33.

384.   SILENCES MAY MEAN DIFFERENT THINGS

A common error of an inexperienced interviewer is to be
embarrassed by silences and to feel that he must fill them with
questions or comments. A decent respect for silences is often
more helpful. Sometimes the person interviewed falls silent
because he is a little reluctant to go on with what comes next
in his story, or because he doesn't quite know how to formulate what he plans to say. A too hasty interruption may leave
this important part of the story forever unsaid. Sometimes, of
course, a silence is due to other causes, and if allowed to continue will only embarrass the person interviewed. In such cases
a pertinent remark or question will encourage him to continue.

Ibid., p. 34.

385.   THE VALUE IN JUST LISTENING

Listening to a client's story is sometimes helpful in and of
itself. Everyone knows the value at times of "letting off
steam." When something happens that upsets a person or
"makes him mad" he tends to get over these feelings more
quickly if he can find a sympathetic friend who will let him
"rave" for awhile. Relieved, he can then go ahead and use his
energy more constructively. Without this opportunity to talk it
out with someone else, he may "boil" for days. He probably
does not want anyone to tell him what to do or what he should
have done differently, but may merely want someone to listen
and understand how upset he is. It is unfortunate that the
average lay person is not a good listener. He usually feels im-

pelled to point out the other person's mistakes and faults or give advice about what to do.

Ibid., p. 34.

386. CENTER ON THE INTERVIEWEE

Sometimes an interviewer deliberately introduces his own personal interests into the discussion. He may admire the in-interviewee's flowers or dog and add comments about his own likes and dislikes. Or to encourage the client to talk about his early experience he may tell the client that he too is from Texas and reminisce with him about the locality and people mutually known, or he may even enter into a discussion of politics, unions, or religion. Although at times such devices may be successful in helping the interviewee to feel acquainted and relaxed, the value of their use except in rare instances is dubious. Their dangers outweigh their possible value. With the introduction of the interviewer's personal opinions and feelings, the relationship may leave the professional level and become a social give and take or, worse, an argument. It is better for the interview to proceed with the client as the focus of attention, for his ideas and opinions rather than the interviewer's are paramount in the professional relationship.

Ibid., p. 42.

387. COUNSELOR LEADS BUT DOES NOT COERCE

From all that has been said thus far it may seem as if the interviewer assumes very little activity and direction, since so much stress has been put upon leaving the client free to express himself in his own way. Indeed, the inexperienced interviewer often feels as if the client were running away with the situation, setting the topics for discussion and determining the pace of the conversation, so that all the poor interviewer can do is try to keep track of what is being said. Actually, however, the skilled interviewer does assume leadership throughout. He consciously decides to allow the client to express himself. He knows the function and policy of his agency; he knows, in general, the areas in which he may be of service to the client; and with these things in mind, he guides the conversation along paths that enable him to determine whether or not he is going to be able to help the client, and if so, in what respects. He first directs his questions along the lines of allowing the interviewee to express his need in sufficient detail so that he may understand him better and know whether he will be able to help or whether he will need later to refer the case to someone else. He unobtrusively directs the interview throughout, deciding when to listen, when to talk, what to observe, and so on. With the over-talkative person who is inclined to ramble, or the old person whose mind tends to wander, he gently but sympathetically leads the interviewee back and redirects him through leading questions to a discussion of the immediate situation.

Ibid., p. 43.

388.   ADVICE IS OFTEN FUTILE

. . . If the interviewer has sound advice to give and if his client is free enough of conflict to be able to accept it, it is probably wise to offer it. In many cases, however, advice is futile because the client is unable to act upon it. A woman in emotional conflict over her husband finds it difficult to accept advice either to divorce him or to remain with him. We can point out in such cases the probable consequences of the various alternatives that are available and stimulate the client to a course of reflection that may enable her to reach a decision for herself.

Ibid., pp. 44-45.

389.   A NICE BALANCE IS NEEDED

If people find their own jobs, look for their own houses, make their own applications to hospitals, or other agencies, they are more likely to carry plans through. One person's way may not always be the same as another's, but each person has to work out his own manner of meeting situations. We must allow people a large measure of self-determination.

On the other hand, a worker should not allow his theory of self-determination to become actually a cloak behind which he withholds giving the client the help really needed. It is possible to give so little direction that the client profits not at all and is not even helped to know what help is available.

Ibid., p. 46.

390. THE INTERVIEWEE MUST ACHIEVE INSIGHT

For an interviewer to interpret for himself is essential; for him to pass his interpretations on to the client is usually inadvisable. It is tempting to reveal our discoveries; for example, to say to a client, "Your blustering shows that you are really afraid." But if an interviewer is interested in helping the client, he will ordinarily keep such interpretations to himself. A client can profit from the interviewer's insight only if it becomes also the client's insight and this transfer cannot usually be made in so many words. The client must arrive at his own conclusions at his own pace. To be told that he feels anxiety, rejection, fear, and so on, will not help him. He must come to recognize the existence of such feelings himself with sufficient conviction so that he can voluntarily acknowledge their presence.

Once an interviewer realizes the existence of such underlying factors he can often help his client to a recognition of them through discreet questions and comments, which include some element of interpretation.

Ibid., pp. 47-48.

---

391. THE CONDUCT OF THE INTERVIEW—DARLEY

For those who are doing interviewing for the first time the situation is a little frightening. The curtain has gone up on their unrehearsed play and they find that they don't even know what lines they are to speak to open the action. As is true of most of us when we are faced with a new social situation, we will do one of two things—shut up like a clam, or talk too much.

At the same time the person being interviewed has a few attitudes of his own. He may be nervous in the presence of a stranger. He may feel that this is just one more step in the run-around he has been getting; he may be particularly anxious for some kind of help; he may give the appearance of arrogance, or anger, merely to cover up his uncertainty; or he may feel that this is another interview during which someone is going to pry into his personal affairs.

This is certainly not an easy situation in which to begin the interview, but it is probably typical. Two strangers are about to do business. If we understand why we like a good movie, or a good play, we have some of the yardsticks by which to measure the interview. It cannot be too dreary or dull; it cannot be too "talky"; it cannot be aimless or vague; it should have one or two dramatic high points; there must be a summary to tie together the loose ends; and there must be a natural and reasonable ending. Any initial awkwardness which both parties may feel is very likely to wear off, just as will actors' stage fright.

An even better way to look at the interview has been mentioned—a situation in which the client learns something about himself and his attitudes, and something about the world into which he is going.

How is such learning brought about? Memory of our own school and educational experiences is valuable here:

1. We do not learn if we are emotionally blocked or if our mind is distracted by personal problems that take our attention away from the classroom.
2. We do not learn if the ideas or vocabulary of the teacher are over our head.
3. We do not learn if too many ideas or facts are thrown at us at one time.
4. Most important, we do not learn if we are given no opportunity to participate in the learning experience.
5. We do not learn if the halting expressions of our deep feelings and attitudes are received with scorn, a casual bit of reassurance, obvious embarrassment, or other attitudes which hinder our expression.

Applied to the interview, these descriptions of bad learning situations become guides for the interviewer, and they may be stated in this way:

1. Do not lecture or talk down to the client.
2. Use simple words and confine the information that you give the client to a relatively few ideas.

3. Make very sure that you know what it is he really wants to talk about before giving any information or answers.
4. Make very sure that you sense or feel the attitudes that he holds, because these will either block the discussion or keep the main problems out of it.

In any discussions of interviewing you will be told that it is necessary to "establish rapport." This is a rather technical term which merely describes the prevailing climate that is achieved and maintained throughout the interview. It implies a harmonious atmosphere in which two people can work together successfully. Broken down into its elements it means the following things:

1. The interviewer should be friendly and interested.
2. The interview room should be comfortable and have the appearance of privacy.
3. The interviewer should appear unhurried, even though many people are waiting to see him.
4. The interviewer should accept whatever hesitant and halting attitudes and ideas the client puts forth and express no moral or ethical judgment, no approval or disapproval of these attitudes and ideas.
5. The interviewer should accept the client as a conversational equal during the interview.
6. The interviewer must always make clear to the client the limitations of the Advisory Center, so that the client will not expect too much.
7. The interviewer must always make clear that the responsibility for planning and final action resides with the client.

It is in a setting so defined that the attitudes, the problems, the bitterness, the self-estimates of the client may possibly emerge. If such a setting does not exist, the interview may be formal and remote from the realities of the individual's problems.

TECHNIQUES DURING THE INTERVIEW

It is always dangerous to try to list things to do and things to avoid in practicing any skill. This is particularly true in interviewing since we do not have very much research to fall back on in proving our points. But such lists are necessary evils at times, and may even be of some assistance as guideposts or rules, if they are not too dogmatic. The list that follows is not to be considered a rigid set of rules for interviewing; it merely attempts to summarize suggestions by which interviewers may study and improve their own technique.

1. *Opening the Interview.*—If both parties in the interview are as nervous as we have indicated earlier, it is important that they both arrive quickly at a more relaxed state. A few of the ordinary rules of good manners, like greeting the client by name and asking him to sit down, come quickly to mind. Then a relatively neutral and casual statement, such as "What do you have on your mind today?" or, "What do you want to see us about?" or, "What can we help you with?" may open up the interview for the client.

2. *Phrasing Questions.*—One of the best ways to cut off any conversational flow from the client is to ask a question that can be answered "Yes" or "No." For example, the question, "So you want to start a small business?" is far less productive than the question, "How did you happen to think of starting your own business?"; and this in turn may not be quite as effective as the simple statement, "Tell me what you have in mind when you talk about starting a small business." Questions that can be answered by "Yes" or "No" or some similar terminal statement should be avoided wherever possible.

3. *The Client's Experiences with Counseling.*—Today, with general enthusiasm about counseling, many clients coming to an Advisory Center will have been "counseled" before, either at a military separation center or at one of many possible governmental agencies. The feeling of your client about you as a counselor will not always be a happy one, especially if he has had a bad time earlier. He will be comparing you with other counselors he has known, good or bad. He will be quoting to you his interpretations of what other counselors have told him. It will often be quite necessary to ask him what others have told him so that you will not be working at cross purposes. On the other hand, it is worth remembering that he will interpret what other people have told him primarily in terms

of his own subjective feeling and attitudes and wants, not with any high degree of objectivity.

4. *Overtalking the Client.*—Many people in an interview may find it difficult to state what they mean concisely, and without some fumbling for words. Do not be in such a hurry that you override or overtalk the client if he is fumbling for the phrases he wants. A very frequent error of beginning interviewers is to put words in a client's mouth or talk faster than the client or in some way take the conversation away from the client.

5. *Accepting the Client's Attitudes and Feelings.*—At various points in the interview the client may be trying to express the more deep-seated attitudes and feelings that control his behavior. He will bog down in the task simply because none of us finds it easy to put into words some of our more private attitudes, resentments, doubts, and uncertainties. He may also fear that the interviewer will not approve of what he says. The interviewer must indicate to the client that he has accepted but not passed judgment on these feelings and attitudes. Merely saying, "I see," or "I understand," or, "Yes," will serve to bridge the conversational gap and to keep the client talking.

6. *Cross Examining.*—Do not fire questions at the client like a machine gun. The interview is not a cross-examination. If you are filling out an interview blank and have to get names, addresses, and other items of fact, spread these items throughout the interview, don't pile them up in a series of questions at the beginning. In any event, when questions are needed, space them out and phrase them in as neutral a manner as possible.

7. *Silences in the Interview.*—Most people are embarrassed if no conversation is going on. Silences seem long and endless. If such silences were actually timed with a stop watch, they would probably be found to last not more than 30 seconds and they do not represent necessarily a real absence of activity. The client may be groping for words or ideas; the interviewer may be studying an earlier bit of conversation that has already taken place. Do not, therefore, be frightened by the silences that sometimes fall in interviews. Do not fill them up with a lot of chattering that breaks the trend of thought or

interrupts the flow of feeling. If it becomes necessary to break a silence, merely ask the client to tell you a little bit more about the point he has just finished covering. This will give him a chance to get in motion again.

8. *Reflecting the Client's Feeling.*—If the client is attempting to put a deeply emotional attitude into words, it may be a difficult and awkward process. He may have a feeling of shame or guilt attached to this attitude, or he may hesitate to appear ridiculous in the eyes of another human being. Whatever his motivations, this flow of emotion will be cut off beyond recovery if the interviewer passes moral judgment on the attitude or turns aside from the underlying feeling that is emerging. The interviewer will have turned aside from the underlying feeling if he asks a question that moves the interview off in another direction.

It is better to say, "You feel that people are being unfair to you," than to tell the complainer, "Everybody has trouble getting along some time." It is better to say, "You would like to get married now but you are not sure that you are still in love with this girl since you have not seen her in so long," than to say, "Go ahead and get married now," or, "Wait awhile until you feel better acquainted." It is better to say, "You feel that the interviewer whom you asked about jobs did not do you any good," than to say, "I am sorry, but you must go back to see the interviewer again since he is the one who must help you." Reflecting feelings and attitudes means that you hold up a mirror, so to speak, in which the client can see the meaning and significance of his deep-seated feelings.

9. *Admitting Your Ignorance.*—If the client asks a question regarding facts and you don't have the facts, it is better to say, "I don't know," than to run off with a lot of vague generalities or in some other way try to cover up your ignorance. The client is likely to have more confidence in the interviewer who does not hesitate to admit his ignorance. It would be desirable for the counselor to get these facts later, and to tell the client where to get them.

10. *Distribution of Talking Time.*—Probably the greatest mistake of beginning interviewers is their tendency to talk the

client into a coma. There are no hard or fast rules regarding the percentage of time that each of the actors in our play should talk. Within the interview itself there are certain places where the interviewer must do most of the talking. But if the interview is to have a successful effect on the client, there are certain points where he must do most of the talking: in developing understanding of himself; in bringing his attitudes to the surface; and in formulating plans of action. Generally speaking, if the interviewer talks considerably more than one-half the time, that interview will be less productive than the one in which the client talks more than one-half the time.

11. *The Vocabulary of the Interviewer.*—We have said earlier that if the ideas and words are beyond the range of the client, he will not learn much. This means that the interviewer must make some judgment of the level of verbal ability and understanding of the person to whom he is talking. He must then choose his words accordingly, striving always to keep the words as simple as possible and to keep the ideas as clear as possible, repeating and rephrasing when necessary.

12. *The Number of Ideas Per Interview.*—It is unlikely that in the usual interview a major miracle can be wrought in the life style of another person. This means that the number of ideas and topics discussed might well be kept to a minimum in most interviews. If a man needs to be referred to four agencies in a community, he can be told all about those agencies and where they are and whom to see in 40 minutes. However, the chances are that if he is told about two of the agencies in each of two 20-minute interviews and then visits two of the agencies between the interviews, he will get more out of it than he will out of the first interview we have described. It may be suggested that a human being does not act like an automobile, all of whose needs can be met in a one-stop filling station. Just as there is a danger of giving the individual a runaround, there is an equal danger in a one-stop system that loads him up with so many ideas that he will forget most of them. Furthermore, the counselor must have time to sort out the ideas which seem relevant to the client's needs.

This same problem of the number of ideas per interview is

particularly important where the ideas involved deal with emotional attitudes, resentments, failures, frustrations, and conflicts. It will do very little good if the interviewer gets the client to "tell all" that is on his mind. If by oversympathetic attention or excessive curiosity the interviewer tricks the client into saying too much about his feelings, the client will go out with a very little likelihood of coming back again, since he will feel guilty and ashamed at having exposed so much to a stranger.

13. *Control of the Interview.*—If the interview is to have the continuity and the end results that will lead to a modification of the client's behavior, the interviewer must keep control of the interview. He may have to pull the client back from conversational byways, from fruitless arguments, or from temporarily insoluble problems. This can be done without interrupting the free flow of the client's attitudes as mentioned in Point 8 above. Expressions like, "We were talking about ——," or, "What was it you said about ——?" or, "How does this fit into what you said earlier?" will serve to bring the conversation back to its normal course.

14. *Avoid the Personal Pronoun.*—Most of us are inclined to use the word "I" much more than we realize. "I think you should go to see Mr. Blank," "If I were you I would do——," "It seems to me that," "I don't see how you can." Generally speaking, the interview will be more effective and will result in a freer conversation if the interviewer will rephrase the above questions or remarks to eliminate the use of "I" or "me" or similar references to himself. The client is not asking the interviewer for his opinion or his experiences. The client is really formulating his own opinions in a way that will permit him to criticize himself.

15. *Bad News in the Interview.*—Not all the facts that the interviewer must give to the client are happy or favorable. It does no good in such situations to reassure the individual by saying that "everything will turn out all right," or "I am sure you won't have any trouble in doing this." If the job situation in the community is tough, nothing is gained by kidding the client about it. If the client wants to do something that can-

not be done in this particular agency, no good is accomplished by agreeing to perform the miracle. If you oversell the client on the agency to which you are going to send him, he is in for a disappointment which could have been avoided by pointing out the difficulties under which that other agency works. If housing is bad, the client will eventually learn so anyhow.

16. *Additional Problems.*—It is not the job of the interviewer to make "problem children" out of his clients. On the other hand, the interviewer must not be misled by assuming that the client's own first statement of his difficulty is either true or complete.

For example, the question may simply involve the place where a pension claim is to be filed. The answer is given and the client does not get up to leave the room. Apparently the interview is over, but the client is still there. It may well be that he has something else on his mind and it is the job of the interviewer to find out what further difficulties need to be discussed. "Was there something else you wanted to ask about?"; "Do you have something else on your mind?" These may produce the desired result.

17. *The Frequent Visitor.*—There is a particular group of people who love to discuss their "problems." They will return periodically for a good heart-to-heart talk with the interviewer. They will give every evidence of intending to do just what the interviewer tells them to do, but for some reason they never quite get around to going to the agencies where they are referred. While it is true that the willingness of the clients to return to the interviewer is one measure of the interviewer's success, it is also true for this group of people that the interviewer is wasting his time in repeated interviews with them. They are the sympathy seekers, the complainers, the overly dependent people that clutter up the crowded time of a busy interviewer.

18. *Setting Limits on the Interview.*—No matter how much an interviewer may be inclined toward lengthy sessions with each client, office routines do not permit them and successful interviewing does not demand them. It is better if the inter-

viewer and the client realize from the beginning that the interview will last for a fixed length of time. It is the job of the interviewer to see that the interview stays approximately within that time. Other interviews may be scheduled later on if the client desires them.

19. *Plans for Action.*—While it is not essential in all cases that the client rush out and do something as a result of the interview, it is generally true that he will complete the learning process about himself and about his particular world if there are certain things that he feels he has to do as a result of the interview discussion. Furthermore, much of our planning in life is based on our flexibility in modifying a course of action, or on building several plans to meet new adjustment problems. Thus it is of assistance for the interviewer and the client to work out alternative plans of action wherever possible. It is not enough for the client to decide to go to school, for instance. He should have some idea which school he is going to and what will happen if he cannot go where he wants to go. If he cannot get into the day school of his choice, will the alternative of night school fill the bill? The working out of alternative plans is important in the over-all interviewing process.

20. *Summarizing the Interview.*—The amount of learning that has gone on in the interview can be roughly estimated from the way in which the client summarizes the interview. When the interviewer sees the time is drawing to a close, it is his job to set the stage for the summary. If possible the client should do the summarizing. "Now suppose we see what we have accomplished in this interview," or "Tell me how you think the situation looks now"—phrases of this kind will be of assistance in calling forth a summary from the client.

21. *Ending the Interview.*—This is not an easy task. In the general relaxation that follows the stress of interviewing, the interviewer may become expansive and start to babble about his own life and his own interests. The interview may degenerate into a most casual social conversation. This is likely to destroy much of the good work that has been done by breaking the quiet, rather objective, and apparently slow pace of

the interview up until that moment. Quite often a phrase such as "Do you think we have done all we can for today?" or, "Is there anything more you would like to talk about today?" will be enough to end the interview. It may help for the interviewer to stand and move toward the door. It is important in any event to learn your own technique of ending an interview when it is really over within the time limit you have set.

> John G. Darley, "Conduct of the Interview," *The Interview In Counseling*. Prepared by the author under the direction of the Retraining and Re-employment Administration, U. S. Department of Labor, 1940. Reprinted by permission of Dr. John G. Darley, pp. 12-19.

392. THE LISTENING-TO VERSUS THE TALKING-TO INTERVIEW

In dealing with young people, adults frequently talk too much and listen too little. A tongue lashing can be more harmful than physical punishment. The adult who hopes to make a point often forgets that he needs to understand a person and his feelings before he can have an effect on his thinking. The method called the "talking-to" interview is based on the premise that a point can be made by an intellectual verbalization of an already known principle.

In the talking-to interview, the adult begins by making a factual statement of the problem. This produces a negative reaction. It arouses usually further guilt, making it necessary to be defensive. The adult does not always recognize this reaction because it is not visible and instead continues his talk by requesting an explanation of the act. This calls for an expression of the guilt and the defensive attitude built up during the interview. In reality, in the talking-to interview, the adult and the youngster talk past each other and never come to grips with the real issue.

The other possibility is to aim at understanding rather than at making a point. For this purpose the "listening-to" interview begins with the adult's attempts to help the youngster to be at ease and opens the way for him to express his troubles. To this the young person can react directly by verbalizing his feelings, perhaps blaming it on others, but always giving the interviewer material about himself. The adult will now try to get closer to the point of real trouble in order to get further help toward understanding. Once the youngster feels accepted and understood, he will give the adult some definite leads as to areas and methods with which he can be helped.

It is the group leader's job to understand individuals in his group. He must be given some time in which to talk with them alone. Where the interview can be informal, the principle of listening for understanding, rather than talking to make a point, is suggested.

> Rudolph M. Wittenberg, *So You Want To Help People*. New York: Association Press, 1947, p. 110.

393. MISTAKES TO BE AVOIDED

The counselor should recognize several ways in which the interview may fail to accomplish its main purpose:

1. The counselor may fail to achieve a warmth of relationship—a "feeling with" the person both intellectually and emotionally. He may feel only sentimentality or pseudo-affection, or even make the contact an outlet for his own ego drives and desire to dominate.

2. The counselor may seize upon a solution and push its acceptance without giving the student a chance to explore the situation more thoroughly; this fault is often attributed to a feeling of pressure—"so much to do and so little time."

3. The counselor may persist in his preferred technic or theory when it is clearly inappropriate in a particular case.

4. The counselor may fail to follow up the clues and leads that the student gives, or neglect important aspects of the case such as a physical impairment or a personality trend, the significance of which he does not recognize.

5. The counselor may evoke confidences that he cannot handle, and that the student will later regret having brought to light. Or he may probe too deeply and too quickly. Prying into another person's private life by methods that do not seem legitimate to him, may have the effect of a boomerang in destroying the relationship that is the *sine qua non* of success. An individual's reticence or resistance may indicate areas of conflict that should be noted, but not necessarily explored immediately.

If the counselor oversteps the boundary line of reticence, he will put the student on his guard. And what doth it profit a counselor though he gain vital information if he thereby antagonize the individual he had hoped to help?

6. The interview may be problem centered or technic centered rather than centered in the person in the setting of his school, home, and community.

> Ruth Strang, *Counseling Technics in College and Secondary School.* New York: Harper and Brothers, 1949, pp. 136-37.

394. COUNSELOR SELF-UNDERSTANDING AIDS HIM AS INTERVIEWER

. . . In so far as an interviewer can discover his own areas of intolerance, his own list of unpardonable sins, he has made a start toward self-disciplined control of his feelings in his relationships with others.

When an interviewer first learns that he should be nonjudgmental, should not become angry, should not become dependent upon the interviewee's affection and response, he tries to suppress his feelings, and as a result he tends to become artificial and stilted in his responses. It would be better to recognize the existence of such feelings and learn to control their expression, for these feelings are not unnatural but merely inappropriate in the professional situation. If an interviewer is aware that he is becoming angry, he is then in a position to regulate his own feelings better than if he denies to himself that he has such feelings. Control of feelings rather than absence of feelings on the part of the worker is the goal.

> Annette Garrett, *Interviewing: Its Principles and Methods.* New York: Family Service Association of America, 1942, p. 22.

395. COUNSELOR ACCEPTANCE OR REJECTION

The Relationship Between Interviewer and Interviewee. Parents are often amused at the enthusiasm their young son shows for his school teacher. He reports her comments on the weather, imitates her mannerisms, wants to take her gifts, is delighted if she asks him to clean the blackboard for her after school, and so on. Another parent whose child has the same teacher may not understand why he seems negativistic toward all the teacher's suggestions, and seems to go out of his way to annoy and irritate the teacher. Similarly adults themselves, when they stop to think about it, find that their rather strong attachments or antagonisms for certain people seem unjustified by any conscious knowledge they have of the other's nature. Such positive and negative feelings toward those we come in contact with are, of course, universal phenomena, always present to some degree. Certain features of interviewing tend to intensify them, and for this reason the wise interviewer will want to understand their nature and effects and will seek to subject them to some measure of self-conscious control. . . .

These feelings are usually not consciously revealed but indications of them may be recognized in such comments from clients as, "It's been such a help to talk with you," "I see you understand," "You're the first person I've ever told this to," "What do you think I should do?" Remarks of this sort occur in case after case.

The opposite sort of situation also arises in interviewing. Again quite independently of the interviewer's actual character, the client, because of his own anxieties, insecurity, and deprivations, may endow him with negative characteristics and build up antagonism toward him. Much depends on the client's previous experiences with his parents or with others in authority.

Negative feelings are often even more concealed than positive ones because of social standards of politeness, but they are revealed sometimes by refusals to talk, by the breaking off of an appointment, by refusal to return to the agency, or by trapping the worker into giving advice which can later be proved wrong. . . .

The development of an inter-relationship of this general sort, positive or negative, between interviewer and interviewee is not all a unique phenomenon but a universal one. It is a commonplace that people tend to become dependent upon their doctors, lawyers, and ministers. Toward the end of her pregnancy a woman often relies more on her physician than on her husband. A patient under psychoanalysis develops a strong emotional attachment to the analyst. The analyst has developed methods of making therapeutic use of such a relationship. He calls it technically "transference." We are concerned with it here only in some of the less intense forms mentioned above.

Annette Garrett, *Interviewing: Its Principles and Methods.* New York: Family Service Association of America, 1942, pp. 18-20.

396. Acceptance—An Essential

. . . The interviewer must learn to counteract this perfectly natural tendency to condemn all behavior that conflicts with his own standards. Toward almost every problem that a client brings, the interviewer has developed an attitude of approval or disapproval based on his own experiences, and he tends to assume that this attitude represents the norm. As his professional training and experience grow he recognizes that there is a wide range of individual variation in human responses to a given situation. This may lead him to try to accept all such behavior, to carefully refrain from evaluating it. But this clearly is an extremely limited understanding of the concept of acceptance, involving as it does only an arid non-judgmental impartiality. Real acceptance is primarily acceptance of the feelings given expression by behavior and does not necessarily involve acceptance of unsocial behavior at all; real acceptance involves positive and active understanding of these feelings and not merely a negative and passive refusal to pass judgment.

A merely negative attitude of not passing judgment on a client's unusual behavior is often interpreted by him as a condoning of that behavior, a repudiation of a standard he himself accepts but has failed to live up to. He tends then either to reject the interviewer as an unfit guide or at the other extreme to continue and increase his undesirable behavior thus trying out the interviewer to see how far he can go in his nonconformity. A man who makes no effort to get a job, for instance, may find his dilatoriness so accepted by the interviewer that he gradually gives up the struggle for self-maintenance entirely. A child whose petty stealing is ignored is not at all reassured, as he would be if he were confronted by the

interviewer with knowledge of this misbehavior and yet convinced that in spite of this the worker accepted him in the
fuller sense of understanding his feelings and the emotional
conflicts which induced his stealing. A child feels that a person who thus understands him is his friend. Such a person's
recognition.of misbehavior will be regarded as a sign that he
wants to help overcome it.

To accept then is not to condone anti-social behavior but to
understand it in the sense of understanding the feeling it expresses. In a worker's early acquaintance with a client it is of
course impossible to know, let alone understand specifically,
all of the various factors responsible for given behavior. In such
early stages we make use of the best knowledge we have available at that time, namely, the general familiarity we have acquired through theory and experience with the basic underlying dynamics of human behavior. We know that a person
who appears angry and belligerent may, in fact, be feeling
anxious and fearful, that one who appears demanding may
have no other way to express his hurt pride and guilt about
asking advice or aid. Understanding of this sort lays the groundwork for real acceptance. As an interviewer's knowledge of
the client deepens, however, his general knowledge is enlarged by an understanding of the particular pressures active
in this specific situation. His general acceptance develops into
more specific understanding. Such detailed understanding is
not always possible, but the more definite it is the more effective the worker can be.

Sometimes an interviewer, relying on his general understanding, says too readily, "I understand," and thus confuses
and blocks the client in his attempt to present the details that
would be needed for more specific understanding. The interviewer means that he wants to understand, or does understand
in general, whereas the client realizes that he certainly does not
yet know about the specific factors of his case. It often would
be far better for the interviewer to say, "I do not understand,"
for then the client would realize that the interviewer wants
to understand but needs more information.

Ibid., pp. 23-24.

397. Interviewing an Art Which Practice and Analysis Can Improve

Probably everyone starting to interview wishes there were a list of rules he could follow, but, unfortunately, it is impossible to enumerate a complete list of infallible rules for all interviewing, or even for any particular kind. Interviewing takes place between human beings who are much too individualized to be reduced to a formula. To be sure, there are certain psychological traits which characterize most people most of the time, and a skilled interviewer will do well to keep some of the more important of these in mind. There are characteristic modes of human action and reaction, and awareness of them tends to increase the satisfactoriness of one's relationships with others. Interviewing involves a close and subtler relation between human beings than may at first be recognized, and skill in conducting this relationship can be increased through knowledge of the fundamental factors involved.

Some people fear that a self-conscious study of the principles of interviewing may detract from the warm friendliness and real interest in other individuals which are so essential for the successful practice of the art. There is certainly no necessity for this to be the case. An informed person need not be unfriendly. One need not be ignorant of human psychology to love human beings. Indeed the opposite is often true. There are few things so frustrating as to love someone but not know how to give the help he desperately needs; and contrariwise, to be able to help those we love increases our affection for them.

Warm human interest does sometimes vanish from interviewing, and when that happens it becomes a monotonous, mechanical sort of thing that is relatively valueless. But the cause of this, when it occurs, is not knowledge of the rich interplay of one human mind with another but the ignorance that regards interviewing as a routine affair of asking set questions and recording answers. If this were all there were to interviewing, a phonograph with a recording device would serve the purpose far better. But with a proper understanding of even some of the intricacies of human personality and of the effective give and take between two complex human beings, our attention and warm interest are aroused in increasing measure, and the process becomes anything but routine.

Interviewing is an art, a skilled technique which can be improved and eventually perfected primarily through continued practice. But mere practice alone is not enough. Skills can be developed to their fullest potentialities only when practice is accompanied by knowledge about interviewing and self-conscious study of our own practice. Knowledge of the theory underlying interviewing gives us certain material in the light of which we can critically examine our present techniques and discern ways in which they can be improved.

The obvious fact about interviewing is that it involves communication between two people. Special problems confront both interviewer and interviewee. We begin to obtain some notion of the complexities involved if we recall some of the feelings we ourselves have had while on the way to be interviewed. Perhaps we were seeking to borrow money, were consulting a doctor or a lawyer, or were applying for a job. We may have felt some fear at the prospect of talking with an unknown person and of revealing our needs to him. We may have been uncertain as to just what about ourselves we might have to tell, fearful that he might wish to know more than we were willing to relate, might not understand us, or might not grant our request.

On the other hand, when we first began to interview, what were some of the worries that plagued us? Would we say the right things to put our client at his ease? Would we be able to draw him out? What would we do if he didn't talk, and if he did, would we be sure to select the significant facts in his remarks and behavior?

For an interview to be successful, the diverse fears of both interviewer and interviewee must be allayed, and the diverse desires of both must be met. Rapport must be established between the two, a relationship that will enable the interviewee to reveal the essential facts of his situation and that will enable the interviewer to be most effective in helping him.

Ibid., pp. 7-9.

398. IMPROVING THE INTERVIEW

The individual counseling interview, which is undoubtedly the most important aspect of the counseling process, is still largely an art rather than a science. However, even the most artistic product, be it in music or in painting, is never accomplished without the artist's firm knowledge of certain relevant objective facts, or without his constant effort to improve his skills. In recent years numerous attempts have been made to improve the counseling interview through analysis, objectification and evaluation by means of the available scientific techniques. Thanks to these attempts our understanding of the counseling interview is greater than ever before. There is no question, however, that our present knowledge and skill in utilizing this very powerful instrument leaves still much to be desired. Constant effort in improving our techniques in interviewing is necessary, and in this the counselor's own self-criticism will probably remain his greatest teacher.

Use of Check List

In training counselors at Springfield College during the past several years we have used a check list which seems to do well in sensitizing students to numerous aspects of the counseling interview and in motivating them to analyze and criticize their own techniques. (This check list was originally developed by Gilbert K. Krulee as part of his Master's project under the writer's supervision. This original form has, however, been revised in several respects through use in our training courses. It is here presented in experimental form subject to further verification and revision.) It is understood, of course, that no mere check list can encompass all that transpires during a counseling interview, nor can it make a good counselor out of one who does not possess an essential degree of human wisdom and warmth. We might say then that, "other things being equal," the check list to be presented in this article can serve as a useful instrument for preparing counselors, for in-service training, and especially for the counselor's own self-evaluation and improvement.

It should be observed that this check list does not subscribe completely to any one of the present-day theories of counseling. Some of the items refer to principles which are agreed upon by the majority of counselors; other items refer to factors which are recognized to be important, even though there may be some disagreement among various writers as to the degree of their importance. The items of observation in the check list are to be recorded in terms of relative degree of occurrence and not on an all-or-none basis. (On the form used in the author's classes each item in the check list is followed by a long horizontal line across the page with designations of "Low" and "High" at the extremes and "Medium" at the middle of the line.) One other observation is in order. It is assumed that all problems whether they are labelled educational, vocational or otherwise are personal problems. Hence the observations are directed not so much to the problem, but to the person himself in the counseling situation.

A Check List for Interviewers

A. Situational Factors
    1. Client seated comfortably
    2. Bright light not shining in client's eyes from window or lamp
    3. Adequate ventilation and temperature
    4. Room simply furnished, not too many distracting features
    5. Cheery and attractive room
    6. Counselor's desk not cluttered, giving the impression of pressure of work
    7. Relative absence of outside distractions and interruptions
    8. Beginning and length of interview definitely scheduled by appointment

B. Observing the Counselor
    1. Counselor neatly dressed
    2. Counselor's diction clear and voice pleasing
    3. Counselor looks alert and interested
    4. Counselor's attitude warm, but not effusive
    5. Counselor is poised and accepting, never shocked by client's remarks and actions
    6. Counselor is prepared or familiar with case material
    7. Counselor's attention is focused on the client and his problem
    8. Counselor does not interrupt or argue with client
    9. Counselor does not talk about own problems

10. Counselor does not introduce irrelevant material interfering with the flow of client's on-going thought or talk
11. Counselor does not minimize client's problems
12. Counselor does not try to "impress" the client
13. Counselor is patient
14. Counselor does not make snap judgments
15. Counselor is unprejudiced
16. Counselor gives information when client is ready for it
17. Counselor gives information in terms understandable to the client
18. Counselor interprets test results cautiously, not dogmatically
19. Counselor does not do most of the talking during the interview
20. Counselor does not moralize
21. Counselor does not challenge the truth of a statement made by the client
22. Counselor willing to admit mistakes or confess ignorance
23. Counselor aware of underlying feelings of client
24. Counselor does not make decisions for the client
25. Counselor knows when and how to make a referral, when such action is necessary

C. Observing the Client
1. Client at ease
2. Client shows signs of emotional disturbances—blushing, stammering, etc.
3. Presence of observable physical deformities or disabilities
4. Client talks freely and volunteers information
5. Client discusses physical ailments which suggest psychological geneses
6. Client submissive toward counselor
7. Client aggressive toward counselor
8. Client having difficulties in more than one area of adjustment
9. Client mentions serious environmental or social handicaps
10. Client successful in some types of activity
11. Client confused; mentions many problems without seeing relationships between them
12. Client continually dependent on counselor; expects counselor to tell him what to do
13. Client shows signs of hostility towards self and others
14. Client is suspicious of the intent of others
15. Client shows signs of defensiveness and inferiority feelings

16. Client shows signs of superiority feelings; genius, bravado, etc.
17. Client's history one of escape from reality; day dreaming, substitute satisfactions, etc.
18. Client shows signs of fear and worry
19. Client is discouraged, dejected, unhappy
20. Client makes no expression of belongingness; talks in terms of "I," rarely in terms of "we"
21. Client thinks in terms of stereotypes
22. Client's thinking very rigid concerning moral ideas and ethical standards
23. Client is a perfectionist
24. Client shows feelings of guilt and sinfulness
25. Client shows a lack of self-esteem
26. Client shows frequent signs of conflict, expresses numerous ambivalences
27. Client's thinking seems to gradually become clearer and more realistic
28. Client begins to see relationships and develop insights
29. Client begins to consider possible courses of action
30. Client makes plans and assumes responsibility

Seth Arsenian, "Improvement in the Counseling Interview," *Counseling*, (Issued by the National Board of the Y.M.C.A., 291 Broadway, N. Y.) Vol. 8, No. 2, February, 1950, pp. 3-4.

15.

Testing

---

399. THERE IS NO MAGIC IN TESTING

In contrast to an attitude of undue expectation among clients as to the magical results to be expected from instruments designed to appraise personality, there is the feeling of fear, present in many clients, of being subjected to the administration of tests and of being confronted with the results. There may be much more to this common disposition than is ordinarily attributed to it by some practitioners who link it to the ordinary human failing of being afraid of new devices of any kind and who liken it to the historic public distaste and fear of early medical devices and practices.

That human superstitions of this type undoubtedly play a role in such situations may be readily agreed. Common feelings of insecurity, also, must undoubtedly be involved in common fears of the test situation. Moreover, some clients may have very good reason to fear the effect of test results upon their level of aspiration. Beyond all these, however, and other motivations that might be mentioned, there may reside an intuitive and deep-seated resentment against an all-embracing belief on the part of some counselors that the whole of the personality can be scientifically appraised, classified, calculated, and assigned an index number. If this is the case, we must recognize the basic validity in the common fear of tests and the need for formulating a philosophy which simultaneously recognizes the correctness of the theoretical scientific view of personality and of the indeterminate and artistic nature of human individuality. (F. S. C. Northrop, *The Meeting of East and West*. New York: The Macmillan Company, 1946). Basically, "man is not a piano key" and will refuse to be regarded as such. Scientific psychometric instruments may be employed for all that they are worth in the problem-situation while, at the same time, their use and results are sufficiently controlled and qualified so that clients are under no delusions as to their proper place in the total scheme.

Robert Hendry Mathewson, *Guidance Policy and Practice.* New York: Harper and Brothers, 1949, p. 89.

400. Tests Have a Distinct Value

Despite their limitations, tests have a place in the total study of an individual's potentialities. As his assets and limitations become clearer, his placement in appropriate learning situations can be made with more certainty. Tests decrease guess work in guidance. Study of the detailed responses on the test paper gives a clearer idea of how the individual's mind works in response to the tasks set by the test. When standardized tests are administered individually by a skillful observer, they yield additional insight into the subject's attitudes, emotional stability, and problem-solving methods. If tests have been given as a routine procedure and their results have been recorded on the cumulative record card, the counselor has an initial background valuable to his understanding of the individual.

When an individual is not speaking freely in an interview, a discussion of test results sometimes unlocks his reticence and helps him to think more freely about his personal problems. Such a discussion may serve as a springboard to a more therapeutic type of relationship. Details from test responses, especially those in personality and interest inventories, suggest possible areas that can be tactfully touched in interviews.

To the individual who needs objective evidence of his abilities or his limitations, test results are more convincing than any general statements made by his friends or his counselor. The tests give the counselee one more bit of evidence that will be useful to him in thinking through his problem or life plan.

Ruth Strang, *The Role of the Teacher in Personnel Work.* New York: Bureau of Publications, Teachers College, Columbia University, 1946, pp. 390-91.

401. Test Results to Supplement Other Available Data

No discussion of procedures for the study of individual students would be complete if testing were omitted. But a discussion of only the essential points would require a book. . . .

Tests are complex devices and should not be incorporated into the guidance program until their proper use is assured. They are not the first step to take in organizing a program for the study of individual students. . . .

Tests should be introduced to supply facts which are supplementary to other evidence or to provide information not otherwise readily available or obtainable. The testing program should be planned in view of the information already available. While from some angles the planning of a testing program which will not duplicate information previously collected is desirable, a certain amount of overlap is advantageous. Test results can serve as a useful gauge of the significance of other items in the cumulative record. At the same time, the usefulness of test scores is increased if they are reviewed in the light of other pertinent data from the individual inventory.

> Clifford P. Froehlich, *Guidance Services in Smaller Schools.* New York: McGraw-Hill Book Company, Inc., 1950, pp. 196-97.

402. Seashore: Psychological Testing

He who interprets psychological tests assumes considerable responsibility for thorough competence in handling highly technical information and for professional skill in translating test information so that the counselee has a meaningful experience of growth in self-understanding. Tests, in and of themselves, are quite simple to administer and score; with rare exceptions, any competent and reliable clerk can "give the tests." It does not follow that interpretation is easy. Every test score is a bit of clinical data about a person and must be clinically interpreted. "Anyone can interpret an Otis I.Q."—this remark is still heard, and it is still a dangerous viewpoint. One still hears of persons who glibly explain to their clients what a low score on the Bernreuter Personality Inventory means. To these persons, neurotic tendency or introversion-extroversion are simple concepts. The trained clinical psychologist is not so sure what they mean!

I.Q.'s percentile ranks, ratings, profiles, and scores on inventories are statistical information that can have meaning only when understood in relation to the experience and personality structure of the particular client, and to the vast experimental and clinical literature in educational and vocational guidance and in the psychology of personality. In our striving for simple and pat answers, and under the pressure of "processing cases," we sometimes forget the modesty which all of us should have in the face of the vast lack of knowledge that still exists about why people are the way they are and our still rather feeble efforts at exact prediction from our testing and interviewing.

Tests are more difficult to interpret today because their scientific use demands that we must realize, not only how test data can help us in counseling, but also what tests cannot do for us.

If agencies want to carry on high-grade, responsible, scientifically oriented counseling and still retain the flavor of "personal work" which has been the genius of some of them, they must face up to the fact that counseling staffs must meet rigorous standards. To provoke discussion of this problem and to provide bases on which thinking can proceed, the writer would like to present some observations based upon his experiences in setting up counseling centers in social agencies and in training counselors. For brevity, the viewpoints are presented rather dogmatically and examples are few.

COUNSELING PROGRAMS INVOLVING TESTS
SHOULD BE ADMINISTERED BY SPECIALISTS

A reasonable minimum standard is that any agency which conducts a formal counseling service for educational and vocational guidance should have one person whose training has been at least at the Master's Degree level in the field of guidance or clinical psychology. This does not mean a few picked-up summer courses, much as these might enhance the competence of the individual who wants to work in guidance. It means a full year's work, specifically and completely, in courses and field work related to psychological guidance: testing, interviewing, statistics, job information, psychology of personality, and so on. This professional goal probably cannot be reached at once, and even when attained it represents a minimum standard. But no organization that claims professional standards can settle for less.

NOT ALL COUNSELORS NEED BE TEST EXPERTS

If the over-all program is under the direction of a technically competent person, there is no reason why many, if not most, of the local staff members cannot function as counselors. In fact, the sheer load of work probably requires that the client contacts be spread among many people. Some agencies will have full-fledged guidance centers with their own staffs; others will operate with a decentralized program, with technical services in one place and departmental staffs actually doing most of the counseling. In either type of organization, it should be considered good policy to train several counselors on the job. The trained psychologist in charge will be responsible for supervision, for in-service training, for special kinds of cases, and for a percentage of the regular clients.

TESTS MUST BE INTEGRATED INTO THE TOTAL COUNSELING PATTERN

The counselor's function is to help the client become better acquainted with himself in such a way that he can evaluate his abilities, interests, and ambitions in a realistic way and can make plans for his life which are possible of attainment. Counseling is effective when it is client-centered. Decisions are the responsibility of the client. This generally accepted viewpoint has implications for the use of tests which should be mentioned here, even though they cannot be adequately elaborated.

First, tests possess an aura of scientific power in the minds of many clients. Care needs to be exercised in order that:

1. The client accepts the need for testing.

2. Having accepted the idea, he is not frightened by them.

3. When he has taken them, the ratings secured do not assume undue prominence in his thinking.

In short, we must neither undersell nor oversell the testing idea to our clients.

Second, the ultimate meaning of test scores is in relation to the purposes for which counseling is being carried on. In in-

terpreting tests, we naturally refer to statistical reference
points: I.Q.'s, percentile ranks, validity co-efficients, and so
forth. These anchorages for interpretations are very important;
and every counselor needs to have some grounding in the statistical concepts involved and have ways of conveying test
information to the clients in terms that are accurate and meaningful to the client. But test scores *per se* have no meaning; they
are just numbers. They acquire meaning only in terms of the
client who is being counseled. From a counseling point of view,
an I.Q. of 110 is not meaningful until one knows what the
ambitions of the client are, what plans he has made or are
being imposed upon him by his family or school, what educational program he is now carrying or contemplates beginning.
If he wants to become a haberdashery salesman, 110 is an
adequate I.Q.; if he wants to be a physician or an engineer or a
biologist, more information and some adept counseling are in
order. Or, since we have mentioned salesmen, what sort of
score on any test should a person have to be a salesman? Among
many factors to consider is this: what kind of salesman?
There are numerous varieties. This simple example points out
that the meaning of a test score appears only in relation to
the client being considered and to the job requirements of the
kinds of work being considered.

> Harold G. Seashore, "Psychological Testing," *Counseling
> Young Adults* (A Symposium), New York: Association Press,
> 1947, pp. 31-33.

403.   DISCUSSION OF THE TESTING PROBLEM—WARTERS

The measurement movement has given personnel work valuable analytical tools and techniques. With the data derived
from these instruments, the personnel worker can make a much
better approach to the student's needs than is possible without them. But these tools, and tests in particular, are probably
the most abused of all the contributions. Personnel workers do
not always make the best use of these instruments for the
most important purposes. Nor do they always use the instruments correctly or evaluate the data properly. This occasional
misuse of tests is not, however, a sin peculiar to personnel
workers. It is a common failing of educators in general.

The history of the use of tests in personnel work is very much the same as that of testing in education as a whole. A period of preliminary exploration was followed by one of rapid growth with greatly exaggerated expectations of the value of tests and with uncritical acceptance of test results. Then came a period of reaction against all tests with a tendency to discount their value entirely. The present period, for the most part, is one of general acceptance of modest but substantial contributions from tests. A more wholesome, critical attitude toward measurement has resulted in a more critical use of tests and a more sensible and intelligent interpretation of the findings.

Today high-school personnel workers have a rich supply of tests from which to draw. They find a number of reliable standardized intelligence and educational-achievement tests useful for discovering exceptional pupils, the slow learner and the gifted; for appraising a pupil's chance at success in a college, in a particular course, or in a job at a particular occupational level, but not in a particular job; for identifying a pupil's special abilities; for diagnosing his disabilities in learning; for appraising his progress; for comparing his present performance with that of other pupils and, more important, with his own past performance; and for determining the contents of a course in accordance with his particular needs.

Tests are also available to the high-school counselor for judging mechanical, clerical, musical, and art aptitudes and for measuring aptitude in particular school subjects and in some occupations. Like tests of general intelligence, however, these tests show what a student can do rather than what he will do. Consequently, the counselor must also know the pupil's personality characteristics, which indicate how well he will use his abilities, general or specific.

To study the pupil's personality, the counselor will rely less upon the test technique than upon such procedures as descriptive ratings, anecdotal records, observation, the case study, and, most important, a synthesis of data from a number of sources. Personality tests are of doubtful value if they are given "to learn a pupil's score" with respect to a particular trait or a general personality pattern. Because scores are dependent upon a student's interpretation of items, upon his understanding of himself, upon his desire to make a good impression, and upon his willingness to give true answers, interpretation of numerical scores is seldom possible. But even though these tests have few quantitative possibilities, they do have a qualitative value. Observation of the pupil while he is taking the test and analysis of his answers to different items can contribute to a better understanding and appreciation of his feelings and attitudes toward himself, toward his problems, and toward the persons involved in his problems. . . .

Many parents and some teachers expect far more from tests than can possibly result from the use of any instrument. High-school counselors should share with others their knowledge of the nature and use of these tools. The counselor is unwise who encourages pupils and parents to believe that he can offer specific advice on the basis of tests. He may find exhilarating the feelings derived from being considered important because all-knowing. He may find less enjoyable the feelings experienced on the day of reckoning when he is classed as a charlatan rather than as a sage. Few of his predictions may come true, for tests cannot be used as fortune-telling devices. Any personnel worker who does not correct misconceptions concerning the magical qualities of tests, who does not point out their limitations as well as the benefits to be derived from their use is helping to make it difficult for other counselors to use tests wisely.

Personnel workers find more helpful than pencil-and-paper tests certain more recent developments of the measurement movement, such as observation techniques, the interview, projective techniques based on psychoanalytic principles, and a new type of measurement generally described by the term "evaluation." Much broader in scope than testing, evaluation emphasizes observation of behavior and the longitudinal study of a pupil to learn how he grows in the various aspects of his total behavior pattern. These techniques have a special value in personnel work because they are focused upon clarifying needs, meanings, processes, and purposes rather than upon appraising general or specific attainments. Furthermore, they make measurement a function of the total situation rather than of a particular part. Such techniques are highly useful to workers concerned with measurement in order to secure improvement in social behavior as well as to test and refine skills, habits, and knowledge.

Jane Warters, *High School Personnel Work Today*. New York: McGraw-Hill Book Company, Inc., 1946, pp. 37-40.

404. DRESHER'S SUMMARY ON USE OF TESTS

A good school is an environment created and directed by teachers, and centered in the growth and development of students at all levels of instruction. "Growth and development" means the attainment of knowledge, skills, appreciation, habits, and attitudes, which helps to make students good citizens in a changing society, limited only by their capacity to acquire these traits. Teachers must have a lasting respect for the personality and individuality of each student enrolled in their classes. There is no fixed formula by which all students can be taught and developed to their fullest capacities. We recognize that certain basic knowledges and skills are important because they are the tools with which students must work. We also recognize that citizenship, character, appreciation, attitudes, and feelings are important, too, because they affect all human behavior. The teacher must deliberately provide situations in which tolerance, honesty, fair play, loyalty, affection, and other desirable human traits, can be constantly emphasized and consistently practiced. All obstacles that will hinder the development of these traits must be removed. The ability of a student to use knowledge in socially significant ways is as important as the amount of knowledge acquired. Assistance in development can be provided only through long and careful observation of each student as he progresses in the school environment and by the use of carefully recorded data which cover his growth in all the phases of his educational, social, physical, and emotional development.

The teacher's knowledge of the growth of each student depends upon the collection, recording, and interpretation of a variety of data in terms of an individual's interests, mental ability, verbal and manual skills, special aptitudes, limitations, personality patterns, health and physical conditions, educational history, and home and community background. Some of this information can be obtained from properly selected tests and instruments. In selecting a test, many things should be considered to make sure that it is useful for the desired purpose. Its type, scope, what it measures, validity, reliability, and practicability should be studied.

Group and individual school-aptitude tests provide a measure of ability that has predictive value, since these tests show the student's ability to progress in his education. Achievement or scholastic proficiency tests should be used for diagnosis, survey, and administrative purposes. While an individual's school aptitude and achievement are important factors, his other aptitudes and interests are significant in connection with his choice of curricula and later, with occupational choices. Although personality is a difficult trait to measure, it is one of the most important factors in a student's background.

In interpreting and evaluating test results, one should keep in mind that many of our tests are not reliable enough for accurate individual prediction. Even if they were, there are so many ways in which students differ that it would be difficult to predict accurately. But by giving tests and collecting all other available information about the individual at different times over a period of years, one gathers data that will have more predictive and diagnostic value and that will be more reliable than will a cross section taken at any one time. In interpreting a number of tests for one individual, the profile is very useful.

If the teacher is to do a good job, she must seek insight into the total development of the student. She may use intelligence, achievement, aptitude, personality, and interest scales. Other useful instruments and techniques are biographies, inventories, questionnaires, graphic scales, rating scales, check lists, and autobiographies. As a result of the use of tests and other measuring instruments of behavior, plus other information about the student's development, the process of education becomes more meaningful.

Clifford E. Erickson, editor, *A Basic Text for Guidance Workers*. New York: Prentice-Hall, Inc., 1947, pp. 83-85. By permission of the publishers. From chapter by Richard H. Drescher.

405. Learning About Pupils Through the Use of Tests and Other Instruments

During the past few years, more emphasis has been placed on the individualization of all educational activities. This trend makes it desirable and necessary to secure adequate data concerning each student. In trying to understand an individual more completely, for whatever purpose, one tries to ascertain all the facts concerning him that might be of value in solving his problem. His interests, desires, abilities, companions, home relationships, and anxieties are taken into consideration. In the process of counseling, the use of properly selected tests, inventories, and rating blanks represents one of the most economical, scientific, and professional techniques for the improvement of education.

THE ROLE OF TESTING

Why of testing. In order to help a pupil, the teacher or counselor must be cognizant of the pupil's characteristics and potentialities. Effective counseling involves the collection, recording, and interpretation, of a variety of data in terms of an individual's interests, mental ability, verbal and manual skills, special aptitudes, limitations, personality patterns, health and physical conditions, educational history, and home and community background. The purpose of employing any test or instrument is to measure some one of these aspects in the most economical way, and to use the results to help students find their best place in the school and in other activities, develop their best abilities, reduce, if possible, their liabilities, and succeed in their educational, social, and vocational aims. Tests give an individual score or rating under standardized conditions and offer, as a general rule, the best method of getting specific information in the most practical and economical way.

What is a test. A test is an objective, organized, and statistically refined, instrument or method to measure some specific skill, behavior, or set of characteristics, under standardized conditions. These skills and abilities may have been acquired by maturation, or they may have been learned. Tests are a valuable aid to good teaching and to good counseling. However, under conditions of poor selection and interpretation, they may become a handicap and do more harm than good. Tests and test results should be used only to supplement other information collected by the teacher or the counselor.

Test interpretation. Even by using the best tests available, we cannot predict individual behavior in complex learning situations with great accuracy. Most of our test results, if used alone, are not reliable enough to be used for accurate individual prediction. . . .

Limitation of tests. By itself, a test score has little meaning and value. Only by supplementing it with other information can one give the score meaning. Is the child working up to capacity? Has he received good instruction? Is he one of the younger pupils in the class? How does he compare with other children of the same age? Is he a slow worker? These should be some of the additional questions asked. Tests do not tell the "why" of a score. Why did this boy receive the lowest score in the class? Why did that student get a lower score than the teacher thought he would? Why did this student get the highest score in the class? These questions are answered by the use of supplementary information, such as study habits, motivation, ability, home environment, and other similar data. Tests do not make decisions. If a student receives the lowest score in the class, the test does not tell what he will do or should do. Because a student received test scores indicating that he is capable of doing very good college work or of taking a highly specialized course, there is no indication that he will make the correct choice, or work up to the limits of his aptitudes.

   Ibid., pp. 47-52.

406. GROUP AND INDIVIDUAL TESTS

Group Tests

Adjustment problems are often revealed or partially explained by a careful study of the measured abilities, achievements, and interests of individual pupils. The tests actually used will vary from grade to grade and school to school, but no modern guidance worker would undertake to deal with pupil problems without the benefits of as much reliable meas-

urement as can be obtained. If only one group test can be
provided, it would normally be a general ability test of such
length and level of difficulty as is appropriate for the child
and the grade. There are dozens of such tests in the market.
Achievement tests, including both general achievement tests in
all subjects and special achievement tests such as achievement
in reading or in mathematics, are frequently of great value in
working on the problem of an individual child. The same can
be said for interest tests when the child is of junior high
school or high school age. While such tests must be interpreted
much more cautiously than general ability tests, they frequently give clues to problems in the total adjustment of the child,
or clues as to what may be done about these problems. When
adequately interpreted, some of the personality tests or scales
now on the market may give very valuable results for the better understanding of a child. The valid use of all group tests
involves accurate administration of tests, careful scoring, and
a systematic comparison of scores. It must always be remembered that test scores represent short samples of pupil achievement, that these samples must be compared with other evidence before they can be used with full confidence.

Individual Tests

Such tests are nearly always given after the need for more
specialized appraisal has been discovered through group tests.
Inconsistencies in test scores may indicate such a need. Thus,
one child will make a very high score in one group test and a
low score on another group test. In such an instance, any worker
would like to have the greater validity of an individual test. Or
it may be that group test results do not correspond well with
class achievement, and here again one would like to compare
the results of the group test with those obtained by carefully
administered individual tests. Ordinarily, only the extreme
deviates such as the marked over-achievers and under-achievers
will be tested with individual tests. Such tests are the sharpest
tools of the guidance worker and must be reserved for children
who require more extended study.

The individual tests which are most frequently used as measures of the ability of a person are the Stanford revision of the

Binet, the Wechsler-Bellevue, and the Arthur Point Scale. All these tests are administered by trained, experienced psychologists who are able to keep the child working at full ability throughout the range of the test. This is the chief advantage of the individual test over the group test. Use is increasingly being made of such individual tests as the Rorschach and the Thematic Apperception Test for probing into the personality patterns of the individual. These tests combine some degree of standardization of an interview situation with a great deal of opportunity for experienced clinical workers to make fruitful observations of the characteristics of a child.

Harl R. Douglass, editor, *Education for Life Adjustment.* New York: The Ronald Press Company, 1950, pp. 320-21. (From chapter by J. W. McDaniel.)

407. INTELLIGENCE TESTING

Summary. Intelligence testing in modern clinical psychology, we have seen, is more than the automatic administration of routine test procedures. It begins with a judicious choice of instruments, suited to the client and constructed to yield valid and reliable results. It requires not only precise knowledge of the characteristics of intelligence scales, but also skill in interpreting test results that are expressed in a variety of ways. It demands an ability to evaluate the results of highly controversial research, and to advance hypotheses to account for a particular client's behavior which go beyond unproductive labeling, but stop short of unfounded speculation. The clinician, in diagnosing general intelligence, plays the dual role of proficient laboratory experimenter and impartial, understanding observer of human behavior.

But however expertly it may be performed, intelligence testing is still only one of many diagnostic tools which the clinical psychologist must use, and general intelligence is only one of many aspects of client behavior which he must study. The test in the hands of a competent clinician raises more questions than it answers; it points out more areas for further study than any single kind of diagnostic technique can encompass. When, therefore, the limits of intelligence testing have been reached for a given client, the responsible clinician must continue his investigation by whatever other methods he has at his disposal. The psychologist who restricts himself to one approach can produce little more than a caricature of his client. It is only by a skillful variation of his diagnostic procedures that the clinician finally arrives at a full and faithful portrayal of the unique individual.

> L. A. Pennington and Irwin A. Berg, editors, *An Introduction to Clinical Psychology*. New York: The Ronald Press Company, 1948, pp. 376-77. (From chapter by Ann Magaret.)

408. ACHIEVEMENT AND APTITUDE TESTS

Summary. One major task of the clinical psychologist is that of appraising the abilities and the aptitudes of his clients so that he may base his diagnosis and remediation upon objective knowledge. Among the available instruments for this purpose are the many standardized measures of achievement and aptitude. In using published tests the clinician must make certain that he knows what the test is actually measuring and that he has familiarized himself with its limitations as well as with its accepted uses. It must be remembered, however, that a test, useful in one situation, may not be in another. The idiosyncrasies of the client must be taken into account when administering a test and interpreting its results.

Considerable overlap exists between tests of achievement and tests of aptitude—they may indeed sometimes be used interchangeably. In selecting either type of test the clinician should keep in mind nine criteria for the selection of such a test: validity, reliability, adequacy, objectivity, administrability, scorability, comparability, economy, and utility. It is particularly important that the practitioners be well acquainted with the concepts of validity and reliability. Information on the standardization of any test, together with a more or less critical analysis, may be obtained from various sources, such as reviews in technical journals and books.

One of the greatest dangers in the use of tests is the tendency on the part of untrained persons to regard the test's results as infallible. The clinician needs to guard against this tendency in announcing test results, and should, in any event, never report the test results or his interpretation of them until in his opinion the client is psychologically prepared to receive the information.

Achievement testing is possible at various age levels, ranging from the preschool years through the adult years; achievement tests are classified as group tests; subject, survey, or analytical in type. Aptitude tests, classified as either paper-pencil or performance in type, have been devised for use in a wide variety of clinical situations. The adequate selection and administration, as well as intelligent interpretation of results of achievement and aptitude tests, can provide the practicing psychologist with valuable information.

Ibid., pp. 350-51. (From chapter by John E. Horrocks.)

409. INTEREST AND PERSONALITY TESTS

Summary. Although the structure of personality is not yet wholly understood, it is possible to use objective devices, such as tests, to measure certain aspects of behavior which we accept as representing personality characteristics. In the full assessment of personality, more information than that obtained from tests which measure its characteristics is needed. The scores earned on interest, adjustment, temperament, and character tests must be interpreted with reference to such other factors as intelligence, achievement, motivation, sex, age, level of aspiration, emotional and physical maturation, social and economic history, educational potentiality and opportunity.

The tests employed to measure personality, just as with any other psychological traits, must be examined for their statistical adequacy. Few of the tests can be relied upon for individual predictive purposes because reliability and validity are too low or they have not been adequately determined. These statistical limitations of the quantitative scores emphasize the importance of examining and making use of the qualitative responses in the clinical use of tests. Interpretation of results should also consider the pattern nature of personality and the balancing of the results of the several tests employed in relation to their critical significance for a particular set of circumstances.

The clinical interpretation of tests is considered by many to be an art. But whether this is true or not, certainly insight, intelligence, and imagination must go into the evaluations of test scores if valid differential diagnoses and practical recommendations are to be made. Indeed, real understanding and skill in the use of the testing instruments depend upon long continued clinical experience with them. In addition, the clinician must be well grounded in the basic principles of psychology and other sciences, and must know a great deal about people and the world in which they live and work.

Ibid., pp. 413-14. (From chapter by Wilma T. Donahue.)

410. PROJECTIVE METHODS

Summary. Projective methods utilize ambiguous stimuli to which subjects are encouraged to respond freely in their own way. On the assumption that attention is selective and that perception is motivated by the wishes and attitudes of the responding person, it is held that the content perceived and the manner of organizing the material reveal significant dynamic aspects of personality. The projective principle, which is grounded in holistic theories of personality, has been applied in the development of a wide variety of tests, including ink blots, pictures, art and drama media, and paper-and-pencil techniques. They have been used for purposes of diagnosis, prognosis, therapy, and research. The most urgent problems in the field are concerned with validation of the methods themselves and with the qualifications of their users.

Ibid., p. 436. (From chapter by Helen Sargent.)

411. THE STUDY OF PERSONALITY NO SIMPLE TASK

Above all, the questionnaires and inventories may be criticized because they suggest that personality study is a simple process. In twenty minutes the personality tester labels conditions that a conscientious counselor might take many days to establish. The personality tester suggests, in his facile use of statistics, that simple addition is the best procedure for collating information about an individual's behavior patterns. He obtains data about one characteristic by forcing into profiles the residuals of other choices. He treats his data as if every characteristic were normally distributed, although social pressures continuously skew such distribution and local mores may distort them. He assumes an atomistic nature of behavior which has not been established, and he lumps the atoms into a total which he names by fiat. The counselor must ask himself whether the understanding of the eternal problems of the behavior of youth seems likely to yield to the application of single instruments of this type.

But if such instruments are rejected, they must be replaced with others (some of which may be subject to the limitations noted above), for the counselor must have some estimates of behavior. He will find that if his counsel is to be good, he must go beyond the level at which the personality questionnaires function. He will use a flexible and varied approach to his problems in the study of behavior and will strive to avoid the error of giving too much weight to any particular theory or data from any one instrument. He will make constant checks on the validity and reliability of any techique (including, of course, the interviews) that he applies. For everything that is said or done he will provide evidence of its basis or present a clear statement of the fact that it is simply a hypothesis. He will strive to be scientific in the true sense of the term, because he will describe his subjects before he takes any action; but he will be aware that the study of human behavior has not yet produced a true, and perhaps unique, science. He will always be very humble and will forever be aware of the limitations of his data. He will be striving to provide as good counsel for every subject as he would for his own son, and he will realize that his counsel will only be as good as his data about behavior permit. And the collection of such data will require the use of several techniques.

John W. M. Rothney and Bert A. Roens, *Counseling the Individual Student*. New York: William Sloane Associates, Inc., 1949, pp. 95-96.

412. PROJECTIVE DEVICES VALUABLE IN TRAINED HANDS

Projective devices make use of the magician's hand-is-quicker-than-the-eye device of misleading. They permit the trained observer to go behind the masks which all of us wear and to observe much of our real selves without our being aware of what is taking place. Sound training and long experience make the clinical psychologist and psychiatrist competent to analyze with more than a fair degree of accuracy what underlying factors are the cause of trouble. It is obvious that this process is perilous for any counselee who is subjected to such probing by an unskilled, awkward amateur. High school and college counselors who deal primarily with the "normal" problem categories from day to day will use projective instruments only with extreme caution unless they are highly trained, and, even then, they will be wary of their interpretations and check them with a specialist.

In any case the skilled general clinical counselor cannot afford to be ignorant of such important tools and the techniques developed for their use. Their values in clinical work cover the whole range from simple educational-vocational to the most complex emotional problems. In the former, they often reveal interests, attitudes, prejudices, and fantasies that inhibit successful achievement in school and college or on the job. In the latter they may speedily uncover areas of fear, rage, and anxiety and give an inkling of their causes.

Examples of projective devices are: free and controlled word association tests, including the psychogalvanometer or lie detector; open-end sentence tests; the various thematic apperception tests; the Rorschach ink blot test; play therapy; and the psychodrama. Despite surface differences among these various types, they are closely akin in their common function of tapping the inner deeps of the counselee's personal life.

> Milton E. Hahn and Malcolm S. MacLean, *General Clinical Counseling*. New York: McGraw-Hill Book Company, Inc., 1950, pp. 157-58. By permission of the publishers.

413. Projective Technics an Encouraging Development in Student Counseling

Because existing tests of personality leave so much to be desired, interest in a new kind of instrument or technic has been keen. Counselors have wanted a technic that would sketch personality structure, that would reveal personality in action,

that would describe "the whole child." The nearest approach
to reaching these objectives has been made by the group of
technics that have been aptly called "projective technics."

As their name implies, these technics induce a person to
project his personality in response to an unfamiliar situation
for which he has no ready-made, conventional responses. Thus
he indirectly discloses his private world of feelings and meanings to the examiner, who records verbatim what he says. Later
the examiner studies the records to see what personality pattern is suggested by the subject's responses.

The best-known and most widely used of the projective technics is the Rorschach. The stimuli presented to the subject
consist of ten selected ink blots, some colored, the majority
black on a white ground. The administration of the technic
is disarmingly simple: the examiner asks with respect to each
card, "What might this be?" The subject may say, "It's a giraffe
sitting down," or he may go on to describe much more that he
sees in the ink blot. The examiner records all responses, including the subject's facial expression, bodily movements, evidences of tension, and side remarks. In interpreting the subject's responses, he avoids implying that any specific responses
indicate certain characteristics. Rather, he tries to get a sense
of structure and organization by studying the subject's total
responses. Although elaborate scoring methods have been developed, the personality picture derived from the ink blots depends a great deal on the clinical insight of the examiner. That
is why it is generally agreed that a person should have at least
three years of clinical training, and experience in the Rorschach
method before he can qualify as a Rorschach expert.

Another of the more widely used projective technics is the
Morgan-Murray Thematic Apperception Test. This consists of
twenty pictures depicting dramatic events. In each picture
there is one person with whom the subject can identify himself. The subject is asked to make up a story for which the
picture could serve as illustration, telling specifically what has
happened, what the persons are thinking and feeling, and what
their relations are to one another. Through his comments the
subject may reveal fears, conflicts, fantasies, disorganization,
or other characteristics.

Other projective technics apply the same principles but employ widely different stimuli: clay, finger paints, and other art materials, nebulous cloud pictures, realistic pictures depicting dramatic events, toy families and furniture, puppet shows, words to which the subject responds by making a simile, and stories. . . .

Although the teacher or teacher-counselor does not have the background and training to use projective technics himself, he is likely to hear more and more about them. If he works with specialists on cases, he should at least have the elementary knowledge of projective technics that has been given here. He will learn more about their interpretation and use from working with clinicians and guidance specialists who include the Rorschach, the Morgan-Murray Thematic Apperception Test, and other projective technics in their diagnostic and therapeutic procedures.

The projective technics are still in an experimental stage. Their apparent simplicity sometimes leads to their use by inexpert persons, whose interpretation of a subject's responses to any of the "unstructured" material may become so far-fetched as to be fantastic. The subjective nature of the interpretation of the subject's responses makes the intuition and clinical psychological background of the examiner a necessity. Despite these limitations, projective technics are a promising new development. They give hope that eventually we shall be able to learn more about the unique, dynamic aspects of individual personality.

> Ruth Strang, *The Role of the Teacher in Personnel Work.* New York: Bureau of Publications, Teachers College, Columbia University, 1946, pp. 391-93.

414.   THREE TYPES OF TEST LIMITATIONS

Many of the limitations actually noted in the use of tests are the result of faulty administration and interpretation rather than of defects inherent in the tests themselves. If the teacher-counselor depends on tests as his main source of information about an individual, he may obtain an incomplete or erroneous picture. If he is not familiar with the particular kind of mental ability measured by a given test, he may make faulty generalizations. If he introduces tests into the counseling process prematurely, instead of in response to a need felt by the counselee, he may block his access to valuable information that the counselee could give directly, if encouraged to do so. The difference of opinion on the role of knowledge obtained from tests in the counseling process seems to stem from conflicting estimates of the counselee's ability to appraise his assets and limitations correctly. Although the counselee has within himself important resources for understanding himself, which should be utilized to the full, his judgment is not always infallible. His self-knowledge may be distorted by such factors as his parents' ambitions and expectations of him, his preconceived idea of himself, his inability to think coherently about himself. He frequently feels the need of more objective information and welcomes the additional data that tests give. Both student and teacher-counselor, however, should recognize these limitations, as well as the possibility of errors in administration and scoring, which, though quite unjustifiable, nonetheless actually occur in practice.

The second type of limitation is within the tests themselves. For the most part, they reward a stereotyped kind of answer and discourage the unique, creative response. They do not adequately measure many important kinds of learning: for example, knowledge of significant current problems that may have been studied intensively by a particular class, or ability to think critically, to appreciate, and to apply knowledge gained.

The third type of limitation may be removed by further research on the relationship between the results of a particular test and achievement in a certain course or vocation. In some industries this kind of relationship has been studied with reference to specific jobs. In education, many correlations have been computed between intelligence test scores and teachers' marks, but practically no information is available on the relationship between test scores and future success in various fields.

Ibid., pp. 389-90.

415. Some Guiding Principles in the Use of Personality Inventories

At the risk of some repetition and perhaps over-simplification, the writer has formulated a dozen generalizations to assist counselors in using *personality inventories:*

Personal adjustment, rather than ability, may sometimes be the key factor in success.

Personality does (and *can*) change, given time and a modified environment.

People are usually willing to attempt a fair self-evaluation, given adequate motivation and assistance.

Personality traits are dynamic, not static—and the interaction between traits must always be considered.

Inventory scores are objective data and probably represent the counselee's feelings more accurately than a judgment obtainable through a counselor's preliminary subjective appraisal.

Inventory data should always be seen against other background information, not as isolated facts.

Inventory data do not comprise a final diagnosis; they supply leads for further investigation.

Because of the preceding statement, one of the most suitable uses of inventories lies in the preliminary screening of larger groups to identify cases needing further individual consideration.

"Normality" in personal adjustment must represent a broader concept than often used for more definable attributes, such as intelligence or achievement.

Consequently, only the bottom (or top) two or three percentiles represent *extreme* cases, when norms are based on a generally representative sample.

Inventory scores can be willfully faked or slanted; hence, always consider the person's motivation and cooperation in taking the test.

Extreme scores should always be verified independently, to guard against faking, malingering, or possible scoring errors.

If these cardinal principles become vital components of the counselor's thinking, he will find personality inventories useful tools in his daily case-work. He will be more sensitive to the role of self-adjustment in the life pattern—and more intelligently prepared to use inventory data in the appraisal of adjustment. By being aware of the known limitations, he can proceed more confidently to profitable utilization of the advantages in a technique so conveniently at his disposal.

> Joseph C. Heston, "Personality Inventories as Tools in Guidance," *Occupations*, Vol. 29, No. 7, April, 1951, p. 501.

416.   A Rule in Using Tests

A good rule of thumb for any counselor who plans to use any test in his program is this: he should delay using it until, at a minimum, he has completed a study of the test manual; taken the test himself; read the basic literature about the instrument; and consulted a competent professional worker who has tried it out experimentally in a quite comparable situation over a period of time. This process can be somewhat speeded up if the counselor has already had extensive training and some experience in the use of a variety of tests.

> Milton E. Hahn and Malcolm S. MacLean, *General Clinical Counseling*. New York: McGraw-Hill Book Company, Inc., 1950, pp. 128-29. By permission of the publishers.

417.   Instructions in the Use of Tests

The Use of Standardized Tests in Counseling.   The function of standardized tests in counseling is to provide counselors and counselees with information attainable in no other convenient way. Standardized tests are constructed so as to provide specific norms for a specific group of individuals. A test which is quite valuable for one particular individual therefore, is not necessarily applicable to another. Backgrounds of culture patterns, schooling, age, experience, and the like, must be taken into account in the selection of tests and in the interpretation of the results. Never assign any test to be administered to a counselee unless there is specific justification for its use in terms of the particular counselee's problem or problems.

Before assigning a test battery, obtain by means of an interview or interviews, and case records (scholastic, personnel files, etc.) an understanding of the counselee's background, schooling, socio-economic status, work and other kinds of experiences, and a clear concept of his particular problem. Never depend upon a test to provide information, not initially predetermined by the selection of the particular tests, which tests should be fully justified in terms of the counselee's particular situation.

Not all counselees need to be given tests to have the results available to the counselees for them to think through their problems. On the other hand, test results can aid materially in indicating to the counselee such things as (1) how his pattern of interest compares with the pattern of interest of successful workers in given vocations, (2) if his intellectual capacity will permit him to profit by further schooling, (3) certain areas of special aptitude, (4) achievement in school subjects and learning skills, and (5) any gross variations in his personality traits from those of his peers.

> Robert C. Woellner, Director of Vocational Guidance and Placement, University of Chicago. A part of the instructions given to counselors, University of Chicago, 1951.

418. TEST USERS NEED PROPER TRAINING

The value of standardized tests for guidance is conditioned by certain shortcomings inherent in these measures. Some of these limitations arise from the manner in which tests are constructed, others grow out of the way in which testing programs are administered, and still others are concerned with basic assumptions underlying their use. No one is in greater need of understanding these limitations than the counselor. Naturally, the guidance worker should have a thorough training in the use of such instruments. Too great emphasis cannot be placed on the importance of the proper psychological background.

> D. Welty Lefever, Archie M. Turrell, Henry I. Weitzel, *Principles and Techniques of Guidance*. New York: The Ronald Press Company, 1941, p. 268.

419. TESTS ARE TOOLS FOR SKILLED WORKERS

Testing is one of the more important devices to help the individual student in solving his problems. It is quite possible that the availability of increasing numbers of tests has contributed to the guidance bandwagon's speed. The job of making tests has gone ahead faster than the job of training people to use and understand them, but it must be remembered that tests are a means to an important end, not an end in themselves.

When you work with a student, you draw on many sources of information about him. You study his grades and talk with his teachers. You look at his health records and his extra-school activities. Often you talk to his parents and others who know what he is like when away from school. Finally, you talk to the student and, with all the skill you possess, try to get him to talk to you.

Somewhere in this total process, test scores can be useful items of information, and that is why many counselors turn to tests so hopefully as a solution to the problems of the individual student. Yet tests are really only tools for the skilled worker in human relations; they cannot help alone or in themselves, but only in relation to all other information obtainable.

What is more, tests are tools which can be harmful as well as useful in their application to the student, depending upon the person who uses or interprets the test. Like another tool, a hammer, the test is an effective instrument for craftsmanship in the proper hands, but in other hands it may play a part in the most wanton destruction.

This possibility bothers neither the maker nor the seller of the "hammer," however, and as you look at the present-day marketing arrangements for psychological tests, you will note that the dangers of misusing tests are often overlooked by some of the makers and sellers of such instruments. To use a test well, one must know something about statistics and research procedures, and one must be familiar with the logic of problems of measuring, predicting, and controlling human behavior. The testing movement in guidance is only about thirty years old and there still is much to learn.

> John G. Darley, *Testing and Counseling in the High School Guidance Program.* Chicago: Science Research Associates, 1943, pp. 20-21.

16.

Recording

---

420. STRAIGHT THINKING ABOUT RECORDS

So you are going to carry some responsibility for records! Be assured it is not just something incidental, a mere chore, perhaps even a bit of drudgery to be gotten out of the way as quickly as possible so as to get on with the real job. It is a *real* responsibility,—and a *fundamental part* of that job. It requires straight thinking. It takes a high degree of ability. It is a test of anybody's workmanship. It can be an exciting adventure.

Some persons, it is true, shy away from having anything to do with responsibility for record-keeping. They are "not interested." They "don't like statistics." They recoil from everything quantitative. They unwittingly exhibit "fear of numbers." They sometimes assume that their own precious capacities are too special to be occupied with "mere clerical tasks."

It may be that most of these attitudes are somewhat fictional, exhibiting more subtle factors that psychologists understand; but to the extent that they are in the foreground and are seemingly real, it may well be a serious administrative error to load the painstaking responsibility of trustworthy record-keeping upon a confused and misplaced person. That would be the surest way to defeat the major purpose.

The case for adequate local records may be stated quite simply: *they are necessary.* Where is the Association that does not need to adopt some systematic plan for current record-keeping that fits its requirements, and to operate that plan with unflagging devotion? Records are never an end in themselves; but from the standpoint of public opinion, they can

never be an optional or unimportant matter. Nor are they so
regarded by staff personnel eager to improve their standards
and product.

Records are documents; and a system of records implies a
series of interrelated documents that record, at the time *when
an event occurs,* whatever facts may later be needed about it.
These documents—comprising cards, papers, and forms—must
tell the story *from source to summary.* There can be no gaps.
Adequate original records must provide the facts needed for
any summary by the local Association, by community agencies
to which it may be related, or for purposes of field and national reporting.

Sound record-keeping practices in local Associations depend
upon establishing and meticulously following certain agreed
day-by-day procedures. Therein, however, lies a real danger.
Established record procedures easily lend themselves to routine. But they should never be left to routine. They will not
run themselves. They should not run on without change forever. They should change as the need changes, but so change
as to carry on the continuity where this is important. If "comparison gives life to statistics," comparisons over a period of
time give most life of all. Record practices thus not only require attention: they also need constant study by those who
use them.

To avoid allowing the local system of current records to become a mere routine, perhaps increasingly burdensome and
complex, staff personnel will do well on occasion to reestablish their perspective and refresh their whole outlook by remembering *why records are kept and what they can do.*

> *Association Records and Accounting—A Manual for Record
> Keeping, Accounting, and Annual Reporting by Y.M.C.A.'s.*
> New York: Association Press, 1950, p. 7.

421. Don't Work in the Dark

These records should make it possible to trace the growth
and development of any particular individual within the
school. Ideally, such records should begin with the entrance of
the pupil into the first school and should bring together the
accomplishments, test results, family background, health rec-

ord, and the accumulated judgments of all individuals who have worked with the pupil as he or she has progressed through the schools. In addition to being complete, records must be efficient. They must be in forms that permit quick perception, can be safely kept, and be easily accessible to the workers who actually contact the child. Without adequate records, guidance workers are likely to be completely frustrated and will surely be making moves in the dark.

> Harl R. Douglass, editor, *Education for Life Adjustment.* New York: The Ronald Press Company, 1950, p. 325. (From chapter by J. W. McDaniel.)

422. DATA ABOUT COUNSELEES ESSENTIAL

Guidance is a highly complex process. Satisfactory guidance can be given to a young person only when the counselor has adequate data about him. (See J. W. M. Rothney and B. A. Roens, *Counseling the Individual Student.* William Sloane Associates, 1949, Chapters 2 and 3.) No adviser, regardless of his skill and experience, can feel confident about the counsel he provides if the data about his counselees are incomplete. Intensive study of a young person to get essential data can be carried out most effectively when detailed and systematic records of his development are maintained. Since there are many educational opportunities and occupational possibilities for each young person, the preparation of records which facilitates the process of selection among them must be begun early in his school career. Records of school achievement, test performances, descriptions of behavior, interests, work accomplishments, and the physical condition of each child should be maintained from the time he enters kindergarten until he graduates from high school.

> John W. M. Rothney and Bert A. Roens, *Guidance of American Youth.* Cambridge: Harvard University Press, 1950, p. 242.

423. RECORDS ADD QUALITY

. . . Adequate records of counseling contribute to the quality of counseling. Without a record of counseling contacts, the service is at best haphazard. With such a record, the counseling program has one of the ingredients of quality.

Clifford P. Froehlich, *Guidance Services in Smaller Schools.* New York: McGraw-Hill Book Company, Inc., 1950, p. 219.

424. RECORDING CHARACTERISTIC OF HIGH-LEVEL WORK

Some persons may protest that the lack of recorded information does not necessarily mean that the information is not had. They may point out that the average high school is small, located in a not very large community, and that in such schools teachers really know their students and the homes. It is true that, in a small school, teachers can collect over a period of 2 or 3 years much important information about a student. Were they, however, to try to record this information, many might find it neither so definite nor so ample as they believe it to be. Besides, unless information is recorded, it is not available to other persons. The teacher does not expect to be on call with this information for everybody at all hours of the day. Furthermore, the information may be needed years after the student has left the school. Teachers do forget. Some go from the school and the community, leaving no heritage of information to their successors. And all die eventually. Doctors and lawyers do not try to carry around in their heads the information collected on their clients. It is absurd for teachers or other professional workers to think that they should try to do so.

Jane Warters, *High School Personnel Work Today.* New York: McGraw-Hill Book Company, Inc., 1946, pp. 61-62.

425. THE PLACE OF RECORDS

Records kept to satisfy someone else are useless. Some records describe activities rather than movement and could be kept by one of the members. If the leader is clear about his purposes and the fact that program is a means and not an end, his notations will become more meaningful as his insight grows. Only if the leader is interested in checking his own activities with the group will a record be useful to him. Records should be written for the leader's own use.

If an agency is interested in meaningful records, it will have to allow time for it in the worker's total schedule. Besides time, it means a quiet place to write, some stenographic help, as well as a folder and a file. The leader alone cannot set such standards without the help of his agency. . . .

A summary of a record kept over a whole season shows the accomplishments objectively. Such a summary can also be used to explain to outsiders, friends, or contributors what the agency is actually doing and accomplishing.

It is possible to trace the growth of several individuals through a period of time by picking out their particular names from a group record and putting them together.

This is most significant if a leader wishes to refer one person for more individual attention. Often referrals fail because no record has been kept.

It is necessary to be selective and record only what seems important to the leader. There are no general rules possible because the form and content of a record will be as different as people's handwriting. To compare records of different clubs often broadens the scope and insight of the individual leader.

Rudolph M. Wittenberg, *So You Want To Help People.* New York: Association Press, 1947, pp. 120-21.

426. THE USE OF RECORDS

One of the questions that arises in a discussion of records is why so much emphasis is placed on their use and maintenance. There are two main reasons:

1. Because of the social nature of the "Y" work—our work is temporary and partial—it is seldom that the "Y" has the opportunity of doing the complete job in any area of guidance, be it educational, vocational guidance, or placement. Our efforts must tie in with work of other organizations. Records facilitate this tie-in. Furthermore, we are working in a relatively new area. We are on the defensive. We need to justify our activities more than would be true of an established activity. Furthermore, our work deals with intangibles.

2. Because of the personal nature of our work, we need objectivity and permanence. In our guidance program, we need organization and continuity. We need to make our work more scientific. We need to evaluate our results. Records provide the best means for taking care of these needs.

We have found it helpful to keep a cumulative record for each student. The record is started at the time of entrance and is continued until the student graduates. Tests, high school grades, questionnaires, and contacts with faculty counselors provide most of the pertinent information placed on the cumulative record form. No attempt is made to duplicate in detail the information of the various departments of the college. Only the general information that is needed to give a comprehensive and continuous picture of the student's characteristics, background, difficulties, achievements, attitudes, and experiences is placed on the record. The record is designed in such a manner that it can be used by the student and the faculty members as well as the guidance leader.

Since records are so important in guidance work, it seems logical that the individuals who are being guided should be taught how to keep their own records of progress. As important as are the records that are now kept by the "Y" for administrative purposes, we can hardly shirk the responsibility of teaching young people to keep their own record of experiences. Properly organized, such a record would be invaluable not only to the individual, but to the counselor that deals with him. We have experimented at the college with what we call the Record and Planning Folder. The experience to date has indicated that it has possibilities of enriching the efforts of an institution in teaching individuals self-guidance.

In conclusion it may be said that the effectiveness of counseling and guidance work is limited largely to the kind and amount of information that is available at the time of the interview. It is the one area in which the guidance department can offer its most outstanding services.

> J. S. Kopas, "Six Aspects of Guidance," *A Primer of Guidance Through Group Work.* New York: Association Press, 1940, pp. 41-42.

427. FUNCTIONS AND PURPOSES OF THE INDIVIDUAL INVENTORY

Students cannot be understood unless they are known. Knowing each student as an individual, therefore, has become a matter of considerable concern in the modern school. Providing for individual differences through individualized instruction, remedial work, adjustment of educational environment, and personal counseling requires first of all that each student be understood as a person.

The individual inventory is the broad, inclusive process of securing those basic facts about a student which distinguish him as an individual from other students. Two commonly found elements in the individual inventory process at the high school level are (1) the cumulative record and (2) the testing program. The cumulative record contains appraisals derived from a variety of sources: questionnaires, interview notes, teachers' written anecdotes, achievement reports, ratings, physical examinations, and psychological test results.

Functions of the individual inventory. The most important function of cumulative records and test data is their effective use by teachers and counselors as the basis for instruction and guidance of students. These data are means to an end—not ends in themselves. Knowledge about students leads to better understanding of their individual potentialities, limitations, handicaps, personal needs, and behavior. One educational leader has said that teachers should spend half their time studying their students as individuals, and the rest of the time using the information thus obtained in the interests of the same students. In fact, careful appraisal of student characteristics and needs is a beginning step, both for effective teaching and for guidance. Comprehensive cumulative records and test data make it possible for the school to begin instruction for each student from the point where he is—rather than from a point where the school would like to have him be.

Purposes of individual appraisal. The individual inventory provides for a more complete understanding of individual differences and needs than it is possible to obtain by less formal means. This understanding in turn, can be the basis for more effective instruction and guidance. Some specific purposes of the inventory are:

1. To provide the school administration and faculty with general information about the characteristics of the total student population.
2. To inform individual teachers regarding the characteristics

of each student with whom they deal and the pattern of characteristics in each class.

3. To provide counselors with needed information about each student.

4. To assist individual students to better self-understanding.

5. To provide a basis for student personnel research, follow-up studies, and a continuing evaluation of guidance services.

> C. Gilbert Wrenn and Willis E. Dugan, *Guidance Procedures in High School.* Minneapolis: The University of Minnesota Press, 1950, pp. 16-17.

428. RECORDS AS MEANS TO ENDS

The guidance program serves individual students by helping them to learn more about themselves. In the process of assisting them, the guidance program makes use of a variety of procedures. Some are appropriate for group use, others can be applied only to one student at a time. In either case, the same objective remains to assist each student to gain a knowledge of himself. This objective requires that first of all the guidance program acquire an understanding of the student. This can be done only if procedures are organized to study the individual student. A knowledge of a student's strengths and weaknesses does not often result from chance happenings or activities incidental to usual school routine. Definite provisions must be made for the *study* of each student. This chapter describes some of the ways in which smaller schools study their pupils.

The cumulative record. The study process yields many data. Some means of organizing and preserving these data must be used. Most schools make use of a cumulative record for this purpose. The cumulative record is, as the term implies, a record of information about the student which is accumulated from many sources over a period of time. The cumulative record is a means of making the data available for use when needed. Unless the data are used, there is no point in keeping a record of them. Unfortunately, in the past some schools have made a ritual of compiling a cumulative record, while at the same time failing to use the information. In schools where the record has been treated as though it were an end rather than a means, much needless effort has been expended. Teachers in these schools have, with just cause, become extremely resentful of the cumulative record program. All proposals for the cumulative record should be weighed in terms of their effect on the probable use of the records. The ultimate criterion must be the contribution of the record to a better understanding of the student.

What is the best type of cumulative record? For each school the best record is the one that meets its needs. Ordinarily, the best record provides for getting maximum information in a minimum space and at the same time displaying significant facts for quick interpretation. In most small schools the record should require a minimum of clerical work to keep it up to date. Each school must decide for itself what type of record it can best use. Cumulative records are of three general types: (1) the packet or folder type, where a variety of record cards are kept together; (2) a single card or folder upon which all data are recorded; and (3) a combination of these two where part of the information is recorded on the folder and the remainder filed inside.

> Clifford P. Froelich, *Guidance Services in Smaller Schools.*
> New York: McGraw-Hill Book Company, Inc., 1950,
> pp. 151-52.

429. DEVELOPMENTAL RECORDS—THEIR CHARACTERISTICS

The name *developmental records* is here substituted for the more usual term *cumulative records* because it directs attention to the use of the records as a means of furthering the student's best development. Any record system should be judged primarily by its efficiency in accomplishing this purpose.

More specifically, the principles that determine the soundness of a record system may be stated as follows:

1. The record is always a means to an end—that of understanding the individual in order to help him understand himself.

2. The record should show past development, present status, and goals and purposes for the future.

3. The record should include information on major aspects

of the individual's development—physical, intellectual, social, and emotional.

4. The record should be in a form useful for counseling.

5. When time is limited, as it invariably is, records should not be kept at the expense of more important values; there should be a nice balance between the amount of time spent on keeping records and the amount of time spent in using the information on them.

6. The ideal record is unified. It is more than a collection of unrelated bits of information. From it the counselor and student can see personality patterns and trends.

7. Provision should be made for continuity of records. If this is done, the understanding of a student will grow as he progresses from one educational level to another.

> Ruth Strang, *The Role of the Teacher in Personnel Work.* New York: Bureau of Publications, Teachers College, Columbia University, 1946, p. 414.

430. Some Records Are Useful—Some Aren't

To many leaders records are a nuisance. Some do not have the time to make notes; others do not see the purpose of writing everything down that happened in a group meeting; and again, others say that nobody reads what they write anyway, so why write it?

There is no question that these are good arguments. It can readily be admitted that too much writing is done and not enough doing, or, as one leader put it: We are erecting paper walls between ourselves and the people whom we serve. . . .

There should be a rule that only those people be asked to keep records who see a purpose in them. Harassed leaders are often found huddled in a corner at closing time, jotting down the activities of their groups because somebody asked them to "keep records." Most of the time leaders have no place to write, because there are not enough desks or offices or light, and often no time allowed in their schedule in which to write.

Those who out of a sense of duty or orderliness keep some kind of records, commonly describe the activities of their club. They write something like this:

11/5/46—The group met at the regular time and voted on the money to be spent for their Christmas party. They played ping-pong and visited the "Leopards" for some dancing. They decided to go swimming next week. Dues were collected and one new member was voted into the club.

This kind of report does not need to be written. If it has meaning to the group, the secretary might well take care of this chore.

If we agree that activities are means to an end, recording of them is useful only if they show how the leader is able to relate ends and means. That the group played ping-pong is not important by itself, or that they voted in one new member.

If leaders are asked to keep records of this kind, it seems clear enough why they consider it a nuisance. Who can blame them if they say: What difference does it make what the club did that night as long as they had a good time?

If the leader knows what he is after in his group and how he is going about accomplishing his aim, his notations become more meaningful and show the growing insight into himself, each individual member of his club, and the interactions between himself and the whole group. Only if the leader is interested in checking his own activity with the group will a record have meaning to him.

We are not speaking here of the statistical records which are kept in many organizations and which measure quantity rather than quality. Statistical facts are meaningful when it comes to fund raising, and for that purpose have their place. We are concerned here with the degree to which the leader can individualize the members of his group, and observe his own growing understanding of their behavior. As long as he is satisfied with the hit-and-miss method, with his own impressions and visitors' encouragements, there is no need to keep records.

If records are not written for the leader's own use, they should not be kept. A leader may have difficulty writing anything down; one may even dislike writing letters. If a leader hands in a report only out of a sense of loyalty, it will mean very little to others because it means little to him. One gets exactly as much out of a record as he puts into it. . . .

It takes time to write things down, particularly if one is selective in what he writes. If an agency is interested in records,
it will have to give the leaders time to write them. They will
need opportunity to concentrate, which means a quiet place.
In addition, it may mean stenographic help, because records,
to have value, should be kept in such form that it is possible
to look back at them after a period of time. It means a folder
for the records of each group; it means a file where they can
be kept, because if they are worthwhile they will be full of
confidential information.

It is plain, then, that facilities must be provided if adequate
group records are to be kept. If the community, board, or administration is not ready to provide them, the leader will not
be in position to keep records. Many leaders have struggled for
standards in record-keeping when the agency or community
was not ready for them. If they throw up their hands and say,
What's the use? Who can blame them?

> Rudolph M. Wittenberg, *So You Want to Help People.*
> New York: Association Press, 1947, pp. 111-13.

431. TEMPER THE IDEAL WITH THE PRACTICAL IN RECORD KEEPING

Personnel records are important only as they contribute to
the development and guidance of individuals. They do this
not only by giving a picture of the individual's needs, abilities, capacities, and interests at any one time, but also by
showing trends in his development—the road by which he has
traveled in reaching a certain status. Moreover, the ideal record has a dynamic effect on the curriculum and on the personnel point of view of every person in the institution, including the teacher, the adviser, and the student himself.

An ideal record system might well combine the American
Council type of cumulative record folder with a supplementary
folder containing detailed observation of the student's behavior, reports of interviews and conferences with him, samples
of his work, and other evidences of his development. The entire folder, containing much or little information, should be
summarized periodically to show the student's potentialities,
the progress he is making toward their realization, and the best

ways to develop them further. This task obviously requires psychological knowledge and skill.

The problem that confronts every personnel worker is to decide how much of this ideal system it is possible and practical to introduce in a particular situation with limited clerical assistance, time and understanding on the part of staff members. Certainly his own limited time and strength should not be diverted to record keeping, to the neglect of other important functions. In general, the personnel worker should not attempt to keep more elaborate records than he can actually use to aid the best development of students.

Ruth Strang, *Counseling Technics in College and Secondary School.* New York: Harper and Brothers, 1949, pp. 204-5.

432.   RECORDING CAN BE DONE

In one school comprehensive, usable records are being developed at a very small cost in terms of time and money. Here all staff members are constantly on the alert for information about all students. Any information obtained is sent to the student's adviser. Questionnaires, time-distribution sheets, autobiography, and other reports made by a student in orientation class are sent to his adviser. Teachers of other classes also send to the adviser all material received from a student that provides any significant information about him. . . .

One semester this faculty made anecdotal records a special subject for study. The teachers became interested in trying to develop skill in detecting significant incidents and in making clear, concise records of them. Incidentally, the study of anecdotal records led the next semester to a study of what to look for in student behavior. The teachers soon found that they could make several records a day without having to give a great amount of time to the work. Some teachers adopted the practice of inserting carbon paper in the record pad so that copies might be sent to the dean, to the nurse, to another class teacher, or to any other interested person as well as to the student's adviser.

The adviser studies all material received on the student and files it in an ordinary Manila folder labeled with the student's name. From time to time, but at least once a year, he prepares a summary sheet for each student. The teachers use different summary forms because the faculty has not yet decided that any one form should be followed by all. The members of the central administrative staff have become interested in this school's experiment and have offered to supply cumulative record cards. The teachers, however, do not believe that they are yet ready to accept the offer. Early in their experiment they developed a card, had it printed, and adopted it for use by all members. Two years later they abandoned the card because they found that its usefulness was not in keeping with the time and effort required for keeping it posted. They are now trying out other cards in mimeographed form. When they find one that proves generally satisfactory, they will have it adopted by the group as a whole. In the meantime they are observing students, are holding conferences with parents and other persons concerned with the students, and are experimenting with various techniques considered useful in collecting and analyzing data. They know that their present method of summarizing and recording the data is somewhat clumsy, but they find it workable. When they find a more useful method, they will adopt it.

Jane Warters, *High School Personnel Work Today*. New York: McGraw-Hill Book Company, Inc., 1946, pp. 75-76.

17.

Referral

---

433. CO-OPERATION WITH COUNSELING EXPERTS

Counseling has become a profession. It is a profession dealing with the life problems of the individual; and since life divides itself into various areas, we find a corresponding variety of specialists in the field of counseling, each group expert in a particular area of life. One of the functions of the lay counselor is to direct individuals who need more expert help than he can give to the proper specialist; but he cannot fulfill this function successfully unless he knows something of the particular contributions of those specialists to the counseling profession. Like the diagnosing physician, he tries to analyze his patient's difficulty thoroughly enough to put him into the hands of the proper therapist. He needs to be in touch with the specialists also so that he may consult with them in regard to those whom he is trying to help. And he can learn much from them, both of understanding and of technique.

> Harrison Sacket Elliott and Grace Loucks Elliott, *Solving Personal Problems.* New York: Henry Holt and Company, Inc., 1936, p. 257. By permission of the publishers.

434. BEWARE OF THE "QUACKS"

A word of caution is important in regard to quacks in the therapeutic field. There are at present no ways of verifying or licensing experts in psychological therapy, non-medical psychotherapy, or psychological counseling. Anybody can apply any one of these titles to his name and take patients. Unfortunately, there are even some who have played on the personality needs of people for their own financial profit, as do quacks in every field. It is important, therefore, that the lay counselor who wishes to place his counselee under the care of an expert should be acquainted with the training and standing of the individual to whom he refers the counselee. (The National Committee for Mental Hygiene, 1790 Broadway, New York City, has on file information concerning psychiatrists, and state as well as private institutions, in all parts of the country, and will answer inquiries about professional help.)

Ibid., p. 279.

435.   SKILL REQUIRED IN MAKING AND RECEIVING REFERRALS

The process of referral to agencies outside the recreation-education agency requires of the group worker an ability to recognize need through symptomatic behavior, a sympathetic skill in dealing with the individual and a thorough knowledge of available resources. Such referral when it is needed is, in fact, one of the most expert aspects of the group worker's job. He must know how to get sufficient rapport to understand what the difficulty may involve, but he must avoid opening up problems too complex or too deep for him to deal with. He must know how to bring in the doctor, case worker or psychiatrist, as the situation may require, without seeming to reject or desert the member who may wish to maintain the relation with him. If the member wants and is able to establish the new relation the group worker must step back to a supportive role and return primarily to his position as leader.

The group worker is likely occasionally to receive referrals, from family or children's agencies, hospitals, churches, or other recreation agencies. The introduction of such people into the group situations available within his agency requires not only the understanding of the individual's needs and interests but the diagnosis of the types of groups available, the interpersonal relations into which he would need to fit and the program that suited his interests. The discovery of what Fritz Redl has called "group relevant" factors must be the joint responsibility of the case worker making the referral and the group worker who receives it.

Grace L. Coyle, *Group Work With American Youth.* New York: Harper and Brothers, 1948, p. 245.

436. Differential Referral

The group worker is frequently asked by members of the group: "Where can I get help on my school program?" "What kind of job should I try to get?" "Should I change jobs?" "Where can I get my eyes examined?" "Do you know why there is so much conflict between my mother and me?" Queries of this kind are symptomatic of unmet needs which neither the worker nor the group can do much about in the setting of the group. They call for the referral of the individual to other resources.

Similarly, the group worker often locates persons who seem to have a need for specialized help but who are unaware of it or unable to ask for help. These instances are difficult to handle. No blanket approach will do because persons are different and their status in the group and with the worker differs. In some cases the group worker may initiate a direct conversation with the individual, saying he has observed what seems to be a need and saying further that there are workers who may be able to help. The extent to which a group worker takes initiative in calling the attention of the individual to his needs and resources depends upon the kind of relationship the worker has with the individual and the timing and circumstances.

No matter whether needs are voluntarily expressed or pointed out by the worker, the process of referral to other resource agencies and workers is a very important one. Referral in social group work is the process of helping an individual in the group become related to another resource. This resource may be a worker within the agency or in another agency. The referral is made for the purpose of providing specific additional service. Designation of referral as a process implies that it has a beginning and an ending. It begins when the group worker and the individual recognize the need for supplementary help from another worker. Following this, there is a joint exploration of available resources and preliminary selection of the specific agency or program. It may be necessary to arrange for a conference with the worker in the receiving agency before the details of the actual referral can be worked out.

A great deal is involved in preparing the individual to make him ready prior to the definite appointment with the other worker. After the individual and the receiving agency have come together it will be necessary to arrange for a follow-up conference between the group worker and the worker in the receiving agency. Decisions must be made as to which worker will assume primary responsibility and in what manner the workers will cooperate so that their separate approaches are mutually understood.

The details of the referral process will vary in terms of the specific case and specific agencies involved. Certain general principles can, however, be stated as guides to the development of skill in this important area of service.

First, the referral must always be individualized. Each referral is different. Group workers must study the individual and his needs, and so interpret the availability of service that it will be voluntarily sought.

Second, the purpose or aim of the referral should be clearly understood by the worker, by the individual who is being referred and by the receiving agency worker. The group worker must be allowed sufficient time for work with the individual and with the receiving agency to define the reason for the referral and to anticipate results. Referral is always a means to an end and that end should be conceived as better service for the person.

Third, to be most effective, referrals should be personalized. When the group worker knows the purpose, function, procedures and personnel of the agency to which the individual is being referred, he can interpret all of this to the person and make the referral easier and less threatening. Referrals should be made to the worker in the receiving agency by name, at a stated time and with a written note of introduction if the individual is not known to the new worker.

Fourth, preparation of the individual for referral and preparation of the agency to receive the individual are very important. The group worker should give a general description of the receiving agency and what the individual will find it to be like when he goes. Naturally, workers must avoid committing the receiving agency to any specific service because they will not know what they can do until they have made a study of the situation. Workers who make referrals should avoid asking the receiving agency for any special privilege or deviation from established policies, procedures and routines they consider necessary for the satisfactory carrying on of their work.

Fifth, the worker should interpret the individual being referred to the receiving agency and should share verbally or by correspondence pertinent information requested by the receiving agency. The individual being referred should know about the exchange of such information and participate in so far as possible in its conveyance.

Sixth, the group worker should be prepared to work with the group at the point of interpretation, especially when referral means the temporary removal of the individual from the group. Though it is neither necessary, nor wise, to magnify or place undue emphasis on referrals which have been made, it is far better to discuss the matter with the group in a matter-of-fact way than to permit lack of knowledge to create group anxiety.

Seventh, immediately after the referral has been made, the follow-up process should begin. The group worker should take the initiative in determining with the receiving agency worker what kind of continuing cooperation between workers is needed.

Harleigh B. Trecker, *Social Group Work—Principles and Practices.* New York: The Woman's Press, 1948, pp. 103-6.

437. SUGGESTIONS FOR INTELLIGENT REFERRALS

Certain problems arise in the matter of referral. One is the danger of sudden confrontation with the idea that a psychiatrist is needed. To some persons, coming to the pastor for help, to hear this in the early part of an interview brings shock and fright. If the pastor has decided to make a referral, he needs to consider how it should be done with each particular person. Certainly he should be aware of the person who will interpret a too sudden referral as indicating fear and rejection on his part, and who will therefore be unable to act on his advice.

Another approach is to help the person to come to the insight that he needs more help than the clergyman is qualified to give. This is done by allowing the person to talk about his problems long enough to get a good picture of them himself and also to get confidence in the pastor's understanding and methods. Unless the pastor shows some real understanding of how the person feels, there is little basis for the person to feel that the psychiatrist will understand him. A referral made on the basis of understanding is more likely to be acted upon. Furthermore, if permitted freedom to talk many people will come to express a fear of psychiatrists. Obviously this feeling needs to be worked out to some extent before an effective referral can be made. Sometimes a person will come to the place of asking the pastor's opinion. Before this is given it would be good to get the person to express his own feelings on the subject. Sometimes a person begins by saying that he could never consult a psychiatrist, but that they do find it possible to talk with a clergyman. Certainly these feelings should be worked through before a referral is made. Technical vocabulary should always be avoided in making a referral. To hear a pastor say, "You are neurotic and need psychiatric treatment," would be devastating to some persons. However, to hear him say with real understanding, "I am not able to help you with these things, but perhaps Dr. So-and-So could help you if you cared to talk it over with him," would have an entirely different effect. It should be remembered that unless a person seeks further help because inwardly he wants it rather than because the pastor says he needs it, help may be impossible to give. Sometimes the approach outlined in this book can be used to help a person accept a deeper level of therapy rather than to give help directly with his problem.

There are times when the pastor must consult the family of the person or some other responsible person. These are situations where a person is too sick mentally to accept responsibility for himself. There are other times in counseling when he must accept the wishes of the person and keep his counseling contacts a secret from the family.

Carroll A. Wise, *Pastoral Counseling, Its Theory and Practice*. New York: Harper and Brothers, 1951, pp. 111-13.

438. Principles of Referral

There are a few positive principles governing the intelligent referral of students:

1. Referral should be made to a person by name, rather than to an agency.

2. Each counselor should know the personnel of each agency sufficiently well that referral can be made to the particular counselor, nurse, doctor, secretary, who will best receive a person of this student's sex, temperament, and state of emotional tension. Sometimes referral is made to a *person* even though that person's title of office may not appear to relate to the student's problem.

3. The first counselor may need to telephone the second counselor in advance of the student's visit in order to prepare the second counselor for the easiest possible accommodation to this student's fears, timidities, or tensions.

4. Referral should be made by personal call (telephone or otherwise) upon the second counselor so that the student will feel that the personal relationship between him and the first counselor is being perpetuated. Sometimes the counselor accompanies the student as a matter of courtesy and psychological support.

5. The referral should be made only after the student sees and accepts the reason for it. If he does not, and seems reluctant, the counselor had better save the time involved in the referral. The student will probably not arrive and, in any event, will feel rejected by the first counselor.

6. An obviously sincere effort should be made by the first counselor to have the student return after the referral to comment upon its effectiveness, to re-establish previous counseling relationships with the first counselor, or to raise new questions as they arise. Few counselors understand how desperately important it is for a student to experience the security of a continued acceptance by some person in whom he has confidence. Each student needs someone who is continuously available to him, even though he seldom makes use of the opportunity.

7. Each referral should be followed up. This is necessary in

order to see if the referral worked and the transfer was made. A follow-up also makes it possible for the second counselor to transmit information that might be of value to the first counselor or to discuss questions that may have arisen.

This latter point raises the question of the confidential nature of counseling. Every effort should be made to safeguard the identity of the student when the nature of the problem must be disclosed in order to get help on procedure, unless the student is willing for you to speak to someone else about his problem. This assumes that the disclosure of his dilemma or need for help is done under conditions that are confidential. When there is any doubt on the matter it is well to consider that the information *is* confidential. Much harm is done by loose talk about individual students, particularly among faculty people. This gets back to the student in more cases than the faculty man ever knows. Another leak resented by students is the secretary or clerk who has access to confidential records or conversations. Too often the dean, professor, or counselor is entirely ignorant of how much a secretary talks. And too often the secretary was not selected in terms of known qualities of discreetness or is not given sufficient recognition to make it unnecessary to gain status by peddling personal information.

If information about a given student is requested from another counselor or agency, it should be possible to secure this without identifying the nature of the problem the student has disclosed. Of course it is necessary at times to transmit personal information, but if the counselor has been given personal information his first responsibility is to the student and not to the college or the institution. *He should not transmit such information to others without the permission of the student, except to prevent injury to the student or to others. He bears the same relationship to a student as does a minister, physician, or lawyer.* These latter ordinarily have a legally privileged status as far as disclosures made by a client are concerned, and while the counselor lacks this he has an *ethical* obligation of the same order.

> C. Gilbert Wrenn, *Student Personnel Work in College*. New York: The Ronald Press Company, 1951, pp. 171-73.

439. REFERRAL OF NEUROTIC PERSONS

When it comes to referring neurotic persons the clergyman is often at a loss. They are not eligible for help in many state hospitals. Many communities have no adequately trained psychiatrists. Furthermore, some ministers have discovered that some psychiatrists who are not oriented psychoanalytically do not understand neurotics and do not help them. Again, we are not trying to give a generalized answer, but rather to indicate where some of the problems and dangers are. Sometimes the best that a pastor can do for these persons is to give them an acceptance and security in his relationship with them, to help them to activities where they can find whatever small degree of satisfaction they are capable of, and not to try to counsel in the sense of getting at the roots of their difficulty.

> Carroll A. Wise, *Pastoral Counseling, Its Theory and Practice.* New York: Harper and Brothers, 1951, p. 109.

440. DANGER SIGNALS

Some girls will of course bring their problems to the secretary, although, as we have already seen in Jane's case, the trouble told of may, even in the girl's mind, be simple compared with her whole situation. Probably every worker has had experience with a girl who "spills over" in the group. Ordinarily this means one of three things: that the girl believes her problems to be common to the group; that she has a real need to be the center of attention; or that her problems occupy so much of her attention that she must get release by talking about them, no matter what the occasion.

Other girls, and frequently those with really serious difficulties, will be able to indicate their problem only indirectly. A flippant or cynical remark regarding sex, marriage, suicide, religion, family life, or insanity may be a girl's only method of indicating that she is facing a difficult situation. Facial expressions during discussion of these subjects may be even more significant, whether they are too expressive or—as would probably have been true of Jane—too carefully controlled. Perhaps most serious of all may be the difficulties of the girl who makes no response but who sits passively and negatively throughout, living in a world of her own because she finds reality too desperately difficult to face.

Overt actions such as marked petting, cheating, untruths, theft, and ignoring the rights of others, as well as unkempt personal appearance and poor health and clothing are too obvious to need more than mention.

In listing these danger signals it is assumed that the workers will use discrimination in their interpretation. A sense of humor and a serenity which is able to judge when a young girl is trying her wings, or exercising her "attention-getting mechanism" by trying to "shock the old maids"—even affectionately regarded ones—are part of the equipment of successful secretaries. Nevertheless there is a real danger that optimism and generosity may overlook danger flags, and it must be remembered that good-natured optimism which assures a girl that "something will surely turn up" when she can see no way ahead, may be sheer cruelty.

Active interest, sympathy, alertness, and a certain outgoing affection on the secretary's part are all the encouragement a girl needs who is facing constructively the ordinary problems of youth. The very fact that in most Y.W.C.A.'s such discussions take place with doors open and with every probability that other girls will join in, tends to help the girl to view them in their proper proportion. Even in such discussions, however, there is a chance that a general question, "Do you believe in free love?" may mask the more personal one, "Shall I live with this man whom I can't marry?"

In general, any deviation from normal behavior in a group, any unusual anxiety, cynicism or bitterness in a casual contact at a special worker's desk, even the tendency to "hang around" an abnormally long time, may indicate a problem which requires individual skilful treatment if danger is to be avoided. To the case work mind, any reaction which has an emotional content (or lack of it) out of proportion to the occasion is significant.

Obviously, for the sake of the group and because serious damage may be done to a girl's self-respect by the attempt to get her to talk of a personal problem which concerns her deeply in a group of her peers, these signals will have to be treated lightly at the time, but the group worker with some case work skill will make the opportunity to suggest casually that the two talk it over alone.

> Mary S. Brisley and Viennie Borton, *Social Case Work*. New York: National Board of the Y.W.C.A., 1934, pp. 11-12.

441. WARNING SYMPTOMS

Retreat from reality is one of the common symptoms of mental ill health. It is found in extreme form in many cases of insanity in which the individual lives wholly, or almost wholly, in a world of make-believe. In its more moderate stages, escape from reality is often achieved thru rationalization, blaming others for one's own mistakes, or attributing failure to develop a satisfactory life to lack of money or lack of appreciation. Sometimes it finds expression in refusal to accept new ideas, in adherence to old prejudices regardless of new information, in undue suspicion of the motives of other people, or in continued and excessive anxiety, pessimism, self-pity, megalomania, (Megalomania is a mental disorder characterized by grandiose delusions) or hypochondria.

Worry is especially prominent among those in need of better mental adjustment. The confirmed worrier requires no situation that calls for real concern; he worries over the most commonplace and harmless details of daily routine. Mole hills in fact become mountains of anticipated disaster in his active but distorted imagination.

Isolationism is another expression of mental ill health and unhappiness, taking the form of retreat from social activities, unsocial attitudes, self-centeredness, self-consciousness, and complete loss of objectivity. Persons so affected, too, are often quick to interpret the actions of other people as deliberate personal insults. Further manifestations of isolationism are found in inability to cooperate with others, extreme aversion to criticism, overintrospection, and the chronic postponement of achievement.

Feelings of inferiority and inadequacy are also symptoms of mental maladjustment. At times the result is withdrawal, extreme timidity, oversensitiveness to one's own mistakes, melancholy, or jealousy. At other times the individual seeks to cover up or compensate for the weakness of which he is so keenly aware by ostentation, sarcasm, or by assuming, wherever possible, a dictatorial or bullying attitude.

Overemphasis on the trivial is another symptom that merits special mention. Persons so affected find it virtually impossible to distinguish what is really significant from that which is of little importance. They are so busy attending to trivialities that they have no time for worthwhile achievements. They lack perspective; they have lost, or failed to acquire, a proper sense of values.

Moroseness in any extreme form should be viewed with suspicion. Chronic dissatisfaction, (Chronic dissatisfaction refers to constant complaining about one's situation without doing anything to improve it. This is to be distinguished from what has been termed "divine discontent." The latter is the mainspring of ambition—a distinctly wholesome attitude.) a continuous train of disappointments, an avid interest in disasters and calamities, concentration on illnesses, moodiness, despondency, querulousness, and other expressions of characteristic unhappiness are often the forerunners, if not the companion traits, of mental illness.

> National Education Association, *Fit to Teach*. Ninth Yearbook of the Department of Classroom Teachers, 1938, pp. 82-83.

442. RED-FLAGS-FLYING

"I Chew My Nails . . . I Twist My Hair"

Are any of these youngsters in your classroom? A child who chews his nails . . . a girl who pulls and twists her hair . . . a youngster who sucks his fingers . . . a boy who picks his nose . . . one who bites his lips . . . another who bites a pencil?

Little mannerisms! And a great many children in a great many classrooms have them.

Unattractive behavior! When you see it you often have a strong urge to STOP it.

You like to think of school-age children as being beyond this baby-stuff.

You think: they *ought* to be beyond it.

Sometimes it even makes you angry when you see a big child

doing such a silly little-child thing. You feel that these children should not be allowed to grow up to adulthood sucking their fingers and twisting their dresses!

Why do they do it anyhow?

Watch the Children

Watch these youngsters and you will see why. Their behavior will tell you.

These mannerisms comfort the child. Somehow they satisfy. It is often hard to know exactly why. Frequently the behavior is identical with or very much like something the child did when he was younger . . . when he was safer and more secure and when life was more serene. He relies on it now because it makes life easier to take.

You can see this. Everyone of us finds something we can turn to when the going is rough. A cigarette . . . chewing gum . . . a walk around the room . . . going home to our wives or husbands or roommate for a cheering word. We find something that carries us over the tough spots. These children pick their noses or bite their nails or pull their hair. It is not too different. . . .

Red-Flags-Flying

These mannerisms are not nice to see but they are warning signals.

They are the red-flags-flying.

They are the symptoms. They tell you that something is wrong.

Doctors learn to look for symptoms. A fever . . . a pain . . . pale skin . . . high white count in the blood. . . . These are the body's danger signs. They tell the doctor that something is wrong.

The emotions and social behavior have warning markers too. Teachers must learn to look for them. Don't be angry at them but be glad.

This is behavior that does not easily go away, despite all talking and persuasion, rewarding and punishment. These mannerisms are signs and the body needs its signs. Despite everything it keeps its red-flags-waving. It is telling you, "There is some trouble here."

Don't Fool Yourself

Once you understand that there is some unhappiness and that these acts are just symptoms, you can avoid some booby traps that others fall into.

1. Many people call these children "nervous" and say they have "nervous habits." But beware. This is a misleading label.

Call a child "nervous" . . . think about him as "a nervous child." The words seem to say: he was born that way; he has to stay that way. He inherited something—"nervousness"—and that is that.

But this is not true. No one *has* to chew the skin around his nails . . . no one *has* to keep his foot tapping on the floor. Not because of his nature. Not because he was born that way.

The feelings inside make children do these things. You can help him improve those feelings.

2. If you call these "habits," it makes them seem easier to deal with than they really are.

Parents, previous teachers, uncles, aunts, friends, neighbors . . . everybody under the sun has reminded the youngster about these "habits." Not once. Not twice. But a thousand times. And still the behavior persists. This nail-biting, thumb-sucking, hair-pulling in the school-age child, these do not just go away.

They are like a habit *but they are more than a habit.* They serve a real purpose in the child's life. You can't talk him out of doing them but you can begin to alter his feelings so he no longer has to do them.

3. Don't fool yourself into thinking: he will out-grow it. Don't hope: this is a stage they all go through.

These really are warning signs, danger signals. Appreciate them for what they are.

You want to steer away from scolding the child in front of others. You won't call him names or be sarcastic or embarrass him or shame him or blame him. (You add pressure when you do these. You make it harder for the child to stop.)

But just because you don't attack these acts with words or in public, don't shrug them off. Don't feel you must do nothing. You can do something to relieve the basic trouble of which these symptoms are the signals.

Help on the Spot

Some children suck their fingers more when they are tired. Some children pull more at their hair when they are in danger of being called on. Some pick their noses more when there is a great deal of excitement. Some twist their dresses when there is stiff competition . . . or the danger of failing . . . or when they are left out in the cold.

Keep watching and you will spot these specific times of strain and stress. Once you spot them, you can ease them. You can cushion them so they do not bear so hard on the child.

Perhaps you can call on the youngster less, until he builds more security.

Perhaps you can stand by him, until he feels more sure of himself.

Perhaps you can overlook some of his minor failings. Correct him less and praise him more. Even assure him in words: "It's not terrible if you don't know. . . . It's no crime to be late (or dirty or wrong or mad . . .)."

Perhaps you can lead him into quieter activities, until he builds up reserves inside of himself.

You will think up your own ideas, and the way will vary with each youngster. But you want the symptom to go away. You will try to lessen any strains that are feeding it. Cut down the times when life grates, and you will help the child.

> James L. Hymes, Jr., *Teacher Listen—the Children Speak* . . .
> Philadelphia: National Mental Health Foundation, 1949,
> pp. 41-45.

443. Conditions Indicating Referral

1. Whenever there are suicidal threats of any kind whatsoever. (Such may turn out not to be real, but it's best to play safe.)

2. Whenever a *depressed* state persists as long as five days. (. . . probably excited states should be included also.)

3. Whenever there seems to be a great change in behavior from what had been previously observed.

4. Whenever there seems to be no adequate situational causes or explanations of markedly inadequate adjustments.

Notes made after a discussion and based on a college psychiatrist's comments. *Circa* 1940.

444. Psychiatrist and Chaplains Discuss Referral

A minister writes:

"My question is how to distinguish between people whom a minister should refer to a psychiatrist and those who do not require psychiatric attention. What symptoms reveal that it is either advisable or imperative for a person to consult a psychiatrist?"

A psychiatrist and two chaplains reply:

"The answer to this question depends a good deal upon a number of factors such as the minister's training, his personality, and his role as a minister. He should consult with a psychiatrist or refer to a psychiatrist when some of the following situations arise:

1. When the religious problem presented by the individual is beginning to reveal a long-standing underlying personality problem with which religious solutions had already proven ineffective.

2. Sudden deterioration in behavior in a middle-aged person, indicating organic changes (paresis, arteriosclerosis, involution, etc.)

3. Severe guilt feelings without a sufficient reality basis.

4. Bizarre behavior or ideas. . . .

5. Monotonously repeated standardized efforts of a person to adjust to all new situations in the same way, disregarding the unique demands of each.

6. Homosexual behavior.

7. Marital conflicts in which the mutual hostility is irrational.

8. Severe maladjustments in children.

In general:

1. A rule of thumb: whether to refer depends on the persistence of the maladjustment, the intensity of feeling expressed, the irrational elements, and the degree of deviation from accepted modes of behavior. Sometimes only one of these factors, sometimes all three must be considered.

2. Referral does not mean desertion. The minister should continue pastoral care for the person he refers and he should work with members of the family as much as possible."

Dr. Karl A. Menninger, Chaplain Charles V. Gerkin,
Chaplain Robert A. Preston.

Karl A. Menninger, *et al.*, "The Consultation Clinic," *Journal of Pastoral Psychology*, November, 1950, pp. 49-50.

445. SOME POSSIBLE "DANGER SIGNALS"

In every grade the teacher should be alert to note those students who give the impression of being "queer" or different from adolescents they have known, those who show sudden changes in their behavior, and those who seem to be becoming increasingly withdrawn, unhappy, moody. Some time ago George K. Pratt gave a useful list of "danger signals" that teacher-counselors should recognize as possible indications of nervous breakdowns. (George K. Pratt, "Nervous Breakdown: A Teen Age Danger," *Parents* 6:14-15, March, 1931.) He mentions as most serious overconscientiousness, various kinds of morbid guilt reactions, and extremely "model" behavior. Second to these, and equally important in some cases, are seclusive, withdrawing, or shut-in tendencies. Individuals showing these tendencies are "poor mixers," retreat into themselves, and brood when criticized or scolded. Marked depression and persistent, pervasive feelings of inferiority or discouragement likewise should be regarded as possible danger signals. An intense, exclusive interest in religion may indicate that all is not well with the individual's emotional life. Certainly the appearance of "queer" habits, such as excessive handwashing, fear of dirt or germs, and a compulsive urge to arrange objects always in a particular order, will cause the teacher-counselor justifiable concern. They indicate the need for more expert help than the teacher has time or training to give. According to one survey, about 20 per cent of the students needed psychiatric treatment. The teacher, however, should try to distinguish between pervasive, persistent tendencies that do not improve under the best environmental conditions he can provide and that require expert help, and behavior that represents merely transitory phases of development and are just as well ignored. It is the responsibility of the teacher-counselor to recognize danger signals, obtain whatever expert service is available, refer the case skillfully, and cooperate intelligently in the treatment.

> Ruth Strang, *The Role of the Teacher in Personnel Work.* New York: Bureau of Publications, Teachers College, Columbia University, 1946, pp. 281-82.

446.   WHEN TO REFER

It is well for teachers to recognize that they should not attempt to deal with certain kinds of cases. Among these are cases involving:

Health and physical conditions that require the attention of a nurse or doctor.

Severe emotional disturbances, indicated by extreme and persistent unhappiness and depression, thoughts of suicide, extreme overconscientiousness, withdrawal from social contacts, feeling of guilt and personal responsibility for everything that goes wrong, extreme neglect of personal appearance, very marked distractability, unfounded suspicion and fears.

Problems deep-seated in home conditions.

To know when to call in a speicalist is difficult. In general if the difficulty is of long standing, if it pervades many areas of life, if it gets worse instead of better despite the teacher's efforts to provide a more suitable school environment and to help the child to understand himself, if physical defects or parents' attitudes make a solution of the problem patently impossible—then the teacher should seek help. It is the responsibility of the principal to acquaint teachers with the guidance resources in the school and to give the best qualified person in the school system the responsibility for making connections with outside agencies.

> *Ibid.,* pp. 72-73.

447.   ALERT FOR PROBLEMS REQUIRING REFERRAL

There are many methods employed by schools for referring counselees to specialists. Whatever method is used, the important thing to keep in mind is the degree of assurance guaranteed by the method or plan that the counselee may have the opportunity to receive the best available counseling at the time it is needed. . . .

. . . One of the first steps is the utilization of all available facilities helpful in detecting counselees' problems or symptoms of problems.

Symptoms of pupil problems or the problems themselves may be more manifest under certain environmental conditions than under others; for instance, the behavior pattern of Johnny may be expressed in a different manner at home, in the community, or at school. He may react in one manner in Miss Jones' class in Social Studies and in another manner in Mr. Smith's class in Shop. On the athletic field, in the halls, or homeroom still other factors about Johnny may be detected which are not noticeable under other environmental conditions. These symptoms or problems may be expressed by the attitude which Johnny displays to his associates, or the questions which he raises and the statements which he makes; or his expressed and manifested interests, observed abilities, indications of aptitudes, likes and dislikes, physical assets and liabilities, and many other symptoms occurring alone or in combination with each other.

If Johnny is to receive the maximum help from the available counseling personnel, his problems must be made known to them and proper steps must be taken for him to receive counseling. Those persons who observe him under varying environmental conditions can render real assistance by noting these symptoms, by evaluating them in terms of significant problems, and by initiating the steps by means of which he can receive assistance. If the best results are to be achieved in discovering these problems or symptoms, there must be an alerted faculty, concerned parents, interested community, informed students and effective guidance personnel working in co-operative effort. In a functioning guidance program the Guidance Director and counseling staff are in a position to detect many of these problems through various counseling tools such as the cumulative record, tests and other various counselee contacts.

Many problems are also discovered by the counselees, themselves, who realize that they have problems and directly request help in the solution of their problems. Critical observation of parents toward their children may result in the discovery of problems with which these children need assistance. Other individuals in the community in various relationships with counselees are also in the position to observe such problems.

> Stewart C. Hulslander, *Referring Counselees to Specialists.* Boston: Research Publishing Company, Inc., 1950, pp. 16-17. (No. 33 in American Guidance Program Monographs.)

448. How to Select the Psychiatrist

A minister writes:

What can you say to the pastor who wants to be able to refer people for more intensive counseling than he can do, but is confused by the variety of psychologists, psychiatrists, and other counselors?

A minister-psychologist replies:

This is a difficult problem, partially because the field is still so unstructured that particular academic degrees are not necessarily a proof of competence in various forms of therapy, and partially because therapy is chiefly an art and therefore dependent upon qualitative personal factors. Some minor principles can be offered. If the person wishes help specifically on a psychosomatic symptom (e.g., ulcers) or if the problems have psychotic aspects, clearly psychiatric help is indicated. If the problems are emotional, but deep-seated, and with a long history, probably psychoanalytic help is indicated. However, these minor principles do not help much because it may be difficult for the pastor to know what the person's problem really is.

This brings me to the main recommendation I would make: that the pastor refer through someone—counselor, psychologist, or psychiatrist—in whose professional integrity he has confidence. In my experience, the personal factors, such as integrity and character of the therapist, are apt to be more crucial than the particular school to which the therapist belongs. Then, if the person referred needs a different kind of treatment from that which that particular therapist can give, the therapist can be expected to make further referral himself.

> Rollo May, Consulting Psychologist.

A minister replies:

I must say that I have sympathy with the minister when he says that he is confused by the variety of psychiatrists, psychologists, and other counselors representing different schools. One possible form of collaboration between a pastor and a psychotherapist involves referring the more serious cases to the latter and letting him make the final decision as to whether long range therapy is indicated, and as to who should undertake it. When the minister succeeds in establishing such a relationship with a psychiatrist or psychotherapist whom he can trust thoroughly, this arrangement works rather well.

Another possibility involves building up a personal list of counselors in whom one has confidence. This may be difficult to do. Even if the minister knows several psychiatrists personally, it may be extremely hard for him to estimate their professional competence. Moreover, even assuming that some of the patients let the pastor know "how things are going" in their therapy, the reports of such patients are not to be taken at face value. A patient can easily over-estimate or under-estimate the professional skill of his own therapist.

Because it takes a great deal of time, and perhaps special opportunity, for a minister to build up a list of counselors in whom he has personal confidence, it occurs to me that Christian ministers with special experience in the field of counseling might well make their knowledge accessible to fellow clergymen for referral purposes. In large communities there might be a bureau with a list of available and competent counselors on whom the parish clergyman might call for assistance. The bureau would take the responsibility for keeping this list up to date and dependable.

Among these various alternatives, the best one seems to me to be that whereby the minister establishes a close working relationship with one or two psychiatrists. The latter can gradually help the minister to avoid two opposite types of error. First, the tendency to refer too much; that is, to pass off to the psychiatrist comparatively trivial problems or the normal difficulties of normal people, where the minister himself should be able to carry the load. Second, the tendency for the minister to be too ambitious, and to try to handle cases which are beyond his depth—possibly without realizing that they are beyond his depth.

It is impossible to escape the fact that the minister will, in any case, be exposed to contradictory advice. Some psychiatrists look favorably upon lay analysis; that is, therapy carried on by non-medical people; others are violently against it. On such problems the minister can form his own opinions only through extensive study and experience.

> David E. Roberts, Professor of Philosophy of Religion, Union Theological Seminary.

Another minister replies:

In the long run, there is no answer to this question which does not include the pastor's getting to know these people personally in his own vicinity, and making up his own mind about them. But a few general comments can be made which he may find helpful.

First, any kind of psychotherapy always involves something more than science, but it needs to be grounded on a solid scientific foundation. Both sides of this statement are important. If there is no evidence that a counselor has studied seriously what science can teach him, this is clearly a mark against him. On the other hand, mere knowledge is not enough. Psychotherapy is an interpersonal relationship of a special kind; and many believe that the kind of person a therapist is will prove as significant as the kind of knowledge he has. Here the cardinal question would seem to be: Is he a genuinely understanding human being?

Second, although it is true that there are schools and groups of psychotherapists, the amount of basic similarity in approach of all those with good training and extensive experience is very great. Like some church denominations, an outsider may see more similarity than the groups see themselves. There are persons of talent, experience, insight, and warmth in several different groups who would approach a patient or client with the same basic skill and understanding.

Third, there is no degree or diploma which in itself will testify to the person's therapeutic skill; but along with other evidence, these things are important. A psychiatrist must have an M.D. But to be trained in psychiatry, he needs work beyond the M.D. And to be trained in intensive psychotherapy or psychoanalysis, he must have had some of this applied to his own life, and have done it himself under supervision.

A psychologist even with a Ph.D. may or may not have training and experience in counseling or psychotherapy. That can easily be discovered by seeing whether he has had a personal therapeutic experience, and has done counseling for some time under supervision—over and above his academic work for his degree.

Fourth, we may be legitimately reassured that no competent counselor or psychotherapist will have a negative attitude toward anything in the religion of his patient which is constructive in character. This is true regardless of the therapist's personal views toward religion. There has been a fundamental change on this point during the past few years. If a therapist now cannot take this attitude toward his client's religion, he is considered to that extent incompetent by his colleagues. If in doubt, we can ask a therapist directly about his attitude toward the religion of his patients. If he tells us that he respects whatever is constructive about it, and believes in helping the patient disentangle that from whatever has become neurotic about it, he is giving the right answer. The pastor cannot expect the psychotherapist to be an evangelist.

There are, and will be, increasing steps by the therapeutic groups for licensing systems of various kinds, designed to protect the public from the incompetent. In the formal sense, the identification of the competent is bound to become simpler in the years ahead. And yet such procedures can never touch more than the externals of competence, helpful though they may be. So long as psychotherapy is a humanistic and not solely a scientific procedure, the real competence of the therapist can never be assessed solely by his degrees, his training, or even his theories. For this we can only say: Know your man.

Seward Hiltner, Associate Professor of Pastoral Theology,
Federated Theological Faculty, The University of Chicago.

Comments by Simon Doniger, editor of the Journal:

All three members of our panel in discussing resources for

referral and treatment of people with emotional difficulties, are referring to individual psychiatrists or psychologists. One other important resource should be added to these, and that is the mental hygiene clinic, operating either as a separate entity under community auspices, or as part of the hospital setup. In a very real sense, the mental hygiene clinic which operates as a team, consisting of psychiatrist, psychologist, and psychiatric caseworker, is often less confusing to the minister who is unacquainted with the quality of resources in his community.

The minister can feel more at ease in his use of the mental hygiene clinic both because the mental hygiene clinic represents a synthesis, frequently of what is best in all the three professional disciplines involved, and also because a community presumably has already spent a good deal of time in evaluating the qualifications of the personnel involved in the team. It is true, of course, that there are still too few such mental hygiene clinics to really meet the need. Their numbers, however, are definitely growing, particularly since the passage of the Federal Mental Health Act.

Rollo May, David E. Roberts, Seward Hiltner, and Simon Doniger, "Consultation Clinic," *Journal of Pastoral Psychology*, December, 1950, pp. 47-50.

449. WHEN NO SPECIALIST IS AVAILABLE

The advice, "Refer case to a specialist," is sometimes given too glibly. Much harm may be done by referring to a specialist a child who shows some slight behavior difficulty. Both child and parents may get the idea that there is something abnormal about him. Antagonizing the parents and giving the child the idea that he is a "mental case" may be fully as serious as not referring a genuinely abnormal case to the specialist. From one point of view it is desirable to call a specialist when deviations appear. From another angle it may be best not to magnify these deviations, for sometimes personality difficulties clear up of their own accord.

In schools having no specialists the teacher needs as much specialized education as he can secure. In this book references on mental hygiene, educational and vocational guidance, and other phases of work with individuals are suggested. These references will supply necessary background but should be supplemented by courses in the special phases of guidance in which the teacher is most interested.

No general answer can be given to the question: Should a teacher do what he can with a case requiring technical knowledge and skill when there is no more expert person to whom to refer it? This situation is somewhat analogous to that of a drowning man viewed from the shore by a person with no life-saving training or equipment. The sensible thing to do in such a case is to try as many measures of rescue as possible that are certain not to endanger further the patient or his would-be helper. For example, in a health problem there are certain general principles of diet and rest that can be recommended. In most emotional problems an individual is usually helped by having an opportunity to "talk it out" in the presence of an understanding person. The teacher should do whatever he can, seeking first the advice of the most competent person in his environment and then getting help from as many other services as may be available. Teachers are frequently accused of making serious mistakes in dealing with their students, but the failures of specialists, if they were all known, would likewise make an alarmingly long list.

Fortunately, the teacher is not wholly alone. Even in schools and communities having the least resources for personnel work, the teacher can count on some help. There is the principal, who is the responsible head of the school. There are fellow teachers with special abilities and training. In the most isolated community there is usually a doctor, a minister, or some other person of natural wisdom to whom a perplexed teacher may occasionally refer baffling cases.

In more adequately staffed schools a counselor, dean of girls, dean of boys, or other broadly trained personnel worker may be employed full time. In school systems, the services of psychologists, visiting teachers or school social workers, vocational guidance experts, psychiatrists, or the staff of a guidance bureau or clinic may be available. Specialists from the county or state department of education may be called upon to assist teachers in local schools.

In the community, social and civic organizations, mental

hospitals, youth-serving agencies, and parents individually and in groups are often eager to work with the teacher in providing the group experiences that students need, in counseling special cases, and in supplying funds to meet emergencies.

> Ruth Strang, *The Role of the Teacher in Personnel Work.* New York: Bureau of Publications, Teachers College, Columbia University, 1946, pp. 73-74.

450. INSTITUTIONAL GUIDANCE RESOURCES

I. NATIONAL

A. *Testing: Vocational Guidance:*
1. Psychological Corporation, 522 Fifth Avenue, New York, N. Y.
2. Science Research Associates, 57 W. Grand, Chicago, Illinois
3. National Vocational Guidance Association, publishes the Journal: "Occupations," 1424 Sixteenth St., N.W., Washington, D. C.

B. *Mental and Social Hygiene, Family Relations:*
1. The National Association for Mental Health, 1790 Broadway, New York, N. Y.
2. American Social Hygiene Assn., 1790 Broadway, New York, N. Y.
3. The American Institute of Family Relations, 607 S. Hill, Los Angeles, California
4. National Council on Family Relations, 1126 E. 59th St., Chicago, Illinois

C. *Religious Emphasis:*
1. Church Boards of Education—Various denominations
2. National Council of the Churches of Christ in the U.S.A., 206 S. Michigan, Chicago, Illinois

D. *General:*
1. Association Press, (Y.M.C.A.), 291 Broadway, New York, N. Y.
2. Women's Press, (Y.W.C.A.), 600 Lexington Avenue, New York, N. Y.
3. Bureau of Documents, Washington, D. C.
4. State Departments of Education——Capitals of various states

5. Office of Education, Washington, D. C.
6. American Red Cross, Washington, D. C.

II. CHICAGO

A. *Testing: Vocational Guidance:*

1. Institute for Psychological Services, Illinois Institute of Technology
2. Chicago Psychological Guidance Center, 55 East Washington
3. Counseling Service, University of Chicago
4. Jewish Vocational Service and Employment Center, 231 S. Wells
5. Employment Bureau, Chicago Y.W.C.A., 59 E. Monroe
6. Counseling Center, University of Chicago, 5737 Drexel (Rogers)
7. Veterans Administration, 366 W. Adams

B. *Mental and Social Hygiene, Family Relations:*

1. Illinois Society for Mental Hygiene, 123 W. Madison
2. Institute for Juvenile Research, 907 S. Wolcott
3. The Association for Family Living, 28 E. Jackson
4. The Illinois Social Hygiene League, 303 E. Chicago

C. *General:*

1. Community Referral Service, 123 W. Madison
2. Cook County Department of Welfare, 160 N. LaSalle
3. Chicago Public Library——Branches throughout the city
4. Catholic Charities, 126 N. Desplaines
5. Jewish Family and Community Service, 231 S. Wells
6. United Charities of Chicago, 123 W. Madison
7. Illinois Employment Service, 73 W. Washington
8. Social Service Department, The Church Federation of Greater Chicago, 77 W. Washington
9. Division of Vocational Rehabilitation, 431 S. Dearborn
10. American Red Cross, 529 South Wabash
11. Veterans' Rehabilitation Center, 2449 W. Washington
12. Travelers Aid Society of Chicago, 443 W. Harrison
13. Chicago Urban League, 3032 S. Wabash
14. Salvation Army Headquarters, 713 N. State

Prepared by editor for class use and as basis upon which a more complete list might be developed. (1951.)

Part V

WORKING WITH THE INDIVIDUAL
IN THE GROUP

18.

Working with the Individual in the Group
(including the Camp)

---

451.   Guidance a Part of All Activities

Guidance is so definitely a part of all activities that center in leading, instructing, and supervising that it is difficult to factor it out of these various functions. The broad view of guidance is that it is coextensive with the educational process itself. From this point of view guidance is inextricably a part of the total educational process. It does not supplement educational method—it is part and parcel of it. But how does one identify guidance as coexistent with the leading, supervising, and administering responsibilities? Practitioners in youth-serving agencies will find an answer, not in speculative pastime, but in focusing some part of their professional time upon the individual. Guidance may become apparent to recreational or group workers who possess an objective point of view about persons and who attempt to meet individual need by using appropriate counseling techniques in their work with individuals. When so viewed and carried on, guidance may be appreciated as an element for definite emphasis.

> John W. Fuhrer, "The Administrator and the Guidance Program," *George Williams College Bulletin,* January 15, 1947, p. 1.

452.   Counseling Touches Group Work at Many Points

. . . An interview with a prospective member is a valuable prelude to the group experience. In such an interview the leader may learn about the student's home background, his expectations with respect to the group, and his feeling about the group. For example, one girl made this significant remark: "Girls

don't like me. I don't know what to do when I'm with girls."
By observing the student in the group, the leader can obtain
useful counseling information: he can note what kind of first
impression the student makes, his appearance and manner, his
special abilities and interests, as well as whether he tends to
be aloof, to dominate, or to refuse cooperation. An examination of the student's cumulative personnel record will yield
information on his academic standing, his work experience,
and other matters relevant to his good adjustment in the group.

The student group offers opportunities for helping individuals who shy away from counseling procedures, who resist the
idea of going to a counselor with their personal problems. They
feel at home with friends in the group and, without being conscious of the group's dynamics, are led to change for the better.

Personal problems that arise in the group must often be
treated on an individual basis apart from the group. The leader
of the group may sometimes call on specialized services to
meet the needs of individuals. The counselor, on his part, needs
to have an understanding of the student's behavior in social
situations; he cannot interpret the student's feelings and conduct without knowing something about the influence of the
groups of which he is a member.

The counselor often turns to campus groups to give students
certain experiences that they need. By contact with other leaders, and even through direct observation if it can be done
naturally and unobtrusively, he studies the available groups
and introduces the individual into the group from which he
will gain most benefit and to which he can make his best contribution. He may even request that special groups be formed
to meet the needs of some of his counselees. Such groups offer
these individuals opportunities for personal development of
which they would otherwise be deprived. In the group they
can channel pent-up feelings into constructive activities. Many
a student has modified his behavior, and possibly his personality, as a result of observing the effects of his behavior on
others. In these and many other ways, group leaders and counselors cooperate to help members achieve better adjustment.

C. Gilbert Wrenn, *Student Personnel Work in College*. New
York: The Ronald Press Company, 1951, pp. 227-28.

453. COUNSELING AND GROUP WORK ARE TWINS

. . . It wasn't called counseling, and it wasn't called group work, but that is what it was—two aspects of helping people with their problems merged into one effort. These two ways of helping people meet life more effectively have always been the main lines of Y.M.C.A. work.

Specialization led to separation

When the purposes and methods of counseling came to be better understood, the need was seen for better preparation on the part of those who did it. There came a tendency on the part of these better trained counselors to conduct guidance activities apart from other program activities. Sometimes this meant a counseling department, the use of scientific methods of diagnosis, record-keeping, and the like, and in consequence a greatly improved counseling service, if only for a small number of persons.

Not quite the same thing has happened in Y.M.C.A. group work. For reasons into which we do not need to go here, the tendency has been to make the group program "activity" centered, rather than "guidance" centered. Thus the guidance content of the group programs has tended to decline. This is at once an important departure from the characteristic early Y.M.C.A. groups and from the best that is now known about modern group work.

There has been a "pattern," therefore, which I think will be short-lived, of counseling that is separated from group work, and of group work that focuses upon the skillful performance of activities rather than on what happens to the individuals engaged in them. Probably no one likes to admit that this is so, but the fact remains that group work in too many Associations does not reveal adequate recognition and control of the factors that affect individuals and their personal adjustments in group situations.

The counseling approach is changing

We have taken time to leave behind us the idea that counseling and guidance in the typical Y.M.C.A. has to be set up as a special program unit with activities that are, in the main, detached from other program units. We have learned that only a few of the larger Y.M.C.A.'s can afford a counseling specialist. This does not mean that counseling is not possible in the smaller Associations, or that they will have to be satisfied with mediocre counseling. Even the Associations that are able to employ a special secretary for counseling are finding it more worthwhile to integrate his activities with the total program of the Association, than to carry on a separate line of activities with a relatively small clientele. Emerging ideas of what counseling is, who does it, under what conditions, lead us to the consideration of just how group work may contribute to it. The discussion that follows assumes that group work is concerned primarily with the development and adjustment of individuals and not simply with the "putting over" of activity programs. Although much group work in Y.M.C.A.'s does not meet this standard, it should do so, and the responsibility rests with both those who are engaged in counseling and those who are engaged in group work.

There can be no very effective personal
adjustment outside of group experience

The role that experience in small groups plays in the development of persons, their adjustments to themselves and to others, the acquisition of productive skills, and attitudes, is too well known to require extended statement. Put negatively, it means that without adequate group experience, or with group experience of the wrong kind, not only do desirable traits and adjustments fail to occur, but undesirable ones often do. Put positively, it means that the solutions of individual problems, if they are to be solved at all, must involve group experience. The normal person is vitally related to at least one small group. In times of greater stability of population, especially before the industrial revolution, or before the fantastic shifts in population that recent wars have brought about, family and neighborhood groups met this need more adequately than now. Smaller families, and the increasing mobility of population, have lessened the likelihood that home and neighborhood will provide all the needed group experience.

The increasing need for individual counseling is a direct

consequence. This emphasizes the importance of the secondary groups that are the particular responsibility of the Y.M.C.A., and similar agencies, to organize and promote, and it emphasizes as well the important point that the essential function of these groups is not the conduct of activities as such, but the contribution to the knowledge, attitudes, and skills that helps persons to become well motivated and well adjusted. A vigorous activity program may have evidences of "success" that conceal its complete failure to do the essential job.

What goes on in small groups

The overworked word "interaction" is as good a word as any to name the active factor in group experience that makes changes in persons—interaction between the leader and members of the group and interaction among the members themselves. Of the two, the latter is by far the more important. This is what it connotes: acceptance, rejection, approval, ridicule, encouragement, tolerance, cooperation, conflict, indifference, dislike, love, stimulation, expectation, confidence, rapport. The list can be extended on and on.

These kinds of "interactions" are strong medicine in the making of personality, especially when they involve relations with one's peers. Their distribution in a group is never uniform. Taken together they make up the group "climate," but the climate affecting certain persons in a group may be quite different from that affecting others. The expression of these interactions (and their effects) in the form of the communication of information, attitudes, and skill among the members of a group, is sometimes called the "group process." The group process goes on whether the group is organized and has a leader and a program in the conventional sense or not. That the group process in a predatory gang, a college fraternity, a well-knit committee with a job to do, an athletic team, a crowd of young adults meeting frequently for bridge and good times, does things to the persons involved is evident to any interested eye.

Now consider *group work*. It is the use of certain techniques in the deliberate direction of group process toward useful personal and social goals. S. R. Slavson, in *Creative Group Education* (Association Press, 1948) states that the four major contributions of all group "education" are (1) to establish effective love relations; (2) to provide ego satisfactions; (3) to give expression to creative-dynamic drives of the individual; and (4) to engender emotions and establish attitudes that dispose the individual to social influences and group participation. These objectives are, of course, honest-to-goodness guidance objectives, and when group processes are so conducted as to lead to them, the programs serve as a phase of the guidance activities of an Association.

Kenneth Norris points out that in practice there are two ways in which group work performs its role in guidance: (1) guidance *in and through* the group process; (2) guidance *arising from* the group process. Concerning the first there is little more to be said. The group process, as directed in group work, is an instrument for the readjustment, rehabilitation, re-education of *each individual* in the group. The observing leader discovers needs, possibilities, problems, and does his best to manage what goes on in the group to the end that these challenges are met. He will see to it that suitable activities engage the interest and efforts of the group but will regard the activities as a sort of "vehicle" for the interactions with the effects of which he is mainly concerned. Probably the most effective guidance in some Associations is done in groups by guidance-minded group leaders. One of the most profitable efforts of those interested in the amount and quality of counseling in our Associations would be to help inject the guidance point of view and the guidance method into the work of those responsible for group programs.

Guidance *arises out of* group work through the discovery of needs and possibilities by the observing leader that cannot be met satisfactorily by the group process alone. The leader supplements the group's influence by his person-to-person relationship with the individual. It may be in the form of special help in learning a needed skill; information that will enable him to understand himself, others, or situations better; help in meeting conflicts; the reassurance of love and interest. These, of course, are standard practices in counseling. They are likely to be all the more effective when the "counselor" is the leader related to the group in which the person is making his adjustments to life and to other people, carrying responsibility, or just having fun. Unfortunately, many group leaders have neither the point of view nor the skill to make use of these opportunities.

The need for help that the usual group leader cannot be expected to provide occasionally arises. In fact, it is my opinion that in an Association with well integrated group and counseling programs, more calls for the specialized services of the expert will come from the group work programs than from any other source. The technique of referral may not be understood by a group leader and may have to be managed by the counseling services.

In addition to the two roles of group work in counseling mentioned by Kenneth Norris, there is a third: the deliberate use of the group by the counselor as a method in meeting certain kinds of problems. Here the referral is reversed. It is *from* the counseling program *to* the group work services. A high degree of skill may be required in introducing a boy who needs a certain kind of group experience into the group that may provide it. Resistance may come from him or from the group, or both. The process calls for unusual insight on the part of the group leader and the counselor should help to develop it.

There is space here for only a brief word about group therapy. The Y.M.C.A. is not usually in a position to conduct therapy groups for deeply disturbed individuals and should not attempt it. A mild kind of therapy is possible with individuals whose needs are not pathological. Work with predatory or near-delinquent gangs is not usually classed as group therapy. In some Associations good results have been attained in rehabilitating and reorienting such groups. Child guidance clinics should be able to get help for clients requiring group experience from the counseling and group work services of Associations when the help can be given without disturbing unduly the on-going programs. Wisdom and restraint should be exercised by Y.M.C.A. leaders in the presence of pressure to assume obligations they are not fitted to fulfill.

Practical ways of increasing the amount and quality of counseling in group work in the Y.M.C.A.

What has been said suggests the possible patterns of coun-

seling in the Y.M.C.A. in relation to group work. To realize it
in practice calls for several rather obvious steps.

1. *The development of counseling services as a part of the* •
total program of the Association, that is, as a responsibility to
be shared with the group work leaders and not carried out as a
detached line of services. This point of view is now quite generally accepted among those interested in counseling. The implications for organization, for leader training, for record keeping, for interdepartmental relations, for the use by the "Y" of
community resources, for the use of the "Y" by community
agencies, will have to be examined carefully by executives and
others responsible for general planning. The approach may be
through staff work on a question like this, "What will the application of the guidance approach mean to the organization,
leader selection, leader training, program planning, record
keeping of our camp? Our young adult work? Our physical
department? Our Hi-Y clubs? Our neighborhood work?"

I have suggested that this may call for a reexamination of
the practical basis on which group work in the Association is
conducted. If the observation is justified that group work
among adults, high school boys, and in the physical program
tends to be activity-centered, rather than guidance-centered,
considerable reorientation of the group work program will be
required. Resistance to it will be met. The cooperation of general secretaries and executives will be needed not only in defining the practical philosophy of the program but in easing
up on pressures that focus the interest of the group work supervisors on numbers of events and attendance, and make them
defensive about considering changes that would put the needs
of individuals at the center. The counseling secretary will have
to look out lest he become a "missionary" for his point of view.
And he will need to look out lest when he encounters his first
rebuff he retreat into a detached program where he can care
for his "clients" in peace.

2. *The planning of leader training to develop the guidance*
point of view and the skills it requires in practice. This is implied in what has just been said. The staff key is of course the
person, or persons, who recruit, train, and supervise the leaders
of groups. He cannot train leaders in the guidance point of

view unless he has it himself. A practical suggestion for Association leaders interested in counseling is that they consider inviting leaders in group work services to join with them in the study of how leaders may be trained for counseling. An unusually good resource at this point is Rudolph M. Wittenberg's *So You Want To Help People* (Association Press, 1947). Dr. Wittenberg emphasizes that many leaders are themselves in need of counsel. Their participation in leadership roles is often a symptom of this need.

3. *The planning of group programs that uncover counseling needs.* Almost any kind of program may reveal to the observant leader the specific needs of the members of this group. The clumsiness of a boy trying to play basketball calls for individual help or he may be thrown out of the group. This is so obvious that one is astonished to see how frequently leaders seem to have their eyes on group achievements at the expense of individuals in the group. This is likely to be true as long as leader prestige depends on group attainments.

But I have in mind something else than alertness to needs discovered casually. Programs can be planned deliberately for the purpose of helping individuals to become aware of their need for counsel and where they can get it. Hi-Y programs that deal from time to time with personal problems: the choice of college and vocation, boy-girl relations, self-understanding, home relations; young adult programs dealing with such matters as preparation for marriage, and young parents' groups concerning the problems of growing children and how to introduce sex education, religion, etc. into the home, are some of the illustrations. Foresight and ingenuity can do much.

4. *The conduct of staff clinics in which cases discovered by the counselor or by the group workers are carefully presented and considered.* To be useful such cases should be as typical as possible in order that their relevance will be obvious to the participants in the discussion. The presence in the group should be planned for, from time to time, of experts related to the cases considered—psychiatrists, consultants from the child guidance clinic, ministers, representatives of the Family Consultation Bureau, psychologists, experts in educational and vocational counseling.

On the following questions the best approach may be a clinical session:

What is the process of making a referral? How get cooperation of the agency and the "client"? Who follows up?

What are the "evidences" that reveal the presence of problems of which the group leader should be aware, i.e., problems *of* individuals as well as those caused *by* individuals?

How does a group leader "talk things over"? What is the difference between a "talking to" interview and a "talking with and listening to" interview?

What arc the resources in the community available for the help of group workers in dealing with individuals?

How does a leader know when he has a case beyond his competence?

5. *Group work supervision that directs the attention of group leaders to individual needs and shows how they can be met.*

6. *Reading for group leaders that carries forward the growing edge of their understanding of the individual and how to help him.*

7. *Records that reveal and preserve essential data without breaking the backs and the hearts of those who must write them.*

8. *Finally, and doubtless this is the most important of these suggestions, the time has come for a reexamination of the preparation of all secretaries for the task of counseling.* The professional courses required for certification include a minimum of one three-semester hour course in counseling and a course in the principles and methods of group work. There is no disparagement of the progress we have made in the comment that the adequacy of these courses would stand looking into, both as to content and as to amount. Do they provide enough? Do they tend toward segregated or toward integrated approaches? Do they reflect the best that is known today in the fields of counseling and group work?

Our in-service training, as well as pre-service training, needs this kind of going-over every so often, and the time is ripe for it now.

In summary

We have seen that good group work is essentially guidance.

We have seen that the group situation is a place in which individual needs and possibilities may be revealed, recognized, and dealt with, both directly and indirectly.

We have seen that counseling in the Y.M.C.A. can become more effective as the guidance point of view and guidance skills are acquired by group leaders.

We have seen that programs can be planned in such a way as to evoke the desire for counsel.

We have seen that the counseling and group work services of the Association are really one, and that the responsibility of making them so is a joint one.

If counseling services in relation to group work should "emerge" in this way and become the common practice among Associations, then their usefulness in the meeting of personal needs would be greatly enhanced.

> L. K. Hall, "Emerging Patterns of Counseling in the Y.M.C.A. in Relation to Group Work," *Counseling*, July, 1949, pp. 1-4.

454. COUNSELING AND GROUP WORK COMPLEMENTARY PROCESSES

It seems to us that the agency engaged in group work should study guidance from two points of view:

First, Guidance *in* and *through* the group-work process—the use of the group and its activities as an instrument for the readjustment, re-habilitation, re-education of the individual member of the group. By this concept of guidance *in* the group-work process, the group is the instrument of the educator, just as the racquet is the instrument of the tennis player. In the skillfully arranged environment of the group, the growth of the individual is stimulated; in it he is enabled to achieve satisfactions; in it he progressively achieves adjustment.

Second, Guidance *arising from* the group-work process. In the activity of the group it becomes apparent that there are within it certain individuals whose growth and adjustment would be furthered by some individual help or attention which the group, as a group, is not able to give. Such persons require individual guidance in addition to the group-educational process, in order to make the group process more effective. Such individuals may be superior or inferior; they may be the usual discipline problems or those too placid to create a disturbance; they may be the perplexed or those too insensitive to become aware of conflict; they may come to the group leader for guidance or they may not be aware that they are in need of any re-adjustment. Whatever the nature of their problem, it is *discovered in* the group-work process, but treated privately and individually apart from it, except for the fact that the group may still be used as *one of* the instruments of re-education.

To repeat: *First,* Guidance *in* and *through* the group-work process, with the group as the instrument of education and adjustment; and *second,* Guidance *arising from* the group-work process, with personal consultation and individual treatment the primary instrument.

In stimulating and guiding the growth of ordinary normal individuals, with the ordinary, normal perplexities, problems, and difficulties of adjustment in an increasingly complex world, there is a point at which the group-work agency or the educational institution must take on a case-work function. There is a point where the guidance problems that arise from a group must be handled individually—as *cases,* if you like, with all the system and efficiency of the case method.

Of course, the agency engaged in group work must know its own limitations. It must realize that it can deal only with normal individuals, and that extreme abnormalities must be referred to psychiatric or case-work agencies, just as the physical director refers cases of physical abnormality or disease to the medical doctor. But even in this regard, the group worker should learn to recognize the symptoms of psychological abnormality, to know when to refer. . . .

In the process of "doing a good group-work job with individual understanding," individual guidance cannot be thought of as something apart from the on-going educational experience of the group. But, as in good formal education, guidance *arising from* the group-work process may provide a good auxiliary service for the work of the group.

K. E. Norris, "Introduction," *A Primer of Guidance Through Group Work*. New York: Association Press, 1940, pp. 10-11.

455. INDIVIDUALS AND THEIR GROUPS ARE INSEPARABLE

No one can escape service to groups, if he helps an individual, nor service to individuals if he helps a group, no matter what be his purpose.

Helping an individual through personal conferences is an integral part of the professional social group worker's skill. The structure of most agencies using the social group work method reveals inherent recognition of face-to-face service as well as service to groups. Registration or intake procedures call for personal interviews to help members understand the program of the agency and find their place in it. Assignment of workers to lounge and lobby services reveals the agency's desire to locate individuals having difficulty in using the agency's program.

The description of the role of group advisers includes skill in interviewing members whose behavior is indicative of need for more personalized help than the group situation affords. These interviews may be casual, or appointments may be made at the request of the member or the worker. From whatever the source and under whatever circumstances, the exploratory interview is one which provides the social group worker with the basis of determining whether, *at this time*, the member is struggling with a "group-related" problem or other personal problems with which help may be secured from some other agency. . . .

While large numbers of people are attached to recreation and educational agencies just because they want fun, relaxation, and new friends, many are unable to use the agencies' resources for these purposes because of the personal and social problems they bring with them. It is the function of the social group worker to help members recognize the nature of the problems which are blocking creative use of their group experiences, to work with them on their group-related problems, and to enable them to use other community agencies which provide services related to other special needs.

Gertrude Wilson, "Work With Individuals in Social Group Work," *Social Work in the Current Scene* (Selected papers

from the 1950 Annual Meeting of the National Conference
of Social Work). New York: Columbia University Press,
1950, pp. 332 and 341.

456. Healthy Individualism in a Framework of Group Democracy

Under leadership, full play is allowed for individual differences that take on meaning in a group. All persons are different. There are no two persons alike. Persons differ physically.
There are differences in mentality and emotional maturity. Individuals respond differently to the same situation. In the reaction to situations, character is formed. Individuals have all
had different experiences out of which their interests and personalities develop. They come to camp with different backgrounds, manners, and modes of behavior. Any program to be
educative and satisfying must be highly flexible to meet these
individual differences, while, at the same time, conserving
group cohesion.

Basic to the individual approach is information about the
camper which will help to create a picture of what the boy is
really like, so that we can better understand him, to the end
of adjusting him to situations arising in the group. We may
employ for this purpose the interest check list, the personal
interview, and the case history. We secure a record of his
physical condition and his social history. We find out how he
gets along at home and at school. During camp we observe
and record the behavior of the boy. We attempt to discover
the camper's interests as well as his needs. There is a distinction between the two. One's interest may not coincide with
one's needs. The cardiac's interest may be to beat the record
in a fifty-yard dash, while his need is for less strenuous activity.

The task of personal guidance is to weave in satisfactorily
the individual differences with group requirements of unity
and harmony. This work with individuals is facilitated by the
breakdown of the mass into small groups. In the small group
the individual has more opportunity to act and react. It is the
intimate contact to which he responds. In responding, he expresses himself, reveals himself, and in this revelation, he finds
himself.

Individual work must sometimes supplant group work in preparing the individual for the group. The boy at camp who feels out of place, who is not wanted, who is teased; the boy who lacks adequate skill in sports, so that he is rarely chosen for the teams—he requires such individual instruction and guidance as will qualify him for acceptable participation in the group. Temporarily, he may be withdrawn from the group.

The status of every camper must be safeguarded. So many of the behavior problems in camp are due to the strong urge on the part of the boy to secure status in camp. He wants to feel that he is a duly recognized member of the group. The blocking of satisfaction of this urge makes for asocial behavior. A carefully selected group in which the camper can find such recognition, is essential.

We cannot leave to chance, or to the whims of the group, such adjustment. The group is no magic instrument that automatically will work beneficial adjustment. If that were true, all children coming to camp would become, by that very fact, socially adjusted, and any environment would be desirable. There are a number of mythical beliefs still existent in group work. We label some agencies character building, and conclude that if a boy participates in their activities, his character will thereby be built. This is wishful thinking that becomes a substitute for the processes that lead to growth.

Group work is purposeful. It stresses leadership, the group and activity in *specific relation* to the individual camper. It individualizes and socializes at every step of the process. It believes in a healthy individualism in the framework of group democracy. Group work acknowledges the unity of self and society and recognizes that one must be on good terms with oneself in order to live satisfactorily with others. Towards the achievement of this as a goal it bends its efforts.

Louis H. Blumenthal, *Group Work in Camping*. New York: Association Press, 1937, pp. 95-97.

457. CAMPS INDIVIDUALIZE THEIR PROGRAM

. . . Camping is becoming more aware of the camper as an individual personality in his own right. One sign of this has been the increased attention to grouping in the light of individual needs, of which mass camping was a denial. Previously the camper was more likely to be lost in the crowd and left to shift as best he could, while now the trend is toward individualization. Once camping is seen as being, basically, community life, the association of persons in a living situation, then the focus of attention begins to shift from an activity program alone to concern with the emotional and social experiences of the child. Camp leaders then become, as they are now more than ever, students of child nature rather than specialists in outdoor nature. This trend is reflected in such growing practices as use of the social service exchange; the pre-camp gathering of case data; the keeping of individual and group records; the exchange of data with case-work agencies; staff conferences centering on the needs and personal problems of campers; individualizing of objectives for each camper; and the use on the staff of guidance counselors, psychologists, and case workers. In some instances, camps set up for diagnostic and therapeutic purposes have been integrated with case-work agencies and psychiatric clinics. These possibilities deserve further study and experimentation by the camping field.

Charles E. Hendry, editor, *A Decade of Group Work*. New York: Association Press, 1948, pp. 12-13. (From chapter by Louis H. Blumenthal.)

458. The Group Worker Sees the Individual

The group worker soon becomes quite well aware of the individuals who compose the group. Though his approach is directed to the group, his aim is to help individuals use their association with the others in the group so that they will grow and develop. For the most part the group worker works with individuals while they are actually with the group. Here the worker's focus is upon the individual *and* the group simultaneously. The group worker also works with the individual outside the group. Prior to, after, or in between group meetings, group workers have frequent contacts with individuals and equally frequent opportunities to be of help to them. In these instances the worker is giving help to the individual *as a member of the group*. He is not assuming a case work relationship; in fact, it is doubtful if it would be desirable or even possible for a worker to be both group worker and case worker to the same individual. The group worker may help the individual to obtain case work service or other kinds of specialized aid outside of the group. In so doing he is utilizing his skill in making a referral. Under such conditions he may work along with the case worker cooperating in a general treatment program but carefully confining his efforts to work with the group aspects of the situation.

Some of the general questions the worker may ask with reference to the individuals in the group are:

(1) How can I tell when the individual is ready for group experience? (2) What kind of group is better for a certain kind of individual personality? (3) What should I try to understand about the individual prior to group placement? (4) How do individuals become a real part of the group? (5) How do they gain acceptance and status? (6) How can I help new members in their efforts to become accepted? (7) What can I do to help the individual who is having difficulty in getting along with others? (8) How can I become sensitive to potential leaders?

No one can honestly claim that social group workers know how to answer all these questions precisely according to formulae. It is heartening, however, that such questions are being asked because it indicates a subtle yet great change in the worker's approach to individuals. For a time it seemed as though group workers tended to insert the word "problem" before the word "individual" whenever they discussed work with individuals in the group. Consequently, emphasis was on understanding the relatively few group members who might have serious personality problems rather than upon trying to achieve a maximum amount of understanding of all members. Individualization in social group work should not be interpreted as being synonymous with a "problem hypothesis." Work is done with individuals in groups not because they are "problems" but because they are persons, and the group is worth while only if it meets their specific needs.

Harleigh B. Trecker, *Social Group Work—Principles and Practices.* New York: The Woman's Press, 1948, pp. 86-87.

459. WHAT EVERY CAMP SHOULD KNOW ABOUT CAMPERS

It is my opinion that one can hardly expect to meet the educational and training needs of growing children unless there is a fairly clear conception as to the nature of this normal developmental course in the emotional life, and an awareness of the effects of the primary family relationships. For the individual child, any deviations or disturbances in his behavior should be regarded as symptomatic of some unfavorable influence emanating from the family circle or, with older children, possibly from other disturbing, social relationships. In order to have some conception of the forces that have been and are being operative, some reasonable amount of information about a child's background and previous experience is required. The essential facts as to health history are frequently illuminating, as actual deterrents toward healthy physical growth and development may be revealed. Reactions of the child or of the parents to problems of ill health may be much more important than the physical factors proper. The child with a history of many difficulties in feeding as an infant, or with a long series of illnesses may be showing no physical evidence whatever of disturbances attributable to the earlier physical difficulties, but may show psychological reactions to the situation of having been excessively cared for and of having been forced to play the invalid role. The actual physical status is important, too, from the mental hygiene point of view. The boy who is less than average in size and strength, or too fat; or the girl who is less attractive physically than her associates, may indeed be quite adequately equipped physically to meet all essential requirements, and still harbor a variety of anxious or resentful attitudes that loom important in determining his behavior and the nature of his adjustment to the camp group.

It is well to know the nature of the child's relationships to other children in his usual school environment, and as well to know about his practical progress in school. His work habits, his customary methods of dealing with other children, his reactions to school authority, all provide a rich background for attaining an authentic picture of the child's success and failure in handling his practical situations. Perhaps most important of all, however, is to know, if possible, the child's own conception of himself and of his relationship to his family and to his social group. If this can be discovered, or constructed correctly, one is in a much more favorable position to deal effectively with the camper. . . .

Perhaps I can emphasize my point through practical illustration: L. J. was a camper who was persistently grouchy, seemed to feel always that someone was putting something over on him, demanded his own way, and readily flared in anger if his will was opposed. Inquiry shows that this is a pattern he evidences outside the camp. In school his attitude is that the teacher is always giving someone else a better "break"; he himself is always getting the small end of every deal. On the playground he is prone to feel that the other fellow cheats, and he argues a great deal if any decision is against him. His family relationships are developed along the same pattern. We find that actually he was not given very close attention by his own mother, but was cared for by a series of nurses during his earliest life period. (His relationship with none of these ever grew to be a close one.) When he was about four years of age, a younger brother was born. He has consistently taken the attitude that this younger brother is indulged and that he is neglected. It seems difficult for him to be satisfied with the really good attention he has received from all members of the family over a period of some years.

For the camp, it is important to realize that the situation can so be handled as to augment this boy's difficulty, or to help him out of his unfortunate attitude. If the counselor and campers react with resentment to his demands, he will have confirmation that he is neglected and cheated. If his demands are met realistically, and in keeping only with what is appropriate, if the counselor develops a good relationship with him instead of permitting the boy to evoke criticism and hostility, he has a good chance, at some time during the course of the camp season, to discuss the boy's attitude with him quite frankly and to win him to a much more secure relationship to both counselor and camp group. In the actual case I am citing, this is what occurred, and two seasons of camp experience did much to alter fundamentally this boy's attitude toward his associates.

George J. Mohr, "The Camp and the Individual Camper," *Character Education in the Summer Camp.* Report of Sixth Annual Camp Institute, George Williams College, Chicago, March, 1935. New York: Association Press, 1935, pp. 39-41.

460.   In Camp the Record Is the Thing

The following types of records are being used in camps either experimentally or as routine and accepted practice. . . .

(1) Anecdotal—description of incidents occurring in various phases of camp life

(2) Diary—running account of a child's or a group's reactions over a period of time

(3) Case Study—careful description and analysis of the camp experience of an individual related to background factors such as family and school experience

(4) Description of Activities—running developmental account of particular activities within the camp program

(5) Interpretive Summary—evaluation of the experiences and adjustments of the individual in all phases of camp life

The following are some suggested uses of camping records. . . .

(1) Child accounting—nature and amount of participation in camp activities

(2) In-service or pre-service counselor training

(3) The adjustment of individual campers

(4) Program planning and development

(5) Research making a contribution to the general field of camping

(6) Evaluation of camp practices

(7) Reports to parents, schools or other community agencies

National Association for the Study of Group Work. *Suggestions for the Study of Group Work in the Field of Camping* (Mimeographed), 1939, pp. 19-20.

461.   Desirable Recording Practices in Camp

A. Each camp should keep the following kinds of records:

1. Program or activity records, to provide a log of all ac-

tivity groups and the experiences of individuals in these activities.

2. Personal records of campers, to afford better understanding of the campers, their backgrounds, and their experience in camp by all who deal with them. (For each camper there should be a record file that includes pertinent data obtained from application blanks, special forms filled in by parents, medical-examination reports, interview records, observation comments or descriptions, treatment suggestions, and program experiences.)

B. Counselors and others should be given training in keeping, using, and interpreting records.

C. The information on record should be used by counselors, interest-group leaders, and others, under competent personnel supervision, throughout the camp period.

D. The camp should use these records:

1. In staff discussions, as an aid in understanding individual campers.

2. In the selection, training, and allocation of the staff.

E. Yearly records of the work of each department of the camp, of inventories, and of supplies needed, together with suggestions for improvement the following year, should be kept, as a basis for planning and improvement. (See source for bibliographical references.)

> American Camping Association. *Marks of Good Camping* (Revised). New York: Association Press, 1950, p. 34.

462. It Is the Individual in the Group

If some group workers have over-emphasized the group, many camp directors have over-emphasized the individual. We have seen that the individual is more the product of group influence than he recognizes, but let us not forget that the individual is the final locus of character, of personality, and of creative effort. The choice is not between the individual or the group. It is the individual and the group.

> Henry M. Busch, "Group Work in Camping," *The Camping Magazine*, October, 1939, p. 5.

463. THE INDIVIDUAL AND THE GROUP

The individual is reached not only as an individual, but also through the group. There seems to be some question about the relationship between the individual and the group. In an analysis of group work, the two are isolated for purposes of discussion, with the result that the emphasis seems to be placed either on the group, or on the individual—on one, to the exclusion of the other. Hence the question "Which is more important, the individual or the group?" Individualization and socialization are two aspects of the same process. When we say that the individual is the starting point of the program, we acknowledge the importance of the individual. When we say that he cannot function fully unless he belongs to a group in which to act and react, we acknowledge the importance of the group. In dealing with the problem child in camp, we do case work with him as an individual, as well as move him around to the group where he has the fullest opportunity of expressing himself. We deal with the individual in relation—in relation to campers, to counselors, to parents, to teachers, to family. It is group opinion, group praise, and group recognition he values.

This seeming conflict becomes resolved in the recognition that what is important is the individual *in* the group. The individual exists as a social being. He cannot be sympathetic, or honest, or antagonistic, unless he is sympathetic to another, honest with his friend, antagonistic to his enemy. A hermit cannot be loyal, because there is no group to which to be loyal. Behavior is socially conditioned. To the extent in which an individual acts and reacts in a group, to that extent does he have the opportunity to practice the so-called character traits.

Camp is made up of individuals in a group and is at the same time a group of individuals. The group becomes a device, if we can use that term, utilized for the more fruitful growth of the individual. The individuals bring to the group their behavior patterns, which, by a "chemical" process, merge into a group pattern. The individuals enrich the group. The group enriches the individual.

This emphasis on the group does not necessarily mean conformity or repression. The regimentation that is found in simple types of society, for example, is not group work. Primitive society was controlled by taboo and custom. Everybody conformed to a simple code of morals. In the army conformity is stressed and individuality submerged. The same uniform, the same manuals, the same central authority permit of no variation. Here individuality is not encouraged; it is frequently penalized. The result is unity in the interest of efficiency and not in the interest of the individual. A command meets with group response, but in the reacting, there is no fulfilment of the individual's needs or interests.

Again, the stressing of the group should not obscure the fact that no one group or number of groups can exhaust the range of one's interest. There are parts of the self that are not expressed in the functioning in groups. Camp directors see the value of the camper's moving away from the group at times to be by himself.

Conversely, the accent on the individual should not subordinate the group. In many situations what is good for the group may be desirable for the individual—even if he does not have his own way. For even in the good life, one must learn to get along with and live with a group. Who enjoys having his own way—apart from a group? One of the most fearful punishments is solitary confinement. In solitary confinement there is freedom from work, freedom to be alone, but nobody wants that kind of freedom. Prisoners would rather work themselves thin on the rock pile, in order that they can associate with other individuals. So fundamental is group life that the normal person rebels against isolation.

Louis H. Blumenthal, *Group Work in Camping.* New York: Association Press, 1937, pp. 92-95.

464.   DESIRABLE GUIDANCE PRACTICES IN CAMP

Every effort should be made to enable the camper to make such adjustment to the life of the camp as will result in a feeling of security and happiness.

A. Individual differences should be recognized and taken into account in the program of the camp:

1. By providing opportunity for the camper to choose the activities in which he wishes to participate. (Having selected

certain activities, the camper should be expected to assume the responsibilities inherent in the activities.)

2. By helping the camper to select those activities that will best meet his needs, and to participate in them in accordance with his abilities and limitations.

3. By helping each camper to gain a sense of achievement that is relative to his own experience, ability, and personality rather than relative to fixed standards. (See source for bibliographical reference.)

B. Objectives for each camper should be set in the light of the following:

1. Information obtained from parents either by interview or a prepared blank

2. Information from school and other agencies

3. Physical and medical examinations

4. Observation of behavior

5. Interviews with camper, at camp, and whenever possible, before camp opens (See source for bibliographical reference.)

C. The resources of the camp should make possible the intelligent individualizing of the program.

1. There should be an adequate number of counselors, and their time program should be so arranged as to permit individual guidance of campers. (See source for cross-reference.)

2. All counselors should be chosen for educational and personality insight and emotional maturity, as well as for skill in camp activities. (See source for cross-reference.)

3. Both the layout of the buildings and the size of the living units should be conducive to an individualized program rather than to mass living. (See source for cross-reference.)

(a) The layout of the cabins and other buildings should be decentralized.

(b) Not more than four to six campers should live in the same room or tent.

(c) Not more than six to eight campers and a counselor should sit at one table in the dining room.

4. There should be a person or persons in camp qualified

to advise counselors and staff and to counsel with campers about personality problems.

5. Personal records should be kept for each camper. (See source for cross-reference and bibliographical items.)

> American Camping Association, *Marks of Good Camping* (Revised). New York: Association Press, 1950, pp. 28-29.

465. Understanding the Individual in the Group

Basic objectives: to help the leader to understand the individual in the group as a total person—his needs; his basic motives; his distinctive abilities, interests, and aptitudes; and his behavior—as a basis for facilitating his growth.

The leader needs:

1. To gain an understanding of the basic urges and needs that motivate behavior; such as the desire for social recognition, for a sense of achievement and success, for a sense of security, for a sense of group belonging, and for new experiences.

2. To gain an understanding of the extent to which, and ways in which the members of the group find satisfaction for these basic urges and needs.

3. To recognize the difference between symptoms and underlying causes of behavior patterns observed in group members or participants.

4. To become familiar with the concept of individual differences as applied to personality, abilities, interests, etc., and to utilize this concept in the understanding of each member as an individual.

5. To gain an understanding of and to utilize elementary principles of mental hygiene in dealing with different personalities.

6. To gain skill in the use of simple techniques, such as the behavior rating scale, anecdotal records, etc., for the observation of the behavior of individuals.

7. To gain an understanding of the elements of the psychology of the particular age group being dealt with, as children, adolescents, young people, adults.

8. To deal with simple behavior difficulties of members of the group.

9. To become familiar with and to use, when necessary, the mental hygiene resources in the community.

10. To become familiar with and to use, where appropriate, vocational guidance resources.

11. To gain skill in using elementary principles of interviewing in dealing with members.

12. To maintain an attitude of objectivity toward various forms of conduct manifested by members of the group.

13. To allow members to grow in their own way, at their own pace.

> Hedley S. Dimock, and Harleigh B. Trecker, *The Supervision of Group Work and Recreation.* New York: Association Press, 1949, pp. 106-7.

466. SERVICE TO THE INDIVIDUAL DEPENDS UPON SERVICE TO THE GROUP AND VICE VERSA

The personal needs of some of the members may be quite different from the collective needs of the group-as-a-whole. This situation presents a dilemma which faces every social group worker. While a group is in session, the worker's first responsibility is to help the group-as-a-whole achieve its purposes. He must keep his attention upon the *relation* of the interaction between the members to the collective purposes of the members. It is in the process by which these purposes are achieved that the value of the group experience is rooted. The end is not so important as the means, yet the end is important. When a group session is over, all the members need to feel that each one, as *part* of a group, has accomplished something; that they, *together*, have accomplished something. The quality of this feeling is dependent upon the means, that is, upon the quality of relationships among all the people involved in the social processes which occurred during the time they had together. During the course of one session personal hostilities are expressed; members unite in expressing group hostility against the worker, the agency, or some cause of common grievance either within the club or without—at school, at work, in the hospital, or in any area of society; conflicts are ironed out (not necessarily eliminated) and decisions are made. Not every member "gets his way"; some may be dissatisfied with group decisions and determined to change them at another meeting; but on the whole the members feel that "it's a good club, it does things." This feeling is essential to the life of an organized group, and it is the worker's responsibility to affect the interpersonal relations in such a way that such feeling results. This the worker does by *being aware* of the personal needs of each of the members but *acting* in response to the needs of the group-as-a-whole.

If the growth and development of each member were normal for his age, the problem of serving the group at the expense of the individual would be minimal. However, groups are seldom composed of people who have achieved somewhere near the same degree of physical, intellectual, or emotional maturity for their age. The social group worker recognizes, in the interacting process, excessive expressions of personal hostility which are natural and normal for a particular individual at the stage of development which he has achieved, but which are harmful to the movement of the group-as-a-whole. As a further complication, the worker may know that this individual needs help in feeling that it is "all right" to express negative feeling. For him at his particular stage of emotional development, a continuously hostile attitude may be a healthy sign. But its expression may be devastating to the group. The worker has a responsibility to help such members, both within the group and outside of it, but his first responsibility during the group session is to protect the group-as-a-whole against the personal hostility of some of its parts. The social group worker must regard the group as something more than a collection of individuals if he is to put the interests of the group-as-a-whole before those of particular individuals. He is unable to do this unless he has a philosophical conviction of the place of groups in the process of social change. He must be able to recognize that many of the difficulties which beset individuals are inherent in social situations which need to be changed and that these social situations are changed through the use of the group process. Therefore, when he is working with a group he is

helping the members to learn how to use the group process for
socially constructive ends. In such a situation, the social purpose, or the good of the whole, must take precedence over the
individual interests and needs of some of the parts.

Society, like the chain in the old adage, is no stronger than
its weakest link. Individuals whose personal hostility is so
great that it blocks them from being able to participate effectively in groups are the weak links in society. They often
belong to groups where the interaction is such that their hostility is increased and the group serves merely to intensify their
problems. These individuals need group experience, but neither
they nor the group benefit unless they can make some positive
contribution. Membership in a group, however, cannot easily
be dissolved. The problem of members who neither help the
group nor are helped by it is a particularly acute one in community agencies offering social group work services through
the medium of recreation and informal education. In these
agencies many of the groups are natural ones, and even the
formed interest groups have been subjected to a large degree
of natural selection in that the members have joined voluntarily
and the membership has become somewhat solidified. The
groups have a large degree of autonomy and determine their
own membership. The individual for whom the group is not a
healthy experience may be a person with high acceptance from
the other members. He may be the clown, the scapegoat, the
person with the most original ideas, the person who is always
willing to do the dirty work, or he may simply be accepted for
reasons difficult to determine. Some individuals for whom the
group is not a good experience make a real contribution to the
movement of the group-as-a-whole. The progress of the group-
as-a-whole, however, should not be advanced through the exploitation of any of its members. The social group worker may
not be able to help members withdraw from groups where
the interaction is harmful to them as persons or to the group-
as-a-whole. In this case, he uses every opportunity to affect the
interacting process so that these individuals will be protected
as much as possible, although his primary object must always
be to safeguard the forward movement of the group.

Both of the purposes—that is, (1) to help individuals personally and (2) to help the group achieve socially acceptable corporate ends—for which the social group work method is used are dependent upon the growth and development of the *group*. Since the group is the vehicle through which the members are served, the survival and achievements of the group are essential to the first purpose. The importance of the survival of the group to the attainment of the second purpose is self-evident. Thus it is seen that the two purposes merge; for service to individuals is predicated upon service to the group-as-a-whole, and service to the group-as-a-whole is possible only through helping individuals.   Through this process individuals and groups contribute to society, whose development is dependent upon the changes which emerge from socially significant groups.

> Gertrude Wilson and Gladys Ryland, *Social Group Work Practice*. Boston: Houghton Mifflin Company, 1949, pp. 63-65.

467.   Ways Group Worker May Help the Individual

Several avenues lie open to the worker as he speculates about how to help the individual. He may decide to try giving help to this individual by means of working with the group. In so doing he assumes that the group is strong enough to "take" the difficult individual and that the individual wants the group enough and has sufficient potentialities for change to subject himself to group controls. Along with this, the worker may decide to work directly with the individual while he is a member of the group and in the actual presence of the group. Thus he may limit the individual's participation, curb his aggression or redirect his energy. Sometimes the group worker will decide to try to help this individual outside and away from the group but in terms of the individual's problem as it affects his group adjustment. A fourth thing he may decide to do is to work for a referral of this person to specialized help such as social case workers can give. Before discussing group work and case work relationships we shall do well to examine the extent to which help can be given by means of the group.

The worker must make a decision as to the nature of the individual's difficulty, the depth of his need and the duration

of the maladjustment. If there is evidence that the individual
has one or two friends in the group it may be that the three
of them can be assigned to some special task, and the individual
can gain status in this way. If the individual has some special
ability which can be displayed for the benefit of the entire
group it may be an entering wedge for a better adjustment.
Rules and conduct regulations made by the group and enforced
by them can be a positive means of correcting individual tendencies to violate group behavior norms.

Sometimes the worker interprets the behavior of the individual to the group by asking the members if they have ever
felt or behaved in a similar manner and what they think the
reasons were. The worker realizes that in so far as possible the
difficult group member should be given protection from the
group if too severe controls imposed by the group would
have a tendency to create more aggression. The worker must
let the group know that he is aware of the bother and discomfort such persons cause the others in the group. He neither
condones nor condemns the individual for his behavior or the
group for feeling the way it does. He does not deny unpleas-
antness but admits that it is present and seeks to find ways of
correcting the situation.

> Harleigh B. Trecker, *Social Group Work—Principles and
> Practices.* New York: The Woman's Press, 1948, pp. 98-99.

468. SEVERAL WAYS OF SERVING THE INDIVIDUAL IN THE GROUP

From the illustrative material presented . . . it is clear that
the leaders of groups have a particular kind of relationship to
group members which at times may prove of special value.
The group leader needs to understand the nature of that relationship and how to use it for the assistance of individuals
when it is needed. It has several facets. Within the group itself the group leader may be aware of the special needs of
individuals as illustrated in the excerpt from the Sub Debs in
this chapter. He may never see them by themselves, no words
may pass between them and yet with this awareness within
the context of the group itself the group leader may help to
see that a person finds the stimulus, the recognition, the affection he is seeking. . . . In such adjustments the group leader

can, within the flow of program and of the relationships, set the stage for many to play their parts with deeper satisfaction. The very diffusion and indirectness of such assistance provides the needed support and encouragement for many who would be threatened by any more individualized approach which broke into their reserve.

The group leader is likely to have many contacts with individuals outside the group. These may run all the way from requests for vocational guidance or medical care to the request for help with individual adjustment problems. In these instances, while the group leader is always a sympathetic listener, he cannot if he is to continue his function as a group leader enter upon a long-continued or deeply involved relationship with a member. This is not only because time will not permit, considering the usual work load of the group worker. It is not even because he may not be qualified to provide the service needed, which is in some instances certainly the case. It is rather that his function as group leader requires him to keep a relation to all members and to the group-as-a-whole. This function is not superficial because he cannot enter upon such deep individual relationships. It is and must remain diffuse in order to be equally available for all. He can give essential but limited assistance like that provided for Art or Ray in getting into the group, or the support given Clarice in time of stress. Such assistance is a vital expression of the worker's warm relation to each member. Its limits are set by the worker's function for the group-as-a-whole. For many leaders who cannot bring about a referral even for those who need long-continued or deeper treatment and for the many leaders in communities where no resources for referral are accessible, this limited type of individual assistance is all they may be able to provide. They will do more harm than good if they attempt the expert service which only the psychiatrist, for example, should attempt. This in no way minimizes the value of the help they can render to boys like Art, or girls like Clarice within the accepted limits of their function.

There are also those situations where the group leader works with another worker in a co-operative relation, as in the case of Rose. The other worker may be a psychiatrist, a doctor, a

vocational counselor, a teacher, or some other professional
person. The contribution of the group worker in such joint assistance may be of value in diagnosis and may through the
relation in the group become, as with Rose, a part of the treatment. Here the group worker needs to be aware both of the
limitations and of the resources that lie within his function.
The contribution of a trained and discerning person who sees
and works with people in the spontaneous social interaction of
the group is a unique and essential one when it can be fully
utilized in co-operative effort to assist those who need and want
it. Like all such assistance, any individualized help can be
useful only when the person involved desires it and co-operates
in it.

> Grace L. Coyle, *Group Work With American Youth*. New
> York: Harper and Brothers, 1948, pp. 246-47.

469.   NEEDS FULFILLED IN GROUP EXPERIENCE

The individual wants to be a part of a group because some
need of his can be met better as a member of a group than
otherwise. (Dorothea F. Sullivan, "Going to Group," *Survey
Midmonthly*, February, 1943.) Though we may not understand exactly what it is we are after when we voluntarily join
groups, there is always a reason or a combination of reasons for
doing so. Sometimes the reasons we express verbally are at
variance with the real reasons which we either do not know or
cannot verbalize. Because of the purposeful nature of human
behavior, the group worker knows that each member of the
group has a need for something which he proposes to get from
his participation with the group. . . . There are numerous
uses to which the individual may put his group experiences
and many shadings of meaning attached to the same experience for different individuals. The group worker tries to find
out what the individual wants and tries to help him satisfy his
wants legitimately by means of the group.

When we discuss the question, "What do we as individuals
want from our group experiences?" we discover that, first and
foremost, we want to belong in a psychological sense. We want
and must get more than symbolic membership identification if
we are to remain in the group very long. To belong we must

be accepted by the group and must accept the others. We become a real part of the group by identifying ourself with it and by playing a role within it. Groups grant or withhold status to individual members on the basis of the role the individual assumes and plays. Differences in individual status are a result of the value the group attaches to a certain role at a certain time.

> Harleigh B. Trecker, *Social Group Work—Principles and Practices.* New York: The Woman's Press, 1948, pp. 87-88.

470. INDIVIDUAL ADJUSTMENT THROUGH GROUP ACTIVITY

There are many theories as to the way in which human attitudes and behavior are developed. Educators, religious leaders, and scientists have all given a great deal of attention to the processes by which personality and character are formed. Emerging from the welter of controversial issues is one concept which is gaining an increasingly large number of adherents—that group experience is the prime determiner of the individual's attitudes and behavior. It is evident to even the most casual observer that the group experience which the individual has in the family is basic in its influence. As a family member, the child participates in such fundamental life activities as eating, sleeping, and affectional interaction. Through these experiences, and others peculiar to the family group, his feelings of belonging, of self-confidence, of justice, or the lack of them, are forged. The family, too, builds in him those ways of feeling, believing, and acting which we call the cultural heritage.

SECONDARY OR DERIVED SOCIAL GROUPS

There are also many secondary or derived groups which play their part in molding the child's attitudes and in conditioning his behavior. Particularly potent are the groups in which he finds himself with others of his own age. As the child begins to broaden the scope of his contacts, he becomes an actively participating member of informal play groups and other more highly organized groups, such as those of the school classroom, the Sunday school, the settlement house, or other character-recreation organizations. Through such activities, through contacts with those who come from families in which there are attitudes and modes of behavior significantly different from those he has developed in his family, his own primary conditionings are somewhat modified.

GUIDANCE OF GROUP ACTIVITIES

Until recently those interested in the broader phases of the child's education have given little intelligent attention or direction to such group influences. Those responsible for his schooling have confined their attention almost entirely to the inculcation of facts or the development of technical skills. Even the guidance experts have thought of guidance as primarily an individual approach not concerned with the group experiences of the individual in any significant way.

Indeed, there are many, parents and educators alike, who would question the desirability of direction or guidance of these group experiences: They see the child already so hemmed in by directed activity that there is little opportunity for spontaneity or freedom of choice. They recall with rose-tinted nostalgia their own childhood experiences in large, relatively unsupervised family groups, and the freedom of neighborhood play groups in a rural or small village environment. Nor can it be denied that children do need to be freed from overmuch of the adult-dominated individual and group activity. If the child is to develop independence, initiative, and self-reliance, opportunities must be afforded that leave children to their own devices and enable them to explore more freely their personal and social environment. But this does not mean a thorough-going *laissez faire* policy as far as group activity is concerned. In the large family of yesteryear, boys and girls did develop many attitudes that stood them in good stead in later life. They learned the importance of co-operation, built up habits of responsibility, and gained genuine insight into the dynamics of human behavior. Unfortunately, they also developed highly competitive attitudes, learned to resent responsibility when it interfered overmuch with their play life, and became biased and warped in their understanding of human needs and desires. Too few of those who hark back to the good old days of the large family have taken this aspect of the picture into account.

In extra-family groups, too, freedom from adult guidance did not, and does not, bring only desirable things in its wake. Individual children are not infrequently exploited by other members of the group for their own personal ends. Cruelty and intolerance are as likely to occur as kindness and understanding. Bullying and other forms of domination are developed. Unhealthy submission occurs in groups where there is no adult leadership as well as in those dominated by grownups. It must also be recognized that the increasing complexity of the environment in which children of today are growing up demands more experienced guidance than was needed a generation or two ago. There are far greater chances that children in groups and as individuals will be exploited and warped in a culture that has become essentially urban than there were in the more simple, rural culture of our fathers.

CAN GROUP ACTIVITY CONTRIBUTE TO INDIVIDUAL ADJUSTMENT?

How then, can group activity contribute most effectively to individual adjustment? In what ways can teachers, club leaders, and other youth leaders, as well as parents, gear in with the group activities of children so as best to develop their potential mental hygiene values? These are questions which should be a challenge to every adult genuinely interested in the optimum development of children.

As the school continues to expand its program to include supervision of what are now called "extra-curricular" activities, it must give careful thought to the processes of social interaction in the group and to the type of leadership, both adult and youth, which will develop potentially constructive experiences rather than destructive ones.

Those social and recreational workers who are sponsoring group activities on playgrounds, in summer camps, in settlement houses, and in other youth organizations, need to re-examine the hypotheses under which they are working. Far too few are consciously aware of the contribution that group activities may make to the individual's adjustment. The conscientious leader attempts to develop activities that will be interesting to the children with whom he is working. He tries to vary these activities so that they will meet the needs and interests

of as many children as possible; but his major emphasis is likely
to be with the activities rather than with the children as growing personalities. Often children do gain much in the way of
personal growth from the sense of accomplishment that comes
from successful activity. They build patterns of behavior that
will stand them in good stead in their contacts with others in
the classroom, on the street, at camp, and in adult life. But far
too often the timid or fearful child, the over-aggressive boy or
girl, the child who needs to learn special skills if he is to feel
secure, will continue to follow old patterns of behavior and get
from the group contacts only the incidental values attendant
on companionship with others. Indeed, he may deepen patterns of undesirable behavior particularly when he is not understood or accepted by the other members of the group.

Nor can parents be relieved from all responsibility though
the school and other community agencies do continue to take
over the supervision of more and more of the child's time. In
the informal play which goes on in and around the home,
whether that home be a small apartment in a crowded city or a
house in the village, children are learning ways of living together that are developmentally significant. The processes of
group interaction do not infallibly lead to the development of
the desirable virtues. Certain combinations of children, certain
kinds of stimulation, may develop distorted asocial ideas of
human interaction. Children may learn that trickery, deceit,
bullying, bribery, or teasing are effective ways of attaining their
objectives. Although no one would advocate minute and rigorous supervision of these informal contacts, the alert parent
will make it his responsibility to be aware of the nature of his
children's contacts with others and will see to it that the more
undesirable relationships and attitudes are not encouraged.

> Ernest Osborne, "Individual Adjustment Through Group
> Activity," *Child Welfare Pamphlets,* No. 65, University of
> Iowa, 1938, pp. 3-6.

471. Some Points at Which the Group Worker Deals With the Individual in the Group

When we analyze recorded experience with a view to high-
lighting the points at which the group worker works with the

individual in the group we soon discover numerous situations repeating themselves. Some examples based on an analysis of several groups are:

1. The group worker is working with the individual when he tells him about various groups to which he might belong and helps him to make a choice from among several group possibilities.

2. The group worker is working with the individual when he helps him to become a part of a group by accepting him and by introducing him to others in the group.

3. Individual work is being done when the group worker works with persons who have assumed leadership responsibilities within the group. The worker aids in planning, defining responsibility, setting standards of performance and in helping individuals to evaluate the way in which they have done their work.

4. The group worker works with individuals who have difficulty in carrying through on responsibilities they have assumed. By helping the person to gain insight at the point of understanding why he has not been able to perform his tasks and by helping the group to understand all that is involved, the group worker is frequently able to convert otherwise negative experiences into positive gains for the individual and the group. Sometimes individual loads must be lightened and responsibilities reallocated.

5. The group worker is called upon to help individuals who have great difficulty in adjusting either because of highly aggressive behavior or because of excessive withdrawal. Frequently, such persons have strong feelings of hostility toward the authority of the agency or adults. They must work out their feelings in the setting of the group but they need help in doing so.

6. The group worker individualizes by encouraging members of great capacity to develop their leadership skills and to take on successively more advanced responsibilities.

7. The group worker may help individuals to withdraw from groups which are not suited to their needs but from

which they cannot depart because of strong guilt feelings associated with "quitting" or "failing to make good."

8. Work with individuals is being done when the group worker works with the group's elected representatives who serve on agency or community intergroup councils.

9. When the worker makes a referral of a member to some other specialized resource agency or worker he is naturally concentrating attention on individual needs.

These examples of individualization are but a few of the possible ways in which the group worker actually works with individuals in the group.

> Harleigh B. Trecker, *Social Group Work—Principles and Practices.* New York: The Woman's Press, 1948, pp. 90-92.

472. The Group Worker in Face-To-Face Relationships With Individuals

The social group worker, on the other hand, works with individuals as well as with groups-as-a-whole; usually, however, he meets the members of groups first as individuals, through the registration process. In an agency which provides individualized registration, the worker interviews the members and thus discovers their expressed interests and the desires which prompted them to come to the agency. He helps them to decide what activities they wish to join and learns about their background—family relationships, school connections, and other group affiliations. The purpose of these interviews is to engage the members in the agency program in order to help them satisfy their interests and needs through the facilities of the agency. The social group worker has many occasions to work with individuals in a face-to-face relationship. The individual who feels uncomfortable in the group may find his adjustment made easier through a personal interview with the worker. Most individuals, of all ages and background, need some help in filling elective offices in their clubs, and social chairmen need assistance in planning for their committee meetings and in learning how to use the members of their committees effectively. Some members' behavior is such that the life of the group is endangered; these must be helped to adjust their behavior to the norms of the group or prevailed upon to leave the group. Others need individualized help in acquiring a skill important to the life of the group and to themselves. The behavior of others may reveal the need for greater understanding of the home situation and thus necessitate visiting the home, perhaps to establish co-operative relations with the family in regard to a member's participation in the group's activities. In all these situations in which the social group worker comes into a face-to-face relationship with individuals, he is not doing social case work; rather, he is using his skill as a professional social worker in serving both the group-as-a-whole and its component individuals through the use of the face-to-face relationships essential to the practice of social group work.

Whether the social worker is serving one individual within the structure of the interview or a collection of individuals within the structure of the organized group, he uses the social work process to help individuals and groups to utilize the service of the agency for the satisfaction of their interests and needs. The service of the particular agency and the specific interests and needs of individuals and groups determine *what* the social worker does, but the profession of social work determines *how* it is done. And this knowledge of HOW is the common possession of all professionally qualified social workers. In fact, it is their possession of a common skill derived from their use of knowledge drawn from the social, psychological, and biological sciences that makes it possible to speak of all social workers as members of a common profession.

Gertrude Wilson, and Gladys Ryland, *Social Group Work Practice*. Boston: Houghton Mifflin Company, 1949, pp. 24-25.

473. "ALL THE WORLD'S A STAGE AND ALL ITS MEN AND WOMEN MERELY PLAYERS"

The individual behavior responses which require considerable understanding and help from the worker are many and varied. One group of workers analyzed their experience with groups and developed the following list of individual adjustment situations with which they were called upon to work during a brief period with so-called "normal groups."

1. Individuals with almost insatiable drives for dominance had to be helped to restrain their tendencies to "take over" the group.

2. Extremely passive individuals who were shy and withdrawn needed help in asserting themselves and in taking some share of responsibility for the group.

3. Markedly dependent individuals, dependent on the worker or other members, indecisive and unable to move, had to have patient help first in making small decisions and then in moving on to larger ones.

4. Individuals who assumed responsibility and then did not carry through, often incurred the wrath of the group and needed help in understanding the meaning of their duties and obligations to other group members.

5. Individuals whose response pattern was highly negativistic, frequently got in the way of group progress and needed help in shifting to a positive response pattern.

6. Some individuals unable to accept limits or in conflict with authority behaved so as to "get the group in trouble" when they violated agency, community or group rules. These ranged from minor incidents to major cases of outright conflict.

7. Individuals sometimes had a false notion of their status in the group and in their anxiety over wanting status they "spoke for the group" or "committed the group" to something different from what the group actually wished to do.

8. Individuals who made excessive use of the group to air their own troubles, grievances or complaints about the world were in need of help in controlling their feelings.

9. Individuals rigid in attitude and conduct and lacking in resiliency required by rapidly changing group situations made for problems requiring special attention.

10. Persons whose performance never measured up to their talk, whose phantasies got in the way of real achievement, represented another category of individual need encountered by the group worker.

Why do individuals behave in this manner? They *say* they want to belong to the group but they *do* many things which annoy the group and hinder their chances of getting acceptance. The answer lies in the person's need to be both dependent and independent, (Arlien Johnson, "Science and Social Work," *The Social Service Review*, September, 1947, pp. 303-4) and in the resultant feelings of ambivalence which arise as persons work through their conflicts. Every individual has conflicting emotions or drives which need resolution. From infancy through the late years the individual needs the love and affection of others. As a baby he is utterly dependent upon the adults in his world to provide physical and psychological care. As a child his needs change and he wishes to become independent from adult care, yet he realizes that it is comfortable to be dependent, and precarious to assume too much independence. Consequently, he wavers back and forth, not fully understanding the dual nature of his feelings. He may struggle to impress upon people the fact that he is independent, yet he feels inwardly that he is not and really wants to be a part of a well-knit group. Eventually, he must work out a style of living or adjustment which allows him to be sufficiently like others to belong, yet sufficiently different to be a person in his own right. Social group work in a sense provides a "proving ground" or "laboratory" in which the individual can try out various means of solving his conflicts without danger to himself or others.

> Harleigh B. Trecker, *Social Group Work—Principles and Practices*. New York: The Woman's Press, 1948, pp. 94-96.

474. CAMPER GROWTH THROUGH GROUP EXPERIENCE

The function of the counselor is to guide the group process of interaction and experience so that it contributes to the growth of each of the members. Specifically, this means that the counselor should understand and facilitate the expression of the interests and purposes of the campers. He should understand the needs of the campers as unique persons, in order to have a basis for individualizing objectives. He must stimulate, refine, and expand the interests and purposes of the campers. He should lead them to discern the deeper and broader issues and implications of their activities and relationships. He must facilitate the satisfying of their basic personality needs for status, friendship, and a sense of worth. This demands that he understand the status of each camper in relation to others: that is, the degree to which he is accepted, ignored, disliked, or rejected. The counselor, further, should utilize democratic or cooperative procedures in the guidance of group experience. He should also be aware of, and utilize, the wider available resources of knowledge or skill that may refine or enrich the experience of his campers.

> Hedley S. Dimock and Taylor Statten, *Talks to Counselors.*
> New York: Association Press, 1947, p. 43.

475. Group and Case Workers Put Their Heads Together at Camp Time

A long felt need in many communities is a closer working relationship between case workers and group workers. There is a fine opportunity in the field of camping of proving through discussion and experimentation that this relationship would be beneficial. Group workers should take the initiative in getting together groups of group workers and case workers who would be concerned with such experimentation and who would work out the details of record-keeping and reporting necessary.

A case worker sets forth this situation and its importance as follows: "In utilizing the summer camp as a resource for its clients, the case work agency seeks, not only a creative developmental experience for the individual, but also help in securing a better understanding of his behavior to serve as a basis for future planning and guidance. Reliable firsthand observations cannot always be secured by the case worker from the family or foster family, and may be difficult to obtain from the school, and the group work agencies in towns where the pressure of numbers and the limited size of the staff make individual study and recording difficult. More and more, therefore, not only is the case work agency coming to regard the summer camp as a resource to provide children with opportunities for growth and development, but also there is increasing recognition of the unique contribution the summer camp can make to an objective understanding of the child and increasing reliance upon this resource for supplementary diagnostic material.

"If the work of the summer camp and the case work agency are to be integrated effectively in the interest of individual development, the summer camp must be provided with knowledge about the individual before he arrives in camp, and the case work agency, in turn, should have a report of the observations of the camp staff on the child referred by them. Conferences between the types of workers and exchange of information in the form of written reports greatly facilitate and seem almost essential for good practice in developing an effective working relationship."

National Association for the Study of Group Work. *Suggestions for the Study of Group Work in the Field of Camping* (Mimeographed), 1939, pp. 19-20.

476. The Camp Provides the Opportunity

What does this mean to us as educators? It means a clinical opportunity to see the growing child's conflicts, and to observe how he is solving them. We must note at the outset: the new freedom does not mean solution of the conflict, though often a child does solve much on his own where the guidance is friendly. Perhaps the fact that he does make a lot of progress in a short time is the reason we hope for too much. You know how often parents send a child to camp to break up behavior patterns of many years' growth, and how disappointed they may be. Sometimes we are tempted as directors to offer camp as a panacea for problems ranging from bed-wetting to lying and stealing. This is an unfortunate attitude because it is not according to the facts of experience, and it is not within the realm of possibility. A camp cannot work miracles, although a camp prospectus or a parental questionnaire may indicate this faith.

An attitude, even more absurd, is to suppose that the child will leave his troubles at home. No one does, the child least of all, because the child is occupied with the business of growth, with the effort to complete each phase of development before the next one is upon him. He rarely does accomplish his maturity in such an orderly fashion. His course is marked with advance and retreat, sometimes a deep retreat to some inner fastness where he has experienced comfort and satisfaction.

Sometimes, this prevails through life; he remains, we say, in an infantile stage of development emotionally, though he may have quite an adult exterior.

If our task as educators is to help the child make an orderly development, to bring him into some good working relationship with the world about him, then we must recognize that he has conflicts, which he is always trying to solve. And we should be able to evaluate these conflicts in the light of his behavior. If we provide an atmosphere in which his behavior has free play, so much the more readily will we see the nature of his difficulty. This brings me back to my original premise: the camp is a clinical opportunity to observe. Accurate observation can be of great value to the school or to the parents, who may request help.

> Helen Ross, "What Can the Camp Contribute to the Emotional Development of the Child?" *The Camping Magazine*, March, 1938, pp. 3-4.

477. The Camp Counselor and the Emotional Needs of Children

So when you ask, what are we going to do to help children solve their conflicts, my first answer is, *let us have good counselors.* A good counselor, I shall not qualify in detail. Suffice it here to say the counselor must be essentially interested in children, must really like them, not just do sentimental lip service to this interest, but prove it in his attitudes and actions. He must have warmth and friendliness, curiosity about and understanding of human beings, with appreciation for their limitations as well as their potentialities; he need not be a paragon; he must be a person. He should be able to enter into the child's faults and difficulties, not sit on the side lines and preach. He should be able to remember his own childhood and adolescent feelings and difficulties. He should be a healthy person emotionally. If clouded with his own troubles, how can he see another's except in distortion?

Why is the counselor so important? Because he stands closest to the child, he becomes the substitute parent, he is the fountain of wisdom every child is looking for in a new situation, the one who can tell him what is done here and what is not, who can save the child from embarrassments before his fellows, who can comfort and encourage him. . . . This is what we hope to find in every counselor. This subject could be greatly expanded, but the time does not allow. Essential to add this: the counselor may not choose this position with reference to the child, i.e., as a substitute parent. That does not alter the case. He is in this position psychologically, and there he remains. Now this is not saying that he will fill the position adequately. To each child he represents a different being, a curious mixture of love and authority. The attitude toward the counselor in the beginning often discloses the attitude toward the parents, a mother or father, as the case may be. If the chosen counselor fails, there grows up a negative relationship which will accomplish nothing and the child goes on a search for one who will fill the bill. He may spend the summer in his search, and never experience the satisfaction he needs as an anchor in this voyage of exploration. Practically, it is of great importance to change a child from one counselor to another if the attitude appears to be hopelessly negative on either side, and it is equally important not to take a child away from a counselor who has become a positive factor in the child's adjustment. I go a step further in this and try to give returning campers to their old counselors, because I believe there is cumulative profit to be derived from a good relationship. Aside from his aid to the camper in general adjustment, he stands as an inspiration to his trying to master new skills or improve himself in old ones. Children first learn for the sake of pleasing someone; it is only later that knowledge and skill take on value per se. Without counselor interest and encouragement, in the absence of the outward stimuli, such as trophies, the child would accomplish little or nothing.

There is danger always that the counselor misuse this subtle position which he holds. This we all recognize. There is danger also that he overestimate his power and qualifications, and therefore attempt to reform the character in his charge. He may want to feel that he is a great influence, he may satisfy his own ego by creating "an interesting case." This is a warning not to be lightly taken. Every child is interesting, but he is not an "interesting case." Even if he were, the counselor may not be qualified to undertake it.

Ibid., pp. 5 and 28-29.

478. EMOTIONAL DEVELOPMENT IN CAMP

What we can do for the emotional development of the child boils itself down to a few statements: we can provide freedom from strain, thus giving a child opportunity to work out some of his own difficulties; we can assume a friendly, permissive, understanding attitude; we can work toward the training of counselors adequate to support and develop this all-important counselor-camper relationship. Reduced to still simpler terms, we can provide the proper atmosphere and the proper attitude, the first largely controlled by the second. So you see, I conclude on the counselor note. Our greatest contribution lies in the quality of counselor we offer the boys and girls who are under our guidance and protection.

Ibid., p. 29.

479. CAMP NOT THE PLACE FOR INTENSIVE THERAPY

This leads me to a discussion of therapy within the camp. I refer now to individual therapy which requires intensive work, a series of interviews with one child. I do not feel that camp is the best place for this type of therapy. My reasons are several: there is not enough time in camp, and there are rarely available counselors sufficiently trained for this work. There is always danger of arousing anxiety in intensive treatment, more anxiety than one can resolve. Another danger lies in the possibility of marking those children as different from the others. Most important of all is the fact that the camp with its directors, counselors, and campers becomes a psychological family, and as a member of this family, each child wants an equal amount of attention. Children are growing and developing in spite of our efforts. We must give them opportunity to work out many things for themselves. Therapy is always going on. Children are good therapists for each other, as you well know.

Ibid., p. 29.

480. THE PLACE OF GROUP METHODS IN A GUIDANCE PROGRAM

Having surveyed the various major types of group guidance and considered their limitations, we should now make an attempt to relate them to each other and to other types of guidance services, in order to see how they fit into a guidance program in an educational institution, a group work agency, or a guidance center. I assume that we are not concerned here with psychotherapy of the more thorough-going sort, nor with the guidance services of mental institutions.

Orientation programs are primarily a function of schools and colleges. Most *factual* orientation work should be integrated with the curriculum, giving students the facts that they need in order to develop legitimate vocational aspirations and sound social attitudes before vocational and social problems become so acute that information cannot effectively be used. As there will inevitably be times in the educational, vocational, and social development of young people at which choices need to be made, and as facts assume a new significance at those points, there is a place for formal orientation activities in educational institutions and in group-work agencies. There is a place for them also in guidance centers which work with people who have no group affiliations and whose orientation problems are closely related to problems on which they are receiving individual counseling. As the need to make decisions heightens the emotional value of facts, formal orientation activities provided at the choice points of development need to be not only factual, but also *attitudinal.* There must be time for members of the group to express their attitudes toward the facts encountered, to work through their related feelings, and to modify their attitudes to make them fit the facts.

Group development and nondirective group therapy seem to me to be techniques which are also appropriate for use with persons who are going through the normal processes of personal development. Late adolescence and early adulthood are periods in which a process of integration is taking place in the individual; it is in these years that he crystallizes, tests out, and revises concepts of himself in relation to other persons, and it is in these years also that internal forces are being organized and synthesized into a more or less integrated personality. The methods of group dynamics appear promising for use with persons who are not completely socialized and who want help in understanding their own rules in relation to other people, so that they may modify their social behavior and be more effective in interpersonal relations. I suspect that we shall find that this approach is most appropriate for persons of post-college age, is useable with many college students, and is definitely less appropriate at the high-school level, for it must require a substantial degree of maturity and insight to profit from a picture of one's behavior in a group.

Nondirective group therapy, on the other hand, should prove useful with high-school age boys and girls as well as with older persons. The technique has been used in college teaching, and may well be adaptable to courses and activities designed to have character-building values with boys and girls of high-school age. It may prove to be the technique par excellence of Hi-Y discussion groups, Sunday school classes, orientation courses dealing with problems of social behavior, and other groups in which an attempt is being made to help adolescents and young adults to achieve self-integration. By providing a permissive situation in which they can express and work through their feelings on problems of importance, discussion groups using nondirective techniques should be able to reach many people who would never see a personal counselor or who could not be served by one if they did seek him out.

Role playing is another method of group therapy which has shown signs of being useful in educational institutions and in guidance centers. It can be used in helping young people to learn social skills and to acquire confidence in social situations, whether the skill be asking a girl to dance or applying for a job; it can be helpful in coaching group leaders, in inducting salesmen, and in training vocational counselors. Role playing involves trying out skills, exercise in putting an emerging self-concept into practice; it involves converting ideas about one's behavior into concrete, criticizable action. It can be used at almost any age level, and in connection with a great variety of needs and problems.

The psychodrama and interpretive group therapy are, I believe, more likely to remain useful with individuals who are more disturbed, more inhibited, and less socialized than those most of us are likely to spend much time with in schools, colleges, group-work organizations and guidance centers. These are more peculiarly clinical techniques, useful in the clinic and in the hospital.

Before concluding this discussion, a few words should be devoted to the relative emphasis which one might expect to find placed on group and individual techniques in a guidance program. One might even ask, is it at all likely that group guidance can meet the needs of the great majority of students and adults, leaving individual counseling for special cases only?

I think the answer to this question must be in the negative, for while group methods can do a great deal of preventive work, and can even do a great deal of creative work, I think it will always be true that most people can benefit from opportunities to discuss their attitudes, aspirations, and plans with a sympathetic listener who has special skill in clarifying issues and who has a perspective on problems and opportunities such as come only with professional training and experience. A good program of group-guidance services should forestall the development of some problems, should assist in the growth of better integrated personalities, improve personal, social and occupational orientation, and finally, should render people better able to make effective use of personal and vocational counseling services when and as they are needed.

Donald E. Super, "Group Techniques in the Guidance Program," *Journal of Educational and Psychological Measurement*, Autumn, 1949, Part 11, pp. 507-10.

481. GROUP GUIDANCE THE PRIMARY FOUNDATION

The need for guidance is great, and the individual approach to guidance is quicker and somewhat more spectacular, but in the long run the most effective guidance program is one in which group-guidance work is the foundation. Outside of pressing cases, group guidance is most effective; in fact, group-guidance work should pave the way for individual guidance activities and should test and carry out the conclusions arrived at in individual counseling. Both types of guidance are needed.

One supplements the other. At the present time there has not
been much done in the area of formal group guidance activities. Because the "Y" is an effective group-work agency, it
should not find a difficult problem in developing formal group-
guidance activities.

The purpose of group-guidance is to teach the individuals
how to assume their share of the responsibility of a guidance
program. To become self-guiding it is necessary that a person
learn certain techniques. This fact should be kept in mind when
the formal group-guidance activities are planned, for they
should provide the practice necessary in learning the techniques of self-guidance. One of the most difficult periods of
adjustment for young people is the step between childhood
and adulthood. This adjustment period might very well provide the theme for the group-guidance activities: namely,
learning how to live successfully in a modern complex society
on the adult level. . . .

Some of the more valuable by-products of such a group-guidance program are:

1. The orientation of the individual to the various adult-life
responsibilities.

2. The teaching of students to analyze some of the more
pressing personal problems and the development of programs
which will help them to solve these problems.

3. A more intimate knowledge by the guidance leader of each
individual.

4. The instructions the individuals get in using the various
guidance techniques, such as tests, cumulative records, and
resource material.

> J. S. Kopas, "Six Aspects of Guidance," *A Primer of Guid-
> ance Through Group Work.* New York: Association Press,
> 1940, pp. 36-37.

482.   Changing From Class or Team to Group

. . . It is, therefore, significant that in the late thirties there
was considerable mention in the literature of how to change
"classes and teams" to "groups." Suggestions similar to the following were made:

1. Reduce the number of members if the class or grouping is too large. Subdivisions may be made on the basis of friendship or of groups that already exist in other activities.

2. The basis of membership should provide for congeniality.

3. Develop a sense of proprietorship in the group by encouraging and stimulating initiative and responsibility on the part of members.

4. Widen the range of shared interests and experience.

5. Encourage significant projects and enterprises that will increase the sense of group unity.

6. Identify and utilize ways of helping members feel a sense of importance and of having a definite role in the group.

7. Encourage the development of an organization structure consonant with a responsible self-propelling group when the actual purposes and plans of the group make this desirable.

> Charles E. Hendry, editor, *A Decade of Group Work*. New York: Association Press, 1948, pp. 27-28. (From chapter by Harry D. Edgren.)

483. A Sound Relationship Between Counseling and Group Work? Try This Test

The following are a few questions by which to test the soundness of relationships between counseling and group work:

1. Does the group worker cooperate with the counselor in forming and developing groups to meet individual needs; does the group worker place individuals in the kinds of groups indicated by the counselor?

2. Does the group worker use the relationships developed during the group-work process to help individuals with their less serious personal problems?

3. Does the group worker obtain counseling service for members whose needs cannot be met by group activity?

4. Does the group worker hold individual or small-group conferences with student leaders and members for the purpose of helping them contribute more effectively to the group—for example, a conference with a student chair-

man to help him improve his technique of leading group discussion?

5. Do counselors and group leaders get together to discuss their common problems and opportunities?

C. Gilbert Wrenn, *Student Personnel Work in College.* New York: The Ronald Press Company, 1951, pp. 230-31.

Part VI

THE RESOURCES OF THE COUNSELOR

19.

The Personality of the Counselor

---

484. Personal Adjustment More Important Than Technique

The teacher's techniques will matter less than his own personal adjustment. The adjustment of the teacher, and his ability to exert a favorable influence on children, will depend, first, upon the way in which he has assimilated his own childhood experiences, and, second, upon his present level of life-satisfaction.

> Paul A. Witty, and Charles E. Skinner, editors, *Mental Hygiene in Modern Education*. New York: Rinehart and Company, Inc., 1939, p. 525. (From chapter by Goodwin Watson.)

485. Unprejudiced Objectivity

Unprejudiced objectivity toward the other person precludes the possibility of the counselor's identifying himself with the counselee in a positive or in a negative manner. A counselor only increases the difficulty the other person is facing if he sympathizes and excuses or condemns and blames him, because of an undiscovered need in himself to do what the counselee is doing. The person seeking help may be to him the one who dares to do what he would like to do but dare not do. Many a reformer takes an undue interest in certain kinds of misconduct because to be associated with the other's misdeeds satisfies a desire to do those things himself. His identification with the other, however, usually adds to the conflict instead of helping towards its elimination. It is always interesting to discover how one's own faults are especially irritating when

found in another person. The person who talks incessantly
cannot stand talkativeness in another; the slow individual is
likely to be overcritical of tardiness; the person quick to make
judgments is intolerant of the same tendency in others. If an
individual comes for help in an area of the counselor's unre-
solved problems, the counselee is likely to be met with unsound condemnation or blame that must cover both his and the
counselor's difficulties. "Judge not, that ye be not judged" is a
canny psychological observation; significant also is the story
of the man with a beam in his own eye who was overconcerned
with the mote in his brother's eye. One does not need to condemn anyone else if his own conduct is free and blameless.

It is evident that the counselor must be emotionally mature
and free enough so that the counselee's manifestations do not
provoke a tumultous response. If he has unsolved problems
himself, he will be vulnerable in the presence of the emotions
of his patient. The individual who has not dared to give expression to certain sexual impulses or desires and who does
not understand them, is a dangerous counselor for one struggling with questions of sex conduct. Likewise he who has
never dared assert his independence from mother or father is
not equipped to deal with another's immature attempts to become free from some hampering bond. If the counselor fears
failure or has made a failure in any area, if he is supersensitive
and easily hurt, the thrusts of the patient will arouse him emotionally, and he will respond personally to them. Therefore,
if he finds that the story of the counselee sets off undue emotion in him, if he cannot sleep for thinking of the counselee's
difficulties, if he is horrified at the counselee's conduct, if deep
sex emotions are aroused within him, he should recognize his
reactions as manifestations of unsolved problems in himself,
and realize that he probably ought not to continue the counseling relationship since he can scarcely hope to attain objectivity in the area under discussion. The discovery of particular
irritation or excessive emotion in the face of another's difficulties is a sign to the wise to examine oneself for the same
unsolved problem.

It needs to be said at this point that many people are attracted to counseling with others because of unsolved problems of their own. There is a fascination to them in problems of others which resemble theirs. Further, if one can spend his time trying to solve other people's problems, it is easier to disregard one's own. Consequently, care must be exercised that vocations dealing with human need, such as social work and the ministry, shall not draw too many people who have been attracted to them by their own unmet personal needs. If the counselor needs to use his relationship with the counselee to extend his personal influence and to dominate another, he will take control or give directions in a manner which will hinder the development of the counselee. However benevolent this domination, it is not sound for the growth of the counselee. (See Van Waters, Miriam, *Youth in Conflict,* p. 251.) The counselor cannot aid successfully in solving another's problems, indeed he becomes an unintentional exploiter of the personality of the other if he undertakes counseling in the attempt to resolve his own conflict. It is because of the difficulty of securing objectivity, when one's own problems have not been explored and solved, that personal analysis has become increasingly recognized as one of the prerequisites for professional therapists.

It is for the above reasons that before any individual dares to accept the responsibility of counseling with another, he must have faced his own life and accepted it. It is no easy requirement to accept one's life as it is, not only one's present and potential strengths, but also his weaknesses and inadequacies, to know the need of forgiveness and to recognize failure and immaturity without excuse or condemnation, but with a patience that is not frightened but challenged by reality. It is to be conscious that within one's own nature are all the potentialities of failure or of achievement that lie in human nature at its best and worst. It is to be honest in attempts at one's own growth. Often by working with another's problems the counselor discovers within himself things that must be faced and dealt with objectively and directly. Unless he is willing to pay the price of facing and dealing objectively and directly with the problems he discovers in himself, he is not equipped to be a counselor. He can help another in an area in which he has not yet attained complete maturity if he is honestly working for his own freedom, but he should not try to help another in the areas of his own unaccepted conduct.

> Harrison Sacket Elliott and Grace Loucks Elliott, *Solving Personal Problems*. New York: Henry Holt and Company, Inc., 1936, pp. 202-5. By permission of the publishers.

486. The Meaning of "Professional Help"

All the professions concerned with individuals, the ministers and priests, the social workers, the psychiatrists and so on, with greater or less effectiveness are taught to provide for those they help what each individually needs without letting their own personal feelings and reactions toward such persons interfere too much with their professional practices. This does not mean that they are impersonal and lack feelings, or that they are "all things to all people." It does mean that they have a professional ideal of serving and helping individuals apart from their moral or ethical or personal judgment of the individual before them. They have become aware of their personal bias and prejudices, of their likes and dislikes, and have learned to give professional help.

> Lawrence K. Frank, "Mental Health in Schools," *Education*, Vol. 66, No. 9, 1946, p. 549.

487. Wanted: An Objective Friend

This relationship of confidence and dependence is one highly charged with emotion and so has potentiality for good or ill. Often the counselee throws himself upon the counselor and wants to be taken charge of. He does everything he can to get direct advice and help, and the temptation of the counselor to yield directly to this appeal for aid is great. His sympathies are stirred and he wants to help the individual. Further, it is very satisfying to become a superior parent, a sort of vice regent of God, and take responsibility for another person. Under such circumstances, many counselors yield to the appeal made to them; others resent the dependent attitude, and rebuff the one who comes for help; while still others recognize the relationship and use it positively in the counseling procedure.

When this relationship of dependence and of confidence has developed, the bars are down. The counselee trusts the counselor and therefore he does not have to act a part. He expresses whatever emotions he has of love or hate, fear or anger, of dependence or inadequacy. If the counselor responds to these emotional manifestations directly, as in ordinary life, an unsound relationship is set up. If the counselor responds to his aggressive thrusts in kind, a fight is begun; if he tries to argue or persuade him out of his pessimistic mood or his disbeliefs, an argument is in progress; if he responds to love protestations in kind, a love affair is developed. Many counselors fail because they respond to the counselee as they would to their fellows in the ordinary affairs of life. It is only as the counselor sympathetically receives the manifestations made to him, but does not respond to them personally, that positive results will take place.

It is thus seen that objectivity is necessary on the part of the counselor if the counseling relation is to be positive and helpful. The reason the counselor must not become involved personally is probably evident. If he responds, the counseling situation becomes merely a repetition of the counselee's difficulties in life's relations and adds to them instead of helping to solve them. Further, if the counselee can get the counselor involved personally, he need not do anything about his own problems. He uses all his energy then, as he has done in life, in getting someone else to take responsibility for him, in blaming others for his conduct, or in using his behavior patterns destructively to accomplish his ends. But if the counseling situation differs from his life situation in that he gets his emotion out but nothing happens in return, then he is impelled to look at his conduct and do something about it himself. If all his efforts to involve the counselor are unavailing, he is thrown more and more upon his own responsibility to face himself as he is and to do something about his difficulties. The counseling relationship becomes an epitome of his life situation under controlled conditions and he has there the chance to work out his own problems, intellectually and emotionally, in his relations with the counselor.

Harrison Sacket Elliott and Grace Loucks Elliott, *Solving Personal Problems*. New York: Henry Holt and Company, Inc., 1936, pp. 197-99. By permission of the publishers.

488. THE IMPORTANCE OF THE COUNSELOR

In any psychotherapy, the therapist himself is a highly important part of the human equation. What he does, the attitude he holds, his basic concept of his role, all influence therapy to a marked degree.

Carl R. Rogers, *Client-Centered Therapy*. Boston: Houghton Mifflin Company, 1951, p. 19.

489. THE SUBTLE INFLUENCE OF THE TEACHER

. . . the viewpoints, prejudices, ambitions, attitudes, and personality make-up of the teacher, because of her position of authority, exert upon every pupil a subtle, irresistible molding influence that makes for mental health or mental disharmony. The teacher's methods of discipline; her basic philosophy of life; the opinions she expresses; her prejudices, emotional fixations, or oddities; the insidious influences that radiate from her appearance, manner of speech, comportment, and emotional poise; her calmness or instability; her mental health or mental discord—all these and many other influences leave a profound impress upon many of her pupils for evil or for good. A dyspeptic teacher may quickly dampen the ardor of a roomful of children so that they come to dislike the teacher and become soured on everything pertaining to the school. This is particularly true of younger children, who tend to transfer their dislike for the teacher to the whole educational system, and who may thus form an aversion to study and begin to fail. The dyspeptic teacher is inclined to radiate impatience, irritability, and cantankerousness, even though she may make a desperate effort to be sweet and even tempered and to hide the disagreeable feelings produced by her upset digestive system.

J. E. Wallace Wallin, *Personality Maladjustments and Mental Hygiene*. New York: McGraw-Hill Book Company, Inc., 1949, p. 97. By permission of the publishers.

490. OBJECTIVE YET SYMPATHETIC

Of equal importance are the teacher-counselor's own motives in helping students. He may find it pleasant to have control over students' decisions. If so, he will find many students wishing to be dominated. These students will grow little in their ability to make their own decisions. Other instructors find it interesting to manipulate student choices in a more subtle way, but still in the same mood of domination. Still other teachers wish to establish their counseling relations with students on a strictly factual basis. They refuse to get involved in the student's problem beyond the point of helping him to discover pertinent facts bearing upon the problem. These are the "detached" counselors. Their point of view has the merit of fostering student initiative, but it lacks the warmth that most students want in their relations with a counselor.

At its best the counselor-student relationship should be objective yet sympathetic. The counselor may genuinely want to assist without indulging in the dubious pleasure of dominating the student. He can assist the student to understand himself without giving the impression that the understanding stems only from the counselor's superior wisdom. He can offer alternatives for the student's choice without prejudicing the choice. Above all, he can permit the student to make a choice even though it be a decision he does not approve.

In short, the teacher-counselor can free himself of self-centered motives in dealing with students. His satisfaction will come from seeing students grow in self-reliance, rather than in dependence upon him. His success will come when the student no longer needs him as a counselor but values him as a friend.

> American Council on Education, *The Teacher as Counselor.* (Donald J. Shank, chairman), October, 1948, p. 13. (From section by George E. Hill.)

491. THE MATURE GROUP LEADER

Once relationship has been established, the leader's ability to function in the group process depends on the degree of understanding and of insight he brings to the group. The leader not only gives but he also receives satisfaction from the group. Where he uses the group, consciously or unconsciously, to meet his own needs and not the needs of the group he is not fully effective and may even be harmful. If the leader is able to meet his major needs outside of the group situation, if he is a person who is well-adjusted in his emotional and social life, he does not have to use the group for satisfaction. He can be more objective and is in a better position to decide whether his own activity is good for him or the group. We have an ideal situation when the leader gets his satisfaction by meeting the group's needs. This will be expressed in practical terms by the way in which he runs his program.

> Rudolph M. Wittenberg, *So You Want To Help People*. New York: Association Press, 1947, p. 39.

492. THE TEACHER STRIVES FOR MATURITY

An important part of the teacher's "way of life" is to achieve emotional maturity, so that she can divest herself of childish survivals, and so that she will avoid, in the attempt to solve her own adjustment problems in the schoolroom, resorting to the immature reaction patterns that brought success in her childhood and that may be used by some of her pupils to solve their schoolroom problems. Such immature response patterns often constitute a bar to normal maturation including for example attitudes of dogmatism, cocksureness, intolerance, prejudice, oversensitiveness, irritability, peevishness, irrational jealousy or hostility, and impulsiveness. Regression to these and other kinds of infantile reaction patterns are often of the nature of defenses against one's inner conflicts and frustrations or the projection of one's difficulties upon someone else. In the schoolroom, the blame projection often involves some pupil who resorts to irritating defense mechanisms for overcoming his unsolved problems or some pupil with whom the teacher has not established sympathetic rapport. The teacher, of course, is not the only one who has to wrestle with the problems of emotional immaturity, but the teacher is confronted with a special hazard in the achievement of mature emotional and intellectual patterns, because she must constantly deal with immature personalities. Because her life is spent in the world of childhood, she may fail to grow up emotionally and may adopt attitudes of complacency or condescension, on the one hand, or supercil- iousness or arrogance, on the other hand, toward the foibles and frailties of her young charges. The teacher must, of course, strive to keep young and plastic, so that she can get down to the level of her pupils in order to maintain effective rapport with them, but not at the cost of emotional fixation and stratification on the childhood level, or of an objective approach toward her prob- lems and those of her pupils. She must strive to maintain a de- tached, objective, but, withal, sympathetic attitude toward her pupils, so that she can accept the child as he is and enter into an understanding relationship with his limitations without emo- tional prepossessions or involvements.

The teacher should balance her association with children by association with adults. To maintain mental equilibrium, we often have to balance one factor against another when we cannot avoid certain deleterious influences in the environment. We can often minimize or counteract inimical influences by balancing factors. We can balance factors that are a hindrance or a liability with factors that make for effective living. One of the important readily available balancing factors for teachers is fraternization with adults, especially with those engaged in other vocations. Contacts with adults from different walks of life develop maturity, adjustability, flexibility, catholicity, and poise.

J. E. Wallace Wallin, *Personality Maladjustments and Men tal Hygiene*. New York: McGraw-Hill Book Company, Inc., 1949, pp. 167-68. By permission of the publishers.

493. THE TEACHER OF THE FUTURE: WELL-ADJUSTED *and* COMPETENT

The Adjustment of the Teacher. The quality of the school's influence for mental hygiene is determined in no small measure by the personal characteristics of its teachers. The attitudes and habits of adjustment that the pupil learns depend more on the social relationships of the classroom than on the more academic aspects of education. Consequently, a teacher whose traits of personality call forth unfavorable reactions from the students can wreck the best-planned curricular provisions for

mental health. Some teachers are overaggressive in their actions toward pupils, bullying them, looking for small infrac-
tions of the rules, and constantly asserting their own mastery
and superiority, often by sarcastic and critical comments. Other
teachers show a lack of emotional balance, being inconsistent
in their treatment of pupils, flying into a rage at misdemeanors,
or displaying "nervousness" and excessive sensitivity to the difficulties of the classroom. On the other hand, there are teachers
who appeal to the class for sympathy, who try to win approval
by granting special favors, or who shower affection on one or
a few pupils while neglecting the rest of the class. All of these
forms of teacher behavior are destructive of good adjustment
for the students.

It is easy to take a moralistic attitude toward teachers who
commit these offenses against mental hygiene, and to advocate
their dismissal. But it must be remembered that teachers are
human beings and, like all others, have their own problems of
adjustment. Teachers who have unfortunate characteristics of
personality are not merely ignorant or perverse, but are suffering from maladjustment. Many adjustive difficulties of
teachers arise from common causes. They suffer the same frustrations of motives as do other people, and may be unable to
adjust constructively because of inadequate habits or developmental defects acquired earlier in life. In addition to the more
general causes of maladjustment the teaching profession provides some special situations that make it hard for teachers
to remain well balanced. It is admittedly a difficult and fa-
tiguing task to deal with forty lively youngsters all day in a
classroom. Teachers are often poorly prepared for their work,
which creates a need for them to be on the defensive. The low
salaries and unesteemed status of teachers also contribute to
an attitude of inferiority. Unmarried teachers away from home
frequently live in rooming houses and do not have the integrating influence of home life and of social outlets. The sexual maladjustments of unmarried teachers, often thoroughly
repressed and unrecognized, undoubtedly make for nervousness and other persistent nonadjustive reactions.

The psychology of adjustment makes clear the relationship
between the frustrations of teachers and their typical undesir-

able classroom habits. Overaggressive behavior and the assertion of mastery are compensatory mechanisms for overcoming an attitude of inferiority. This attitude may have been built up by the teacher's childhood or adolescent experiences, by the struggle necessary to gain an education, or may result from recent factors such as a sense of inadequacy for the task of teaching, or an unfulfilled desire to enter some other profession. The control of children in school offers an exceptional opportunity for compensatory behavior. In fact, it has even been suggested that some persons enter teaching in order to gain the motive satisfaction that results from lording it over the helpless pupils. Appeals for sympathy from the class are often the result of the emotional maldevelopment of the teacher that causes an excessive need for love and favorable attention. Persistent nonadjustive reactions result from many serious thwartings of motives for which no outlets can be found. When a teacher says that a class makes her nervous or "drives her wild," it is, of course, her inability to adjust to the situation that is the real source of the emotional response.

Most of the personality handicaps of teachers are remediable. First, all teachers should make a critical analysis of their own behavior from the point of view of mental hygiene. The motives underlying the teacher's methods of handling pupils should be clearly recognized, and modifications made if needed. The teacher should ask, "Am I just gratifying my own drives, or am I directing the school activities objectively, for the benefit of the pupils themselves?" Improvement in competence assists in maintaining an adjustive attitude, for the teacher who is sure of her subject matter and methods will have less need to act defensively. Principals and supervisors have as great a responsibility for the personalities of teachers as for their methods of instruction. Reprimands and orders are no more effective for a maladjusted teacher than for a maladjusted pupil, but a cordial relationship between teacher and supervisor and the making of tactful and psychologically considered suggestions can do much to assist the teacher in working out her own problems. The provision of psychiatric service for teachers in connection with the school health department can, if skillfully administered, turn some teachers from liabilities into educational assets. Even with the best of facilities for mental health, however, there will remain a few teachers so hopelessly handicapped in personal adjustment that they can be nothing but a menace to their pupils. Since the mental health of a generation of children is more important than is the vocational advantage of one teacher, these individuals must be guided into another occupation for which they may be less poorly adapted.

The teacher of the future must be as much a specialist in mental hygiene as in subject matter or method. Increasing recognition is being given in schools of education to the importance of mental hygiene in the curriculum for prospective teachers. While an intelligent and informed attitude toward problems of personality and behavior will do much good, it is not sufficient. Teachers must be exceptionally well-adjusted persons themselves. This end can be accomplished in part by selection and in part by clinical service. Some candidates for the teaching profession should be debarred because of a lack of good adjustment, no matter what their other accomplishments. A psychiatric examination should be as important in the selection of teachers as are the physical examinations and educational attainments now required. Well-administered vocational guidance can eliminate many misfits among prospective teachers, for few persons wish to enter an occupation for which they know themselves to be poorly qualified. Mental hygiene clinical service for teachers in training can remedy some of the less fixed defects of personality. Selective methods alone are not enough, however, for some persons who were well adjusted when they entered the profession may become maladjusted later. Teachers must be educated to make use of mental hygiene facilities that should be provided for them. By these various means teachers can be supplied who are adequate not only in scholarship and intelligence but also in emotional balance, adaptability and integration.

Laurance Frederic Shaffer, *The Psychology of Adjustment*. Boston: Houghton Mifflin Company, 1936, pp. 512-15.

494. IMPORTANCE OF THE TEACHER'S OWN ADJUSTMENT

A fair proportion of the adjustment problems which teachers

find in children arise really in the teacher-child relationship and are caused in part by the teacher's own personality. "Stubbornness" usually arises in two persons, not just in one, and so also does irritation. Classroom observation shows a vicious circle in which a teacher may unintentionally annoy some pupil, the pupil's outburst irritates the teacher, whose voice then further upsets the pupil, who then goes in for more extreme provocation of the teacher. The unhappy affair may just as often begin with the child's reaction to trouble at home or on the playground, but the teacher's personality, instead of relieving the child's tension, adds to the irritation and strain, making matters worse for everyone. It is not strange that Boynton and associates found more unstable children in the classrooms of unstable teachers. (P. L. Boynton, H. Dugger, and M. Turner, "The Emotional Stability of Teachers and Pupils," *Journal of Juvenile Research*, XVIII, October, 1934, 223-32.) Mental hygiene is more a matter of the human environment than of the material world or the school requirements. The teacher whose soft answer not only "turneth away wrath" but gives the child a stronger sense of security in a friendly world, is the acme of emotional hygiene.

The ability of teachers to exert a favorable influence on children's adjustments depends very largely on two factors: the way in which the teacher has assimilated his own childhood, and the adequacy with which his present life-needs are being met. No professional techniques or mastery of academic subject matter can make a good teacher out of a person who is coerced by infantile behavior patterns and distorted by present emotional deprivations.

Freedom of the self from the coercion of childhood responses does not depend upon having had no childhood difficulties. Some of the best teachers and mental hygienists had serious problems in their own youth, but they have made an asset out of those potential handicaps. A hunger for affection which may have been denied in early years, if it no longer drives blindly toward intense, too demanding, and unwholesome attachments, but has become understood, accepted, and allowed for in conscious adjustments, leaves the adult teacher better equipped to appreciate what love may mean in a child's life.

A childhood experience of isolation which prevented easy social relationships, if it no longer drives blindly toward competition and self-assertion, may help to keep the adult teacher
constantly alert to the pupil's need for "belonging."

There is a difficult but extremely important distinction between the wise use of our own past experience, and the common tendency to identify other people's problems with our
own. The teacher's experiences should have given a general
sensitivity to pupil needs and to the complex phantasy life beneath unexpressive masks, but should not lead the teacher to
say, "Aha! I know just what's wrong with you because I went
through just the same thing!" No two people, being different
in hundreds of important ways, ever go through what is *psychologically* the same experience. The teacher should always remember that differences in personality and situation make it
likely that what worked well in his own life may work very
poorly as a course of action for the worried child. The attempted solution that failed and hurt us badly may be very
successful in the child's case. His life is his own; his problems
are unique; a natural tendency toward identification must not
be allowed to prevent a new and fresh attack on his present situation. Adult experience cannot contribute cut-and-dried remedies. The teacher, as a wiser and sometimes sadder person,
places at the disposal of the child, not a set of tested answers
to life problems, but a deeper appreciation of needs and a
broader awareness of relationships.

> Paul A. Witty and Charles E. Skinner, editors, *Mental Hy-
> giene in Modern Education.* New York: Rinehart and Com-
> pany, Inc., 1939, pp. 520-22. (From chapter by Goodwin
> Watson.)

495. THE ROLE OF THE COUNSELOR

In addition to having a clear conception of the camper and
his experience, there is at least one other important necessity
for constructive dealing with the individual camper. For children who in any sense require any individualization in treatment at camp, the counselor must have an awareness of *his
own* role, of what the camper finds in *him,* and of what the effect of his attitudes toward the camper may be. I have indicated

that the child tends to carry over into the camp situation his characteristic methods of dealing with the persons about him. In relation to the *counselor,* he is very likely to carry over specific attitudes that have developed toward important persons in his own family. The boy whose father is overly strict, and toward whom he reacts with resentment and rebelliousness, may tend initially to regard the counselor as another such father, and his initial attitude tends to be the same as toward his own father. The too-dependent child will see in the counselor the protective parent in relation to whom he has developed his dependency reaction, and will attempt to exploit the counselor on this basis.

The counselor is in a position to minimize or to augment the intensity of these reactions and relationships. If he is aware of what is happening, his responses can be such as to force the child to deal with him on a more mature basis. If the child can achieve this in relation to the counselor, he is very likely to find it easier to do likewise in other relationships, and a step forward in his development has been made. If, on the other hand, the counselor is not aware of what is happening, he may find himself inveigled into a role that involves a continuation of the old customary pattern for the child. An appreciation by the counselor of the very salutary effect he may have in aiding children through their difficulties in giving up the older and socially less useful patterns pays good dividends in real growth on the part of the camper.

Occasionally a counselor fails to see the essential elements in a situation, and may aggravate rather than aid some irritating situation. Some time ago, a camp counselor was considerably disturbed about the difficult plight of one of the adolescent girls in her charge. This girl confided quite fully in the counselor, and recounted the difficult situation in her home in which a sister, some two or three years older, played a favored role. The younger girl was constantly in the position of playing second fiddle, felt her style was considerably cramped, had no real freedom, and was under the constant domination of the older sister. (All this is according to the camper's statement.) The counselor felt this was an unhealthy situation, sympathized with the camper, and promised to help her to better arrangements in the family at the end of the season. Actually, the situation was one in which very alert parents carefully provided as well as was humanly possible for the special needs of the younger girl, who was by far the more aggressive of the two; and the real requirement was to aid the younger sister in overcoming her envy and resentment of the elder sister. The reception her complaint received in camp, however, tended to crystallize her resentments rather than to aid in dispersing them, since the counselor's acceptance of her version of the situation constituted a confirmation of her own interpretation of the family relationships. This same reliance in the counselor, which increased her difficulty, would have permitted an effort to undermine her resentful feelings and the establishment of a more realistic response to her actual home situation.

> George J. Mohr, "The Camp and the Individual Camper,"
> *Character Education in the Summer Camp*. Report of Sixth
> Annual Camp Institute, George Williams College, Chicago,
> March, 1935. New York: Association Press, 1935, pp. 41-42.

496. MENTAL HYGIENE FOR THE COUNSELOR

The psychological condition of the counselor is so significant for the outcomes of counseling that he needs to pay careful attention to his own mental health program. The observation of a few simple principles of good mental health will pay large dividends, not only in counselor satisfactions but in counseling effectiveness. The first principle relates to the possibility that a counselor may take clients *too* seriously and professionally and lose any sense of enjoyment in the experience. *He should have joy from the sheer human companionship involved*, that is, if he is correctly placed in counseling and teaching! To take all such human relationships too seriously is to lose one of the motivations that counselors need to keep them at their task. People who are casual and relaxed in their relationships with others are sought out because it is easy for others to enjoy that atmosphere. Counselors and other personnel workers, on the other hand, may become so tense and preoccupied in developing their programs or in seeking personal goals that clients and associates feel tense when around them.

Perhaps this principle could be adopted in terms of the counselor *learning* more from others and *instructing* them less. This would put him in a different relationship to many people, particularly his students and his associates. No one should have entered the field of personnel work unless he enjoyed constant human contact with people. This enjoyment may have been evident in the beginning of some careers, but some have become so engrossed with programs, public relations, publications, and promotions that the joy that they once had from simple human contacts has been greatly diminished. Once this happens, they become less effective in all of their personal relationships. People enjoy less being around such individuals, since they in turn do not enjoy being around others. Any uniqueness they may have had as far as an understanding and sensitive personality are concerned has been merged in the common pattern of personal ambition and drive. Such people take themselves too seriously and in this engrossment of self they miss much of the pleasure of life.

A second point is that the counselor should *recognize his fatigue point* and deliberately avoid any extensive contact with people once that point has been reached. He certainly is not effective after he has reached this fatigue point. It is at this time that the voice becomes sharp, attention wanders, patience with the slow progress of others falters, and effectiveness drops to the vanishing point. This fatigue point will be different with each individual. Various fatigue studies have indicated high fatigue points at about eleven o'clock in the morning and four o'clock in the afternoon. This, of course, relates to people who keep regular office or factory hours. For others, the fatigue point may come either earlier or later, but it is the personal problem of each to select his own fatigue point. Furthermore the counselor must learn to recognize the symptoms of that approaching state of tension. For some there is respite in a candy bar or a hot drink (coffee will do for the writer). Others read something light, and still others will look out the window. Someone else may stretch for a moment or two or shadow box and then sprawl in a chair with every muscle relaxed. All of these have a combined effect of releasing physical tensions and at the same time bringing new associations into one's intellectual existence. This breaks the synapse, so to speak, of well-established paths, and by this process tension levels apparently are reduced.

A third principle is to *avoid setting up impossible goals for oneself* in terms of the amount to be accomplished each day. If a counselor plans on *less* than he actually expects to do each day, the unexpected things that always arise will fill in the chinks of time without strain. On the contrary, many people plan on more than they can do and then feel frustrated and unhappy because the impossible has not been accomplished. A counselor, or other professional person, would be practicing good mental hygiene if he blocked out a small amount of professional reading each day and thereby reduced the feeling of frustration that develops because he is not making professional progress. Journals and new books pile up with the consequence that any professional person always has several hours' reading ahead of him any day and seldom gets more than a fraction of it done. Rather than carry about a feeling of frustration and pressure constantly, a pressure that will affect counseling relationships, a counselor could block out a schedule of one-half hour a day of professional reading and strictly observe that minimum. By this procedure he will make slow but steady progress on a schedule that he can actually accomplish.

Another practical mental hygiene procedure is that of *deliberately practicing small courtesies in all relations with other people.* This is easier on others and will pay large dividends in social effectiveness. Beyond this, by practicing these small social courtesies the counselor is actually demonstrating that he believes in the integrity of each human personality with whom he deals. He will avoid a guilt tension arising from a gap between his theory and practice. If courtesy and consideration for the welfare and dignity of the other person in small affairs is practiced, then it will be easier to measure up to high ideals in major human relationships. Courtesies in crowded traffic, in stores, in restaurants, or remembering birthdays and personal honors that have come to friends seem small indeed, but it is of such small incidents that major patterns are made. Many people give verbal support to high-sounding social responsibility, but actually live in cramped, self-centered fashion as far as their day-to-day social contacts are concerned.

Finally, the counselor, who is essentially an idealist, should remember that *ultimate values persist regardless of what happens to his personal life.* Things that he deeply believes in, that have permanent significance, do not change no matter how much the world about him deteriorates. In the face of fears about international relations, domestic economy, and personal advancement, certain basic values do not change. Human rights and dignities, the integrity of each human personality, the warmth of love and friendship, the beauty of the earth, the eternal significance of the spiritual—these things endure. The physical and the political world may cause suffering of body and mind, but the things of the human spirit do not die, and it is with these eternals of human life that the counselor must be concerned if he is to live up to his high calling as a specialist in human relationships and as a trustee of human values.

C. Gilbert Wrenn, *Student Personnel Work in College.* New York: The Ronald Press Company, 1951, pp. 187-90.

497. Insights for the Counselor
PRINCIPLES OF MENTAL HYGIENE

1. A sound physical basis makes easier the development of constructive emotional responses. Rest, exercise, sleep, play, sunshine, reasonable diet, with regular physical examinations are helpful. Unhappiness and poor health travel together.

2. Recognition of reality as the state of affairs with which one must deal, changing it perhaps, but not ignoring it or pretending that the facts have altered themselves to fit wishes, is fundamental to mental health. When things can't be changed, effort is better used at making the best of what is, rather than at bewailing what is not.

3. The most wholesome enterprises are those into which the whole self can enter without scruples or conflicts.

4. When conflict arises among desires and standards, a solution often can be found which satisfies all demands. It is worth the effort and intelligence to find a way to keep one's cake and eat it too. . . .

6. Comparison and competition is usually a vicious habit. The worth of any mode of living can be found more happily

apart from the endeavor to surpass some one else. There is all the difference between heaven and hell in the distinction between trying to do something well and trying to beat someone else at it.

7. Each individual can discover through tests, ratings, interviews, and especially through his own past experience, some things he does better than he does other things. Usually greater satisfaction comes from achieving within one's range of ability, than from failing attempts at unattainable goals. Choose, don't drift.

8. A strong urge toward vague yet marvelous greatness may often be recognized as compensation for some sense of lack, inferiority, or deprivation which is emotionally strong although practically of little consequence. A demand for perfection at one point may be the unfortunate result of failure in a different area of life. . . .

10. Some people enjoy the sympathy they obtain so much that they continue to try to deserve this commiseration. Ailments may be exaggerated, "busyness" aggravated, minor troubles talked about until they seem large, because of the satisfaction of having others seem solicitous. Don't enjoy your misery too much.

11. It is frequently possible to become aware of previously unrecognized prejudices or weaknesses in oneself, by noticing the behavior of others which arouses most irritation or most unusual emotional excitement in one's own reactions. Be suspicious of the points to which you continually react with strong emotional feeling. They probably aren't what they seem to you to be.

12. There is a common tendency to attribute major responsibility for one's likes or dislikes to the persons or things liked or disliked, rather than to recognize these feelings as characteristic only of the one who feels them. A person's judgments of others tell more about himself than about the others.

13. Growth comes most easily to the person who can ignore the common impulse to save his face, to show that he has been right from the beginning, to try to make the other

person admit fault or error first. Mistakes are occasions for learning, not for deceit or lamentation.

14. Day dreams about the future are not harmful when they end in carefully planned and executed "next steps." Don't let the engine race, put in the clutch.

15. The emotional maturity, which enables one to face the world alone, sufficient for whatever may happen, to make the best of it, independent of any particular person or type of persons, is probably a result of successfully assuming this self-reliance in many specific situations over a period of years.

16. Some people are handicapped by the false assumption that they have problems and peculiarities which normal persons do not have. Human nature and experience is such that few serious problems arise which have not been faced more or less victoriously by thousands of other persons. Don't be ashamed of your feelings.

17. Disagreeable obligations are made worse by attempts to ignore them, or put them off. Done promptly and with dispatch, as a matter of course, they consume much less energy. The more disagreeable, the more promptly it should be done.

18. Darwin and others have avoided some of the common consequences of prejudice, by looking with especial care for evidence against the theories and practices which they tended most warmly to espouse. A strong emotional preference may be evidence of inadequate rational support. . . .

19. Persistent patterns, such, for example, as a preference for the radical, a dislike of the new, an aversion to some persons others admire, a fondness for actions others eschew, loyalty to unusual causes, etc., always have some reason for existence. Often the real reason is neither obvious nor connected with the objective value of the pattern response. When the behavior drive is thoroughly understood, it may or may not seem advisable to retain it. . . .

21. It is possible definitely to limit the pleasant practice of reliving past glories and achievement. Better mental health seems to come from creating new experiences each new day, rather than from romanticizing the past. Don't rest on your laurels. Tackle the next thing.

22. Love contributes most to those who do not have to gratify their demands for recognition and importance, demands for protection and security, demands for romantic super-human perfection, demands for effusive sympathy, through the love relationship. Be grown up if you would discover true love.

23. Making things, writing, drawing, dancing, creating sometimes for one's own taste alone, are among the commonly accepted aids to satisfactory living. Don't be dependent on others for your tastes. . . .

25. It is usually easier to change a habit by altering the cue or stimulus situation than by conscious effort to build a new response while the old setting persists unchanged. Change in surroundings, conversations, companions, reading, recreations, jobs, may be wholesome if these are useful steps in a plan, not simply evasions and running away. . . .

29. The person who blames his heredity, the way his parents treated him, his teachers, his luck, the social order, the trivial events of the day, his associates, or fate in general for the mishaps of his life, may be surrendering his major hope; that is, intelligent reconstruction of his own responses.

30. Headaches, homesickness, temper outbursts, crying spells and many other disorders may, if they succeed once, continue to come at "convenient" times.

31. The most troublesome fear is the fear of a fear. Getting to the bottom of the uneasy feeling may dispel it.

32. The friend who is most helpful may be critical rather than flattering, abrupt rather than tactful. Objectivity is a better gift than sympathy; insight is more to be desired than advice.

33. Sensitiveness to criticism is not a mark of fine breeding. It is often the result of brooding over slights, self-pity, working up feelings over fancied wrongs, generally mis-applying energy in melancholy pleasures. Success in social relationships is the best stimulant to a healthier attitude.

34. The most satisfactory life attitudes include a place for difficult, tiresome, monotonous, and unheroic activities. Sometimes the satisfaction which carries one through such enter-

prises comes from the remote end which is being sought. Sometimes satisfaction comes from the ever-varying details, from new ways of getting at the job, creative elaborations. Usually success in doing the dull commonplaces of existence is a matter of simple habituation, a result of many refusals to give up and run away.

35. Smug satisfaction with everything as it is, is the lowest level. The neurotic has progressed at least to the point of being restless and unhappy about things as they are. At the highest level is the well-adjusted person, freely using his powers without internal friction, in the creation of a world nearer heart's desire.

> Goodwin Watson and Ralph B. Spence, *Educational Problems for the Psychological Study*. New York: The Macmillan Company, 1930, pp. 331-36. (Selected.)

498. Unaware of Our Own Motives

. . . Sometimes a teacher, for no apparent reason, "simply can't stand that child!" The feeling has real consequences, even though the cause cannot be permitted in consciousness. There are other teachers who "play baby," and whine for sympathy, but who have never realized the childhood origins of this pattern. There are teachers who retreat from any discussion of certain topics highly charged with emotion. They are still carrying out a visceral response painfully developed in scenes they have long since "forgotten." There are even a few teachers who get a tense, greedy, gloating satisfaction, which they themselves hardly recognize, out of giving some child a severe tongue-lashing, or practicing corporal punishment, or successfully outwitting some hapless offender. Flushed face, rapid breath, and hard-clenched jaws betray excitement. However the punishment may be rationalized and projected as well deserved by the child, the real reason for it is in obscure emotional cravings of the teacher.

> Paul A. Witty and Charles E. Skinner, editors, *Mental Hygiene in Modern Education*. New York: Rinehart and Company, Inc., 1939, p. 222. (From chapter by Goodwin Watson.)

499. COUNSELOR: KNOW THYSELF

The day has already passed when the Christian minister
can be considered trained by knowing the Bible (and other
books), the Lord, and the people. He must know himself. The
fact is, he will not properly use the Bible nor know people
adequately if his emotions are not operating correctly. We
tend to see things as we are, not as they are. We react to books
or people in a given manner because we have a given emotional
make-up. Therefore, the emotions need training as well as the
intellect.

For example, it is too well known to need argument that a
person who has a great deal of trouble with sex will find himself getting "all steamed up" in his fierce condemnation of sen-
sual sinners. The reformed drunkard is hardest against drinking, the converted adulterer is suspicious of anyone who is not
ultra-conservative in his social relations with the opposite sex,
and often extreme denunciation of worldliness reveals primarily the preacher's problem with his sly envy of the world.
The preacher may not know why he finds himself emphasizing
one doctrine or virtue above all others, or even avoiding the
discussion of certain doctrines and problems. Much, if not
all, of our thinking is colored by our emotions. Our loves, our
hates, our fears, our longings, our unconscious wishes, are as
important as our memories, our philosophies, our factual
knowledge, and our logic. . . .

Most modern ministers are called upon to do a certain
amount of counseling. This is not new, of course. But poorly or
well, with skill or crudity, the contemporary pastor must discuss with all sorts of people their problems. If the pastor has
an emotional "kink," it is amazing how frequently he will
project it into an interview. In other words, if the minister has
an "illness of the unconscious" he may study all of the books
on psychotherapy and yet be a poor, even harmful, counselor.
The basic preparation for healing is to be a healthy person
yourself.

> R. Lofton Hudson, "The Emotions of the Minister," *Pastoral
> Psychology*, May, 1951, pp. 32 and 36.

500. ALL OF US HAVE PREJUDICES

It is necessary to state again that everyone has prejudices. Each of us has formed judgments on an intuitive basis, and thus gives expression to the fact that feelings of an earlier period in our life are still operating in the present. Prejudice might be against a red dress, stewed pears, or the cello; against Shakespeare, Balzac, or Chaucer. It might be directed against individuals, groups of individuals, nations. Since leaders are concerned with helping young people to overcome their prejudices, they may well begin by recognizing their own. As long as we go around believing that our minds are free and open, and that we never judge anybody or anything without having all the "facts," we will fail to be helpful to our young people. They either will not believe our insistence on freedom from prejudice or, if they do, it will make them far removed from the high, pure level we profess to have attained. Moreover, even if we actually have reached that rare stage where we can meet any situation without preconceived hostility, we still have to overcome the most difficult hurdle: the prejudice against the prejudiced persons. As leaders of groups, we may have developed to a point of emotional maturity where we can be reasonably fair with everybody, but we cannot help becoming emotionally involved when we meet with a person who wears his prejudices on his sleeve.

Rudolph M. Wittenberg, *So You Want To Help People*. New York: Association Press, 1947, p. 163.

501. THE EFFECT OF BIAS

The effect of an interviewer's bias upon the information that he obtains in an interview was effectively illustrated by Rice.[2] In his investigation, two investigators interviewed approximately two thousand homeless applicants at the New York municipal lodging house. The schedule called for a statement of the applicant's own explanation of his destitution and also of the investigator's explanation. Investigator A, who was an ardent believer in prohibition, was informed by the men he interviewed that their downfall was due to drink in more than three times as many instances, relatively, as was B, who was an ardent socialist. Investigator B, however, was given "industrial" explanations of their poverty by half again as many men as gave this type of explanation to A. [2] (Stuart A. Rice, "Contagious Bias in the Interview." *American Journal of Sociology.* 35:420-423, November, 1929.)

> Ruth Strang, *The Role of the Teacher in Personnel Work.* New York: Bureau of Publications, Teachers College, Columbia University, 1946, p. 410.

502.   THE BEAM IN THE COUNSELOR'S EYE

Judge not, that you may not be judged yourselves; for as you judge so you will be judged, and the measure you deal out to others will be dealt out to yourselves.

Why note the splinter in your brother's eye, and fail to see the plank in your own eye? How can you say to your brother, "Let me take out the splinter from your eye," when there lies the plank in your own eye? You hypocrite! take the plank out of your own eye first, and then you will see properly how to take the splinter out of your brother's eye.

> James Moffatt, *The New Testament: A New Translation.* New York: Harper and Brothers, 1922, Matthew 7:1-5.

503.   REACTIVATING LONG-FORGOTTEN DRIVES

Our deepest needs, determined in the first few years of our lives in both pleasant and unpleasant experiences, have gone deep down into our unconscious. We have forgotten about them but they are still with us. Nature helps us forget many of the earlier feelings and impressions, and, perhaps, without this ability to forget things, we couldn't function. But, sometimes, when we work with people, some of these earlier and basic needs are brought to the surface and made conscious. As raised temperature is a sign of infection in our bodies, sudden emotional reaction to people is a sign of reactivation of long-forgotten and often unconscious drives. We usually call this state of affairs "getting emotionally involved." The effect of the basic childhood pattern is often seen in the way in which a leader gets emotionally involved in his relationships with the group.

Rudolph M. Wittenberg, *So You Want To Help People.* New York: Association Press, 1947, pp. 28-29.

504.   SELF-KNOWLEDGE BASIC IN HELPING PEOPLE

Self ignorance has defeated many highly trained, well-informed, and widely experienced social case workers. Frustration day after day in dealing with people because one does not truly know or understand them in spite of extensive information about them, can react in such a way as to deepen personal need and further complicate and confuse the worker in his professional relationships. It is essential for us to realize that we can have much knowledge about people without really knowing people. Self-knowledge is basic in knowing people. Penetrating insight enables us to be penetrating and deepens our understanding of those to whom we relate ourselves. We see the world through our own eyes and what we see is subject to the limitations of our range of vision and to any dis-function in our visual capacity. Likewise, as we relate ourselves to people, the reaction we induce is not solely the reaction of the other individual, but is the product also of what we inject. His reaction is the composite interplay of two personalities, each of whom is the product of his total life experience. An individual's reaction to a given social case worker is not his reaction in general, but his reaction to that social worker as an individual. That is why the same client may be free with one worker and constrained with another, secure with one, and defensive with another, or amenable and hostile by turn in response to the individual worker. Therefore, since the worker determines the client's response, he cannot understand the client unless he understands himself. He must see himself in others, and be aware of his own part in the client's response in order to see the client more nearly as he is. It is essential that he see himself as he is not only for a more adequate understanding of the client, but in order that he may handle his own needs, and inclinations, in short, deal with his tendency to project in such a way as to interfere as little as possible with the client's full and free expression of himself.

Charlotte Towle, "The Mental Hygiene of the Social

Worker," *Report, Illinois Conference on Social Work.* 1935, pp. 209-10.

505. THE IMPORTANCE OF THE TEACHER'S BEING "OBJECTIVE" AND HAVING INSIGHT REGARDING POSSIBLE INVOLVE-MENT OF HER OWN EMOTIONS

. . . it is of prime importance that a teacher should not let her own emotions become so involved in her relations with her pupils that she acts to satisfy her own feelings rather than their needs. A pupil's inattention, stubborness, or insolence naturally arouses irritation and countering aggressive responses in the teacher, and to indulge her own feelings by sarcastic remarks and get other aggressive responses is a release and satisfaction to her. But it usually only adds to the tension. Instead of reacting subjectively in terms of her own feelings, she should maintain an objective attitude of calm, friendly open-mindedness and desire to understand what the trouble really is. Often nothing more is needed to handle a disciplinary situation than easy good nature and refusal to take a bit of excitement seriously. . . .

"Objectivity" means further that the teacher will not be shocked or upset by various types of distressing information which may come to her. For instance, a desperate youngster may blurt out to her a story of some sex episode which seems to her very disgusting. But she must not show that feeling, any more than a physician should show disgust when he sees a sick person. Nor should she go into a dither of sympathy for the unhappy youth, any more than a physician should exhaust his feelings in sympathy for his patient. An important contribution of a good physician is his calm, unemotionalized cheerfulness in the sickroom—the implication he gives that things after all are not so bad as the patient thinks, that many people have been ill before and recovered, that one shouldn't worry, that if the patient will only keep calm and follow the doctor's directions everything will be better before long. Similarly the distraught young person needs calm reassurance, understanding of his problem, and common-sense suggestions as to what he should do. The well-informed teacher will know that various episodes and habits not uncommon among children are not so abnormal as was once supposed. . . . She will not be prudish or moralistic; she may give directly, or in suggested reading, information which will be helpful; she will have helpful suggestions or suggest where they may be obtained (perhaps from physician, nurse, or psychologist).

Very important but little mentioned is the fact that a teacher should be objective and on guard as to possible involvement of her own emotions in connection with her pupil's likes and accomplishments as well as their antagonisms and wrongdoings. Mabel's interest in history . . . was at first greatly encouraged by her teacher in large part because this teacher much enjoyed the girl's admiring attentions. The English teacher encouraged Ruth's ideas of becoming an author and helped her obtain publication of a story in the local paper, because it added to the teacher's own self-feeling and reputation as the one who had discovered and developed this girl's "unusual talents." The mathematics teacher did not like Algernon much better than John did, and encouraged John in part for that reason. In fact, probably most of the time, the average teacher, being human, deals with her pupils' emotional problems on the basis of her own feelings rather than theirs.

> Sidney L. Pressey and Francis P. Robinson, *Psychology and the New Education (Revised)*. New York: Harper and Brothers, 1944, pp. 190-92.

506. SEEK THE CAUSES OF INTENSE EMOTIONAL NEEDS

"I Want You . . . I Need You . . . I Love You"

Do the children in your class like you? They probably do! And you are pleased.

But what about the children who like you too much?

Do you have a youngster who clutches your hand? He holds you so tight that it hurts.

Do you have a youngster you can't shake off? He is your shadow every minute of the time.

Do you have a youngster who doesn't know when to stop? He hangs on you and demands . . . demands . . . demands.

Do you have a youngster who is so dependent on you that he gets upset when you pay attention to others?

In most classrooms there are some children like this. Boys and girls who drain you dry because they want you to give so much. Sometimes you are not pleased with their friendliness. You feel smothered by it . . . even irritated.

"Why Don't They Grow Up?"
"Why don't they leave me alone?"
"Why don't they get some friends their own age?"

You may have an urge to push them off, to make them stand on their own two feet, to *stop* them from being clinging vines.

But wait! These children are in trouble! Adults have been pushing them off and trying to get away from their needs. If you do it too, you may make it more necessary than ever for these children to over-seek love. . . .

Before you make a quick judgment, investigate.

Sometimes when you find out enough about a child's background, you can see the picture: a parent dead or missing or ill . . . a mother working . . . father travelling all the time . . . divorce . . . constant quarrelling . . . many children in the family . . . busy, busy adults.

> James L. Hymes, Jr., *Teacher Listen—the Children Speak . . .*
> Philadelphia: National Mental Health Foundation, 1949,
> pp. 27-28.

507. Leader's Needs or Member's Needs?

It is necessary again to point out that this leader's motivations were on an unconscious level and that it would be false to accuse him of selfishness. As far as he knew he had the best of intentions; he was unselfishly trying to help the boys, to show them a good time, to get to know them individually. This illustration of a leader's unconscious use of the group to meet his own needs, without objective awareness of the group's own needs, can be duplicated in many different cases.

Very often, however, a leader may meet his own needs and those of his group at the same time. There does not necessarily have to be conflict between them. The important thing is for the leader to recognize how frequently the effort to meet his own needs is rationalized as a desire to "help others." In situations where young people and their parents disagree, this danger is sometimes clearly demonstrated. Some leaders habitually take the side of the parents, others the side of the children. It is necessary for a leader to learn to accept a youngster's complaint against his parent, or a parent's complaint against his child, without his own feelings getting involved.

> Rudolph M. Wittenberg, *So You Want To Help People.* New York: Association Press, 1947, pp. 26-27.

508. THE NEEDS OF COUNSELOR AND CLIENT ARE CLOSELY RELATED

There is no need to elaborate the changes which have come in our philosophy of social case work through recognition of this tendency on the part of the social worker to project his own need into the lives of others, thereby defeating his well-intentioned efforts to help individuals realize basic growth. Present day trends which emphasize the identity of the client and which stress the opportunity for self determinism as his inalienable right in any case work situation are based on our growing awareness of how the worker's personal needs have interfered and may continue to obstruct the client's development. In this connection it is well to note that because of the reciprocal nature of the relationship between worker and client that in frustrating the client, the worker inevitably has interfered with his own development. In so far as the worker enables the client to develop, he himself realizes growth. In so far as he projects his own needs, he entangles himself in the other individual, and experiences the frustration, the defeat which is almost inevitable when the client is exposed to the ensnaring experience of being lived in and through by another, rather than left free to live his own life.

> Charlotte Towle, "The Mental Hygiene of the Social Worker," *Report, Illinois Conference on Social Work,* 1935, p. 211.

509. THE COUNSELOR ALSO HAS EMOTIONAL NEEDS

... the idea that "teachers are also people" is stressed to highlight the fact, often overlooked, that teachers have basic personality needs which inevitably affect their activities, purposes, and beliefs. Perhaps in no other single activity of the teacher is this emphasis upon needs more important than in counseling. For counseling is, by definition, interaction between persons. Hence, the needs of each party to the counseling experience may be expected to affect it most noticeably. Sometimes the needs of the faculty member are such that he cannot be an effective counselor; sometimes they permit him to counsel only with regard to certain areas of living; sometimes his adjustments are sufficiently adequate to permit him to work therapeutically with students.

An illustration or two will recall to any faculty member's mind instances where the significance of these considerations is apparent. Mr. M's most obvious need was for security. On the faculty of X college for twenty years, he had been shifted about from one department to another; he still had not developed for himself a valued role in the life of the institution. Currently, he was head of a new struggling department. Mr. M's personal insecurity—his basic feeling of not "belonging"—coupled with the need of his new department for students, combined to make him a poor counselor who registered freshmen for advanced courses in his department; who maneuvered things so that he was assigned a larger number of counselees; who assumed a dictatorial attitude toward students, confidently telling them what courses they should and should not take, what specifically to do about their problems, and so on. In all his counseling, his insecurity manifested itself in dogmatism which alienated more independent students, but which ingrained the dependence of others more deeply still. He filled his classes, but at what a cost in the growth of students!

Miss L was a competent teacher in that she was a well-informed and stimulating lecturer. As a counselor, however, her own needs in the area of adjustment to the opposite sex militated against her effectiveness. At forty-five she was a good-looking spinster whose indifference toward men hid a fierce bitterness over her own experience as a college student. At twenty, just graduated from a midwest university, she had fallen in love with an intern who had an exceptionally promising future as a neural surgeon. They had postponed marriage because he put his training first. She waited for him, meanwhile earning her own Ph. D. degree in biology. Then suddenly he married the office secretary of a brain surgeon with whom he was working. Miss L never fully recovered from being jilted. In her counseling she inevitably felt tense when discussing heterosexual adjustments. Her own protective cynicism distorted the conversation and tended to prevent in students a fine exploration of the feelings, emotions, and ideas related to boy-girl relations.

> Paul J. Brouwer, *Student Personnel Services in General Education.* Washington: American Council on Education, 1949, pp. 27-28.

510.   SELF-UNDERSTANDING CAN BE ACHIEVED

One of the first steps in the improvement of adjustments is the understanding of one's own behavior. It is inconceivable that any person can study the psychological principles of adjustment with real comprehension and fail to gain some degree of greater insight into his own life. From the study of psychology the individual gets a clearer conception of his own motives, of their origins and of the ways in which they are satisfied. An examination of the varieties of adjustive behavior causes each person to detect minor inadequate mechanisms in his own conduct that were often unrecognized before. The study of the development of personality traits may reveal the sources of characteristics that the individual did not understand in himself. A knowledge of the methods of mental hygiene clinics can assure any maladjusted person that he can achieve a solution for his difficulties. It is especially important that all persons be informed of the existence of clinical facilities and persuaded of the importance of consulting them when they or their friends display symptoms of maladjustment.

One common pitfall inherent in the study of the psychology of adjustment must be avoided. A partial knowledge of psychology can serve as a means of self-deceit and self-justification, whereas a full comprehension should result in understanding. Unless sparingly used, the diagnostic terms of psychology can cover more than they reveal. One student protests his inability to achieve because of his "inferiority complex," which he seems to be cherishing proudly. Another points to the assertion that he is the product of his heredity and his environment and so asks how should he be expected to improve! Such statements must be recognized as forms of rationalization rather than reasoning. They cannot be regarded as blameworthy, but merely indicate that in a smattering of psychology the individual has found a new means for justifying inferior types of adjustment. A more serious damage is sometimes done by persons inadequately trained in psychology who go about diagnosing and labeling the maladjustments of their acquaintances. This is, of course, a compensatory mechanism for asserting the person's own superiority, a form of showing off. One who has learned a really psychological attitude will keep his guesses at diagnosis to himself, and will try to help maladjusted individuals to make better responses. Considerable good may be accomplished by inviting a shy, seclusive person to a party and seeing that he has a good time; much harm may be done by summarily labeling him an "introvert." The cure for the errors that inadequate psychological knowledge may cause is not to abandon instruction in this subject, but is to teach more and better psychology.

It is sometimes believed that a study of one's own thought and behavior is morbid. This is not necessarily true. A morbid attitude is a nonadjustive one that leads to phantasy or anxiety. Mental hygiene for one's self should be positive rather than diagnostic. The hygienic consideration of one's own adjustments is a necessary first step, to be followed by a planned course of action. If self-examination is made the basis of a persistent effort to live according to principles of positive mental hygiene, each person can achieve a more satisfying and worthy existence.

Laurance Frederic Shaffer, *The Psychology of Adjustment.* Boston: Houghton Mifflin Company, 1936, pp. 534-35.

511. Need Something to Give

Can one blind man lead another?
Will they not both fall into a pit?

James Moffatt, *The New Testament: A New Translation.* New York: Harper and Brothers, 1922, Luke 6:39.

20.

Self-Guidance and Growth

---

512. WHO ARE YOU?

Who are you who go about to save them that are lost?
Are you saved yourself?
Do you not know that who would save his own life must lose it?
Are you then one of the lost?

Be sure, very sure, that each one of these can teach you as much as, probably more than, you can teach them.

Have you then sat humbly at their feet, and waited on their lips that they should be the first to speak—and been reverent before these children—whom you so little understand?

Have you dropped into the bottomless pit from between yourself and them all hallucination of superiority, all flatulence of knowledge, every shred of abhorrence and loathing?

Is it equal, is it free as the wind between you?

Could you be happy receiving favors from one of the most despised of these?

Could you yourself be one of the lost?

Arise, then, and become a savior.

> Edward Carpenter, "Who Are You?" *Towards Democracy.*
> London: George Allen and Unwin Ltd., 1921, p. 180. (First published, 1883.)

513. TAKE THE DIMNESS OF MY SOUL AWAY

> I ask no dream, no prophet ecstacies,
> No sudden rending of the veil of clay,
> No angel visitant, no opening skies;
> But take the dimness of my soul away.

George Croly (1854) and Frederic C. Atkinson (1870). From the hymn, "Spirit of God, Descend upon My Heart."

514. Man Has Great Capacity for Self-Help

The more one works with people in trouble, the greater his confidence in human kind and his respect for human beings becomes. Seeing what they accomplish in overcoming their difficulties brings an ever deepening faith in their capacity for self-help. Let a man be free to be himself and his success is almost assured. Aid him, if he asks it, to a realization of the adjustment which he must make, interpreting to him, if need be, those with whom he is associated. Quicken his desires, if quickening they require, or show him that from which he can derive stability and inspiration. Encourage him to make his own plans, and to do his own thinking, and through it all strive to see him as he is and to understand and appreciate him.

This is the point of view from which social case workers approach the difficulties of the men and the women who come to them for help. It is a point of view to be sought by every person who is so placed that he may influence other people. It is as applicable in the daily relationships of life as it is in the most complicated forms of trouble. It is a philosophy that any one may apply to the making of his own adjustments.

To him who thus strives to understand his fellows and their problems life begins to reveal itself in deepening richness and wonder. The old fears, the old prejudices disappear leaving him free to perceive the truth, the truth whose facets are myriad so that one may gaze upon it through eternity and not make an ending. Out of life's very difficulties, out of our own frailty comes renewed appreciation of all that living can mean and the privilege that is ours in its practice. Who does not thrill at the miracle of being alive and of holding comradeship with that most marvelous of creatures, his fellow man! Transcending the vicissitudes of experience is the challenge of the greatest of the arts.

Karl de Schweinitz, *The Art of Helping People Out of Trouble*. Boston: Houghton Mifflin Company, 1924, pp. 229-31.

515. RESOURCES WITHIN EACH MAN ARE GREAT

. . . The physician assumes that the curative powers are within the body itself, and that his function is that of providing them a chance to work. In medical care, he does use remedies to control the fever, but he turns his attention chiefly toward providing for the body the maximum chance to eliminate the infection and work its own cure; and in surgery, after guarding against the danger of infection, he closes the wound and trusts the body to do its own healing. Nor does this involve an irreverent or irreligious attitude. He is in the presence of curative powers beyond his understanding and in the presence of the mystery of healing before which he may bow in reverence. If he is a religious man he may subscribe definitely to the motto: "The physician furnishes the conditions; God works the cure," even though he recognizes that these God-given possibilities are resident within the body. So also the counselor believes that the person who comes to him has available the curative powers for the restoration of his personality, and it is his business to furnish the conditions through his counseling under which these have a chance to operate. He believes that the individual is capable of a life different from that which he has lived; and he tries to help him to utilize his available resources. In the capacity of the individual to remake his life through the discovery and utilization of these resources, he recognizes the presence of a mystery as wonderful as that of the curative powers of the body. He too may say that of the Most High comes this healing.

An individual's religion, when viewed from this dynamic functional approach, represents the inclusive and supreme basis of his life. Every individual, however mature, is dependent in countless ways upon nature and upon human beings. His religious faith is his interpretation of that dependence. Every individual has to find a basis for security if he is to face the morrow without devastating dread. Many factors contribute to his security or its lack. His religious faith represents the grounds for his confidence in life. Every individual whose existence has meaning has purposes and values around which his life is organized and which give direction and inspiration to his endeavors. His religious faith represents the supreme goal of his life. Every individual who experiences the fullness of life knows what it is to love and be loved. His religious faith is his conviction that God is love. The goal of all counseling is to help an individual find an adequate personal religion and the counseling process is not complete until this end has been attained.

> Harrison Sacket Elliott and Grace Loucks Elliott, *Solving Personal Problems.* New York: Henry Holt and Company, Inc., 1936, pp. 303-4. By permission of the publishers.

516. HUMAN NATURE IS PLASTIC

Human beings by original nature seem to be neither good nor bad, responsible nor irresponsible, but they have in their original equipment the capacities for developing either or both kinds of characteristics. Whatever habits and attitudes they have, have been learned and relearned in their experience. The same human equipment may develop suspicion, distrust, and ruthless ways of protecting itself and robbing others; or confidence, good will, respect for the rights of others and various forms of co-operative action. The basis for the most significant present-day work with individuals as well as for the newer methods in education is a recognition of the possibilities of human nature.

> *Ibid.,* pp. 287-88.

517. HUMAN NATURE SUBJECT TO CHANGE

. . . As we are progressively emancipated from the older beliefs about human nature as fixed and unchangeable, as innately wicked, sinful, and antisocial, and begin to realize that the process of socialization creates the warped, twisted, and distorted individuals, and that this process of personality development can and will be changed, then it would appear that the present pessimism, and in some cases defeatism, will be replaced by a broader and more balanced viewpoint with a longer time perspective.

> Lawrence K. Frank, "Freud's Influence on Western Thinking and Culture," *American Journal of Orthopsychiatry,* Vol. 10, 1940, pp. 881-82.

518. A Prayer For Bill

Please, God,
  Give me wisdom and judgment and understanding;
  Give me knowledge of when to help,
      and when to leave him alone
      to solve his own problems.
Keep me
  From overemphasizing activity
  And underemphasizing silence and solitude.
Help me
  To awaken in him
      a wholesome curiosity about this world;
  To be sensitive to and interested in others.
Help him
  To meet his disappointments and failures;
  To accept his successes.
Help him
  To be glad and anxious
      to do a little more than his share;
  To be willing at times
      to be part of the chorus
      and not always the center of the stage.
Help him
  To know he is loved and needed
      for the little things he does;
  To be self-reliant
      but to know when to ask for help.
Help him
  To grow and to stand on his own two feet
  And to be happy about it.

> Theodora Jane Van De Mark, "A Prayer for Bill," *Childhood Education*, Vol. 25, January, 1949, p. 209.

519. To My Teacher

> Put learning in my way, then stand aside
> To guide my footsteps.
> But do not push—
> My steps are small because my legs are short
> And there is much to see that you have seen
> But see no more—too bad!

When I have traveled all the road through books
Up hill and down,
My head will overflow with so much knowing.
Don't make me go too fast to see and hear
This lovely world.
Let joy keep pace with growing.

Audrey M. Linaberry, "To My Teacher," *Childhood Education*, Vol. 25, May, 1949, p. 416.

520. LEADER HAS GOALS AND STANDARDS

Above all, a leader should have goals, standards, ideals which are tested and which function in her own life. This does not assume dogmatic insistence upon conformity by others to those ideals; but nothing is more important in the deflated, value-less, rudderless stage of much of the present social milieu than that there should be offered to young people access to that which the generation ahead of them lives by in the realm of motive and goal. Related to this, the leader should be able to live by and act according to her convictions while she gives to the led the opportunity to act differently.

Grace L. Elliott, "The Importance of Maturity and a Social Philosophy for Group Leaders and Supervisors," *Proceedings of the National Conference of Social Work*. Chicago: The University of Chicago Press, 1937, p. 271.

521. STRENGTH FOR THE COUNSELOR

Dear Lord and Father of Mankind,
Forgive our feverish ways;
Re-clothe us in our rightful mind;
In purer lives Thy service find,
In deeper reverence, praise.

Drop Thy still dews of quietness
Till all our strivings cease;
Take from our souls the strain and stress,
And let our ordered lives confess
The beauty of Thy peace.

John G. Whittier and Frederick C. Maker. From the hymn, "Dear Lord and Father of Mankind." (1887.)

522. A Mental Hygiene Creed

1. I shall adapt to life, immediately, completely and gracefully.

2. I shall exercise, rest, work and play—every day.

3. I shall avoid undue fatigue.

4. I will discount harmful emotional urges, avoid emotional orgies, keep away from emotionally undisciplined people.

5. The five useless sentiments are: self-pity, suspicion, envy, jealousy, and revenge. The three dependable sentiments are: loyalty, courage, and kindness.

6. I shall work at a worthwhile job.

7. I face facts, discount my likes and dislikes, and cultivate an objective point of view.

8. I make clear-cut decisions and abide by them. I ask for counsel, consider it without argument, but let *no one* make up my mind for me.

9. I form good habits of living, acting, thinking, speaking and feeling.

10. I *choose* to see the good aspects and meanings of life. I do not deny that unfortunate facts exist and I do not overlook them, but having seen them *I choose to look for the good aspects.*

11. Knowing myself, I accept my liabilities and cultivate my assets.

12. I do not expect to get what I want in this world, and I cannot be sure that I shall in the next. I will not kick against the pricks of life. I expect trouble and have accepted inevitable difficulty, that I may be free to accept opportunity unhandicapped by the sense of the difficult.

13. Fear, anxiety and worry cannot hurt me. They threaten to destroy, but they possess no weapons other than the ones I give them. Even though afraid, anxious and worried, I shall say "I'll get by," and continue with my normal activities, knowing that fear is the normal stimulus to courage. When the reality of courage walks with me fear is only a shadow.

14. I believe that I am one of God's Disciples; it is intended that my life have significance. God's hand is on my shoulder.

15. I am going to laugh *more* every day. . . .

William Terhune, "The Doctor's Wife," *The Connecticut State Medical Journal,* July, 1947.

523.   RELIGIOUS FAITH

Finally, the mature leader should have achieved for herself a dynamic religious faith. This faith may not and probably will not be expressed in orthodox beliefs or statements. Because of the pressure upon her spirit from the needs of others, as well as from her becoming aware of her own life, she cannot stand alone and without resources. These resources cannot be the creation of her subjective imagination or will. She needs to see herself and others integrally a part of whatever process is universal. She must be able to accept the limitations as well as the resources that are hers, not only as a part of the human race but as a part of the totality of life which is the universe. With that grounding for her faith, she can the more effectively work for the accomplishment of that which she may not live to see.

> Grace L. Elliott, "The Importance of Maturity and a Social Philosophy for Group Leaders and Supervisors," *Proceedings of the National Conference of Social Work.* Chicago: The University of Chicago Press, 1937, p. 275.

524.   AN INTEGRATING FAITH NEEDED FOR TODAY

Living in a world of motion, flux, and change, we must have an integrating faith within and without which will hold us together against split personalities as well as against split atoms. We need a sense of "belonging" to dispel the haunting loneliness which one sometimes feels in a crowd as well as amidst the awful, impersonal majesty of nature.

An adequate faith for today will have to release our full power for personal and social growth in co-operation with the laws of the universe which make that life possible. Furthermore, a man must be related to whatever eternal values there may be, and moved to action on their behalf. All this must be worthy of subjection to the tests of reason and modern knowledge. Religious faith can make contributions beyond those of science, but certainly science and religion must not be in direct conflict, or religion in the end will suffer.

Charles C. Noble, *Faith for the Future.* New York: Association Press, 1950, p. 114.

525.   THE GOOD LIFE

It is difficult, indeed, for one who has followed children and has seen at first hand the vitality, energy, and strength of the young human being to believe that their existence is without purpose and that humans are tiny bits of matter in a universe that is without meaning and significance. Through and through, the developmental process seems to be creative; the problems and situations which are old and hackneyed to the adult are new and interesting to the child. And the social organizations of adolescents, even though they are like those of earlier generations, are new creations to those who form them. Neither the person nor society is quite the same at successive moments—life goes on even while we think about it.

In the enchantment and enrichment of personality and the mutual creation of a good life for all is found the measure of a full life. Some make money a symbol of a good life; some make power, some material goods, some social position. As more is learned about personality, the primary goal becomes the desirability of using the capacities of persons to the fullest degree, and of searching out the talents which all possess and giving them opportunities to manifest themselves. Society proceeds most rapidly when it utilizes its human resources most fully and gives each member some opportunity for self-realization through the essentially creative process of broadening his own life space and finding in interests and activities the opportunities for development and appreciation. Wasted ability is forever lost, both for the person and for society. Emphasis, then, goes to living a full life, not so much in terms of status and rewards as in terms of contribution, development, and personality enhancement. Thus, we seek a society in which there will not only be a concept of the dignity of the human being, but also the opportunity for the person to manifest that dignity.

Somewhere in the area of symbolic manipulation and social reinforcement that separates man from the animal there is generated what has been called the "divine discontent" that makes of man what he is and is constantly becoming. In the release of energy for the achievement of remote goals, man becomes a creator. Interwoven and reinforcing stimulation sets the atmosphere in which humans strive for the heights. What matter if from time to time they pass through the depths?

> John E. Anderson, *The Psychology of Development and Personal Adjustment.* New York: Henry Holt and Company, Inc., 1949, p. 675. By permission of the publishers.

526. "Physician: Heal Thyself!"

. . . A teacher who is worried over poor health, loneliness, criticism by superiors, jealousy of friends, possible loss of his job, insufficient savings for emergencies and retirement, or other deprivations, is not free to keep his mind on his teaching. Fear is always a paralyzing influence. Chronic hunger for some basic personality satisfaction introduces a persisting bias into the way in which the teacher responds to people and to books. The teacher who tries to escape from himself or to justify his existence by overwork is not in a position to help children toward happy adjustments. "Physician, heal thyself!" is hard doctrine to practice, but it is the essence of mental hygiene.

To some extent the teacher can control his own life. He can provide the recreation, diet, and sleep which makes for higher levels of physical vitality. He can refuse to let his life be badgered into bits by the pressure of an excessive number of assumed obligations. He can go out of his way to make friends, inside and outside the teaching profession. He can keep the spirit of adventure alive in his work and avoid falling into a rut. He can cultivate some of the creative arts, as consumer and also as producer. He can throw his efforts into some causes and institutions which seem to him of greater significance than his own life, and so, in Scriptural terms, may lose his life to find it.

> Paul A. Witty and Charles E. Skinner, editors, *Mental Hygiene in Modern Education.* New York: Rinehart and Company, Inc., 1939, pp. 522-23. (From chapter by Goodwin Watson.)

527. The Counselor Is the Key

. . . The central element in pastoral counseling, as in all pastoral care, is the relationship that the pastor creates with his people. His ministry stands or falls on this. Through his relationship the pastor may give a great deal that is vital to the growth, welfare and salvation of persons. He may give an understanding and acceptance of the painful and disturbing aspects of life as well as the positive, creative side. He may give reality to a reverence for persons, a faith in persons and a love toward persons. In this way, he not only ministers in the name of God: he brings God to men in a real way. He makes the spirit of Christ a living resource for others. He does not try to become God; he rather tries to create conditions through which the grace of God can operate to produce healing and growth. His is a humble service for which mankind today stands in great need.

> Carroll A. Wise, *Pastoral Counseling, Its Theory and Practice*. New York: Harper and Brothers, 1951, p. 221.

528. A ROCK IN A WEARY LAND

One of the greatest contributions that can be made by the counselor to any individual is his own faith that life is worth the price one pays for it. In these days of an "Eat, drink, and be merry" philosophy and of opportunist action, people are sick for want of a reason for living that will call for the degree of heroism which is an intrinsic part of human equipment. To fail to be summoned into action is to miss the meaning of life. The old antithesis which held that one to be "unselfish" must give up his chance to cultivate his own "selfish" interest, developed human beings so meager in their own personalities that they were of little value to others. Youth in a rapidly changing world needs more than anything else interests about which someone has conviction, as a point around which to orient their questions. To be without convictions is to be useless to another struggling for his own. This does not mean imposition of one's convictions upon another, but rather the maturity of having thought far enough to have arrived at tentative conclusions from which to go on to the next step of having finished experiments sufficiently to have a new hypothesis for the next test.

Because the help one person gives another is likely to be more intangible than tangible, the honesty, spontaneity, and freedom of the counselor's life are likely to be much more important than his words. In a time of such tension and restlessness, of such fear and confusion, and of such lack of any aim or goal in life as the present represents, it is of immeasurable help to the baffled individual to sit down beside another who has faced what needs to be faced, who has found life good, and who has achieved within himself "constructive composure" and the "power to maintain uniformity and continuity of feeling."

> Harrison Sacket Elliott and Grace Loucks Elliott, *Solving Personal Problems*. New York: Henry Holt and Company, Inc., 1936, p. 211-12. By permission of the publishers.

529. Some Seeds Fall on Good Soil

. . . A sower went out to sow, and as he sowed some seeds fell on the road and the birds came and ate them up. Some other seeds fell on stony soil, where they had not much earth, and shot up at once because they had no depth of soil; but when the sun rose they were scorched and withered away, because they had no root. Some other seeds fell among thorns, and the thorns sprang up and choked them. Some other seeds fell on good soil and bore a crop, some a hundredfold, some sixty, and some thirtyfold.

> James Moffatt, *The New Testament: A New Translation.* New York: Harper and Brothers, 1922, Matthew 13:4-8.

530. Love You *Must* Have

I may speak with the tongues of men and of angels,
   but if I have no love,
     I am a noisy gong or a clanging cymbal;
I may prophesy, fathom all mysteries and secret lore,
I may have such absolute faith that I can move hills from their place,
   but if I have no love,
     I count for nothing;
I may distribute all I possess in charity,
I may give up my body to be burnt,
   but if I have no love,
     I make nothing of it.

Love is very patient, very kind. Love knows no jealousy; love makes no parade, gives itself no airs, is never rude, never selfish, never irritated, *never resentful;* love is never glad when others go wrong, love is gladdened by goodness, always slow to expose, always eager to believe the best, always hopeful, always patient. Love never disappears. As for prophesying, it will be superseded; as for "tongues," they will cease; as for knowledge, it will be superseded. For we only know bit by bit, and we only prophesy bit by bit; but when the perfect comes, the imperfect will be superseded. When I was a child, I talked like a child, I thought like a child, I argued like a child; now that I am a man, I am done with childish ways.

At present we only see the baffling reflections in a mirror, but then it will be face to face; at present I am learning bit by bit, but then I shall understand, as all along I have myself been understood.

Thus "faith and hope and love last on, these three," but the greatest of all is love.

James Moffatt, *The New Testament: A New Translation.* New York: Harper and Brothers, 1922, I Corinthians 13:1-13.

531. A FRIEND OF MAN

Let me live in my house by the side of the road—
    It's here the race of men go by.
They are good, they are bad, they are weak, they are strong,
    Wise, foolish—so am I;
Then why should I sit in the scorner's seat,
    Or hurl the cynic's ban?
Let me live in my house by the side of the road
    And be a friend to man.

Sam Walter Foss, "The House by the Side of the Road," from *Dreams in Homespun,* New York: Lothrop, Lee, and Shepard Co., Inc.

BIBLIOGRAPHY

CONTENT INDEX

AUTHORS INDEX

Bibliography

BOOKS

American Camping Association. *Marks of Good Camping*. New York: Association Press, 1950 (revised).

American Council on Education. *Helping Teachers Understand Children*. Washington, D. C.: American Council on Education, 1945.

————. *The Student Personnel Point of View*, Series 1, No. 3. Washington, D. C.: American Council on Education, 1937.

Anderson, John E. *The Psychology of Development and Personal Adjustment*. New York: Henry Holt and Co., Inc., 1949.

Averill, Lawrence A. *Mental Hygiene for the Classroom Teacher*. New York: Pitman Publishing Corporation, 1939.

Baruch, Dorothy W. *New Ways in Discipline*. New York: McGraw-Hill Book Co., Inc. (Whittlesey House), 1949.

Bell, Howard M. *Youth Tell Their Story*. Washington, D. C.: American Council on Education, 1938.

Bell, Hugh M. "Counseling and Guidance," *The American College*, edited by P. F. Valentine. New York: Philosophical Library, 1949.

Blumenthal, Louis H. *Group Work in Camping*. New York: Association Press, 1937.

Brisley, Mary S., and Borton, Viennie. *Social Case Work*. New York: National Board of Y.W.C.A.'s, 1934.

Britt, Stuart H. *Social Psychology of Modern Life*. New York: Rinehart and Co., Inc., 1949 (revised).

Brouwer, Paul J. *Student Personnel Services in General Education*. Washington, D. C.: American Council on Education, 1949.

Carpenter, Edward. *Toward Democracy*. London: George Allen and Unwin, Ltd., 1921. (Ruskin House. First published 1883.)

Carroll, Herbert A. *Mental Hygiene*. New York: Prentice-Hall, Inc., 1947.

623

Cassidy, Rosalind, and Kozman, Hilda C. *Counseling Girls in a Changing Society*. New York: McGraw-Hill Book Co., Inc., 1947.

Cole, Lawrence E., and Bruce, William F. *Educational Psychology*. New York: World Book Co., 1950.

Coleman, James C. *Abnormal Psychology and Modern Life*. Chicago: Scott, Foresman and Co., 1950.

Counseling Young Adults (a symposium). New York: Association Press, 1947.

Coyle, Grace L. *Group Work with American Youth*. New York: Harper and Bros., 1948.

Cruze, Wendell W. *Educational Psychology*. New York: The Ronald Press Co., 1942.

Darley, John G. *The Interview in Counseling*. Washington, D. C.: U. S. Department of Labor, 1940.

————. *Testing and Counseling in the High-School Guidance Program*. Chicago: Science Research Associates, 1943.

de Schweinitz, Karl. *The Art of Helping People Out of Trouble*. Boston: Houghton Mifflin Co., 1924.

Dewey, John. *Democracy and Education*. New York: The Macmillan Co., 1920.

————. *Experience and Education*. New York: The Macmillan Co., 1938.

Dimock, Hedley S., and Statten, Taylor. *Talks to Counselors*, 2nd ed. New York: Association Press, 1946.

Dimock, Hedley S., and Trecker, Harleigh B. *The Supervision of Group Work and Recreation*. New York: Association Press, 1949.

Donahue, Wilma T., Coombs, Clyde H., and Travers, Robert M. W., eds. *The Measurement of Student Adjustment and Achievement*. Ann Arbor: University of Michigan Press, 1949.

Douglass, Harl R., ed. *Education for Life Adjustment*. New York: The Ronald Press Co., 1950.

Edwards, Richard H. *The Place of Persons in the Educational Process*. Chambersburg, Pa.: The Kerr Printing Co., 1933.

Eliot, George. "Stradivari," *Poems*. New York: P. F. Collier and Son, n.d.

Elliott, Grace Loucks. "The Importance of Maturity and a Social Philosophy for Group Leaders and Supervisors," *Proceedings of National Conference of Social Work*. Chicago: University of Chicago Press, 1937.

Elliott, Harrison Sacket, and Elliott, Grace Loucks. *Solving Personal Problems*. New York: Henry Holt and Co., Inc., 1936.

Erickson, Clifford E., ed. *A Basic Text for Guidance Workers.* New York: Prentice-Hall, Inc., 1947.

Finch, F. H., and Yowell, Velma. "Guidance for the Exceptional Child," *The Education of Exceptional Children.* Forty-ninth Yearbook of the National Society for the Study of Education, Part II. Chicago: University of Chicago Press, 1950.

Froelich, Clifford P. *Guidance Services in Smaller Schools.* New York: McGraw-Hill Book Co., Inc., 1950.

Garrett, Annette. *Counseling Methods for Personnel Workers.* New York: Family Service Association of America, 1945.

————. *Interviewing—Its Principles and Methods.* New York: Family Service Association of America, 1942.

Gates, Arthur I., Jersild, Arthur T., McConnell, T. R., and Challman, Robert C. *Educational Psychology.* New York: The Macmillan Co., 1942.

Goetting, M. L. *Teaching in the Secondary School.* New York: Prentice-Hall, Inc., 1942.

Griffin, J. D. M., Laycock, S. R., and Line, W. *Mental Hygiene.* New York: American Book Co., 1940. (Toronto: W. J. Gage and Co., Ltd.)

Hagedorn, Hermann. *The Bomb That Fell on America.* New York: Association Press, 1950 (revised).

Hahn, Milton E., and MacLean, Malcolm S. *General Clinical Counseling.* New York: McGraw-Hill Book Co., Inc., 1950.

Hamrin, Shirley A., and Paulson, Blanche B. *Counseling Adolescents.* Chicago: Science Research Associates, 1950.

Hendry, Charles E., ed. *A Decade of Group Work.* New York: Association Press, 1948.

Hilgard, Ernest R., and Russell, David H. "Motivation in School Learning," *Learning and Instruction.* Forty-ninth Yearbook of the National Society for the Study of Education, Part I. Chicago: University of Chicago Press, 1950.

Hobson, C. V., ed. *Mental Hygiene in the Classroom.* Joint Committee on Health Problems in Education of the National Education Association and the American Medical Association, 1939.

Hulslander, Stewart C. *Referring Counselees to Specialists.* Boston: Research Publishing Co., Inc., 1950.

Hymes, James L., Jr. *Teacher Listen—The Children Speak.* Philadelphia: National Mental Health Foundation, 1949.

Jones, Arthur J. *Principles of Guidance,* 3rd ed. New York: McGraw-Hill Book Co., Inc., 1945.

————, and Hand, Harold C. "Guidance and Purposive Living,"

Guidance in Educational Institutions. Thirty-seventh Yearbook of the National Society for the Study of Education, Part I. Bloomington, Ill.: Public School Publishing Co., 1938.

Kelley, Janet A. *College Life and the Mores*. New York: Bureau of Publications, Teachers College, Columbia University, 1949.

Kopas, J. S. "Six Aspects of Guidance," *A Primer of Guidance Through Group Work*. New York: Association Press, 1940.

Landis, Paul H. *Adolescence and Youth*. New York: McGraw-Hill Book Co., Inc., 1947.

Lefever, D. Welty, Turrell, Archie M., and Weitzel, Henry I. *Principles and Techniques of Guidance*. New York: The Ronald Press Co., 1941.

Lindesmith, Alfred R., and Strauss, Anselm L. *Social Psychology*. New York: The Dryden Press, Inc., 1949.

Lloyd-Jones, Esther, and Fedder, Ruth. *Coming of Age*. New York: McGraw-Hill Book Co., Inc. (Whittlesey House), 1941.

Mathewson, Robert H. *Guidance Policy and Practice*. New York: Harper and Bros., 1949.

Menninger, William C. *Psychiatry*. Ithaca: Cornell University Press, 1948.

Mohr, George J. "The Camp and the Individual Camper," *Character Education in the Summer Camp III*. New York: Association Press, 1935.

Munroe, Ruth L. *Teaching the Individual*. New York: Columbia University Press, 1942.

Murphy, Gardner. *A Briefer General Psychology*. New York: Harper and Bros., 1935.

Mursell, James L. *Educational Psychology*. New York: W. W. Norton and Co., Inc., 1939.

National Education Association. *Fit to Teach*. Ninth Yearbook of the Department of Classroom Teachers. Washington, D. C.: National Education Association, 1938.

New Testament. A New Translation by James Moffatt. New York: Harper and Bros., 1922.

Noble, Charles C. *Faith for the Future*. New York: Association Press, 1950.

Norris, K. E. "Introduction," *A Primer of Guidance Through Group Work*. New York: Association Press, 1940.

Olson, Willard C. "General Methods—Case Study," *The Scientific Movement in Education*. Thirty-seventh Yearbook of the National Society for the Study of Education, Part II. Chicago: University of Chicago Press, 1938.

Osborne, Ernest. *Individual Adjustment Through Group Activity*, Child Welfare Pamphlet No. 65. Iowa City: State University of Iowa, 1938.

Outler, Albert C. *A Christian Context for Counseling*. New Haven, Conn.: Edward W. Hazen Foundation, 1945.

Pennington, L. A., and Berg, Irwin A., eds. *An Introduction to Clinical Psychology*. New York: The Ronald Press Co., 1948.

Prescott, Daniel A. *Emotion and the Educative Process*. Washington, D. C.: American Council on Education, 1938.

Pressey, Sidney L., and Robinson, Francis P. *Psychology and the New Education*. New York: Harper and Bros., 1944 (revised).

Remmers, H. H., and Hackett, C. G. *Let's Listen to Youth*. Chicago: Science Research Associates, 1950.

Rivlin, Harry N. *Educating for Adjustment*. New York: Appleton-Century-Crofts, Inc., 1936.

Rogers, Carl R. *Client-Centered Therapy*. Boston: Houghton Mifflin Co., 1951.

————. *Counseling and Psychotherapy*. Boston: Houghton Mifflin Co., 1942.

————. *Dealing with Social Tensions*. Danville, Ill.: The Interstate Printers and Publishers, 1948.

Rothney, John W. M., and Roens, Bert A. *Counseling the Individual Student*. New York: William Sloane Associates, Inc., 1949.

————. *Guidance of American Youth*. Cambridge, Mass.: Harvard University Press, 1950.

Sargent, S. Stansfeld. *Social Psychology*. New York: The Ronald Press Co., 1950.

Senn, Milton J. E., ed. *The Healthy Personality*. New York: Josiah Macy, Jr., Foundation, 1950.

Shaffer, Laurence Frederic. *The Psychology of Adjustment*. Boston: Houghton Mifflin Co., 1936.

Shank, Donald J., ed. *The Teacher as Counselor*, Series 6, No. 10. Washington, D. C.: The American Council on Education, October, 1948.

Sherif, Muzafer. *An Outline of Social Psychology*. New York: Harper and Bros., 1948.

Sherman, Mandel. "Contributions to Education of Scientific Knowledge in Mental Hygiene," *The Scientific Movement in Education*. Thirty-seventh Yearbook of the National Society for the Study of Education, Part II. Chicago: University of Chicago Press, 1938.

Shore, Maurice J., *et al. Twentieth Century Mental Hygiene.* New York: Social Sciences Publishers, 1950.

Strang, Ruth. *Counseling Technics in College and Secondary School.* New York: Harper and Bros., 1949 (revised).

————. *The Role of the Teacher in Personnel Work.* New York: Bureau of Publications, Teachers College, Columbia University, 1946 (revised).

Thorpe, Louis P. *Psychological Foundations of Personality.* New York: McGraw-Hill Book Co., Inc., 1938.

Towle, Charlotte. "The Mental Hygiene of the Social Worker," *Report of Illinois Conference on Social Welfare.* Chicago: State of Illinois, 1935.

Traxler, Arthur E. *Techniques of Guidance.* New York: Harper and Bros., 1945.

Trecker, Harleigh B. *Social Group Work—Principles and Practices.* New York: The Woman's Press, 1948.

Tyler, Leona E. *The Psychology of Human Differences.* New York: Appleton-Century-Crofts, Inc., 1947.

Wallin, J. E. Wallace. *Minor Mental Maladjustments in Normal People.* Durham, N. C.: Duke University Press, 1939.

————. *Personality Maladjustments and Mental Hygiene.* New York: McGraw-Hill Book Co., Inc., 1949 (revised).

Warner, W. L., Havighurst, R. J., and Loeb, Martin B. *Who Shall Be Educated?* New York: Harper and Bros., 1944.

Warters, Jane. *High School Personnel Work Today.* New York: McGraw-Hill Book Co., Inc., 1946.

Watson, Goodwin, and Spence, Ralph B. *Educational Problems for Psychological Study.* New York: The Macmillan Co., 1930.

Williamson, E. G. *How to Counsel Students.* New York: McGraw-Hill Book Co., Inc., 1939.

————, ed. *Trends in Student Personnel Work.* Minneapolis: University of Minnesota Press, 1949.

————, and Foley, J. D. *Counseling and Discipline.* New York: McGraw-Hill Book Co., Inc., 1949.

Wilson, Gertrude. "Work with Individuals in Social Group Work," *Social Work in the Current Scene.* New York: Columbia University Press, 1950.

————, and Ryland, Gladys. *Social Group Work Practice.* Boston: Houghton Mifflin Co., 1949.

Wise, Carroll A. *Pastoral Counseling: Its Theory and Practice.* New York: Harper and Bros., 1951.

Wittenberg, Rudolph M. *So You Want to Help People*. New York: Association Press, 1947.

Witty, Paul A., and Skinner, Charles E., eds. *Mental Hygiene in Modern Education*. New York: Rinehart and Co., Inc., 1939.

Wood, Ben D., and Haefner, Ralph. *Measuring and Guiding Individual Growth*. New York: Silver Burdett Co., 1948.

Woodworth, Robert S. *Psychology*, 4th ed. New York: Henry Holt and Co., Inc., 1940.

————, and Marquis, Donald G. *Psychology*, 5th ed. New York: Henry Holt and Co., Inc., 1947.

Wrenn, C. Gilbert. *Student Personnel Work in College*. New York: The Ronald Press Co., 1951.

————, and Dugan, Willis E. *Guidance Procedures in High School*. Minneapolis: University of Minnesota Press, 1950.

Wright, Barbara H. *Practical Handbook for Group Guidance*. Chicago: Science Research Associates, 1948.

Articles

Arsenian, Seth. "Improvement in the Counseling Interview," *Counseling*, Vol. 8, No. 2, February, 1950.

Averill, Lawrence A. "Case Studies in the Schools," *Mental Hygiene*, Vol. 25, January, 1941.

Baker, Helen Cody. "No Bad Boys? The Court Helps Prove It," *Chicago Daily News*, date unestablished.

Baxter, Edna D. "What Is Guidance?" *Childhood Education*, Vol. 25, No. 5, January, 1949.

Berdie, Ralph F. "Counseling: An Educational Technique," *Journal of Educational and Psychological Measurement*, 9, 1949.

Brunner, Edmund de S. "The Social Scene and Personal Adjustment," *Occupations*, April, 1939.

Busch, Henry M. "Group Work in Camping," *The Camping Magazine*, October, 1939.

Butler, John M., and Seeman, Julius. "Client-Centered Therapy and the Field of Guidance," *Education*, April, 1950.

Crampton, C. Ward, and Partridge, E. DeAlton. "Social Adjustments Associated with Individual Differences Among Adolescent Boys," *Journal of Educational Sociology*, Vol. 12, No. 2, October, 1938.

Davis, Frank G. "Pupil Personnel Service in the Public Schools," *Education*, April, 1950.

Frank, Lawrence K. "Freud's Influence on Western Thinking and

Culture," *The American Journal of Orthopsychiatry*, Vol. 10, October, 1940.

————. "Mental Health in Schools," *Education*, Vol. 66, No. 9, May, 1946.

————. "Society as the Patient," *The American Journal of Sociology*, Vol. 42, November, 1936.

Fuhrer, John W. "The Administrator and the Guidance Program," George Williams College *Bulletin*, January 15, 1947.

Ginsburg, Sol W. "Mental Health and Social Issues of Our Times," *The American Journal of Orthopsychiatry*, Vol. 20, No. 2, April, 1950.

Gioseffi, William. "The Relationship of Culture to the Principles of Social Casework," *Social Casework*, Vol. 32, No. 5, May, 1951.

Hall, L. K. "Emerging Patterns of Counseling in the Y.M.C.A. in Relation to Group Work," *Counseling*, July, 1949.

Harris, Sydney J. "Freud Is Father of Our Age," from column "Strictly Personal," *Chicago Daily News*, May 25, 1951.

Healy, William, Bronner, Augusta F., and Shimberg, Myra E. "The Close of Another Chapter in Criminology," *Mental Hygiene*, Vol. 19, No. 2, April, 1935.

Heath, C. W., and Gregory, L. W. "Problems of Normal College Students and Their Families," *School and Society*, May 18, 1946.

Heston, Joseph C. "Personality Inventories as Tools in Guidance," *Occupations*, Vol. 29, No. 7, April, 1951.

Hudson, R. Lofton. "The Emotions of the Minister," *Pastoral Psychology*, May, 1951.

Keliher, Alice V. "The Professional Person—A Mental Hygiene Resource in Education," *Mental Hygiene*, Vol. 34, No. 2, April, 1950.

Leonard, Margaret, *et al.* "A Project Study of Mental Hygiene," *Journal of Health and Physical Education*, February, 1942.

Linaberry, Audrey M. "To My Teacher," *Childhood Education*, Vol. 25, May, 1949.

Lloyd-Jones, Esther. "Some Current Issues in Guidance," *Teachers College Record*, November, 1947.

Low, Camilla M. "The Neglect of the Personal-Social Needs of Youth," *Progressive Education*, Vol. 28, No. 2, November, 1950.

Malamud, Daniel. "The Counselor Says 'M—HM,'" *Science Monthly*, February, 1948.

Malmberg, A. O. "Human Relations and Business Success," *Guideposts*, No. 52, 1947.

Murphy, J. Fred, chmn. "Characteristics of a High School Guidance and Counseling Program," *North Central Association Quarterly,* Vol. 22, No. 2, October, 1947.

Pope, Liston, and Hall, Clarence W. "The Man Who Founded a People," *Christian Herald,* March, 1951.

Pratt, George K. "Seeing the Individual Whole," *Occupations,* Vol. 13, No. 2, November, 1934.

Rogers, Carl R. "A Current Formulation of Client-Centered Therapy," *The Social Service Review,* Vol. 24, No. 4, December, 1950.

Ross, Helen. "What Can the Camp Contribute to the Emotional Development of the Child," *The Camping Magazine,* March, 1938.

Super, Donald E. "Group Techniques in the Guidance Program," *Journal of Educational and Psychological Measurement,* Part II, Autumn, 1949.

Swartz, Philip G. "Counseling in a Smaller Y.M.C.A.," *Counseling,* April, 1951.

Terhune, William. A Mental Hygiene Creed in "The Doctor's Wife," *Connecticut State Medical Journal,* July, 1947.

Towle, Charlotte. "Client-Centered Case Work," *The Social Service Review,* Vol. 24, No. 4, December, 1950.

Traxler, Arthur E. "Emerging Trends in Guidance," *The School Review,* Vol. 58, No. 1, January, 1950.

Van De Mark, Theodora Jane. "A Prayer for Bill," *Childhood Education,* Vol. 25, January, 1949.

Watson, Goodwin. "Areas of Agreement in Psychotherapy," *The American Journal of Orthopsychiatry,* Vol. 10, 1940.

Weislogel, Robert L. "Counseling in a Social Framework," *Counseling,* April, 1948.

Wrenn, C. Gilbert. "Client-Centered Counseling," *Journal of Educational and Psychological Measurement,* Winter, 1946.

Wright, Herbert F. "How the Psychology of Motivation Is Related to Curriculum Development," *The Journal of Educational Psychology,* March, 1948.

Zerfoss, Karl P. "Counseling as Cooperative Experience," *Counseling,* May, 1949.

———. "Guidance—Central or Peripheral?" (unpublished).

———. "The Sphere of the General Counselor," George Williams College *Bulletin,* Vol. XL, No. 4, January, 1946.

Miscellaneous

Association Records—A Manual for Record-Keeping and Annual Reporting by Y.M.C.A.'s. New York: Association Press, 1945.

Counsel of Guidance and Personnel Associations. *Fundamental Beliefs.* 1939.

Family Service Association of America. News release. New York, June 7, 1951.

Highlights. New York: Family Service Association of America, November, 1950.

Illinois Society for Mental Hygiene. Report. Chicago, 1951.

Institute of Counseling, Testing, and Guidance, Michigan State College, East Lansing. "The Role of the Staff in the Guidance Program" (mimeographed release), 1951.

May, Rollo, Roberts, David E., Hiltner, Seward, and Doniger, Simon. Consultation Clinic, *Journal of Pastoral Psychology*, December, 1950.

Menninger, Karl A., *et al.* Consultation Clinic, *Journal of Pastoral Psychology*, November, 1950.

Mooney, Ross L. Mooney Problem Check List. Published by the American Psychological Corporation, New York.

National Association for the Study of Group Work. "Records and Reports." Suggestions for the study of group work in the field of camping. New York: National Association for the Study of Group Work, 1939 (mimeographed).

Purdue Opinion Pole, Report of. *Chicago Sun Times,* 1948.

Report from a Chicago social settlement, January, 1945. (Editor's files.)

Report in *Chicago Sun,* March 24, 1947.

Rogers, Carl R. "A Counseling Viewpoint for the U.S.O. Worker," mimeographed release *circa* 1944, pp. 1-2.

Woellner, Robert C. "Instructions to Counselors" (mimeographed). University of Chicago, 1951.

Zerfoss, Karl P. Class notes and other materials.

———. Diagram of Counselor's Sphere.

———. "Mental Hygiene in the Activity Program" (lecture notes).

Content Index

Figures refer to the numbers of the selections in the Readings.
Numbers in parentheses refer to extended treatment of the topic.

Authors Index